# The First Resource

Wild Species in the
North American Economy

**Christine Prescott-Allen**
**and Robert Prescott-Allen**

# The
# First
# Resource

Published with support from
the World Wildlife Fund
and Philip Morris Incorporated

Yale University Press
New Haven and London

Research for *The First Resource* was funded by
World Wildlife Fund and Philip Morris Incorporated,
whose generous support the authors gratefully acknowledge.
The authors also thank the many persons, listed in
Appendixes A–D, who kindly gave them help and information.
All royalties from the sale of *The First Resource*
go to World Wildlife Fund. The opinions expressed
in this book are those of the authors and are not
necessarily endorsed by World Wildlife Fund
or Philip Morris Incorporated.

Designed by Sally Harris
and set in Trump Mediaeval type by
The Composing Room of Michigan, Inc.
Printed in the United States of America by
Vail-Ballou Press, Binghamton, N.Y.

Library of Congress Cataloging-in-Publication Data

Prescott-Allen, Christine, 1949–
    The first resource.

    Bibliography: p.
    Includes index.
    1. Biology, Economic—United States. 2. Biology,
Economic—Canada. 3. Animal products—United States.
4. Animal products—Canada. 5. Plant products—United
States. 6. Plant products—Canada. 7. Food, Wild—
United States. 8. Food, Wild—Canada. I. Prescott-Allen,
Robert. II. Title.
QH705.P74 1986      333.95′097      86–1657
ISBN 0-300-03228-5

The paper in this book meets the guidelines for
permanence and durability of the Committee on
Production Guidelines for Book Longevity
of the Council on Library Resources.

10  9  8  7  6  5  4  3  2  1

# Contents

# List of Figures

# List of Tables

# 1

# Wildlife as a Resource and Other Values

Wildlife is the first resource: the exclusive source of food, fiber, fuel, and medicines for the first 99% of human history.* During the latest 1%, however, wildlife has become the forgotten resource. Agriculture, the use of fossil fuels, and industrial development have transformed the human economy, relegating wildlife to a supporting role. Nowhere does this transformation appear more complete than in the industrialized countries, where the primary values of wild plants and animals are widely regarded as aesthetic, emotional, and recreational. It is easy to be left with the impression that in developed economies wildlife may nourish the soul but it no longer keeps body and soul together. This impression is reinforced by the anti-utilitarian spirit of some campaigns to protect wild animals.

Wildlife conservationists often claim this is not so. They affirm the intangible values of wildlife but argue that, no matter how developed the economy, wild species remain a significant source of raw materials and other consumable commodities. That wild resources continue to make an economic contribution is obvious and undeniable (commercial fisheries are an example). But just how large the contribution is (and hence whether it is significant), and whether it is increasing, stable, or on its way to becoming an economic curiosity, no one can say because data have not been assembled to support any of these conclusions.

In the absence of such data, land managers, businesspeople, politicians, civil servants, conservationists, and others who make decisions that affect wildlife do so in ignorance of the possible consequences not only for wildlife but also for the people who benefit from wildlife. Recognizing the lack of information, the *World Conservation Strategy* (produced by the International Union for Conservation of Nature and Natural Resources [IUCN] in 1980) called for "well documented accounts of the extent and manner in which societies at different stages of development depend on . . . conservation" (G-391). This book is a response to this call.

---

* Recognizably human beings have existed for at least 2 million years (J-627). Prior to the development of agriculture some 10,000 years ago (S-323), they lived entirely by hunting wild animals and gathering wild plants (J-627).

## What Is Wildlife?

Logically, *wildlife* means "all life that is wild." The term is usually used in a variety of less encompassing senses; in some circles it is understood to mean wild animals (but not wild plants) and may be restricted further to apply only to those wild animals that are the objects of recreational hunting or fishing. For the purposes of this book we define *wildlife* as wild plants and animals (kingdoms Plantae and Animalia according to the concept of Whittaker [V-341]), therefore excluding fungi, protists, and prokaryotes such as bacteria and blue-green algae. We use the phrases *wildlife, wild species*, and *wild plants and animals* interchangeably.

A wild plant or animal is one that reproduces without human intervention and whose critical habitats (the habitats required for reproduction and nutrition) can regenerate without human intervention. A wild plant or animal propagates itself. It is not sown or planted, put to stud, or given the assistance of a veterinarian at delivery. Wild species are adapted to closed, primary habitats; to open, naturally disturbed habitats; or to range or forest disturbed by human activity (the ecological extension of open, naturally disturbed habitats). Species are not wild if they survive largely or only in cultivated fields and gardens or urban areas, or as the parasites of human beings or of their domesticated animals or plants.

The distinction between wild and domesticated is not always clear-cut. Deer and other wild game animals are often given supplementary winter feed; scrupulous collectors of wild ginseng sow the seeds of plants they dig at collection sites; sugar bushes (maple groves) may be thinned; wild stands of timber trees may be sprayed with pesticides. Although we give these organisms a helping human hand from time to time, we regard them as wild because they and their habitats retain the capacity for independent regeneration. By contrast, we regard as domesticated salmon that spawn in confinement (even though they are released to the ocean to grow to maturity) because both reproduction and the habitat critical for reproduction are under human management. A species is wild if both elements of our definition are met (that is, independent regeneration both of the species and of its critical habitats); it is semiwild (or semidomesticated) if only one element is met; it is domesticated if neither is met.

Although distinguishing between wild and domesticated species may sometimes be difficult, it has important consequences for resource management. The different users of wild species may find themselves relying on the same habitats. For example, a mountain area may be used for wildlife watching, logging, spawning streams for salmon, and the maintenance of wild genetic resources for crop improvement. Usually, such potential conflicts can be avoided. The need for habitat conservation, in fact, is the common denominator uniting otherwise separate interest groups.

## Aim and Scope of This Book

As far as we know, this book is the first systematic analysis of the contributions of wild plant and animal species to a developed economy. Its aims are to assess the contributions of wild species and gene pools to the supply of resources used in an industrialized society, to compare them with the contributions of domesticated species and gene pools, to determine the relative importance of different kinds of contributions, and to identify major trends in the use of wild plant and animal resources. The book is not intended to be comprehensive: we have limited its scope by focusing only on plants and animals (not on other organisms) and on those contributions at the levels of species and gene to which dollar values can readily be assigned. We have also limited the book's geographical scope (to resources produced or imported by the United States and Canada) and the period covered (1976–1980), thus providing an explicit framework in which to make comparisons between the contributions of wild species and domesticated species. The dollar sums we cite are not important in themselves but as indicators of the relative importance (a) of different wild species as origins of a particular type of resource; (b) of different types of wild resources; and (c) of wild and domesticated species to the total resource supply of an industrialized economy. We have found that these proportions (unlike the dollar figures themselves) change rather slowly. It is because we have adhered to this geographical and temporal framework (further defined below) that we describe this report as systematic rather than selective or anecdotal.

Our research covers the wild resources that are produced or consumed in the United States and Canada. We had originally intended to treat the two countries separately, but their economies are so similar (in nature, not in scale) and so closely linked that to do so would have led to considerable repetition. Instead we use the United States as our model and introduce Canadian data occasionally for comparative purposes or to fill gaps. An exception is chapter 5, for which we were able to obtain more comprehensive data from Canada. The geographical scope of the resource-consumption picture is therefore exclusively North American and based largely on the United States. Because the United States imports a great variety of wild resources, the scope of the resource-supply picture is global.

This book is concerned with contemporary uses of wildlife. We believe that an understanding of present uses and their evolution provides the most useful guide to the potential contribution of wildlife. We therefore have concentrated on the present and the immediate past. To reduce distortion by unusual years we have tried to assemble data for a five-year period. We chose the period 1976–1980 because it is the latest for which the most comprehensive statistics are available. Wherever we refer without qualification to annual production, consumption, or imports, we mean the annual average for 1976–1980. Where we have been unable to obtain data for the five-year period, we use statistics for as many years as possible within the period or, failing that, for the year nearest the period.

The contributions of wildlife to the human economy can be typified in several ways, but they fall into two broad categories: biological and psychological (fig. 1.1). Biological contributions comprise the provision of raw materials (food, medicines, and industrial materials such as timber) and services (such as the recycling of nutrients, watershed protection, and pollination). They also include the provision of germplasm (genetic material) for the selection and improvement of domesticated plants and animals (a contribution that can be regarded as either a raw material or a service). Psychological contributions include: recreational, both consumptive (hunting, fishing, plant collecting) and nonconsumptive (watching, enjoying via film or print media); intellectual and scientific (including educational); aesthetic, artistic, and cultural; and religious and symbolic.

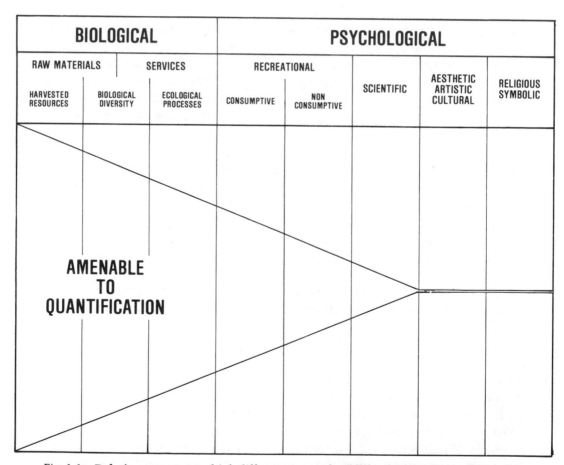

Fig. 1.1   **Relative extents to which different types of wildlife contribution are amenable to economic quantification (illustrative only)**

Figure 1.1 illustrates the point that these contributions differ markedly in the extent to which they can be economically quantified. Expressing value in monetary terms distorts the value of biological contributions less than it does that of psychological ones. For biological contributions, dollar values can be assigned more easily to harvested resources (raw materials), which are bought and sold on the market, than to ecological processes, which are not. The products of biological diversity (genetic resources) are intermediate: their dollar value can be estimated via the new domesticates derived from them or the improvements they confer on established domesticates. For psychological contributions, nonconsumptive recreation is more difficult to quantify monetarily than is consumptive recreation; and quantification becomes progressively more difficult (and absurd) as the material component of the contribution diminishes.

Although our analysis contains both quantitative and qualitative assessments of the contributions of wildlife, we felt it advisable to concentrate on those types of contributions whose value could be quantified (see below). Accordingly, it is restricted to biological and recreational contributions.

The biological and recreational contributions of wildlife are made at three levels of biotic organization: ecosystem, species, and gene. We illustrate this typology (with respect to biological contributions) in figure 1.2. Similar examples can be given for recreation: wilderness lovers relate to certain landscapes

| CONSERVATION COMPONENTS / LEVELS OF BIOTIC ORGANIZATION | MAINTENANCE OF | | |
|---|---|---|---|
| | HARVESTED RESOURCES | BIOLOGICAL DIVERSITY | ECOLOGICAL PROCESSES |
| ECOSYSTEM | e.g. rangeland | | e.g. watershed forests |
| SPECIES | e.g. commercial fish 2, 3, 4, 5, 6 | e.g. new domesticates 7 | e.g. pollinators 9 |
| GENE | | e.g. in crop improvement 8 | |

Fig. 1.2  **Biological contributions of wildlife by conservation component (vertical columns) and level of biotic organization (horizontal columns). This book covers the contributions of wildlife at the levels of species and gene (shaded area). The numbers in the boxes indicate the chapters concerned.**

and communities of plants and animals, such as mountains, wetlands, forests, and coral reefs (the ecosystem level); bird-watchers, whale-watchers and wild-flower lovers relate to the wildlife they are interested in at the species level; sportfishing people can benefit at the gene level through stock enhancement programs.

Human beings are components, beneficiaries, and modifiers of the biosphere, the film of life that coats this planet. Apart from humans and their domesti-cates, the biosphere is entirely wild. Accordingly, human economies, regardless of their stage of development, are utterly dependent on wildlife. Natural biota foster the conditions for life, including human life, by maintaining planetary biochemical equilibria and providing other essential ecological services: degra-dation of organic wastes, nitrogen fixation, soil and water conservation, pollina-tion, and pest control (P-792). All these processes except for pollination and pest control are made at the ecosystem level of organization. Pimentel et al. (P-792) have reviewed the contributions of these ecological processes to the United States. They conclude that maintenance of the processes and of the participat-ing ecosystems calls for precise description and quantification of the processes and identification of species groups that could serve as indicators of the condi-tion of the ecosystems concerned. Beyond those measures, maintenance of the processes themselves requires conservation of ecosystems and not of particular species or habitats.

Contributions to human survival and well-being at the ecosystem level are essentially contributions of the natural biota (of which the three kingdoms not included in this study—fungi, protists, and prokaryotes—are extremely impor-tant members). The contributions are so all encompassing that there is little point in attaching a dollar value to them; and the wild component is so domi-nant that the comparative approach adopted in this study is scarcely applicable. Instead we focus on the economic contributions of wild plants and animals at the two remaining levels of biotic organization: species and gene. At these levels the impact of domestication is so great that the role of wild resources can easily be underestimated or overlooked altogether.

### Resource Values versus Intrinsic Values

This book treats wildlife as a resource and concentrates on those contributions to which monetary values can be assigned. We have encountered two objections to this approach: first, that it underestimates the value of wildlife and hence will lead people to think less of wild species; second, that it is time wild plants and animals were thought of not as commodities but as companions—with intrin-sic rights and values—needing no justification of human utility to be accorded the freedom of the planet we share with them. The first objection is tactical, the second philosophical.

All evaluations are incomplete. The price of a house does not express its value as a home to the people living in it, yet a real-estate market does exist and people do put prices on homes. The accumulated costs and value added of growing, processing, and selling corn in the United States do not take into account the pleasure of eating cornbread or the cultural importance of corn to Pueblo Indians; yet agricultural statistics are published and the data put to good use. A price tag on a work of art reflects neither the essential artistic value of the piece nor the sheer delight that it may give another human being; yet art galleries do not decline to take out insurance because assigning a monetary value to the art would diminish it.

The value of goods and services has both a quantitative aspect that is measurable and a qualitative aspect that is not. The goods and services provided by wild species are no different in this respect from those of any other source. The problem is not that assessing the quantitative values will lead to underestimating the overall contribution of wildlife to society. Rather, it is that the contribution is already being underestimated because quantitative assessments are not available. Decisions are made on the basis of comparisons, and comparisons are made largely on the basis of figures: so many dollars here, so many votes there. Knowing that wild sunflowers make a significant contribution to the U.S. economy does not detract from the beauty of the flowers or the pleasure they give. Describing that contribution and estimating its dollar value so that people can judge its significance for themselves do not change the aesthetic and other unquantifiable arguments for conserving wild sunflowers.

Our response to the philosophical objection to the approach adopted in this study is similar. We agree that other species do not exist to serve human ends, and we hope for the evolution of a more biocentric, less anthropocentric view of life. But such an evolution will not diminish the contributions other species make to human survival and well-being. Other species will remain a resource. Many aboriginal peoples live with this dichotomy well enough, expressing strong spiritual bonds with the species that feed, clothe, and cure them as well as with those that make no identifiable contribution to their lives. Improving our understanding of how people benefit from wild plants and animals should not impede the development of a sense of companionship with them. Rather, it could increase our sense of obligation to them.

The literature on the nonresource values of wildlife is large. By contrast, there are very few assessments of the resource values of wildlife (although there are several general reviews) and none, as far as we know, for a developed economy. This is surprising, given the strongly utilitarian cast to decision making in industrialized societies. The implication is that wildlife is of no account as a resource—that it is of great interest to small numbers of highly opinionated people, but that an advanced economy can take it or leave it.

Our hope is to redress this imbalance and to demonstrate the value of the material contributions of wild species. As possessor of the world's biggest economy, the United States may seem perhaps the least likely to be influenced by wild resources. On the contrary, wildlife plays an important role in this economy, and although the mixture of contributions is changing, the need for wildlife is likely to persist. We have concentrated on the resource contributions to describe this role as clearly and objectively as possible.

# 2

# Logging

The timber industry gets its wood either from logging wild trees or by practicing silviculture, the cultivation of domesticated trees. Wild trees may be protected from fire, pests, and diseases and otherwise tended from time to time. Nevertheless they are wild as defined in chapter 1 and as compared with the true domesticates of silviculture, which, like crops in agriculture, are tended from cradle to grave. This chapter is concerned with the products of logging wild trees: wood, pulp, and fuel. The chemical by-products of manufacturing wood and pulp are also covered in this chapter, as are related biochemicals obtained from living trees (rosin, turpentine, and terpenes). Other exudates from living trees are discussed in chapter 6.

Logging is the world's biggest wildlife industry, far outstripping in value the next biggest, fishing. World trade in timber products (most from wild trees) is $40 billion a year; in fishery products, $12 billion a year (note 1). The United States is both the world's leading timber producer (by volume) and the biggest importer (by value). Canada ranks sixth as a producer by volume (after the United States, the People's Republic of China, India, Brazil, and Indonesia) but is the world's top timber exporter by value; the United States is second (D-384).

The United States produces 13,757 million cubic feet of timber products a year, 2,000 million cubic feet of which is exported, but the country also imports 3,364 million cubic feet. Annual timber consumption is therefore 15,122 million cubic feet, with each person in the United States consuming 67.8 cubic feet of timber products a year (S-797, S-817).

The most recent official estimate of the value of timber production is for 1972: that year's production of 11,812 million cubic feet has been estimated by the Forest Service of the U.S. Department of Agriculture to be worth $6.4 billion (P-475). Since 1972, timber prices have risen steeply. Our own estimate of the current annual value of timber production in the United States is $16.4 billion (see table 2.1 and note 2). Imports are worth an additional $7.5 billion a year (note 3). These figures are summarized in table 2.2.

The total economic contribution of the $23.9 billion of timber products produced and imported by the United States is several times greater. In 1972 timber

Table 2.1  Volume (roundwood equivalent) and estimated value (current U.S.$) of U.S. timber production

| | 1976 | | 1977 | | 1978 | | 1979 | | 1980 | | ANN. AVE. |
|---|---|---|---|---|---|---|---|---|---|---|---|
| | Million ft³ | U.S.$ million | Million ft³ | U.S.$ million | Million ft³ | U.S.$ million | Million ft³ | U.S.$ million | Million ft³ | U.S.$ million | 1976–1980 U.S.$ million |
| Lumber | | | | | | | | | | | |
| Softwood | 4,415 | | 4,625 | | 4,665 | | 4,475 | | 3,685 | | |
| Hardwood | 1,060 | | 1,105 | | 1,160 | | 1,205 | | 1,175 | | |
| All | 5,475 | | 5,730 | | 5,825 | | 5,680 | | 4,860 | | |
| Logs | | | | | | | | | | | |
| Softwood | 535 | | 505 | | 560 | | 640 | | 530 | | |
| Hardwood | 20 | | 20 | | 25 | | 25 | | 30 | | |
| All | 555 | | 525 | | 585 | | 665 | | 560 | | |
| TOTAL LUMBER AND LOGS | 6,030 | 6,977 | 6,255 | 8,100 | 6,410 | 9,705 | 6,345 | 12,823 | 5,420 | 10,612 | 9,643 |
| Plywood and veneer | | | | | | | | | | | |
| Softwood | 1,270 | | 1,335 | | 1,370 | | 1,280 | | 1,115 | | |
| Hardwood | 85 | | 90 | | 90 | | 90 | | 80 | | |
| All | 1,355 | 2,637 | 1,425 | 2,732 | 1,460 | 3,558 | 1,370 | 4,411 | 1,195 | 3,807 | 3,429 |
| Pulp products | | | | | | | | | | | |
| Softwood | 2,635 | | 2,475 | | 2,450 | | 2,770 | | 3,020 | | |
| Hardwood | 1,175 | | 1,175 | | 1,295 | | 1,335 | | 1,370 | | |
| All | 3,810 | | 3,650 | | 3,745 | | 4,105 | | 4,390 | | |
| Pulpwood chips | | | | | | | | | | | |
| Softwood/all | 245 | | 250 | | 225 | | 280 | | 275 | | |
| TOTAL PULP PRODUCTS AND CHIPS | 4,055 | 1,719 | 3,900 | 1,747 | 3,970 | 1,914 | 4,385 | 2,543 | 4,665 | 2,883 | 2,161 |
| Other industrial | | | | | | | | | | | |
| Softwood | 240 | | 240 | | 245 | | 245 | | 225 | | |
| Hardwood | 140 | | 145 | | 155 | | 160 | | 160 | | |
| All | 380 | 190 | 385 | 218 | 400 | 268 | 405 | 305 | 385 | 341 | 273 |
| Fuelwood | | | | | | | | | | | |
| Softwood | 130 | | 240 | | 380 | | 565 | | 780 | | |
| Hardwood | 470 | | 785 | | 1,190 | | 1,710 | | 2,340 | | |
| All | 600 | 235 | 1,025 | 460 | 1,570 | 736 | 2,275 | 1,156 | 3,120 | 1,950 | 907 |
| TOTAL OTHER PRODUCTS | 980 | 425 | 1,410 | 678 | 1,970 | 1,004 | 2,680 | 1,506 | 3,505 | 2,291 | 1,181 |
| TOTAL SOFTWOOD | 9,470 | | 9,670 | | 9,895 | | 10,255 | | 9,630 | | |
| TOTAL HARDWOOD | 2,950 | | 3,320 | | 3,915 | | 4,525 | | 5,155 | | |
| TOTAL ALL* | 12,420 | 11,758 | 12,990 | 13,257 | 13,810 | 16,181 | 14,780 | 21,283 | 14,785 | 19,593 | 16,414 |

Sources: Volumes: S-817; fuelwood values: S-817, remainder: table 2.3.
*Data may not add due to rounding.

Table 2.2   **Average annual consumption, production, imports, and exports of timber products by the United States, 1976–1980**

| CONSUMPTION | | PRODUCTION | | IMPORTS | | EXPORTS |
|---|---|---|---|---|---|---|
| Total | Per capita | Volume | Value | Volume | Value | Volume |
| (million ft³) | (ft³) | (million ft³) | ($ million) | (million ft³) | ($ million) | (million ft³) |
| 15,122 | 67.8 | 13,757 | 16,414 | 3,364 | 7,525 | 2,000 |

Sources: Volume: S-797, S-817. Value: note 2.
Note: Data do not add due to independent rounding.

was estimated to have contributed $48.5 billion to the gross domestic product (GDP), or 4.1%, which is higher than the percentage of 1967 (3.9%) but lower than that of 1963 (4.4%) (P-475). The contribution to GDP is calculated by adding the estimated value added attributable to timber at each level of economic activity—from management of the growing tree through logging, primary manufacturing (for example, making pulpwood logs into wood pulp and wood pulp into paper), and secondary manufacturing (for example, making paper into paper products) to construction (the biggest single consumer), transportation, wholesaling, and retailing. We estimate that timber currently contributes about $84 billion to the GDP, or 3.9% (see table 2.6, fig. 2.1, and note 4). In chapter 7 we estimate that some 96% of the timber produced and imported by the United States comes from wild (naturally regenerated) trees. That proportion of the combined value of timber production and imports amounts to $23 billion. The corresponding contribution to GDP is $80.6 billion, or 3.8%.

## Main Uses and Markets

Timber was North America's most used raw material from the time human beings first settled the continent until the twentieth century. In the late 1920s other living resources (chiefly agricultural) displaced timber as the top industrial raw material in the United States, and in the early 1940s timber was also overtaken by minerals. Since then, timber continued to decline in importance, although not as sharply as did other living resources, which reached their peak use in 1935. Today minerals are the nation's preeminent source of raw materials, supplying more than half the dollar value of raw materials consumed. Timber has been the number-two source since the early 1960s. Its decline appears to have ended, and it now contributes more than a quarter (by value) of the industrial raw materials consumed in the United States (fig. 2.2). Per capita

(text continued on page 17)

**Table 2.3  Timber production in the United States, 1972, and price calculations, 1976–1980**

| | 1972 | | | 1976 | | 1977 | | 1978 | | 1979 | | 1980 | |
|---|---|---|---|---|---|---|---|---|---|---|---|---|---|
| | Value ($1,000) | Volume (1,000 ft³) | Price ($) | % Change | Price ($) | % Change | Price ($) | % Change | Price ($) | % Change | Price ($) | % Change | Price ($) |
| SAWLOGS | 3,716,500 | 5,897,750 | 0.630 | | | | | | | | | | |
| North | 274,450 | 575,550 | 0.477 | 35.12 | 0.645 | 13.53 | 0.732 | 17.55 | 0.860 | 20.21 | 1.034 | −11.63 | 0.914 |
| South | 1,054,450 | 1,979,850 | 0.533 | 49.20 | 0.795 | 13.08 | 0.899 | 21.45 | 1.092 | 21.21 | 1.324 | −3.51 | 1.278 |
| West | 2,387,600 | 3,342,350 | 0.714 | 119.59 | 1.568 | 11.38 | 1.746 | 15.32 | 2.013 | 37.66 | 2.815 | −1.96 | 2.760 |
| VENEER LOGS | 1,302,700 | 1,389,700 | 0.937 | | | | | | | | | | |
| North | 21,250 | 24,400 | 0.871 | 54.50 | 1.346 | 2.96 | 1.386 | 16.53 | 1.615 | 16.99 | 1.889 | 4.65 | 1.977 |
| South | 321,250 | 507,000 | 0.634 | 42.56 | 0.904 | 16.95 | 1.057 | 32.19 | 1.397 | 25.27 | 1.750 | −5.12 | 1.660 |
| West | 960,200 | 858,300 | 1.119 | 139.74 | 2.683 | −5.80 | 2.527 | 25.99 | 3.184 | 34.51 | 4.283 | −0.02 | 4.282 |
| PULPWOOD | 993,650 | 3,644,250 | 0.273 | | | | | | | | | | |
| North | 176,300 | 667,300 | 0.264 | 50.68 | 0.398 | 3.78 | 0.413 | 2.63 | 0.424 | 11.24 | 0.472 | 7.17 | 0.506 |
| South | 719,150 | 2,628,600 | 0.274 | 48.05 | 0.406 | 5.52 | 0.428 | 6.80 | 0.457 | 16.09 | 0.531 | 8.75 | 0.577 |
| West | 98,200 | 348,350 | 0.282 | 111.53 | 0.597 | 10.60 | 0.660 | 16.31 | 0.768 | 48.08 | 1.137 | −0.61 | 1.129 |
| OTHER PRODUCTS | 347,550 | 950,000 | 0.366 | | | | | | | | | | |
| North | 125,000 | 259,100 | 0.482 | 1.75 | 0.490 | 8.60 | 0.532 | 8.44 | 0.577 | 13.87 | 0.657 | 11.97 | 0.736 |
| South | 157,800 | 514,250 | 0.307 | 43.66 | 0.441 | 12.56 | 0.496 | 23.48 | 0.612 | 20.88 | 0.740 | −0.95 | 0.733 |
| West | 64,750 | 176,650 | 0.367 | 87.70 | 0.689 | 23.11 | 0.848 | 21.12 | 1.027 | 59.81 | 1.641 | 0.58 | 1.651 |
| TOTAL | 6,360,400 | 11,881,700 | 0.535 | | | | | | | | | | |
| AVERAGE PRICE (based on the above) | | | | | | | | | | | | | |
| Lumber and logs | | | 0.630 | | 1.157 | | 1.295 | | 1.514 | | 2.021 | | 1.958 |
| Plywood and veneer | | | 0.937 | | 1.946 | | 1.917 | | 2.437 | | 3.220 | | 3.186 |
| Pulp products and chips | | | 0.273 | | 0.424 | | 0.448 | | 0.482 | | 0.580 | | 0.618 |
| Other products | | | 0.366 | | 0.499 | | 0.567 | | 0.670 | | 0.863 | | 0.887 |

Sources: 1972 data: P-475. 1976–1980 data: calculated from tables 2.4 and 2.5 as follows. See note 2 for explanation.

SAWLOGS
North: mean of items 15–18
South: mean of items 10 + (mean of 12–14), weighted 2:1 in favor of 10
West: mean of items 11 + (mean of 42–46)

VENEER LOGS
North: mean of items 20–27
South: mean of items 2 + 5
West: mean of items 19 + (mean of 42–46)

AVERAGE PRICE
Lumber and logs = sawlogs—North:South:West weighted in ratio of 1:2:3
Plywood and veneer = veneer logs—North:South:West weighted in ratio of 1:15:22
Pulp products and chips = pulpwood—North:South:West weighted in ratio of 2:7:1
Other products* —North:South:West weighted in ratio of 2:3:1
*Excludes fuelwood, calculated direct from average prices in S-817

PULPWOOD
North: mean of (mean of items 32–36) + (mean of 40–41)
South: mean of (mean of items 28–31) + (mean of 37–39), weighted 3:1 in favor of former
West: mean of items 1 + 3 + 4 + 42–46

OTHER PRODUCTS
North: item 6
South: mean of (mean of items 2 + 5) + (mean of 6–9)
West: mean of items 1 + 3 + 4

13

Table 2.4  Average prices per thousand board feet of U.S. timber products, 1972 and 1976–1980, with percentage change on previous entry

| PRODUCT AND SPECIES | 1972 Price ($) | 1976 Price ($) | 1976 % Change | 1977 Price ($) | 1977 % Change | 1978 Price ($) | 1978 % Change | 1979 Price ($) | 1979 % Change | 1980 Price ($) | 1980 % Change |
|---|---|---|---|---|---|---|---|---|---|---|---|
| SOFTWOOD SAWTIMBER STUMPAGE | | | | | | | | | | | |
| 1. Douglas fir (W. Washington and W. Oregon) | 71.7 | 176.2 | 145.75 | 225.9 | 28.21 | 250.3 | 10.80 | 394.4 | 57.57 | 432.2 | 9.58 |
| 2. Southern pine (Southern region) | 65.6 | 87.0 | 32.62 | 100.3 | 15.29 | 134.5 | 34.10 | 155.2 | 15.39 | 155.4 | 0.13 |
| 3. Ponderosa pine (Pacific S. W. region) | 65.8 | 101.8 | 54.71 | 131.4 | 29.08 | 164.7 | 25.34 | 239.0 | 45.11 | 206.1 | −13.77 |
| 4. Western hemlock (Pacific N. W. region) | 49.0 | 79.7 | 62.65 | 89.3 | 12.05 | 113.6 | 27.21 | 200.8 | 76.76 | 212.7 | 5.93 |
| 5. Southern pine (Louisiana private) | 66.3 | 101.1 | 52.49 | 119.9 | 18.60 | 156.2 | 30.28 | 211.1 | 35.15 | 189.2 | −10.37 |
| HARDWOOD SAWTIMBER STUMPAGE | | | | | | | | | | | |
| 6. All eastern hardwoods (National Forests) | 34.3 | 34.9 | 1.75 | 37.9 | 8.60 | 41.1 | 8.44 | 46.8 | 13.87 | 52.4 | 11.97 |
| 7. Gums (Louisiana private) | 23.9 | 37.2 | 55.65 | 39.7 | 6.72 | 46.2 | 16.37 | 51.9 | 12.34 | 53.2 | 2.50 |
| 8. Oaks (Louisiana private) | 23.1 | 37.3 | 61.47 | 40.6 | 8.85 | 46.5 | 14.53 | 53.4 | 14.84 | 55.5 | 3.93 |
| 9. Ash (Louisiana private) | 28.6 | 45.8 | 60.14 | 49.7 | 8.52 | 59.5 | 19.72 | 74.3 | 24.87 | 70.2 | −5.52 |
| SOFTWOOD SAWLOGS | | | | | | | | | | | |
| 10. Southern pine (Louisiana private) | 93.1 | 138.0 | 48.23 | 160.8 | 16.52 | 201.2 | 25.12 | 251.9 | 25.20 | 230.6 | −8.46 |
| 11. Douglas fir (W. Washington and N. W. Oregon) | 95.1 | 202.9 | 113.35 | 242.8 | 19.66 | 284.6 | 17.22 | 382.2 | 34.29 | 379.8 | −0.63 |
| HARDWOOD SAWLOGS | | | | | | | | | | | |
| 12. Gums (Louisiana private) | 57.4 | 86.8 | 51.22 | 90.7 | 4.49 | 101.9 | 12.35 | 116.0 | 13.84 | 122.6 | 5.69 |
| 13. Oaks (Louisiana private) | 56.0 | 87.0 | 55.36 | 91.6 | 5.29 | 101.8 | 11.14 | 116.3 | 14.24 | 126.4 | 8.68 |
| 14. Ash (Louisiana private) | 63.4 | 93.1 | 46.85 | 101.3 | 8.81 | 120.4 | 18.85 | 134.4 | 11.63 | 140.7 | 4.76 |
| 15. Hard maple (Wisconsin) | 75.3 | 99.4 | 32.01 | 103.6 | 4.23 | 131.3 | 26.74 | 144.1 | 9.75 | 132.6 | −7.98 |
| 16. Basswood (Wisconsin) | 62.6 | 80.9 | 29.23 | 91.4 | 12.98 | 112.9 | 23.52 | 128.8 | 14.08 | 123.1 | −4.43 |
| 17. Yellow birch (Wisconsin) | 68.4 | 92.5 | 35.23 | 106.6 | 15.24 | 120.9 | 13.41 | 155.3 | 28.45 | 124.4 | −19.90 |
| 18. Aspen (Wisconsin) | 37.5 | 54.0 | 44.00 | 65.7 | 21.67 | 70.0 | 6.54 | 90.0 | 28.57 | 77.2 | −14.22 |
| SOFTWOOD VENEER LOGS | | | | | | | | | | | |
| 19. Douglas fir (W. Washington and N. W. Oregon) | 148.9 | 377.7 | 153.66 | 322.2 | −14.69 | 446.4 | 38.55 | 571.3 | 27.98 | 584.4 | 2.29 |
| HARDWOOD VENEER LOGS | | | | | | | | | | | |
| 20. Hard maple (Wisconsin) | 182.5 | 244.0 | 33.70 | 259.0 | 6.15 | 300.0 | 15.83 | 332.5 | 10.83 | 307.5 | −7.52 |
| 21. Basswood (Wisconsin) | 120.5 | 199.0 | 65.15 | 180.0 | −9.55 | 200.0 | 11.11 | 266.5 | 33.25 | 280.0 | 5.07 |
| 22. Aspen (Wisconsin) | 101.5 | 134.0 | 32.02 | 101.5 | −24.25 | 106.5 | 4.93 | 147.5 | 38.50 | 166.5 | 12.88 |
| 23. Yellow birch (Wisconsin) | 212.5 | 320.0 | 50.59 | 354.0 | 10.63 | 327.5 | −7.49 | 350.0 | 6.87 | 270.0 | −22.86 |
| 24. Walnut (Illinois) | 957.0 | 1,253.5 | 30.98 | 1,350.0 | 7.70 | 1,639.5 | 21.44 | 1,931.5 | 17.81 | 2,072.0 | 7.27 |
| 25. White oak (Illinois) | 231.0 | 496.0 | 114.72 | 662.5 | 33.57 | 893.5 | 34.87 | 1,109.0 | 24.12 | 1,123.5 | 1.31 |
| 26. Black walnut (Indiana) | 1,436.8 | 2,149.3 | 49.59 | 2,366.3 | 10.10 | 2,564.8 | 8.39 | 2,691.0 | 4.92 | 3,561.3 | 32.34 |
| 27. Tulip poplar (Indiana) | 135.3 | 215.5 | 59.28 | 192.5 | −10.67 | 275.5 | 43.12 | 274.5 | −0.36 | 298.5 | 8.74 |

Sources: Items 1–27: S-797, S-817. See note 2 for explanation.

Table 2.5  Average prices per standard cord of U.S. timber products, 1972 and 1976–1980, with percentage change on previous entry

| PRODUCT AND SPECIES | 1972 Price ($) | 1976 Price ($) | 1976 % Change | 1977 Price ($) | 1977 % Change | 1978 Price ($) | 1978 % Change | 1979 Price ($) | 1979 % Change | 1980 Price ($) | 1980 % Change |
|---|---|---|---|---|---|---|---|---|---|---|---|
| SOFTWOOD PULPWOOD | | | | | | | | | | | |
| 28. Southern pine (Midsouth) | 20.8 | 29.75 | 43.03 | 31.4 | 5.55 | 33.15 | 5.57 | 40.1 | 20.92 | 43.3 | 7.98 |
| 29. Southern pine chips (Midsouth) | 17.9 | 28.5 | 59.22 | 30.95 | 8.60 | 33.7 | 8.89 | 42.25 | 25.37 | 48.5 | 14.79 |
| 30. Southern pine (Southeast) | 22.85 | 33.6 | 47.05 | 34.65 | 3.13 | 36.25 | 4.62 | 40.65 | 12.14 | 43.9 | 8.00 |
| 31. Southern pine (Louisiana) | 19.25 | 30.45 | 58.18 | 31.65 | 3.94 | 34.55 | 9.16 | 38.95 | 12.74 | 41.45 | 6.42 |
| 32. Pine (Wisconsin) | 21.35 | 36.6 | 71.43 | 38.4 | 4.92 | 37.75 | -1.69 | 41.25 | 9.27 | 42.7 | 3.52 |
| 33. Spruce (Wisconsin) | 29.9 | 41.75 | 39.63 | 40.45 | -3.11 | 38.45 | -4.44 | 48.35 | 25.75 | 47.95 | -0.83 |
| 34. Hemlock (Wisconsin) | 21.8 | 34.25 | 57.11 | 33.4 | -2.48 | 34.0 | 1.80 | 35.9 | 5.59 | 37.65 | 4.87 |
| 35. Spruce and fir (N. New Hampsh re) | 23.75 | 31.5 | 32.63 | 36.5 | 15.87 | 39.0 | 6.85 | 44.0 | 12.82 | 46.0 | 4.55 |
| 36. Hemlock and pine (N. New Hampshire) | 19.25 | 30.4 | 57.92 | 32.5 | 6.91 | 34.5 | 6.15 | 36.65 | 6.22 | 36.65 | 0.00 |
| HARDWOOD PULPWOOD | | | | | | | | | | | |
| 37. Hardwoods (Midsouth) | 18.55 | 26.5 | 42.86 | 28.1 | 6.04 | 30.35 | 8.01 | 33.9 | 11.70 | 36.7 | 8.26 |
| 38. Hardwoods (Southeast) | 18.95 | 24.55 | 29.55 | 26.55 | 8.15 | 28.15 | 6.02 | 30.4 | 7.99 | 32.9 | 8.22 |
| 39. Hardwoods (Louisiana) | 19.0 | 26.1 | 37.37 | 27.2 | 4.21 | 28.3 | 4.04 | 32.05 | 13.25 | 33.6 | 4.84 |
| 40. Aspen (Wisconsin) | 16.25 | 25.25 | 55.38 | 25.75 | 1.98 | 26.0 | 0.97 | 30.0 | 15.38 | 33.5 | 11.67 |
| 41. Hardwoods (N. New Hampshire | 22.0 | 31.65 | 43.86 | 33.0 | 4.27 | 35.0 | 6.06 | 37.0 | 5.71 | 41.5 | 12.16 |
| LOGS, W. WASHINGTON AND N. W. OREGON (per thousand board feet) | | | | | | | | | | | |
| 19. Douglas fir peeler | 148.9 | 377.7 | 153.66 | 322.2 | -14.69 | 446.4 | 38.55 | 571.3 | 27.98 | 584.4 | 2.29 |
| 11. Douglas fir sawmill | 95.1 | 202.9 | 113.35 | 242.8 | 19.66 | 284.6 | 17.22 | 382.2 | 34.29 | 379.8 | -0.63 |
| 42. Western hemlock | 105.6 | 213.6 | 102.27 | 234.6 | 9.83 | 250.6 | 6.82 | 355.8 | 41.98 | 376.5 | 5.82 |
| 43. Noble fir | 164.1 | 441.6 | 169.10 | 409.6 | -7.25 | 482.0 | 17.68 | 708.8 | 47.05 | 543.0 | -23.39 |
| 44. White fir | 126.4 | 256.0 | 102.53 | 258.9 | 1.13 | 290.6 | 12.24 | 411.8 | 41.71 | 431.3 | 4.74 |
| 45. Western red cedar | 113.2 | 264.7 | 133.83 | 320.8 | 21.19 | 391.1 | 21.91 | 503.5 | 28.74 | 380.2 | -24.49 |
| 46. Western white pine | 85.1 | 188.4 | 121.39 | 170.6 | -9.45 | 185.0 | 8.44 | 269.5 | 45.68 | 352.2 | 30.69 |

Sources: Items 28–41: S-797, S-817. I.ems 11, 19, and 42–46: F-478. See note 2 for explanation.

Table 2.6  Estimate of the average annual value added attributable to timber, 1976–1980, using the value added attributed to timber as a percentage of the gross product in 1963, 1967, and 1972 (U.S. $ million)

| Economic Activity (SIC No.) | 1963 Gross product | 1963 Value added (timber) | 1963 % | 1967 Gross product | 1967 Value added (timber) | 1967 % | 1972 Gross product | 1972 Value added (timber) | 1972 % | ANN. AVE. 1976–1980 Gross product | ANN. AVE. 1976–1980 % | ANN. AVE. 1976–1980 Value added (timber) |
|---|---|---|---|---|---|---|---|---|---|---|---|---|
| Agricultural services, forestry, and fisheries (07–09) | | | | | | | | | | | | |
| Timber management | 1,504 | 1,336 | 88.8 | 2,146 | 1,470 | 68.5 | 3,522 | 2,864 | 81.3 | 7,234 | 81.0 | 5,860 |
| Construction (15–17) | 27,355 | 6,237 | 22.8 | 37,489 | 6,733 | 18.0 | 59,364 | 11,947 | 20.1 | 99,208 | 20.0 | 19,842 |
| Lumber and wood products (24) | | | | | | | | | | | | |
| Harvesting | | 1,533 | | | 1,762 | | | 3,065 | | | | |
| Sawmills and planing mills | | 1,254 | | | 1,449 | | | 2,876 | | | | |
| Veneer and plywood plants | | 476 | | | 584 | | | 1,073 | | | | |
| All other primary | | 132 | | | 141 | | | 264 | | | | |
| Millwork, etc., products | | 599 | | | 779 | | | 1,951 | | | | |
| Wooden containers | | 146 | | | 197 | | | 324 | | | | |
| All other secondary | | 409 | | | 600 | | | 718 | | | | |
| SUBTOTAL | 4,444 | 4,549 | | 5,569 | 5,512 | | 9,623 | 10,271 | | 17,469 | | |
| Chemical and allied products (28) | 12,463 | | | 15,424 | | | 21,996 | | | 39,711 | | |
| TOTAL | 16,907 | | 26.9 | 20,993 | | 26.3 | 31,619 | | 32.5 | 57,180 | 32.5 | 18,584 |
| Furniture and fixtures (25) | 2,445 | 1,024 | 41.9 | 3,353 | 1,375 | 41.0 | 4,662 | 1,820 | 39.0 | 7,297 | 36.5 | 2,663 |
| Textile-mill products (22) | 5,197 | | | 6,989 | | | 9,613 | | | 14,743 | | |
| Apparel and related products (23) | 5,794 | | | 7,693 | | | 10,157 | | | 15,130 | | |
| TOTAL FIBERS, PLASTICS, TEXTILES | 10,991 | 1,762 | 16.0 | 14,682 | 2,189 | 14.9 | 19,770 | 2,629 | 13.3 | 29,873 | 11.5 | 3,435 |
| Paper and allied products (26) | | | | | | | | | | | | |
| Pulp, paper, and paperboard mills | | 2,932 | | | 3,454 | | | 4,583 | | | | |
| Paper and paperboard products | | 2,698 | | | 3,626 | | | 5,063 | | | | |
| TOTAL | 6,316 | 5,630 | 89.1 | 8,132 | 7,080 | 87.1 | 11,413 | 9,646 | 84.5 | 20,676 | 84.0 | 17,368 |
| Transportation | 24,948 | 1,837 | 7.4 | 32,075 | 1,835 | 5.7 | 45,596 | 2,729 | 6.0 | 80,758 | 6.0 | 4,845 |
| Wholesale trade | 39,733 | 1,573 | 4.0 | 53,632 | 1,761 | 3.3 | 83,403 | 2,997 | 3.6 | 153,992 | 3.5 | 5,390 |
| Retail trade | 56,382 | 2,130 | 3.8 | 76,482 | 2,813 | 3.7 | 116,081 | 3,561 | 3.1 | 202,584 | 3.0 | 6,078 |
| TOTAL | 186,581 | 26,079 | 14.0 | 248,984 | 30,768 | 12.4 | 375,430 | 48,464 | 12.9 | 658,802 | 12.8 | 84,065 |
| GROSS DOMESTIC PRODUCT | 591,765 | | 4.407 | 793,654 | | 3.877 | 1,175,022 | | 4.125 | 2,132,955 | 3.941 | |

Sources:  1963, 1967, 1972, 1976–1980 gross products: S-819–S-822. 1963, 1967, 1972 value added attributed to timber: P-476 (data may not add due to rounding). 1976–1980 average annual value added attributed to timber: our estimate (see note 4).

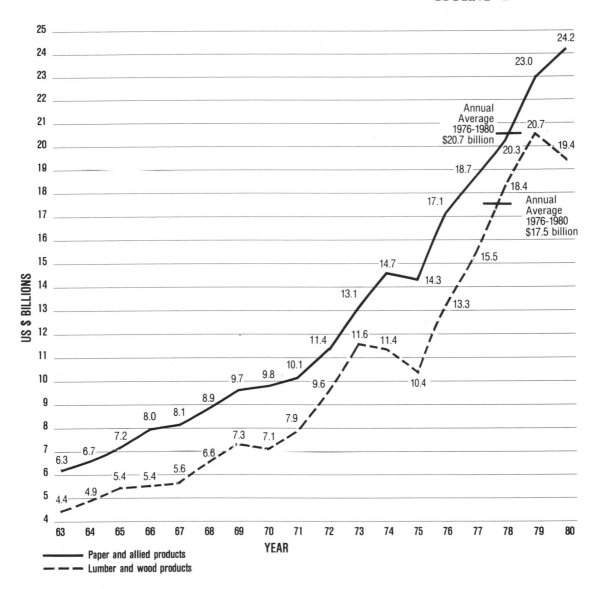

Fig. 2.1   **Annual gross products (current U.S. dollars) of paper and allied products and lumber and wood products from 1963 to 1980. Source: U.S. Department of Commerce, Bureau of Economic Analysis. See note 4 for explanation.**

consumption of timber products was in decline until 1970 and is now rising (fig. 2.3). Total timber consumption reached a low of 11,741 million cubic feet in the early 1960s and has risen steadily since then (fig. 2.4).

Timber is consumed primarily in three ways. It is burned for fuel; it is pulped and turned into paper and other reconstituted products; and it is used as wood as a raw material in its own right. In many developing countries most of the timber

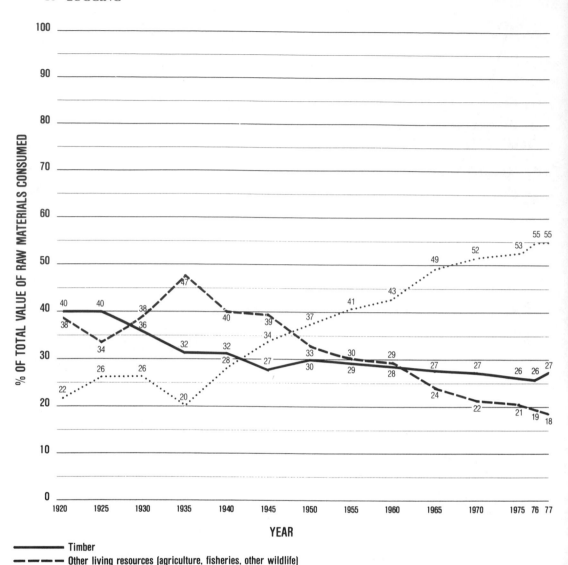

Fig. 2.2  **Relative importance (in terms of dollar value) of timber, other living resources, and minerals as sources of raw materials in the U.S. economy. Source: S-800**

consumed is burned for fuel (D-384, P-365). In the United States and Canada (as in other industrialized countries) the opposite is the case. Of the 15,122 million cubic feet that the United States currently consumes each year, 8,766 million cubic feet (58.0%) is used as wood (lumber, plywood and veneer, and other industrial wood products), 4,637 million cubic feet (30.6%) is converted into pulp products, and 1,719 million cubic feet (11.4%) is burned as fuel (figs. 2.4 and 2.5). Every year each person in the United States consumes an average of 39.3

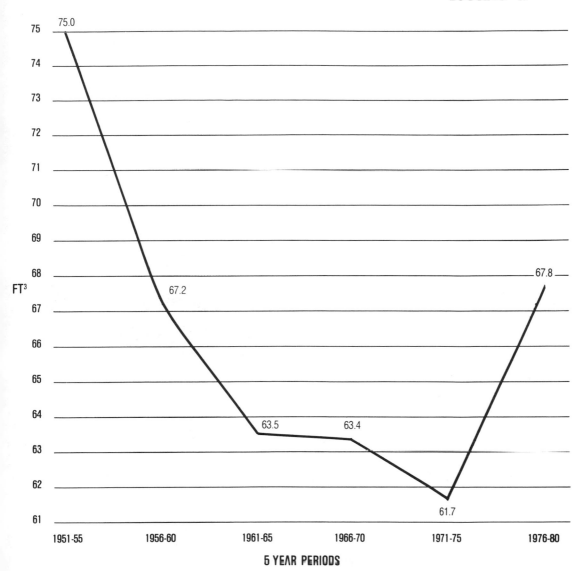

FT³

Fig. 2.3   **Per capita consumption of timber products in the United States in cubic feet: annual average per 5-year period from 1951–55 to 1976–80. Source: S-797**

cubic feet of wood products, 20.8 cubic feet of pulp products, and 7.7 cubic feet of fuelwood (fig. 2.6). To clarify this distinction among the three main uses of timber, we use the word *wood* unqualified by the prefixes *pulp-* or *fuel-* to mean only lumber, plywood and veneer, other industrial wood (cooperage logs, poles and piling, mine timbers, shingle bolts, and so on), and their products. We use the word *timber* to refer collectively to wood as defined above plus pulpwood and its products plus fuelwood.

Figures 2.4 and 2.6 show that in the United States wood consumption as a

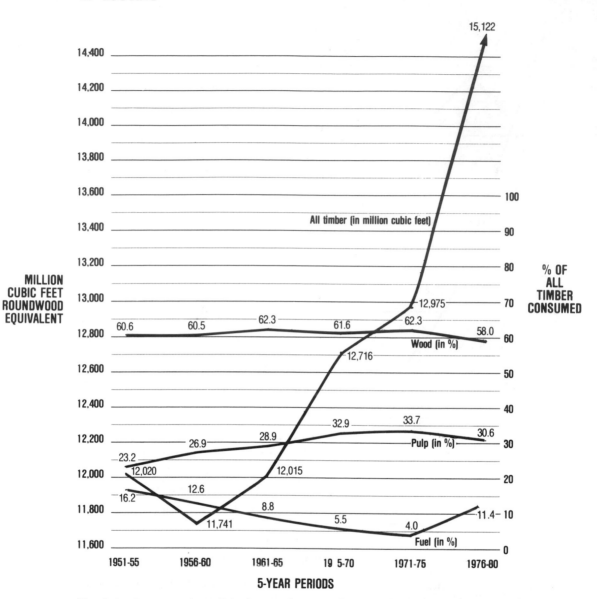

Fig. 2.4  Consumption of timber products in the United States: annual average per 5-year period from 1951–55 to 1976–80; and percentage consumed as wood products, pulp products, and fuelwood. Source: S-797

proportion of total timber consumption has been fairly stable over the past 25 years. Consumption of pulp products, however, rose steadily from around 3,000 million cubic feet (a quarter of the total) in the mid-1950s to almost one-and-a-half times that (and a third of the total) in the early 1970s. Since then the relative importance of pulp has declined, but consumption remains much above the

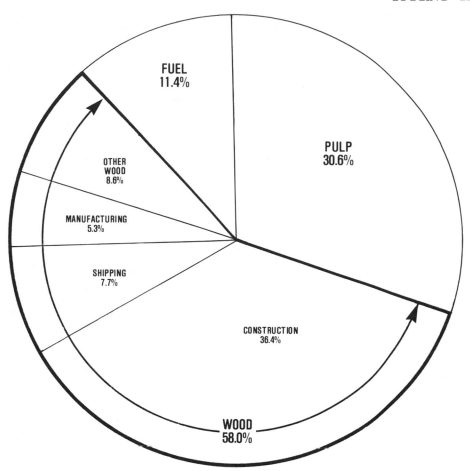

Fig. 2.5 **Consumption of timber by major product group in the United States, 1976–1980. Source: S-797**

level of a quarter century ago and is expected to resume its growth. By contrast, fuelwood consumption (overall and as a proportion of the total) continued its sharp decline until the early 1970s, reaching an all-time low of 475 million cubic feet (3.5% of the total) in 1972 (S-797). Since then it has been rising very rapidly. Broadly speaking, the three main groups of timber products—wood, pulp, and fuel—demonstrate three contrasting trends: an apparent stability masking changes in the relative importance of different wood products; fairly steady growth as a result of innovation in pulp products; and rescue from imminent obsolescence in the case of fuel. These trends have a great impact on the types of timber used, hence on the kinds of trees that are in demand, and hence on the current and future proportion of timber production from wild (naturally regenerated) trees. The following sections discuss the three main uses of timber with the question of demand and production in mind. Unless stated otherwise, all

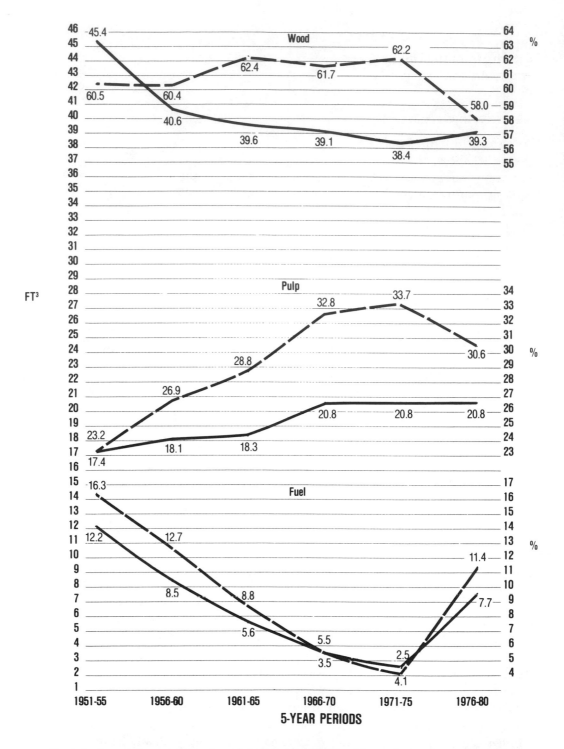

Fig. 2.6  **Per capita consumption of timber in the United States by major product group: annual average per 5-year period from 1951–55 to 1976–80. Solid lines: ft³, dashed lines, %. Source: S-797**

22

data are from the USDA Forest Service's statistics (S-797, S-817) and its major study, *An analysis of the timber situation in the United States, 1952–2030* (S-800).

*Wood Products*

As shown in figures 2.4–2.6, most timber is consumed in the form of wood. Figure 2.7 shows the main U.S. domestic markets for wood products. The construction industry is by far the biggest consumer, accounting for just under 63% of total wood consumption (and just over 36% of total timber consumption). The next largest markets are shipping, which accounts for 13% of wood consumption (almost 8% of timber consumption), and manufacturing, which accounts for 9% of wood consumption (5% of timber consumption). The

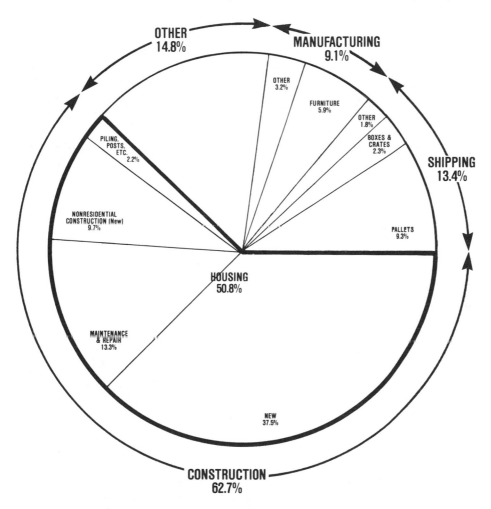

Fig. 2.7 **Consumption of wood (lumber, plywood, and veneer and other industrial wood) by major market in the United States, 1976–1980. Source: S-797**

Table 2.7  **Wood consumption in the United States by major sectors, 1962, 1970, 1976, with extrapolation to annual average, 1976–1980**

| SECTOR | LUMBER Million bd. ft. | % | Million ft³ | PLYWOOD Million ft² | % | Million ft³ | TOTAL Million ft³ | % of wood | % of timber | OTHER INDUSTRIAL % of timber | million ft³ | million ft² | BOARD million ft² | % |
|---|---|---|---|---|---|---|---|---|---|---|---|---|---|---|
| *1962* | | | | | | | | | | | | | | |
| New housing | 13,940 | 37.4 | 2,156 | 4,180 | 35.7 | 312 | 2,468 | 37.2 | | | | | 2,760 | 28.7 |
| Housing maintenance and repair | 4,400 | 11.8 | 680 | 1,030 | 8.8 | 77 | 757 | 11.4 | | | | | 1,415 | 14.7 |
| HOUSING TOTAL | | | | | | | | 48.6 | | | | | | |
| New nonresidential construction | 4,200 | 11.2 | 646 | 1,690 | 14.4 | 126 | 772 | 11.6 | | | | | 1,050 | 10.9 |
| CONSTRUCTION TOTAL | | | | | | | | 60.2 | | | | | | |
| Manufacturing | 4,240 | 11.4 | 657 | 1,870 | 16.0 | 140 | 797 | 12.0 | | | | | 1,790 | 18.7 |
| Shipping | 4,340 | 11.6 | 669 | * | * | | 669 | 10.1 | | | | | | |
| All other | 6,180 | 16.6 | 957 | 2,946 | 25.1 | 220 | 1,177 | 17.7 | | | | | 2,593 | 27.0 |
| TOTAL | 37,300 | | 5,765 | 11,716 | | 875 | 6,640 | | | | 465 | | 9,608 | |
| *1970* | | | | | | | | | | | | | | |
| New housing | 12,270 | 31.1 | 1,857 | 6,330 | 35.5 | 415 | 2,272 | 31.8 | | | | | | |
| Housing maintenance and repair | 4,690 | 11.9 | 710 | 2,510 | 14.1 | 165 | 875 | 12.3 | | | | | | |
| HOUSING TOTAL | | | | | | | | 44.1 | | | | | | |
| New nonresidential construction | 4,700 | 11.9 | 710 | 1,939 | 10.9 | 127 | 837 | 11.7 | | | | | | |
| CONSTRUCTION TOTAL | | | | | | | | 55.8 | | | | | | |
| Manufacturing | 4,670 | 11.8 | 705 | 1,656 | 9.3 | 109 | 814 | 11.4 | | | | | | |
| Shipping | 5,720 | 14.5 | 866 | 591 | 3.3 | 39 | 905 | 12.7 | | | | | | |
| All other | 7,450 | 18.8 | 1,122 | 4,796 | 26.9 | 315 | 1,437 | 20.1 | | | | | | |
| TOTAL | 39,500 | | 5,970 | 17,822 | | 1,170 | 7,140 | | | | 425 | | | |
| *1976* | | | | | | | | | | | | | | |
| New housing | 16,555 | 38.8 | 2,512 | 8,410 | 40.9 | 614 | 3,126 | 39.2 | | | | | 3,540 | 26.2 |
| Housing maintenance and repair | 5,690 | 13.3 | 861 | 3,350 | 16.3 | 245 | 1,106 | 13.9 | | | | | 2,160 | 16.0 |
| HOUSING TOTAL | | | | | | | | 53.1 | | | | | | |
| New nonresidential construction | 4,470 | 10.5 | 680 | 1,875 | 9.1 | 136 | 816 | 10.2 | | | | | 1,095 | 8.1 |
| CONSTRUCTION TOTAL | | | | | | | | 63.3 | | | | | | |
| Piling | | | | | | | | | | | 27 | | | |
| Poles | | | | | | | | | | | 90 | | | |
| Mine timber | | | | | | | | | | | 24 | | | |
| Posts | | | | | | | | | | | 46 | | | |
| "Construction" | | | | | | | | | | | | | | |
| Total | | | | | | | | | | 1.3 | 187 | | | |

24

| | | | | | | | | | | | | |
|---|---|---|---|---|---|---|---|---|---|---|---|---|
| Manufacturing | 4,300 | 10.1 | 654 | 1,550 | 7.5 | 112 | 766 | 9.6 | 0.1 | 16 | 3,480 | 25.7 |
| Shipping | 6,900 | 16.1 | 1,043 | 738 | 3.6 | 54 | 1,097 | 13.8 | 1.2 | 177 | 3,248 | 24.0 |
| All other | 4,725 | 11.2 | 725 | 4,638 | 22.6 | 339 | 1,064 | 13.3 | 2.6 | 380 | | |
| TOTAL | 42,700 | | 6,475 | 20,561 | | 1,500 | 7,975 | | | | 13,523 | |

Cooperage
Other

*1976–1980*

| | | | | | | | |
|---|---|---|---|---|---|---|---|
| New housing | | | | | 39.2 | 21.7 | |
| Housing maintenance and repair | | | | | 13.9 | 7.7 | |
| HOUSING TOTAL | | | | | 53.1 | 29.4 | |
| New nonresidential construction | | | | | 10.2 | 5.7 | |
| CONSTRUCTION TOTAL | | | | 192 | 63.3 | 35.1 | 1.3 |
| Manufacturing | | | | 16 | 9.6 | 5.3 | 0.1 |
| Shipping | | | | 182 | 13.8 | 7.6 | 1.2 |
| All other | | | | | 13.3 | 7.4 | 2.6 |
| | | | | | | 55.4 | |
| TOTAL | 6,846 | 1,507 | 8,376† | 390 | | 100.0 | |

Sources: S-797, S-800, S-817.
*Included in "All other."
†Includes logs (imports).

25

proportion of wood consumption accounted for by construction has been fairly stable over the past two decades, ranging from 55% to 63% (table 2.7). It is in fact even larger than figure 2.7 suggests, because the "Other" category of markets includes uses of wood for construction—such as nonresidential maintenance and repair, roof and siding shingles and shakes, and made-at-home products such as furniture and boats—for which data on the amounts consumed are not available.

Table 2.7 shows that manufacturing has declined in importance and that shipping has replaced it as the number-two market for wood. However, this decline applies only with respect to volume. In terms of value of production and contribution to gross domestic product, manufacturing remains a larger wood market than shipping, since it uses wood with a higher average unit cost and its products require more processing. It is not possible to provide a breakdown of value corresponding to that in figure 2.7, but table 2.8 provides a rough indication of the relative contribution of value added of the three major markets. All three major wood markets (construction, shipping, and manufacturing) illustrate the two great strengths of the wood-products industry: its conservatism, in that the industry relies on wood's intrinsic qualities; and its capacity for innovation, in that new products and technologies are developed in response to competing materials, rising costs, and fewer choice trees. This paradoxical combination is the basis of wood's continuing importance as a raw material.

Housing is by far the most important construction market, particularly the building of new housing. It is the largest single market for timber products in the United States, in 1976 using some 39% of the lumber, 41% of the plywood, and large amounts of wood- and pulp-based panel products such as hardboard, insulating board, and particle board. Wood use per square foot in single-family housing units (the biggest of the housing markets, the others being multifamily housing units and mobile homes) has been dropping, mainly because of the decline in lumber use (from 8.5 board feet per square foot in 1962 to 6.8 board feet in 1976). Although use of plywood and board products is growing, it has not made up the difference. The drop is partly due to competition from other materials. Aluminum and steel can be used instead of wood for framing, although since 1973 aluminum has been so much more expensive that it has ceased to be competitive. Similarly, the use of carpeting, either on a concrete-slab floor or over particle board, has led to a decline in the use of oak flooring.

Competing materials probably had their greatest effect as a factor in timber's general decline up to the early 1970s. Since then, however, changes in the types of wood products used have probably been more important. The three most important changes are a greater use of prefabricated housing components, the increasing substitution of plywood for lumber, and the rise of new panel products, all of which have tended to lower the average use of lumber largely through better design and reduced waste. The substitution of plywood for lumber in sheathing, subflooring, and similar uses is probably close to the saturation

Table 2.8 **Value added attributable to timber in construction, shipping, and furniture manufacturing in the United States, 1972, and annual average, 1976–1980 (U.S.$ million)**

|  | 1972 | ANN. AVE. 1976–1980 |
|---|---|---|
| Construction | 11,947 | 19,842 |
| Wooden containers* | 324 | 745 (est.) |
| Furniture and fixtures† | 1,820 | 2,663 |

*Includes all the industries included as "Shipping" in fig. 2.7.
†Principal "Manufacturing" market in fig. 2.7.
Source: Table 2.6.

point. For example, in 1972 more than 90% of new single-family houses were built with plywood roof sheathing, as compared with 50% in 1959. Since 1972, in fact, the proportion has dropped to 85%, largely because of the resurgence of lumber as a substrate for shingles. The trends of greater prefabrication and use of new panel products are expected to continue. Almost all doors, windows, and cabinets are now factory-made rather than constructed on site; but there is room for further growth with respect to structural components such as roof and floor trusses, beams and lintels, exterior and interior wall panels, and roof and floor panels. Panels are likely to be made of structural flakeboard, waferboard, and other types of particle board. These are widely used in Canada and are increasingly being used in the United States.

Despite the drop in timber use per square foot of floor area, wood consumption by the housing industry is expected to grow. Several factors are involved (apart from those, such as population growth and the state of the economy, that are external to the industry), but the most important is floor area itself. The unit size of an average single-family house grew from 1,340 square feet in 1962 to 1,750 square feet in 1978 and is expected to grow to 1,975 square feet by 2010. Corresponding increases in multifamily housing units and mobile homes are also projected. Such growth in the past has contributed to the increased consumption of plywood and other panel products. In addition, more new houses use wood as the main exterior siding material and more are built with wooden decks. The popularity of decks continues to rise and has partly offset the drop in wood use caused by the virtual disappearance of the porch, once a standard feature.

The resulting increase in wood consumption is not expected to be directly proportional, because a number of countertrends are likely partly to offset the effect of growth in floor area. More single-family houses are being built on concrete-slab foundations (thus eliminating the wood-joist floor system): 16% of new houses in 1956; 36% in 1970; 40% in 1978. With the shift in population to the South and Southwest, where slab foundations predominate, this trend could well continue. In other parts of the country, however, concrete may give way to the preserved-wood foundation, essentially an extension of the conventional wood frame below the surface, except that the lumber and plywood are treated with preservatives. The advantages of preserved wood over concrete or masonry foundations are that wood foundations can be built by carpenters (not requiring special subcontractors), they can be built year-round (concrete does not set in freezing weather), they provide better insulation, and they are easier and cheaper to finish (P-476).

Another trend that will probably reduce the effect of the growth in floor area is the increasing proportion of two-story houses: from fewer than 10% of new single-family dwellings in 1956 to 28% in 1978. Two-story houses have a smaller roof-area-per-floor-area ratio (lowering the construction cost per square foot and allowing bigger houses on smaller lots), thereby reducing the wood requirement per square foot of floor area. Similarly, more housing is being built with at least one common wall (townhouses, for example), which cuts down on the amount of wood framing, sheathing, and siding needed. All in all, over the next half-century wood use is not expected to grow by more than 2–3%, except for board products generally and except for lumber and plywood in mobile homes (because these are growing very much bigger and presumably very much less mobile). The Forest Service projects that consumption of hardboard, insulating board, and particle board (including waferboard, flakeboard, composite board, and medium-density fiberboard) will at least double by the year 2010. Otherwise, wood consumption by the housing industry is likely to be controlled largely by factors external to the timber industry, notably housing demand and the general condition of the economy.

In addition to new housing there are three construction markets for wood—housing maintenance and repair, nonresidential construction, and a category identified in figure 2.7 as "Piling, posts, etc." The first is self-explanatory. The second includes the construction of new utilities, water and sewer systems, highways and airports, offices, stores, hotels, and other nonresidential buildings. The third, which is basically a category of nonresidential construction, includes wood piling used in the construction of docks, bridges, and buildings; roof supports and other construction in mines; utility poles; and fence posts.

Figure 2.8 shows that, except for board, consumption of wood products per dollar of nonresidential construction declined until 1970. Thereafter lumber consumption virtually stabilized while plywood and board consumption rose. Total consumption of all products grew between 1962 and 1973 but dropped after that. As with housing, many offsetting factors contributed to these trends. Lumber use suffered due to the growing use of plywood and metal to make the structures in which concrete slabs are formed (concrete-forming is the second

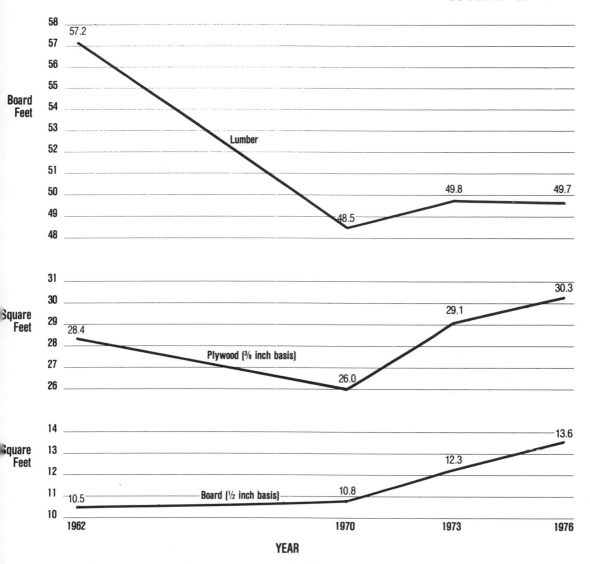

Fig. 2.8   Consumption of lumber, plywood, and board in nonresidential construction per $1,000 of construction expenditure in the United States. Source: S-800

most important use of timber in nonresidential construction—after beams, decking, and other structural components—and the most important use of plywood); the substitution of precast and prestressed concrete beams for concrete formed on site; and increases in the use of metal studs, joists, and decking. Conversely, there has been greater use of large wood trusses, beams, arches, and other structural members in some types of building; of wood siding in some of the smaller buildings; and of interior paneling.

Both conservatism and innovation are at work here. Hardwood flooring has been outsold by wall-to-wall carpeting and synthetic tiles in buildings where initial cost is the main consideration. Where lowest annual maintenance is more important (in bowling alleys, for example), the greater ruggedness and durability of hardwood floors have enabled them to hold their own (J-626). The development of glue-laminated beams and arches (and more recently of press-laminated members) has provided builders of large buildings with greater free-dom of design, uninhibited by the sizes of available sawlogs (P-476). The Forest Service expects that by the year 2010, the consumption of lumber per $1,000 of nonresidential construction expenditure will fall from 49.7 board feet in 1976 to 39.2 board feet; that of plywood will rise from 30.3 square feet in 1976 to between 33.5 and 34.3 square feet; and that of board will rise from 13.6 square feet to 20.6 square feet. Only slightly different projections are made for wood consumption in housing maintenance and repair. Lumber and plywood use per $1,000 expenditure are expected to drop (lumber from 280 board feet in 1976 to 260 board feet in 2010, plywood from 165 square feet in 1976 to 150 square feet in 2010), but board consumption is projected to grow from 80 square feet in 1976 to 115 square feet in 2010.

All told, the construction industry seems likely to remain the most important market for wood for the foreseeable future, and its share of the market will probably not change significantly. The Forest Service's low, medium, and high projections for the year 2010 show the industry accounting for 59–61% of wood consumption—much the same for the next quarter century as for the last (table 2.9).

Shipping, the largest consumer of wood products after construction, has been the fastest growing market for wood during the last two decades and the one that has experienced the greatest changes: the steady decline of wooden boxes and crates, the virtual extinction of slack cooperage, and the rise of the wooden pallet. Wooden boxes and crates are still the preferred means of shipping es-pecially bulky and fragile goods (such as delicate instruments, glass, and ce-ramics) and certain fruits and vegetables; but increased shipping costs and auto-mation have favored containers made of paper, plastic, or metal. In 1948, boxes and crates accounted for 80% of the lumber used in shipping; today they ac-count for 16%. Between 1970 and 1976 the share for boxes and crates of all wood used by shipping dropped from a third to less than a fifth. Cooperage has de-clined even more: from 214.7 million board feet in 1970 to 93.9 million board feet in 1976. Slack cooperage (loose wooden barrels used mainly for shipping food and hardware) has almost disappeared; and tight cooperage (watertight barrels used for storing liquids) has been reduced chiefly to those uses in which the intrinsic qualities of the wood itself are indispensable—for example, white oak barrels for aging bourbon and wine. The "Other" shipping category in figure 2.7 includes cooperage and wood used in blocking, bracing, and dunnage (a splendid word for the material wedged between or beneath goods being shipped to prevent damage or spoilage) in railroad cars, trucks, and ships.

Table 2.9  USDA Forest Service low, medium, and high projections of U.S. wood consumption in 2010

| Sector | LUMBER | | | PLYWOOD | | | TOTAL | | BOARD | |
|---|---|---|---|---|---|---|---|---|---|---|
| | Million bd ft | % | Billion bd ft | Million ft² | % | Billion bd ft | Billion bd ft | % | Million ft² | % |
| *Low* | | | | | | | | | | |
| New housing | 20,170 | 33.9 | 18.8 | 10,005 | 33.3 | 4.3 | 23.1 | 33.9 | 6,895 | 23.8 |
| Housing maintenance and repair | 8,140 | 13.7 | 7.6 | 4,760 | 15.8 | 2.0 | 9.6 | 14.1 | 4,800 | 16.5 |
| HOUSING TOTAL | | 47.6 | | | 49.1 | | | 48.0 | | |
| New nonresidential construction | 6,240 | 10.5 | 5.8 | 4,210 | 14.0 | 1.8 | 7.6 | 11.1 | 3,350 | 11.5 |
| CONSTRUCTION TOTAL | | 58.1 | | | 63.1 | | | 59.1 | | |
| Manufacturing | 6,050 | 10.2 | 5.6 | 1,900 | 6.3 | 0.8 | 6.4 | 9.4 | 6,805 | 23.5 |
| Shipping | 11,650 | 19.6 | 10.9 | 1,370 | 4.6 | 0.6 | 11.5 | 16.9 | | |
| All other | 7,190 | 12.1 | 6.7 | 7,805 | 26.0 | 3.3 | 10.0 | 14.6 | 7,150 | 24.6 |
| TOTAL | 59,440 | | 55.4 | 30,050 | | 12.8 | 68.2 | | 29,000 | |
| *Medium* | | | | | | | | | | |
| New housing | 23,010 | 35.2 | 21.5 | 11,430 | 34.8 | 4.9 | 26.4 | 35.2 | 7,805 | 24.4 |
| Housing maintenance and repair | 8,390 | 12.3 | 7.8 | 4,900 | 14.9 | 2.1 | 9.9 | 13.2 | 4,950 | 15.5 |
| HOUSING TOTAL | | 47.6 | | | 48.4 | | | 48.4 | | |
| New nonresidential construction | 6,810 | 10.4 | 6.3 | 4,540 | 13.8 | 1.9 | 8.2 | 10.9 | 3,650 | 11.4 |
| CONSTRUCTION TOTAL | | 58.1 | | | 59.3 | | | 59.3 | | |
| Manufacturing | 6,790 | 10.4 | 6.3 | 2,150 | 6.6 | 0.9 | 7.2 | 9.6 | 7,730 | 24.2 |
| Shipping | 12,570 | 19.3 | 11.8 | 1,480 | 4.5 | 0.6 | 12.4 | 16.5 | | |
| All other | 7,740 | 11.9 | 7.3 | 8,340 | 25.4 | 3.6 | 10.9 | 14.5 | 7,815 | 24.5 |
| TOTAL | 65,310 | | 61.0 | 32,840 | | 14.0 | 75.0 | | 31,950 | |
| *High* | | | | | | | | | | |
| New housing | 27,190 | 37.5 | 25.5 | 13,525 | 37.2 | 5.7 | 31.2 | 37.4 | 9,190 | 26.0 |
| Housing maintenance and repair | 8,730 | 12.0 | 8.1 | 5,100 | 14.0 | 2.2 | 10.3 | 12.4 | 5,150 | 14.5 |
| HOUSING TOTAL | | 49.5 | | | 49.8 | | | 49.8 | | |
| New nonresidential construction | 7,430 | 10.2 | 6.9 | 4,900 | 13.4 | 2.1 | 9.0 | 10.8 | 3,990 | 11.3 |
| CONSTRUCTION TOTAL | | 59.7 | | | 60.6 | | | 60.6 | | |
| Manufacturing | 7,500 | 10.3 | 7.0 | 2,370 | 6.5 | 1.0 | 8.0 | 9.6 | 8,590 | 24.3 |
| Shipping | 13,440 | 18.5 | 12.6 | 1,590 | 4.4 | 0.7 | 13.3 | 15.9 | | |
| All other | 8,310 | 11.5 | 7.8 | 8,905 | 24.5 | 3.8 | 11.6 | 13.9 | 8,480 | 23.9 |
| TOTAL | 72,600 | | 67.9 | 36,390 | | 15.5 | 83.4 | | 35,400 | |

Source: S-800.

The rise in wood use in shipping is entirely due to the growth in demand for pallets. In 1948, pallets accounted for 4% of the lumber used in shipping; today they account for 71%. Between 1970 and 1976 the share for pallets of all wood used in shipping rose from just over half to well over two-thirds. In 1978, 270 million pallets were produced, as compared with 196 million in 1976 and 62 million in 1960. On average, each pallet required 25 board feet of lumber and 2 square feet of plywood. The Forest Service projects continued increases in pallet output to between 445 and 525 million by 2010. Although lumber consumption per pallet is expected to fall slightly (to 22 board feet), plywood consumption is expected to increase (to 2.5 square feet). Overall, by 2010 shipping is projected to require between 11.5 and 13.3 billion board feet of lumber and plywood, most of it for use in pallets, and to account for 16–17% of wood consumption in the United States.

The manufacturing sector is the third major domestic market for wood by volume and the second by value. It includes the making of sports equipment, games and toys, musical instruments, agricultural implements, and a great variety of other products. Together these markets account for about a third of the wood consumed in manufacturing and just over 3% of total wood consumption. Several of them, notably sports equipment and musical instruments, although tiny compared with housing or shipping, have specialized requirements that commit them to particular timber species. For example, baseball bats are made from ash (*Fraxinus* species); hockey sticks from extremely tough species such as rock elm (*Ulmus thomasii*), white ash (*Fraxinus americana*), and hickory (*Carya* species); and bowling pins are made of hard maple (*Acer saccharum* and *A. nigrum*), which provides maximum resistance to splitting. Hard maple is also regarded as the only flooring material able to withstand the constant, heavy wear of bowling alleys (J-626).

In gross terms the only significant consumer of wood in the manufacturing sector is the furniture industry. Furniture making takes two-thirds of the wood used by this market and accounts for 6% of wood consumption in the United States. However, wood use in furniture has been gradually falling over the past two decades, reflecting wood's replacement by plastics and fiberglass and the growing use of particle board instead of lumber as corestock. There are signs of consumer resistance to plastic, so the former trend may not continue. The latter almost certainly will, however, since particle board is cheaper and easier to use than lumber.

Collectively, construction, shipping, manufacturing, and other U.S. markets consume almost 9 billion cubic feet of wood products. The Forest Service projects that consumption will continue to grow, reaching 12–14.5 billion cubic feet by the year 2010. At those levels wood products will make up about 52% of total timber consumption, a significantly smaller proportion than that prevailing between the 1950s and today (around 60%). The difference is accounted for by pulp products, whose remarkable growth since the early 1950s is expected to continue, and by fuelwood, whose resurgence has just begun.

*Pulp Products*

Currently pulp products make up almost 31% of timber consumption; by 2010 they are expected to account for 40%. Total and per capita consumption of pulp products have been rising steadily since 1920. Today the average annual consumption of paper and board is 68.9 million tons—twice the amount in the 1950s and more than eight times the amount in 1920 (when it was under 8 million tons). Each person in the United States consumes 618 pounds of pulp products a year—one-and-a-half times per capita consumption in the 1950s and more than four times the 145 pounds each person consumed in 1920 (table 2.10).

This growth is due in part to increases in economic activity and disposable personal income, but it is also due to the development of new paper products, such as milk cartons and computer paper, and to the substitution of paper products for lumber and metals in shipping, construction, and other industries. The rate of growth has been declining since 1966–1970, when per capita consumption grew by almost 18% more than in the period 1961–1965; currently the growth rate is about 5%, and it is expected to decline further as a result of saturation of some markets for paper products and penetration of others by plastics and other rival materials. However, the growth is not expected to end; the Forest Service projects that per capita consumption of paper and board will rise to between 1,042 and 1,082 pounds by the year 2010 and will have doubled (to at least 1,260 pounds) by 2030.

The raw materials used to make paper and board are wood pulp, waste paper, and other fibers, such as cotton and bagasse (cane or beet refuse from sugar-making). Dollar bills, for example, are made from a cotton- and linen-rag pulp. The amount of fibrous material needed to make a ton of paper has slowly but surely dropped from more than a ton in the 1940s to less than a ton today (table 2.11).

At the same time, the proportion of wood pulp used in the production of paper and board has risen from 59% to 79%, while the proportions of waste paper and other fibers have dropped correspondingly. Probably the chief reason for this trend is the concentration of the paper and board industry into large, vertically integrated complexes designed to use as much as possible of the timber that is logged. This concentration also partly accounts for the gradual reduction in the amount of pulpwood required to produce a ton of wood pulp (table 2.12), although the shift from sulfite and soda pulping processes to the higher yielding sulfate and semichemical processes is probably a larger factor. The reduction in pulpwood required per ton of wood pulp would likely be greater were it not for the increase in the proportion of bleached and semibleached grades. For these reasons, and also because of the increasing use of hardwoods (which yield more

Table 2.10 **Consumption of pulp products in the United States, 1951–55 to 1976–80**

| | PAPER (INCL. BUILDING PAPER) | | PAPERBOARD (INCL. WET MACHINE BOARD) | | BUILDING BOARD (HARDBOARD, INSULATING BOARD, ETC.) | | TOTAL | |
|---|---|---|---|---|---|---|---|---|
| | Total (1,000 tn) | Per capita (lb) | Total (1,000 tn) | Per capita (lb) | Total (1,000 tn) | Per capita (lb) | Total (1,000 tn) | Per capita (lb) |
| 1951–55 | 17,904 | 223 | 12,160 | 151 | 1,424 | 18 | 31,488 | 393 |
| 1956–60 | 20,738 | 237 | 14,512 | 166 | 1,783 | 21 | 37,033 | 424 |
| 1961–65 | 24,343 | 257 | 17,882 | 189 | 2,255 | 24 | 44,479 | 470 |
| 1966–70 | 30,259 | 301 | 22,580 | 225 | 2,692 | 27 | 55,532 | 553 |
| 1971–75 | 33,613 | 317 | 25,217 | 238 | 3,505 | 33 | 62,335 | 588 |
| 1976–80 | 37,650 | 338 | 27,546 | 247 | 3,717 | 33 | 68,913 | 618 |

Source: S-797, S-817.
Note: Data may not add due to independent rounding.

Table 2.11   **Consumption of fibrous materials per ton of paper and board produced in the United States: annual average per 5-year period, 1941–45 to 1976–80**

| | TOTAL | WOOD PULP | | WASTE PAPER | | OTHER | |
|---|---|---|---|---|---|---|---|
| | *tn* | *tn* | *% of total* | *tn* | *% of total* | *tn* | *% of total* |
| 1941–45 | 1.072 | 0.629 | 58.7 | 0.366 | 34.1 | 0.077 | 7.2 |
| 1946–50 | 1.069 | 0.652 | 61.0 | 0.351 | 32.8 | 0.066 | 6.2 |
| 1951–55 | 1.067 | 0.702 | 65.8 | 0.317 | 29.7 | 0.049 | 4.6 |
| 1956–60 | 1.046 | 0.736 | 70.4 | 0.276 | 26.4 | 0.035 | 3.3 |
| 1961–65 | 1.031 | 0.764 | 74.1 | 0.242 | 23.5 | 0.025 | 2.4 |
| 1966–70 | 1.023 | 0.798 | 78.0 | 0.207 | 20.2 | 0.018 | 1.8 |
| 1971–75 | 1.015 | 0.802 | 79.0 | 0.200 | 19.7 | 0.014 | 1.4 |
| 1976–80 | 0.988 | 0.781 | 79.0 | 0.195 | 19.7 | 0.012 | 1.2 |

Sources: S-797, S-817.
Note: Data may not add or percentages total 100 due to rounding.

pulp per unit of wood than do softwoods), the Forest Service estimates that pulpwood consumption per ton of wood pulp produced will continue its slow decline to about 1.4 cords by the year 2030.

*Fuelwood*

Firewood was the main source of household energy in the United States until the 1880s, after which it was progressively displaced by fossil fuels and electricity. By 1970 fewer than 2% of U.S. households used wood as their primary heating fuel and fewer than 1% used it as their primary cooking fuel. Since 1973, rises in the costs of crude oil, coal, and natural gas have transformed the picture of fuelwood from one of virtual extinction as a commodity to that of a bright "new" resource. A growing number of households use wood as the primary

Table 2.12   **Consumption of pulpwood per ton of wood pulp produced in the United States: annual average per 5-year period, 1941–45 to 1976–1980**

| | PULPWOOD CORDS | | PULPWOOD CORDS |
|---|---|---|---|
| 1941–45 | 1.63 | 1961–65 | 1.56 |
| 1946–50 | 1.64 | 1966–70 | 1.53 |
| 1951–55 | 1.61 | 1971–75 | 1.53 |
| 1956–60 | 1.61 | 1976–80 | 1.51 |

Sources: S-797, S-817.

source of heating, and many more use it as a supplementary source. In 1969, 44% of new single-family houses were built with fireplaces; in 1976, 58% were. The number of woodstoves in use is also going up.

Fuelwood's sudden and rapid recovery took analysts unawares. In the late 1970s annual fuelwood consumption was estimated to be around 674 million cubic feet (or 4.7% of total timber consumption) and rising. The Forest Service projected this growth to continue into the next century, reaching between 1,600 million cubic feet (low projection) and 2,300 million cubic feet (high projection) by the year 2010, when fuelwood would make up 7–8% of the nation's total timber consumption. In fact it is now believed that these levels had already been reached by the time these projections were being made. It is now estimated that average annual fuelwood consumption for 1976–1980 was 1,719 million cubic feet—or 11.4% of total timber consumption. In a period of sharp decline our annual averages overestimate, in one of rapid growth they underestimate: by 1980 fuelwood consumption was well above our average for the period—3,120 million cubic feet (or 20% of total timber consumption), which happens to equal the Forest Service's high projection for the year 2030 (when it was expected to account for 9% of total consumption).

Projection is the art of going out on a limb. Every resource analyst is aware that the chain saw of reality can suddenly lop off the limb and bring him or her back down to earth. The Forest Service's estimates were the best that could be made on the basis of the available data; with new data come revised estimates. The resurgence of fuelwood consumption in response to higher fossil-fuel prices was taken into account but proved to be of much more importance than realized. Will current growth rates be maintained? Probably not. Table 2.13 shows

Table 2.13  **Estimated rate of growth of U.S. annual fuelwood production and consumption, 1972–1980**

|  | MILLION FT$^3$ | CHANGE (%) |
|---|---|---|
| 1972 | 475 | — |
| 1973 | 505 | 6.3 |
| 1974 | 535 | 5.9 |
| 1975 | 570 | 6.5 |
| 1976 | 600 | 5.0 |
| 1977 | 1,030 | 71.7 |
| 1978 | 1,570 | 52.4 |
| 1979 | 2,275 | 44.9 |
| 1980 | 3,120 | 37.1 |

Source: S-817.

that the biggest jump in consumption (about 72%) occurred between 1976 and 1977 and that, although comparatively they are still very high, growth rates have been declining since then. With the softening of oil prices in the early 1980s it is likely that this decline is continuing. Does this mean that the apparent comeback of fuelwood is a flash in the pan? Again, probably not. The softening of fossil-fuel prices is due to a fall in demand caused first by readjustment of the global economy to the previous high prices and then by recession. The consequent glut of oil is expected to be temporary. Fossil-fuel prices are virtually certain to rise again, and fuelwood consumption will probably continue growing as a result. In due course the supply of competitively priced firewood will become a problem and could quickly become a major constraint if growth in consumption does not fall below 10%.

More than three-quarters of current fuelwood consumption is domestic; the rest is industrial, primarily located in pulpmills and other timber-processing plants. Fuelwood used by the timber industry consists mainly of wastes from the manufacturing process: sawdust, shavings, odds and ends, and pulping residue. In 1976 pulpmills used 5 million tons (dry weight) of bark and 61 million tons of spent liquor solids for fuel. In the future most of the bark and wood wastes not sold for pulp or particle board is likely to be burned in order to meet as much as possible of the energy needs of the timber industry. Utilities and other industries use only a small amount of wood wastes and bark. If fuelwood is to make a significant contribution to industrial energy needs, it will have to be harvested expressly for the purpose. Not enough is known about either the economies or the environmental effects of large-scale use of wood for fuel to say with confidence that fuelwood could or should be a major energy source for industry or for power utilities. For the time being the Forest Service is assuming that almost all the anticipated growth in fuelwood consumption will come from the residential sector.


## Chemical By-products

Some of the wastes from pulp and board manufacture are processed into valuable chemical products. In 1977 (the latest year for which there are comprehensive economic data) the U.S. timber industry produced $449.8 million of biochemicals (A-922). Biochemical by-products also accounted for an annual average of $34.5 million (0.5%) of the $7,524.9 million a year of timber imports during 1976–1980 (S-450–S-454). These figures include rosin, turpentine, and terpenes obtained from living trees and from steam-distilled wood. In the following discussion we refer to these biochemicals and to biochemical by-products collectively as silvichemicals. Silvichemicals fall into three main groups: naval stores, lignin products, and other products. They are listed in table 2.14 together with the value of their U.S. production in 1977.

Naval stores is by far the largest of the three groups, accounting for 76% of the value of U.S. silvichemical production (table 2.14). Originally the term meant the pitch and rosin obtained from pine trees to caulk the timbers and preserve the rigging of sailing ships. Now it is applied to four types of silvichemicals (tall oil, rosin, turpentine, and terpenes) derived largely from pines. Naval stores are obtained in three ways: by tapping the gummy exudate (oleoresin) of living trees; by steam-distilling wood (chiefly stumps); and as a by-product of the sulfate pulping process. More than 85% of world production of oleoresin from living trees comes from six species of pine: slash pine (*Pinus elliottii*) and longleaf pine (*P. palustris*) in the United States; Scots pine (*P. sylvestris*) in the USSR and northern Europe; Masson pine (*P. massoniana*) and *P. tabulaeformis* in China; and maritime pine (*P. pinaster*) in France, Italy, Portugal, and Spain (A-1170). Slash and longleaf pines are the only two species that have ever been important for gum (oleoresin) production in the United States because the oleoresins of the other southern pines tend to crystallize quickly once exposed to air and moisture and do not flow freely when tapped regularly (G-536).

Production of naval stores in the United States has remained stable through-out this century but the relative importance of the three sources has changed (A-922, G-536, J-110). In the early 1900s all U.S. naval stores were obtained by tapping. From the 1930s steam distillation of stumps became the more impor-tant source (J-110). Today both these sources have been virtually replaced by the sulfate process, which now provides 79% of the value of U.S. naval stores' production (compared to 18% from pine stumps and 3% from living trees) (table 2.14).

Tall oil (including tall oil rosin) accounts for 67% of the value of U.S. naval stores' production (table 2.14). It is recovered from the spent cooking liquors of the sulfate pulping process and distilled into rosin (discussed below with the other sources of rosin), fatty acids, and an intermediate material (a mixture of rosin and fatty acids) called distilled tall oil. Currently about half the tall oil fatty acid production is used to make polyamide resins for adhesives, coatings, and inks; about a quarter is used in paints, varnishes, and other protective coatings; and the remainder goes into soaps and detergents, hard floor coverings, and other products. Distillation of tall oil also produces a volatile "heads" fraction (used as a cheap chemical in ore flotation, particularly in the phosphate industry) and a "pitch" fraction at the bottom of the still (which has little use except as boiler fuel) (S-800).

Rosin is the next most valuable naval stores' product, accounting for 42% of U.S. production (including tall oil rosin) (table 2.14). The three sources of rosin (tall oil from sulfate pulping, pine stumps, and pine tree tappings) are essentially interchangeable for many uses, although not for all since the sulfur impurities in tall oil rosin inactivate certain catalysts (S-800). The two major uses of rosin, together making up about 70% of U.S. consumption, are in the manufacture of chemicals and synthetic rubber (as emulsifying and tackifying agents) and in paper sizing (to control water absorptivity). Another 20% is used in ester gums (for example, chewing gum) and synthetic resins; the rest goes into paint varnishes, lacquers, and adhesives (A-922, S-800).

Turpentine and terpenes account for 8% and 6%, respectively, of the value of U.S. naval stores' production (table 2.14). Most (more than 80%) turpentine is obtained from the relief gases during sulfate pulping; and the same proportion of terpenes is produced from sulfate turpentine (A-922, S-800). The rest of both types of product come from pine stumps and pine tree tappings (table 2.15). Traditionally used as a paint thinner, turpentine today is primarily employed in the synthesis of pine oil (about 50%), the manufacture of terpene resins (15%) and chlorinated insecticides (15%), and in flavors and fragrances (10%). In turn, pine oil is used in disinfectants and cleaners, deodorants, and textile processing; and terpene resins are used mainly in the compounding of pressure-sensitive adhesives (such as Scotch tape) (A-922, S-800). Other uses of terpene resins are in rubber cements, solvents, emulsion-based adhesives, sealants, inks, casting waxes, paints, varnishes, waterproofing agents, and chewing gum bases. Turpentine has been employed as the feedstock for bulk production of synthetic fragrances since the 1950s, notably hydroxycitronellal (lily of the valley), geraniol (rose), ionones (violet), and citral (lemon) (M-1025). Synthetic flavors from turpentine include lemon, lime, peppermint, spearmint, and nutmeg (S-800). Menthol from turpentine is used to flavor cigarettes, chewing gum, toothpaste, and pharmaceuticals (G-832). Turpentine is also the feedstock for synthesis of vitamin A (A-134).

Lignin products are the next most valuable group of silvichemicals after naval stores, making up 13% of the value of U.S. silvichemical production (table 2.14). Virtually all lignosulfonates are produced from the spent liquor from the sulfite pulping process (although about 5% is made from lignin from the sulfate process) (A-922). Lignosulfonates are used as dispersants in oil-drilling muds and as binders for roads and animal-feed pellets. They are also used in vat dyestuffs in the textile industry, agricultural sprays, ore flotation, and in the cement and ceramic industries (D-804).

Last comes a miscellaneous group of products, of which the most important is vanillin. The United States produced $30 million of vanillin in 1977 (table 2.14) and imported another $15 million a year (on average) during 1976–1980, mostly from Canada (S-450–S-454). This silvichemical could with justice be included among the lignin products because it is obtained from sulfite lignosulfonates. North American (United States plus Canada) production of vanillin has grown rapidly, from 700 tons a year in the early 1960s to 8,800 tons a year by the late 1970s (A-922, A-2029). Vanillin is in great demand as a flavor and as an intermediate material for the manufacture of pharmaceuticals; for example, lignosulfonate vanillin is the starting material in the synthesis of L-dopamine, which is used to treat Parkinson's disease (A-2029). Other miscellaneous silvichemicals include torula food yeast, which is grown on the sugars in waste

Table 2.14  Chemical by-products of pulp and wood manufacture and related silvichemicals produced in the United States in 1977 (U.S.$ million)

| PRODUCT GROUP | PULP MANUFACTURE *Relief gases and spent pulping liquor* | | OTHER MANUFACTURE | | PINE STUMPS | PINE TREE TAPPINGS | TOTAL |
|---|---|---|---|---|---|---|---|
| | *Sulfate process* | *Sulfite process* | *Effluent from board manufacture* | *Bark* | | | |
| NAVAL STORES | | | | | | | |
| Gum rosin | | | | | | 7.0 | |
| Steam-distilled rosin | | | | | 56.6 | | |
| Tall oil rosin | 81.2 | | | | | | 144.8 |
| Rosin (total) | | | | | | | |
| Gum turpentine | | | | | | 1.1 | |
| Steam-distilled turpentine | | | | | 3.2 | | |
| Sulfate turpentine | 22.7 | | | | | | |
| Turpentine (total) | | | | | | | 27.0 |
| Pine oil | | | | | | | (19.0) |
| Other terpenes | | | | | | | ( 2.3) |
| Terpenes (total) | 17.9* | | | | 2.6* | 0.8* | 21.3 |
| Distilled tall oil† | 19.6 | | | | | | |
| Tall oil fatty acids | 96.9 | | | | | | |
| Tall oil heads and pitch fractions | 15.0 | | | | | | |

| | | | | | | | |
|---|---|---|---|---|---|---|---|
| Crude tall oil | 19.3 | | | | | | 150.8 |
| *Tall oil (total)* | 272.6 | | | | | | |
| *Total Naval Stores* | | | 62.4 | 8.9 | | | 343.9 |
| LIGNIN PRODUCTS | | | | | | | |
| Sulfate lignin | 3.0 | | | | | | |
| Lignosulfonate, Ca-base | | 26.7 | | | | | |
| Lignosulfonate, Na-base | | 6.5 | | | | | |
| Lignosulfonate, other | | 20.6 | | | | | |
| *Total Lignin Products* | 3.0 | 53.8 | | | | | 56.8 |
| OTHER PRODUCTS | | | | | | | |
| Dimethylsulfide | 3.0 | | | | | | |
| Dimethylsulfoxide | 0.5 | | | | | | |
| Ethyl alcohol, 190-proof | | 5.0 | | | | | |
| Vanillin | | 30.0 | | | | | |
| Torula food yeast | | 6.4 | | | | | |
| Acetic acid, glacial | | 1.6 | | | | | |
| *Other Pulp By-products (total)* | | | | | | | 46.5 |
| Hemicellulose extract | | | | | 0.2 | | |
| Bark wax and bark powder | | | | | | 2.4 | |
| *Other By-products (total)* | | | | | 0.2 | 2.4 | 2.6 |
| *Total Other Products* | 3.5 | 43.0 | | | 0.2 | 2.4 | 49.1 |
| TOTAL | 279.1 | 96.8 | 62.4 | 8.9 | 0.2 | 2.4 | 449.8 |

Source: A-922.

*Proportions derived by using same proportions as for turpentine.

†Includes acid-refined tall oil.

Table 2.15  **Proportion of U.S. timber production supplied by softwoods and hardwoods, by major product group: annual average per 5-year period, 1951–55 to 1976–80**

| | TOTAL | | WOOD PRODUCTS | | | | | | | | | | PULP PRODUCTS | | FUELWOOD | |
| | | | ALL | | LUMBER | | PLYWOOD AND VENEER | | OTHER INDUSTRIAL | | LOGS | | | | | |
| | Million ft³ | % | Million ft³ | % | Million ft³ | % | Million ft³ | % | Million ft³ | % | Million ft³ | % | Million ft³ | % | Million ft³ | % |
|---|---|---|---|---|---|---|---|---|---|---|---|---|---|---|---|---|
| **1951–55** | | | | | | | | | | | | | | | | |
| Softwoods | 7,315 | 67.7 | 5,246 | 75.9 | 4,621 | 80.4 | 290 | 61.6 | 319 | 47.1 | 16 | 76.2 | 1,619 | 83.4 | 450 | 23.1 |
| Hardwoods | 3,490 | 32.3 | 1,670 | 24.1 | 1,125 | 19.6 | 181 | 38.4 | 359 | 52.9 | 5 | 23.8 | 322 | 16.6 | 1,498 | 76.9 |
| All | 10,805 | | 6,916 | | 5,746 | | 471 | | 678 | | 21 | | 1,941 | | 1,948 | |
| **1956–60** | | | | | | | | | | | | | | | | |
| Softwoods | 7,361 | 70.1 | 5,176 | 78.1 | 4,401 | 81.5 | 473 | 74.1 | 276 | 49.5 | 26 | 76.5 | 1,880 | 78.8 | 305 | 20.6 |
| Hardwoods | 3,133 | 29.9 | 1,455 | 21.9 | 1,001 | 18.5 | 165 | 25.9 | 282 | 50.5 | 7 | 20.6 | 505 | 21.2 | 1,173 | 79.4 |
| All | 10,494 | | 6,631 | | 5,402 | | 638 | | 558 | | 33 | | 2,385 | | 1,478 | |
| **1961–65** | | | | | | | | | | | | | | | | |
| Softwoods | 7,627 | 71.4 | 5,435 | 78.9 | 4,301 | 80.5 | 732 | 82.7 | 269 | 52.3 | 133 | 91.1 | 1,990 | 72.8 | 202 | 19.1 |
| Hardwoods | 3,058 | 28.6 | 1,456 | 21.1 | 1,045 | 19.5 | 153 | 17.3 | 245 | 47.7 | 13 | 8.9 | 745 | 27.2 | 857 | 80.9 |
| All | 10,685 | | 6,891 | | 5,346 | | 885 | | 514 | | 146 | | 2,735 | | 1,059 | |
| **1966–70** | | | | | | | | | | | | | | | | |
| Softwoods | 8,531 | 73.8 | 5,848 | 79.6 | 4,298 | 79.2 | 919 | 87.5 | 268 | 54.8 | 363 | 95.5 | 2,543 | 72.2 | 140 | 20.1 |
| Hardwoods | 3,030 | 26.2 | 1,497 | 20.4 | 1,128 | 20.8 | 131 | 12.5 | 221 | 45.2 | 17 | 4.5 | 977 | 27.8 | 556 | 79.9 |
| All | 11,561 | | 7,345 | | 5,426 | | 1,050 | | 489 | | 380 | | 3,520 | | 696 | |
| **1971–75** | | | | | | | | | | | | | | | | |
| Softwoods | 8,907 | 75.4 | 6,066 | 81.8 | 4,263 | 80.2 | 1,105 | 90.4 | 233 | 58.1 | 465 | 96.5 | 2,737 | 70.5 | 104 | 20.1 |
| Hardwoods | 2,913 | 24.6 | 1,354 | 18.2 | 1,052 | 19.8 | 117 | 9.6 | 168 | 41.9 | 17 | 3.5 | 1,146 | 29.5 | 413 | 79.9 |
| All | 11,820 | | 7,420 | | 5,315 | | 1,222 | | 401 | | 482 | | 3,883 | | 517 | |
| **1976–80** | | | | | | | | | | | | | | | | |
| Softwoods | 9,784 | 71.1 | 6,440 | 82.1 | 4,373 | 79.3 | 1,274 | 93.6 | 239 | 61.1 | 554 | 95.8 | 2,925 | 69.7 | 419 | 24.4 |
| Hardwoods | 3,973 | 28.9 | 1,404 | 17.9 | 1,141 | 20.7 | 87 | 6.4 | 152 | 38.9 | 24 | 4.2 | 1,270 | 30.3 | 1,299 | 75.6 |
| All | 13,757 | | 7,844 | | 5,514 | | 1,361 | | 391 | | 578 | | 4,195 | | 1,718 | |

Sources: S-797, S-817.

sulfite liquor and is used to fortify breakfast cereals and other processed foods with amino acids and B-complex vitamins (A-922, A-2029, S-880); hemicellulose extract, concentrated from the effluent from hardboard and insulating board manufacture and sold as feed molasses to fatten cattle; and bark wax (used mainly as a release agent for press platens, as a binder for fireplace logs, and in molding or casting compounds) and bark powder (used as an extender for phenolic plywood glue and for oil-drilling muds) (A-992).

## The Most Important Species

The timber industry divides trees into two species groups—softwoods and hardwoods—depending on whether they are conifers (Coniferae) or flowering plants (Angiospermae). The terms are not completely accurate. Hardwoods include both the hardest woods (woods of the highest relative density), such as lignum vitae of the *Guaiacum* species, and the softest, such as balsa from *Ochroma lagopus* (A-732). The densest North American softwoods, such as slash pine (*Pinus elliottii*) and longleaf pine (*P. palustris*), are considerably harder than low density hardwoods such as quaking aspen (*Populus tremuloides*) and American basswood (*Tilia americana*) (J-256). However, the terms are well established and in this book we use them together with the botanically more descriptive terms, *conifers* (for softwoods) and *broad-leaved trees* (for hardwoods).

Softwoods are much more important than hardwoods to the economies of the United States and Canada. They account for more than 71% of U.S. domestic timber production, providing 82% of the wood and almost 70% of the pulp products (table 2.15). The reason for the dominance of conifers is simple: there are more of them and they are easier to use. As table 2.16 shows, conifers make up 64% of the volume of growing stock on commercial timberland in the United States (see note 5), broad-leaved trees the remaining 36%. Conifers tend to grow in concentrations of one species or in simple communities of a few species. The species that grow together often have similar characteristics and can therefore be logged, sold, and processed together. For example, Douglas fir (*Pseudotsuga menziesii*) and western larch (*Larix occidentalis*) produce lumber that is similar in strength and weight (P-477). Broad-leaved trees tend to grow in mixtures and are more diverse. Because of their comparative uniformity and interchangeability, softwoods are better suited than hardwoods to the demands of the modern timber industry for mass production of standard goods, such as paper and panel products, from standard materials.

Table 2.15 shows that the proportion of hardwoods to softwoods in U.S. domestic timber production declined from 32.3% in the early 1950s to 24.6% in the early 1970s. During these two decades total hardwood production fell, while for most of the period softwood production (and overall production) rose. The decline in hardwood production apparently has ended. During the period 1976–

Table 2.16  **Major tree groups accounting for U.S. timber production**

| TREE GROUPS | GROWING STOCK | | REMOVALS | |
| --- | --- | --- | --- | --- |
| | Million ft³ | % | Thousand ft³ | % |
| Major *Pinus* species | | | | |
| Southern yellow pines | 92,624.4 | 13.0 | 4,421,858 | 31.1 |
| Ponderosa & Jeffrey pines | 38,219.6 | 5.4 | 724,399 | 5.1 |
| Eastern white and red pines | 10,734.8 | 1.5 | 204,877 | 1.4 |
| Western white and sugar pines | 7,420.2 | 1.0 | 165,738 | 1.2 |
| SUBTOTAL | 148,999.0 | 20.9 | 5,516,872 | 38.8 |
| Other major Pinaceae | | | | |
| Douglas fir | 93,501.6 | 13.2 | 1,964,800 | 13.8 |
| Western hemlock | 51,357.7 | 7.2 | 753,398 | 5.3 |
| True firs (western) | 43,496.3 | 6.1 | 503,198 | 3.5 |
| Eastern spruce and balsam fir | 18,969.1 | 2.7 | 249,759 | 1.8 |
| SUBTOTAL | 207,324.7 | 29.2 | 3,471,155 | 24.4 |
| MAJOR PINACEAE SUBTOTAL | 356,323.7 | 50.1 | 8,988,027 | 63.2 |
| Redwood | 4,393.0 | 0.6 | 139,757 | 1.0 |
| Other western conifers | 77,816.9 | 10.9 | 618,353 | 4.3 |
| Other eastern conifers | 19,245.5 | 2.7 | 299,983 | 2.1 |
| TOTAL CONIFERS (SOFTWOODS) | 455,779.1 | 64.1 | 10,046,120 | 70.6 |
| White and red oaks | | | | |
| Select | 38,785.2 | 5.5 | 704,201 | 4.9 |
| Other | 47,903.6 | 6.7 | 904,087 | 6.4 |
| SUBTOTAL | 86,688.8 | 12.2 | 1,608,288 | 11.3 |
| Sweet gum | 13,649.6 | 1.9 | 302,345 | 2.1 |
| Yellow poplar | 11,770.2 | 1.7 | 223,564 | 1.6 |
| Hickory | 14,763.8 | 2.1 | 222,011 | 1.6 |
| Ash, black cherry, and black walnut | 13,587.0 | 1.9 | 204,186 | 1.4 |
| Hard maple | 13,658.1 | 1.9 | 162,832 | 1.1 |
| Yellow birch | 3,366.4 | 0.5 | 50,576 | 0.4 |
| Other eastern broad-leaved trees | 75,959.9 | 10.7 | 1,279,792 | 9.0 |
| Western broad-leaved trees | 21,745.0 | 3.1 | 129,309 | 0.9 |
| TOTAL BROAD-LEAVED TREES (HARDWOODS) | 255,188.8 | 35.9 | 4,182,903 | 29.4 |
| TOTAL SOFTWOODS AND HARDWOODS | 710,967.9 | 100.0 | 14,229,023 | 100.0 |

Source: S-818.

1980 hardwood production rose for the first time in a quarter century, and its share of total production is now higher than it has been since the 1950s. The USDA Forest Service (S-800:69) attributes the change to "increases in furniture and pallet manufacture, and rising fuelwood consumption, the bulk of which comes from hardwoods." The resurgence of fuelwood is clearly a major factor, but a look at table 2.15 suggests that the increased use of hardwood lumber for pallets has been largely offset by declines in other products, such as hardwood flooring. Hardwood lumber production (overall and as a proportion of total lumber production) has fluctuated around the same level since the 1950s. Any recovery has been counterbalanced almost completely by the steady and continuing declines of hardwood plywood and veneer and other industrial wood products. The most impressive and consistent growth in hardwood production has been in production of pulp products: from 322 million cubic feet (16.6%) in the early 1950s to 1,270 million cubic feet (30.3%) today.

Softwoods have long been the preferred raw material for pulp products because of their longer fibers, greater strength, and lighter color. The growing use of hardwoods is due to four factors: increased competition for softwoods and a consequent rise in prices; availability close to mills and major markets in the East of large volumes of hardwoods that are cheaper per ton of fiber than softwoods; improvements in the technology of pulping that enable the industry to take greater advantage of this abundant, low-cost resource; and growth in demand for grades of paper and board that are improved by addition of hardwood pulps (S-800). A typical mix of pulps in a Louisiana mill, for example, might consist of loblolly pine (*Pinus taeda*), or loblolly plus shortleaf pine (*P. echinata*), as the main pulping material giving strength to the product, supplemented with a mixture of hardwoods, such as soft maple (*Acer* spp.), sweet gum (*Liquidambar styraciflua*), tulip tree or yellow poplar (*Liriodendron tulipifera*), and magnolia (*Magnolia* spp.), to make it smooth (R. T. Carter, pers. com., 11 August 1982).

The tree family that makes the greatest contribution to U.S. domestic timber production is the Pinaceae or pine family, which includes douglas fir, the hemlocks (*Tsuga* spp.), spruces (*Picea* spp.), firs (*Abies* spp.), and larches (*Larix* spp.), as well as the pines (*Pinus* spp.) themselves. The influence of the pine family is even greater than its size. Together the major species in the family account for half the growing stock on commercial timberland in the United States, yet they make up almost two-thirds of the removals (table 2.16). The difference is due to the popularity of the pines, particularly of the four main southern yellow pines: loblolly, shortleaf, longleaf, and slash. These species, douglas fir, the western white and sugar pines (*Pinus monticola* and *P. lambertiana*), redwood (*Sequoia sempervirens*), and the sweet gum, are the only species in the United States that account for a higher percentage of timber removals than of the total growing stock.

The southern yellow pines are the principal reason that almost 70% of the pulpwood produced in the United States comes from the South (S-818). The two most important species are loblolly and shortleaf, which together make up 71% of the volume of southern yellow pine growing stock; loblolly alone accounts for more than half (S-800). Douglas fir plays a similar though less dramatic role in the West, where it accounts for the West's predominance as the nation's supplier of sawlogs (51% of the total) and veneer logs (58%) (S-818).

The other important softwood families are the Taxodiaceae (redwood and bald cypress, *Taxodium distichum*) and the Cupressaceae (western red cedar, *Thuja plicata*, for example). However, their contributions are smaller than those of either of the top two hardwood families, the Fagaceae (beech, *Fagus grandifolia*, and oaks, *Quercus* spp.) and the Altingiaceae (sweet gum). The oaks are the only timber species of commercial importance in the Fagaceae family. They alone account for 11.3% of U.S. timber removals and as such are the most important genus after the pines. Their value is due largely to their abundance. In the South they are avoided in favor of softwoods and other hardwoods because their tannins spoil the pulp (R. T. Carter, pers. comm., 11 August 1982), but there are "select" white and red oaks that are sought after for their special qualities. Oak is the wood of choice in hardwood flooring and is also popular for furniture; it is the leading wood for railroad crossties and is prescribed by law as the only wood for barrels for storing and aging bourbon. Sweet gum is very much less abundant, making up only 1.9% of the volume of growing stock (compared with the oaks' 12.2%), but it is so highly valued, particularly for veneer and furniture (J-228), that it accounts for 2.1% of timber removals.

Conifers also dominate U.S. imports. They account for at least $5,302.6 million (70%) of the annual average of $7,524.9 million of timber products imported by the United States in 1976–1980. Hardwoods account for $987.1 million (13%). The remaining $1,235.2 million (16%) may be either. Assuming that the remainder comprises softwoods and hardwoods in the same proportion, the conifers' share of imports would be 84% and the broad-leaved trees' share would be 16%.

The reason for this emphasis on softwoods is that most U.S. timber imports come from Canada, which accounts for 97% of the lumber, 50% of the hardwood veneer, and 90% of the pulp and paper products (S-797). The value of timber imports from Canada is $6,410.8 million, or 85% of the total (our calculations from S-450–S-454). Virtually all the Canadian supplies come from conifers. For example, in 1976 (the last year that statistics were published on the composition of pulpwood species) softwoods made up 92% of the pulpwood produced (S-823). It is unlikely that the proportion has changed significantly since then.

As in the United States, the most important family in Canada is the Pinaceae, but the pines themselves are not as important as the spruces. Annual imports of spruce lumber from Canada are worth more than $1 billion. In addition, most of the newsprint from Canada is derived from spruce, which is also the major constituent of Canadian pulpwood generally. We estimate that the five spruce species—Engelmann spruce (*Picea engelmannii*), white spruce (*P. glauca*), black spruce (*P. mariana*), red spruce (*P. rubens*), and Sitka spruce (*P. sitchensis*)—together account for more than half of U.S. imports from Canada (by value) and half of all timber imports, or $3,750 million a year. The other species that are major contributors to Canadian pulpwood are (in order of importance) western hemlock (*Tsuga heterophylla*), jack pine (*Pinus banksiana*), balsam fir (*Abies balsamea*), and—among the hardwoods—the poplars (*Populus* spp.) (S-823).

After Canada, the biggest supplier to the United States of timber products is the tropical rain forest region of Southeast Asia. The timber originates in four countries—Indonesia, Malaysia, the Philippines, and Thailand—but the contribution of these nations is obscured because much of the timber they supply is processed in the Republic of Korea and Taiwan, which are then listed as the exporting countries. Making due allowance for this, we estimate that annual timber imports from Southeast Asia are worth almost $480 million. Veneer and plywood are the main products: the region supplies 34% of the hardwood veneer and 91% of the hardwood plywood (the United States imports very little softwood plywood and veneer, being virtually self-sufficient) (S-797). All Southeast Asian plywood and veneer comes from the Dipterocarpaceae family, the most important of the hardwoods in the import group. The main genera, marketed under the collective trade name of lauan or Philippine mahogany, are *Shorea*, *Parashorea*, *Dipterocarpus*, *Dryobalanops*, and *Pentacme*. These make up some three-quarters of the region's timber exports (D-242). A large proportion of the decorative plywood on the market, the standard interior finish for mobile homes, uses lauan prefinished with wood-grain patterns and textures (A-1375).

Taken together, production and imports in the United States present a picture of conservatism with respect to relatively high-value, low-volume species whose wood is intrinsically suitable for particular uses. Examples are: western red cedar (*Thuja plicata*), whose very high durability, fine texture, high thermal insulation, and large diameter are the features that make the species so suitable as a source of shingles; and select white and red oaks, hard maple, yellow birch, sweet gum, tulip tree (yellow poplar), ash, black walnut (*Juglans nigra*), black cherry (*Prunus serotina*), true mahogany (*Swietenia* and *Khaya* spp.), and teak (*Tectona grandis*), which are among the preferred species for cabinetwork, paneling, furniture, and similar uses in which surface appearance is one of the main considerations (J-626, S-800). Otherwise, timber users are opportunistic, taking advantage of such species as the douglas fir, the southern pines, the spruces, and lauan because of their abundance as well as their utility. With technological innovation, timber users will be able to take advantage of North America's rich resource of low value hardwoods, such as the poplars. A large proportion of the poplars are unsuitable for lumber or plywood because young trees (under 70 years old) tend to be small and crooked, whereas older trees are often badly decayed. The construction industry's increasing substitution of panel products for lumber has effectively removed these obstacles. No matter how poor the poplar, it can now be converted into waferboard; the entire stem is shredded into tiny (1.5–3 inches × 0.2 inch) wafers coated with resin and hot-pressed at high heat and pressure (A-1375).

Softwoods are sure to remain more important than hardwoods; but with changes in consumer behavior (for example, the return to fuelwood) and innovations in technology (greater use of hardwoods in pulp production, as well as the rise of panel products), hardwoods are likely to continue their comeback. This change in market share has implications for the domestication of timber trees and the share of production accounted for by wild timber (as we will discuss in chapter 7).

# 3

# Fishing

Between 1976 and 1980, commercial fishery landings in the United States for both edible and industrial products averaged 5.9 billion pounds worth $1.8 billion per year; during the same period, American imports of edible and industrial fishery products annually averaged 5.5 billion pounds valued at $2.3 billion (A-1206, P-432–P-435; see figs. 3.1 and 3.2). Edible products account for 94% of the combined value of the commercial domestic catch and imports.

An annual value of $4.1 billion makes fisheries (the catching of fish and other aquatic animals for food or biochemicals) the second largest wildlife-based industry in the United States after logging (chap. 2); and the contribution of fisheries to the gross domestic product is greater still. The contribution to GDP is calculated by adding the estimated value added attributable to fisheries at each level of economic activity—from fishery landings through processing, wholesale distribution, retail stores, and public eating places. We estimate that fisheries currently contributes about $6.5 billion (or 0.31%) annually to the GDP of the United States (table 3.1), of which about $6.3 billion (or 0.30% of GDP) is attributable to wild fish and shellfish (see chap. 7). This figure does not include imports of shell, coral, natural pearls, pearl essence, pearl products, ornamental hydroids, sponges, and sharkskin leather (see chap. 4); domestic harvests and imports of seaweed (see chaps. 5 and 6); recreational fishing (see chap. 10).

## Commercial Landings in the United States

For the period 1976–1980, almost 5.9 billion pounds of fish and shellfish worth $1.8 billion were taken on average each year in U.S. commercial landings (A-1206, P-432–P-435). Alaska, California, Louisiana, Texas, Massachusetts, and Florida all averaged annual fishery landings worth more than $100 million (table 3.2). Together these six states contributed 67% of the total value of U.S. commercial landings. Fourteen other states had annual landings worth between

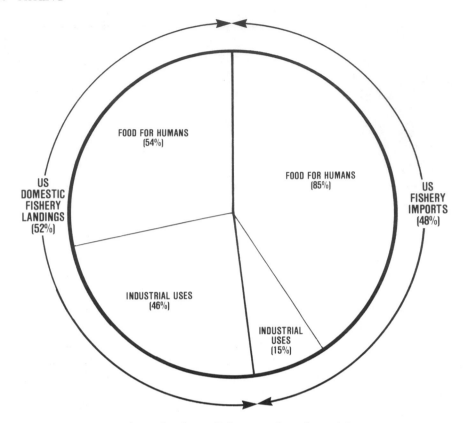

Fig. 3.1   **Average annual supply of U.S. fishery products by weight, 1976–1980. Sources: A-1206, P-432–P-435**

$10 and $100 million (table 3.3); nine others between $1 million and $10 million (table 3.4); 13 had annual landings worth under $1 million (table 3.5).

Shellfish (clams, crabs, lobsters, oysters, scallops, shrimp, squid, and other invertebrates) made up only 20% of the U.S. commercial catch but was worth about 50% of the value (fig. 3.3). Five groups of species had a landed value of more than $100 million a year: shrimp, $389 million; salmonids, $288 million; crabs, $240 million; scombrids (tunas, mackerels), $183 million; and clupeids (menhadens, herrings, alewives), $118 million. Except for the last group, and in particular the menhadens (*Brevoortia* spp.), most of the species in these categories were caught largely for edible consumption. (The industrial products derived from menhaden are discussed later in this chapter.)

Figure 3.4 illustrates the disposition of U.S. commercial landings by weight for 1976–1980. About 54% went to the food industry; the remaining 46% to a range of uses, such as fish glue, fish leather, cuttlefish bone, and reduction to meal, solubles, and oil. Whereas food and industrial products each account for about half of the landings by weight, the picture changes dramatically with respect to value—landings for human food are worth $1,717 million, or 93% of

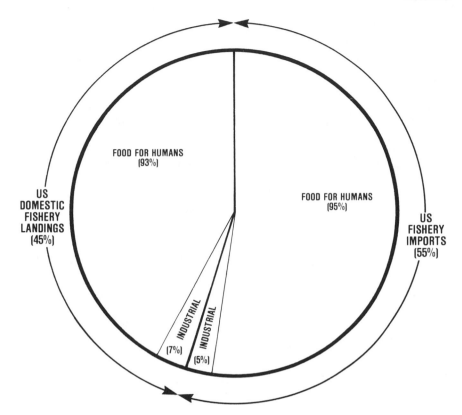

Fig. 3.2 **Average annual supply of U.S. fishery products by dollar value, 1976–1980.**
Sources: A-1206, P-432–P-435

U.S. commercial fishery, and landings for industrial products are worth only $121 million, or 7% (fig. 3.5).

## Fishery Imports to the United States

Between 1976 and 1980, the United States imported on average 5.5 billion pounds of fishery products valued at $2.3 billion each year (A-1206, P-432–P-435). In terms of both weight and value these imports consisted largely of products for human consumption (see figs. 3.1 and 3.2). Imports of five groups of species (largely for edible consumption) were valued at more than $100 million a year: shrimp, $562 million; gadids (cods, haddocks, pollocks), $474 million; scombrids (tunas, mackerels), $328 million; lobster, $277 million; and flounder, $121 million (S-450–S-454). About $104 million (or 5%) of American fishery imports were for uses other than human consumption (A-1206, P-432–P-435). Industrial products include fish meal and scrap, solubles, oils, fish scales, shark leather, fish glue, fish sounds, isinglass, and so forth (S-450–S-454). Table 3.6

Table 3.1 **Value added from fisheries to the gross domestic product of the United States (U.S.$ million)**

| ECONOMIC ACTIVITY (SIC NO.)* | 1976 | 1977 | 1978 | 1979 | 1980 | Ann. Ave. 1976–1980 |
|---|---|---|---|---|---|---|
| Edible Products† | | | | | | |
| Landings level (09) | 835 | 950 | 1,185 | 1,448 | 1,464 | 1,176 |
| Processing level (20) | 1,020 | 1,143 | 1,344 | 1,268 | 1,275 | 1,210 |
| SUBTOTAL | 1,855 | 2,093 | 2,529 | 2,716 | 2,739 | 2,386 |
| Wholesale level | 492 | 577 | 645 | 703 | 720 | 627 |
| Retail stores | 510 | 604 | 654 | 735 | 760 | 653 |
| Public eating places | 2,123 | 2,176 | 2,414 | 2,456 | 2,479 | 2,330 |
| Institutions | 103 | 108 | 121 | 129 | 132 | 119 |
| SUBTOTAL | 3,228 | 3,465 | 3,834 | 4,023 | 4,091 | 3,729 |
| TOTAL | 5,083 | 5,558 | 6,363 | 6,739 | 6,830 | 6,115 |
| PERCENTAGE OF U.S. GDP | 0.30 | 0.29 | 0.30 | 0.28 | 0.27 | 0.29 |

| | 1977 | 1978 | 1979 | Ann. Ave. 1977–1979 |
|---|---|---|---|---|
| Industrial Products‡ | | | | |
| Landings level (09) | 89 | 103 | 114 | 102 |
| Processing level (20) | 161 | 185 | 169 | 172 |
| SUBTOTAL | 250 | 288 | 283 | 274 |
| Wholesale level | 37 | 39 | 36 | 37 |
| Retail stores | 91 | 94 | 87 | 91 |
| SUBTOTAL | 128 | 133 | 123 | 128 |
| TOTAL | 378 | 421 | 406 | 402 |
| PERCENTAGE OF U.S. GDP | 0.02 | 0.02 | 0.02 | 0.02 |
| COMBINED TOTAL | 5,936 | 6,784 | 7,145 | 6,517 |
| COMBINED PERCENTAGE OF GDP | 0.31 | 0.32 | 0.30 | 0.31 |

*SIC = Standard Industrial Classification.
†Sources: A-1206, P-432–P-435.
‡Source: P-439.

Table 3.2 **U.S. commercial fishery landings by state: average annual value of more than $100 million, 1976–1980**

| STATE | AVERAGE ANNUAL VALUE (U.S.$) |
|---|---|
| Alaska | 429,941,000 |
| California | 231,942,000 |
| Louisiana | 168,315,000 |
| Texas | 144,958,000 |
| Massachusetts | 143,604,000 |
| Florida | 106,031,000 |

Sources: A-1206, P-432–P-435.

Table 3.3  **U.S. commercial fishery landings by state: average annual value of $10 million to $100 million, 1976–1980**

| STATE | AVERAGE ANNUAL VALUE (U.S.$) |
|---|---|
| Washington | 92,075,000 |
| Maine | 71,520,000 |
| Virginia | 65,738,000 |
| Oregon | 54,966,000 |
| North Carolina | 44,833,000 |
| New Jersey | 44,074,000 |
| Alabama | 36,618,000 |
| New York | 36,217,000 |
| Maryland | 35,410,000 |
| Rhode Island | 30,957,000 |
| Mississippi | 27,316,000 |
| South Carolina | 17,168,000 |
| Georgia | 16,767,000 |
| Hawaii | 10,209,000 |

Sources: A-1206, P-432–P-435.

Table 3.4  **U.S. commercial fishery landings by state: average annual value of $1 million to $10 million, 1976–1980**

| STATE | AVERAGE ANNUAL VALUE (U.S.$) |
|---|---|
| Wisconsin | 4,524,000 |
| Connecticut | 4,169,000 |
| Michigan | 3,865,000 |
| Arkansas | 3,054,000 |
| New Hampshire | 2,563,000 |
| Ohio | 2,532,000 |
| Tennessee | 2,124,000 |
| Minnesota | 1,686,000 |
| Delaware | 1,135,000 |

Sources: A-1206, P-432–P-435.

Table 3.5 **U.S. commercial fishery landings by state: average annual value under $1 million, 1976–1980**

| STATE | AVERAGE ANNUAL VALUE (U.S.$) |
|---|---|
| Kentucky | 996,000 |
| Illinois | 949,000 |
| Iowa | 853,000 |
| Oklahoma | 465,000 |
| South Dakota | 306,000 |
| Pennsylvania | 266,000 |
| Missouri | 175,000 |
| Indiana | 98,000 |
| North Dakota | 85,000 |
| Idaho | 32,000 |
| Nebraska | 28,000 |
| Kansas | 20,000 |
| West Virginia | 11,000 |

Sources: A-1206, P-432–P-435.

lists the top fishery exporters (of both edible and industrial products) to the United States.

## Food Products

Americans are eating more fish and shellfish today than during any other period this century. Between 1976 and 1980, fish and shellfish consumption averaged 13 pounds per person a year. Most (62%) of the fish and shellfish consumed is fresh or frozen; 35% is canned; only 3% is cured (fig. 3.6). Fish and shellfish consumption is still small, however, when compared with meat consumption, which averaged 185 pounds per person a year for the period 1976–1980 (table 3.7).

Since the beginning of their history, Americans have been great meat-eaters; even in 1854, *Harper's Weekly* reported that the most common meal in America—from coast to coast—was steak (P-304). Vast expanses of open land in the West supplied all the beef the nation needed; the Midwest (in particular Chicago) developed the industrial organization, capital, and know-how required to butcher, process, and deliver beef to consumers; and the East provided the market. The American Civil War (1861–1865) stimulated the building of railroads, and the development of the railroads revolutionized the way in which meat, especially beef, could be moved from the producers to the consumers. By

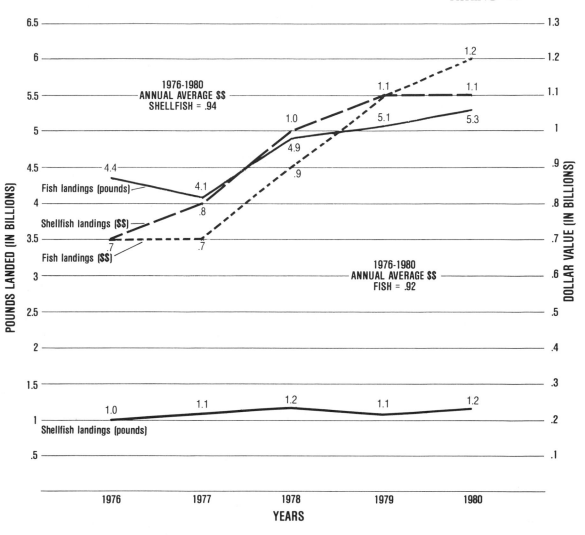

Fig. 3.3   **Commercial landings of fish and shellfish in the United States, 1976–1980. Solid lines: billions of pounds; broken lines: billions of dollars. Sources: A-1206, P-432– P-435**

1880, the United States was even exporting beef to the United Kingdom. One hundred years later, Americans lead the world in per capita meat consumption and pay less for meat, in terms of proportion of total income, than do consumers in any other country. The United States contains less than one-fifteenth of the world's population but eats one-third of its meat (P-304).

There has been much speculation about why the average American consumer continues to shy away from fish. One hypothesis is that since World War II steak was seen as a sign of upward mobility while fish was a reminder of ethnic heritage and poverty (J-489). Another is that meat (and poultry) producers in the

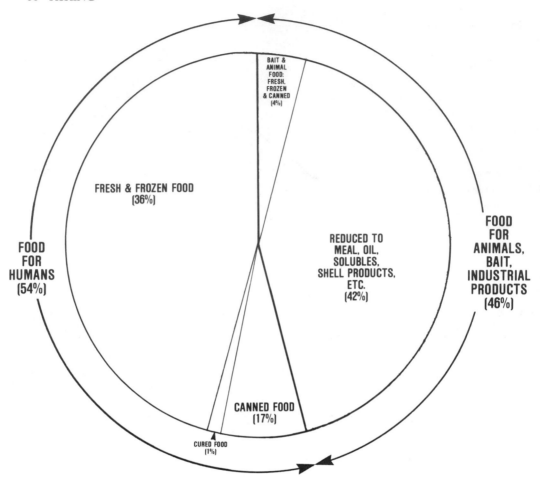

Fig. 3.4 **Average annual percentage disposition of commercial fishery landings by weight in the United States, 1976–1980. Sources: A-1206, P-432–P-435**

United States, as recipients of subsidies, price supports, and other beneficial programs, were subject to mandatory inspections that assured consumers a product of reasonably consistent high quality. The fishing industry, however, remained unregulated. Fishermen were given no economic incentives to provide a fresher product (J-489) even though fish and shellfish are among the most perishable of foods (M-348). Fish lacks the clean, sterile, and odorless appearance of supermarket-packaged meat, and consumers, uneducated about quality and preparation of fish, view it with suspicion (J-489).

No information was available for the period between 1976 and 1980 on the value or major groups of unprocessed edible fish and shellfish consumed. Data

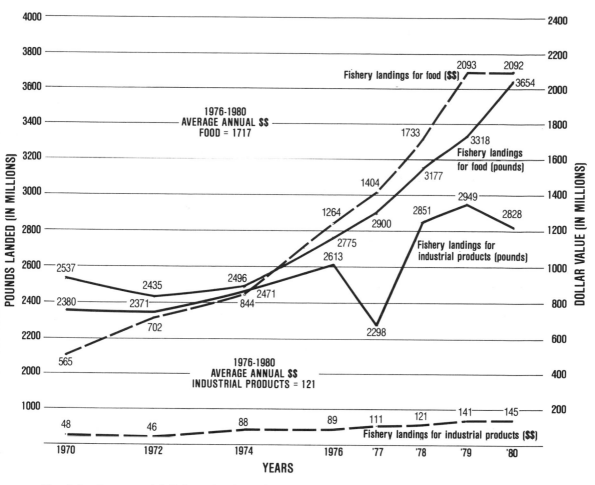

Fig. 3.5   Commercial fishery landings for food and industrial products in the United States, 1970, 1972, 1974, 1976–1980. Solid lines: millions of pounds, dashed lines: millions of dollars. Sources: A-1206, P-432–P-435

on the major categories of processed edible fish and shellfish are listed in table 3.8. The value of processed products (from both the domestic catch and imports) annually averaged $3.75 billion. The most important fish and shellfish groups— accounting for 95%, 97%, and 94% of the total value of all fillets/steaks, canned, and cured products, respectively—are listed in table 3.9 in the order of their total value (all three product groups combined). (There are no data on the species used in fish sticks and portions.) The list provides a revealing indication of American consumer preferences. Tuna, salmon, and shrimp are the favored species, followed by flounder (flatfish), herring, clams, cod, haddock, and crabs.

---

Table 3.6  **Leading exporters of fishery products to the United States, 1976–1980**

| EXPORTERS | PERCENTAGE OF U.S. IMPORTS |
|---|---|
| *Edible fishery products (by weight)* | |
| Canada | 22 |
| Japan | 13 |
| Iceland | 7 |
| Mexico | 6 |
| Republic of Korea | 5 |
| Others | 47 |
| *Edible fishery products (by value)* | |
| Canada | 21 |
| Mexico | 12 |
| Japan | 9 |
| Iceland | 7 |
| Republic of Korea | 3 |
| Others | 48 |
| *Industrial fishery products (by value)* | |
| Italy | 41 |
| Hong Kong | 8 |
| Japan | 8 |
| West Germany | 5 |
| Switzerland | 5 |
| Canada | 4 |
| United Kingdom | 4 |
| Others | 25 |

Sources: A-1206, P-432–P-435.

---

## Industrial Products

About 75–80% of fish caught by U.S. commercial fisheries for nonedible, industrial purposes is reduced to meal and scrap, solubles, and oils (P-439). The remaining 20–25% is used for such products as fish glue, fish leather, fish sounds, and fish scales. As table 3.10 indicates, menhaden (*Brevoortia* spp.) is the fish most often used for reduction to meal and scrap, solubles, and oils. Between 1976 and 1980, menhaden accounted for 77% of the average annual value of scrap and meal from U.S. industrial fisheries, 76% of the value of solubles, and 94% of the value of oils.

Fish meal is mixed with other ingredients, such as grain (particularly soybean) meals and synthetic supplements, in the preparation of animal feed. About 78% of the fish meal sold goes into poultry feed, 9% into aquaculture feed (especially for warm-water species), 6% into pet feed, and 5% into hog feed. Like fish meal

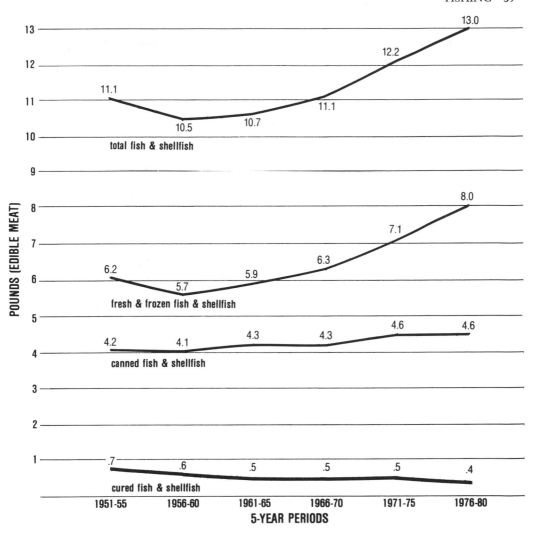

Fig. 3.6 **Per capita consumption of commercial fish and shellfish in the United States in pounds: annual average per 5-year period from 1951–55 to 1976–80. Sources: A-1206, P-432–P-435**

and scraps, fish solubles are almost exclusively used in the animal feed industries. About 80% of all fish solubles sold ends up in poultry (especially turkey) feed, 8% in pet feed, 7% in hog feed, and 5% in aquaculture feed (again in particular for warm-water species) (P-439).

Almost half (49%) of the industrial fish oil traded in the United States goes into the production of paints used for protective coatings. (Paint- and lubricant manufacturers have been more inclined recently to use mammal, fish, and plant

Table 3.7 **Average per capita meat consumption (lb) in the United States**

|                 | 1951–55 | 1956–60 | 1961–65 | 1966–70 | 1971–75 | 1976–80 |
|-----------------|---------|---------|---------|---------|---------|---------|
| Beef            | 71.6    | 83.4    | 94.1    | 108.9   | 114.3   | 115.7   |
| Pork            | 66.9    | 64.2    | 63.0    | 71.0    | 67.4    | 64.3    |
| Veal            | 8.5     | 7.4     | 5.3     | 3.6     | 2.6     | 2.9     |
| Lamb and mutton | 4.3     | 4.5     | 4.6     | 3.7     | 2.7     | 1.6     |
| All meat        | 151.3   | 159.5   | 167.0   | 187.2   | 187.0   | 184.5   |

Sources: S-725, S-801.

oils as substitutes for petrochemically derived materials, which are higher in price.) Another 7% of industrial fish oil is used by the poultry- and pet-food industries. The remaining 44% finds a wide variety of applications—in insecticides, hot-melt adhesives, caulks, putty, leather treatment, buffing compounds, and nitrogen derivatives. Fish oils are also used as additives to other oils, as reagents and pigments to produce oil blends for such final products as lubricants, printing ink, and resins (P-439).

Table 3.8 **Processed edible fishery products from U.S. domestic catch and imported products: average annual value and percentage, 1976–1980**

| ITEM | VALUE (U.S. $) | PERCENTAGE OF TOTAL |
|------|---------------|---------------------|
| FRESH AND FROZEN   | 2,066,290,400 | 55.0  |
| Fillets and steaks | 224,467,400   | 6.0   |
| Fish sticks        | 83,434,600    | 2.0   |
| Fish portions      | 372,297,200   | 10.0  |
| Breaded shrimp     | 241,946,600   | 6.5   |
| Other              | 1,144,144,600 | 30.5  |
| CANNED             | 1,558,002,000 | 42.0  |
| CURED              | 121,252,800   | 3.0   |
| TOTAL              | 3,745,545,200 | 100.0 |

Sources: A-1206, P-432–P-435.

Table 3.9  **Top species (by value) in U.S. processed fishery products (from both domestic catch and imported products): 1976–1980 average annual value**

| SPECIES PROCESSED (U.S.$ value) | FILLETS AND STEAKS* (U.S.$ value and %) | CANNED† (U.S.$ value and %) | CURED‡ (U.S.$ value and %) |
|---|---|---|---|
| Tuna (1,056,348,000) | — | 1,056,142,600 (68%) | 205,400 (.2%) |
| Salmon (348,904,800) | 7,308,400 (3%) | 275,769,000 (18%) | 65,827,400 (54%) |
| Shrimp§ (301,320,000) | — | 57,209,200 (4%) | 2,164,200 (2%) |
| Flounder (80,196,000) | 80,196,000 (36%) | — | — |
| Sea herring (64,493,600) | 8,492,200 (4%) | 32,739,200 (2%) | 23,262,200 (19%) |
| Clams (64,490,800) | — | 64,490,800 (4%) | — |
| Cod (36,104,800) | 34,315,000 (15%) | — | 1,789,800 (2%) |
| Haddock (23,621,200) | 23,621,200 (11%) | — | — |
| Crabs (20,572,600) | — | 20,572,600 (1%) | — |
| Atlantic perch (9,472,800) | 9,472,800 (4%) | — | — |
| Rockfish (9,369,600) | 9,368,600 (4%) | | 1,000 (1980 only) (.001%) |
| Pollock (6,946,600) | 6,821,800 (3%) | — | 124,800 (.1%) |
| Halibut (6,663,200) | 6,254,000 (3%) | — | 409,200 (.3%) |
| Whitefish (6,393,800) | 1,543,000 (1%) | — | 4,850,800 (4%) |
| Sablefish (6,151,600) | 1,367,600 (1%) | — | 4,784,000 (4%) |
| Chub (5,534,600) | — | — | 5,534,600 (5%) |
| Yellow perch (5,493,600) | 5,493,600 (2%) | — | — |
| Sturgeon (2,274,800) | — | — | 2,274,800 (2%) |
| Whiting (1,976,400) | 499,200 (.2%) | — | 1,477,200 (1%) |
| Pacific perch (1,831,200) | 1,831,200 (1%) | — | — |
| Cusk (1,777,400) | 1,777,400 (1%) | — | — |

(continued)

Table 3.9 (*Continued*)

| SPECIES PROCESSED (U.S.$ value) | FILLETS AND STEAKS* (U.S.$ value and %) | CANNED† (U.S.$ value and %) | CURED‡ (U.S.$ value and %) |
|---|---|---|---|
| Yellow pike (1,620,800) | 1,620,800 (1%) | — | — |
| Carp (1,558,400) | 1,466,000 (1%) | — | 92,400 (.1%) |
| Hake (1,334,200) | 1,334,200 (1%) | — | — |
| Lingcod (1,328,000) | 1,328,000 (1%) | — | — |
| Red snapper (1,325,000) | 1,325,000 (1%) | — | — |
| Swordfish (1,289,800) | 1,289,800 (1%) | — | — |

*Sources: A-1206, P-432–P-435.
†Sources: S-806–S-810.
‡Sources: S-811–S-815.
§Between 1976 and 1980, breaded shrimp was worth an average of $241,946,600 each year.

## The Most Important Fishery Groups

Six families of fishes (gadids, scombrids, salmonids, flatfishes [chiefly bothids and pleuronectids], and clupeids) and four groups of invertebrates (shrimps, lobsters, crabs, and scallops) together make up 84% of the combined value of U.S. fishery landings and imports. Each family or group has an average annual landed plus import value of $100 million or more (table 3.11). The other economically significant families and groups are listed in tables 3.12 and 3.13.

Table 3.10  **U.S. industrial fishery products—scrap and meal, solubles, and oils: average annual percentage of value, 1976–1980**

| SPECIES | SCRAP AND MEAL | SOLUBLES | OIL |
|---|---|---|---|
| FISH | | | |
| Menhaden | 77 | 76 | 94 |
| Tuna and mackerel | 11 | — | 1 |
| Anchovy | 4 | — | 1 |
| Other fish | 8 | — | — |
| SHELLFISH | 1 | — | — |
| UNCLASSIFIED | — | 24 | 4 |

Percentages may not add to 100 because of rounding.
Sources: A-1206, P-432–P-435.

Table 3.11  **Average annual value of fishery families commercially caught and imported by the United States: value more than $100 million, 1976–1980**

| FAMILY<br>*Average annual value (U.S.$)* | U.S. COMMERCIAL LANDINGS*<br>*Average annual value (U.S.$)* | U.S. IMPORTS†<br>*Average annual value (U.S.$)* |
|---|---|---|
| SEVERAL FAMILIES<br>(Shrimp)<br>951,652,000 | 389,262,000 | 562,390,000 |
| GADIDAE<br>(Cods)<br>521,744,000 | 47,359,000 | 474,385,000 |
| SCOMBRIDAE<br>(Mackerels and tunas)<br>511,276,000 | 183,046,000 | 328,230,000 |
| SEVERAL FAMILIES<br>(Lobsters)<br>352,700,000 | 75,390,000 | 277,310,000 |
| SALMONIDAE<br>(Salmonids)<br>314,215,000 | 287,591,000 | 26,624,000 |
| SEVERAL FAMILIES<br>(Crabs)<br>262,966,000 | 240,018,000 | 22,948,000 |
| SEVERAL FAMILIES<br>(Flatfishes)<br>212,195,000 | 91,241,000 | 120,954,000 |
| CLUPEIDAE<br>(Herrings, shads,<br>sardines, menhadens)<br>186,744,000 | 118,362,000 | 68,382,000 |
| PECTINIDAE<br>(Scallops)<br>148,545,000 | 79,357,000 | 69,188,000 |

*Sources: A-1206, P-432–P-435.
†Sources: S-450–S-454.

Table 3.12 **Average annual value of fishery families commercially caught and imported by the United States: value $10 million to $100 million, 1976–1980**

| FAMILY<br>*Average annual<br>value (U.S.$)* | U.S. COMMERCIAL LANDINGS[*]<br>*Average annual<br>value (U.S.$)* | U.S. IMPORTS[†]<br>*Average annual<br>value (U.S.$)* |
|---|---|---|
| SEVERAL FAMILIES<br>(Clams)<br>88,100,000 | 77,742,000 | 10,358,000 |
| OSTREIDAE<br>(Oysters)<br>83,508,000 | 60,444,000 | 23,064,000 |
| SCORPAENIDAE<br>(Rockfishes)<br>65,687,000 | 18,699,000 | 46,988,000 |
| MERLUCCIIDAE<br>(Merluccid hakes)<br>23,634,000 | 6,006,000 | 20,628,000 |
| ENGRAULIDAE<br>(Anchovies)<br>20,459,000 | 9,502,000 | $10,957,000 |
| XIPHIIDAE<br>(Swordfish)<br>16,181,000 | 15,848,000 | 333,000 |
| HALIOTIDAE<br>(Abalone)<br>15,846,000 | — | 15,846,000 |
| ESOCIDAE<br>(Pikes)<br>15,545,000 | — | 15,545,000 |
| SCIAENIDAE<br>(Drums)<br>13,679,000 | 13,679,000 | — |

Dash indicates no data.
[*]Sources: A-1206, P-432–P-435.
[†]Sources: S-450–S-454.

Table 3.13  **Average annual value of fishery families commercially caught and imported by the United States: value under $10 million, 1976–1980**

| FAMILY<br>*Average annual value (U.S.$)* | U.S. COMMERCIAL LANDINGS*<br>*Average annual value (U.S.$)* | U.S. IMPORTS†<br>*Average annual value (U.S.$)* |
|---|---|---|
| LUTJANIDAE<br>(Snappers)<br>9,806,000 | 9,806,000 | — |
| SEVERAL FAMILIES<br>(Catfish)<br>9,710,000 | — | 9,710,000 |
| PERCIDAE<br>(Perches)<br>8,291,000 | — | 8,291,000 |
| SERRANIDAE<br>(Sea basses)<br>7,692,000 | 7,692,000 | — |
| ANOPLOPOMATIDAE<br>(Sablefishes)<br>7,292,000 | 7,292,000 | — |
| ANARHICHADIDAE<br>(Wolffishes)<br>6,896,000 | 170,000 | 6,726,000 |
| SPARIDAE<br>(Porgies)<br>5,607,000 | 5,607,000 | — |
| MUGILIDAE<br>(Mullets)<br>5,221,000 | 5,221,000 | — |
| OSMERIDAE<br>(Smelts)<br>4,553,000 | — | 4,553,000 |
| LOLIGINIDAE<br>(Squid)<br>4,497,000 | 4,497,000 | |
| PERCICHTHYIDAE<br>(Temperate basses)<br>4,091,000 | 4,091,000 | — |
| CARANGIDAE<br>(Jacks and pompanos)<br>3,539,000 | 3,539,000 | — |
| SEVERAL FAMILIES<br>(Sharks)<br>2,916,000 | 1,954,000 | 962,000 |

(*continued*)

65

Table 3.13  (*Continued*)

| FAMILY<br>*Average annual<br>value (U.S.$)* | U.S. COMMERCIAL LANDINGS*<br>*Average annual<br>value (U.S.$)* | U.S. IMPORTS†<br>*Average annual<br>value (U.S.$)* |
|---|---|---|
| STROMATEIDAE<br>(Butterfishes)<br>2,122,000 | 2,122,000 | — |
| POMATOMIDAE<br>(Bluefishes)<br>1,728,000 | 1,728,000 | — |
| ACIPENSERIDAE<br>(Sturgeons)<br>1,678,000 | — | 1,678,000 |
| HEXAGRAMMIDAE<br>(Greenlings)<br>1,589,000 | 1,589,000 | — |

Note: Dash indicates no data.
*Sources: A-1206, P-432–P-435.
†Sources: S-450–S-454.

# 4

# Trapping and Collecting

Economically, logging and fishing are the two most important ways in which the United States obtains wild species from native and imported sources. Third is trapping and collecting. Although economically the least important of the three means of harvesting resources from the wild, trapping and collecting yield a greater diversity of products. They are discussed in this and the next two chapters. This chapter covers wild species used in the ornamental and pet trades: animals used for their skins or for other decorative or ornamental purposes (such as shells and ivory); animals used as pets (such as birds and aquarium fish); and ornamental plants (such as wild orchids). Chapter 5 deals with wild species used in medicines, pharmaceuticals, and biomedical research. Chapter 6 discusses wild species used for food and industrial sources of fibers and biochemicals (except for wood, which is covered in chap. 2, and aquatic animals, covered in chap. 3).

Trade in ornamental and pet species is complicated by the large numbers of species involved, indirect trade routes (so that the exporting country is not necessarily the originating country), and statistics that are often vague and inconsistent. This makes it very difficult to determine the main species included in a given trade statistical category, whether or not they are wild, and their relative economic importance. A great many wild species enter the marketplace, but trade in most of them is economically significant only to the actual participants: the hunter or trapper, the customer, and the smuggler or other intermediary. Hundreds of these microeconomic species are threatened with extinction as a result of overexploitation compounded by habitat destruction.

International trade in wild species and their products is controlled under the Convention on International Trade in Endangered Species of Wild Fauna and Flora (officially abbreviated to CITES). Species placed on Appendix I of CITES may not be traded commercially. Species placed on Appendix II may be traded commercially, but all trade must be licensed and monitored. CITES has become a valuable generator of data on trade in Appendix II species. Conservation-oriented organizations—notably the Conservation Monitoring Centre of the International Union for Conservation of Nature and Natural Resources (IUCN) and TRAFFIC (USA) of World Wildlife Fund–US—have developed increasingly sophisticated methods of analyzing and verifying these data. We have relied on the bulletins and reports of both organizations in our interpretation of U.S. import statistics and have not attempted to duplicate or amplify their work.

Between 1976 and 1980 the United States imported an annual average of about $346 million of ornamental and pet species and their products in 16 import categories that might include wild species (table 4.1). Of this sum we estimate that at least $90 million a year comes from unequivocally wild sources (see tables 4.1–4.3 and notes 1–6). In addition, U.S. domestic production of wild furs and skins during this period had an average annual value of $122.4 million (see tables 4.4 and 4.5); and U.S. freshwater pearl production had an average landed value of $0.6 million a year. The combined customs and production values for the United States of imported and domestically trapped/collected ornamental and pet species from the wild were $213.8 million a year, of which furs and skins accounted for $173.5 million (81%). This category, together with the six other import categories whose wild component had an average annual import value of $1 million or more (listed above the dashed line in table 4.1), are discussed below.

## Furs and Skins from North American Species

During the period 1976–1980, the average annual value (at harvest) of furs and skins from wild North American mammals and reptiles was some $176 million: $122 million from animals harvested in the United States and $54 million from animals harvested in Canada (tables 4.4 and 4.5). The U.S. figure is probably an underestimate. In Canada, information on wild furbearers is gathered and published yearly by the federal government (S-554–S-558). (We have converted all currency to U.S. dollars.) In the United States, the Fur Resources Committee of the International Association of Fish and Wildlife Agencies (IAFWA) collects the American statistics, but as our five-year period was more recent than its last published records (D-320), we obtained the information for the United States through our own mail survey of the 50 state wildlife agencies (listed in appendix A). All except Maryland responded. However, the data supplied by the states varied greatly in scope and detail. Many states had only partial information over the five-year period (for example, harvest statistics but no dollar value) or no information at all.

The trade in furs and skins from wild North American animals is concentrated on a small number of relatively abundant species. The eleven families with an average annual harvest value higher than $1 million are shown in table 4.4. Six of them together accounted for more than 90% of the value of produc-

Table 4.1  **Imports by the United States of wild (and wild plus domesticated) ornamental and pet species and/or their products obtained by trapping and collecting, 1976–1980**

| AVERAGE ANNUAL VALUE (U.S.$)* Wild + domesticated sources | AVERAGE ANNUAL VALUE (U.S.$)† Wild sources only | SPECIES/PRODUCT DESCRIPTION |
|---|---|---|
| 219,739,000 | 51,103,000 | Furs and fur products, reptilian skins and skin products, shark skin leather |
| 10,980,000 | 10,980,000 | Crude shells, shell articles |
| 17,405,000 | 7,989,000 | Aquarium fish |
| 6,369,000 | 6,369,000 | Raw ivory, worked ivory |
| 4,895,000 | 4,895,000 | Crude coral, worked coral and cameos |
| 5,997,000 | 4,887,555 | Birds for pet trade |
| 1,880,000 | 1,880,000 | Natural pearls, pearl parts, pearl buttons |
| 1,029,000 | 1,029,000 | Sponges, sponge articles |
| 55,342,000 | ? | Feathers and down |
| 17,876,000 | ? | Live plants nspf‡; orchids |
| 2,822,000 | 807,000 | Live animals nspf‡ |
| 727,000 | 727,000 | Ornamental hydroids |
| 580,000 | ? | Alpaca, llama, vicuña hair |
| 534,000 | ? | Articles of bone, horn, hoof, whalebone, quill |
| 66,000 | 66,000 | Tussah or wild silk |
| 31,000 | 31,000 | Live turtles |

*Sources: S-450–S-454.
†Source: Notes 1–6.
‡Not specified.

tion: Procyonidae (raccoons), Canidae (dogs, foxes), Muridae (mice, rats), Felidae (cats), Mustelidae (weasels), and Castoridae (beavers). Raccoon (*Procyon lotor*), the species with much the highest overall value (harvest number × pelt value), alone accounted for one-third of the value of North American wild fur and skin production; and the top three species—raccoon, muskrat (*Ondatra zibethicus*), and beaver (*Castor canadensis*)—made up more than half this value. As much as 90% of annual production value was accounted for by only a dozen species: the first three, together with red fox (*Vulpes vulpes*), coyote (*Canis latrans*), bobcat (*Felis rufus*), lynx (*Felis lynx*), gray fox (*Vulpes*

Table 4.2 **Fur and skin imports by the United States of wild or wild plus domesticated species for 1976–1980:** average annual value more than $1 million

| AVERAGE VALUE (U.S. $) | DESCRIPTION OF IMPORT | SOURCE W | SOURCE W + D | SOURCE ? | MAJOR EXPORTERS (% U.S. imports) | |
|---|---|---|---|---|---|---|
| 81,723,000 | Mink fur skin | | X | | Denmark | 29 |
| | | | | | Finland | 20 |
| | | | | | Canada | 16 |
| | | | | | Sweden | 12 |
| | | | | | Other | 23 |
| 32,631,000 | Hides and skins except fur skins; nspf; leather and leather nspf | | X | | Argentina | 26 |
| | | | | | Canada | 17 |
| | | | | | Brazil | 10 |
| | | | | | United Kingdom | 10 |
| | | | | | Other | 37 |
| 23,445,000 | Fur skins nspf | | X | | Canada | 24 |
| | | | | | New Zealand | 22 |
| | | | | | Greece | 9 |
| | | | | | Spain | 7 |
| | | | | | Other | 38 |
| 19,466,000 | Fox skins except silver, black, platinum | | X | | Norway | 47 |
| | | | | | Finland | 24 |
| | | | | | Canada | 11 |
| | | | | | Other | 18 |
| 10,890,000 | Reptile skins and leather | X | | | Argentina | 37 |
| | | | | | France | 15 |
| | | | | | Other | 48 |
| 8,571,000 | Sable fur skins: whole, raw, undressed | | X | | USSR | 79 |
| | | | | | Canada | 11 |
| | | | | | Other | 10 |

| Value | Description | | | Country | % |
|---|---|---|---|---|---|
| 8,222,000 | Rabbit fur skins | X | | France | 78 |
| | | | | Other | 22 |
| 6,403,000 | Chamois leather | X | | United Kingdom | 57 |
| | | | | Belgium | 32 |
| | | | | Other | 11 |
| 5,230,600 | Fur articles nspf of fur skins nes | X | | Peru | 17 |
| | | | | New Zealand | 12 |
| | | | | South Africa | 12 |
| | | | | Argentina | 8 |
| | | | | Other | 51 |
| 4,524,000 | Lynx fur skins | | X | Canada | 92 |
| | | | | Other | 8 |
| 3,981,000 | Beaver, ocelot, wolf, sable, and other skins | | X | West Germany | 57 |
| | | | | Canada | 17 |
| | | | | Argentina | 13 |
| | | | | Other | 13 |
| 3,371,000 | Reptile leather: billfolds, letter cases, other flat goods, luggage, handbags, pocketbooks, leather articles nspf, wearing apparel nspf | | X | Italy | 31 |
| | | | | Spain | 21 |
| | | | | Argentina | 14 |
| | | | | France | 9 |
| | | | | Other | 25 |
| 3,138,000 | Fur wearing apparel nspf of mink skins | | X | Canada | 34 |
| | | | | Italy | 13 |
| | | | | Republic of Korea | 9 |
| | | | | Other | 44 |
| 1,940,000 | Marten fur skins: whole, raw, undressed | | X | France | 37 |
| | | | | Canada | 34 |
| | | | | West Germany | 19 |
| | | | | Other | 10 |

(continued)

Table 4.2 (*Continued*)

| AVERAGE VALUE (U.S.$) | DESCRIPTION OF IMPORT | SOURCE | | | MAJOR EXPORTERS (% U.S. imports) | |
|---|---|---|---|---|---|---|
| | | W | W + D | ? | | |
| 1,442,000 | Beaver fur skins | X | | | Canada | 99 |
| | | | | | Other | 1 |
| 1,254,000 | Coney rabbit fur skins | | | X | Belgium | 36 |
| | | | | | Spain | 29 |
| | | | | | France | 26 |
| | | | | | Other | 9 |
| 1,196,000 | Deer, buck, doe skins | | X | | Sweden | 42 |
| | | | | | West Germany | 15 |
| | | | | | Canada | 13 |
| | | | | | Other | 30 |

Sources: S-450–S-454.
Notes: W = wild, W + D = wild + domesticated, ? = unknown, nspf = not specified, nes = not elsewhere specified.

Table 4.3  **Fur and skin imports by the United States of wild or wild plus domesticated species for 1976–1980: average annual value under $1 million**

| AVERAGE VALUE (U.S.$) | DESCRIPTION OF IMPORT | W | W + D | ? | MAJOR EXPORTERS (% U.S. imports) | |
|---|---|---|---|---|---|---|
| 921,000 | Hare fur skins: whole, raw, undressed | | | X | Argentina<br>Other | 68<br>32 |
| 652,000 | Sharkskin leather | X | | | Mexico<br>Other | 96<br>4 |
| 288,000 | Carpincho (capybara) hides and skins: raw, cured | X | | | Paraguay<br>Other | 87<br>13 |
| 121,200 | Fur apparel and articles nspf of silver, black, or platinum fox skins | | | X | Other | 100 |
| 98,000 | Otter fur skins | X | | | Canada<br>Other | 84<br>16 |
| 85,500 | Squirrel fur skins: whole, raw, undressed | X | | | USSR<br>Other | 95<br>5 |
| 55,000 | Fox skins: silver, black platinum | | | X | Other | 100 |
| 48,000 | Seal fur skins: whole, raw, undressed | X | | | Other | 100 |
| 35,000 | Ocelot fur skins | X | | | Canada<br>Other | 66<br>34 |
| 7,000 | Leopard fur skins | X | | | Other | 100 |

Sources: S-450–S-454.

cinereoargenteus), mink (*Mustela vison*), northern fur seal (*Callorhinus ursinus*), harp seal (*Pagophilus groenlandicus*), and marten (*Martes americana*).

Table 4.6 classifies North American furbearers (plus the American alligator) by average annual harvest volume and pelt (or skin) value. The top two species economically—raccoon and muskrat—are both high volume species, being harvested in the millions. The muskrat harvest is more than twice that of raccoon but the latter has the more valuable pelt. Hence its economic preeminence both in the United States and in North America as a whole. The popularity of raccoon pelts has fluctuated widely during this century. The 1920s marked the heyday of the coonskin coat; for a time demand was so great there were even a number of raccoon ranches (A-769). Then fashion changed and the fad passed. Coonskin reemerged as a hot item in the 1950s, ushered in on the head of a television superstar, Davy Crockett (P-408). This craze, too, passed. In the 1972–73 season raccoon overtook muskrat as the top dollar value

Table 4.4 **North American furbearing families with average annual mean harvest of more than $1 million, 1976–1980 (mean value U.S.$)**

| FAMILY | SPECIES | NORTH AMERICA: HARVEST | UNITED STATES: HARVEST* | CANADA: HARVEST† |
|---|---|---|---|---|
| PROCYONIDAE (3,258,908) $58,631,000 | *Procyon lotor* Common raccoon | (3,139,796) $57,763,000 | (3,019,945) $54,679,000 | (119,851) $3,084,000 |
| | *Bassariscus astutus* Ring-tailed cat | (119,112) $868,000 | (119,112) $868,000 | NO |
| CANIDAE (936,188) $36,518,000 | *Vulpes vulpes* Red fox | (291,385) $13,649,000 | (214,789) $8,516,000 | (76,596) $5,133,000 |
| | *Canis latrans* Coyote | (371,305) $12,889,000 | (303,209) $8,625,000 | (68,096) $4,264,000 |
| | *Vulpes cinereoargenteus* Gray fox | (114,596) $5,061,000 | (114,596) $5,061,000 | NH |
| | Unspecified fox | (118,173) $3,279,000 | (118,173) $3,279,000 | ND |
| | *Alopex lagopus* Arctic fox | (31,713) $1,037,000 | ND | (31,713) $1,037,000 |
| | *Canis lupus* Wolf | (6,005) $477,000 | ND | (6,005) $477,000 |
| | *Vulpes velox* Swift fox | (1,675) $16,000 | (1,675) $16,000 | NH |
| | *Vulpes macrotis* Kit fox | (1,336) $11,000 | (1,336) $11,000 | NO |
| MURIDAE (6,552,821) $27,821,000 | *Ondatra zibethicus* Muskrat | (6,552,821) $27,821,000 | (4,573,486) $18,738,000 | (1,979,335) $9,083,000 |

| | | | |
|---|---|---|---|
| MUSTELIDAE (813,028) $12,618,000 | | | |
| *Mustela vison* American mink | (314,467) $4,676,000 | (201,624) $2,259,000 | (112,843) $2,417,000 |
| *Martes americana* American marten | (122,468) $2,731,000 | (5,047) $46,000 | (117,421) $2,685,000 |
| *Lutra canadensis* Canadian otter | (48,148) $2,558,000 | (27,807) $1,160,000 | (20,341) $1,398,000 |
| *Martes pennanti* Fisher | (15,585) $1,179,000 | (5,254) $85,000 | (10,331) $1,094,000 |
| *Taxidea taxus* American badger | (40,183) $842,000 | (33,628) $585,000 | (6,555) $257,000 |
| Unspecified skunks | (86,706) $247,000 | (86,706) $247,000 | ND |
| *Gulo gulo* Wolverine | (863) $133,000 | (28) $4,000 | (835) $129,000 |
| Unspecified weasels | (99,796) $119,000 | (13,726) $8,000 | (86,070) $111,000 |
| *Mephitis mephitis* Striped skunk | (76,498) $84,000 | (74,961) $79,000 | (1,537) $5,000 |
| *Spilogale putorius* Eastern spotted skunk | (8,314) $49,000 | (8,314) $49,000 | NO |
| FELIDAE (109,174) $14,941,000 | | | |
| *Felis rufus* Bobcat | (83,825) $9,469,000 | (79,956) $8,984,000 | (3,869) $485,000 |
| *Felis lynx* Lynx | (25,319) $5,467,000 | (2,563) $80,000 | (22,756) $5,387,000 |
| *Felis concolor* Puma | (30) $5,000 | ND | (30) $5,000 |

(continued)

75

Table 4.4 (*Continued*)

| FAMILY | SPECIES | NORTH AMERICA: HARVEST | UNITED STATES: HARVEST* | CANADA: HARVEST† |
|---|---|---|---|---|
| CASTORIDAE (641,409) $13,917,000 | *Castor canadensis* American beaver | (641,409) $13,917,000 | (204,382) $1,863,000 | (437,027) $12,054,000 |
| OTARIIDAE (38,880) $3,160,000 | *Callorhinus ursinus* Northern fur seal | (38,880) $3,160,000 | (33,200) $2,831,000 | (5,680) $330,000 |
| PHOCIDAE (179,508) $2,992,000 | *Pagophilus groenlandicus* Harp seal and *Cystophora cristata* Hooded seal | (179,508) $2,992,000 | NO | (179,508) $2,992,000 |
| DIDELPHIDAE (908,961) $2,104,000 | *Didelphis virginiana* Virginian opossum | (908,961) $2,104,000 | (908,961) $2,104,000 | ND |
| ALLIGATORIIDAE‡ (19,000) $1,925,000 | *Alligator mississippiensis* American alligator | (19,000) $1,925,000 | (19,000) $1,925,000 | NO |
| SCIURIDAE (826,273) $1,072,000 | Unspecified squirrels | (826,273) $1,072,000 | ND | (826,273) $1,072,000 |

* Source: Mail survey (appendix A) except for northern fur seal (S-699).

† Sources: S-554–S-558; Canadian dollars converted to U.S. dollars at the average annual exchange rate of .91 for 1976–1980 (D-450).

‡ Data only for 1979–1980.

Notes: ND = no data, NH = not harvested, NO = does not occur.

Table 4.5  **North American furbearing families with average annual mean harvest of under $1 million, 1976–1980 (mean value U.S.$)**

| FAMILY | SPECIES | NORTH AMERICA: HARVEST | UNITED STATES: HARVEST* | CANADA: HARVEST† |
|---|---|---|---|---|
| URSIDAE (4,267) $531,000 | *Thalarctos maritimus* Polar bear | (467) 332,000 | ND | (467) $332,000 |
| | *Ursus americanus* American black bear | (3,784) $194,000 | ND | (3,784) $194,000 |
| | *Ursus arctos* Brown bear | (16) $5,000 | ND | (16) $5,000 |
| CAPROMYIDAE (38,719) $231,000 | *Myocastor coypus* Coypu | (38,719) $231,000 | (38,719) $231,000 | NH |
| LEPORIDAE (2,132) $1,000 | Unspecified rabbits | (2,132) $1,000 | ND | (2,132) $1,000 |

Notes: ND = no data, NH = not harvested.
* Source: Mail survey (appendix A).
† Sources: S-554–S-558; Canadian dollars converted to U.S. dollars at the average annual exchange rate of .91 for 1976–1980 (D-450).

furbearer in the United States. As of this writing it still has this position. Between 1976 and 1980 an average of about 3 million raccoons were harvested annually for a value exceeding $54 million.

Beaver, red fox, coyote, gray fox, mink, northern fur seal, harp seal, and marten are medium-volume, medium-value species. Red fox and mink are also farmed, but domesticated red fox accounts for only a small proportion of the value of production (2% of U.S. production, 12% of Canadian production, 6% of combined North American production). The picture is quite different for mink, which when farm and wild production are combined is the most valuable furbearer on the continent. The average annual value of North American mink production during the period was $117.8 million (United States, $86.8 million; Canada, $31.0 million), of which farmed animals accounted for $113.1 million (96%) and wild animals for $4.7 million (4%). The domestication of furbearers is discussed in chapter 7.

The American beaver, the second largest rodent in the world (after the capybara of South America), was one of Canada's first natural resources to be exploited. The quest for its pelt was the driving force behind the exploration and settlement of New France by Europeans and the cornerstone of the vast northern empire of the Hudson's Bay Company (A-769, P-408). It was the unit of currency in the new land (A-769). In 1763, about 75,000 beaver pelts were ex-

Table 4.6 **Classification of North American wild furbearers and skinbearers by average annual harvest volume and pelt/skin value, 1976–1980**

| | |
|---|---|
| High volume, high value | — |
| High volume, medium value | raccoon |
| High volume, low value | muskrat |
| Upper-medium volume, high value | — |
| Upper-medium volume, medium value | beaver, red fox, coyote, gray fox, mink, harp seal, marten |
| Upper-medium volume, low value | opossum, red squirrel, ringtail |
| Lower-medium volume, high value | bobcat, lynx, American alligator, fisher |
| Lower-medium volume, medium value | northern fur seal, otter, Arctic fox, badger |
| Lower-medium volume, low value | ermines/weasels, skunks |
| Low volume, high value | polar bear, wolverine, brown bear, cougar |
| Low volume, medium value | wolf, black bear |
| Low volume, low value | swift fox, kit fox, rabbits |

Sources: Tables 4.4 and 4.5.

Notes: High volume = millions, Upper-medium volume = hundreds of thousands, Lower-medium volume = tens of thousands, Low volume = fewer than ten thousand. High value = U.S. $100 + per pelt/skin,* Medium value = U.S. $10–99 per pelt/skin,* Low value = under U.S. $10 per pelt/skin.*

* Average value in the United States and Canada; values vary with origin (e.g., Canadian lynx and beaver fetch higher prices than U.S. lynx and beaver): the higher value category is chosen throughout.

ported from North America (G-449). By the early 1920s, this rotund national symbol of Canada had disappeared from large regions of the country, primarily because of uncontrolled trapping and the contagion of tularemia virus from rabbits (A-1013, A-1098). Between 1930 and 1950, provincial and federal governments initiated and implemented beaver conservation plans and established strict trapping regulations. Remnant populations from many national and provincial parks and game preserves were used to reestablish beaver colonies in the depleted areas (A-1098). The beaver responded. It is estimated that there are more beavers in Canada today than there were when Europeans first arrived (A-982). In the late 1950s, the beaver displaced the muskrat as Canada's most valuable wild furbearer. For the five-year period from 1976 to 1980, an annual average of 400,000 beavers worth more than $12 million were trapped in Canada, making this historically important animal a continuing economic force.

Bobcat and lynx are medium-volume, high-value species whose economic importance has increased dramatically in recent years. Bobcat fur is soft and not very durable, and prior to 1970 a pelt was seldom bought for more than $10. Then in 1971–72 the average price per pelt rose to $30. By 1975–76 it had leaped to $125 (D-320), with better quality pelts fetching prices as high as $300 and $400 (P-408). Lynx is more valuable than bobcat, having a long, lax, and thick pelage, and is now considered one of the high style furs (A-769). However, its average price per pelt, double that of bobcat, has risen almost as sharply (S-558). These changes reflect the shift in the fur trade from the big cats to smaller cats that began in the early 1970s. Overhunting threatened the survival of tiger, leopard, jaguar, cheetah, snow leopard, and other big cats, many of which were placed on Appendix I (banning all trade) when CITES came into force in 1975. As trade in these species came under more stringent control, the industry switched to the smaller cats to meet consumer demand (M-1021). There is a substantial North American demand for lynx and bobcat fur. Fewer than 50% of the 84,000 bobcat pelts harvested annually from 1976 to 1980 were exported; the main importing countries were West Germany, Switzerland, Denmark, France, and Italy (S-428).

Overexploitation of certain species and consequent restriction of their trade and substitution for other species—together with changes in fashion—are the two factors influencing the rising demand for some North American species and the declining value of others. The trend can be illustrated from the Canadian statistics on harvests and average pelt values (S-558). In the quarter century between the periods 1951–1955 and 1976–1980 there have been

1. increased harvests of beaver (up by 83%), raccoon (282%), marten (572%), coyote (427%), lynx (104%), and bobcat (630%)
2. reduced harvests of muskrat (down by 47%), ermine (77%), and Arctic fox (40%)
3. much increased average pelt values of lynx (up by 3,872%), bobcat (13,159%), red fox (1,296%), coyote (2,508%), and raccoon (1,290%).

As a result of these changes, beaver became Canada's most valuable wild furbearer (switching 1st and 2d places with muskrat), lynx moved from 11th to 3d, red fox from 8th to 4th, coyote from 13th to 5th, and raccoon from 12th to 6th; while squirrel dropped from 4th to 12th, Arctic fox from 6th to 13th, and ermine from 5th to 20th.

A third factor, public opinion, emerged as a decisive force in the market for particular species during the late 1970s and early 1980s. By 1983 the public outcry against the killing of pups of harp seals (*Pagophilus groenlandicus*) prompted the European Economic Community to impose a two-year ban on imports of furskins both of this species and of the hooded seal (*Cystophora cristata*). Since the countries of the EEC were the principal markets for harp and hooded seal products, the effect of this ban has been virtually to end trade in the fur and leather of these species (D-811).

Wolf (*Canis lupus*) and polar bear (*Thalarctos martimus*) are listed as vulnerable by IUCN, and two subspecies of cougar (*Felis concolor*)—eastern (*F. c. cougar*) and Florida (*F. c. coryi*)—are listed as endangered (S-625). These are the only North American furbearing/skinbearing species considered threatened, but none makes a major contribution to trade. Wolf, the most valuable of the three species, had an average annual harvest value during our period of $477,000. This represented 0.3% of the total value of production (table 4.4).

These three species and five other North American species entering the fur and skin trades have been placed on Appendix II of CITES (G-486). This means that trade in these species and their products is monitored and subject to federal regulation. Of the five other species, brown bear (*Ursus arctos*) is of negligible economic significance, but the remaining four make major contributions to the fur and skin trades: bobcat and lynx (already discussed), Canadian otter (*Lutra canadensis*), and American alligator (*Alligator mississippiensis*).

With an annual value of $2.6 million, the Canadian otter is the 13th most valuable North American furbearer (table 4.4). On average, 48,000 otters were trapped each year in North America between 1976 and 1980. Major European importing countries of otter skins include West Germany, Switzerland, Italy, and Austria (D-272). Like bobcat and lynx, the Canadian otter is not threatened but is covered by CITES largely because of its similarity to related species that are at risk.

The range of the American alligator is the southeastern United States from central North Carolina to Texas and north along the Mississipii River drainage to extreme southeast Oklahoma and southern Arkansas (G-478). The alligator was exterminated over large areas because of excessive hunting and poaching (P-406) and drastic alteration of its habitat by human activities (A-797). In 1967 the American alligator was classified as "endangered" throughout its range under the U.S. Endangered Species Act. Between 1970 and 1974 the wild population increased by 47%; it continued to increase with the result that by 1978 the species had made a comeback to 800,000 in the wild. Another 25,000 animals were to be found on farms in Louisiana, Florida, and Georgia (G-478). By 1979, the alligator was reclassified in every state to "threatened" or "threatened by similarity of appearance" and transferred from CITES Appendix I to Appendix II. As a result, skins from Florida and Louisiana (the two states with the largest wild populations) could again enter international trade (P-406). The American alligator is now classified by IUCN as out of danger. In 1979 and 1980 an average of 19,000 wild alligators were harvested annually in Louisiana and Florida for a value of about $2 million. France was the leading importer for both years. The species remains on Appendix II because of the need to monitor its status closely and because of the similarity of its appearance to other crocodilians, most of which are either endangered or vulnerable (vulnerable = threatened = likely to become endangered if present trends persist) (G-828).

## Furs and Skins Imported into the United States

During the period 1976–1980, U.S. imports of furs and skins from wild and domesticated species had an average customs value of some $220 million a year (see tables 4.2 and 4.3). We estimate that at least $51 million of this sum comes from wild populations (see table 4.1 and note 1). Wild furs and skins from Canada account for $21 million (41%), wild furs and mammal, bird, and shark skins from other countries for $16 million (31%), and reptile skins for $14 million (28%).

Determination of what comes from wild and what from domesticated sources is complicated by interchangeable use of the terms *farmed* and *ranched* and application of either term to animal-raising operations that rely wholly or largely on reproductive stock from the wild. In 1979 the parties to CITES defined as *farmed* animals born or hatched from parents mated in a captive environment. In 1981 they defined as *ranched* animals taken from the wild and reared in a controlled environment. International trade in endangered species is permitted under CITES if the stocks are farmed or if they are ranched by an operation deemed "primarily beneficial to the conservation of the local population" and whose products are "adequately identified and documented to ensure that they can be readily distinguished from products of Appendix I populations" (M-329).

The CITES definition of farmed corresponds with ours. Populations defined as ranched fall within our definition of wild. According to a detailed study of farmed and ranched wildlife undertaken for CITES by the IUCN Conservation Monitoring Centre (personal communication, April 1984), the commercial domestication status of the nine mammal groups classified by us as W (from the wild) in tables 4.2 and 4.3 is as follows.

1. Squirrel, seal, ocelot, leopard. Not farmed at all.
2. Lynx, marten, otter. A few small farms. Commercial fur supplies still 100% from the wild.
3. Capybara (carpincho [*Hydrochaeris hydrochaeris*]). Farmed experimentally. Ranched in Venezuela to the extent that wild populations occurring on ranches are harvested regularly, but with no/negligible habitat management. Commercial skin supplies 100% from the wild.
4. Beaver. An incipient domesticate (chap. 7). Several large farms, all in the United States and hence not contributors to U.S. imports, which are 100% from the wild.

Reptiles are in a similar position. Although to date no snake or lizard farms have been established, crocodilians and turtles are increasingly being ranched and many of the ranches are called farms. As far as we can determine, however, no large-scale reptile "farm" has yet become completely independent of wild-collected eggs.

During the period 1976–1980 the United States imported an annual average of $14.3 million of reptile skins and their products (table 4.2). An analysis of U.S. imports of crocodilian skins and their products in 1981 (P-406) reports a total declared value of $9 million—15% of the total value of reptile skin imports that year. The year 1981 was unusual, its $60.7 million of reptile skin imports being almost three times the level of 1980 ($23.3 million) and almost twice that of 1983 ($33.4 million). We assume, however, that the proportion accounted for by crocodilian skins is representative of recent years. Once the mainstay of the reptile-leather industry, crocodilians have declined in importance since the 1960s, owing to trade restrictions and much reduced populations following two decades of heavy overexploitation (G-1199). All 21 species are now covered by CITES.

Three species make up virtually all U.S. crocodilian imports: spectacled caiman (*Caiman crocodilus*), New Guinea crocodile (*Crocodylus novaeguineae*), and estuarine crocodile (*Crocodylus porosus*). In 1981 spectacled caiman accounted for 89% of imports of crocodilian skins and 91% of imports of manufactured products; New Guinea crocodile accounted for the remaining 11% of the skins and for 7% of the manufactured products; and estuarine crocodile accounted for 1% of the manufactured products. The remaining 1% of manufactured products was supplied by a miscellany of minor species, notably African crocodiles (*Crocodylus* spp. and *Osteolaemus tetraspis*) and smooth-fronted caimans (*Paleosuchus* spp.) from South America (P-406).

Although New Guinea and estuarine crocodiles supplied only 11% of the crocodilian skins and 8% of the manufactured products imported by the United States in 1981, they accounted for 50% of the value of crocodilian skin imports. The estuarine crocodile is highly valued by the reptile leather trade for the small size of its belly scales and the large area of belly skin without osteoderms (bony protuberances). The New Guinea crocodile is somewhat less valuable than the estuarine crocodile but commands a higher price than the spectacled caiman, which (like other caimans) has well-developed osteoderms on its belly skin (G-828). Osteoderms generally cannot be eliminated and make it difficult or impossible for processors to achieve a fine horn back or smooth, glazed finish (J-292, V-317). Hence, although caimans made up 90% of the volume of U.S. crocodilian skin imports in 1981, they accounted for 47% of the value.

The estuarine crocodile is classified by IUCN as endangered throughout its range (Sri Lanka to Micronesia and northern Australia). It is on Appendix I of CITES, which bans trade in all populations of the species except those in Papua New Guinea, which have been placed on Appendix II. The aim of this measure is to allow trade in skins from so-called farms in Papua New Guinea, which rear in captivity young collected from the wild. The New Guinea crocodile is found on the island of New Guinea and is classified as vulnerable. It is a CITES Appendix II species, and most of the U.S. supply comes from wild (including wild-caught young reared in captivity) populations in Papua New Guinea; the remainder comes from Irian Jaya (the Indonesian portion of New Guinea). The spectacled caiman is a widespread (Mexico to Argentina) and variable species whose taxonomy is confused. The nominate subspecies (which makes up virtually all the trade in caimans) is considered vulnerable and is listed on CITES Appendix II (G-828). In 1981 many of the caiman skins and caiman skin products came from Colombia (19% of the total value of U.S. crocodilian skin imports). Other important suppliers were Paraguay (8%), French Guiana (6%), Bolivia (5%), and Peru (4%) (P-406).

A small proportion of U.S. reptile skin imports (probably not more than 5% of the total value) during 1976–1980 consisted of the skin and leather of the green turtle (*Chelonia mydas*) and olive ridley turtle (*Lepidochelys olivacea*). Both species are classified as endangered by IUCN and listed on Appendix I of CITES (G-828). The United States banned imports of sea turtle products in June 1979, but before the ban it was a major consumer both of sea turtle skin and of the meat of green turtle. Between 1976 and 1979 the United States imported several large consignments of olive ridley turtle skins from Mexico and green turtle skins from Mexico and the Cayman Islands, as well as 3,000 turtle leather shoes from Mexico. Imports continued even after the two species were listed in the Endangered Species Act in 1978 but appear to have ended with the outright ban on all sea turtle imports in mid-1979 (M-329).

The bulk of U.S. reptile skin imports (80% of the value) comes from snakes and lizards. The main snake species in trade are the oriental rat snake, or whip-snake (*Ptyas mucosus*), largely from India; the boa constrictor (*Boa constrictor*), chiefly from Paraguay; the anaconda (*Eunectes anaconda* and *E. murinus*), from several South American countries; and the python (*Python molurus, P. sebae,* and *P. reticulatus*), largely from Southeast Asia (except for African *P. sebae*) (G-792, G-1199). Most of the lizard skins imported by the United States come from tegu and monitor lizards. Between 1977 and 1980 world trade in tegu lizard (*Tupinambis teguixin*) averaged more than 1 million skins a year, most originating from Argentina and Paraguay (G-1178). (Data for 1976 are not available, because the genus was not then monitored under CITES.) World trade in monitor lizards (*Varanus* spp.) averaged 450,000 skins a year between 1976 and 1980. The three main species in trade are Nile monitor (*V. niloticus*), largely from Nigeria, Sudan, Mali, and Cameroon; Malayan monitor (*V. salvator*), largely from Indonesia, Thailand, the Philippines, Malaysia, and China; and African savanna monitor (*V. exanthematicus*), largely from Nigeria (A-2040, G-1201). Common snake and lizard products include belts, handbags, wallets, shoes, jewelry, garments, and briefcases. Lizard skin is also often used in watchbands.

## Shells and Shell Articles Imported by the United States

Shell collecting as a hobby reached a peak of popularity in the nineteenth century during the Victorian "golden age of natural history." Recently there has been a resurgence in the number of amateur conchologists (A-1027, V-274). Although European countries are among the principal shell importers (V-274), the United States also imports impressive quantities of both crude marine shells and articles of shell. From 1976 to 1980, the United States imported an average of $11 million worth of shells annually—of which approximately one-third was crude marine shells and the remaining two-thirds articles of shell (fig. 4.1).

Mexico was the leading exporter of crude shells to the United States, followed by the Philippines. Each exported more than $1 million worth a year to the United States. The Mexican shells included rock shells (*Murex* spp.), olives (*Oliva* spp.), conches (*Strombus* spp.), and abalone (*Haliotis* spp.) (A-1027, V-274). The Philippine shell exports were largely composed of four species of mother-of-pearl (*Pinctada maxima, P. margaritifera, Trochus niloticus,* and *Turbo marmoratus*) plus the capiz shell, or windowpane oyster (*Placuna placenta*) (V-274).

Other big exporters included Haiti, Australia, and India. Among the Haitian shells, collected mainly from the Gulf of Gonâve, were helmet shells (*Cassis* spp.), tritons (*Cymatium* spp.), rock shells (*Murex* spp.), and conchs (*Strombus* spp.). Haiti is the poorest nation in the Western Hemisphere. Its prominence in shell exportation is due to organized wholesalers on La Gonâve Island, cheap labor, a scarcity of jobs, and the fact that much-needed protein is provided by the mollusks that are removed when the shells are cleaned (A-1027). For over 100 years, Australia has had a mother-of-pearl industry based on *Pinctada maxima.* In the 1960s the Arafura Sea region was producing 80–90% of the world's mother-of-pearl (V-274). India's rise in shell exports is due to recent exploitation of offshore beds of shells (A-1027). The Gulf of Mannar and Palk Bay supply most of the ornamental shells collected. About two dozen species are involved, including chanks (*Turbinella pyrum*) and cowries (*Cypraea* spp.) (V-274).

More than half ($4,944,000) of the $7,166,000 of shell articles imported annually into the United States comes from the Philippines. Many articles are made of mother-of-pearl or capiz shells. Mother-of-pearl is often used for buttons, jewelry, cutlery handles, and decorative inlay work. Capiz shell is used for lampshades, wind chimes, coasters, boxes, and so forth (V-274). Shells are also used in figurines, dolls, boats, animal figures, napkin rings, mobiles, and as borders on wall mirrors and place mats. A recent item on the market from the Philippines is a woman's purse made of leatherwork and the chambered nautilus (*Nautilus pompilius*) (A-1027).

The impact of shell collecting is not well documented. The following Caribbean (and Floridian) species are now uncommon in certain localities as a result

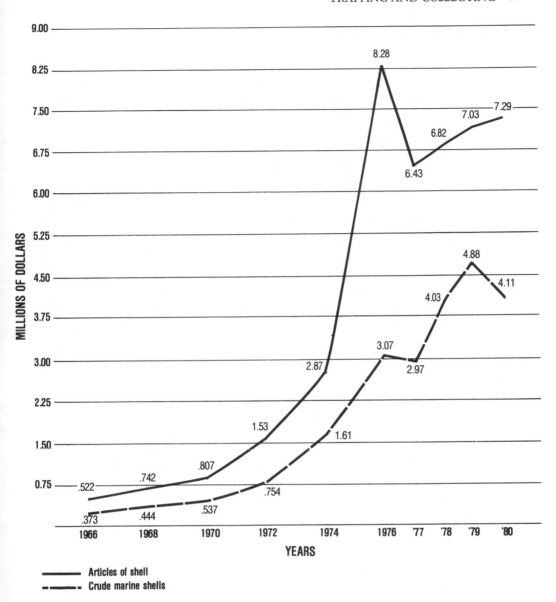

Fig. 4.1   **Imports of articles of shell and crude marine shells to the United States, 1966, 1968, 1970, 1972, 1974, 1976–1980. Sources: A-1027, S-450–S-454**

of overcollection: pink conch (*Strombus gigas*), queen helmet (*Cassis madagas-carensis*), Florida horse conch (*Pleuroploca gigantea*), Triton's trumpet (*Charonia variegata*), angel wing (*Cyrtopleura costata*), flamingo tongue (*Cyphoma gibbosum*) and king's crown (*Melongena corona*) (A-1027). Overcollection has also become a problem in East Africa, the Seychelles, and Australia (V-274).

## Ornamental Fish Imported by the United States

Prior to 1945, the world trade in ornamental fish was not significant. The limited demand was met most often through domestic breeding. Any imported (largely freshwater) species usually served as breeding stock. By the late 1960s, trade in tropical fish assumed new dimensions as a result of the introduction of jets in civil aviation, which reduced transport time, and the economic boom in industrialized countries. Aquarists wanted a greater number of fish from a greater number of species. It became more profitable for the wholesaler to import, rather than to breed, exotic fish. By 1979, 85% of all tropical aquarium fish sold in industrialized countries was imported (G-432). Between 1976 and 1980, the United States imported an average of $17.4 million worth of aquarium fish each year; wild species accounted for $8 million (see table 4.1 and note 4).

World trade in exotic fish totaled $4 billion in 1973. (This figure includes all elements of the trade, including, for example, tanks and accessories.) Sales of fish were worth $1 billion retail and $300 million wholesale. Overall trade figures increased to $6 billion in 1979, with fish sales estimated at $1.8 billion retail and $600 million wholesale. Hobbyists account for nearly 95% of the world market. By far the highest percentage of aquarium fish tanks is purchased by apartment dwellers in industrial urban centers (G-432). The United States, with 22 million exotic-fish enthusiasts (A-757), is by far the largest world market (G-432). The total population of ornamental aquarium fish in U.S. homes, stores, and fish farms has been estimated to be 1–3 billion. According to a 1981 survey of 300 pet retailers, freshwater and saltwater fish sales make up 45% of all pet store livestock sales, more than the sales of dogs, cats, and birds combined (G-1200). Imports supply about half the fish sold in the United States. The other half comes largely from farms in Florida (some are wild-caught from the coastal waters of Florida and Hawaii) (G-1200).

Ornamental fish imports by the United States increased from less than $1 million a year in 1963 to more than $18 million a year in 1982. In the early 1960s almost 90% of ornamental fish imports came from tropical America. By the mid-1970s supplies from Asia accounted for more than half the total import value. In the period 1976–1980 South and East Asia contributed 74% of the total import value; South America and the Caribbean contributed 21% (table 4.7). Imports from mainland Asia, Taiwan, and Japan consist almost entirely of freshwater species. Most are captive bred, but the proportion of captive-bred to wild-caught fish varies among the individual countries of the region (G-432). For example, 80% of Thailand's exotic fish export trade is from wild-caught fish (A-757). Virtually all the ornamental fish coming from the Philippines are saltwater species (G-432). Indonesia supplies both freshwater and saltwater species (G-1200). Imports from tropical America are predominately of freshwater species, except for those from Central America and Haiti, which are mainly of saltwater species (A-757, G-1200). South American and Caribbean supplies

come almost entirely from the wild (G-432). This reliance on wild-caught specimens will probably continue because only 15% of the more popular Latin
American species can be bred successfully. Imports from Africa are of freshwater species obtained from the wild (A-757, G-432).

Table 4.7  **Countries from which United States imported an annual average of ornamental fish worth $17.4 million, 1976–1980**

| REGION (% of total value) | COUNTRY* (% of total value) | VALUE (U.S.$ million) |
|---|---|---|
| South and East Asia (74) | Hong Kong (19) | 3.4 |
| | Singapore (19) | 3.3 |
| | Thailand (17) | 3.0 |
| | Philippines (8) | 1.4 |
| | Taiwan (5) | 0.9 |
| | Japan (4) | 0.7 |
| | Indonesia (1) | 0.2 |
| South America and Caribbean (21) | Colombia (10) | 1.8 |
| | Peru (5) | 0.8 |
| | Brazil (3) | 0.4 |
| | Guyana (2) | 0.2 |
| | Haiti (1) | 0.1 |
| | Trinidad and Tobago (1) | 0.1 |
| | Panama (1) | 0.1 |
| | Jamaica (1) | 0.1 |
| Africa (2) | Nigeria (2) | 0.3 |
| | Malawi (1) | 0.1 |
| Other countries (3) | | 0.5 |

Sources: S-450–S-454.
*Country percentages may not add to regional percentages due to rounding.

In terms of quantity, freshwater species account for 90% of the world market (G-432) and 95% of the U.S. market (G-1200). United States imports during 1977 and 1980 included some 250 freshwater species and more than 230 marine species. The native regions of the freshwater species were South and Central America (50%), Asia (34%), and Africa (16%). The native regions of the marine species were the Indo–West Pacific (74%) and the Caribbean–West Atlantic (23%) (G-1200).

Demand for marine fish is now growing more rapidly than is the demand for freshwater fish (G-432). For example, during 1972 and 1973, saltwater species comprised a mere 1% of all U.S. imports of ornamental fish (A-757); by 1979 this figure had jumped to 10–15%. Although the volume of trade may be low at present, the value is high—25–30% of the value of the entire U.S. ornamental-fish trade is generated from the sale of saltwater species. The reasons for this expanding market include increased supplies of marine fish in recent years, the development of new products to facilitate maintenance of saltwater tanks, and wide dissemination of information on how to keep saltwater fish. The United States imports its saltwater (and brackish-water) species primarily from the Philippines (G-432).

## Ivory Imported by the United States

"White gold" is the traditional (and economically apt) nickname for ivory. Today the world trade in ivory—raw and worked, wholesale and retail—is worth more than $222 million annually (P-391). The United States does not import much raw ivory—just over $400,000 worth annually. It is, however, a big consumer of worked ivory—importing almost $6 million worth of beads and other articles each year (fig. 4.2).

Ivory articles range from carvings to jewelry, billiard balls, chess sets, knife handles, and ivory-black paint (derived from ivory crisped to an ebony powder). Eighty-eight percent of U.S. imports in 1976–1980 of worked ivory came from Hong Kong, for which the United States—with more than 30% of the share—is the biggest market. Other exporters to the United States were Japan, the People's Republic of China, and India. Historically, India has been a center of ivory-working, but the Indian government, trying to conserve foreign exchange by restricting the import of luxury goods, levied a duty of 120% on the declared value of imported African ivory. This tax, in combination with the endangered status of the Asian elephant (*Elephas maximus*), which has been listed on CITES Appendix I, has contributed to the decline of the Indian ivory industry (P-391).

The species that now provides almost all the ivory traded is the African elephant (*Loxodonta africana*), which is found south of the Sahara (S-426). Current estimates of the wild population range from 1.3 million to 2.6 million

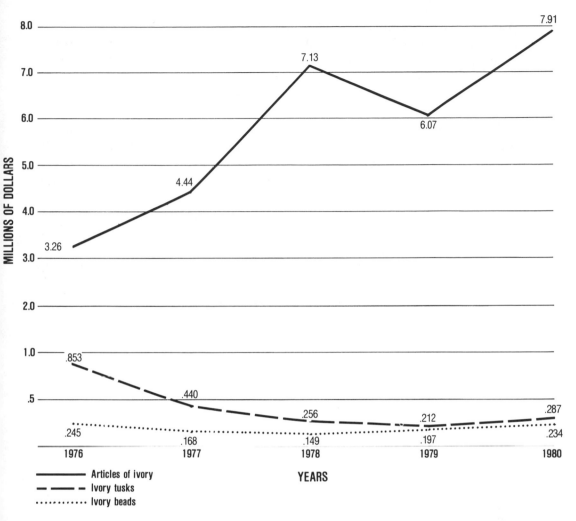

Fig. 4.2   **Imports of articles of ivory, ivory tusks, and ivory beads to the United States, 1976–1980. Sources: S-450–S-454**

(M-611). The African elephant, classified as vulnerable by IUCN (S-426), is an Appendix II species, so trade in it or its by-products is subject to regulation and monitoring by countries party to CITES. Each year the ivory from 44,000 to 60,000 elephants is exported from Africa (P-797). During the period 1976–1980 an estimated 83% of this ivory was bought by Japan and Hong Kong. Much of Japan's imports are destined for the home market; most of Hong Kong's are reexported in manufactured form (A-2041, P-797). The major exporters of raw ivory are Sudan, the Central African Republic, and Congo, which together accounted for 60–80% of Hong Kong's supplies between 1979 and 1983 (A-2042).

A substantial proportion of the ivory from Sudan is believed to originate in Zaire (P-797). Kenya (until 1977), South Africa, and Botswana were the main exporters of tusks to the United States during 1976–1980, but the quantity of U.S. imports was small (an average of 30,000 pounds a year) compared to Hong Kong's imports (an average of more than a million pounds a year) (A-2041, A-2042, S-450–S-454).

Raw elephant ivory is used in the United States by scrimshaw engravers, principally in New England and Hawaii, and by Inuit carvers in Alaska. Traditionally, the former group used teeth from the sperm whale, which are now banned from trade by all CITES members; the latter group relied on walrus the catch of which is limited by strict hunting regulations (P-391). Table 4.8 lists some average import values for raw ivory over the last 70 years. Since the mid-1970s the price of ivory has been falling, but the volume of raw ivory in trade has not diminished. Parker and Martin (P-797) believe that the supply of ivory is likely to remain high through the 1980s, regardless of fluctuations in demand or of attempts at regulating trade, because intensifying habitat competition between elephants and humans will result in a continued heavy kill of elephants.

Table 4.8  **Average world ivory prices**

| PERIOD | PRICE (U.S.$ per pound) |
|---|---|
| Pre-World War I | 2.25 |
| 1960s | 7.25–11.00 |
| Mid-1970s | 45.00–50.00 |
| Late-1970s | 37.00 |
| 1983 | 29.00 |

Sources: M-611, P-391.

## Coral and Coral Products Imported by the United States

Between 1976 and 1980, the United States imported an average of about $5 million worth of crude coral and coral and cameos each year for use in jewelry (fig. 4.3). Almost 50% of the crude coral was imported from the Philippines, even though a 1977 presidential decree banned coral exports. Precious corals (order Gorgonacea) and black or semiprecious corals (order Antipatharia) are found in Philippine waters but are not exploited very much because the local people lack the necessary expertise to fish at great depths (V-273). The Philippines exports mainly stony corals (of the order Scleractinia). These include the blue coral (*Heliopora coerulea*), the organ-pipe coral (*Tubipora musica*), several

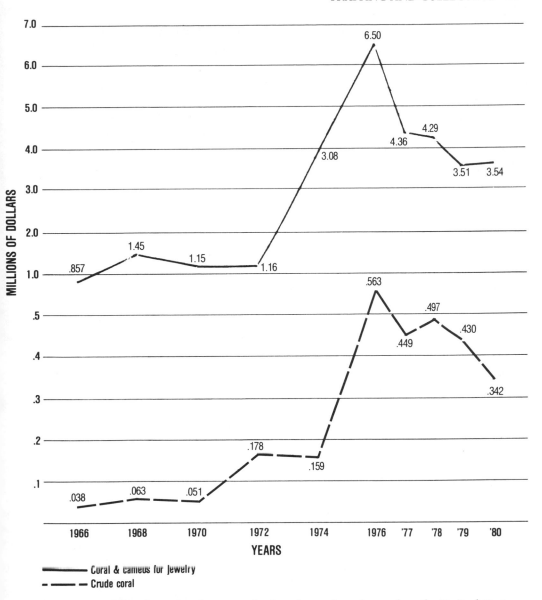

Fig. 4.3   **Imports of coral and cameos for jewelry and crude coral to the United States, 1966, 1968, 1970, 1972, 1974, 1976–1980. Sources: A-1027, S-450–S-454**

species of Acropora (*A. arcuata, A. humilis, A. millepora, A. multiacuta, A. rotumana, A. vaughani*), *Pocillopora* (*P. danae, P. verrucosa*), and *Fungia* (V-273; I. A. Ronquillo, pers. comm. 18 Jan. 1982).

Unfortunately, U.S. statistics combine worked coral with cameos cut for use in jewelry. As cameos can be made of coral or shells, it is not possible to know what proportion of this import category, valued at $4,439,000, is attributable to coral and what proportion to shells. Two countries—Italy, the largest exporter, and Taiwan—exported to the United States on average each year more than $1 million worth of coral and cameos cut for use in jewelry. Once easily obtainable (A-1027), *Corallium rubrum* has been the mainstay of the Mediterranean precious coral industry, which has been in existence since the Neolithic period. It is still collected off the west and north coasts of Sardinia and off the coasts of Sicily, but the harvests can no longer meet the current demand and Italy now imports large quantities of precious coral mainly from the Indo-Pacific. Large specimens of *C. rubrum* are said to be scarce in accessible sites, and the beds off Sardinia are becoming depleted. There may be, however, a few isolated places that have not yet been exploited (V-273).

Taiwan's importance stems not only from its production of carvings and cutouts from helmet shells (*Cassis* spp.), turban shells (*Turbo* spp.), and (wild) pearl oysters (A-1027) but also from its exports of large quantities of gem-quality coral. Its coral-collecting fleets range far into the Pacific and down into Australian waters in search of both precious and stony corals. Taiwan is a major world center for the coral-carving industry (V-273).

## Birds Imported by the United States for the Pet Trade

The international trade in birds is a high-volume business—a conservative estimate puts the figure at 5,000,000 birds per year. Most of the animals destined for the cage bird trade are wild caught from Asia, Africa, and South America. The major importing nations are the United States, Great Britain, France, Japan, the Federal Republic of Germany, Belgium, and the Netherlands. These last three countries are not only big importers but also big reexporters of foreign birds (G-697). Wild-caught birds suffer an extremely high mortality rate—40% on average—during capture and shipment. For delicate species the death rate may be as high as 80% (D-474, cited in M-616). Given these attrition rates, we estimate that at least 12–13 million birds are taken from the wild each year for the pet trade. Even though many birds are lost, the profit margin is still enticingly high for importers. A Thai collector may be paid only 60 cents to one dollar per mynah brought in. The wholesaler then sells the bird for $30. At the retail level the animal fetches $350 (M-616). A blue-and-yellow macaw (*Ara ararauna*) can be purchased from hunters in Bolivia for $40. Wholesale prices in the United States range from $525 to $775 and retail prices from $950 to $2,000 (M-379).

About 40 million Americans own at least one bird (V-62). Canaries and budgerigars are still the best sellers, but there is an increasing demand for exotic species, such as cockatoos, cockatiels, finches, mynahs, parrots, toucans, and tanagers (M-616, V-62). Between 1976 and 1980, the United States imported on average each year about 500,000 birds worth $6 million (see table 4.1). Although we cannot state for certain what percentage of these imported birds was wild caught as opposed to captive bred, we can estimate that wild birds account for approximately $5 million. This is based on analyses for 1971 and 1972 showing that U.S. imports come largely from the wild—77% and 86%, respectively (A-1197, A-1198). A rough breakdown of the annual $6 million bird import trade is as follows: $2.75 million from Latin America and the Caribbean; $1.25 million from Africa; $1 million from Southeast Asia; and $1 million from Europe (table 4.9).

In the early 1970s, waxbills and finches comprised the majority of birds imported into the United States, but by 1980 the import business was dominated by members of the family Psittacidae (parrots) (M-379). The neotropical region is the top exporter to the United States, and a 1979–1980 study of U.S. imports of live birds revealed that 99% of the birds declared as originating in the New World were psittacines (P-260). The neotropical psittacine trade illustrates a

Table 4.9   **Live bird imports to the United States worth $6 million: annual average, 1976–1980**

| EXPORTING REGION<br>*(Average value U.S.$)* | EXPORTING COUNTRIES*<br>*(Average value U.S.$)* | |
|---|---|---|
| Latin America and Caribbean<br>(2,750,000) | Bolivia | (680,000) |
| | Paraguay | (500,000) |
| | Mexico | (470,000) |
| | Guyana | (470,000) |
| | Peru | (200,000) |
| | Nicaragua | (170,000) |
| | Argentina | (160,000) |
| | Trinidad and Tobago | (110,000) |
| Africa<br>(1,250,000) | South Africa | (580,000) |
| | Ghana | (200,000) |
| | Cameroon | (200,000) |
| | Tanzania | (200,000) |
| | Senegal | (150,000) |
| Southeast Asia<br>(1,000,000) | Indonesia | (840,000) |
| | Singapore | (180,000) |
| | Taiwan | (80,000) |
| | Malaysia | (70,000) |
| Europe<br>(1,000,000) | Belgium | (320,000) |
| | Sweden | (300,000) |
| | Netherlands | (200,000) |
| | West Germany | (200,000) |
| | Italy | (80,000) |

Sources: S-450–S-454.
*Country values do not add to regional values because of rounding.

feature of the trade in wild pets in general: although the total value of the trade is relatively low, it involves a huge number of species.

There are seven major groups of birds (and more than 70 species) involved in the neotropical psittacine import trade with the United States: macaws (see table 4.10), conures (table 4.11), parakeets (table 4.12), parrotlets (table 4.13), caiques (table 4.14), parrots (table 4.15), and amazons (table 4.16). Table 4.10 lists the 12 major macaw species imported into the United States between 1976 and 1979 and their countries of origin. The most popular species—with almost 1,000 animals imported annually—is the blue-and-yellow macaw, which has been imported regularly into Europe and the United States since the sixteenth century. In 1979, an average retail price for a blue-and-yellow macaw was about $1,200, third in expense among the eight species of macaw for which we have 1979 average retail figures: hyacinthine, $3,783; scarlet, $1,635; blue-and-yellow, $1,240; red-fronted, $1,149; military, $867; red-and-green, $648; chestnut-fronted, $412; golden-collared, $375 (M-379). Thousands of psittacines are smuggled into the United States from Mexico. The U.S. Department of Justice estimates that from 25,000 to 50,000 are smuggled across the border every year (S-429).

## Natural Pearls and Pearl Parts Produced and Imported by the United States

The pearl trade includes cultured pearls, natural pearls, the nuclei for cultured pearls, and mother-of-pearl. Since 1891 there has been a U.S. pearl button industry using freshwater bivalves from the Mississippi drainage. There are about 40 useful species and 17 species of major importance, all in the genera *Actinonaias*, *Amblema*, *Fusconaia*, *Lampsilis*, *Legumia*, *Megalonaias*, *Plagiola*, and *Quadrula* in the family Unionidae. The industry prospered until the 1940s, when plastics replaced pearl as the raw material for most button manufacture. In the early 1950s the Japanese cultured-pearl industry found that small pellets from the American Unionidae provided ideal nuclei for cultured pearls. Freshwater mussel production revived, only to slump in the 1970s as a result of overharvesting (P-788). In 1976, 3 million pounds of freshwater mussel shells were produced, with a landed value of $595,000, chiefly from the Arkansas, Tennessee, and Cumberland rivers and their tributaries. The main producing states were Tennessee and Oklahoma, with smaller amounts coming from Alabama, Arkansas, and Kentucky (A-1229).

The United States imported an annual average of $1,586,000 of natural pearls and pearl parts during 1976–1980. Most came from India (41% of the value), Japan (25%), and Burma (12%). Imports of cultured pearls during this period averaged $34,230,000 a year (S-450–S-454). The United States also imported an annual average of $294,000 of pearl buttons, manufactured from mother-of-pearl.

Table 4.10  **Major neotropical macaw species imported into the United States, 1976–1979**

| MACAW SPECIES | AVERAGE NUMBER IMPORTED ANNUALLY | EXPORTING COUNTRIES |
|---|---|---|
| *Ara ararauna* Blue-and-yellow macaw | 993 | Guyana (286); Bolivia (238); Trinidad and Tobago (114); Paraguay (67); Panama (38); Guatemala (36); others (214) |
| *Ara severa* Chestnut-fronted macaw | 974 | Bolivia (783); others (191) |
| *Ara auricollis* Golden-collared macaw | 873 | Bolivia (728), Indonesia—reexporter (24); Paraguay (13); others (108) |
| *Ara chloroptera* Red-and-green macaw | 275 | Paraguay (108); Guyana (44); Bolivia (39); Panama (14); others (70) |
| *Ara nobilis* Red-shouldered macaw | 220 | Guyana (99); Bolivia—reexporter (34); Suriname (13); others (74) |
| *Ara macao* Scarlet macaw | 199 | Guyana (26); Italy—reexporter (25); Trinidad and Tobago—reexporter (24); Panama (23); Guatemala (21); Sweden—reexporter (17); El Salvador (15); Bolivia (10); others (38) |
| *Anodorhynchus hyacinthinus* Hyacinthine macaw | 168 | Brazil (illegally smuggled from Brazil and reexported from Paraguay [127] and Bolivia [34]); others (7) |
| *Ara manilata* Red-bellied macaw | 97 | Guyana (31); Bolivia (20); Paraguay (18); others (28) |
| *Ara rubrogenys* Red-fronted macaw | 56 | Bolivia (all) |
| *Ara maracana* Blue-winged macaw | 39 | Paraguay (37); others (2) |
| *Ara militaris* Military macaw | 31 | Mexico (13); Panama (6); El Salvador (3); Guatemala (3); others (6) |
| *Ara ambigua* Great green macaw | 10 | Panama (4); Nicaragua (3); Italy—reexporter (3) |

Source: M-379.

Table 4.11  **Major neotropical conure species imported into the United States, 1977–1979**

| CONURE SPECIES | AVERAGE NUMBER IMPORTED ANNUALLY | EXPORTING COUNTRIES |
|---|---|---|
| *Nandayus nenday*<br>Black-hooded parakeet | 3,322 | Paraguay (2,705); Guyana (303); others (314) |
| *Aratinga mitrata*<br>Mitred parakeet | 1,999 | Bolivia (1,708); others (291) |
| *Pyrrhura devillei*<br>Blaze-winged parakeet | 1,865 | Paraguay (all) |
| *Aratinga aurea*<br>Peach-fronted parakeet | 1,800 | Paraguay (1,297); others (503) |
| *Aratinga pertinax*<br>Brown-throated parakeet | 1,080 | Guyana (715); Suriname (203); others (162) |
| *Aratinga leucophthalmus*<br>White-eyed parakeet | 846 | Bolivia (718); Paraguay (67); others (61) |
| *Aratinga acuticauda*<br>Blue-crowned parakeet | 569 | Bolivia (474); Paraguay (77); others (18) |
| *Pyrrhura frontalis*<br>Reddish-bellied parakeet | 374 | Paraguay (283); others (91) |
| *Cyanoliseus patagonus*<br>Burrowing parrot | 361 | Argentina (226); Paraguay (124); others (11) |
| *Aratinga weddellii*<br>Dusky-headed parakeet | 337 | Bolivia (103); others (234) |
| *Aratinga holochlora*<br>Green parakeet | 314 | Paraguay (292); others (22) |
| *Pyrrhura picta*<br>Painted parakeet | 305 | Nicaragua (200); Guyana (88); others (17) |
| *Aratinga jandaya*<br>Jandaya parakeet | 302 | Paraguay (272); others (30) |
| *Aratinga auricapilla*<br>Golden-capped parakeet | 183 | Paraguay (131); others (52) |
| *Enicognathus leptorhynchus*<br>Slender-billed parakeet | 140 | Chile (all) |
| *Aratinga canicularis*<br>Orange-fronted parakeet | 107 | Bolivia (75); Mexico (23); others (9) |
| *Pyrrhura rhodocephala*<br>Rose-headed parakeet | 105 | Paraguay (all) |
| *Pyrrhura molinae*<br>Green-cheeked parakeet | 100 | Bolivia (81); others (19) |

Source: S-429.

**Table 4.12  Major neotropical parakeet species imported into the United States, 1977–1979**

| PARAKEET SPECIES | AVERAGE NUMBER IMPORTED ANNUALLY | EXPORTING COUNTRIES |
|---|---|---|
| *Brotogeris versicoloris* Canary-winged parakeet | 959 | Paraguay (557); Bolivia (314); others (88) |
| *Myiopsitta monachus* Monk parakeet | 551 | Paraguay (451); Trinidad and Tobago (100) |
| *Brotogeris chrysopterus* Golden-winged parakeet | 387 | Paraguay (219); Trinidad and Tobago (100); others (68) |
| *Brotogeris jugularis* Orange-chinned parakeet | 177 | Panama (150); Paraguay (23); others (4) |

Source: S-429.

**Table 4.13  Major neotropical parrotlet species imported into the United States, 1977–1979**

| PARROTLET SPECIES | AVERAGE NUMBER IMPORTED ANNUALLY | EXPORTING COUNTRIES |
|---|---|---|
| *Forpus passerinus* Green-rumped parrotlet | 812 | Suriname (263); Trinidad and Tobago (175); others (374) |
| *Forpus xanthopterygius* Blue-winged parrotlet | 180 | Bolivia (50); others (130) |
| *Forpus sclateri* Dusky-billed parrotlet | 10 | Guyana (all) |

Source: S-429.

**Table 4.14  Major neotropical caique species imported into the United States, 1977–1979**

| CAIQUE SPECIES | AVERAGE NUMBER IMPORTED ANNUALLY | EXPORTING COUNTRIES |
|---|---|---|
| *Pionites melanocephala* Black-headed parrot | 312 | Guyana (200); Suriname (48); others (64) |
| *Pionites leucogaster* White-bellied parrot | 158 | Bolivia (120); Guyana (20); others (18) |

Source: S-429.

Table 4.15   **Major neotropical parrot species imported into the United States, 1977–1979**

| PARROT SPECIES | AVERAGE NUMBER IMPORTED ANNUALLY | EXPORTING COUNTRIES |
|---|---|---|
| *Pionus maximiliani* Scaly-headed parrot | 393 | Paraguay (259); Bolivia (92); others (42) |
| *Pionus menstruus* Blue-headed parrot | 327 | Trinidad and Tobago (107); Bolivia (51); Suriname (40); Guyana (23); others (106) |
| *Pionus fuscus* Dusky parrot | 48 | Guyana (11); others (37) |
| *Pionus tumultuosus* Plum-crowned parrot | 25 | Bolivia (all) |
| *Pionus senilus* White-crowned parrot | 11 | Guatemala (1); others (10) |
| *Hapalopsittaca melanotis* Black-eared parrot | 10 | Bolivia (7); Guyana (3) |
| *Deroptyus accepitrinus* Red-fan parrot | 7 | Suriname (4); Paraguay (2); others (1) |
| *Triclaria malachitacea* Blue-bellied parrot | 4 | Bolivia (all) |
| *Pionus sordidus* Red-billed parrot | 1 | Bolivia (all) |

Source: S-429.

## Sponges and Sponge Articles Imported by the United States

The United States imported an annual average of just over $1 million of sponges and sponge articles during 1976–1980. The main suppliers were Greece (49% of the value), Japan (12%), and the Bahamas (7%). The percentage accounted for by the Bahamas was probably somewhat greater because it is the main supplier of tropical sponges, which represent 16% of U.S. sponge imports by value (S-450–S-454).

Table 4.16  **Major neotropical amazon species imported into the United States, 1977–1979**

| AMAZON SPECIES | AVERAGE NUMBER IMPORTED ANNUALLY | EXPORTING COUNTRIES |
|---|---|---|
| *Amazona aestiva* Turqoise-fronted parrot | 2,915 | Paraguay (1,438); Bolivia (709); Guyana (174); others (594) |
| *Amazona ochrocephala* Yellow-headed parrot | 2,896 | Trinidad and Tobago (828); Guyana (403); Bolivia (402); Panama (119); Guatemala (108); Honduras (101); Mexico (100); others (835) |
| *Amazona amazonica* Orange-winged parrot | 2,261 | Guyana (1,611); Trinidad and Tobago (110); others (540) |
| *Amazona pretrei* Red-spectacled parrot | 976 | Guyana (466); Trinidad and Tobago (260); Panama (250) |
| *Amazona farinosa* Mealy parrot | 863 | Guyana (620); others (243) |
| *Amazona viridigenalis* Red-crowned parrot | 525 | Mexico (all) |
| *Amazona autumnalis* Red-lored parrot | 307 | El Salvador (73); Panama (30); Guatemala (13); others (191) |
| *Amazona finschia* Lilac-crowned parrot | 225 | Mexico (all) |
| *Amazona albifrons* White-fronted parrot | 146 | Mexico (83); Honduras (23); Guatemala (14); others (26) |

Source: S-429.

# 5

# Medicine

Throughout their lives, North Americans reach into the medicine cabinet for products to treat everything from diaper rash to menopause. A remarkable number of these familiar remedies contain ingredients that come from the wild.

Much attention in the literature has been devoted to the contribution of plant-derived products to the drug industry, but the distinction between cultivar-derived sources versus wild-derived sources is seldom addressed. For example, a 1976 paper by Farnsworth and Morris (D-135), the one most often cited when the dollar value of wild plants in medicine is discussed, gives the 1973 value as $3 billion, but this value is based on sales of prescription drugs with plant-derived ingredients, regardless of whether the plants are wild or domesticated. (A 1982 update by Farnsworth [D-404] projected a 1980 value of $8 billion.) A great number of the most widely used products are from cultivated plants, such as morphine from the opium poppy (*Papaver somniferum*), cocaine from coca (*Erythroxylum coca*), colchicine from the autumn crocus (*Colchicum autumnale*), vincristine and vinblastine from the Madagascar periwinkle (*Catharanthus roseus*), bromelin from the pineapple (*Ananas sativus*), papain from the papaya (*Carica papaya*), alseroxylon fraction from serpentwood (*Rauvolfia serpentina*), digitoxin from foxglove (*Digitalis purpurea*), and digoxin from Grecian foxglove (*D. lanata*).

We were unable to obtain adequate data to estimate the dollar value of wild species—both plant and animal—to the North American drug industry. Production statistics are not compiled for most of the species used in pharmaceuticals. Many of the species for which statistics—largely import statistics—are available are used by industries other than the pharmaceutical. Examples are carrageenan, gum arabic, and tragacanth. We present customs' value data for these species in the section on industrial products in chapter 6. Data on species and products imported by the United States primarily for medicinal purposes are found in table 5.1. Many of the general drug import categories include both wild and cultivated species, making it impossible to know what percentage of the value is attributable to wild species. Other import categories probably include synthesized products in addition to wild and cultivated species; again, the

Table 5.1  **Imports by the United States for largely medicinal purposes of species/products with possibly wild component, 1976–1980**

| PRODUCT DESCRIPTION | AVERAGE ANNUAL IMPORT VALUE (U.S.$) | EXPORTING COUNTRIES (% of U.S. imports) | |
|---|---|---|---|
| Natural drugs of vegetable origin, crude and advanced; drug compounds of vegetable origin nes | 37,634,500* | India | 40 |
| | | Netherlands | 15 |
| | | Republic of Korea | 9 |
| | | France | 8 |
| | | Sweden | 5 |
| | | Poland | 4 |
| | | Others | 19 |
| Adrenocortical hormones, synthetic nspf | 16,545,000 | France | 34 |
| | | Bahamas | 29 |
| | | United Kingdom | 15 |
| | | Netherlands | 5 |
| | | Others | 17 |
| Synthetic hormones nspf | 16,387,000* | Bahamas | 18 |
| | | Denmark | 17 |
| | | Mexico | 15 |
| | | France | 14 |
| | | West Germany | 14 |
| | | Netherlands | 10 |
| | | Others | 12 |
| Synthetic steroid hormones nspf | 12,879,000† | Denmark | 50 |
| | | Bahamas | 22 |
| | | Mexico | 10 |
| | | France | 7 |
| | | West Germany | 5 |
| | | Others | 6 |
| Other natural drugs: crude and advanced | 12,139,000 | Canada | 41 |
| | | Taiwan | 24 |
| | | Ivory Coast | 16 |
| | | Others | 19 |
| Hydrocortisone | 8,254,000‡ | Bahamas | 41 |
| | | France | 39 |
| | | Canada | 13 |
| | | Others | 7 |
| Natural drugs of animal origin, crude and advanced; drug compounds of animal origin nes | 8,146,000 | Canada | 66 |
| | | Argentina | 9 |
| | | Others | 25 |
| Natural hormones | 6,136,000 | Netherlands | 37 |
| | | Denmark | 18 |
| | | Argentina | 18 |
| | | France | 10 |
| | | Others | 17 |

(continued)

101

Table 5.1  (*Continued*)

| PRODUCT DESCRIPTION | AVERAGE ANNUAL IMPORT VALUE (U.S.$) | EXPORTING COUNTRIES (% of U.S. imports) | |
|---|---|---|---|
| Animal glands and organs and bile and other animal secretions | 2,757,000† | France | 18 |
| | | United Kingdom | 11 |
| | | New Zealand | 10 |
| | | Mexico | 4 |
| | | Others | 57 |
| Estrogens | 2,120,000† | West Germany | 54 |
| | | Canada | 9 |
| | | Others | 37 |
| Annato, archil, cochineal, cudbear, litmus | 1,761,000 | Peru | 45 |
| | | Kenya | 29 |
| | | Dominican Republic | 11 |
| | | Others | 15 |
| Natural vitamins | 1,725,000 | Japan | 44 |
| | | West Germany | 18 |
| | | United Kingdom | 14 |
| | | Others | 24 |
| Prednisolone | 1,702,000‡ | France | 64 |
| | | Netherlands | 27 |
| | | Others | 9 |
| Alkaloids and natural compounds nspf | 1,541,000 | Brazil | 20 |
| | | Italy | 20 |
| | | France | 7 |
| | | Others | 53 |
| Prednisone | 1,352,000‡ | France | 91 |
| | | Netherlands | 5 |
| | | Others | 4 |
| Tannic acid | 1,291,000 | Belgium | 62 |
| | | Italy | 15 |
| | | Others | 23 |
| Aloes, aconite, asafetida, buchu leaves, cocculus indicus, digitalis (lanata), ipecac, jalap, manna, marshmallow, or althea: crude and advanced | 1,246,000 | Netherlands | 75 |
| | | Nicaragua | 10 |
| | | South Africa | 10 |
| | | Others | 5 |
| Anabolic agents and androgens | 1,108,000† | West Germany | 28 |
| | | Mexico | 22 |
| | | Netherlands | 15 |
| | | Others | 35 |
| Progestins nspf | 865,000‡ | Bahamas | 83 |
| | | Others | 17 |

Table 5.1  (*Continued*)

| PRODUCT DESCRIPTION | AVERAGE ANNUAL IMPORT VALUE *(U.S.$)* | EXPORTING COUNTRIES *(% of U.S. imports)* | |
|---|---|---|---|
| Strychnine and salts; brucine and compounds; nux vomica | 468,000 | India<br>Others | 83<br>17 |
| Camphor | 447,000 | Taiwan<br>Others | 78<br>22 |
| Gallnuts | 353,000 | Turkey<br>People's Republic of China<br>Iraq<br>Republic of Korea<br>Others | 45<br>20<br><br>19<br>15<br>1 |
| Gallic acid | 269,000 | France<br>Others | 61<br>39 |
| Gentian | 29,000 | Others | 100 |
| Natural drugs in forms such as tablets and pills | 10,000§ | Others | 100 |
| Santonin and its salts | 2,000* | Others | 100 |

Sources: S-450–S-454.
* 1976–1977 only.
† 1978–1980 only.
‡ 1980 only.
§ 1977–1978 and 1980 only.

percentage from wild sources cannot be estimated. Therefore, in light of inadequate statistical data, we have not attempted to assess the dollar value of wildlife in medicine. Instead we have chosen to analyze the extent to which wild species are sources of particular medical ingredients. Determination of which drug ingredients are currently obtained from wild plants and animals provides a useful indication of the contribution of wildlife to the drug industry, and is the necessary basis of any assessment of the dollar value of that contribution.

## Active Ingredients

To assess the importance of wild species in both prescription and nonprescription drugs for human and veterinary use in North America, we reviewed the active ingredients of 15,871 drug products described in Health and Welfare Canada's publication *Canadian Drug Identification Code, 1981* (G-724) (note 1). Our analysis showed that 247 active ingredients (comprising more than 300 plant and animal species) could be classified as originating from one of three sources: first, exclusively wild sources, a category that includes such ingredients as cascara sagrada and halibut and accounts for 193 ingredients, or 78%; second, wild plus cultivated sources, of which senna and buchu are examples; third, sources about which there was not enough information in the literature for a definite assessment but that might include wild components, such as boldo and pasqueflower. Each of these last two categories is represented by 27 ingredients, or 11% of the total.

Many (152) of the 247 active ingredients occur in fewer than 10 products (listed in tables 5.2–5.4). Most of the discussion presented here centers on the remaining 95 ingredients, which we consider significant because of their occurrence in 10 or more drug products. The origins of these ingredients are illustrated in figure 5.1.

*Exclusively Wild Species*

Tables 5.5–5.7 list 71 active ingredients each of which comes exclusively from wild species and occurs in 10 or more drug products sold in Canada. Cod (*Gadus morhua*), unspecified fish, and halibut (*Hippoglossus hippoglossus*) are the only animal species represented. It is the liver oil, a rich source of vitamins A and D, that accounts for these species' significance to medicine. Tannic acid can be considered a combined animal and plant effort, as gallnuts, the source of tannin, are the result of egg deposits of insects (*Cynips* and *Schlechtendalia*) in the young twigs of certain tree species (*Quercus* and *Rhus*). Fish-liver oil, introduced into medicine only 200 years ago, is a relative newcomer compared with gallnuts, whose medical use has been known since 450 B.C. (S-433).

All remaining 67 ingredients in our tables come from plants. Two of these—kelp and bladder wrack—are marine; the rest are terrestrial. About one-quarter of the species are native only to North America; another quarter are species native only to countries outside North America, so they must be imported. The remaining half is a combination of imported species not found in North America plus natives plus species introduced to North America (fig. 5.2).

The top wild species in terms of number of products is cascara sagrada, the bark of *Rhamnus purshiana*, a tree native to British Columbia, Washington, Oregon, Idaho, Montana, and California. Cascara sagrada had been used for centuries by Pacific Northwest Indians as a traditional remedy for constipation and became known to white settlers in the early 1800s. By 1900 the plant was officially listed in the Pharmacopoeia of the United States.

In 1977 the annual U.S. retail value of cascara sagrada reached $75 million (J-213). Cascara sagrada accounts for about 20% of the U.S. laxative market, which is estimated to be worth between $350 and $400 million annually (D-135). Bulk-forming laxatives and emollient (stool-softening) laxatives account for a major portion of all laxatives sold (J-213). Stimulant (or cathartic) laxatives, which "increase the propulsive peristaltic activity of the intestine by local irritation of the mucosa or by a more selective action on the intramural

## Table 5.2 Ingredients used in 1–9 drug products in Canada that come from the wild exclusively

| INGREDIENTS | PRINCIPAL SPECIES INVOLVED | NUMBER OF PRODUCTS |
|---|---|---|
| Hydrangea | *Hydrangea arborescens* | 9 |
| Lungwort | *Sticta pulmonaria;* *Pulmonaria officinalis* | 9 |
| Butternut | *Juglans cinerea* | 9 |
| White willow | *Salix alba* | 9 |
| Cuttlefish | *Sepia officinalis* | 9 |
| Eastern white cedar | *Thuja occidentalis* | 9 |
| Balsam fir | *Abies balsamea* | 9 |
| Lady's slipper | *Cypripedium pubescens* | 9 |
| Willow | *Salix?* | 9 |
| Poison oak | *Toxicodendron diversilobum* | 8 |
| Soapwort | *Saponaria officinalis* | 8 |
| Cone flower | *Echinacea pallida;* *E. angustifolia* | 8 |
| Boneset | *Eupatorium perfoliatum* | 8 |
| Iceland moss | *Cetraria islandica* | 7 |
| Ignatius bean | *Strychnos ignati* | 7 |
| Iris | *Iris versicolor;* *I. caroliniana* | 7 |
| Culver's root | *Veronicastrum virginicum* | 7 |
| Mayapple | *Podophyllum peltatum* | 7 |
| Spikenard | *Aralia racemosa* | 7 |
| Wintergreen | *Gaultheria procumbens* | 7 |
| Speckled alder | *Alnus rugosa* | 7 |
| Bayberry | *Myrica cerifera* | 7 |
| Winterberry | *Ilex verticillata* | 7 |
| Carrageenan | *Chondrus crispus;* *Gigartina mammillosa;* *G. stellata* | 7 |
| Eastern hemlock | *Tsuga canadensis* | 7 |
| Aspidium | *Dryopteris filix-mas;* *D. marginalis* | 6 |
| Spermaceti | *Physeter catodon* | 6 |
| Restharrow | *Ononis spinosa* | 6 |
| Asafetida | *Ferula assafoetida* | 6 |
| Dwarf elder | *Sambucus ebulus* | 6 |
| Eyebright | *Euphrasia officinalis* | 6 |
| Heather | *Calluna vulgaris* | 5 |
| Poison ivy | *Toxicodendron radicans* | 5 |
| Spanish moss | *Tillandsia usneoides* | 5 |
| White hellebore | *Veratrum viride* | 5 |
| Yohimbine | *Pausinystalia yohimbe* | 5 |
| Aletris | *Aletris farinosa* | 5 |
| Giant ragweed | *Ambrosia trifida* | 5 |

*(continued)*

105

Table 5.2 (*Continued*)

| INGREDIENTS | PRINCIPAL SPECIES INVOLVED | NUMBER OF PRODUCTS |
|---|---|---|
| Spruce | *Picea*? | 5 |
| Lamb's quarters | *Chenopodium album* | 4 |
| Pinkroot | *Spigelia marilandica* | 4 |
| Dwarf ragweed | *Ambrosia elatior* | 4 |
| Snake root | *Polygonum bistorta* | 4 |
| Twinberry | *Mitchella repens* | 4 |
| Wild strawberry | *Fragaria virginiana* | 4 |
| Algaroba | *Prosopis juliflora* var. *velutina* | 4 |
| Cantharides | *Cantharis vesicatoria* | 4 |
| Blue cohosh | *Caulophyllum thalictroides* | 4 |
| Cedar wood oil | *Juniperus virginiana; J. mexicana; Cedrus atlantica* | 4 |
| American mountain ash | *Sorbus americana* | 4 |
| Gravel root | *Eupatorium purpureum* | 3 |
| Helonias | *Chamaelirium luteum* | 3 |
| Liverwort | *Hepatica nobilis* | 3 |
| Mugwort | *Artemisia vulgaris* | 3 |
| Muira-puama | *Liriosma ovata; Acanthea virilis; Ptychopetalum olacoides; P. uncinatum* | 3 |
| Sponge | *Spongia tosta* | 3 |
| Stillingia | *Stillingia sylvatica* | 3 |
| Sweet sumac | *Rhus aromatica* | 3 |
| Tamarack | *Larix laricina* | 3 |
| Wild ginger | *Asarum canadense* | 3 |
| Chickweed | *Stellaria media* | 3 |
| Fish-berry | *Anamirta cocculus* | 3 |
| Herb Robert | *Geranium robertianum* | 3 |
| Dog's mercury | *Mercurialis perennis* | 3 |
| Germander | *Teucrium chamaedrys; T. scordium* | 3 |
| Maple | *Acer*? | 3 |
| Wasp | ? | 3 |
| Kalmia | *Kalmia latifolia* | 2 |
| Karaya gum | *Sterculia urens; S. villosa; S. tragacantha; Cochlospermum gossypium* | 2 |
| Labrador tea | *Ledum palustre* | 2 |
| Pareira brava | *Chondrodendron tomentosum* | 2 |
| Pilocarpus | *Pilocarpus jaborandi; P. pennatifolius; P. microphyllus;* | 2 |

Table 5.2  (*Continued*)

| INGREDIENTS | PRINCIPAL SPECIES INVOLVED | NUMBER OF PRODUCTS |
|---|---|---|
| Pilocarpus (*continued*) | *P. trachylopus;* | |
| | *P. spicatus* | |
| Rock rose | *Helianthemum canadense* | 2 |
| Sea lettuce | *Ulva lactuca* | 2 |
| Solomon's seal | *Polygonatum officinale* | 2 |
| Sundew | *Drosera rotundifolia;* | 2 |
| | *D. anglica;* | |
| | *D. longifolia* | |
| Maidenhair fern | *Adiantum capillus-veneris;* | 2 |
| | *A. pedatum* | |
| Common arum | *Arum maculatum* | 2 |
| Flowering dogwood | *Cornus florida* | 2 |
| Dwarf pine needle | *Pinus mugo* | 2 |
| Goat's rue | *Galega officinalis* | 2 |
| Gamboge | *Garcinia morella;* | 2 |
| | *G. hanburyi* | |
| Strophanthus | *Strophanthus gratus;* | 2 |
| | *S. hispidus; S. kombe* | |
| Common sagebrush | *Artemisia tridentata* | 2 |
| Hazel | *Corylus?* | 2 |
| Seaweed | ? | 2 |
| Wild plum | *Prunus?* | 2 |
| Yellow jacket | ? | 2 |
| Larch agaric | *Fomes laricis* (fungus) | 1 |
| Milkweed | *Asclepias syriaca* | 1 |
| Mountain avens | *Dryas octopetala* | 1 |
| New Jersey tea | *Ceanothus americanus* | 1 |
| Pitcher plant | *Sarracenia purpurea* | 1 |
| Poison sumac | *Toxicodendron vernix* | 1 |
| Quebracho | *Schinopsis balansae;* | 1 |
| | *S. quebracho-colorado* | |
| Red sandwort | *Spergularia rubra* | 1 |
| Rocket candytuft | *Iberis amara* | 1 |
| Scurvy grass | *Cochlearia officinalis* | 1 |
| Sneezewort | *Helenium autumnale;* | 1 |
| | *H. amarum* | |
| Smooth sumac | *Rhus glabra* | 1 |
| European toad | *Bufo vulgaris* | 1 |
| Wild cranesbill | *Geranium maculatum* | 1 |
| Trillium | *Trillium erectum* | 1 |
| Turtle bloom | *Chelone glabra* | 1 |
| Western ragweed | *Ambrosia psilostachya* | 1 |
| White poplar | *Populus alba* | 1 |
| Wild bergamot | *Monarda punctata;* | 1 |
| | *M. fistulosa* | |

(continued)

Table 5.2 (*Continued*)

| INGREDIENTS | PRINCIPAL SPECIES INVOLVED | NUMBER OF PRODUCTS |
|---|---|---|
| Wild indigo | *Baptisia tinctoria* | 1 |
| Yerba santa | *Eriodictyon californicum* | 1 |
| Hickory | *Carya?* | 1 |
| Lobster | *Homarus?* | 1 |
| | *Palinurus?* | |
| | *Panulirus?* | |
| Oyster | *Ostrea?* | 1 |
| | *Crassostrea?* | |
| Salmon | *Salmo salar;* | 1 |
| | *Oncorhynchus?* | |
| Shrimp | *Peneaus?* | 1 |
| | *Pandalus?* | |
| | *Crangon?* | |
| Sycamore | *Platanus?* | 1 |
| Yellow ragweed | *Ambrosia?* | 1 |
| Yellow hornet | ? | 1 |
| Conch | ? | 1 |
| Red coral | ? | 1 |
| Crab | ? | 1 |
| Hornet | ? | 1 |
| Pacific weed | ? | 1 |

Table 5.3 **Ingredients used in 1–9 drug products in Canada that come from wild and cultivated sources**

| INGREDIENTS | PRINCIPAL SPECIES INVOLVED | NUMBER OF PRODUCTS |
|---|---|---|
| Hyoscyamine | *Hyoscyamus muticus* | 7 |
| Night-blooming cactus | *Selenicereus grandiflorus* | 7 |
| Ginseng | *Panax ginseng;* | 6 |
| | *P. quinquefolium* | |
| Gum arabic | *Acacia senegal;* | 5 |
| | *A. seyal* | |
| Grindelia | *Grindelia camporum;* | 4 |
| | *G. humilis; G. robusta;* | |
| | *G. squarrosa* | |
| Gotu kola | *Centella asiatica* | 3 |
| Wild patience | *Rumex obtusifolius* | 1 |

Table 5.4  **Ingredients used in 1–9 drug products in Canada with state of domestication unknown**

| INGREDIENTS | PRINCIPAL SPECIES INVOLVED | NUMBER OF PRODUCTS |
|---|---|---|
| Catnip | *Nepeta cataria* | 9 |
| Damiana | *Turnera diffusa* | 9 |
| Bittersweet | *Solanum dulcamara* | 9 |
| Centaurein | *Centaurea jacea* | 8 |
| Blackberry | *Rubus villosus; R. allegheniensis; R. sativus; R. cuneifolius* | 7 |
| Lily-of-the-valley | *Convallaria majalis* | 7 |
| Celandine | *Chelidonium majus* | 6 |
| Ammoniacum | *Dorema ammoniacum* | 2 |
| Balsam mecca | *Commiphora opobalsamum* | 2 |
| Box elder | *Acer negundo* | 2 |
| Cat thyme | *Teucrium marum* | 2 |
| Daisy | *Bellis perennis* | 2 |
| Diadem spider | *Aranea diadema* | 2 |
| East Indian balmony | *Swertia chirata* | 1 |
| Black horehound | *Ballota nigra* | 1 |
| Black widow spider | *Latrodectus mactans* | 1 |
| Cascarilla | *Croton eluteria; C. cascarilla* | 1 |
| Cedron | *Quassia cedron* | 1 |
| Condurango | *Marsdenia reichenbachii* | 1 |
| Dragon's blood | *Daemonorops propinquus; D. draco* | 1 |

nerve plexus of intestinal smooth muscle, thus increasing motility" (A-687), figure next in market share. Cascara sagrada is a cathartic whose principal use is in the correction of habitual constipation (S-433, V-345). It acts not only as a laxative but also as a tonic laxative—it strengthens the peristaltic muscles of the intestinal wall so that after a period of use natural tone will be restored to the colon and the laxative will no longer be necessary (D-205).

Cascara sagrada has been called the most widely used cathartic on earth (V-224, V-345). Although recent publications (M-317, S-433) state that most of the present-day market supply is from Oregon, Washington, and British Columbia, we were able to trace cascara suppliers only in Washington. The collecting season begins about the middle of April and ends late August. Dry-bark yields per tree range from 5 pounds for a 3-inch-diameter tree to 175 pounds for a 17-inch tree (D-378). Most trees are destroyed in the collection of cascara because they are peeled to such an extent that no new bark is formed (G-589). On average, a harvester peels 100–250 pounds a day (M-317). The young men we

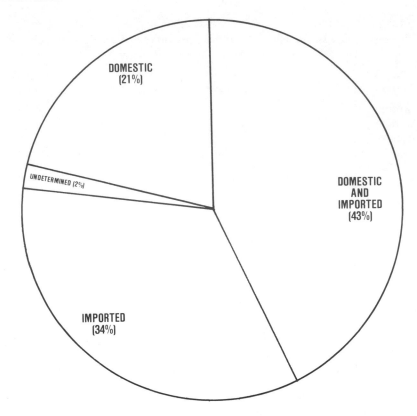

DOMESTIC
(21%)

UNDETERMINED (2%)

DOMESTIC
AND
IMPORTED
(43%)

IMPORTED
(34%)

Fig. 5.1   **Origins of 95 ingredients occurring in 10 or more drug products sold in Canada: combined percentages. Domestic: Canada and/or United States. Sources: chap. 5 tables**

interviewed in Washington said on a good day each of them could bring in 280–300 pounds. The price harvesters get per pound depends on whether the bark is wet or has been dried in the open air for 4–5 days; the latter fetches about double the price. The bark is aged for at least one year before being used as a laxative. Table 5.8 shows that since the turn of the century the market demand for cascara sagrada has risen substantially. Cascara sagrada is an active ingredient in 199 products sold in Canada, including Cascara Sagrada Tab 200 mg (Parke Davis and Co. Ltd.), Aromatic Cascara Fluid Extract (Shoppers Drug Mart), Laxatif aux Herbages Tab (Bioforce Canada Ltee), and Sachet pour Infusion Laxative (Frega Inc., Produits Naturels). Three veterinary products for cattle, horses, dogs, and cats contain cascara sagrada: Purgex Inj. (Fatro Inc. [Canada]), Laxative Injectable (Veterinary Labs Inc.), and Laxative Inj. 20% W/V (Armitage Carroll Ltd.).

Uva ursi from *Arctostaphylos uva-ursi* is an active ingredient in the greatest number of products for a wild species from domestic plus imported sources, 112 (all for human patients). Four of these products are Relaxatone Herbs Garden of Eden (Nu Life Nutrition Ltd.), Bladder Tonic Formula Tab (General Nutrition

(text continued on page 123)

**Table 5.5  Ingredients used in 30+ drug products in Canada that come from the wild exclusively**

| INGREDIENTS | PRINCILAL SPECIES INVOLVED | ORIGIN OF SPECIES | NUMBER OF PRODUCTS* | THERAPEUTIC CATEGORY† |
|---|---|---|---|---|
| Cascara sagrada | *Rhamnus purshiana* (D-205, D-378, G-453, J-213, J-217, J-325, J-337, M-307, M-317, S-41, S-433, V-150, V-224, V-232, V-234, V-345) | Canada; United States Oregon, Washington, and British Columbia main producers (M-317, S-433) | 199 (196/3/0) | *Human*: cathartic *Vet*: laxative |
| Uva ursi | *Arctostaphylos uva-ursi* (A-686, G-453, J-325, J-337, M-317, S-337, S-433, V-224, V-234) | North America; Europe; Asia | 112 (112/0/0) | *Human*: antiseptic (urinary) *Vet*: has been used as a diuretic |
| Cod liver oil | *Gadus morrua* | | 101 (96/5/0) | *Human*: vitamins A and D source *Vet*: vitamins A and D source; locally to promote healing |
| Gentian | *Gentiana aeaulis* (A-839, G-452, J-337) | Appenines; Alps; Pyrenees; Juras; Vosges‡ | 81‡ (81/0/0) | *Human*: bitter tonic‡ *Vet*: bitter tonic‡ |
| | *Gentiana lutea* (A-686, G-452, G-453, J-235, J-337, M-307, M-317, S-433, V-224) | | | |
| Juniper berry | *Juniperus communis* (J-325, J-337 M-307, M-317, S-337, S-433, V-224, V-232, V-234) | North America; Europe; Asia Italy, Hungary, France, Yugoslavia, Austria, Czechoslovakia, Germany, Poland, USSR, and Spain main producers (J-337) | 77 (77/0/0) | *Human*: diuretic |
| Limetree | *Tilia americana* (A-839, G-8 , S-337, V-232, V-234) | Canada; United States | 68 (68/0/0) | |
| | *Tilia spp.* (A-839, J-217, S-433) | | | |

(continued)

Table 5.5 *(Continued)*

| INGREDIENTS | PRINCIPAL SPECIES INVOLVED | ORIGIN OF SPECIES | NUMBER OF PRODUCTS* | THERAPEUTIC CATEGORY† |
|---|---|---|---|---|
| Kelp/algin | *Macrocystis pyrifera* (M-317, M-319) Principal source of world's supply of algin (M-319) *Laminaria hyperborea* (M-319) Most important of smaller kelps as source of algin (M-319) Several other spp. | Temperate zones of Pacific Ocean California main producer (M-319) | 65 (65/0/0) | |
| Hawthorn | *Crataegus oxycantha* (A-686, A-839, S-337, S-433, VG-234) | Europe; Asia; introduced to North America | 59 (59/0/0) | *Human:* cardiotonic, coronary vasodilator |
| Burdock | *Arctium lappa* (A-839, G-453, J-325, J-337, S-337, S-433, V-224, V-234) *Arctium minus* (J-325, J-337, S-337, V-234) | Europe; Asia; introduced to North America | 54 (54/0/0) | *Human:* dermatologic |
| Fish liver oil | Unspecific; could be cod, halibut, menhaden, shark, herring, and so forth | | 49 (45/4/0) | ? |
| Mallow | *Malva sylvestris* (A-839, G-453, J-217, S-337, V-234) *Malva rotundifolia* (G-453, S-337, V-234) | Europe; Asia; introduced to North America‡ | 44‡ (44/0/0) | |
| Passionflower | *Passiflora incarnata* (A-686, A-839, J-217, J-337, S-337, S-433, V-234, V-345) | United States | 43 (43/0/0) | *Human:* sedative, analgesic |
| Horsetail | *Equisetum arvense* (S-337, V-224) | Temperate | 41 (41/0/0) | |

| Common name | Scientific name | Distribution | Rank | Uses |
|---|---|---|---|---|
| Common barberry and Oregon grape | *Mahonia aquifolium* (A-686, J-217, J-337, S-337, V-224, V-345) | Canada; United States | 40‡ (40/0/0) | *Human:* bitter; antipyretic‡ |
| | *Berberis vulgaris* (J-337, S-337 V-224) | Europe; introduced to North America | | |
| Yarrow | *Achillea millefolium* (A-686, A-839, G-453, J-217, J-325, J-337, S-337, S-433, V-224, V-234) | Europe, Asia; introduced to North America | 40 (40/0/0) | *Human:* sudorific |
| Witch hazel | *Hamamelis virginiana* (A-686, A-839, G-453, G-479, J-217, J-325, J-337, M-307, M-317, S-41, S-337, S-433 V-150, V-224, V-232, V-234) | Canada; United States | 39 (39/0/0) | *Human:* astringent<br>*Vet:* has been used as astringent, homostatic, sedative |
| European white birch | *Betula alba* (S-337, V-234) | Europe; Greenland, Asia | 39 (39/0/0) | *Human:* pharmaceutic aid (flavor) |
| Tannic acid/gallnuts | *Quercus infectoria* (S-337) —caused by *Cynips acicalata* (S-337) | United States | 39‡ (15/24/0) | *Human:* astringent‡<br>*Vet:* astringent, hemostatic, in solutions for burns; has been used internally as an astringent and as a heavy metal antidote‡ |
| | *Q. lusitanica* (S-41, S-337) —caused by *Cynips gallae-tinctoriae* (S-337) | Mediterranean region | | |
| | *Q. ilex* (S-41, S-337, V-232) —caused by *Cynips gallae-tinctoriae* (S-337) | Mediterranean region | | |
| | *Q. infectoria* (J-337, M-317, S-433, V-234) —caused by | Greece to Iran | | |

*(continued)*

## Table 5.5 (Continued)

| INGREDIENTS | PRINCIPAL SPECIES INVOLVED | ORIGIN OF SPECIES | NUMBER OF PRODUCTS* | THERAPEUTIC CATEGORY† |
|---|---|---|---|---|
| | *Cynips gallae-tinctoriae* [M-317] | | | |
| | *Q. cerris* [S-337, V-232] —caused by ? | Europe; Asia | | |
| | *Q. tauriola* [S-41, S-337] —caused by *Cynips insana* [S-337] | Europe; Asia | | |
| | *Q. robur* [S-337, V-232] —caused by *Cynips calcies* [S-337] | Europe; Asia; northern Africa | | |
| | *Rhus chinensis* [S-337, S-433] —caused by *Schlechtendalia chinensis* [S-935] | China; Japan | | |
| Halibut liver oil | *Hippoglossus hippoglossus* [M-307, S-433, V-234] | Atlantic and Pacific oceans | 38 (38/0/0) | *Human:* source of vitamins A and D *Vet:* source of vitamins A and D |

| Cornflower | *Centaurea cyanus* (G-453, J-217, S-337) | Mediterranean region; widely naturalized | 38 (38/0/0) | |
|---|---|---|---|---|
| Bloodroot | *Sanguinaria canadensis* (A-686, J-217, J-325, J-337, M-317, S-337, S-433, V-224, V-232, V-234, V-345) | Canada; United States | 37 (36/1/0) | |
| Scullcap | *Scutellaria lateriflora* (A-686, J-325, S-337, S-433, V-234, V-345) | Canada; United States | 37 (37/0/0) | |
| Sassafras | *Sassafras albidum* (A-686, G-453, G-479, J-217, J-325, J-337, M-307, M-317, S-41, S-337, S-433, V-150, V-224, V-232, V-234, V-345) | Canada; United States | 35 (32/3/0) | *Human:* sudorific |
| Mistletoe | *Phoradendron tomentosum* (A-839, S-337, S-433, V-224) | Canada; United States | 32‡ (32/0/0) | |
| | *Viscum album* (A-686, A-839, G-453, J-217, S-337, S-433, V-224, V-232) | Europe; Asia | | |
| Nettle | *Urtica dioica* (A-686, A-839, G-453, J-217, S-337, V-224) | North temperate | 31 (31/0/0) | |

*Human use/veterinary use/disinfectant.
†Source: V-234.
‡These characteristics apply to all species supplying this ingredient.

Table 5.6 Ingredients used in 20–29 drug products in Canada that come from the wild exclusively

| INGREDIENTS | PRINCIPAL SPECIES INVOLVED | ORIGIN OF SPECIES | NUMBER OF PRODUCTS* | THERAPEUTIC CATEGORY† |
|---|---|---|---|---|
| Black cohosh | *Cimicifuga racemosa* (A-686, G-453, J-325, J-337, S-337, V-224, V-232, V-234, V-345) | Canada; United States Blue Ridge Mountains main producer (V-224) | 29 (29/0/0) | *Human:* astringent bitter |
| Wall pellitory | *Parietaria officinalis* (A-839, G-453, S-337) | Europe | 29 (29/0/0) | |
| Wild cherry | *Prunus serotina* (A-686, A-839, G-453, G-479, J-217, J-325, J-337, M-317, S-41, S-337, S-433, V-224, V-234, V-345) | Canada; United States | 28 (27/1/0) | *Human:* pharmaceutic aid (flavoring) |
| Queen-of-the-meadow | *Filipendula ulmaria* (J-217, S-337) | Europe; Asia, introduced to North America | 28 (28/0/0) | |
| Coltsfoot | *Tussilago farfara* (G-453, J-325, S-337, S-433, V-224, V-232, V-234) | Temperate Eurasia (excluding China and Japan); northern Africa; introduced to North America | 28 (28/0/0) | |
| Bladderwrack | *Fucus vesiculosis; F. serratus; F. siliquosus* (A-686, G-453, S-337, V-234) | Atlantic and Pacific oceans | 27 (27/0/0) | |
| Elder flower | *Sambucus canadensis* (A-686, G-479, J-217, J-325, J-337, V-224, V-234) | Canada; United States | 26‡ (26/0/0) | *Human:* diaphoretic; diuretic; cathartic‡ |
| | *Sambucus nigra* (A-686, A-839, J-217, J-337, S-337) | Europe | | |
| Slippery elm | *Ulmus rubra* (G-453, G-479, J-217, J-325, M-317, S-337, V-224, V-345) | Canada; United States | 24 (24/0/0) | |
| St. John's wort | *Hypericum perforatum* (A-686, G-453, S-337, V-224, V-234) | Europe; Asia; northern Africa; introduced to North America | 24 (24/0/0) | *Human:* antidepressant |

| Common name | Species | Distribution | No. | Uses |
|---|---|---|---|---|
| Squill | *Urginea maritima* (A-839, G-453, J-217, J-337, M-307, M-317, S-41, S-337, S-433, V-224, V-234) | Spain; France; Italy; Greece; Algeria; Morocco | 24‡ (22/2/0) | *Human:* diuretic, emetic, expectorant, cardiotonic‡ *Vet:* has been used as expectorant, emetic‡ |
| | *Urginea indica* (A-839, G-423, G-453, J-217, M-307, S-337, S-433) | India | | |
| White pine | *Pinus strobus* (G-479, J-325, J-337, S-41, S-337, S-433, V-234) | Canada; United States | 23 (23/0/0) | *Human:* bark as expectorant |
| Buckbean | *Menyanthes trifoliata* (A-686, A-839, G-453, J-217, J-325, S-337, V-224, V-232, V-234) | North America; Europe; Asia | 23 (23/0/0) | |
| Centaury | *Centaurium erythraea* (A-839, G-453, J-235, J-337, S-337) | Europe; Asia; northern Africa; introduced to North America | 23 (23/0/0) | *Human:* bitter tonic |
| Vervain | *Verbena hastata* (A-686, G-453, J-325, S-337, S-433) | United States | 22‡ (22/0/0) | |
| | *Verbena officinalis* (A-686, G-453, S-337) | Mediterranean region | | |
| Myrrh | *Commiphora molmol* (J-337, M-307, S-337, S-433, V-224) | Ethiopia to Somalia Somalia main producer (S-433) | 22‡ (22/0/0) | *Human:* carminative‡ |
| | *Commiphora abyssinica* (J-337, M-307, M-317, S-337, S-433, V-234) | Sudan; Somalia; Ethiopia; southern Arabia Somalia main producer (S-433) | | |
| | *Commiphora schimperi* (M-307, S-337) | Ethiopia; Yemen | | |

*(continued)*

Table 5.6 (*Continued*)

| INGREDIENTS | PRINCIPAL SPECIES INVOLVED | ORIGIN OF SPECIES | NUMBER OF PRODUCTS* | THERAPEUTIC CATEGORY† |
|---|---|---|---|---|
| Yellow jasmine | *Gelsemium sempervirens* (A-686, G-81, G-453, J-217, J-325, J-337, M-317, V-224, V-232, V-234) | United States: Mexico | 21 (19/2/0) | *Human:* central stimulant |
| Blackhaw | *Viburnum prunifolium* (A-686, J-217, J-325, J-337, S-337, V-234, V-345) | United States | 20 (20/0/0) | |
| Yellow dock | *Rumex crispus* (A-686, G-453, J-325, S-337, V-224, V-234, V-345) | Europe; Asia; introduced to North America | 20 (20/0/0) | *Human:* cathartic, astringent |
| Juniper tar/cade oil | *Juniperus oxycedrus* (J-337, M-307, M-317, S-337, S-433, V-232) | From Portugal and Spain to Balkans; Aegean Islands; Cyprus; Morocco; Algeria; Tunis; Syria; Lebanon; Turkey; Caucasus; Iran; Iraq; introduced to North America Yugoslavia, France, and Spain main producers (M-317) | 20 (13/7/0) | *Human:* topical antieczematic |

*Human use/veterinary use/disinfectant.
†Source: V-234.
‡These characteristics apply to all species supplying this ingredient.

Table 5.7  Ingredients used in 10–19 drug products in Canada that come from the wild exclusively

| INGREDIENTS | PRINCIPAL SPECIES INVOLVED | ORIGIN OF SPECIES | NUMBER OF PRODUCTS* | THERAPEUTIC CATEGORY† |
|---|---|---|---|---|
| Stoneroot | Collinsonia canadensis (A-686, G-453, J-325, S-337, S-433, V-232, V-234) | Canada; United States | 19 (19/0/0) | |
| Peru balsam | Myroxylon balsamum var. pereirae (D-246, G-453, J-217, J-337, M-307, M-317, S-41 S-337, S-433, V-224, V-234) | Mexico; Belize; El Salvador, Nicaragua; Guatemala; Honduras; Panama El Salvador (D-246, M-307, M-317, S-41, S-337, S-433), Honduras (D-246, S-433), Nicaragua (D-246), and Belize (M-317) main producers | 19 (10/9/0) | *Human:* scabicide; skin ulcer therapy *Vet:* miticide; to aid in healing of indolent wounds |
| Mullein | Verbascum thapsus (A-686, A-839, G-453, J-217, J-325, S-337, V-224, V-234) | Europe; Asia; introduced to North America | 18 (18/0/0) | |
| Common motherwort | Leonurus cardiaca (A-839, G-453, J-217, J-325, S-337, V-224) | Europe; Asia | 18 (18/0/0) | |
| Ash | Fraxinus sp? | ? | 18 (18/0/0) | |
| Cocillana | Guarea guidonia (G-453, J-337, S-337, S-433, V-234) | Bolivia | 17 (17/0/0) | *Human:* expectorant *Vet:* has been used as an expectorant |
| Immortal | Gnaphalium obtusifolium (A-686, S-337) | Canada; United States | 16 (16/0/0) | |
| Creosote | Fagus grancifolia (G-479, J-217, J-325, S-337, S-433) Fagus sylvatica (J-217, S-337, V-232) Other unspecified species | Canada; United States Europe | 16‡ (12/4/0) | *Human:* antiseptic; expectorant‡ *Vet:* antiseptic, parasiticide, deodorant; has been used as expectorant, gastric sedative, and gastrointestinal antiseptic; do not use in cats‡ |

(continued)

# Table 5.7 (Continued)

| INGREDIENTS | PRINCIPAL SPECIES INVOLVED | ORIGIN OF SPECIES | NUMBER OF PRODUCTS* | THERAPEUTIC CATEGORY† |
|---|---|---|---|---|
| Pipsissewa | *Chimaphila umbellata* (A-686, G-453, J-217, J-325, J-337, S-337, V-224, V-234) | North America; Europe; Asia | 15 (15/0/0) | *Human:* urinary antispetic |
| Agrimony | *Agrimonia eupatoria* (A-839, J-235, S-337) | Europe; Asia; introduced to North America | 15 (15/0/0) | |
| Bryony | *Bryonia cretica; B. alba* (A-686, A-839, G-453, J-235, V-232, V-234) | Europe | 15 (15/0/0) | *Human:* cathartic<br>*Vet:* formerly as a purgative |
| Speedwell | *Veronica officinalis* (G-453, J-217, S-337) | Europe; Asia; introduced to North America | 14 (14/0/0) | |
| Poke root | *Phytolacca americana* (A-686, A-839, G-453, J-217, J-325, S-41, S-337, S-433, V-150, V-234, V-345) | Canada; United States; introduced to southern Europe and northern Africa | 14 (14/0/0) | *Human:* antirheumatic; topical antiparasitic |
| Shepherd's purse | *Capsella bursa-pastoris* (A-686, A-339, G-453, J-325, S-337, V-224, V-232) | Cosmopolitan | 14 (14/0/0) | |
| Billberry | *Vaccinium myrtillus* (G-453, J-235, S-337, V-232) | Europe | 13 (13/0/0) | |
| Pill-bearing spurge | *Euphorbia pilulifera* (G-453, J-217, J-337, S-337, V-234) | India; Australia; widely distributed | 13 (12/1/0) | |
| Goldenrod | *Solidago virgaurea* (A-686, A-839, G-453, J-217, S-41, S-337, V-232) | Europe; Asia; introduced to North America | 12 (12/0/0) | |
| Pine needle oil | *Pinus mugo* (J-217, J-337, M-307, M-317, S-337) | Alpine Europe Austria, Yugoslavia, and Italy main producers (J-337) | 12‡ (9/3/0) | *Human:* pharmaceutic aid (flavor and perfume); expectorant‡ |
| | *Pinus sylvestris* (J-337, S-337, V-234) | Europe; Asia; widely cultivated Austria, USSR, Yugoslavia, and Scandinavia main producers (J-337) | | |

| | | | | |
|---|---|---|---|---|
| Prickly ash | *Zanthoxylum americanum* (G-453, J-217, J-325, J-337, S-337, V-224, V-234) | Canada, United States | 11‡ (11/0/0) | *Human*: carminative; anti-diarrheal‡ |
| | *Zanthoxylum clava-herculis* (G-453, J-217, J-325, J-337, S-41, S-337, V-234) | United States; perhaps Mexico | | |
| Saw palmetto | *Serenoa serrulata* (A-686, G-453, J-325, S-41, S-337, V-232, V-234) | United States; West Indies | 11 (11/0/0) | |
| Storax | *Liquidambar styraciflua* (J-217, J-325, J-337, M-307, M-317, S-41, S-433 V-232, V-234) | United States; Mexico; Nicaragua; Honduras; Guatemala Honduras (J-337, M-307, M-317, S-433, V-234) and Guatemala (J-337) main producers | 11‡ (10/1/0) | *Human*: topical protectant; expectorant† *Vet*: as component of compound benzoin tincture; has been used as a parasiticide‡ |
| | *Liquidambar orientalis* (G-453, J-337, M-307, M-317, S-41, S-433, V-232, V-234) | Asia Minor Turkey main producer (M-317, S-433) | | |
| Scouring rush | *Equisetum hyemale* (A-686, S-337, S-433) | Temperate | 11 (11/0/0) | |
| Sweet woodruff | *Asperula odorata* (A-839, G-453, J-337, S-337, V-234) | Europe; Asia; northern Africa, introduced to North America West Germany main producer (J-337) | 11 (11/0/0) | *Human*: flavoring agent; the fresh leaves in flavoring May wine, the dried leaves in sachets |
| Life root | *Senecio aureus* (A-686, J-217, J-325, S-337, S-433, V-234) | Canada; United States | 10 (10/0/0) | *Human*: emmenagogue |
| White oak | *Quercus alba* (G-479, J-325, S-41, S-337, V-232, V-234) | Canada; United States | 10 (10/0/0) | *Human*: astringent |
| Pilewort | *Ranunculus ficaria* (A-839, G-453, S-337, S-433) | Europe; Asia; northern Africa | 10 (9/1/0) | |

*Human use/veterinary use/disinfectart.
†Source: V-234.
‡These characteristics apply to all species supplying this ingredient.

121

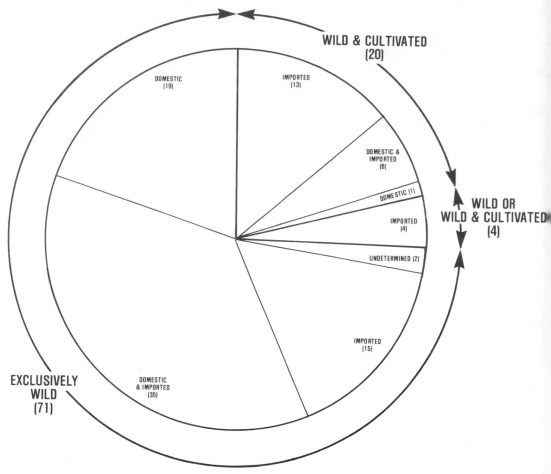

Fig. 5.2  Origins of 95 ingredients occurring in 10 or more drug products sold in Canada: wild, wild and cultivated, wild or wild and cultivated. Domestic: Canada and/or United States. Sources: chap. 5 tables

Table 5.8  **Cascara sagrada: quantity harvested and value to harvesters**

|  | QUANTITY HARVESTED (Pounds) | DRY BARK PRICE (Cents per pound) |
|---|---|---|
| 1909 | 2,000,000 | 3–4½ |
| 1931–41 | ? | 5–6 |
| 1947 | ? | 22 |
| 1977 | 4,000,000 | ? |
| 1982 | ? | 25 |

Sources: A-915, G-589, M-317; pers. comm.

Corp.), Rheumatism Tabs (Heath and Heather Ltd.), and Pancreas Tonic Tea (A. G. Kuenzle Kraeuterpfarrer).

Gentian (*Gentiana* spp.) is the leading wild species from entirely imported sources. It is found in 81 products, including 7 for veterinary use. Two of the veterinary products are Zev Appetizer & Conditioner for cattle, horses, lamb, swine, dogs, and cats (W. K. Buckley Ltd.) and Herbageum Condiment for cattle, horses, lamb, swine, poultry, dogs, cats, chinchilla, mink, and wild animals such as deer, moose, and bison (Galt Chemical Products Ltd.).

*Wild and Cultivated Species*

Tables 5.9–5.11 list 20 active ingredients each of which comes from wild and cultivated sources and occurs in 10 or more drug products sold in Canada. All are terrestrial plants. The biggest subdivision, with 13 ingredients, consists of exclusively imported species (see figure 5.2). The second largest subdivision—of North American and imported species—includes 6 ingredients. A single ingredient—goldenseal—represents the subdivision of strictly North American natives. Senna, turpentine, and goldenseal are the top ingredients in each of the source subdivisions. Examples of these products include the following: for senna—Senokot Suppositories (Purdue Frederick Co. [Canada] Ltd.), Vegetable Herb Laxative Tab (Hilcoa Corporation), Naran Reducing Plan (Wilton Drug Products), and Special Balsam Bedwetting (Thuna Herbal Remedies Ltd.); for turpentine, pine oil, pine tar, and rosin—veterinary products such as Udder Balm for cattle (Austin Laboratories [Canada] Ltee) and Hoof Conditioner with Lanolin for cattle, horses, lamb, and swine (APA, Inc.) and disinfectant products such as Pincguard Disinfectant (Avmor Ltd.) and W333P Liquid Pine Disinfectant (Wyant Chemical Company Ltd.); for goldenseal—Golden Seal Pure Herb Tea No. 22 (Alphian Herbs) and Detoxification No. 3 Tab (Carrefour Sante Enrg.).

Ginseng, which is used as a tonic, stimulant, and demulcent, is listed as occurring in only six drug products for sale in Canada (table 5.3). However, because ginseng is such a heavily traded international market commodity, we have selected it to exemplify medicinal species from wild and cultivated sources. Two principal species make up the ginseng of commerce—*Panax ginseng* and *P. quinquefolium. P. ginseng* grows wild or is cultivated in the People's Republic of China, Japan, Taiwan, the Republic of Korea, the Democratic People's Republic of Korea, and the Pacific coastal regions of the USSR (A-642, M-112). Its use in Chinese medicine dates back 4,000 years (A-890). Kirin Province in the People's Republic of China is the major center of cultivation. Although much of the cultivated *P. ginseng* is used in the countries in which it is grown, a considerable amount is exported. Wild ginseng, collected primarily in Kirin and Liaoning provinces, is in demand in major Chinese cities, such as Canton, Shanghai, and Peking, and for export (S-503). From 1976 to 1980, Canada imported an annual average of U.S. $881,244 of ginseng. Two-thirds of

(*text continued on page 129*)

Table 5.9  Ingredients used in 30+ drug products in Canada that come from wild and cultivated sources

| INGREDIENTS | PRINCIPAL SPECIES INVOLVED | ORIGIN OF SPECIES | NUMBER OF PRODUCTS* | THERAPEUTIC CATEGORY† |
|---|---|---|---|---|
| Senna | *Cassia angustifolia* (G-423, J-337, M-307, M-317, S-41, S-337, S-433, V-234) | Somalia; Arabian peninsula, Yemen; Pakistan; India Mostly from cultivated sources (J-337, S-41, S-433) Cultivated in India and Pakistan (J-337, M-317, S-41) | 175‡ (175/0/0) | *Human:* cathartic‡ *Vet:* has been used as a purgative‡ |
| | *Cassia acutifolia* (D-246, G-423, J-337, M-307, M-317, S-337, S-433, V-234) | Egypt; Sudan From wild and cultivated sources (D-246, J-337, M-307, M-317) Cultivated in Egypt, Sudan, India, and China (J-337, M-317) | | |
| Turpentine/pine tar/pine oil/rosin | *Pinus elliottii* (A-1170, G-536, J-110, J-337, M-317, S-433, S-485) | United States Cultivated in United States and Brazil (M-317) | 119‡ (43/55/21) | Turpentine: *Human:* rubefacient, counterirritant‡ *Vet:* internally: antiseptic, carminative, expectorant; externally: counterirritant, rubefacient‡ |
| | *Pinus palustris* (A-1170, G-536, G-76, J-110, J-325, J-337, M-317, S-337, S-433, S-485, V-234) | United States Cultivated in United States (M-317) | | Pine tar: *Human:* topical antieczematic; rubefacient‡ *Vet:* mild irritant, antiseptic in chronic skin conditions; expectorant‡ |
| | *Pinus caribaea* (G-76, J-170, S-337, S-485) | Belize; Guatemala; Honduras; Nicaragua; Bahamas; Turks and Caicos; Cuba | | |
| | *Pinus pinaster* (A-1170, V-232) | Mediterranean region | | Pine oil: *Human:* pharmaceutic aid (flavor and perfume)‡ |

| Common name | Species | Origin | Human use/veterinary use/disinfectant* | Uses |
|---|---|---|---|---|
| | *Pinus sylvestris* (E-1170, V-232) | Europe; Asia | | Rosin:<br>*Human*: pharmaceutic aid (stiffening agent)‡ |
| | *Pinus massoniana* (E-1170) | People's Republic of China | | |
| Dandelion | *Taraxacum officinale* (A-839, G-453, J-217, J-235, J-337, M-307, S-337, V-150, V-232, V-234) | Europe; introduced to North America<br>Cultivated sometimes for salad (J-235, S-337) | 86 (86/0/0) | |
| Buchu | *Barosma betulina;*<br>*B crenulata* (G-453, J-337, M-307, M-317, S 41, S-337, S-433, V-232, v-234) | South Africa<br>From wild and cultivated sources (J-337, S-41)<br>Cape Province main producer (J-337) | 75 (75/0/0) | *Human*: antiseptic (urinary)<br>*Vet*: has been used as a urinary antiseptic, diuretic |
| Sage | *Salvia officinalis* (A-686, A-839, J-325, J-337, S 41, S-337, V-150, V-234) | Mediterranean region<br>Cultivated extensively worldwide (A-686, J-337, S-337, V-150, V-234)<br>Yugoslavia main producer (S-41, V-150) | 53 (53/0/0) | *Human*: antisecretory agent |
| | *Salvia triloba* (S-337) | Greece; Turkey | | |
| | *Salvia lavandulaefolia* (G-76, J-337) | Spain, France<br>Collected from the wild in Spain (G-76, J-337) | | |
| Sarsaparilla | *Smilax regelii* (-337, M-307, M-317, S-337, S-433, V-234) | Guatemala; Honduras<br>Cultivated in Jamaica (M-317) | 43‡ (43/0/0) | *Human*: pharmaceutic aid (flavoring agent)‡ |
| | *Smilax aristolochiifolia* (-337, M-307, M-317, S-337, S-433, V-234) | Mexico; Guatemala; Honduras | | |
| | *Smilax febrifuga* (-337, M-317, S-433) | Ecuador; Peru | | |

*Human use/veterinary use/disinfectant.
†Source: V-234.
‡These characteristics apply to all species supplying this ingredient.

125

Table 5.10 **Ingredients used in 20–29 drug products in Canada that come from wild and cultivated sources**

| INGREDIENTS | PRINCIPAL SPECIES INVOLVED | ORIGIN OF SPECIES | NUMBER OF PRODUCTS* | THERAPEUTIC CATEGORY† |
|---|---|---|---|---|
| Tolu balsam | *Myroxylon balsamum* var. *balsamum* (D-246, G-453, J-337, M-307, M-317, S-433, V-234) | Venezuela; Colombia; Peru Colombia main producer (D-246, M-307) Cultivated in West Indies (J-337, S-433) | 29 (29/0/0) | *Human:* expectorant *Vet:* has been used as an expectorant |
| Goldenseal | *Hydrastis canadensis* (A-686, G-453, J-217, J-325, J-337, M-307, M-317, S-41 S-337, S-433, V-150, V-224, V-232, V-234) | Canada, United States Collected from wild in West Virginia, Tennessee, North Carolina, Ohio, Kentucky, and Indiana (M-307) Most of goldenseal on market wild (V-345) In 1976 fewer than 100 acres under cultivation in United States (V-345) Cultivated in Washington and Oregon (J-337, M-307, M-317, S-41, V-150) | 25 (25/0/0) | *Human:* uterine hemostatic |
| Lobelia | *Lobelia inflata* (A-686, A-839, G-453, J-217, J-325, J-337, M-307, M-317, S-337, S-433, V-224, V-234, V-345) | Canada; United States Collected from the wild in North Carolina, Virginia, and Tennessee (S-433) Cultivated in Europe (M-317), in eastern North America (S-337), in several places (V-150) | 24 (21/3/0) | *Human:* expectorant *Vet:* has been used as an expectorant |
| Ipecac | *Cephaelis ipecacuanha* (G-453, J-217, J-337, M-307, M-317, S-41, S-337, S-433, V-224, V-234) | Brazil; Bolivia Brazil main producer (M-317, S-433) Most of roots for drug trade from wild plants (M-317) Cultivated in India, Burma, and Malaysia (J-337, M-317, S-433, V-234) | 22‡ (21/1/0) | *Human:* antiamebic‡ |
| | *Cephaelis acuminata* (J-337, M-307, M-317, S-41, S-337, S-433, V-234) | Nicaragua and Panama to Colombia | | |
| Reserpine | *Rauvolfia vomitoria* (J-217, M-317, S-337, S-433) Main source of reserpine (J-217, M-317, S-433) | West Africa from Senegal and the Congo to Mozambique No commercial plantations (M-317, S-433) | 22‡ (21/1/0) | *Human:* antihypertensive‡ *Vet:* hypotensive, tranquilizer; has been used to prevent aortic rupture in turkeys‡ |

| | | | |
|---|---|---|---|
| | *Rauvolfia serpentina* (J-217, M-317, S-41, S-337, S-433) | India; Bangladesh; Burma; Thailand; Sri Lanka; Malaysia; Andaman Islands; Indonesia. Cultivated in India and Thailand (S-433) | | |
| | *Rauvolfia tetraphylla* (J-217, M-317) | Mexico to Colombia and Venezuela; Trinidad and Tobago; Barbados; St. Thomas, Jamaica; Cuba | | |
| Thyme | *Thymus vulgaris* (J-337, M-307, M-317, S-337, V-224, V-234) | Mediterranean region; introduced to North America. Extensively cultivated (J-337, M-307, M-317, V-234). France, Germany, and Greece main producers (M-317) | 22‡ (22/0/0) | *Human:* carminative‡ |
| | *Thymus zygis* (M-307, M-317) | Spain: Portugal, Balearic Islands. Collected in Spain from wild for oil (M-307). Cultivated most extensively in Spain (M-317) | | |
| | *Thymus serpyllum* (A-90, S-337) | Europe; Asia; Africa. Collected from wild in France, Germany, Yugoslavia, Italy, and Poland (A-90). Cultivated sometimes (S-337) | | |
| Arnica | *Arnica fulgens; A. sororia; A. cordifolia* (J-337, M-307, M-317) | Canada; United States. Rarely cultivated (V-150). Collected from wild chiefly in Montana, Wyoming, North Dakota, and South Dakota (M-307) | 20‡ (16/4/0) | *Human:* topical counterirritant‡  *Vet:* counterirritant‡ |
| | *Arnica montana* (G-453, J-337, M-307, M-317, S-337, S-433, V-224) | Europe. Cultivated in northern India (J-337) | | |
| Nux vomica | *Strychnos nux-vomica* (A-686, G-453, J-217, M-307, M-317, S-41, S-337, S-433, V-232, V-234) | India; Sri Lanka; Southeast Asia; Australia. Mostly from wild (S-41, S-337). Cultivated in Africa and United States (Hawaii) (M-317) | 20 (0/20/0) | *Human:* formerly as bitter tonic  *Vet:* has been used as bitter tonic |

*Human use/veterinary use/disinfectant.
†Source: V-234.
‡These characteristics apply to all species supplying this ingredient.

Table 5.11   Ingredients used in 10–19 drug products in Canada that come from wild and cultivated sources

| INGREDIENTS | PRINCIPAL SPECIES INVOLVED | ORIGIN OF SPECIES | NUMBER OF PRODUCTS* | THERAPEUTIC CATEGORY† |
|---|---|---|---|---|
| Calamus | *Acorus calamus* (A-839, J-217, J-337, S-337, V-234) | North America; Europe; Asia Collected from wild in Britain, Germany, Netherlands, USSR, United States (S-337) Cultivated in Burma and Sri Lanka (S-337, V-234) | 18 (18/0/0) | *Human*: carminative, anthelmintic |
| Horse chestnut | *Aesculus hippocastanum* (A-686, G-81, G-453, J-325, S-337, V-224) | Middle East and Caucasus to Himalayas; introduced to North America Cultivated for timber (S-337) Cultivated as ornamental (G-453) | 15 (15/0/0) | |
| Club moss | *Lycopodium clavatum* (A-686, G-453, J-325, M-307, M-317, S-337, V-224, V-234) *Lycopodium annotinum* (V-234) *Lycopodium anceps* (V-234) | North America; Europe; Asia Collected from wild in United States, Canada, Ukraine, Poland, Switzerland, Germany, Japan (M-307) Cultivated in USSR (V-234) | 14‡ (14/0/0) | *Human*: adsorbent‡ |
| Seneca snakeroot | *Polygala senega* (A-686, G-453, J-217, J-325, M-307, M-317, S-41, S-433, V-150, V-234, V-345) | Canada; United States Collected from wild in North America; cultivated in Japan (S-935) | 13 (13/0/0) | *Human*: expectorant, emetic *Vet*: has been used as expectorant |
| Colocynth | *Citrullus colocynthis* (J-217, M-307, M-317, S-41, S-337, V-150, V-232, V-234) | Asia; Africa Sudan main producer (M-307, V-150) Cultivated in India and Mediterranean region (S-337) | 12 (12/0/0) | *Human*: cathartic *Vet*: has been used as purgative |
| Lavender | *Lavandula vera* (A-90, A-839, J-337, S-41, V-224, V-232, V-234) | France; Spain; Italy Mostly from wild sources in southern Europe (S-41) Cultivated elsewhere (A-90, J-337) | 11 (11/0/0) | *Human*: pharmaceutic aid (perfume) |

*Human use/veterinary use/disinfectant.
†Source: V-234.
‡These characteristics apply to all species supplying these ingredients.

128

Canada's ginseng imports were from the Republic of Korea and Hong Kong (S-409–S-411). From 1978 to 1980, the United States imported an annual average of almost $8 million of ginseng (S-450–S-454), 80% of which was from the Republic of Korea.

*Panax quinquefolium* is native to North America. It was first discovered in 1715 in Quebec, near Montreal, and today it can still be found in the wild in Ontario and Quebec (A-1187, A-1188). In Canada it is cultivated mainly in Norfolk County, Ontario. In 1979, Canada exported about 80,000 pounds of ginseng (about 1% of which was wild) with a value of U.S. $4.3 million (A-1187). Ginseng grows wild in the United States from New England south to the Appalachian Mountains and Georgia and west to Oklahoma, Michigan, and Wisconsin (J-325). Since the turn of the century Marathon County, Wisconsin, has accounted for 90% of the annual American cultivated crop (A-1063). (*P. quinquefolium* is also cultivated in the Republic of Korea [D-470] and in the People's Republic of China [J-337].)

From 1976 to 1980, an annual average of 400,000 pounds of ginseng was exported from the United States (table 5.12), about 30%, or 120,000 pounds, of which came from the wild. Between 50 and 60 wild ginseng plants are required to make up one pound of dry root for export (A-1188). Therefore, in the late 1970s approximately 6 million wild ginseng plants were collected annually in the United States for export. The amount collected for domestic purposes is unknown.

Most North American ginseng, both from wild and cultivated sources, is exported. From 1976 to 1980, about 85% of U.S. ginseng exports went to Hong Kong. Since 1980, however, Hong Kong's percentage share has declined slightly due to Japan's emergence as a big new market for American ginseng.

In both species of ginseng, the wild root is always more highly valued than the

Table 5.12    **Exports of ginseng (*Panax quinquefolium*) by the United States**

|  | % WILD/% CULTIVATED | QUANTITY *(Pounds)* | VALUE *(U.S.$)* |
|---|---|---|---|
| 1862 | 100% w/0% c | 625,000 | 625,000 |
| 1962 | ? | 100,000 | 2,750,000 |
| 1972 | ? | 200,000 | 9,000,000 |
| 1976 | ? | 300,000 | ? |
| 1977 | ? | 350,000 | ? |
| 1978 | 30% w/70% c | 350,000 | 25,000,000 |
| 1979 | 30% w/70% c | 325,000 | 22,200,000 |
| 1980 | 30% w/70% c | 575,000 | 39,000,000 |

Sources: M-577, P-171, S-41, S-433, S-683.

cultivated (M-112, V-347). The selling price of wild ginseng can be one-third to two-thirds higher than the cultivated variety (P-171). The reasons for this cachet are not clear. One study has indicated that cultivated ginseng is one-and-a-half to two times less active than wild (M-112); and it is reported that connoisseurs consider cultivated ginseng inferior in taste and efficacy (P-171).

High demand for wild ginseng and destruction of its habitat have put severe pressure on both species. During the last two or three decades, the supply of wild *P. ginseng* has rapidly declined as a result of intensive digging of the roots, felling of the forests, and forest fires (A-890). In 1972, *P. quinquefolium* was listed on Appendix II of CITES as a species requiring monitoring because of its high demand in international trade and its declining populations (A-1187, A-1188). In Canada the decline in wild populations is suspected to be the result of four factors: collection of young and immature plants; failure to plant seeds when harvesting roots; clearance of hardwood forests; and land development for such purposes as sand mining, road and commercial construction, and home construction (A-1188). In the United States, overharvesting and clearance of the eastern deciduous forest are reasons cited (M-577).

Table 5.13 lists four active ingredients—frangula, boldo, pasqueflower, and lachesis—that may come from wild or wild plus cultivated species and that occur in 10 or more drug products sold in Canada. Not enough information was available in the literature to determine their state of domestication.

### The Most Important Families

Tables 5.14 and 5.15 list the plant families supplying ingredients from wild or wild plus domesticated species for products that figure prominently in the drug industries of Canada and the United States, respectively. The two tables are not strictly comparable, because the Canadian data cover both prescription and over-the-counter drugs (including herbal remedies) whereas the U.S. data are restricted to prescription drugs. Nonetheless there are nine families in common: Cupressaceae, Ericaceae, Fagaceae, Leguminosae, Pinaceae, Rhamnaceae, Rosaceae, Rubiaceae, and Rutaceae.

Table 5.15 also provides a means of assessing the relative importance of wild species as sources of the plant-derived ingredients in U.S. prescription drugs. Farnsworth (D-404) has identified 87 ingredients and ingredient groups (different ingredients from the same species, for example, leurocristine and vincaleukoblastine from *Catharanthus roseus*) that are derived from plants and were used in prescription drugs sold in the United States in 1980. On the basis of our review of the current origins of active drug ingredients, we estimate that 26 (30%) of the 87 ingredients are obtained from wild species, 15 (17%) from sources that are both wild and domesticated, and the remaining 46 (53%) from exclusively domesticated sources.

*(text continued on page 138)*

**Table 5.13 Ingredients used in 10+ drug products in Canada with state of domestication unknown**

| INGREDIENTS | PRINCIPAL SPECIES INVOLVED | ORIGIN OF SPECIES | NUMBER OF PRODUCTS* | THERAPEUTIC CATEGORY† |
|---|---|---|---|---|
| Frangula | *Rhamnus frangula* (A-686, G-453, J-217, M-317, S-41, S-337, S-433, V-232, V-234) | Europe; Asia; northern Africa Cultivated in Southeast Europe (S-41) and North America (J-217) | 89 (88/1/0) | *Human*: cathartic *Vet*: has been used as a laxative |
| Boldo | *Peumus boldus* (A-839, G-453, J-337, S-337, V-232, V-234) | Chile; Peru; introduced to Europe | 36 (36/0/0) | *Human*: in hepatic dysfunction, cholelithiasis |
| Pasqueflower | *Anemone pulsatilla* (A-839, G-453, J-217, S-337, V-232) | Europe Czechoslovakia main producer (S-337) | 35 (35/0/0) | |
| Lachesis/snake venom | *Bothrops jararaca* (A-686, S-632, V-234) | Brazil; Paraguay; Argentina | 12 (12/0/0) | |

*Human use/veterinary use/disinfectant.
†Source: V-234.

Table 5.14  **Plant families supplying two or more ingredients in 10 or more drug products for sale in Canada in 1981 that come from wild and/or wild and cultivated (W + C) species**

| FAMILY | NUMBER OF INGREDIENTS | INGREDIENTS | | |
|---|---|---|---|---|
| | | *From wild* | *From W + C* | *From W or W + C* |
| COMPOSITAE | 9 | Burdock<br>Yarrow<br>Cornflower<br>Coltsfoot<br>Immortal<br>Goldenrod<br>Life root | Dandelion<br>Arnica | |
| LABIATAE | 6 | Scullcap<br>Stoneroot<br>Common motherwort | Sage<br>Thyme<br>Lavender | |
| ROSACEAE | 4 | Hawthorn<br>Wild cherry<br>Queen-of-the-meadow<br>Agrimony | | |
| FAGACEAE | 3 | Tannic acid<br>Creosote<br>White oak | | |
| PINACEAE | 3 | White pine<br>Pine needle oil | Turpentine<br>and others | |
| RANUNCULACEAE | 3 | Black cohosh<br>Pilewort | | Pasqueflower |
| LEGUMINOSAE | 3 | Peru balsam | Senna<br>Tolu balsam | |
| CUPRESSACEAE | 2 | Juniper berry<br>Cade oil | | |
| EQUISETACEAE | 2 | Horsetail<br>Scouring rush | | |
| ERICACEAE | 2 | Uva ursi<br>Bilberry | | |
| FUCACEAE | 2 | Kelp<br>Bladderwrack | | |
| GENTIANACEAE | 2 | Gentian<br>Centaury | | |
| SCROPHULARIACEAE | 2 | Mullein<br>Speedwell | | |
| URTICACEAE | 2 | Nettle<br>Wall pellitory | | |
| CUCURBITACEAE | 2 | Bryony | Colocynth | |
| RUBIACEAE | 2 | Sweet woodruff | Ipecac | |
| RUTACEAE | 2 | Prickly ash | Buchu | |
| RHAMNACEAE | 2 | Cascara sagrada | | Frangula |

Table 5.15 **Plant families supplying ingredients in prescription drugs sold in the United States in 1980 that come from wild and/or wild and cultivated (W + C) species**

| FAMILY | NUMBER OF INGREDIENTS | INGREDIENTS FROM WILD *(Species)* | INGREDIENTS FROM W + C *(Species)* |
|---|---|---|---|
| LEGUMINOSAE | 6 | Peru balsam (*Myroxylon balsamum*) Physostigmine (*Physostigma venenosum*) | Gum acacia (*Acacia senegal*) Senna (*Cassia* spp.) Licorice (*Glycyrrhiza glabra*) Tolu balsam (*Myroxylon balsamum*) |
| APOCYNACEAE | 2 | Deserpidine/reserpine/ rescinammine (*Rauvolfia vomitoria*) | Alseroxylon/rauwolfia (*Rauvolfia serpentina*) |
| CUPRESSACEAE | 2 | Cade oil (*Juniperus oxycedrus*) Cedar leaf oil (*Thuja occidentalis*) | |
| ERICACEAE | 2 | Uva ursi (*Arctostaphylos uva-ursi*) Wintergreen (*Gaultheria procumbens*) | |
| LILIACEAE | 2 | Squill (*Urginea maritima*) Veratrum (*Veratrum viride*) | |
| PINACEAE | 2 | White pine (*Pinus strobus*) | Sitosterols (*Pinus* spp.)* |
| RUBIACEAE | 2 | Yohimbine (*Pausinystalia yohimbe*) | Ipecac (*Cephaelis ipecacuanha*) |
| RUTACEAE | 2 | Pilocarpine (*Pilocarpus* spp.) | Buchu (*Barosma betulina*) |
| SALICACEAE | 2 | Poplar bud (*Populus balsamifera*) | Saligenin (*Salix alba*) |
| ARALIACEAE | 1 | Aralia (*Aralia racemosa*) | |
| BERBERIDACEAE | 1 | Berberine (*Berberis vulgaris*) | |
| BURSERACEAE | 1 | Myrrh (*Commiphora* spp.) | |

(*continued*)

Table 5.15 (*Continued*)

| FAMILY | NUMBER OF INGREDIENTS | INGREDIENTS FROM WILD (*Species*) | INGREDIENTS FROM W + C (*Species*) |
|---|---|---|---|
| DIOSCOREACEAE | 1 | | Diosgenin (*Dioscorea* spp.) |
| EPHEDRACEAE | 1 | | Ephedrine (*Ephedra sinica*)† |
| FAGACEAE | 1 | Tannic acid (*Quercus infectoria*) | |
| HAMAMELIDACEAE | 1 | Witch hazel (*Hamamelis virginiana*) | |
| LAURACEAE | 1 | Sassafras (*Sassafras albidum*) | |
| LOGANIACEAE | 1 | Gelsemium (*Gelsemium sempervirens*) | |
| MELIACEAE | 1 | | Cocillana (*Guarea guidonia* [= *G. rusbyi*]) |
| PALMAE | 1 | Saw palmetto (*Serenoa serrulata*) | |
| PAPAVERACEAE | 1 | Sanguinaria (*Sanguinaria canadensis*) | |
| PODOPHYLLACEAE | 1 | Podophyllum (*Podophyllum peltatum*) | |
| POLYGALACEAE | 1 | | Senega (*Polygala senega*) |
| POLYGONACEAE | 1 | | Rhubarb (*Rheum palmatum*) |
| RHAMNACEAE | 1 | Casanthranol/cascara sagrada (*Rhamnus purshiana*) | |
| ROSACEAE | 1 | Wild cherry (*Prunus virginiana*) | |
| STERCULIACEAE | 1 | Karaya gum (*Sterculia urens*) | |
| STRYCHNACEAE | 1 | | Strychnine (*Strychnos nux-vomica*) |

Sources: D-404 (U.S. prescription drug ingredients from plants); tables of this chapter (wild or wild and cultivated origin of ingredients).

*When produced from tall oil (sitosterols also produced from domesticated soybean).

†Also produced by synthesis.

# Table 5.16 Major ingredients used in 10 or more drug products for sale in Canada that are synthesized and come from wild and/or wild and cultivated species

| INGREDIENT | SYNTHESIS PROCEDURE | PRINCIPAL SPECIES INVOLVED | STATUS OF SPECIES | ORIGIN OF SPECIES IF WILD OR WILD AND CULTIVATED |
|---|---|---|---|---|
| Steroids | Most of steroids produced synthetically (A-671)<br>Synthetic steroids may be manufactured either by<br>(1) total synthesis—such as norgestrel and norethisterone<br>(2) semisynthesis—majority of steroid drugs made by partial synthesis (A-671)<br>from percursors such as | Natural steroids from pregnant mares' urine; accounts for most of steroidal estrogens in use today (A-671) | Domesticated | |
| | (a) stigmasterol (since early 1960s) and sitosterol (since late 1970s) | Stigmasterol from soya bean, *Glycine max* (A-671, M-35)<br>Sitosterol from residue of stigmasterol (A-671, M-33) | Cultivated | |
| | (b) hecogenin (since mid-1950s) | Hecogenin from sisal, *Agave sisalana* (A-324, A-671, M-33, M-35) | Cultivated | |
| | (c) cholesterol (since late 1970s) | Cholesterol from sheep wool grease via wool scouring industry (A-671, M-33, M-35) | Domesticated | |
| | (d) solasodine (since late 1970s) | Solasodine from certain species of *Solanum* such as *S. khasianum* (A-671, M-33)<br>*S. laciniatum* (A-324, A-671, M-33)<br>*S. aviculare* (A-61, A-671, M-33, M-35, P-125, P-126) | Cultivated esp. in India<br>Cultivated esp. in USSR<br>Cultivated esp. in New Zealand | |

(continued)

## Table 5.16 (*Continued*)

| INGREDIENT | SYNTHESIS PROCEDURE | PRINCIPAL SPECIES INVOLVED | STATUS OF SPECIES | ORIGIN OF SPECIES IF WILD OR WILD AND CULTIVATED |
|---|---|---|---|---|
| Steroids (*continued*) | (e) diosgenin (since late 1950s) | Diosgenin from certain species of *Dioscorea* such as the following: | | |
| | | *Dioscorea composita* (A-324, A-662, A-671, M-35, M-48, M-317, M-403, M-461) | Wild | Mexico; Central America; introduced to United States |
| | | *D. spiculiflora* (A-324, A-662, M-35, M-48, M-317, M-403, S-433) | Wild; cultivated (S-433) | Mexico |
| | | *D. floribunda* (A-324, A-662, A-671, M-35, M-48, M-317, M-403, M-461, S-433) | Wild; cultivated in India (A-671) | Mexico; Guatemala; introduced to United States |
| | | *D. deltoidea* (A-324, A-662, A-671, M-35, M-48, M-317, M-403, M-461) | Wild | India; Nepal; China |
| | | *D. sylvatica* (A-324, A-662, M-35, M-48, M-317, M-403) | Wild | South Africa |
| Camphor | More than $\frac{3}{4}$ of camphor sold in United States produced synthetically (V-234) Synthetic camphor may be manufactured either by (1) total synthesis—from vinyl chloride and cyc-opentadiene | Nautral camphor from *Cinnamomum camphora* (M-317, S-337, S-433, V-234) | Mostly cultivated (M-317, S-337) Taiwan and Japan main producers (M-317, S-433) | |

136

| Substance | Preparation / synthesis | Source | Wild/cultivated | Geographic distribution |
|---|---|---|---|---|
| | (2) semisynthesis—from pinene (S-433) Usually camphor sold in United States manufactured by semisynthesis (V-234) | Pinene—principal constituent of turpentine oil (S-433) See table 5.9: turpentine/pine tar/pine oil/rosin | Wild and cultivated (see table 5.9: turpentine/pine tar/pine oil/rosin) | (See table 5.9: turpentine/pine tar/pine oil/rosin) |
| Methyl salicylate | Mostly prepared by total synthesis—esterification of salicylic acid with methanol (S-433, V-234) | Natural methyl salicylate from wintergreen, *Gaultheria procumbens* A-686, J-217, J-325, J-337, M-317, S-41, S-337, S-433, V-150, V-224, V-232, V-234, V-345) | Wild | (Canada); United States Pennsylvania main producer (V-150) |
| | | and sweet birch, *Betula lenta* (J-217, J-325, J-337, M-317, S-41, S-337, S-433, V-234) | Wild | (Canada); United States |
| Ephedrine + pseudoephedrine | Recently most ephedrine and pseudoephedrine used in Western world manufactured synthetically (M-317) Total synthesis—reductive condensation between L-1-phenyl-1-acetylcarbinol and methylamine (S-433) | Natural ephedrine and pseudoephedrine from: | | |
| | | *Ephedra major* | Wild or wild and cultivated | Mediterranean region of Spain, Sicily, Afghanistan, and Pakistan (M-317) |
| | | *E. equisetina* | Wild or wild and cultivated | Northern China (M-317) |
| | | *E. sinica* | Wild or wild and cultivated | Northern China to Mongolia (M-317) |
| | | *E. intermedia* | Wild or wild and cultivated | Northern China to Pakistan (M-317) |
| | | *E. gerardiana* | Wild or wild and cultivated | India; Pakistan; Tibet; China (M-317) Pakistan, India, and China main producers (M-317, S-433) |

*Synthesized Products*

Table 5.16 lists four major active ingredients—steroids, camphor, methyl salicylate, and ephedrine—found in more than 10 drug products sold in Canada. All are synthesized, although each may also be obtained from wild or wild plus cultivated sources. Most important of these ingredients are the steroids.

Two classes of natural steroid hormones occur in the body: the sex hormones and the adrenocortical hormones. The sex hormones, produced primarily in the gonads, fall into three categories: estrogens and progestins (female sex hormones) and androgens (male sex hormones). The adrenocortical hormones (or corticosteroids) are produced by the outer cortical portion of the adrenal glands. There are at least 70 corticosteroids, which include cortisone, hydrocortisone, desoxycorticosterone, and aldosterone (S-433).

Steroid drugs are used for several reasons: principally they are more potent than steroids normally found in the body, and they are suitable for use in a wide range of circumstances—from the treatment of inflammatory conditions and certain hormone-dependent disorders and cancers to use as oral contraceptives (A-671). In 1973, steroid drugs constituted almost 15% of all prescriptions filled in the United States (D-135).

Steroid drugs can be produced by three methods:

1. derivation from natural sources: estrogens, for example, are produced from urine from pregnant mares (estrogen from this source is among the top-selling drugs and accounts for most steroidal estrogens in use today) (A-671);
2. total synthesis: such as norethisterone and norgestrel, two of the most widely used components of oral contraceptives (A-671);
3. semisynthesis: the majority of steroid drugs are made by a chemical modification of a natural product (A-671, S-433).

Semisynthesis is the method of relevance to this book. It relies on three main sources: sterols (principally cholesterol, stigmasterol, and sitosterol); sapogenins (principally diosgenin, hecogenin, and solasodine); and bile acids from animals (mostly oxen [D-238]). All bile acids and sterols come from domesticated species. Among the sapogenins, hecogenin is derived from long-cultivated sisal (*Agave sisalana*) and solasodine from more recently cultivated species of *Solanum*. Only diosgenin is derived from the wild.

The most important commercially exploited source of diosgenin is the genus *Dioscorea* (the yams) (A-671). Five species of wild yams are the major precursors used to make diosgenin. (The cultivated, edible yams do not contain diosgenin [A-671].) *Dioscorea spiculiflora* is native to Mexico, *D. floribunda* to Mexico and Guatemala, and *D. composita* to Mexico and Central America. *D. sylvatica* is harvested from the wild in South Africa and *D. deltoidea* from the wild in India.

In the 1940s a company began production of progesterone from Mexican sources of diosgenin. By the early 1960s Mexican diosgenin accounted for 75% of world steroid production. During this same 20-year period the potential of first hecogenin and then stigmasterol as precursors for the steroid industry was discovered. In the mid-1970s a largely governmental organization took control of the collection, drying, and sale of wild *Dioscorea* in Mexico, and within two years it had raised the price by more than 250% (A-671). Producers of Mexican diosgenin were faced with a price hike and uncertainty about the amounts that would be available (A-666). The multinationals turned away from Mexican diosgenin—largely not to alternative sources of diosgenin but to cheaper raw materials. Not only were hecogenin and stigmasterol available but by the late

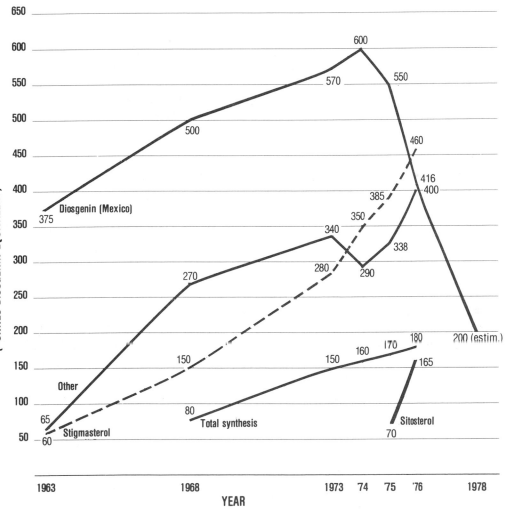

Fig. 5.3 **World steroid production (tons), 1963, 1968, 1973–1976, 1978. Other: other sapogenins, cholesterol, and bile acids. Source: A-671**

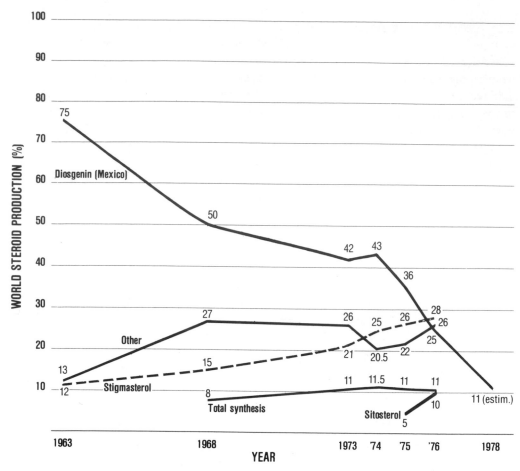

Fig. 5.4  **World steroid production (percentages), 1963, 1968, 1973–76, 1978. Other: other sapogenins, cholesterol, and bile acids. Source: A-671**

1970s sitosterol and solasodine had come onto the market and cholesterol (which had been used in the 1930s) reemerged as a steroid precursor. By 1978 diosgenin's share of the market had dropped to about 11%. Figures 5.3 and 5.4 chart the fall from favor of diosgenin and the concomitant reduced input from the wild to the steroid industry. This drastic decrease in *Dioscorea* use is contrary to the impression often given in the literature on wild plants in medicine.

*Essential Drugs*

In 1979, the World Health Organization (WHO) published a list of 245 drugs it considered essential (V-206). Table 5.17 lists nine of these active ingredients that might qualify for one of the following three categories: exclusively wild sources—pilocarpine and tubocurarine; wild plus cultivated sources—senna, reserpine, and ipecacuanha; synthesized and wild plus cultivated sources—ephedrine, hydrocortisone, dexamethasone, and prednisolone.

## Auxiliary Ingredients

Auxiliary ingredients are used by the drug industry in key but nonactive roles as stiffeners, emulsifiers, emollients, demulcents, disintegraters, binders, thickeners, suspending agents, and so forth. In this section we will discuss these ingredients.

### Exclusively Wild Species

Some major wild species used as auxiliary agents include algin, carrageenan, agar, furcellaran, tragacanth, and karaya. The first four of these are derived from marine species; the last two from terrestrial species. Information on the species involved and the nonmedical uses of all these ingredients (except furcellaran, since it is not important in North America for its nonmedical uses) is presented in chapter 6.

Algin is used as a suspending agent, protective colloid, emollient, tablet binder, and tablet disintegrater. It gives body, spreadability, and emulsion stability to pharmaceutical ointments and has found an application in the formation of a firm gel for preparing dental impressions (M-317, M-319, S-433, V-234).

About 20% of the present world production of carrageenan is used in pharmaceuticals and cosmetics (S-369). Carrageenan, a demulcent, is used to form gels and give stability to emulsions and suspensions. It may be employed to give bulk in laxatives (Kondremul, Kondremul with Cascara, and Kondremul with Phenolphthalein—all products by Fisons [A-687, A-739]). It is a particularly desirable component of toothpastes and powder formulations as it imparts firm texture, good rinsability, and better foam than other agents (S-369, S-433); it is an ingredient in Lever Brothers Pepsodent Tooth Powder and Pepsodent Ammoniated Powder (A-687).

Agar furnishes a smooth, nonirritating bulk in laxatives, such as in Petrogalar made by Wyeth (A-687), Agarol by P.D. & Co., and Agarphen by Harris (A-739). (Bulk in the laxatives Agoral and Agoral Plain by Warner-Chilcott is provided by tragacanth and acacia in addition to agar gel [A-687].) Agar is a suspending agent for barium sulfate in radiology, an ingredient in slow-releasing capsules, suppositories, and surgical lubricants, and a disintegrating agent in tablets (M-307, S-370, V-234).

Furcellaran (or Danish agar) is derived from the seaweed *Furcellaria fastigiata*, which is found along the coasts of the North Atlantic and adjacent seas. Only 10% of furcellaran harvested is used in pharmaceuticals (the food industry is the major market). Danish agar is used particularly in Europe for suspensions, emulsions, foams, and tablet disintegration (A-1186, M-317, S-433, V-234).

Tragacanth is widely used as a natural emulsifier and thickener by the drug industry. It is also valuable as a suspending agent for insoluble powders in mixtures, as an adhesive or binding agent in pills, tablets, and lozenges, and as

# Table 5.17 Wild species in drugs considered essential by the World Health Organization (WHO)

| DRUG | SOURCE* | | | PRINCIPAL WILD SPECIES INVOLVED | ORIGIN OF WILD SPECIES |
|---|---|---|---|---|---|
| | W | W + C | S + W + C | | |
| Pilocarpine | X | | | Opthalmological preparation: miotic | *Pilocarpus jaborandi;* *P. microphyllus;* *P. spicatus;* *P. trachylophus;* *P. pennatifolius* | Brazil (M-307, M-317)<br><br>Brazil, Paraguay (M-307, M-317) |
| Tubocurarine | X | | | Muscle relaxant: (peripherally acting) and cholinesterase inhibitor | *Chondrodendron tomentosum* | Brazil, Peru, Colombia; Panama (M-317) |
| Senna | | X | | Gastrointestinal drug: cathartic | *Cassia acutifolia* (Co-source of senna; please refer to table 5.9 for other species) | Egypt, Sudan (D-246, J-337, M-307, M-317) |
| Reserpine | | X | | Cardiovascular drug: antihypertensive | *Rauvolfia vomitoria* (Main source of reserpine; please refer to table 5.10 for other species) | West Africa from Senegal and the Congo to Mozambique (M-317) |
| Ipecacuanha | | X | | Antidote | *Cephaelis ipecacuanha* (Please refer to table 5.10 for more information)<br><br>*C. acuminata* | Brazil, Bolivia (J-337, M-317, S-433, V-234)<br><br>Nicaragua and Panama to Colombia (J-337, M-307, M-317, S-337, S-433) |
| Ephedrine | | | X | Drug acting on respiratory tract: antiasthmatic | *Ephedra major*<br><br>*E. equisetina*<br><br>*E. sinica* | Mediterranean region of Spain, Sicily, Afghanistan, and Pakistan (M-317)<br><br>Northern China (M-317)<br><br>Northern China to Mongolia (M-317) |

142

| Drug | Status | Medicinal use | Source species | Distribution (references) |
|---|---|---|---|---|
| | | | E. intermedia | Northern China to Pakistan (M-317) |
| | | | E. gerardiana | India; Pakistan; Tibet; China (M-317) |
| Hydrocortisone | X | Dermatological drug: anti-inflammatory; Opthamological preparation: anti-inflammatory; Hormone: adrenal hormone and synthetic substitute | Dioscorea composita | Mexico; Central America (A-324, A-662, A-671, M-35, M-48, M-317, M-403, M-461) |
| | | | D. spiculiflora | Mexico (A-324, A-662, M-35, M-48, M-317, M-403, S-433) |
| | | | D. floribunda | Mexico; Guatemala (A-324, A-662, A-671, M-35, M-48, M-317, M-403, M-461, S-433) |
| | | | D. deltoidea | India; Nepal; China (A-324, A-662, A-671, M-35, M-48, M-317, M-403, M-461) |
| | | | D. sylvatica (Source of diosgenin; please refer to table 5.16 for other species used in steroid drugs) | South Africa (A-324, A-662, M-35, M-48, M-317, M-403) |
| Dexamethasone | X | Hormone: adrenal hormone and synthetic substitute | (May be derived from diosgenin [A-671]; please refer to hydrocortisone above and table 5.16) | |
| Prednisolone | X | Hormone: adrenal hormone and synthetic substitute | (May be derived from diosgenin [A-671]; please refer to hydrocortisone above and table 5.16) | |

*W = wild; W + C = wild plus cultivated; S + W + C = synthesized plus wild plus cultivated.

143

a base for jelly lubricants—especially spermicidal jellies (D-246, M-107, M-317, S-433). In Canada two of the products in which tragacanth is found are the lotion Alphosyl (Reed & Carnrick), used in keratolytic-psoriasis therapy, and Aci-Jel (Ortho), a vaginal acidifier (A-739).

Much of the gum karaya imported by the United States is used in the pharmaceutical industry (G-45). Karaya is employed primarily as a bulk laxative (for example, in Saraka by Plough [A-687]) and, in this class of product, is second only to psyllium seed (which is cultivated) (G-45). Another important pharmaceutical application of karaya is as a denture adhesive (G-45, V-234). Karaya is found in the following denture-adhesive products: Corega Powder (Block), Fasteeth (Vicks), Firmdent (Moyco), Orafix (Norcliff Thayer), Orafix Medicated (Norcliff Thayer), Poli-Grip (Block), and Wernet's Powder (Block) (A-687).

### Wild plus Cultivated Species

Acacia (or gum arabic) is the one major auxiliary drug ingredient that comes from wild and cultivated sources (D-246, G-44, G-300, S-433). Approximately 5% of the gum arabic imported into the United States is used for pharmaceutical purposes (G-44). Gum arabic is used as an emollient and demulcent in cough drops and syrups to produce a smooth syrup and prevent crystallization of sugar in both these products (G-44, V-234); as a suspending agent (M-307, M-317, S-433) for calamine-kaolin suspensions and liquid petrolatum and cod-liver-oil emulsions (G-44); as an adhesive or binding agent in tablets and pills (G-44, M-307, M-317, S-433); and as an excipient in the manufacture of pills and plasters (G-44).

## Medical Research

### Nonhuman Primates

In 1977, an estimated 34,000 nonhuman primates were used in the United States by the biomedical community in health-related activities (G-425). (The projected figures for 1982 were about 22,500.) Tables 5.18 and 5.19 list the species used, their major biomedical uses, the numbers needed annually in the United States (and how many of these are from wild versus captive-bred animals), and the origins of the wild species.

Several trends in nonhuman-primate use are worth noting. The first is the big decrease (by more than 30%) in the total number of animals used—from about 34,000 in 1977 to 22,500 in 1982. The second is the slight decrease (by two species, the common marmoset and the common gibbon) in the number of species used—from about 26+ species in 1977 to 24+ species in 1982. The third is the decrease in the number of wild animals used due to captive-breeding programs. Of the projected 22,650 animals used in 1982, demand for the

**Table 5.18 Nonhuman primates used in biomedical activities in the United States in 1977 and 1982: each genus contributes more than 2,000 individuals annually**

| SPECIES | MAJOR BIOMEDICAL USES* | NUMBER USED IN UNITED STATES† | | ORIGIN OF WILD SPECIES |
|---|---|---|---|---|
| | | 1977 (Number U.S. captive bred) | 1982 (est.) | |
| *Macaca mulatta* (Rhesus macaque) | 1. General purpose 2. Production and testing of biological products 3. Vaccines (i.e., poliomyelitis) | 14,015 (6,049 U.S. captive bred in 1981) (V-350) | 6,000 | Afghanistan to the People's Republic of China (A-1189) In 1977, most of U.S. imports from India (G-425); in 1978 India banned all rhesus exports (G-735) |
| *Macaca fascicularis* (Long-tailed/crab-eating macaque) | 1. General purpose 2. Drug safety testing | 6,005 (433 U.S. captive bred in 1981) (D-476) | 8,000 | Burma, Thailand, Indonesia; Malaysia; Philippines (A-1189, M-355) U.S. imports from Indonesia, Malaysia, and Philippines (G-425, M-605) |
| Other *Macaca* spp: | 1. Neuroscience 2. Behavioral studies 3. Many other research areas | 995 (907 U.S. captive bred in 1981) (V-350) | 900 | |
| *M. nemestrina* (Pigtail macaque) | | | | India; Burma; Thailand; Indonesia; Malaysia (A-1189, G-425, M-355) |
| *M. arctoides* (Bear macaque) | | | | Burma, Thailand; Indonesia; Malaysia; People's Republic of China (A-1189, M-355) |
| *M. cyclopis* (Tawian macaque) | | | | Taiwan (A-1189) |
| *M. fuscata* (Japanese macaque) | | | | Japan (A-1189) |
| *M. radiata* (Bonnet macaque) | | | | India (A-1189, G-425) |

(continued)

# Table 5.18 (*Continued*)

| SPECIES | MAJOR BIOMEDICAL USES* | NUMBER USED IN UNITED STATES† | | ORIGIN OF WILD SPECIES |
|---|---|---|---|---|
| | | 1977 (*Number U.S. captive bred*) | 1982 (*est.*) | |
| *Saimiri sciureus* (Common squirrel-monkey) | 1. General research<br>2. Drug testing<br>3. Nutrition<br>4. Cardiovascular research | 4,445 (518 U.S. captive bred in 1981) (D-476) | 1,800 | Colombia to Amazon Basin (A-1189)<br>U.S. imports from Bolivia; Peru; Guyana (M-605) |
| *Saguinus* spp.: | 1. Virology<br>2. Immunology<br>3. Dental studies<br>4. Reproductive physiology<br>5. Behavioral studies<br>6. Other research | 2,190 (20 U.S. captive bred in 1981) (D-476) | 2,000 | U.S. imports from Bolivia; Peru; Guyana (M-605) |
| *S. fuscicollis* (Saddle-back tamarin) | | | | Brazil, Bolivia, Peru, Ecuador, Colombia |
| *S. nigricollis* (Black and red tamarin) | | | | Brazil, Bolivia, Peru, Ecuador, Colombia |
| *S. labiatus* (White-lipped tamarin) | | | | Central Amazon (A-1189) |
| *S. mystax* (Moustached tamarin) | 1. Hepatitis A virus studies | | | Peru; Brazil (A-1189) |
| *S. oedipus* (Cotton-top tamarin) | 1. Viral oncology | | | Colombia; Panama (A-1189) |
| *Cercopithecus aethiops* (Savanna/green/vervet monkey) | 1. Production of biological material (e.g., for tissue culture)<br>2. Toxicology testing | 2,075 (165 U.S. captive bred in 1981) (D-476) | 1,500 | Senegal to Somalia to South Africa (A-1189)<br>U.S. imports from Kenya; Somalia; Ethiopia; Tanzania (M-605) |

Note: Each genus contributes more than 2,000 individuals annually.
* Source: G-425.
† Source: G-735.

## Table 5.19 Nonhuman primates used in biomedical activities in the United States in 1977 and 1982: each genus contributes fewer than 2,000 individuals annually

| SPECIES | MAJOR BIOMEDICAL USES* | NUMBER USED IN UNITED STATES† | | ORIGIN OF WILD SPECIES |
|---|---|---|---|---|
| | | 1977 *(Number U.S. captive bred)* | 1982 *(est.)* | |
| Aotus trivirgatus (Night monkey) | 1. Malaria chemotherapy<br>2. Immunology studies<br>3. Vision research | 1,465 (44 U.S. captive bred in 1981) (D-476) | 500 | Panama to Paraguay (A-1189) U.S. imports from Bolivia; Peru; Guyana (M-605) |
| Papio spp. (Baboon) | 1. General purpose<br>2. Experimental surgery<br>3. Reproductive physiology | 1,282 (515 U.S. captive bred in 1981) (V-350) | 1,300 | Sub-Sahara Africa (A-1189, G-425) U.S. imports from Kenya; Somalia; Ethiopia; Tanzania (M-605) |
| Other primate spp. | 1. General research<br>2. Many specific applications | | 600 | |
| Erythrocebus patas (Patas monkey) | | | | Senegal to Ethiopia to Tanzania (A-1189) |
| Ateles spp. (Spider monkey) | | | | Mexico to Bolivia (A-1189) |
| Cebus spp. (Capuchin monkey) | | | | Honduras to Argentina (A-1189) U.S. imports from Bolivia; Peru; Guyana (M-605) |
| Galago spp. (Bushbaby) | | | | Africa (A-1189) |
| Callithrix jacchus (Common marmoset) | 1. General research<br>2. Reproductive physiology<br>3. Teratology<br>4. Drug safety testing | 170 (Supply from Europe all captive bred) (G-735) | — | Brazil (A-1189) |
| Pan troglodytes (Chimpanzee) | 1. Hepatitis research<br>2. Psychobiology | 180 (90 U.S. captive bred in 1981) (V-350) | 50 | Guinea to Zaire to Uganda and Tanzania (A-1189) |
| Hylobates lar (Common gibbon) | 1. Cancer viruses<br>2. Hepatitis B research<br>3. Behavioral studies | 100 | — | Burma; Thailand; Kampuchea; Indonesia; Malaysia (A-1189, M-355) |

Note: Each genus contributes fewer than 2,000 individuals annually.
*Source: G-425.
†Source: G-735.

following species is apparently met entirely by captive-bred animals: rhesus monkeys, some of the other *Macaca* species, and chimpanzees. One-third of the common squirrel-monkeys and one-fifth of the baboons are also apparently supplied from captive-bred stock.

The species now in highest demand—about 7,000 animals a year—and the only one still largely taken from the wild is the long-tailed macaque (*Macaca fascicularis*), which the United States imports from Indonesia, the Philippines, and Malaysia (G-425, M-605). In December 1981, we interviewed the owners of two of the top three Indonesian exporting firms—C. V. Primaco Indonesia (which has about 60% of the Indonesian trade) and C. V. Primates Indonesia (about 11% of the trade). (The number two company—with 14% of the trade—is C. V. Inquatex Indonesia.) Both exporters reported that 95% of their animals were trapped in Sumatra. The remaining 5% came from western Java.

*Wild Species Other Than Nonhuman Primates*

Between 1976 and 1980, the biomedical community in the United States used an average each year of 60,795 wild animals other than nonhuman primates (S-691–S-693, S-695, S-696). We repeatedly requested a list of the major species in use from USDA's Animal and Plant Health Inspection Service, but these data were never sent.

# 6

# Food and Industrial Products

Between 1976 and 1980, the United States produced and imported on average each year $229 million worth of food and industrial products from wild sources. This includes food items from native species such as maple syrup and sugar, pecans, blueberries, and wild rice (table 6.1; notes 1–3) as well as food and industrial items from foreign species such as Brazil nuts, oregano, rattan, gum arabic, and chicle (tables 6.2 and 6.3; notes 2, 4–10). Not included in this sum are industrial products from wood (chap. 2) or food and industrial products from aquatic animals (chap. 3). Figure 6.1 shows the breakdown of the $229 million: 18 different foods account for 38% (or $87 million) and 31 different industrial products account for 62% (or $142 million).

## Food

Eighteen different food items, either domestically produced or imported by the United States during the period 1976 to 1980, came from wild species. They were worth an average of $87 million each year. As figure 6.2 illustrates, five nuts and fruits accounted for 60%: pecans ($22 million), Brazil nuts ($17 million), blueberries ($13 million), pine nuts ($800,000), and lingonberries ($3,000); five specialty products for 31%: maple sugar and syrup ($23 million), wild rice ($3 million), edible seaweeds ($900,000), hearts of palm ($400,000), and fiddleheads ($20,000); eight herbs and spices for the remaining 9%: oregano ($3 million), sage ($1.5 million), rosemary ($900,000), thyme ($700,000), allspice ($600,000), bay leaf ($400,000), winter savory ($100,000), and Bombay mace ($20,000).

### Nuts and Berries

#### PECANS
Between 1976 and 1980, U.S. harvests of wild pecans were worth $22 million annually (table 6.1). The pecan (*Carya illinoensis*) is considered the all-American nut (M-566). Native trees grow in wide areas of Texas, Oklahoma, Arkansas,

(*text continued on page 159*)

149

Table 6.1  Domestic production of food in the United States from wild or wild and cultivated sources: average annual value more than $1 million, 1976–1980

| PRODUCT | AVERAGE ANNUAL VALUE OF DOMESTIC PRODUCT (U.S. $) | PRODUCT FROM WILD (%) | PRODUCER STATES OF WILD PRODUCT (%) | |
|---|---|---|---|---|
| Pecans | 121,575,000* | 18† | Texas | (50) |
| | | | Louisiana | (26) |
| | | | Oklahoma | (16) |
| | | | Mississippi | (5) |
| | | | Arkansas | (3) |
| Blueberries | 48,797,000* (1978–1980 only) | 15‡ | Maine | (99) |
| | | | Oregon | |
| | | | Michigan | (1) |
| | | | New Jersey | |
| | | | Washington | |
| Maple syrup and sugar | 13,616,000* | 100 | Vermont | (36) |
| | | | New York | (25) |
| | | | Wisconsin | (9) |
| | | | Michigan | (8) |
| | | | New Hampshire | (7) |
| | | | Ohio | (7) |
| | | | Others | (8) |
| Wild rice | 4,177,000§ | 32§ | Minnesota | (95+) |
| | | | Wisconsin | (rest) |

*Sources: S-724, S-726–S-728.
†Source: See note 1.
‡Source: See note 2.
§Source: See note 3.

**Table 6.2   Imports of food and industrial products by the United States from wild or wild and cultivated sources: average annual value more than $1 million, 1976–1980**

| IMPORT *(Food or industrial use)* | AVERAGE ANNUAL VALUE OF IMPORT *(U.S. $)\** | % OF IMPORT FROM WILD | EXPORTING COUNTRIES PERCENTAGE OF U.S. IMPORTS* | |
|---|---|---|---|---|
| Rattan (I) | 58,396,000† | 91 (4)‡ (G-428) | Hong Kong | 40 |
| | | | Philippines | 34 |
| | | | Taiwan | 7 |
| | | | People's Republic of China | 5 |
| | | | Singapore | 3 |
| | | | Indonesia | 2 |
| | | | Thailand | 2 |
| | | | Others | 7 |
| Cork (I) | 23,631,000 | 75 (5)‡ (A-532) | Portugal | 69 |
| | | | Spain | 21 |
| | | | Others | 10 |
| Brazil nut (F) | 17,679,000 | 97 (6)‡ (V-208) | Brazil | 75 |
| | | | Bolivia | 16 |
| | | | Peru | 7 |
| | | | Others | 2 |
| Arabic gum/gum acacia (I) | 11,134,000 | 75 (5)‡ | Sudan | 95 |
| | | | Others | 5 |
| Maple syrup and sugar (F) | 9,314,000 | 100 (M-373) | Canada | 99 |
| | | | Others | 1 |
| Blueberries (F) | 7,883,000 | 70% of Canadian production (2)‡ | Canada | 99 |
| | | | Others | 1 |
| Agar (I) | 7,275,000 | 75 (5)‡ | Spain | 31 |
| | | | Chile | 20 |

*(continued)*

Table 6.2 (**Continued**)

| IMPORT (Food or industrial use) | AVERAGE ANNUAL VALUE OF IMPORT (U.S. $)* | % OF IMPORT FROM WILD | EXPORTING COUNTRIES PERCENTAGE OF U.S. IMPORTS* | |
|---|---|---|---|---|
| Agar (continued) | | | | |
| Seaweeds nes (I) | 6,545,000 | 75 (5)‡ | Chile | 24 |
| | | | Philippines | 23 |
| | | | Canada | 15 |
| | | | Mexico | 14 |
| | | | Japan | 12 |
| | | | Others | 12 |
| Carnauba (I) | 5,434,000 | 100 (S-41) | Brazil | 99 |
| | | | Others | 1 |
| Istle/tampico (I) | 4,798,000 | 100 (S-684) | Mexico | 99+ |
| | | | Others | (under 1) |
| Quebracho and red quebracho (I) | 4,569,000 | 100 (P-258) | Argentina | 78 |
| | | | Paraguay | 18 |
| | | | Others | 4 |
| Jelutong (I) | 4,344,000 | 100 (V-276) | Singapore | 94 |
| | | | Malaysia and Indonesia | 6 |
| Lac (I) | 4,338,000 | 100 | Thailand | 41 |
| | | | India | 34 |
| | | | Others | 25 |

| Commodity | Production | Source | Country | % |
|---|---|---|---|---|
| Oregano/origanum; origanum oil (F) | 4,126,000 (4,010,000 = herb) (116,000 = oil) | *Herb:* 75 (5)‡ (A-1120, G-83, J-337, M-579, P-183, S-413) | *Herb* Greece / Mexico / Turkey / Others | 44 / 29 / 20 / 7 |
| | | *Oil:* 100 (G-76, P-151) | *Oil* Spain / Others | 80 / 20 |
| Chicle/sapodilla (I) | 4,072,000 | 100 (P-258) | Mexico / Belize / Guatemala / Others | 79 / 12 / 7 / 2 |
| Gutta balata, Gutta percha, and Gutta nes (I) | 3,989,000 | 85 (7)‡ Some cultivation in Indonesia (V-277) | Malaysia / Indonesia / Brazil / Others | 72 / 15 / 7 / 6 |
| Carrageenan (I) | 3,895,000 | 100 | Denmark / Spain / Canada / Others | 48 / 20 / 12 / 20 |
| Karaya gum (I) | 3,760,000 | 100 (G-45, G-300) | India / Others | 96 / 4 |
| Seaweeds and other marine plants (prepared for edible uses) (F) | 3,433,000 | 25 (8)‡ | Japan / Republic of Korea / Others | 76 / 15 / 9 |
| Leche-caspi/sorva (I) | 3,068,000 | 100 (V-315) | Brazil / Others | 99+ / (under 1) |

*(continued)*

Table 6.2  (*Continued*)

| IMPORT<br>*(Food or industrial use)* | AVERAGE ANNUAL VALUE<br>OF IMPORT *(U.S.$)** | % OF IMPORT FROM WILD | EXPORTING COUNTRIES | PERCENTAGE OF U.S. IMPORTS* |
|---|---|---|---|---|
| Tragacanth (I) | 3,043,000 | 100<br>(G-556) | Iran<br>Turkey<br>Others | 88<br>4<br>8 |
| Sage (F) | 3,019,000 | 50 (9)‡<br>(G-83) | Albania<br>Yugoslavia<br>Turkey<br>Others | 55<br>37<br>3<br>5 |
| Sodium alginate (I) | 2,315,000 | 100 | United Kingdom<br>Canada<br>Norway<br>Others | 44<br>30<br>17<br>9 |
| Wild rice (F) | 1,904,000 | 100 | Canada<br>Others | 99<br>1 |
| Pignolia nut/pine<br>nut/piñon nut (F) | 1,671,000 | 50 (9)‡<br>(V-208) | Portugal<br>Spain<br>People's Republic of China<br>Others | 41<br>27<br>26<br>6 |

| | | | | |
|---|---|---|---|---|
| Hearts of palm (F) | 1,494,000 | 25 (8)‡ (M-229) | Brazil | 98 |
| | | | Others | 2 |
| Candelilla wax (I) | 1,349,000 | 100 (G-263, M-229) | Mexico | 99+ |
| | | | Others | (under 1) |
| Allspice/pimento (F) | 1,268,000 | About 50 (10)‡ (P-183, P-256) | Jamaica | 52 |
| | | | Guatemala | 18 |
| | | | Mexico | 15 |
| | | | Honduras | 13 |
| | | | Others | 2 |
| Thyme (F) | 1,108,000 (878,000 = herb) (230,000 = oil) | Herb: 50 (9)‡ (G-83) | Herb | |
| | | | Spain | 77 |
| | | | France | 19 |
| | | | Others | 4 |
| | | Oil: 100 (G-76, G-83, P-151) | Oil | |
| | | | Spain | 77 |
| | | | Others | 23 |
| Brazilian sassafras (I) | 1,081,000 | 100 (A-90) | Brazil | 99+ |
| | | | Others | (under 1) |

*Sources: S-450–S-454.

†The value of imported rattan products was $58,396,000; another $25,527,000 in two combined categories (bamboo, rattan and willow) was also imported.

‡Numbers in parentheses refer to notes.

Table 6.3 **Imports of food and industrial products by the United States from wild or wild and cultivated sources: average annual value under $1 million, 1976–1980**

| IMPORT (Food or industrial use) | AVERAGE ANNUAL VALUE OF IMPORT (U.S.$)* | PERCENTAGE OF IMPORT FROM WILD | EXPORTING COUNTRIES* | PERCENTAGE OF U.S. IMPORTS |
|---|---|---|---|---|
| Bois de rose (I) | 980,000 | 100 (G-76, M-30) | Brazil | 84 |
| | | | Others | 16 |
| Rosemary (F) | 926,000 | 100 (G-83, P-151) | Tunisia | 40 |
| | | | Spain | 26 |
| | | | France | 12 |
| | | | Others | 22 |
| Bay leaf (F) | 528,000 | 75+ (G-83) | Turkey | 95 |
| | | | Others | 5 |
| Styrax natural balsam (I) | 367,000 | 100 | Honduras | 84 |
| | | | Turkey | Minor |
| Babassu (I) | 361,000 (1976–1979 only) | 100 (A-316, M-229, V-85) | Brazil | Major |
| | | | Paraguay | Minor |
| Cedar leaf oil (I) | 253,000 | 100 | Canada | 96 |
| | | | Others | 4 |
| Civet (I) | 237,000 | 100 (in Africa) (D-221) | France | 49 |
| | | | Others | 51 |
| Tolu balsam (I) | 179,000 | 100 (A-90, A-109, D-246, G-76) | Colombia | Major |

| Product | Quantity | | Country | |
|---|---|---|---|---|
| Palmarosa (I) | 168,000 | 75† | India | Major |
| Musk (I) | 165,000 | 75† | India | Major |
| | | | Hong Kong | Major |
| Valonia (I) | 154,000 | 100 | Turkey | 99 |
| | | | Others | 1 |
| Tonka bean (I) | 139,000 | 75† (D-246) | Venezuela | 27 |
| | | | Brazil | 26 |
| | | | Others | 47 |
| Savory (F) | 127,000 | 75† (G-83) | Yugoslavia | Major |
| Castoreum (I) | 67,000 | 100 | Canada | Major |
| Copaiba balsam (I) | 45,000 | 100 (A-90, A-109, G-76) | Brazil | Major |
| Ouricury wax (I) | 27,000 | 100 (S-41) | Brazil | Major |
| Fiddlehead ferns (F) | 24,000 (1980 only) | 100 (S-780) | Canada | Major |
| Bombay mace (F) | 23,000 | 100 (G-363) | India | Major |
| Lingonberry/partridgeberry (F) | 3,000 | 100 (S-796) | Canada | Major |

* Sources: S-450–S-454.
† Source: See note 5.

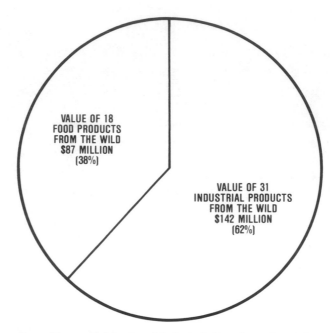

Fig. 6.1  **Domestic and imported food and industrial products from the wild (excluding items covered in other chapters) in the United States: 1976–1980 average annual value $229 million. Sources: tables 6.1–6.3**

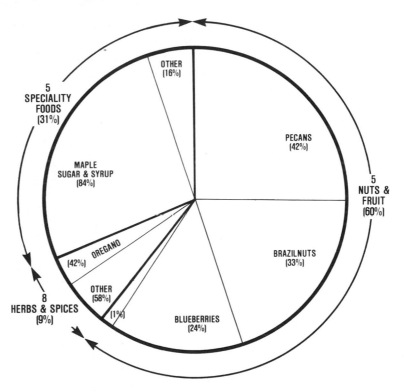

Fig. 6.2  **Eighteen wild food items native to and imported by the United States: 1976–1980 average annual value $87 million. Sources: tables 6.1–6.3**

Louisiana, and Mississippi. They are also found in smaller numbers in Kansas, Missouri, Tennessee, Kentucky, Indiana, Illinois, Iowa, and Nebraska (J-342, M-624). The selection and propagation of superior trees began around 1850 (M-22, M-624). Most of the commercial trees grown today were developed between 1915 and 1930—the period when big expansion of the pecan industry created a demand for improved cultivars (M-625).

Canada is the chief foreign buyer of American pecans (P-302, S-782). Pecans are now also grown outside the United States, principally in Mexico, Australia, Israel, Brazil, and South Africa (M-624, V-208). For the 1976–1980 period, the United States imported each year an average of about $2 million worth of pecans: Mexico supplied 72% of the imports; Australia 26% (S-450–S-454).

From 85 to 90% of pecans sold are shelled. The remainder is sold in the shell or precracked. Bakery products consume more than one-third of the shelled pecan crop (M-624, V-208). Pecans are used in fruitcakes (for which Georgia and Texas are especially celebrated [M-566]); coffee cakes; cinnamon buns; nut breads; cookies; and brownies (J-310, V-208). A regional speciality of Kentucky is whiskey or bourbon cake with pecans (M-566). However, probably the most famous of all pecan specialties is pecan pie made with molasses or corn syrup. One appropriately named recipe for this super-rich dessert is Utterly Deadly Pecan Pie (M-566). The confectionery industry is the next biggest consumer of pecans, which are widely used in candy bars and eaten salted, spiced, or sugared as snacks (J-310, M-566). Pecans are also used in ice creams by the dairy industry (J-310, M-624) and are popular in stuffings, salads, vegetable dishes, and main dishes (M-566).

### BRAZIL NUTS

Between 1976 and 1980, the United States imported approximately $17 million worth of Brazil nuts annually. Brazil was the top supplier (75% of imports originating from this country), followed by Bolivia (16%) and Peru (7%) (table 6.2). The United States, West Germany, and the United Kingdom are the largest consumers of Brazil nuts (V-208, S-372). Brazil nuts (*Bertholletia excelsa*) are native to the Amazon Basin (S-372, V-208). The northern limit to their range is Venezuela and Guyana, the western limit Colombia and Peru, the southern limit Bolivia and Brazil (V-208).

Commercial supplies of Brazil nuts are derived almost entirely from wild trees (M-57, V-208). There are only three plantations in existence—all are in Brazil—and together they contribute less than 1% of Brazil's output (V-208). Trade reports indicate that Brazil nut production is on the decline for two reasons: development of other economic activities in the Amazon Basin, which have created other opportunities for the available labor force; and large cattle-raising operations, which, in creating pastures, have destroyed many of Brazil's wild nut groves (S-372, V-208). Brazil nuts are eaten raw and used in brittles and crunches, caramel-type candies, cream centers, fudge-type candies, hard candies, nougats, marshmallow candies, toppings, and chocolate (V-208).

BLUEBERRIES

The quintessential North American fruit is the blueberry. At present three domesticated species and four primarily wild species enter trade. The domesticated species are discussed in chapter 7. Two wild species of minor commercial importance are the evergreen blueberry (*Vaccinium ovatum*) and the mountain blueberry (*V. membranaceum*), which are harvested primarily in Oregon and Washington (D-339). (In addition, small quantities of wild highbush blueberries (*V. australe* and *V. corymbosum*) may be harvested in Michigan and New Jersey (D-339).) The two most important wild blueberries are the lowbush blueberry (*V. angustifolium*) and the Canadian blueberry (*V. myrtilloides*). Their average annual value between 1978 and 1980 in the United States was approximately $7.3 million (table 6.1). Another $5.5 million of wild blueberries were imported from Canada (table 6.2).

The major harvests of these two species of wild blueberry take place in eastern Canada—in order of harvest size the provinces are Nova Scotia, Quebec, New Brunswick, Newfoundland, and Prince Edward Island—and in the northeastern United States—particularly the state of Maine. The annual production of the five Canadian provinces equals that of Maine (G-127). The two species grow together, in a 50:50 ratio in New Brunswick and western Maine and in an 80:20 ratio (in favor of *V. angustifolium*) east of these points (A. Ismail, pers. comm., 3 September 1982). They therefore are harvested and processed together as lowbush types.

There has been a long association between people in this region of North America and wild blueberries. For hundreds of years, the Micmac, Abnaki, Penobscot, Passamaquoddy, and Malecite—all tribes of the Algonkin language family—ritually gathered the berries in late summer (J-598, S-744). In 1866 wild blueberries began to be canned in Maine (G-744). In 1883 the first metal blueberry rake was invented by Abijah Tabbutt of Columbia Falls (Maine) (S-407). The Tabbutt rake, modified since the prototype, is still being manufactured today—by Tabbutt's grandson—and the demand for it is tremendous (A. Ismail, pers. comm., 3 September 1982). Jasper Wyman and Sons, located in Cherryfield (Maine), is the largest American processor of wild blueberries (P-373); its Canadian counterpart is Oxford Frozen Foods Ltd. of Oxford (Nova Scotia) (A-912).

Native lowbush blueberry stands represent a successional stage. They are often fields in which other forms of agriculture have been attempted and abandoned (G-124). These fields are brought into blueberry stands and improved through weed control (by herbicide applications) and burn-pruning—an Indian tradition (A-171, A-172, G-121). In burn-pruning, the fields are burned either after every harvest or after every second harvest (G-611). The only other boost commonly given to the native stands is the introduction of honeybees during bloom to increase the fruit set (G-121).

Each year about 18–20 million pounds of wild lowbush-type blueberries are harvested in Maine (and an equivalent amount in Canada) between July and

September (G-127, G-611). The pickers are schoolchildren, university students, and entire families. They are usually paid by the box—which holds 22–24 pounds of berries. In 1982 the Washington County (Maine) price to rakers ranged from 12 to 14 cents per pound—so the average box of berries was worth about $3. A good raker can pick anywhere from 30 to 50 boxes a day.

About 80% of the Maine wild blueberry crop is frozen (G-611). Most of the remainder is canned—with only a negligible amount sold fresh (G-611). New export markets are being developed in Japan, Hong Kong, and Singapore. Wild blueberries are very popular supplements to muffin, pancake, and waffle mixes (G-127, S-407). Their size is smaller than that of cultivated varieties. The advantage in this is more berries to the muffin (or pancake or waffle). Furthermore, the smaller wild berries look less messy after baking. Wild blueberries are used by such major food companies as Sarah Lee and Duncan Hines in their blueberry cakes and by McCains in its blueberry pies. Wild blueberry juice is also fermented into table and dessert wines or fortified to make brandies and cordials (A-912, G-744).

## PINE NUTS

During the period 1976 to 1980, the United States imported on average each year about $800,000 of wild pine nuts, primarily from Portugal (41%), Spain (27%), and China (26%) (table 6.2). Edible pine nuts (also called piñon nuts or pignolias) are harvested in several countries around the world from several species of pine. In terms of U.S. consumption, the two most important species are imported nuts from the stone pine (*Pinus pinea*)—native to the Mediterranean region—and nuts from the Colorado pine (*P. edulis*)—native to Colorado, Utah, Arizona, and New Mexico (J-306, J-342, J-529, M-57, M-631). Recent statistics on the quantity and value of American wild harvests are not available, as autumn gathering is done on an informal basis by natives of piñon country—Indians (particularly Navaho), Hispanic Americans, and other groups (J-529). (In 1960 it was estimated that 125 tons of wild piñon nuts were harvested in the United States [J-529].)

Pine nuts were always an important source of food—highly prized for their smooth texture and delicate evergreen flavor—for the six Indian language families of the southwest United States: the Uto-Aztecan (which includes the Hopi and Pima tribes); the Tanoan (which includes the Rio Grande Pueblos); the Keresan (which includes seven other Pueblo groups); the Zunian (the Zuni tribe); the Athabascan (which includes the Apache and Navaho tribes); and the Yuman (which includes the Havasupai, Walapai, and Yuma (J-598, S-744). At present, the pine nut harvest has attained some importance as a source of revenue on Navaho land (V-208). Up to 150 pounds of piñons (approximately 200,000 nuts) can be collected in a day by a two-person team (J-529, V-208).

Rich, sweet pine nuts are eaten in a variety of ways: raw or toasted as snacks; in soups, salads, and appetizers; as a ground meal used to thicken stews, gravies, and sauces (such as the famous Italian pesto sauce for pasta); as a pounded paste used to make flat fried cakes; baked in cookies, cakes, and pies (G-594, J-442, M-477, V-208).

### LINGONBERRIES

Between 1976 and 1980, the United States imported on average each year $3,000 worth of wild lingonberries (table 6.3). Most of this probably originated in the Canadian province of Newfoundland. Lingonberries (*Vaccinium vitis-idaea*), also called lowbush cranberries or partridgeberries, are harvested from the wild in the fall throughout their native range—the temperate northern hemisphere (S-337, S-796). They are most commonly used as a substitute in sauces for commercial cranberries. Lingonberries also make good jellies, jams, sauces, pies, tarts, and cakes (S-796).

*Speciality Foods*

### MAPLE SYRUP AND SUGAR

Between 1976 and 1980, Canada and the United States produced about $38 million worth of maple products, 58% of which came from the province of Quebec (S-517–S-520, S-622). The top U.S. producing state—Vermont—contributed 13% (S-448, S-449, S-699). Table 6.1 lists the other major American maple syrup states. During this five-year period the United States each year produced $13.6 million worth of maple sugar and syrup and imported (largely from Canada) another $9.3 million worth (table 6.2) for a total of approximately $23 million.

The sugar maple (*Acer saccharum*), found in the northeastern United States and adjacent provinces in Canada, aptly has been called "a standing miracle of goodness" (A-1273 cited by M-373). Its sap provides 75% of the maple syrup and sugar of commerce (G-479, M-373). The remaining 25% comes from silver maple (*A. saccharinum*), red maple (*A. rubrum*), and black maple (*A. nigrum*) (M-373).

Maple syrup and sugar making were established Indian customs long before the first Europeans arrived in North America (J-550, M-373). The syrup and sugar were highly prized by the tribes of the Algonkin, Siouan, and Iroquoian language families (J-442, J-598). Maple syrup was their principal confection and both the syrup and sugar were used—in place of salt—to flavor cooked vegetables, fruits, and stews (J-416, P-304).

In early colonial days, the availability of this native sweetener freed the new settlers from dependence on expensive and unreliable supplies of imported cane sugar (J-550, M-373, P-304), and maple products were also used by them as bartering foods (J-550). Information on the benefits and practice of maple sugaring was even included in tracts, written in the early 1800s, for immigrants to Canada and the United States (M-373). Maple sugar remained the major sweetener in the northeast until the end of the nineteenth century (P-302, P-304).

There is an old Indian legend that once upon a time the maple trees gave forth a sap that was almost pure syrup, but when the good Ne-naw-Bo-zhoo tasted it he found it too good and too easy to obtain, so he diluted the sap of the maple until the sweetness was barely discernible. From then on people had to work hard to make sugar from sap, and so the maple sugar was much more valuable to them (M-373). There is no question that the work involved is heavy and intensive and the profit margin small (P-302). The present trend appears to be that fewer and fewer maples are being tapped. Further reductions in maple sugar production may occur as more sugarbushes are sold to lumberers and more farms are bought by "summer people" (M-373).

The sugar season lasts only four to six weeks a year (J-550)—anytime from mid-February to the first of May (M-373). Our late March visit to a working sugarbush in Quebec came just near the end of that year's harvest. The most important single factor in sugaring is the weather (M-373)—sap is available in quantity only after a severe freezing. The best syrup is made while the ground is snow covered, the nights are very cold and the days sunny with temperatures above freezing but low enough to prevent sap fermentation (J-550, M-373).

It takes 40 years before a maple reaches a tappable size—eight inches in diameter (J-310, J-550, M-373). For each six inches more of diameter, another tap can be added. At the beginning of the season, the sugar content of sap is at its highest—with 20 gallons of sap yielding perhaps 1 gallon of syrup (J-550). By the end of the season, 35–50 gallons of sap may be required to yield 1 gallon of syrup (J-321, J-550, M-373). The sap is collected either in buckets that are then emptied periodically and the sap transported to storage tanks, or by pipes that run directly from the trees to the storage tanks. From the storage tanks the sap is moved to the sugarhouse, where it is boiled. The water evaporates and the syrup is obtained. There are often state and provincial laws that set the minimum percentage of sugar content of all maple syrup sold commercially. It is usually around 66% (J-550).

WILD RICE

Between 1976 and 1980, United States' harvest of (wild) wild rice were worth an average of $1.3 million annually (table 6.1) and imports (almost exclusively from Canada) another $1.9 million (table 6.2) for a total of $3.2 million. Wild rice (*Zizania aquatica*), an annual aquatic grass, is North America's only native cereal. It was probably first consumed as a food item by native Americans 10,000 years ago (D-512; M-654) and became an extremely important part of the diet of the Indian tribes of the Great Lakes area, supplying up to one-quarter of their caloric intake (G-269, M-653). Wild rice was used as a staple and substituted for maize by these tribes (S-744). The Indian wild rice gatherers belonged to two of the great North American language families: the Siouan language family (a 12-tribe family that includes the Dakotas) and the Algonkin language family (a 6-tribe family that includes the Ojibwas) (A-387, J-598, S-744). The Ojibwas moved west into Dakota territory as the French expanded their trade routes in the New World (S-744). Between 1500 and 1750 many tribal battles were waged between the Ojibwas and Dakotas over possession of the wild rice stands (G-269, M-652). In the end, the Dakotas were pressured by the Ojibwas to move south and west onto the plains (J-598).

During the pioneer days in North America, wild rice was also a common food of hunters, traders, and settlers, and in combination with maple syrup, wild fruits, bison, deer, partridge, and other game formed a diet as rich as any served in the Old World (D-420). Later interest was shown in wild rice by sportsmen, hunting preserve owners, and park caretakers as a means of attracting game. (Many birds such as ducks, geese, and waders, in addition to deer, muskrat, and beaver, are avid consumers of wild rice (A-387, D-512, G-269, M-652).)

The distribution of wild rice stretches from the northern end of Lake Winnipeg eastward along the northern shores of the Great Lakes and the St. Lawrence River, and southward to the central Dakotas, western Nebraska, and eastern Texas to the Atlantic Ocean and along the east coast as far south as central Florida (M-654). The best wild rice stands, however, are along margins of tidewater rivers (above the saline zone) of the Middle Atlantic states and in shallow lakes, ponds, and sluggish streams in northern Minnesota, Wisconsin, and southern Manitoba and Ontario (M-654).

Wild rice usually grows in water two to three feet deep (D-512, M-652). The seeds lie on lake, pond, and stream bottoms throughout the winter and germinate in the spring. Around the end of June stalks appear above the water (D-512, M-653). Harvesting takes place from about late August to mid-September (A-387, D-512, G-269). Today in the United States, Minnesota is the top wild-rice producer: over 95% of the wild rice harvested comes from this state (table 6.1). (The leading Canadian producer is Manitoba [D-512, S-595].) Under Minnesota, Manitoba, and Wisconsin laws, wild rice growing in public waters must be handharvested. Anyone may purchase a license to harvest wild rice from public waters, but wild rice on Indian land may be harvested only by Indians (E. A. Oelke, pers. comm., 17 September 1981).

Harvesting is done by the canoe and flail method. There are two persons per ricing boat. One person propels the canoe by hand with a long pole through the stands—in this way the wild rice is not damaged (G-269, M-652). The other person, seated, uses two small sticks to bend the stalks over the canoe and tap the seed heads so that the ripe grain falls into the boat. In one hour, 25 to 100 pounds can be harvested per canoe (M-654). The average harvest from natural wild-rice stands is 50 pounds per acre (M-264) compared to more than 300 pounds per acre now being harvested from cultivated wild rice paddies (E. A. Oelke, pers. comm., 17 September 1981). (Domestication of wild rice is described in chap. 7.)

SEAWEED

Between 1976 and 1980, the United States imported on average annually $900,000 worth of wild seaweeds and other marine plants for edible purposes (table 6.2). About 75% of this came from Japan. The three main seaweed food products eaten in (and presumably exported from) Japan are nori, wakame, and konbu (M-313). The most important of these is the red algae nori, which is derived almost entirely from five cultured *Porphyra* species: *P. angusta, P. kuniedai, P. pseudolinealis, P. tenera,* and *P. yezoensis* (A-1150, M-313). Cultivation of nori began in the seventeenth century in Tokyo Bay (A-1150, J-268). By the 1970s, between 60,000 and 70,000 Japanese fishermen were cultivating nori (M-313). Nori has been labeled not only "the most profitable of all fisheries in Japan" (S-803 cited by M-313) but also Japan's "single most commercially valuable marine product" (A-1150). Nori is used to wrap around sushi, rice balls, rice crackers, and so forth or crumbled and added as a flavoring to soups, sauces, and broths (M-313, S-805).

Less important than nori but still consumed on a major scale are the two brown algae wakame and konbu. Like nori, most—more than 80%—of Japan's present production of wakame (*Undaria pinnatifida*) comes from cultured plants (A-1150, M-313). Prized for its flavor and texture, wakame is widely used in soups and salads (S-805). Of the three major Japanese edible seaweeds, only konbu is still derived largely from wild sources. Various *Laminaria* species are included such as *L. angustata, L. japonica, L. longissima,* and *L. ochotensis.* Konbu is used as a soup stock, or eaten boiled, deep fried, or sauteed as a vegetable, or in dried strips as a snack food (M-313, M-332, S-805).

### HEARTS OF PALM

Between 1976 and 1980 the United States imported on average each year about $400,000 of wild hearts of palm. Brazil supplied 98% (table 6.2). Hearts of palm are the growing tips of palm trees (M-229). They are usually eaten fresh in the countries of origin but are always canned for export (M-482). Brazil is the principal supplier of canned hearts of palm for the North American market. Hearts of palm are eaten in salads and soups or served as a vegetable (M-229, M-482).

Several species of palm may be used, but the two principal ones are pejibaye (*Bactris gasipaes*) and assai (*Euterpe edulis*) (A-913, G-421, M-229). Pejibaye is grown in commercial plantations in both Central and South America (A-316, A-332, A-913, J-21, J-26, M-229, S-55, S-74). Brazilian assai palms—a source of palm hearts since the mid-1960s—are both wild and cultivated (M-229).

As the tree must be killed to obtain the heart (which may be several inches in diameter and several feet long) and as world demand for this speciality food is increasing, Brazil's wild palms are being threatened with extinction. To ease this threat, replanting has become mandatory in Brazil and cultivation is being encouraged (M-229).

### FIDDLEHEADS

In 1980, the United States imported about $24,000 worth of fiddleheads, probably largely from Canada (table 6.3). Fiddleheads are the green tightly curled fronds of newly emerging ferns. Fiddlehead harvests are considered by wild food enthusiasts one of the most outstanding gastronomic events of the spring season (J-322). In fact, parties of fiddlehead hunters have been known to demolish entire local populations of ferns and in the process disturb much of the spring forest floor (V-270).

The fronds of several fern species have been eaten at the fiddlehead stage, but the ostrich fern (*Matteuccia struthiopteris*) is the best-known species. It is a very tasty species, unlike the cinnamon fern (*Osmunda cinnamomea*) and the lady fern (*Athyrium filix-femina*), which are inclined to be bitter and unpalatable. The ostrich fern is also the safest species to eat. Recent studies on consumption of bracken ferns (*Pteridium aquilinum*) have indicated possible carcinogenic effects in many animal species, and there have been suggestions that the high incidence of human stomach cancer in Japan may be linked to the wide consumption of bracken ferns in that country (S-780). Ostrich fern grows in Canada from Newfoundland to eastern and northern British Columbia and north as far as Great Slave Lake. It also is found in central and northern United States and in Eurasia (S-780).

The heart of the industry is in New Brunswick (Canada), which produces an annual wild harvest of 200 tons—4 times that of Maine. In 1977 harvesters were paid 50–60 cents (U.S.) a pound, averaging a daily income of $55 (A-2038). Fiddleheads are marketed both frozen and canned.

## Herbs and Spices

The United States is the world's largest importer and consumer of herbs and the largest producer and consumer of herb oleoresins (G-83). Most of the herbs (and spices) imported by the United States come from entirely cultivated species—such as cinnamon, clove, coriander, dill, parsley, pepper, saffron, tarragon, turmeric, and vanilla. Eight commercially important herbs and spices, however, still are harvested from wild or wild and cultivated sources—oregano, sage, rosemary, thyme, allspice, bay leaf, winter savory, and Bombay mace.

### OREGANO

Before 1940, the United States showed little interest in oregano (P-183). More than 40 years later, this perennial ranks as the top U.S. imported herb with an average annual value of more than $4 million for the period 1976–1980. Of this, we estimate $3 million worth came from wild plants (table 6.2). Greece was the leading exporter to the United States (44%), followed by Mexico (29%) and Turkey (20%). This dramatic change—estimated by Rosengarten to represent an increase in demand of at least 6,000%—is thought to be the result of American G.I. exposure to pizza in Italy during World War II (P-183). The returning warriors created a hungry market that quickly was catered to by the U.S. food industry.

Two genera—*Origanum* and *Lippia*—and several species are traded under the name of oregano. The main European *Origanum* species is *O. heracleoticum*, which in Greece is collected from the wild by shepherds (D-697). Two of the major *Lippia* species are *L. graveolens* and *L. palmeri*. Both are indigenous to the warmer areas of the Western Hemisphere, especially Mexico, and are often sold as "Mexican oregano" (G-83, P-183). In the United States, the European oreganos are used in Italian-style foods—spaghetti, pizza, and so forth—and the Mexican oreganos in Mexican-style foods: chili con carne, enchiladas, and tamales (G-83, P-183). Oregano is also used in flavoring soups, salads, egg dishes, meat, pork, fish, poultry, game, and a variety of vegetables such as tomatoes, eggplant, zucchini, potatoes, peppers, and beans (G-83, M-129, P-183, P-303).

Origanum oil, distilled only from wild *Thymus capitatus* (native to the Mediterranean region and Asia Minor), is produced mainly in Spain and Israel (P-151). lt is used to a limited extent in flavoring food products such as meats, sausages, sauces, and canned goods (G-76). The major applications of origanum oil are in perfumery and pharmaceutical products—soaps, dental preparations, mouthwashes, colognes, and after-shave lotions (P-151).

SAGE

Sage, another perennial, is probably the world's most popular flavoring and seasoning herb and the world's second most important herb oleoresin (after celery seed). The United States is already the world's biggest consumer of sage and biggest producer of sage oleoresin (G-83). The United States imported about $1.5 million of wild sage on average annually between 1976 and 1980. Of this, 55% came from Albania, 37% from Yugoslavia, and 3% from Turkey (table 6.2). The two major species involved are *Salvia officinalis* and *S. triloba*. Both are native to the Mediterranean region (P-183).

Yugoslavia is the leading producer of dried sage leaf, sage oil (and sage honey) from both wild and cultivated *S. officinalis* (G-83). Traders consider Dalmatian sage the best (J-235) and some even specify a preference for wild Dalmatian sage over the cultivated Dalmatian herb (G-83). Turkey and Greece are the major sources of *S. triloba* (G-83).

The dominant American use of sage oleoresin is in the meat industry, particularly in poultry stuffing and sausage and hamburger seasoning (G-83, M-129). The herb is used to flavor soups, sauces, fish, cheese, meats, and vegetables such as onions, tomatoes, leeks, peas, and eggplant (G-76, P-303).

ROSEMARY

Between 1976 and 1980, the United States imported each year an average of about $900,000 worth of wild rosemary (of which 83% was in oil form): 40% came from Tunisia, 26% from Spain (table 6.3). Rosemary (*Rosmarinus officinalis*), a perennial, is native to the Mediterranean region (P-183, P-303). Most of the herb, and virtually all of the oil, entering trade is gathered from wild plants (G-83, P-151). The major producers of rosemary oil are Spain, Tunisia, and Morocco (P-151). Tunisian oil is regarded at present as the best available high volume oil (P-151). Rosemary oil is most frequently used in cosmetic and pharmaceutical products such as soaps, shampoos, bath essences, eau de colognes, high class perfumes, deodorants, inhalants, room sprays, insecticides, and disinfectants (G-76, G-83, P-151). lt also has minor applications in flavoring a range of meat and baked products (P-151). Rosemary, as a herb, is used most extensively in Italian cooking. Italy is the major market for the herb (G-83).

### THYME

Thyme may come from cultivated sources or from the wild (G-83). The oil is derived almost entirely from wild growing plants (G-76, G-83, P-151). Between 1976 and 1980, the United States imported an average of approximately $700,000 of wild thyme each year. About 80% of this was in herb form, 20% in oil. Seventy-seven percent of the total thyme imports was from Spain and 19% from France (table 6.2).

Many species are traded commercially under the name of thyme. Two of the most important are *Thymus vulgaris* (garden thyme) and *T. zygis* (white thyme) (G-83). Both these perennials are native to the Mediterranean region (J-235, J-337, P-183). Spain is the major exporter of both the herb and oil (G-76, G-83, P-151).

The market for thyme is growing in the United States due to increased demand for its use in herb mixtures (especially in stuffings) and in the meat industry (G-83). Thyme is used in soups, sauces, gravies, salads, sausages, poultry, game, fish, oils, vegetables, baked goods, and beverages such as Benedictine liqueur (J-337, M-129, P-183, P-303). Because thyme is a powerful germicide it is also an ingredient in several pharmaceutical products such as gargles, mouthwashes, cough drops, cough syrups, and cold treatment preparations (G-76, P-151).

### ALLSPICE

Between 1976 and 1980, the United States imported on average each year about $600,000 worth of wild allspice. Approximately one-third of this came from Guatemala, one-third from Mexico, and one-third from Honduras (table 6.2). Allspice comes from a tree (*Pimenta dioica*) native to the West Indies and Central America (J-235, P-183, P-256, P-275). It is called allspice because its flavor and aroma are said to resemble a combination of cinnamon, nutmeg, clove, and pepper (P-164, P-275). It is the only spice produced entirely in the Western Hemisphere (P-183, P-256).

Long before the arrival of the Spanish in the sixteenth century, the Mayans had used allspice to embalm the bodies of important persons. From the seventeenth to the nineteenth century, allspice was used aboard ships to preserve meat during long voyages (P-183). At present, allspice is used to flavor broths, gravies, sauces, relishes, pickles, preserves, mincemeats, fruitcakes, pies, puddings, and beverages such as Benedictine and Chartreuse liqueurs (P-183, P-275). The oil is used not only in food but also in men's spice-based cosmetics such as after-shave lotions and colognes (P-256).

Allspice trees start to bear at 7 or 8 years of age and continue to produce up to

100 years of age or more (J-235, P-183). The average yield per tree is $2\frac{1}{2}$ pounds of dried berries a year (P-183). Most allspice traded today is from Jamaica, where the crop has been cultivated to a considerable extent—particularly since the 1950s—and is subject to careful husbandry (P-164, P-183, P-256). The bulk of Mexican, Guatemalan, and Honduran allspice comes from wild trees (P-183, P-256). The wild allspice has a different flavor, lower oil content, and less consistent quality than the Jamaican berries (P-256), which are considered to be of the highest quality (J-235).

### BAY LEAF

Between 1976 and 1980, the United States imported an annual average of approximately $400,000 worth of wild bay leaves—95% of which came from Turkey (table 6.3). The bay leaf (*Laurus nobilis*) is native to the Mediterranean region and Asia Minor (G-83, P-183). In ancient Greece and Rome, bay wreaths were the symbol of military, scholastic, and athletic achievement (P-183). Today the leaves appear more often in gastronomic events. Turkey and Greece are the two major exporters of bay leaves—most of which come from wild sources. Bay leaves are used in flavoring soups, sauces, pickles, stews, game dishes, milk puddings, and various types of canned and preserved fish, meat, and vegetables (G-83).

### WINTER SAVORY

Between 1976 and 1980, the United States annually imported on average $127,000 worth of unspecified savory. As 1979 and 1980 U.S. imports from Yugoslavia were valued at $114,000, it is estimated that $100,000 of the savory imported each year during this period by the United States was wild winter savory (table 6.3).

There are a number of species of savory, but the two most often traded are summer savory (*Satureja hortensis*) from cultivated sources and winter savory (*S. montana*) from largely wild plants (G-83). Winter savory, a perennial, is native to southern Europe (J-235). It is the most common savory exported by Spain, Yugoslavia, Morocco, and central Europe (G-83). Savory is used to flavor soups, sauces, gravies, salads, fish, eggs, and cheese dishes, meats, poultry, game, and vegetables such as lima beans, onions, peas, carrots, lentils, and chick-peas (P-303).

### BOMBAY MACE

Between 1976 and 1980, the United States imported an average of about $20,000 worth of wild Bombay mace each year (table 6.3). Bombay (or false) mace is produced from a tree (*Myristica malabarica*) that grows wild on the southwest coast of India (G-363). Bombay mace, used as an adulterant of genuine nutmeg and mace from *M. fragrans*, possesses a very low essential oil content, is virtually devoid of aroma, and is considered inferior for cooking (P-256, S-413).

## Industrial Products

Thirty-one different industrial products imported by the United States during the period 1976 to 1980 came from wild species. Each year they were worth an average of $142 million. As figure 6.3 illustrates, three fibers accounted for 53%: rattan ($53 million), cork ($18 million), and istle or tampico ($5 million); four seaweeds for 12%: agar ($5.5 million), unspecified seaweeds ($5 million), carrageenan ($4 million), and sodium alginate ($2 million); three gums for 11%: arabic or acacia ($8 million), karaya ($4 million), and tragacanth ($3 million); four balatas for 10%: jelutong ($4 million), chicle ($4 million), gutta ($3 million), and lechi-caspi ($3 million); and finally a mixed grouping of 17 products for

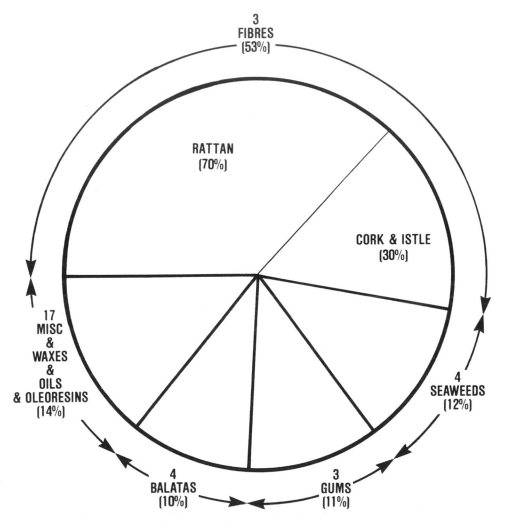

Fig. 6.3   **Thirty-one wild industrial products imported by the United States: 1976–1980 average annual value $142 million. Sources: tables 6.2, 6.3**

14%. This last category includes miscellaneous products—quebracho ($4.5 million), lac ($4 million), civet ($200,000), valonia ($150,000), tonka bean ($100,000), and castoreum ($70,000); waxes—carnauba ($5.5 million), candelilla ($1 million), and ouricury ($30,000); oils—Brazilian sassafras ($1 million), bois de rose ($1 million), babassu ($400,000), cedar leaf ($250,000), and palmarosa ($125,000); oleoresins—styrax ($400,000), tolu balsam ($200,000), and copaiba balsam ($50,000).

Some of the supply information on several industrial products was supplemented by data gathered from our own mail survey. Our survey was sent to 321 companies—largely U.S. based—listed in one of two major directories (A-1367, A-1368) as suppliers of specific wild ingredients in which we were interested. We received replies from 97 companies (30%). Appendix B lists the names of the persons with whom we corresponded.

*Fibers*

RATTAN

Between 1976 and 1980, the United States imported about $53 million worth of wild rattan and rattan products (note 4) from Hong Kong (40%), the Philippines (34%), Taiwan (7%), the People's Republic of China (5%), Singapore (3%), Indonesia (2%), and Thailand (2%) (table 6.2). Rattans are, in general, spiny climbing palms. They include 12–14 genera and about 600 species (D-69, D-248). The richest concentration—11 genera—occurs in Southeast Asia between Thailand and Papua New Guinea (D-68, D-69, D-248, G-428). Rattan is the second most important forest product after timber in Southeast Asia (D-68, G-428). In 1977, for example, trade in raw rattan amounted to U.S. $50 million; and the end value was over U.S. $1.2 billion (D-68, G-428, S-373). Most of the rattan entering world trade is collected from the wild (D-248).

About 20 species of rattan are regarded as elite commercial species, but recent shortages of these canes have resulted in the collection and use of species formerly regarded as useless (D-68). *Calamus*, the largest and most widespread genus (ranging from West Africa to Fiji and southern China to Australia), provides much of the rattan of commerce. Two *Calamus* species—*C. trachycoleus* and *C. caesius*—are intensively cultivated (and have been for more than a century) in Kalimantan, Indonesia (D-68, D-70, G-428).

Indonesia is the top supplier of rattan. In 1977, Indonesia provided 90% of the world's supply (S-373). About 95% of Indonesian rattan is exported in the raw, unworked form (S-786). In recent years, measures have been taken in the Philippines, Thailand, Malaysia, and Indonesia to control the export of raw rattan (D-68, G-428). The measures range from export royalties on unprocessed cane to complete bans (D-68). In this way the producer countries hope to ensure more employment for their own rural people (G-428).

According to 1975 data, the two largest importers of raw rattan—accounting for 85% of the market—were Hong Kong (57%) and Singapore (28%). Singapore processes, rather than manufactures, rattan. This involves such steps as curing, cleaning, straightening, sorting, and grading (S-373). Hong Kong is a manufacturing center for wicker and weave products (S-373) and is considered one of the traditional Southeast Asian manufacturers and exporters (along with Taiwan and the Philippines) of rattan furniture in particular (A-1360, S-786). The final major markets for rattan products are the United States, Japan, and Europe (S-373).

Harvesting rattan consists of dragging rattan out of the forest canopy, removing debris and useless parts, and cutting the cane into lengths suitable for bundling and transport out of the forest to the processor (D-69). Between 100 and 120 extractors (or harvesters) supplied rattan to the factory we visited in Sabah, Malaysia. In 1982, these extractors were paid about U.S. $8 a bundle for 18-foot lengths of rattan and about U.S. $9 a bundle for 20-foot lengths (K. K. Poh, pers. comm., 11 January 1982). In one day an extractor can gather 3–4 bundles (S. Jaima, pers. comm., 12 January 1982). The average bundle contains 100 sticks of rattan with diameters in the small to medium range ($\frac{1}{8}$–$\frac{3}{8}$ inches).

The diameter of each piece of rattan often determines its end use. The large-diameter canes (more than $\frac{5}{8}$ inches) include such species as *Calamus manan* and *C. scipionum*. *C. manan*, native to Malaysia, Indonesia, and Thailand, is described as "the premier large size furniture cane of unsurpassed quality." Its present range is reduced due to overexploitation. *C. scipionum*, native to Malaysia, Singapore, and Indonesia, is much prized and is the source of Malacca cane for walking sticks, umbrella handles, and so forth. The very best cane of medium diameter ($\frac{1}{4}$–$\frac{5}{8}$ inches) is *C. caesius*, native to Malaysia and Indonesia. It is regarded as "supreme for all types of binding and weaving in the furniture industry and widely used locally in the finest basket ware." An example of the small-diameter canes (those under $\frac{1}{4}$ inch) is *C. viridispinus*, native to Malaysia, which is considered "a good cane for tying purposes" (D-69).

In addition to furniture, walking sticks, and umbrella handles, rattan is made into bags, baskets, brooms, bird cages, curtains, fish traps, hammocks, mats, ornamental wares, ropes, sporting goods, and toys (A-1360, G-428, S-786).

CORK

The biggest cork importing countries are France, West Germany, the United Kingdom, the United States, and Japan (A-363). Between 1976 and 1980, the United States imported each year about $18 million worth of wild cork and cork products primarily from Portugal (69%) and Spain (21%) (table 6.2).

Most of the cork of commerce is provided by the cork oak (*Quercus suber*) (A-532, M-149, M-277, P-157, S-41, S-337). (Minor amounts of *Q. occidentalis* may also enter trade (A-532).) *Q. suber* is native to Portugal, Spain, France, Italy, Algeria, Morocco, and Tunisia (A-363, A-532, M-149). Portugal, the top cork producer, supplies more than 50% of the 390,000 tons marketed each year (A-363, A-532, P-157). Cork is Portugal's largest export industry after textiles.

About 90% of Portugal's cork trees grow in the southern part of the country in the Alentejo region (A-363). Spain is second in importance in corkwood production; Algeria is the largest of the North African cork producing countries (A-532).

Cork has been an article of commerce since 400 B.C. (A-532). The real cork industry, however, did not begin until the mid-1700s—2,000 years later—when worldwide demand for cork stoppers had increased dramatically, spurred by the fifteenth-century invention of the glass bottle (A-532). By the late nineteenth century, cork factories had been established (A-363). Most cork production comes from wild trees, although the natural cork forests may be managed in various ways: clearance of undergrowth and dead wood to reduce the possibility of forest fires; pruning of trees to facilitate stripping of cork; thinning of trees to allow each sufficient nourishment from the ground yet at the same time leaving trees near enough to each other to shade the ground and cut down evaporation (A-363; A-532). The cork trees, however, largely are left to reproduce themselves from the nuts that fall to the ground (A-363, A-532). There is no planned reforestation (A-363).

Information varies on the age at which trees begin to produce appreciable amounts of cork—from 20 years (A-532) to 30 years (P-157) to 45 years (A-363). The cork is stripped first by making circular cuts at the base of the tree and just below the first branches and then making vertical cuts. (In large trees, cork is stripped also from a portion of the lower branches.) The bark is removed in slabs as big as possible because they fetch a higher price than smaller pieces. A young tree may yield 35 pounds of cork, whereas a large old tree may provide several hundred pounds. A skilled harvester can gather 300–800 pounds of cork a day (A-532). Cork may be removed periodically—every 8–10 years—from the same tree without affecting its vitality (A-532; P-157). In fact especially high quality cork is obtained from the third stripping on. The average productive life of cork trees is 150 years (A-532).

Cork has certain natural qualities that make it "virtually irreplacable." The air-filled cells make cork lightweight and buoyant, compressible and resilient, slow burning, an ideal thermal and sound insulating material (A-363). Clean commercial cork is "not affected or changed in composition by contact with water, vegetable, animal or mineral oils, gasoline, many organic solvents and many gases, such as carbon dioxide, hydrogen, nitrogen and air." "No other untreated naturally occurring plant product can be used in contact with so many different materials" (A-446).

Numerous articles are manufactured from natural cork. Cork bottle stoppers are the oldest and most famous (A-446, A-532). For most wine drinkers, a cork stopper is a sign of quality (A-363). Wine kept in a tightly corked bottle lasts much longer than wine kept in a barrel and ages in a different way, acquiring a bouquet (J-620). Without a superior cork stopper, champagne would have "no creamy foam, no pale-gold sparkle and none of the wine's characteristic 'crisp and flinty' taste" (P-157). Natural cork is also used in life preservers, buoys, fishing net floats, and the following sporting goods: fishing rod handles, duck decoys, badminton birdies, top quality baseballs—even whistles often contain small cork balls (A-446, A-532).

A wide range of articles is made from composition cork—which consists of natural cork and a binding adhesive (A-446, A-532). Composition cork is molded into rods, flat blocks, round blocks, and special shapes (A-446). The rods, for example, then may be cut into disks, which are used as sealing liners in beverage crown caps and other kinds of closures (A-446, A-532). The next most important use of composition cork (after sealing liners) is in the manufacture of industrial gaskets. Cork gaskets keep oil in and moisture, air, and dust out. Composition cork is also widely used in footwear, for both outer and inner soles (A-532).

Corkboard is made by baking cork particles under pressure to bind them together in a single mass. This increases cork's natural resistance to heat transfer, and consequently corkboard insulation has become a major industrial commodity (A-532). Corkboard is also valuable for machinery isolation—the resilient corkboard absorbs shock, reduces vibration, and prolongs the life of the machine (A-446, A-532). In addition, corkboard is used for acoustical purposes as it absorbs sound waves and reduces noise (A-532). Miscellaneous cork products include cork tiles (which make quiet, warm, resilient, and durable floors); cork bulletin boards; abrasive cork wheels used to polish glass and ceramic products; and cork cots used by the textile industry in the spinning of cotton and other fibers (A-446; A-532).

ISTLE

Between 1976 and 1980, the United States imported on average each year 8.6 million pounds of wild istle fibers valued at about $5 million. Mexico provided over 99% (table 6.2). The hard fiber istle (also called tampico) is derived from two wild Mexican desert species—*Agave lecheguilla* (lechuguilla) and *Yucca carnerosana* (palma samandoca) (S-41, S-337, S-684). Commercial harvesting of the fiber takes place in what is known locally as the Zona Ixtlera. This includes part of five states: Coahuila, Nuevo León, Zacatecas, San Luis Potosí, and Tamaulipas (S-684).

Istle's commercial history dates from the nineteenth century. By the beginning of the twentieth century, large quantities were being marketed both domestically and internationally. At present the number of persons whose livelihood depends upon istle varies from year to year. When there has been good rainfall, the harvesters turn instead to crop cultivation and the number drops to 400,000. During years when farming is limited, the number climbs to 650,000. The fact that istle continues to be an important item of international commerce is attributed to its "particular qualitative aspects of resiliency, texture and water absorbency that make it a superior fiber for some applications, and an indispensable one for others." Istle is often converted into power-driven cylinder brushes used in steel mills and metal fabricating plants for cleaning and buffing operations. It is also widely used alone or mixed with horsehair in floor sweeps, counter dusters, calcimine brushes, roofing brushes, and pastry brushes. No satisfactory replacement for istle has been found for either industrial or household rotary floor scrubbers and polishers (S-684).

## Seaweeds

Agar, carrageenan, algin, and furcellaran are the four most important seaweed extracts in commercial use in the world today (M-313). Only the first three extracts, however, are of significance to North America. Both agar and carrageenan are extracted from genera of red (or purple) algae (Rhodophyceae), while algin is derived from brown algae (Phaeophyceae) (A-661, M-313).Rhodophytes and phaeophytes are almost exclusively marine (M-313).

During the period 1976 to 1980, the United States imported each year an average or $16.5 million worth of wild seaweed and wild seaweed extracts for industrial purposes: agar ($5.5 million); unspecified seaweeds ($5 million); carrageenan ($4 million); and sodium alginate ($2 million) (table 6.2).

### AGAR

Between 1976 and 1980, the United States imported on average each year about $5.5 million worth of agar, principally from Spain (31%), Chile (20%), Mexico (13%), and Morocco (13%) (table 6.2). *Gelidium corneum* is a primary agar-yielding algae from Spain and Morocco; Morocco also exports quantities of *G. sesquipedale* and *G. spinulosum. G. lingulatum* is traded by Chile and *G. cartilagineum* and *G. coulteri* by Mexico (S-370). Respondents to our supplier survey indicated that they also relied on U.S. domestic production of *Gelidium cartilagineum* plus imports of *Gracilaria* species from Japan, Chile, and Taiwan and imports of *Pterocladia* species from Portugal.

Agar has been known to commerce since the late 1860s (M-110, S-370). It comes from several species of seaweed. Of primary commercial value are the following: *Gelidiella acerosa* (Japan, India), *Gelidium amansii* (Japan), *G. cartilagineum* (United States, Mexico, South Africa), *G. corneum* (South Africa, Portugal, Spain, Morocco), *G. liatulum* (Japan), *G. lingulatum* (Chile), *G. pacificum* (Japan), *G. pristoides* (South Africa), *G. sesquipedale* (Portugal, Morocco), *Gracilaria confervoides* (South Africa), *Pterocladia capillacea* (Egypt, Japan, New Zealand), and *P. lucida* (New Zealand) (S-370). More than three-quarters of the world production of agar comes from Japan, Spain, the USSR, and Portugal (M-313).

Agar is used in bacteriological and fungal culture work because, after nutrient materials have been added, even a dilute solution sets to a firm jelly upon which the bacteria or fungi can grow (A-661). In chemical laboratories agar is used to cause flocculation of barium sulfate precipitates. Microtechnicians find agar valuable both as an embedding medium for small pieces of plant or animal tissues that might otherwise be lost in solutions, and for cutting material with a freezing microtome (G-684). In low concentrations agar prevents the entry of oxygen into liquid media, making the cultivation of anaerobes feasible in air-exposed broths (S-370).

The baking industry uses agar as a stabilizer in chiffon pies, meringues, pie fillings, icings, toppings, and related products (G-527). Agar is also used in cookies, cream shells, piping gels, and pie fillings where gel strength is most important (G-527) and as an antistaling agent in breads and cakes (S-370). In the confectionery business, agar is used in agar-jelly candies such as fig-agar and in the manufacture of marshmallows (G-527, G-684, S-370). In the canning of pickled tongue, fish, poultry, and other soft meats, agar is used to gel the meats to prevent their becoming mushy and to eliminate transit damage of fragile tissues (G-527, S-370). Agar has also been applied as an edible, protective coating for extending the shelf life of poultry and has been used to gel meat pies and artificial sausage skins (G-527). Agar, in combination with tragacanth or other gums, serves as a stabilizer in sherbets and ices and is used in the fining of juices and vinegars (G-527) and as a clarifying agent in the brewing of beer and the manufacture of wines and coffee. Health food products that may contain agar include prepared cereals, meat substitutes, and desserts (S-370).

Agar is used in areas such as prosthetic dentistry, criminology, tool making, and sculpting where it is necessary to make accurate casts of intricate undercut objects (S-370). Miscellaneous uses of agar include the following: in photographic stripping films and papers that serve as sensing elements in mechanical and electrical hygrometers; in media for orchid culture; in shoe and leather polishes and dressings; in dyed coatings for paper, textiles, and metals; in pressure-sensitive tape adhesives; in the electroplating of lead; in batteries for use in boats; and as a flash inhibitor in sulfur mining explosives (G-684, S-370). The role of agar in laxatives and other pharmaceuticals is discussed in chapter 5.

CARRAGEENAN

Between 1976 and 1980, the United States imported each year an average of almost $4 million worth of carrageenan from Denmark (48%), Spain (20%), and Canada (12%) (table 6.2). About 600 years ago, residents of County Carragheen in Ireland found uses for Irish moss (*Chondrus crispus*) in foods, medicines, and fertilizers (S-369). Irish emigrants settling in America in the 1700s created a demand for carrageenan (as it is sometimes called) (S-369), and it was imported from Europe as a standard commodity until 1835 (G-527). Then *Chondrus crispus* was discovered to be a component of the natural flora off the coast of Massachusetts, and a U.S.-based industry began.

Today the principal species traded under the name of carrageenan are *Chondrus crispus* (the most important species) and *Gigartina stellata* (A-661, M-313). The North American Atlantic coast distribution of *Chondrus crispus* is from Newfoundland to New Jersey (S-359). Other known concentrations are off Portugal, France, the United Kingdom, the Republic of Korea, and Japan (M-313). The three maritime provinces of Canada—Prince Edward Island, Nova Scotia, and New Brunswick—account for about three-quarters of the world's supply of carrageenan (A-1207). Of all the seaweeds, *Chondrus crispus* is the most important commercially for Canada (M-358). Irish moss harvesting and gathering is the primary source of income for more than 750 families in Atlantic Canada; another 1,000–1,500 families depend on it as a secondary source of income (A-1203). Figure 6.4 illustrates the size and value of Canadian harvests of carrageenan. Between 1976 and 1980, the average annual harvest of carrageenan was 59.4 million pounds: 58% from Prince Edward Island, 39% from Nova Scotia, and 3% from New Brunswick. The average annual dollar value was $3.2 million (Canadian currency was converted to U.S. at an exchange rate of .91, which was the average annual rate for the period [D-450]). The two carrageenan producer states in the United States are Maine and Massachusetts (A-661, G-527, S-359). Whereas the United States is only a small producer of carrageenan, it leads the world in the extraction phase of the industry. Two other major centers of extraction are Denmark and France (M-313).

Approximately 80% of the present world production of carrageenan goes to food and food-related industries. A large proportion of the remainder is used in pharmaceuticals and cosmetics (S-369). In the dairy industry, carrageenan is used as follows: to thicken and stabilize chocolate milk products; to prevent fat or whey separation in cheese spreads and to provide good spreading properties; to give body so that the creaming mixture clings to the curds in cottage cheese; to thicken and stabilize milkshakes and instant breakfast powders and to impart a richer mouth feel; to impart body and flow characteristics to chocolate sauces, fudge, and butterscotch syrup toppings; to promote a light body to eggless custards and blanc mange desserts; and to improve colloidal solubility of protein in liquid coffee whiteners, which results in a better shelf life (G-527, S-369).

In the bakery industry the uses of carrageenan include the following: yielding a moister texture in fruitcake and helping maintain a uniform distribution of fruit throughout the cake; improving dough strength, loaf volume, loaf shape, and texture in bread; strengthening and extending protein ingredients in breading and batter mixes, which permits uniform coverage and adhesion of the batter to chicken, shrimp, fish sticks, and so forth (G-527). Carrageenan is also used in making pie fillings, cake frostings, jelly fillings, and jams (S-359). It stabilizes mustard sauces, cocktail sauces, spaghetti sauces, white sauces, and gravies (G-527). Carrageenan protects fatty meat and fish products from oxidative rancidity after freezing (G-527) and is effective as a gel binder in ground meat packs—such as pet foods—or a gel coating for whole meat packs. The addition of carrageenan to macaroni allows the incorporation of nonfat milk solids for added nutritional value and enhanced flavor (S-369). Carrageenan is a fining agent for the clarification of beer, coffee, honey, and wine (A-661). It is used in dietetic foods to maintain and stabilize the suspension of insoluble powder ingredients and to impart body and creamy mouth feel and texture (G-527).

The textile industry uses carrageenan as a stiffener and binder. It produces a

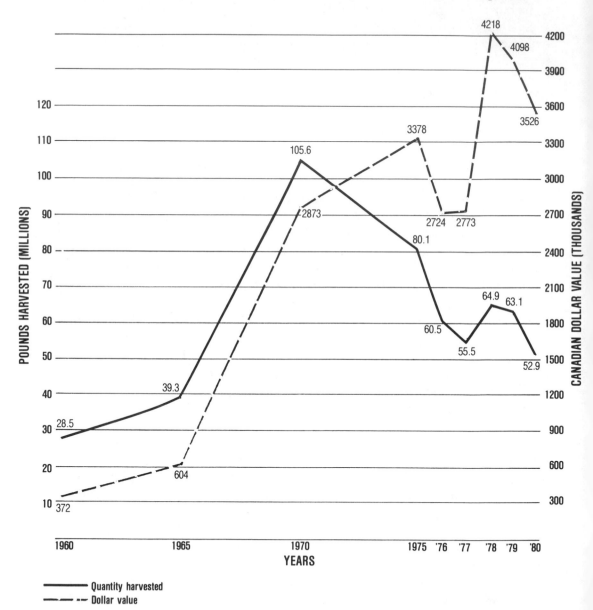

Fig. 6.4    **Quantity and dollar value of carrageenan (*Chondrus crispus*) harvested in Canada, 1960, 1965, 1970, 1975, 1976–1980. Sources: A-1203, P-430; G. J. Sharp, pers. comm., 1983**

soft finish and surface to which printing will adhere. Carrageenan is used extensively in shoe polish because the mucilage holds down and smooths out the tiny rough projections on the surface of shoe leather. Carrageenan is used to bind briquettes of vegetable charcoal powder (A-661). The emollient and demulcent properties of carrageenan make it an important ingredient in hand lotions and cough syrups (M-111). In toothpastes, it enhances shape retention and promotes good rinseability; in toothpowders it provides body and better foam characteristics (S-369). The medicinal uses of carrageenan are discussed in chapter 5.

SODIUM ALGINATE

The United States is a world leader in the production of algin from its own domestic beds of *Macrocystis pyrifera* (kelp) along the coast of southern California. Between 1976 and 1980, the United States harvested over 310 million pounds of *M. pyrifera* annually (fig. 6.5). (We were not able to determine the value of the harvests, because this information is considered privileged in the United States.) In addition it yearly imports more than $2 million of sodium alginate, principally from the United Kingdom (44%), Canada (30%), and Norway (17%) (table 6.2).

Commercial products of algin (a generic name for the salts of alginic acid and most commonly applied to sodium alginate) were introduced in the United States and United Kingdom in the early 1930s. The major genera used include *Macrocystis*, *Ascophyllum*, and *Laminaria* (M-313). Also used are *Ecklonia*, *Nereocystis*, *Sargassum*, and *Fucus* (A-661, M-313).

Until 1979, Alginate Industries Ltd. was Britain's only manufacturer of alginic acid (V-198). This company relies mainly on *Laminaria hyperborea* but also uses lesser quantities of other *Laminaria* species together with *Ascophyllum nodosum* (A-661). Supplies from Canada are made up largely of *Ascophyllum nodosum* and *Laminaria* species (M-313), those from Norway of *Ascophyllum nodosum* and *Laminaria digitata* (A-661). Our supplier survey revealed that U.S. firms import their sodium alginate from France as well. The species involved include *Laminaria digitata* and *Ascophyllum nodosum*.

Sodium alginate fills many roles in the food-related industries. It is used in bakery icings, cake and pie fillings, and toppings; in sauces and salad dressings; in meat, sausage, and fish preparations; in canned foods; in dietetic foods; and in frozen fruit (G-527, M-313). Algin prevents the sedimentation of pulp in fruit drinks, stabilizes cocoa powder in chocolate milk, clarifies wine, removes the haze in beer (resulting in a brilliant beer), and stabilizes and lengthens the foam persistence of beer (G-527). Half the entire U.S. output of sodium alginate is reported to be used as a stabilizer for ice cream and as a suspending agent for milkshakes (M-313).

Sodium alginate is used by the textile industry because it forms an excellent dressing and polishing material (A-661). Algin has wide industrial applications. A range of these include the following products: fire-extinguishing foams,

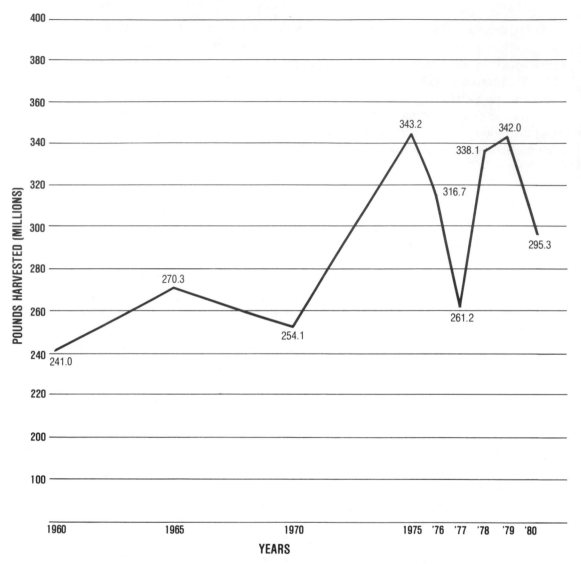

Fig. 6.5 **Quantity of kelp (*Macrocystis pyrifera*) harvested in California, 1960, 1965, 1970, 1975, 1976–80. Source: E. J. Smith, pers. comm., 24 May 1983**

paints, dyes, car polishes, photographic coatings, insecticides, herbicides, explosives, oil-drilling lubricants and coolants, and building materials (tar and asphalt, artificial wood, insulation products, sealing compounds) (M-313).

The cosmetic industry also finds uses for sodium alginate in hand jellies, hand lotions, as ointment bases, in pomades and other hair preparations, in greaseless creams, and in dentifrices. The advantage of using sodium alginate in hand creams is that it increases the body of the mixture without requiring an increase in the solid content. In brushless shaving creams, algin makes the cream easier to spread, easier to rinse from the razor, and, by increasing the water-holding power of the cream, it stabilizes the lather, retards drying of the skin, and reduces the bubble size. In toothpastes, algin acts as a suspending agent for the powder, increases the wetting action of the paste, and will not corrode the tube (J-465).

## Gums

According to Whistler (V-382), the "term gum is applied to a wide variety of substances with 'gummy' characteristics and cannot be precisely defined . . . (It is technically employed in industry to refer) to plant or microbial polysaccharides or their derivatives that are dispersible in either cold or hot water to produce viscous mixtures or solutions." This definition includes exudate gums such as gum arabic, karaya, and tragacanth and seaweed gums such as agar, carrageenan, and sodium alginate. Not covered by this definition are lactiferous products such as jelutong, chicle, guttas, and leche-caspi, which are discussed under the heading Balatas.

### GUM ARABIC

The United States—the world's largest market for gum arabic (A-5)—imported an average of about $8 million of the wild gum each year between 1976 and 1980. Sudan supplied 95% (fig. 6.6, table 6.2). Gum arabic (or gum acacia) has been an article of commerce since 4000 B.C. (V-367). It is the exudate obtained from several *Acacia* species, two of which are of special commercial significance—*A. senegal* and *A. seyal*. *A. senegal* grows wild in tropical Africa from Mozambique and Zambia to Somalia, Sudan, Ethiopia, Kenya, and Tanzania (D-246). *A. seyal* is found in abundance from Nigeria to Egypt and Sudan (M-317). Sudan is not only the leading supplier of gum arabic but also the only country in which gum arabic is a significant contributor to foreign exchange (A-5, G-44, P-11, P-108). *Acacia senegal* makes up the bulk—about 90%—of the Sudanese output, *A. seyal* the remaining 10% (A-5, G-44, M-317). Most of the gum is collected from wild trees, but *A. senegal* is also cultivated in plantations on government land and private holdings in Sudan (A-5, M-317).

Originally all gum arabic marketed was the result of natural exudations, but over 50 years ago tapping was introduced. The tree's bark is pulled away to form 2–3-foot wounds from which the gum exudes (G-44, G-527, M-317, P-108, S-41). About one month later the gum has crystallized and is ready for collection (M-317, P-108). Annual yields average half a pound per tree (V-367).

Most (65%) of the gum arabic imported into the United States is used by the food industry to impart desirable qualities to the body, texture, and viscosity of various foodstuffs (A-5, A-500, G-44, M-317). Gum arabic is nontoxic, odorless, colorless, tasteless, and completely water-soluble. In confectionary products, gum arabic performs two main functions. It retards or prevents crystallization of sugar in jujubes, pastilles, and the like, and it acts as a fat emulsifier in caramels, toffees, and so forth (G-44, G-527, V-367). Gum arabic is also a component of chewing gum (G-527, V-367). In beverages, the gum acts as a foam

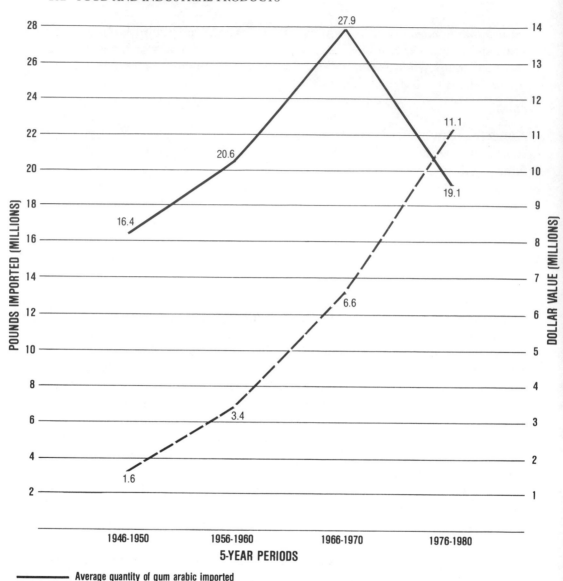

Fig. 6.6  **Quantity and dollar value of U.S. imports of gum arabic: annual averages per 5-year period, 1946–50, 1956–60, 1966–70, 1976–80. Sources: G-44, S-450–S-454**

stabilizer in soft drinks and beer (G-44, G-527, V-367). It is responsible for the lace curtain effect on a glass when the beer is consumed (G-44, G-527). It also may be used as a clouding agent to produce eye-appealing opacity in some beverages and beverage dry mixes. In bakery products gum arabic is used as a stabilizer and for its viscosity and adhesive properties in glazes and toppings (G-44, G-527, V-367). Gum arabic is used as a flavor fixative, especially with citrus oils and imitation flavors—it forms a thin film around each flavor particle, thereby protecting it from oxidation, evaporation, and absorption of moisture. It is also the preferred flavor emulsifier in the preparation of orange, lemon, lime, cherry, root beer, and cola flavor emulsions (G-44, G-527).

Another 5% of the gum arabic imported by the United States is used for pharmaceutical purposes, which are discussed in chapter 5. The remaining 30% finds a wide variety of applications: in cosmetics (as a binding agent in the formulation of compact cakes and rouges; an adhesive in the preparation of facial masks); in adhesives (particularly in the manufacture of adhesive for postage stamps); in inks (particularly special purpose inks such as soluble ink used by textile workers to mark cloth for cutting or sewing, water-color ink, white- and bronze-pigmented inks; decorative gloss-finish inks for showcards and other display purposes); in textiles (as a sizing agent for cloth; for finishing silk and rayon) (A-5, A-500, D-246, G-44, J-337, M-317).

### GUM KARAYA

The United States imports 75–80% of the world supply of karaya (G-45). These imports, largely from India, averaged more than 6 million pounds (worth about $4 million) a year during the period 1976–1980 (S-450–S-454). Karaya is native to India. The gum is collected from at least three species of *Sterculia* and one species of *Cochlospermum*. The major species of commerce is *Sterculia urens* (G-45, M-317, S-41, S-433). The demand for karaya on world markets developed in the early 1930s (G-300). At present there are some commercial plantations in tropical Africa, but in India the gum is still collected from wild trees. The trees are either tapped or blazed. The gum begins to flow immediately and exudation continues for several days (G-45, M-317, V-367). The exuded gum, solidified in tear shapes or wormlike strips, is collected every few days. A single tree yields 2–10 pounds of gum per season. With appropriate rest intervals between tappings, the same tree may be tapped up to five times during its life (M-317).

A large part of the American imports is utilized in the pharmaceutical industry (discussed in chap. 5). The three major nonmedical industries that use gum karaya are paper, textile, and food. In the paper industry, karaya acts as a binder in long-fibered, light-weight papers (such as condenser tissues). In the textile industry, karaya is used as a thickening agent for dye in direct color printing on cotton fabrics. In the food industry, karaya is used to stabilize whipped cream, meringues, and French dressing; to prevent the formation of large ice crystals in ice pops and sherbets; to increase spreadability and prevent water separation in cheese spreads; to help retard staling in breads and other baked foods; to provide water retention and cohesion in bologna and other ground meat preparations, which gives the products a good, smooth appearance (G-45, G-527, J-337).

### GUM TRAGACANTH

The United States and United Kingdom are the biggest importers of tragacanth, accounting for about 50% of world production (D-246, M-107). Between 1976 and 1980, the United States imported on average each year about half a million pounds of tragacanth (worth about $3 million) from Iran (88%) and Turkey (4%) (table 6.2). Tragacanth gum comes from several species of *Astragalus* (V-367). Most important among them is *Astragalus gummifer* (M-317, S-433), which grows wild in Greece, Corsica, Turkey, Syria, Lebanon, and Iran (M-317). Iranian tragacanth is considered the best (M-107).

Tragacanth was known to Greek physicians from the seventh century B.C. By A.D. 1300 it was an article of commerce to Europe. Tragacanth is not cultivated; all collections are from the wild (G-556, M-317). Plants are tapped at two years of age and every other year thereafter for six to eight years (G-556). The best gum is derived from the roots, although the stems and branches are also tapped (M-317, V-367). The exudate is allowed to harden and then is scraped off.

Tragacanth is one of the most widely used natural emulsifiers and thickeners available to the food, drug, and allied industries (M-107). (The medicinal uses of tragacanth are discussed in chap. 5.) Tragacanth serves many functions in the food industry. It is used in the preparation of salad dressings because it forms a creamier, more natural looking dressing and imparts excellent shelf life and good refrigerator stability once the dressing has been opened (M-107). Tragacanth acts as a stabilizer in ice cream, ice pops, sherbets, and water ices (G-527) and as a stabilizer and thickener in condiments and sauces (M-107). Tragacanth provides clarity and brilliance to frozen pie fillings (G-527) and body to liqueurs (D-246).

In the textile industry, tragacanth is used in print pastes and sizes because of its good release properties (M-107). It is also used to stiffen silk, crepe, and felt goods and in the dressing of leather and the preparation of leather polishes (G-556, M-107).

## Balatas

Some plant exudates are in the form of latex—a milky liquid which is a complex colloidal mixture of water, salts, hydrocarbons, and various other organic compounds. Lactiferous products can be divided into two general categories: rubbers, which contain a high percentage of an elastic polymer; and balatas, of which the principle hydrocarbon is an inelastic polymer (S-41). The four wild lactiferous products of commercial importance are jelutong, chicle, gutta, and leche-caspi.

### JELUTONG

The United States is the major importer of jelutong (V-209, V-276). Between 1976 and 1980, the United States imported on average each year about $4 million worth. Singapore provided more than 90% (table 6.2).

Jelutong may be derived from both species of *Dyera*—*D. polyphylla* and *D. costulata*—the latter supplying the better grade of gum. The two species are native to Indonesia, Malaysia, and Brunei. Production of jelutong has always been entirely from wild trees (V-276; T. C. Whitmore, pers. comm., 9 February

1981). The tapped trees yield on average eight pounds of coagulate per tree per season. The same panel of a tree may be retapped after two years (V-276). Final refinement of jelutong and shipping take place in Singapore (V-209). Jelutong collection and production are currently on the decline (V-209, V-276). Two possible reasons include a decrease in productivity of certain areas after years of exploitation and competition from other forest and plantation crops, particularly in Central and South America (V-276).

Since about the 1920s, jelutong has been used almost exclusively in the manufacture of chewing gum (V-276). The rubbery characteristics of jelutong render it particularly suitable as a basis for bubble gum (P-258; T. C. Whitmore, pers. comm., 9 February 1981).

CHICLE

Between 1976 and 1980, the United States—the major importer of chicle—imported on average each year 2.1 million pounds of chicle worth about $4 million. Mexico supplied 79%, Belize 12%, and Guatemala 7% (table 6.2).

The sapodilla tree (*Manilkara zapota*), which provides the chicle of commerce, is native to Mexico (especially the Yucatan Peninsula), Guatemala, and Belize (G-380, J-252). The trees are tapped in zigzag gashes—a modified herringbone system—and the latex drains down the channels to the base, where it is caught in bags (G-380, J-252, J-337, S-41). It is then boiled until coagulated. At least 5% of the trees die after each tapping. The size of the tree is no indication of its potential yield (J-252). Information in the literature varies on the average yield per tree—from one pound (J-252) to 2–10 pounds (S-41). All production is from wild trees (G-380, J-252, P-258, S-41). The sapodilla does not seem to be a tree for plantation culture because of its slow growth rate (trees should not be tapped until 20 years old); the 3–5-year healing or rest period between tappings; and the death of the trees after 5–6 tappings (G-380, J-252).

The primary use of chicle is as a gum base in chewing gum (J-252, J-337, P-258). The chewing gum industry has been looking for a substitute for a long time, and although it has managed to reduce the amount of chicle used, it still is not possible to do without the substance entirely. It is chicle that gives gum its elasticity (G-380, J-252). In a strip of chewing gum, 10–20% is chicle (G-380, J-337).

GUTTA

Between 1976 and 1980, the United States imported each year an average of about $3 million of wild gutta: 72% from Malaysia, 15% from Indonesia, and 7% from Brazil (table 6.2). Several species enter trade under the category of *guttas*. Three genera—*Palaquium, Ganua,* and *Payena*—provide gutta from Southeast Asia; and two genera—*Manilkara* and *Lucuma*—provide gutta from South America (P-258, S-422, V-277).

Commercial exploitation of *Palaquium gutta* began in Singapore in 1847 when considerable quantities of the raw material were shipped to England.

Gutta percha was found to be admirably suited to insulate the underground and underwater cable systems being established in both Europe and the United States (P-258, V-277). By 1857, almost all the adult gutta percha trees in Singapore had been felled for the export market. Harvesting then shifted to other forested regions on the Malay Peninsula, Indonesian islands, and Borneo. Finally these too failed to provide sufficient quantities of *P. gutta*, and other species began to be harvested. These included eight *Palaquium* species: *P. calophyllum, P. hexandrum, P. hispidum, P. leiocarpum, P. maingayi, P. obovatum, P. oxleyanum, P. treubii*; two *Ganua* species: *G. motleyana* and *G. pallida*; and one *Payena* species: *P. leerii*. All these species are considered inferior to *P. gutta* and provide lower grade guttas. The genus *Palaquium* ranges from western India and Sri Lanka to the south central Pacific (P-258, V-277). *Ganua* is found in Malaysia and Indonesia; *Payena* in Malaysia, Indonesia, and the Philippines (V-277).

Originally the latex was extracted by felling the trees and girdling the trunk and main branches. This destructive practice was later replaced by tapping standing trees. At present some of the Southeast Asian output is from mechanical or chemical treatment of the leaves from plantation-grown trees. The average yield from tapped standing trees ranges from a few ounces to three pounds per tree per tap; the yield from cultivated leaf gutta may go up to 10,000 pounds per acre. It has been estimated that by 1914, 50 million *Palaquium* trees had been felled to supply the gutta percha consumed in the manufacture of a submarine cable net of about 3,000 miles (V-277). At present gutta's use is almost entirely restricted to the manufacture of golf balls; a little is believed to be used in industrial transmission belting. In both these areas, gutta faces competition from synthetics (P-258).

Malaysia gutta comes mostly from wild trees. From about 1900 to 1920, 15,000 acres of natural forests were managed but only to the extent that other species were felled, resulting in almost pure gutta percha forests. Indonesian gutta is derived from wild trees and from trees grown in plantations started in the late 1800s (V-277).

Some South American trees also yield a material—often called gutta balata—that is almost identical to the Southeast Asian gutta perchas (P-258). One such tree is *Manilkara bidentata*, which grows in the forests of the Amazon and Orinoco basins and the Guianas (V-277). Species of the genus *Lucuma*, native to the Amazon region, are also harvested (P-258). We suspect that gutta production from these South American trees is entirely from wild trees.

### LECHE-CASPI

The United States is the major importer of leche-caspi, which is used primarily as a base in the manufacture of chewing gum or as a supplement to other balata products (S-41, S-337, V-315). Between 1976 and 1980, the United States imported on average each year 2.7 million pounds of leche-caspi worth about $3 million. Almost all of this was supplied by Brazil (table 6.2).

There are six known *Couma* species concentrated mainly in the rainforest area of northern South America. The most important species is *C. macrocarpa*, the major source for the last 50 years of leche-caspi (or sorva) balata gum for the Western Hemisphere. *C. macrocarpa* grows wild in Brazil, Peru, Ecuador, Colombia, Venezuela, and Guyana. All latex collection is from wild sources. The trees are not considered suitable for plantation cultivation for two major reasons: a slow growth rate (the trees must be 20 years old to reach tappable size); and an inability to maintain a uniformly high yield of latex in repeated tappings. The herringbone system of tapping is one of the collection methods used; another is single-channel tapping plus felling and girdling. The average yield from an adult felled tree is 4 pounds of coagulum (V-315).

## Miscellaneous Products

### QUEBRACHO

Table 6.4 summarizes American imports of major tannins for the period 1976–1980. Quebracho heads the list with average annual imports (largely from Argentina) worth about $4.6 million. (Valonia imports are discussed later.)

The bark used to produce the industrial tannin called quebracho comes from two South American trees—*Schinopsis balansae* (white quebracho) and *S. quebracho-colorado* (red quebracho) (J-337, P-258). The use of quebracho in

Table 6.4 **Imports of major tannins by the United States, 1976–1980**

| TANNIN(S) | AVERAGE ANNUAL IMPORT VALUE *(U.S.$)* | EXPORTING COUNTRIES PERCENTAGE OF U.S. IMPORTS | |
|---|---|---|---|
| Quebracho | 4,569,000 | Argentina | 78 |
| | | Paraguay | 18 |
| | | Others | 4 |
| Wattle | 3,914,000 | South Africa | 85 |
| | | Brazil | 14 |
| | | Others | 1 |
| Canaigre, chestnut, curupay, divi-divi, eucalyptus, hemlock, larch, tara | 970,000 | Italy | 31 |
| | | Peru | 12 |
| | | Others | 57 |
| Mangrove, myrobalan, oak, sumac, urunday | 639,000 | Turkey | 26 |
| | | Italy | 21 |
| | | France | 20 |
| | | Others | 33 |
| Valonia | 154,000 | Turkey | 99 |
| | | Others | 1 |

Sources: S-450–S-454.

tanning was discovered in the early 1870s (G-301, P-258). The first factory opened in Paraguay in 1889. Within 35 years, 20 quebracho factories were in operation in Paraguay and Argentina (G-301).

During this period of rapid growth, the wild stands of quebracho—particularly the white quebracho—were heavily exploited and natural regeneration was inhibited by livestock grazing practices that destroyed many young trees (G-301, P-258, S-178). Most quebracho still comes from wild trees, as the species' slow growth rate has discouraged the development of plantations (P-258). These factors, plus the absence of aggressive export strategies, have contributed to quebracho's not being used—in spite of its special qualities—on the same scale world wide as some of its traditional tannin competitors, especially wattle (which is cultivated) (P-258, S-178). The two features of quebracho tannin that make it so valuable are a weight-giving characteristic particularly useful in tanning of sole leather and the speed with which it tans—in one-third the time required by oak tannin (G-301).

### LAC

Between 1976 and 1980, the United States each year imported an average of about $4 million worth of lac in various forms: seed lac ($1,996,000); stick, button, and other lacs ($1,416,000); bleached shellac ($910,000); and shellac ($16,000) (S-450–S-454). Although traditionally India has been the world's largest producer of lac (A-325, G-300), Thailand has developed a strong industry since World War II. The United States now imports about 40% of its lac from Thailand and 35% from India (table 6.2). Other lac-producing countries are Burma, Sri Lanka, and Pakistan (A-325).

Lac, the hardened secretion of a tiny insect, is the only known commercial resin of animal origin (A-325). No superior modern substitute has been found. The United States imports annually about 12 million pounds of lac (S-450–S-454). It requires 150,000 lac insects to yield 1 pound of lac (M-133).

A number of species of the genus *Laccifer* occur in lac-producing countries, but by far the most important is *Laccifer lacca*, which contributes the major portion of commercial lac. Young larvae of lac insects emerge from the dead shell of the mother and crawl about in search of a feeding place (A-325, G-300). They settle on any available succulent tender shoot of a suitable host plant. Indian host plants include *Schleichera oleosa*, *Butea monosperma*, *Zizyphus jujuba*, *Z. xylopyra*, *Shorea talura*, *Acacia catechu*, and *Cajanus cajan* (A-325, G-300, V-232). One Thai host plant is *Samanea saman* (A-325). The larvae anchor themselves to the host plants by piercing the bark with their mouths in order to suck the sap for nourishment. Then they start to secrete resin from their backs. (The natural function of the resin is to protect the motionless insect from predators and adverse weather [M-133].) The resin hardens on contact with the air (M-133) and forms cells with pores for breathing and excretion (A-325).

For 8 to 14 weeks the larvae grow under the lac. Then the insects reach sexual maturity. Winged and unwinged males emerge, seek out, and fertilize the females, who remain anchored to the host plant for life (A-325, G-300). During the next two to three months, the fertilized females continue to grow and secrete more lac (A-325, G-300). Where females are closely crowded together, the lac cells coalesce and form a continuous thick encrustation (A-325, G-300, M-133). Each female then withdraws part of her body from her hardened resinous covering to create a space into which she lays her eggs. The eggs hatch and the new generation emerges in search of a host plant.

Although lac insects are not domesticated, lac production is promoted by three methods: cultivation of suitable host plants, pruning of host plants to time emergence of tender shoots with emergence of larvae, and cutting down branches that bear the broodlac encrustations and tying them near the new young shoots of the pruned potential host plants (A-325). In India the bulk of commercial lac is obtained from wild host trees of the species *Butea monosperma* and *Schleichera oleosa*, although cultivation of these and other host species is being promoted (J-1039).

Several forms of lac are traded: sticklac—the lac encrustations broken off the branches by hand or scraped off with a knife or sickle; seedlac—large lac grains that emerge after sticklac is crushed and cleaned; shellac—sheets of refined lac broken into flakes; and button lac—circular disks or buttons that result when molten lac is dropped on smooth metal sheets (A-325).

There are many present-day industrial applications of lac. It is used for decorative varnishes as it is capable of giving a smooth finish and taking a high polish. It is often used as a first coating on wood to fill the pores and seal knots likely to exude resin and disfigure or spoil finished paint work (G-300). Aqueous varnishes containing lac are used by leather-dressing and -finishing industries and by milliners to stiffen hat materials (A-325, G-300, M-133). Lac is used by electrical industries to bind mica and to produce insulating sealing waxes (A-325, G-300). Lac serves as an adhesive and cement in laminated paper and jute boards, plate sealer, gasket cement, general cements, optical cement (A-325). Lac is used in lithographic ink, waterproof ink, and colored ink; in making phonograph records; and in antifouling and anticorrosive paints used on ships' bottoms (A-325, G-300). The light color of bleached lac makes it ideally suited for colorless polishes and quick-drying paints that may be tinted to any shade. Bleached lac polishes have a wide number of uses—finishing of wooden floors, playing cards, pottery, sporting goods, ivory articles, and imitation fruits; glazing of chocolate; and protective coating of pills (A-325, G-300, M-133).

CIVET

Between 1976 and 1980, the United States imported on average each year about $200,000 worth of civet (table 6.3). African countries (primarily Ethiopia—according to our supplier survey and the literature) are reported to be the major suppliers of crude civet; minor suppliers include India, Indonesia, Malaysia, and the People's Republic of China (J-337).

The secretion called civet is taken from two species: *Viverra civetta* (the

African civet), native from Senegal and Somalia to the Transvaal; and *V. zibetha* (the large Indian civet), native from India through Burma to the People's Republic of China, and south to Malaysia (A-924, A-1189, D-221, G-635, J-337, M-355). The oily secretion is produced by glands located between the anus and genitalia in both males and females (A-90, D-221, V-234). Some articles on civet suggest that collection from males is preferable (A-90, D-221).

Most commercial civet is taken from animals kept in cages (D-221). This does not mean, however, that the animals can be considered truly farmed (both bred and raised in captivity)—a false impression often given in the literature (A-924, D-322, G-635, J-337). African civets, all of whom are taken from the wild, will not breed in captivity (D-221). We were not able to determine if the situation with the large Indian civet was similar.

The African civet begins to yield commercially profitable amounts of secretion (10–12 ounces per animal per year) at about four years of age. This continues throughout the life of the animal, which may live 10–12 years in captivity. The secretion is collected, at regular intervals, by scraping the glands with a spatula. This may occur every 7–9 days for the African civet and 2–3 times a week for the large Indian civet. Civet is extensively used as a fixative and fragrance component in perfumes (especially oriental and rose types), soaps, detergents, creams, and lotions (A-90, A-924, D-221, D-322, G-635, J-337, V-234).

### VALONIA

Between 1976 and 1980, the United States imported on average each year about $150,000 worth of valonia—99% of which was from Turkey (table 6.3).

Valonia, a tannin, comes from an oak (*Quercus aegilops*) native to eastern Europe and western Asia (G-301, S-337, V-232). Unlike quebracho, this tannin is extracted not from the bark but from the acorn (S-41, S-337, S-469). Valonia, a trade product by the eighteenth century, is today one of the more commonly used vegetable tannins. The acorns are collected almost entirely from wild trees in Turkey; and extraction is carried out mainly in Izmir. The chief value of valonia is in the production of high grade heavy leather (such as sole leather), where weight and water resistance are important (G-301, S-41, S-469).

### TONKA BEAN

Each year between 1976 and 1980, the United States imported an average of about $100,000 worth of wild tonka beans from Venezuela (27%), Brazil (26%), and other countries (47%) (table 6.3). According to our supplier survey, Trinidad and Tobago also exported tonka beans to the United States.

The tonka bean tree (*Dipteryx odorata*), native to South America, is found in particular abundance in Venezuela and Brazil. The bulk of the crop is harvested from wild trees, with an average yield per tree of 2–8 pounds of beans a year. The seed of the tonka bean yields coumarin, which may be used in several ways: as a substitute for vanilla, as a fixing agent in the manufacture of coloring materials, as a fragrance ingredient in toilet soaps, and as a piquant flavoring in liqueurs. In recent years, the demand for tonka beans has declined due to competition from synthetic coumarin and vanillin. The United States is the top importer of tonka beans. The biggest American consumer of coumarin is the tobacco industry, which uses it to give tobacco a pleasant fragrance (D-246, S-41).

CASTOREUM

Between 1976 and 1980, the United States each year imported an average of about $70,000 worth of castoreum from unspecified sources (table 6.3). Respondents to our supplier survey indicated that most U.S. imports were from Canada.

Two species of beaver are used to provide castoreum—*Castor canadensis* (the American beaver) native to Canada and the United States; and *C. fiber* (the Eurasian beaver) native to Europe through to Altai (A-90, A-769, A-1189, J-337, P-408). Castoreum (from *C. fiber*) has been considered a valuable product since Grecian times (A-769). At present, most castoreum comes from wild caught animals that have been trapped for their furs.

Castoreum is the secretion accumulated in scent glands located between the anus and genitalia. Both male and female beavers have two large (3–5 inches) scent glands on both sides of the cloaca. The scent glands are removed from the dead animal and dried. Extracts are prepared by solvent extraction (J-337, P-408).

Castoreum is rarely used in pharmaceuticals. Its main use is in cosmetics as a fragrance component or fixative in perfumes, especially men's fragrances and oriental types, and in soaps, creams, and lotions. In food, castoreum has found a particular application in vanilla flavor compounds (A-90, J-337).

*Waxes*

The two most important vegetable waxes in the world are carnauba and candelilla. Ouricury is considered of less significance (V-380).

CARNAUBA

For the period 1976–1980, the United States imported on average each year about $5 million worth of carnauba, 99% of which came from Brazil (table 6.2). Brazil is the almost exclusive producer of carnauba wax, which comes from a tree (*Copernicia cerifera*) native to that country (V-380). The palm grows wild in large numbers in some of Brazil's northeastern states. In the last 50 years, plantings of the carnauba palm have been made, but most of the production still comes from the wild (S-41). The wax is obtained from the leaves (A-1079); each tree yields about six ounces (S-41).

Carnauba has special properties for which the wax is held in high esteem: hardness, high melting point, ability to take a lasting polish, and compatability (S-41). Carnauba is primarily used for carbon paper, floor and car polishes, and cosmetics (V-380). It may also be an ingredient in lubricants, insulating materials, chalk, matches, candles, phonograph records, plastics, protective coatings, photographic films, and leather dressings (A-1079, S-41).

CANDELILLA

Between 1976 and 1980, the United States imported about $1 million worth of candelilla wax on average each year—virtually all of it from Mexico (table 6.2).

The candelilla wax of commerce may come from several species of *Euphorbia* and *Pedilanthus*. The most commonly used species, however, is *E. antisyphilitica* (G-263, M-229). *Pedilanthus pavonis* is a distant second—our supplier survey revealed that US imports of *E. antisyphilitica* outnumbered imports of *P. pavonis* by a 2:1 ratio.

Candelilla shrubs are stem succulents native primarily to the deserts of northern Mexico. *Euphorbia antisyphilitica* is found throughout the Coahuilan Desert formation: in Mexico this includes the states of Nuevo Leon, Coahuila, Durango, Hidalgo, Puebla, Zacatecas, and San Luis Potosí. In the United States, the species occurs in the Big Bend area of Texas, mostly within the boundaries of Big Bend National Park (G-263, M-229, S-41, V-327).

The development of candelilla as a Mexican export product began about 1930. To date, all wax has been obtained from wild plants; no effort has been made to cultivate candelilla. The wild plants are usually pulled from the ground by hand. They must be at least two to five years of age to produce wax in commercial quantities. The wax is obtained by boiling the plants in acidified water. One ton of candelilla plants yields 50 pounds of wax (G-263, M-229, M-312, S-41, V-70).

In the past, the United States used half its candelilla imports for coating and polishing preparations and another third in chewing gum (G-263, M-229, M-312). A recent report published in 1979 (V-380) indicated that the present major user of candelilla wax is the American chewing gum industry. We have not been able to verify this. Candelilla is also used to harden soft waxes, and in the manufacture of candles, leather goods, varnishes and lacquers, paper sizing, dental molds, sealing waxes, and electrical insulating material (M-229, M-312, M-601).

OURICURY

Ouricury wax, often a substitute for carnauba, comes from a wild palm (*Syagras coronata*) found frequently in stands in northeastern Brazil (S-41). Between 1976 and 1980, the United States imported an annual average of about $30,000 worth of ouricury from unspecified countries (table 6.3). All respondents to our supplier survey indicated that Brazil was the exporting country from which they obtained their ouricury wax.

*Oils*

Five major imported oils—largely from wild sources—were used in industrial products in the United States during the period 1976–1980: Brazilian sassafras, bois de rose, babassu, cedar leaf, and palmarosa.

## BRAZILIAN SASSAFRAS

Between 1976 and 1980, the United States each year imported an average of about $1 million of Brazilian sassafras oil—almost all of which came from Brazil (table 6.2). The wild tree (*Ocotea cymbarum*), from which Brazilian sassafras oil is taken, ranges from Brazil and Paraguay to Colombia. Commercial production of the oil began in 1938. Principally the oil is used for the isolation of its main component—safrole—and for conversion of safrole into heliotropin. Safrole and heliotropin are used to perfume insecticides, disinfectants, floor waxes, polishes, soaps, and deodorants. The antiseptic effect of safrole contributes to its inclusion in glues, gummed papers, library pastes, and so forth by preventing deterioration from mold and fungus (A-90, G-76, P-258).

## BOIS DE ROSE

Between 1976 and 1980, the United States imported on average each year about $1 million of bois de rose oil—84% of which was supplied by Brazil (table 6.3). The essential oil bois de rose is obtained, primarily by steam distillation, from a wild-growing tree (*Aniba rosaeodora*) found in the Amazon region of South America. Brazil and Peru are major producers of bois de rose, but the best quality oil is reported to come from French Guiana. Formerly, bois de rose was used for the isolation of its major component—linalool—but after the advent of synthetic linalool, rosewood's attraction became its own unique and useful notes. Bois de rose is used extensively to perfume soaps, detergents, creams, lotions, and perfumery of the floral type. It is also a flavor ingredient in most major food categories: alcoholic and nonalcoholic beverages, baked goods, meat and meat products, frozen dairy desserts, and candies (A-90, G-76, J-337, M-30, S-41).

## BABASSU

Between 1976 and 1979, the United States imported an annual average of about $400,000 of babassu oil (table 6.3). Nuts from three wild palm species provide the babassu oil of commerce: *Orbignya martiana*, found in the Amazon basin; *O. oleifera*, found in Brazil outside Amazonia; *O. speciosa*, found in tropical South America, especially Brazil (A-316, M-229, V-85). Brazil, the major supplier of babassu oil, began production in the early 1920s. Before World War II, most of the oil was exported. But after the war, the United States and various European countries began to develop other vegetable oil industries such as copra, palm kernel, and palm oil. At present, the babassu oil industry of Brazil meets mostly domestic demand. Even so, it is thought to be probably the largest vegetable oil industry in the world wholly dependent on wild plants (M-229, M-644). Four factors hinder further development of the babassu industry: first, a labor shortage for collection of the wild nuts; second, inadequate transportation facilities; third, low yields per tree due to the high density of the wild palms; fourth, the difficulty of cracking the hard shell (or endocarp) without damaging the kernel (A-316, M-229). Babassu oil, a rich lauric acid type, can be used for the same purposes as coconut oil—for the production of fatty acids and the manufacture of toilet soap, detergents, lubricants, margarine, shortening, and general edibles (A-316, M-229, M-644, V-85).

### CEDAR LEAF

Between 1976 and 1980, the United States imported on average each year about $250,000 of cedar leaf oil, presumably mostly from Canada (table 6.3). Cedar leaf oil is obtained from steam distillation of the leaves (and twigs) of the North American white cedar (*Thuja occidentalis*) (A-90, J-337, S-433). The tree's Canadian distribution includes Nova Scotia, New Brunswick, Quebec, Ontario, and Manitoba (G-479); the American distribution includes Maine, New Hampshire, Vermont, New York, Michigan, Wisconsin, and Minnesota (J-342). The uses of cedar leaf oil are as follows: a counterirritant in over-the-counter drugs; a fragrance in high class perfumes and in soaps, lotions, creams, detergents, disinfectants, room sprays, insecticides, and paints; a flavor ingredient in most food categories—alcoholic and nonalcoholic beverages, meat and meat products, condiments and relishes, baked goods, gelatins and puddings, frozen dairy desserts, and candies (A-90, J-337, S-433).

### PALMAROSA

Between 1976 and 1980, the United States imported on average each year about $125,000 of wild palmarosa oil, all of which came from India (table 6.3). Palmarosa (*Cymbopogon martinii*), a member of the grass family, grows wild and is cultivated in India. It also has been planted in Indonesia, the Seychelles, and the Comoros. India, however, remains the most important producer. Palmarosa oil is used in several ways: as one of the best natural sources of the terpene geraniol; as a fragrance in cosmetics—particularly soap; and as a flavoring in tobacco (A-90, G-76, P-258, S-337).

## Oleoresins

Natural oleoresins are mixtures of mostly resins and essential oils found in exudations from tree trunks, bark, and so forth. Chemically, resins are complex oxidation products of terpenes and are insoluble in water. Essential oils generally represent the odoriferous principles of the plants from which they are obtained; most are terpenes at different stages of oxidation (A-90, A-109, J-337). Three oleoresins, obtained primarily from wild trees, are imported by the United States: styrax (or storax), tolu balsam, and copaiba balsam.

### STYRAX

Between 1976 and 1980 the United States each year imported an average of about $400,000 worth of styrax, mostly from Honduras (table 6.3). The styrax traded on world markets comes from two tree species: *Liquidambar orientalis* (Asian styrax) and *L. styraciflua* (American styrax). There are no commercial plantations of either species; collection is from wild trees only. Asian styrax is native to Asia Minor (A-90, A-109, G-300, J-337, M-317). Turkey is the major producer of Asian styrax (A-1079, G-683). Bruising the trees by pounding or puncturing induces the sapwood to secrete the balsam, which accumulates in the inner bark. This bark is then stripped, pressed, and boiled. American styrax is native to the United States (from Connecticut west to Oklahoma and Texas and south to central Florida), Mexico, Guatemala, Honduras, and possibly Nicaragua (A-109, G-300, J-337, M-317, S-41). Honduras is the chief source of American styrax, followed by Guatemala. American styrax is collected by tapping the naturally formed pockets of exudate occurring between the wood and the bark. Styrax is used by three principal industries: pharmaceuticals (as an ingredient in compound tincture of benzoin in the United States); perfumery (in floral and oriental-type perfume compounds; in incense, soap, and talcum powder perfumery); and food (as a flavoring in soft drinks, candy, desserts, and chewing gum) (A-90, A-109, A-1079, J-337, M-317, S-41).

TOLU BALSAM

Between 1976 and 1980, the United States imported an annual average of about $200,000 worth of Tolu balsam, largely from Colombia (table 6.3). The tree (*Myroxylon balsamum*) from which Tolu balsam is obtained grows wild in Argentina, Paraguay, Brazil, Bolivia, Venezuela, Peru, and Colombia (D-246, J-337, M-317). It is particularly abundant in the Tolu province of Colombia, which is the major supplier (A-90, A-109, A-1079, D-246, M-317). Tolu balsam is obtained by making incisions through the bark and sapwood; the oleoresin then drips into gourd cups (J-337, M-317). The average yield per tree is 17–22 pounds (M-317).

Tolu balsam has applications in several industries: in pharmaceuticals it is an ingredient in compound tincture of benzoin, an expectorant and flavoring in cough mixtures, an inhalant for catarrh and bronchitis; in the food industry it is a fixative for rum, a flavoring in chewing gum, soft drinks, candy, baked goods, and frozen dairy desserts (A-90, A-109, D-246, J-337, M-317).

COPAIBA BALSAM

Between 1976 and 1980, the United States imported on average each year about $50,000 worth of copaiba balsam from unspecified countries (table 6.3). Brazil was the only country named by respondents to our mail survey as a U.S. supplier.

Copaiba balsam is extracted from several species of *Copaifera: C. reticulata* yields most of Brazil's copaiba and *C. officinalis* most of the copaiba from northern South America and Central America (J-337, S-41). Collection is from wild trees, which are tapped either by drilling several holes or hacking incisions into the trunks; the exudate accumulates in and about the cavities. Yield per tree may go as high as 11 gallons (S-41). The chief producers of copaiba balsam are Brazil and Colombia (A-90, A-109).

Copaiba is used as a flavoring in most major categories of food; the oil is also used as a blender-modifier in fragrances and perfumes; the oleoresin itself has no perfumery value but may be used as a fixative (A-90, A-109, J-337).

# 7

# New Domesticates

The supply of consumable products is just one of the ways in which wildlife benefits people. Another is by providing raw materials and services in support of crop and livestock production—including the most basic of raw materials, the domesticates themselves. New (twentieth century) domesticates in the United States already have an annual combined farm sale and import value of $1.2 billion. In this chapter we review first the domestication of new agricultural and horticultural crops, and then newly domesticated timber trees, livestock, and aquaculture species.

People began domesticating plants and animals about 10,000 years ago (S-323). Although the process is still going on, several authorities consider it an essentially prehistoric phenomenon. Schery, in his textbook of economic botany *Plants for Man* (S-41) writes: "There exist today few economically important plants or animals that have been domesticated within historic times." By contrast, Simmonds (S-123), analyzing 127 crops discussed in his *Evolution of Crop Plants* (S-384), concludes that domestication has not been limited to specific historical periods but has been "continuously spread over time, a reflection of the ever-changing demands of human societies for new and improved agricultural products. . . . Allowing for a good deal of guesswork and uncertainty, it looks as though rate of domestication (per 1,000 years, say) has not changed very greatly over time." Simmonds' findings are summarized in table 7.1.

Table 7.1 does not respond to Schery's point that, although the rate of domestication may be roughly constant, few of the species domesticated in historic times are economically important. Indeed, Simmonds includes in his list of crops some that are clearly minor, such as *Amaranthus caudatus*, quinoa (*Chenopodium* spp.), Jerusalem artichoke (*Helianthus tuberosus*), and Ethiopian mustard (*Brassica carinata*). At the same time, he leaves out major crops like cashew (*Anacardium occidentale*), walnut (*Juglans regia*), and celery (*Apium graveolens*). Perhaps if the list were different the picture—even of the rate of domestication—would change.

To provide an economic as well as a historic perspective to the question, we reviewed 160 domesticated vascular plant species (excluding timber trees) of

Table 7.1  **Places and times of domestication of Simmonds' sample of 127 crops**

| TYPE | AGE* | NEAR EAST AND EUROPE | CENTRAL AND EAST ASIA | AFRICA | AMERICA | TOTAL |
|---|---|---|---|---|---|---|
| Cereals and pulses | A | 7 | 0 | 0 | 0 | 7 |
| | E | 4 | 4 | 6 | 9 | 23 |
| | L | 0 | 1 | 0 | 0 | 1 |
| | R | 0 | 0 | 0 | 1 | 1 |
| | Total | 11 | 5 | 6 | 10 | 32 |
| Tubers, vegetables, and fruits | A | 0 | 1 | 2 | 2 | 5 |
| | E | 10 | 17 | 2 | 7 | 36 |
| | L | 6 | 3 | 1 | 3 | 13 |
| | R | 2 | 0 | 0 | 1 | 3 |
| | Total | 18 | 21 | 5 | 13 | 57 |
| Other crops | A | 1 | 0 | 1 | 0 | 2 |
| | E | 7 | 10 | 3 | 4 | 24 |
| | L | 2 | 0 | 2 | 1 | 5 |
| | R | 2 | 2 | 2 | 1 | 7 |
| | Total | 12 | 12 | 8 | 6 | 38 |
| TOTAL | | 41 | 38 | 19 | 29 | 127 |

| | A | E | L | R |
|---|---|---|---|---|
| TOTAL | 14 | 83 | 19 | 11 |

Source: S-123.
*A = ancient (7000–5000 B.C.), E = early (5000–0 B.C.), L = late (A.D. 0–1750), R = recent (after A.D. 1750). Rate of domestication per 1000 years: A = 7, E = 17, L + R = 15 (rough estimates).

economic importance to the United States. We categorized each species according to its combined domestic (farm sales) plus import (customs) value as follows: super (more than $1,000 million), major ($100 million–$1,000 million), medium ($10 million–$100 million), and minor ($1 million–$10 million). Anything with a value of less than $1 million we regarded as a microresource and have not included (except with respect to certain incipient crops discussed later in this chapter).

We followed Simmonds in dividing the period between the earliest evidence of plant domestication (around 7000 B.C.) and the present into these eras: ancient (7000–5000 B.C.), early (5000–0 B.C.), and late (A.D. 0–1700). We split Simmonds' recent into two divisions: recent (A.D. 1700–1900) and new (A.D. 1900 to the present). (In table 7.1 Simmonds gives 1750 as the year of transition between late and recent, but in the analysis of which the table is the summary he gives the year 1700. We have chosen 1700 for convenience.)

Our sample of 160 species is drawn from the list of 226 species given in tables 7.2 and 7.3 (see note 1). The results are summarized in tables 7.4 and 7.5. The

(text continued on page 203)

Table 7.2  **Crop species (226) grown or imported by the United States with an annual value of $1 million or more**

| CROP CATEGORY (Number of crops) | AVERAGE ANNUAL VALUE OF CROP U.S. farm sales and imports (U.S. $ million) | CROP | CROP FAMILY |
|---|---|---|---|
| SUPER (15 crops) | 11,278.4 | Soybean | Leguminosae |
| | 10,412.4 | Corn | Gramineae |
| | 6,475.1 | Wheat | Gramineae |
| | 4,233.0 | Cotton (G. hirsutum) | Malvaceae |
| | 3,925.3 | Coffee | Rubiaceae |
| | 2,851.4 | Tobacco | Solanaceae |
| | 1,722.5 | Sugarcane | Gramineae |
| | 1,524.9 | Grape | Vitidaceae |
| | 1,206.0 | Potato | Solanaceae |
| | 1,163.1 | Rice | Gramineae |
| | 1,150.3 | Sweet orange | Rutaceae |
| | 1,146.5 | Sorghum | Gramineae |
| | 1,053.7 | Alfalfa | Leguminosae |
| | 1,051.0 | Tomato | Solanaceae |
| | 1,016.0 | Cacao | Sterculiaceae |
| MAJOR (42 crops) | 814.6 | Apple | Rosaceae |
| | 786.9 | Timothy | Gramineae |
| | 759.5 | Beet/beetroot/sugarbeet | Chenopodiaceae |
| | 746.8 | Peanut/groundnut | Leguminosae |
| | 706.4 | Rubber | Euphorbiaceae |
| | 672.3 | Barley | Gramineae |
| | 527.3 | Lettuce | Compositae |
| | 516.6 | Common bean/green bean/ French bean/snap bean/dry bean | Leguminosae |
| | 393.4 | Sunflower | Compositae |
| | 368.2 | Banana/plantain | Musaceae |
| | 365.2 | Broccoli/brussels sprout/ cabbage/cauliflower/kale/ kohlrabi/collard | Cruciferae |
| | 354.5 | Almond | Rosaceae |
| | 349.3 | Peach | Rosaceae |
| | 314.3 | Coconut | Palmae |
| | 304.2 | Oats | Gramineae |
| | 286.9 | Onion | Alliaceae |
| | 251.9 | Strawberry | Rosaceae |
| | 218.8 | Grapefruit | Rutaceae |
| | 197.5 | Chrysanthemum | Compositae |
| | 192.3 | Cucumber | Cucurbitaceae |
| | 189.4 | Melon | Cucurbitaceae |
| | 186.0 | Pineapple | Bromeliaceae |

Table 7.2 (*Continued*)

| CROP CATEGORY (Number of crops) | AVERAGE ANNUAL VALUE OF CROP U.S. farm sales and imports (U.S. $ million) | CROP | CROP FAMILY |
|---|---|---|---|
| MAJOR (continued) | 179.4 | Roses | Rosaceae |
| | 166.7 | Celery | Umbelliferae |
| | 163.9 | Walnut/Persian walnut/English walnut | Juglandaceae |
| | 158.1 | Peppers/chilis | Solanaceae |
| | 155.6 | Jute | Tiliaceae |
| | 155.0 | Plum/prune | Rosaceae |
| | 147.7 | Sweet cherry/sour cherry | Rosaceae |
| | 145.6 | Pear | Rosaceae |
| | 143.9 | Olive | Oleaceae |
| | 143.3 | Oil palm | Palmae |
| | 142.3 | Carrot | Umbelliferae |
| | 142.0 | Pea | Leguminosae |
| | 135.5 | Lemon | Rutaceae |
| | 130.0 | Bermuda grass | Gramineae |
| | 128.0 | Tea | Theaceae |
| | 116.3 | Watermelon | Cucurbitaceae |
| | 116.1 | Cashew | Anacardiaceae |
| | 109.6 | Sweet potato | Convolvulaceae |
| | 101.5 | Pecan | Juglandaceae |
| | 100.0 | Azaleas/rhododendrons | Ericaceae |
| MEDIUM (85 crops) | 93.8 | Avocado | Lauraccac |
| | 91.4 | Ornamental geranium | Geraniaceae |
| | 90.3 | Asparagus | Liliaceae |
| | 85.8 | Poinsettia | Euphorbiaceae |
| | 85.3 | Hops | Cannabidaceae |
| | 81.2 | Flax/linseed | Linaceae |
| | 76.2 | Ornamental junipers | Cupressaceae |
| | 75.0 | Cotton (*G. barbadense*) | Malvaceae |
| | 69.7 | Carnation | Caryophyllaceae |
| | 66.2 | Tangerine/mandarin | Rutaceae |
| | 55.2 | Peppermint | Labiatae |
| | 54.8 | Black pepper/white pepper | Piperaceae |
| | 52.7 | Philodendron | Araceae |
| | 52.1 | Safflower | Compositae |
| | 51.8 | Cranberry | Ericaceae |
| | 50.6 | Lima bean | Leguminosae |
| | 49.1 | Ornamental pines | Pinaceae |
| | 45.2 | Ornamental maples | Aceraceae |
| | 44.0 | Highbush blueberry | Ericaceae |
| | 40.5 | Castor | Euphorbiaceae |
| | 39.4 | Ornamental yews | Taxaceae |

(*continued*)

Table 7.2 (*Continued*)

| CROP CATEGORY (Number of crops) | AVERAGE ANNUAL VALUE OF CROP U.S. farm sales and imports (U.S. $ million) | CROP | CROP FAMILY |
|---|---|---|---|
| MEDIUM (*continued*) | 39.1 | Ornamental palms | Palmae |
| | 38.6 | Dracaena | Agavaceae |
| | 38.0 | Italian ryegrass/annual ryegrass | Gramineae |
| | 37.5 | Cinchona/quinine/quinidine | Rubiaceae |
| | 37.4 | Apricot | Rosaceae |
| | 35.5 | Tall fescue/meadow fescue/red fescue | Gramineae |
| | 34.7 | Opium poppy | Papaveraceae |
| | 33.9 | Rye | Gramineae |
| | 33.1 | Cacti | Cactaceae |
| | 33.0 | Dieffenbachia | Araceae |
| | 32.2 | Spinach | Chenopodiaceae |
| | 32.2 | Petunia | Solanaceae |
| | 31.8 | Garlic | Alliaceae |
| | 31.8 | Lime | Rutaceae |
| | 30.4 | Sesame | Pedaliaceae |
| | 29.3 | Globe artichoke/artichoke | Compositae |
| | 28.1 | Begonia | Begoniaceae |
| | 27.9 | Ginseng | Araliaceae |
| | 27.8 | Easter lilies/other. lilies | Liliaceae |
| | 27.7 | Ornamental ash | Oleaceae |
| | 27.5 | Guar | Leguminosae |
| | 27.5 | Holly | Aquifoliaceae |
| | 26.9 | Pistachio | Pistaciaceae |
| | 26.8 | Ornamental oak | Fagaceae |
| | 26.6 | Sericea/perennial lespedeza/ Korean lespedeza/Japanese lespedeza/annual lespedeza | Leguminosae |
| | 25.8 | Orchids | Orchidaceae |
| | 25.4 | Marigold | Compositae |
| | 24.8 | Bamboo | Gramineae |
| | 24.7 | Kentucky bluegrass | Gramineae |
| | 22.8 | Abaca | Musaceae |
| | 22.7 | Ornamental spruce | Pinaceae |
| | 22.4 | Spearmint | Labiatae |
| | 21.9 | Fig | Moraceae |
| | 21.3 | Gladiolus | Iridaceae |
| | 21.3 | Tulip | Liliaceae |
| | 21.1 | Vanilla | Orchidaceae |
| | 19.3 | Date | Palmae |
| | 19.1 | Japanese mint/corn mint | Labiatae |
| | 19.0 | Filbert | Corylaceae |
| | 18.8 | Tangelo | Rutaceae |

Table 7.2  (*Continued*)

| CROP CATEGORY (Number of crops) | AVERAGE ANNUAL VALUE OF CROP U.S. farm sales and imports (U.S. $ million) | CROP | CROP FAMILY |
|---|---|---|---|
| MEDIUM (*continued*) | 18.6 | Ornamental apple | Rosaceae |
| | 18.5 | Lentil | Leguminosae |
| | 18.0 | Endive/escarole | Compositae |
| | 17.7 | Impatiens | Balsaminaceae |
| | 17.7 | Brown mustard/mustard greens/white mustard | Cruciferae |
| | 17.2 | Euonymus | Celastraceae |
| | 17.1 | Red clover | Leguminosae |
| | 16.6 | Red raspberry/black raspberry | Rosaceae |
| | 16.4 | Proso millet | Gramineae |
| | 15.0 | Cowpea/black-eyed pea | Leguminosae |
| | 13.9 | Licorice | Leguminosae |
| | 13.7 | Eggplant | Solanaceae |
| | 13.3 | Macadamia nut | Proteaceae |
| | 12.9 | African violet/saintpaulia | Gesneriaceae |
| | 11.9 | Pyrethrum | Compositae |
| | 11.8 | Squashes/pumpkin | Cucurbitaceae |
| | 11.4 | Cassia | Lauraceae |
| | 10.9 | Tung | Euphorbiaceae |
| | 10.3 | Papaya | Caricaceae |
| | 10.3 | Dogwood | Cornaceae |
| | 10.3 | Clove | Myrtaccac |
| | 10.3 | Blackberry | Rosaceae |
| | 10.2 | Ornamental cherry/plum | Rosaceae |
| | 10.0 | Hydrangea | Hydrangeaceae |
| MINOR (84 crops) | 9.3 | Cassava/manioc/tapioca | Euphorbiaccac |
| | 9.3 | Pansy | Violaceae |
| | 9.1 | Chickpea/garbanzo bean | Leguminosae |
| | 9.1 | Pittosporum | Pittosporaceae |
| | 8.9 | Water chestnut | Cyperaceae |
| | 8.9 | Basket willow | Salicaceae |
| | 8.8 | Gloxinia | Gesneriaceae |
| | 8.7 | Fuchsia | Onagraceae |
| | 8.7 | Snapdragon | Scrophulariaceae |
| | 8.6 | Mango | Anacardiaceae |
| | 7.9 | Narcissus/daffodil | Amaryllidaceae |
| | 7.8 | Hyacinth | Liliaceae |
| | 7.7 | Buckwheat | Polygonaceae |
| | 7.6 | Gypsophila | Caryophyllaceae |
| | 7.3 | Zinnia | Compositae |
| | 7.3 | Psyllium | Plantaginaceae |
| | 6.9 | Coleus | Labiatae |
| | 6.6 | Iris | Iridaceae |

(*continued*)

Table 7.2 (*Continued*)

| CROP CATEGORY (Number of crops) | AVERAGE ANNUAL VALUE OF CROP U.S. farm sales and imports (U.S. $ million) | CROP | CROP FAMILY |
|---|---|---|---|
| MINOR (continued) | 6.5 | Rapeseed/rape/rutabaga/swede | Cruciferae |
| | 6.5 | Vetivert | Gramineae |
| | 6.5 | Nutmeg/mace | Myristicaceae |
| | 6.3 | Anthurium | Araceae |
| | 6.3 | Velvet bentgrass/creeping bentgrass/colonial bentgrass | Gramineae |
| | 6.1 | Ageratum | Compositae |
| | 6.1 | Magnolia | Magnoliaceae |
| | 6.0 | Salvia | Labiatae |
| | 6.0 | Cyclamen | Primulaceae |
| | 5.9 | Cumin | Umbelliferae |
| | 5.9 | Cork | Fagaceae |
| | 5.8 | Alyssum | Cruciferae |
| | 5.3 | Orchard grass/cocksfoot | Gramineae |
| | 5.3 | Ornamental pear | Rosaceae |
| | 5.2 | Taro/dasheen | Araceae |
| | 5.2 | Turnip/Chinese cabbage | Cruciferae |
| | 5.2 | Rattan | Palmae |
| | 5.2 | Ginger | Zingiberaceae |
| | 4.9 | Chestnut | Fagaceae |
| | 4.9 | Patchouli | Labiatae |
| | 4.7 | Locust bean/carob | Leguminosae |
| | 4.6 | Ladino clover/white clover | Leguminosae |
| | 4.2 | Caraway | Umbelliferae |
| | 4.1 | Geranium oil | Geraniaceae |
| | 4.1 | Portulacca | Portulacaceae |
| | 4.0 | Chicory/witloof/Belgian endive | Compositae |
| | 3.9 | Sisal | Agavaceae |
| | 3.9 | Black wattle | Leguminosae |
| | 3.8 | Asparagus plumosus | Liliaceae |
| | 3.7 | Kapok | Bombacaceae |
| | 3.7 | Okra | Malvaceae |
| | 3.7 | Sandalwood | Santalaceae |
| | 3.6 | Sour orange/Seville orange | Rutaceae |
| | 3.5 | Citrus fruits, juices, and oils nspf | Rutaceae |
| | 3.1 | Citronella | Gramineae |
| | 2.8 | Wild rice | Gramineae |
| | 2.7 | Henequen | Agavaceae |
| | 2.7 | Gum arabic | Leguminosae |
| | 2.6 | Sweet clover | Leguminosae |
| | 2.5 | Ylang ylang/cananga | Annonaceae |
| | 2.4 | Pomegranate | Punicaceae |

Table 7.2  (*Continued*)

| CROP CATEGORY (Number of crops) | AVERAGE ANNUAL VALUE OF CROP *U.S. farm sales and imports* (U.S. $ million) | CROP | CROP FAMILY |
|---|---|---|---|
| MINOR (*continued*) | 2.3 | Guava | Myrtaceae |
| | 2.1 | Caper | Capparidaceae |
| | 2.0 | Lavender oil/spike lavender oil | Labiatae |
| | 2.0 | Cinnamon | Lauraceae |
| | 2.0 | Mungbean | Leguminosae |
| | 1.9 | Wheatgrass | Gramineae |
| | 1.9 | Ornamental crocus | Iridaceae |
| | 1.9 | Common vetch/hairy vetch | Leguminosae |
| | 1.8 | Chinese gooseberry/kiwi fruit | Actinidiaceae |
| | 1.8 | Statice | Plumbaginaceae |
| | 1.8 | Calceolaria | Scrophulariaceae |
| | 1.6 | Crimson clover | Leguminosae |
| | 1.5 | Sage | Labiatae |
| | 1.5 | Litchi | Sapindaceae |
| | 1.5 | Coriander | Umbelliferae |
| | 1.4 | Pigeon pea | Leguminosae |
| | 1.4 | Eucalyptus | Myrtaceae |
| | 1.3 | Birdsfoot trefoil | Leguminosae |
| | 1.3 | Turmeric | Zingiberaceae |
| | 1.2 | Jicama | Leguminosae |
| | 1.1 | Radish | Cruciferae |
| | 1.1 | Meadow brome/California brome/smooth brome | Gramineae |
| | 1.1 | Hearts of palm | Palmae |
| | 1.0 | Saffron | Iridaceae |
| | 1.0 | Cardamon | Zingiberaceae |

Note: See note 1 for explanation.

apparent rate of domestication per millennium has increased in terms of the number of species domesticated but has declined in terms of the current combined value of the crops. The picture changes significantly when we examine the apparent rate of domestication per century. The number of species domesticated every 100 years was roughly constant until A.D. 1700, when it shot up from 1.4 species/century to 17.0 species/century. The twentieth century (with 6 species so far), is substantially below the eighteenth and nineteenth centuries but well above the prehistoric rate of domestication. In terms of the value of the crops domesticated, however, the recent period is not notably greater than the ancient and early periods; but the new (twentieth century) period marks an all-time low. The reasons for the sharp increase in the number of species domesti-

(*text continued on page 226*)

Table 7.3  **Periods of domestication and average annual values (1976–1980) of 226 crop species grown or imported by the United States**

| | CROP | PERIOD WHEN DOMESTICATED | | | | |
|---|---|---|---|---|---|---|
| FAMILY | SPECIES | Ancient/B.C. before 5000 | Early/B.C. 5000–0 | Late/A.D. 0–1700 | Recent/A.D. 1700–1900 | New/A.D. 1900 on |
| ACERACEAE | *Acer* spp. Ornamental maple | | | | | |
| ACTINIDIACEAE | *Actinidia chinensis* Chinese gooseberry/kiwi fruit | | | | | S-497 |
| AGAVACEAE | *Agave fourcroydes* Henequen | | V-122, V-123 | | | |
| | *Agave sisalana* Sisal | | | | V-122 | |
| | *Dracaena* spp. Dracaena | | | | | |
| ALLIACEAE | *Allium cepa* Onion | | M-83, S-123 | | | |
| | *Allium sativum* Garlic | | S-123 | | | |
| AMARYLLIDACEAE | *Narcissus* spp. Narcissus/daffodil | | | G-746 | | |
| ANACARDIACEAE | *Anacardium occidentale* Cashew | | | | | Page 233 |
| | *Mangifera indica* Mango | | M-182, M-186, M-191 | | | |
| ANNONACEAE | *Cananga odorata* Ylang ylang/cananga | | | | G-76 | |
| AQUIFOLIACEAE | *Ilex* spp. Holly | | | | | |
| ARACEAE | *Anthurium* spp. Anthurium | | | | | |
| | *Colocasia esculenta* Taro/dasheen | | P-39 | | | |
| | *Dieffenbachia maculata* D. seguine Dieffenbachia | | | | | |
| | *Philodendron scandens* Monstera deliciosa Philodendron | | | | | |
| ARALIACEAE | *Panax ginseng* Ginseng | | | | | |
| | *P. quinquefolium* American ginseng | | | | M-577 | |
| BALSAMINACEAE | *Impatiens balsamina* Impatiens | | | | | |
| BEGONIACEAE | *Begonia* spp. Begonia | | | | G-14 | |
| BOMBACACEAE | *Ceiba pentandra* Kapok | | | Y-24, Y-25 | | |
| BROMELIACEAE | *Ananas comosus* Pineapple | | | S-123 | | |

| U.S. farm sales | U.S. imports (customs value) | Total farm sales and imports | Category |
|---|---|---|---|
| 45.2 (1978 only) | — | 45.2 | Medium |
| ? | 1.8 | 1.8 | Minor |
| — | 2.7 | 2.7 | Minor |
| — | 3.9 | 3.9 | Minor |
| 38.6 | — | 38.6 | Medium |
| 264.8 | 22.1 | 286.9 | Major |
| 23.0 | 8.8 | 31.8 | Medium |
| 4.0 (1978 only) | 3.9 | 7.9 | Minor |
| — | 116.1 | 116.1 | Major |
| ? | 8.6 | 8.6 | Minor |
| — | 2.5 | 2.5 | Minor |
| 27.5 (1978 only) | — | 27.5 | Medium |
| 6.3 (1978 only) | — | 6.3 | Minor |
| 1.0 | 4.2 | 5.2 | Minor |
| 33.0 (1978 only) | — | 33.0 | Medium |
| 52.7 (1978 only) | — | 52.7 | Medium |
| 20.1 | 7.8 | 27.9 | Medium |
| 17.7 | — | 17.7 | Medium |
| 26.0 | 2.1 | 28.1 | Medium |
| — | 3.7 | 3.7 | Minor |
| 65.2 | 120.8 | 186.0 | Major |

(*continued*)

Table 7.3 (**Continued**)

| FAMILY | SPECIES | Ancient/B.C. before 5000 | Early/B.C. 5000–0 | Late/A.D. 0–1700 | Recent/A.D. 1700–1900 | New/A.D. 1900 on |
|---|---|---|---|---|---|---|
| | | | | PERIOD WHEN DOMESTICATED | | |
| CACTACEAE | Cacti | | | | | |
| CANNABIDACEAE | Humulus lupulus Hops | | | M-243 | | |
| CAPPARIDACEAE | Capparis spinosa Caper | | | | | |
| CARICACEAE | Carica papaya Papaya | | S-226 | | | |
| CARYOPHYLLACEAE | Dianthus caryophyllus Carnation Gypsophila arrostii G. muralis Gypsophila | | | | | |
| CELASTRACEAE | Euonymus Euonymus | | | | | |
| CHENOPODIACEAE | Beta vulgaris Beet/beetroot/sugar beet | | Vegetable beet A-267 | | Sugar beet A-267 | |
| | Spinacia oleracea Spinach | | | G-833, P-302, S-171 | | |
| COMPOSITAE | Ageratum houstonianum Ageratum | | | | | |
| | Carthamus tinctorius Safflower | | J-137 | | | |
| | Chrysanthemum cinerariifolium Pyrethrum | | | | A-443, M-101 | |
| | Chrysanthemum morifolium Chrysanthemum | | G-746 | | | |
| | Cichorium endivia Endive/escarole | | S-171 | | | |
| | Cichorium intybus Chicory/witloof/Belgian endive | | S-171 | G-467 | | |
| | Cynara scolymus Globe artichoke/ artichoke | | Y-83 | | | |
| | Helianthus annuus Sunflower | | A-330, A-376, G-219 | | | |
| | Lactuca sativa Lettuce | | J-225, P-217 | | | |
| | Tagetes erecta T. lucida T. patula Marigold | | | G-746 | | |
| | Zinnia elegans Zinnia | | | | M-646 | |
| CONVOLVULACEAE | Ipomoea batatas Sweet potato | Y-10 | | | | |
| CORNACEAE | Cornus florida Dogwood | | | | | |

AVERAGE ANNUAL VALUE, 1976–1980 (U.S.$ MILLION)

| U.S. farm sales | U.S. imports (customs value) | Total farm sales and imports | Category |
|---|---|---|---|
| 33.1 (1978 only) | ? | 33.1 | Medium |
| 63.8 | 21.5 | 85.3 | Medium |
| — | 2.1 | 2.1 | Minor |
| 8.4 | 1.9 | 10.3 | Medium |
| 67.1 (1978 only) | 2.6 (1980 only) | 69.7 | Medium |
| 7.6 (1978 only) | — | 7.6 | Minor |
| 17.2 (1978 only) | — | 17.2 | Medium |
| 719.5 | 40.0 | 759.5 | Major |
| 32.1 | 0.1 (Seed only) | 32.2 | Medium |
| 6.1 | — | 6.1 | Minor |
| 52.1 (1974 only) | ? | 52.1 | Medium |
| — | 11.9 | 11.9 | Medium |
| 197.5 | — | 197.5 | Major |
| 18.0 | — | 18.0 | Medium |
| ? | 4.0 | 4.0 | Minor |
| 20.1 | 9.2 | 29.3 | Medium |
| 391.4 | 2.0 | 393.4 | Major |
| 526.2 | 1.1 | 527.3 | Major |
| 25.4 (1978 only) | — | 25.4 | Medium |
| 7.3 (1978 only) | — | 7.3 | Minor |
| 107.9 | 1.7 (1978–1980 only) | 109.6 | Major |
| 10.3 (1978 only) | — | 10.3 | Medium |

*(continued)*

# Table 7.3 (*Continued*)

| FAMILY | SPECIES | Ancient/B.C. before 5000 | Early/B.C. 5000–0 | Late/A.D. 0–1700 | Recent/A.D. 1700–1900 | New/A.D. 1900 on |
|---|---|---|---|---|---|---|
| | | | | **PERIOD WHEN DOMESTICATED** | | |
| CORYLACEAE | *Corylus avellana*<br>*C. colurna*<br>*C. maxima*<br>Filbert | | | S-171 | | |
| CRUCIFERAE | *Brassica campestris*<br>Turnip/Chinese cabbage | | G-334, P-322 | | | |
| | *Brassica juncea*<br>Brown mustard/mustard greens | | Brown mustard<br>M-224, P-322 | | | |
| | *Sinapis alba*<br>White mustard | | | | | |
| | *Brassica napus*<br>Rapeseed/rape/rutabaga/swede [Rapeseed also comes from *B. campestris* (turnip)] | | Swede P-322 | Swede M-102<br>Rape M-102 | Rape G-334, P-322, S-686<br>Rutabaga G-334, S-686 | |
| | *Brassica oleracea*<br>Broccoli/brussels sprouts/cabbage/cauliflower/kale/kohlrabi/collards | | Broccoli P-322<br>Cabbage P-322<br>Kale P-322<br>Collards P-322 | Brussels sprouts P-322<br>Cauliflower G-334, S-279<br>Kohlrabi S-686 | Brussels sprouts S-279, S-686 | |
| | *Lobularia maritima*<br>Alyssum | | | | | |
| | *Raphanus sativus*<br>Radish | | A-202 | S-686 | | |
| CUCURBITACEAE | *Citrullus lanatus*<br>Watermelon | | G-421, S-123, V-106 | | | |
| | *Cucurbita maxima*<br>*C. moschata*<br>*C. pepo*<br>Squashes/pumpkins | | *C. maxima* V-368<br>*C. moschata* A-482<br>*C. pepo* A-482 | | | |
| | *Cucumis melo*<br>Melon | | | G-467, V-106 | | |
| | *Cucumis sativus*<br>Cucumber | | V-105, V-106 | | | |
| CUPRESSACEAE | *Juniperus* spp.<br>Ornamental juniper | | | | | |
| CYPERACEAE | *Eleocharis dulcis*<br>Water chestnut | | | | | |
| ERICACEAE | *Rhododendron* spp.<br>Azalea/rhododendron | | | | | |
| | *Vaccinium ashei*<br>Rabbiteye blueberry | | | | Rabbiteye (G-744, M-633) | |
| | *V. australe*<br>*V. corymbosum*<br>Highbush blueberry | | | | | Highbush (A-909) |
| | *Vaccinium macrocarpon*<br>Cranberry | | | | G-744 | |

| U.S. farm sales | U.S. imports (customs value) | Total farm sales and imports | Category |
|---|---|---|---|
| 10.6 | 8.4 | 19.0 | Medium |
| ? | 5.2 | 5.2 | Minor |
| 4.7 (1974 mustard seed only) | 13.0 | 17.7 | Medium |
| ? | 6.5 | 6.5 | Minor |
| 104.8 (Broccoli only) | 4.6 (Broccoli: 1978–80 only) | 365.2 | Major |
| 21.8 (Brussels sprouts only) | 1.5 (Brussels sprouts: 1977–80 only) | | |
| 155.4 (Cabbage only) | 2.3 (Cabbage only) | | |
| 72.4 (Cauliflower only) | 2.4 (Cauliflower only) | | |
| 5.8 (1978 only) | — | 5.8 | Minor |
| ? | 1.1 | 1.1 | Minor |
| 107.2 | 9.1 | 116.3 | Major |
| ? | 11.8 | 11.8 | Medium |
| 164.5 | 24.9 | 189.4 | Major |
| 158.5 | 33.8 | 192.3 | Major |
| 76.2 (1978 only) | — | 76.2 | Medium |
| — | 8.9 | 8.9 | Minor |
| 100.0 (1978 only) | — | 100.0 | Major |
| ? | — | ? | |
| 41.6 | 2.4 | 44.0 | Medium |
| 51.0 | .8 | 51.8 | Medium |

(*continued*)

Table 7.3  (*Continued*)

| FAMILY | SPECIES | Ancient/B.C. before 5000 | Early/B.C. 5000–0 | Late/A.D. 0–1700 | Recent/A.D. 1700–1900 | New/A.D. 1900 on |
|---|---|---|---|---|---|---|
| EUPHORBIACEAE | *Euphorbia pulcherrima* Poinsettia | | | | | |
| | *Hevea brasiliensis* Rubber | | | | V-185 | |
| | *Manihot esculenta* Cassava/manioc/tapioca | | P-166, P-167 | | | |
| | *Ricinus communis* Castor | | S-132 | | | |
| | *Vernicia fordii* *V. montana* Tung | | S-123 | | | |
| FAGACEAE | *Castanea sativa* Chestnut | | J-567, S-171 | | | |
| | *Quercus* spp. Ornamental oak | | | | | |
| | *Quercus suber* Cork | | | | A-532 | |
| GERANIACEAE | *Pelargonium graveolens* *Pelargonium* spp. Geranium oil | | | | G-76 | |
| | *Pelargonium* spp. Ornamental geranium | | | | | |
| GESNERIACEAE | *Saintpaulia ionantha* African violet/saint-paulia | | | | | |
| | *Sinningia speciosa* Gloxinia | | | | | |
| GRAMINEAE | *Agropyron* spp. Wheatgrass | | | | | |
| | *Agrostis canina* Velvet bentgrass | | | | | |
| | *A. stolonifera* var. *palustris* Creeping bentgrass | | | | | |
| | *A. tenuis* Colonial bentgrass | | | | | |
| | *Avena sativa* Oats | | A-211, A-435 | | | |
| | *Bambusa* spp. *Dendrocalamus* spp. *Gigantochloa* spp. *Phyllostachys* spp. *Schizostachyum* spp. Bamboo | | | | | |
| | *Bromus biebersteinii* Meadow brome | | | | | G-142 |
| | *B. carinatus* California brome | | | | | G-142 |
| | *B. inermis* Smooth brome | | | | G-142 | |
| | *Cymbopogon nardus* *C. winterianus* Citronella | | | | G-76 | |
| | *Cynodon dactylon* Bermuda grass | | | | G-142 | |

| U.S. farm sales | U.S. imports (customs value) | Total farm sales and imports | Category |
|---|---|---|---|
| 85.8 (1978 only) | — | 85.8 | Medium |
| — | 706.4 | 706.4 | Major |
| — | 9.3 | 9.3 | Minor |
| — | 40.5 | 40.5 | Medium |
| — | 10.9 | 10.9 | Medium |
| ? | 4.9 | 4.9 | Minor |
| 26.8 (1978 only) | — | 26.8 | Medium |
| — | 5.9 | 5.9 | Minor |
| — | 4.1 | 4.1 | Minor |
| 91.4 (1978 only) | — | 91.4 | Medium |
| 12.9 (1978 only) | — | 12.9 | Medium |
| 8.8 (1978 only) | — | 8.8 | Minor |
| 1.5 (1974: seed only) | .4 | 1.9 | Minor |
| 6.3 (Seed only) | .03 | 6.3 | Minor |
| 301.3 | 2.9 | 304.2 | Major |
| — | 24.0 | 24.8 | Medium |
| 1.1 (1974: seed only) | — | 1.1 | Minor |
| — | 3.1 | 3.1 | Minor |
| 130.0 (1974: hay) | — | 130.0 | Major |

(*continued*)

## Table 7.3  (*Continued*)

| FAMILY | SPECIES | Ancient/B.C. before 5000 | Early/B.C. 5000–0 | Late/A.D. 0–1700 | Recent/A.D. 1700–1900 | New/A.D. 1900 on |
|---|---|---|---|---|---|---|
| GRAMINEAE (continued) | *Dactylis glomerata* Orchard grass/cocksfoot | | | | A-266 | |
| | *Festuca arundinacea* Tall fescue | | | | Tall and meadow (A-299, G-142) | |
| | *F. pratensis* Meadow fescue | | | | | |
| | *F. rubra* Red fescue | | | | | |
| | *Hordeum vulgare* Barley | G-170, G-834 | | | | |
| | *Lolium multiflorum* Italian ryegrass/annual ryegrass | | | A-266 | | |
| | *L. perenne* Perennial ryegrass | | | | | |
| | *Oryza sativa* Rice | | A-390 | | | |
| | *Panicum miliaceum* Proso millet | P-124 | | | | |
| | *Phleum pratense* Timothy | | | | A-266 | |
| | *Poa pratensis* Kentucky bluegrass | | | | | |
| | *Saccharum officinarum* Sugarcane | | A-971, S-123 | | | |
| | *Secale cereale* Rye | | J-97 | | | |
| | *Sorghum bicolor* Sorghum/broomcorn | | D-31, V-96 | | | |
| | *Triticum aestivum* subsp. *compactum* Club wheat | D-144 | | | | |
| | *T. a.* subsp. *spelta* Spelt | | | | | |
| | *T. a.* subsp. *vulgare* Common wheat | | | | | |
| | *T. turgidum* subsp. *turgidum* conv. *durum* Durum wheat | | | | | |
| | *Vetiveria zizanoides* Vetivert | | | | | |
| | *Zea mays* Corn/maize | Around 5000 B.C. (G-4–G-6, M-29, M-458, V-144) | | | | |
| | *Zizania aquatica* Wild rice | | | | | M-654 |
| HYDRANGEACEAE | *Hydrangea* spp. Hydrangea | | | | | |
| IRIDACEAE | *Crocus sativus* Saffron | | | G-368, P-183 | | |
| | *Crocus* spp. Ornamental crocus | | | | | |

| U.S. farm sales | U.S. imports (customs value) | Total farm sales and imports | Category |
|---|---|---|---|
| 5.2 (Seed only) | .1 | 5.3 | Minor |
| 28.4 (Seed only) | 7.1 (Seed only) | 35.5 | Medium |
| 636.9 | 35.4 | 672.3 | Major |
| 37.7 (Seed only) | .3 (Seed only) | 38.0 | Medium |
| 1,159.4 | 3.7 | 1,163.1 | Super |
| 16.4 (1974 only) | — | 16.4 | Medium |
| 5.0 (Seed only) | .6 (Seed only) | 786.9 | Major |
| 781.3 (1974: hay and clover) | | | |
| 24.3 (Seed only) | .4 | 24.7 | Medium |
| 485.9 | 1,236.6 | 1,722.5 | Super |
| 31.9 | 2.0 | 33.9 | Medium |
| 1,133.3 | 13.2 | 1,146.5 | Super |
| 6,450.5 (Excludes spelt and triticale) | 24.6 | 6,475.1 | Super |
| — | 6.5 | 6.5 | Minor |
| 10,391.7 | 20.7 | 10,412.4 | Super |
| 2.8 | — | 2.8 | Minor |
| 10.0 (1978 only) | — | 10.0 | Medium |
| — | 1.0 | 1.0 | Minor |
| — | 1.9 | 1.9 | Minor |

(*continued*)

# Table 7.3 (*Continued*)

| | CROP | PERIOD WHEN DOMESTICATED | | | | |
|---|---|---|---|---|---|---|
| FAMILY | SPECIES | Ancient/B.C. before 5000 | Early/B.C. 5000–0 | Late/A.D. 0–1700 | Recent/A.D. 1700–1900 | New/A.D. 1900 on |
| IRIDACEAE (continued) | *Gladiolus* spp. Gladiolus | | | | | |
| | *Iris* spp. Iris | | | G-14 | | |
| JUGLANDACEAE | *Carya illinoensis* Pecan | | | | M-22, M-625 | |
| | *Juglans regia* Walnut/Persian walnut/ English walnut | | G-467, P-302 | | | |
| LABIATAE | *Coleus blumei* Coleus | | | | | |
| | *Lavandula angustifolia* Lavender oil | | | | | G-76 |
| | *L. latifolia* Spike lavender oil | | | | | |
| | *Mentha arvensis* Japanese mint/corn mint | | | G-76 | | |
| | *Mentha* × *piperita* Peppermint | | | | G-832, P-183 | |
| | *Mentha spicata* Spearmint | | P-183, P-302 | | | |
| | *Mentha* × *gentilis* Scotch spearmint | | | | | |
| | *Pogostemon cablin* Patchouli | | | | G-76 | |
| | *Salvia* spp. Salvia | | | | | |
| | *Salvia officinalis* *S. triloba* Sage | | P-302 | | | |
| LAURACEAE | *Cinnamomum aromaticum* *C. burmannii* Cassia | | | | | |
| | *Cinnamomum verum* Cinnamon | | | | P-256 | |
| | *Persea americana* Avocado | By 5000 B.C. (A-233) | | | | |
| LEGUMINOSAE | *Acacia mearnsii* Black wattle | | | | S-96 | |
| | *Acacia senegal* *A. seyal* Gum arabic | | | | | |
| | *Arachis hypogaea* Peanut/groundnut | | G-69 | | | |
| | *Cajanus cajan* Pigeon pea | | A-342, D-12, P-206 | | | |
| | *Ceratonia siliqua* Locust bean/carob | | G-527 | | | |
| | *Cicer arietinum* Chickpea/garbanzo | J-164, P-100, Y-58 | | | | |
| | *Cyamopsis tetragonoloba* Guar | | | G-742 | | |

| U.S. farm sales | U.S. imports (customs value) | Total farm sales and imports | Category |
|---|---|---|---|
| 20.1 (1978 only) | 1.2 | 21.3 | Medium |
| 5.0 (1978 only) | 1.6 | 6.6 | Minor |
| 99.7 | 1.8 | 101.5 | Major |
| 163.4 | .5 | 163.9 | Major |
| 6.9 (1978 only) | — | 6.9 | Minor |
| — | 2.0 | 2.0 | Minor |
| — | 19.1 | 19.1 | Medium |
| 54.5 | .7 | 55.2 | Medium |
| 22.3 | .06 | 22.4 | Medium |
| — | 4.9 | 4.9 | Minor |
| 6.0 | — | 6.0 | Minor |
| ? | 1.5 | 1.5 | Minor |
| — | 11.4 | 11.4 | Medium |
| — | 2.0 | 2.0 | Minor |
| 93.4 | .4 | 93.8 | Medium |
| — | 3.9 | 3.9 | Minor |
| — | 2.7 | 2.7 | Minor |
| 746.3 | .5 | 746.8 | Major |
| — | 1.4 (1980 only) | 1.4 | Minor |
| — | 4.7 | 4.7 | Minor |
| 1.9 | 7.2 | 9.1 | Minor |
| 1.4 (1974 only) | 26.1 | 27.5 | Medium |

(continued)

**215**

Table 7.3  (*Continued*)

| FAMILY | SPECIES | Ancient/B.C. before 5000 | Early/B.C. 5000–0 | Late/A.D. 0–1700 | Recent/A.D. 1700–1900 | New/A.D. 1900 on |
|---|---|---|---|---|---|---|
| | | | PERIOD WHEN DOMESTICATED | | | |
| LEGUMINOSAE (continued) | *Glycine max* Soybean | | G-317 | | | |
| | *Glycyrrhiza glabra* Licorice | | S-171 | | | |
| | *Lens culinaris* Lentil | Y-40 | | | | |
| | *Lespedeza cuneata* Sericea/perennial lespedeza | | | | | |
| | *L. stipulacea* Korean lespedeza | | | | | |
| | *L. striata* Japanese lespedeza/ annual lespedeza | | | | | |
| | *Lotus corniculatus* Birdsfoot trefoil | | | | S-731 | |
| | *Medicago sativa* Alfalfa/lucerne | | A-1421, J-338 | | | |
| | *Melilotus alba* *M. officinalis* Sweet clover | | | | G-53 | |
| | *Pachyrhizus erosus* Jicama | | | | | |
| | *Phaseolus lunatus* Lima bean | | D-104, J-51 | | | |
| | *Phaseolus vulgaris* Common bean/green bean/French bean/ snap bean/dry bean | D-104, J-51, J-593 | | | | |
| | *Pisum sativum* Pea | Y-58 | | | | |
| | *Trifolium incarnatum* Crimson clover | | | | D-105, J-594 | |
| | *Trifolium pratense* Red clover | | | D-105 | | |
| | *Trifolium repens* Ladino clover/white clover | | | | D-105 | |
| | *Vicia sativa* Common vetch | | | | | |
| | *V. villosa* Hairy vetch | | | | | |
| | *Vigna radiata* Mungbean | | | | | |
| | *Vigna unguiculata* Cowpea/black-eyed pea | | S-207 | | | |
| LILIACEAE | *Asparagus officinalis* Asparagus | | S-171 | | | |
| | *Asparagus plumosus* Asparagus plumosus | | | | | |
| | *Hyacinthus orientalis* Hyacinth | | | | | |
| | *Lilium longiflorum* Easter lily | | | | | |

| U.S. farm sales | U.S. imports (customs value) | Total farm sales and imports | Category |
|---|---|---|---|
| 11,271.6 | 6.8 | 11,278.4 | Super |
| — | 13.9 | 13.9 | Medium |
| 18.1 (1974 only) | .4 | 18.5 | Medium |
| 22.4 (1974: hay) 4.2 (Seed only) | — | 26.6 | Medium |
| 1.3 (1974: seed) | — | 1.3 | Minor |
| 1,053.6 | .1 | 1,053.7 | Super |
| 1.0 (1974: seed) | 1.6 (Seed only) | 2.6 | Minor |
| — | 1.2 | 1.2 | Minor |
| 50.6 | .04 | 50.6 | Medium |
| 505.9 | 10.7 | 516.6 | Major |
| 129.8 | 12.2 | 142.0 | Major |
| 1.6 (Seed only) | .01 (Seed only) | 1.6 | Minor |
| 14.9 (Seed only) | 2.2 (Seed only) | 17.1 | Medium |
| 4.2 (Seed only) | .4 (Seed only) | 4.6 | Minor |
| 1.9 (Seed only) | .03 (Seed only) | 1.9 | Minor |
| — | 2.0 | 2.0 | Minor |
| 14.5 | .5 | 15.0 | Medium |
| 82.1 | 8.2 | 90.3 | Medium |
| 3.8 | — | 3.8 | Minor |
| 4.2 (1978 only) | 3.6 | 7.8 | Minor |
| 27.2 (1978 only) | .6 (Bulbs only) | 27.8 | Medium |

(*continued*)

# Table 7.3  (*Continued*)

| FAMILY | SPECIES | Ancient/B.C. before 5000 | Early/B.C. 5000–0 | Late/A.D. 0–1700 | Recent/A.D. 1700–1900 | New/A.D. 1900 on |
|---|---|---|---|---|---|---|
| | | | PERIOD WHEN DOMESTICATED | | | |
| LILIACEAE (continued) | *Lilium* spp. Other lilies | | *L. candidum* S-594 | | | |
| | *Tulipa gesneriana* Tulip | | | G-746, S-493 | | |
| LINACEAE | *Linum usitatissimum* Flax/linseed | D-14 | | | | |
| MAGNOLIACEAE | *Magnolia* spp. Magnolia | | | | | |
| MALVACEAE | *Abelmoschus esculenta* Okra | | | | | |
| | *Gossypium hirsutum* | | P-269 | | | |
| | *G. barbadense* Cotton | | P-269 | | | |
| MORACEAE | *Ficus carica* Fig | | Y-46 | | | |
| MUSACEAE | *Musa acuminata* *M. balbisiana* Banana/plantain | | S-122, S-123 | | | |
| | *Musa textilis* Abaca | | | | | |
| MYRISTICACEAE | *Myristica fragrans* Nutmeg/mace | | | | | |
| MYRTACEAE | *Eucalyptus globulus* Eucalyptus | | | | G-76 | |
| | *Psidium guajava* Guava | | S-171 | | | |
| | *Syzygium aromaticum* Clove | | V-166 | | | |
| OLEACEAE | *Fraxinus* spp. Ornamental ash | | | | | |
| | *Olea europaea* Olive | | A-248, Y-46 | | | |
| ONAGRACEAE | *Fuchsia* spp. Fuchsia | | | | G-746 | |
| ORCHIDACEAE | *Cattleya* spp. *Cymbidium* spp. *Cypripedium* spp. *Vanda* spp. Orchids | | | | | |
| | *Vanilla planifolia* Vanilla | | | P-257 | | |
| PALMAE | *Calamus* spp. Rattan | | | | D-69 | |
| | *Cocos nucifera* Coconut | | | | | |

| U.S. farm sales | U.S. imports (customs value) | Total farm sales and imports | Category |
|---|---|---|---|
| 9.4 | 11.9 | 21.3 | Medium |
| 59.3 | 21.9 | 81.2 | Medium |
| 6.1 (1978 only) | — | 6.1 | Minor |
| ? | 3.7 | 3.7 | Minor |
| 3,794.0 | 439.0 | 4,233.0 | Super |
| 45.0 | 30.0 | 75.0 | Medium |
| 11.2 | 10.7 | 21.9 | Medium |
| 1.0 | 367.2 | 368.2 | Major |
| — | 22.8 | 22.8 | Medium |
| — | 6.5 | 6.5 | Minor |
| — | 1.4 | 1.4 | Minor |
| — | 2.3 | 2.3 | Minor |
| — | 10.3 | 10.3 | Medium |
| 27.7 (1978 only) | — | 27.7 | Medium |
| 29.0 | 114.9 | 143.9 | Major |
| 8.7 (1978 only) | — | 8.7 | Minor |
| 8.5 (1978: *Cymbidium*) 3.5 (1978: *Cattleya*) .8 (1978: *Vanda* and *Cypripedium*) 1.3 (1978: other cut orchids) 11.5 (1978: potted orchids) | .2 (Orchid plants) | 25.8 | Medium |
| — | 21.1 | 21.1 | Medium |
| — | 5.2 | 5.2 | Minor |
| — | 314.3 | 314.3 | Major |

*(continued)*

# Table 7.3 (*Continued*)

| FAMILY | SPECIES | Ancient/B.C. before 5000 | Early/B.C. 5000–0 | Late/A.D. 0–1700 | Recent/A.D. 1700–1900 | New/A.D. 1900 on |
|---|---|---|---|---|---|---|
| | | CROP | | PERIOD WHEN DOMESTICATED | | |
| PALMAE (continued) | *Elaeis guineensis* Oil palm | | | | G-189, S-186 | |
| | *Phoenix dactylifera* Date | | Y-46 | | | |
| | ? Ornamental palms *Bactris gasipaes* *Euterpe edulis* Hearts of palm (main sources) | | | | | |
| PAPAVERACEAE | *Papaver somniferum* Opium poppy | | S-171, S-433 | | | |
| PEDALIACEAE | *Sesamum indicum* Sesame | | M-238, M-239 | | | |
| PINACEAE | *Picea* spp. Ornamental spruce *Pinus* spp. Ornamental pine | | | | | |
| PIPERACEAE | *Piper nigrum* Black pepper/white pepper | | P-256 | | | |
| PISTACIACEAE | *Pistacia vera* Pistachio | | S-171 | | | |
| PITTOSPORACEAE | *Pittosporum undulatum* Pittosporum | | | | | |
| PLANTAGINACEAE | *Plantago ovata* Psyllium | | | | | |
| PLUMBAGINACEAE | *Limonium* spp. Statice | | | | | |
| POLYGONACEAE | *Fagopyrum esculentum* Buckwheat | | | A-368 | | |
| PORTULACACEAE | *Portulaca grandiflora* Portulaca | | | | | |
| PRIMULACEAE | *Cyclamen persicum* Cyclamen | | | | | |
| PROTEACEAE | *Macadamia integrifolia* Macadamia nut | | | | S-720 | |
| PUNICACEAE | *Punica granatum* Pomegranate | | Y-46 | | | |
| ROSACEAE | *Fragaria* × *ananassa* Strawberry | | | Page 230 | | |
| | *Malus pumila* Apple | | A-1236, V-46 | | | |
| | *Malus* spp. Ornamental apple | | | | | |
| | *Prunus armeniaca* Apricot | | V-47 | | | |
| | *Prunus avium* Sweet cherry | | D-499, V-47 | | | |
| | *P. cerasus* Sour cherry | | | | | |

AVERAGE ANNUAL VALUE, 1976–1980 (U.S.$ MILLION)

| U.S. farm sales | U.S. imports (customs value) | Total farm sales and imports | Category |
|---|---|---|---|
| — | 143.3 | 143.3 | Major |
| 10.3 | 9.0 | 19.3 | Medium |
| 39.1 (1978 only) | — | 39.1 | Medium |
| — | 1.1 | 1.1 | Minor |
| — | 34.7 | 34.7 | Medium |
| — | 30.4 | 30.4 | Medium |
| 22.7 (1978 only) | — | 22.7 | Medium |
| 49.1 (1978 only) | — | 49.1 | Medium |
| — | 54.8 | 54.8 | Medium |
| ? | 26.9 | 26.9 | Medium |
| 9.1 (1978 only) | — | 9.1 | Minor |
| — | 7.3 | 7.3 | Minor |
| 1.8 | — | 1.8 | Minor |
| 7.4 (1974 only) | 0.3 | 7.7 | Minor |
| 4.1 (1978 only) | — | 4.1 | Minor |
| 6.0 (1978 only) | — | 6.0 | Minor |
| 13.3 | — | 13.3 | Medium |
| 2.4 | — | 2.4 | Minor |
| 218.9 | 33.0 | 251.9 | Major |
| 751.4 | 63.2 | 814.6 | Major |
| 18.6 (1978 only) | — | 18.6 | Medium |
| 32.5 | 4.9 | 37.4 | Medium |
| 146.7 | 1.0 | 147.7 | Major |

(continued)

## Table 7.3 (*Continued*)

| FAMILY | SPECIES | Ancient/B.C. before 5000 | Early/B.C. 5000–0 | Late/A.D. 0–1700 | Recent/A.D. 1700–1900 | New/A.D. 1900 on |
|---|---|---|---|---|---|---|
| | | | | PERIOD WHEN DOMESTICATED | | |
| ROSACEAE (continued) | *Prunus domestica* *P. salicina* Plum/prune | | V-358 | | | |
| | *Prunus dulcis* Almond | | G-467, P-302, V-47 | | | |
| | *Prunus persica* Peach/nectarine | | G-755, V-50 | | | |
| | *Prunus* spp. Ornamental cherry and plum | | | | | |
| | *Pyrus communis* Pear | | J-587 | | | |
| | *Pyrus* spp. Ornamental pear | | | | | |
| | *Rosa* spp. Roses | | G-746 | | | |
| | *Rubus idaeus* Red raspberry | | | J-17, M-641 | | |
| | *R. occidentalis* Black raspberry | | | | | |
| | *Rubus lacinatus* *R. ursinus* Blackberry | | | | D-366 | |
| RUBIACEAE | *Cinchona calisaya* *C. officinalis* *C. pubescens* Cinchona/quinine/ quinidine | | | | G-187, G-188 | |
| | *Coffea arabica* *C. canephora* Coffee | | | D-148, V-78 | | |
| RUTACEAE | *Citrus aurantiifolia* Lime | | A-367, S-708, S-730 | | | |
| | *Citrus aurantium* Sour orange/Seville orange | | A-367, S-708, S-730 | | | |
| | *Citrus limon* Lemon | | A-367, S-708, S-730 | | | |
| | *Citrus paradisi* Grapefruit | | Page 230 | | | |
| | *Citrus paradisi* × *reticulata* Tangelo | | | | | |
| | *Citrus reticulata* Tangerine/mandarin | | A-367, S-708, S-730 | | | |
| | *Citrus sinensis* Orange/sweet orange | | A-367, S-708, S-730 | | | |
| | *Citrus* spp. Citrus fruits, juices, and oils nspf | | | | | |
| SALICACEAE | *Salix vimanalis* Basket willow | | | | | |
| SANTALACEAE | *Santalum album* Sandalwood | | | | | |

| U.S. farm sales | U.S. imports (customs value) | Total farm sales and imports | Category |
|---|---|---|---|
| 151.5 | 3.5 | 155.0 | Major |
| 353.6 | 0.9 | 354.5 | Major |
| 347.0 | 2.3 | 349.3 | Major |
| 10.2 | — | 10.2 | Medium |
| 142.4 | 3.2 | 145.6 | Major |
| 5.3 | — | 5.3 | Minor |
| 173.2 (1978 only) | 4.7 (1980: fresh roses) 1.5 (Rose oil) | 179.4 | Major |
| 13.5 | 3.1 | 16.6 | Medium |
| 10.3 | — | 10.3 | Medium |
| — | 37.5 | 37.5 | Medium |
| 2.9 | 3,922.4 | 3,925.3 | Super |
| 12.8 | 19.0 | 31.8 | Medium |
| — | 3.6 | 3.6 | Minor |
| 124.5 | 11.0 | 135.5 | Major |
| 215.4 | 3.4 | 218.8 | Major |
| 18.8 | — | 18.8 | Medium |
| 35.2 | 30.9 | 66.1 | Medium |
| 1,075.4 | 74.9 | 1,150.3 | Super |
| — | 3.5 | 3.5 | Minor |
| — | 8.9 | 8.9 | Minor |
| — | 3.7 | 3.7 | Minor |

(continued)

Table 7.3  (*Continued*)

| | CROP | PERIOD WHEN DOMESTICATED | | | | |
|---|---|---|---|---|---|---|
| FAMILY | SPECIES | Ancient/B.C. before 5000 | Early/B.C. 5000–0 | Late/A.D. 0–1700 | Recent/A.D. 1700–1900 | New/A.D. 1900 On |
| SAPINDACEAE | *Litchi chinensis*<br>Litchi | | J-436 | | | |
| SCROPHULARIACEAE | *Antirrhinum majus*<br>Snapdragon<br>*Calceolaria crenatiflora*<br>Calceolaria | | | | | |
| SOLANACEAE | *Capsicum annuum*<br>*C. frutescens*<br>Peppers/chilis | | P-27, P-28 | | | |
| | *Lycopersicon esculentum*<br>Tomato | | J-14 | | | |
| | *Nicotiana tabacum*<br>Tobacco | | G-28, S-123 | | | |
| | *Petunia × hybrida*<br>*P. axillaris*<br>*P. violacea*<br>Petunia | | | | | |
| | *Solanum melongena*<br>Eggplant | | A-413, S-123 | | | |
| | *Solanum tuberosum*<br>Potato | G-835 | | | | |
| STERCULIACEAE | *Theobroma cacao*<br>Cacao/chocolate/cocoa | | S-181, S-183 | | | |
| TAXACEAE | *Taxus* spp.<br>Ornamental yew | | | | | |
| THEACEAE | *Camellia sinensis*<br>Tea | | V-24 | | | |
| TILIACEAE | *Corchorus capsularis*<br>*C. olitorius*<br>Jute | | | | *C. capsularis*<br>S-131 | |
| UMBELLIFERAE | *Apium graveolens*<br>Celery | | P-302 | G-467 | | |
| | *Carum carvi*<br>Caraway | | | G-467, P-183 | | |
| | *Coriandrum sativum*<br>Coriander | | P-302 | | | |
| | *Cuminum cyminum*<br>Cumin | | P-183 | | | |
| | *Daucus carota*<br>Carrot | | | A-201 | | |
| VIOLACEAE | *Viola tricolor*<br>Pansy | | | | | |
| VITIDACEAE | *Vitis vinifera*<br>*V. labrusca*<br>Grape | | *V. vinifera*<br>M-324 | | | |
| ZINGIBERACEAE | *Curcuma domestica*<br>Turmeric | | | | | |
| | *Elettaria cardamomum*<br>Cardamon | | | | P-257, S-13 | |
| | *Zingiber officinale*<br>Ginger | | P-257 | | | |

Notes: — = none or negligible; ? = not determined; super = more than $1,000 million; major = $100–$1,000 million; medium = $10–$100 million; and minor = $1–$10 million. See note 1 for explanation and sources of value data.

| U.S. farm sales | U.S. imports (customs value) | Total farm sales and imports | Category |
|---|---|---|---|
| — | 1.5 | 1.5 | Minor |
| 8.7 | — | 8.7 | Minor |
| 1.8 | — | 1.8 | Minor |
| 104.4 | 53.7 | 158.1 | Major |
| 893.0 | 158.0 | 1,051.0 | Super |
| 2,437.8 | 413.6 | 2,851.4 | Super |
| 32.2 | — | 32.2 | Medium |
| 8.6 | 5.1 | 13.7 | Medium |
| 1,195.8 | 10.2 | 1,206.0 | Super |
| — | 1,016.0 | 1,016.0 | Super |
| 39.4 (1978 only) | — | 39.4 | Medium |
| — | 128.0 | 128.0 | Major |
| — | 155.6 | 155.6 | Major |
| 164.8 | 1.9 | 166.7 | Major |
| — | 4.2 | 4.2 | Minor |
| — | 1.5 | 1.5 | Minor |
| — | 5.9 | 5.9 | Minor |
| 135.8 | 6.5 | 142.3 | Major |
| 9.3 (1978 only) | — | 9.3 | Minor |
| 985.2 | 539.7 | 1,524.9 | Super |
| — | 1.3 | 1.3 | Minor |
| — | 1.0 | 1.0 | Minor |
| .8 | 4.4 | 5.2 | Minor |

Table 7.4 **Periods of domestication of 160 crop species grown or imported by the United States with a minimum annual value of $1 million**

| PERIOD OF DOMESTICATION | VALUE CATEGORY* | CROP SPECIES | COMBINED VALUE ($million) |
|---|---|---|---|
| Ancient (7000–5000 B.C.) | Super | 3 | 18,093.5 |
| | Major | 4 | 1,440.5 |
| | Medium | 5 | 221.7 |
| | Minor | 1 | 9.1 |
| | | 13 | 19,764.8 |
| Early (5000–0 B.C.) | Super | 11 | 28,190.8 |
| | Major | 25 | 7,666.2 |
| | Medium | 28 | 905.6 |
| | Minor | 19 | 77.5 |
| | | 83 | 36,840.1 |
| Late (A.D. 0–1700) | Super | 1 | 3,925.3 |
| | Major | 5 | 936.3 |
| | Medium | 11 | 322.6 |
| | Minor | 7 | 37.6 |
| | | 24 | 5,221.8 |
| Recent (A.D. 1700–1900) | Super | 0 | 0.0 |
| | Major | 6 | 2,023.7 |
| | Medium | 9 | 271.5 |
| | Minor | 19 | 70.4 |
| | | 34 | 2,365.6 |
| New (A.D. 1900–present) | Super | 0 | 0.0 |
| | Major | 1 | 116.1 |
| | Medium | 1 | 44.0 |
| | Minor | 4 | 8.5 |
| | | 6 | 168.6 |
| TOTAL | | 160 | 62,360.9 |

Source: Table 7.3.

*Super = more than $1,000 million; major = $100–$1,000 million; medium = $10–$100 million; minor = $1–$10 million.

cated in the last two centuries and the relatively low value of those species domesticated in this century are discussed in the section on incipient crops.

## The Domestication Process

Domestication is a process, not an event. Harvesting imposes selection pressures on wild populations that may alter their genetic constitution; and people

Table 7.5 **Apparent rates of domestication of 160 crop species grown or imported by the United States with a minimum annual value of $1 million**

| PERIOD OF DOMESTICATION | APPARENT RATE PER MILLENNIUM | | APPARENT RATE PER CENTURY | |
|---|---|---|---|---|
| | Number of crop species | Combined value ($million) | Crop species | Combined value ($million) |
| Ancient (7000–5000 B.C.) | 6.5 | 9,882.4 | 0.65 | 988.2 |
| Early (5000–0 B.C.) | 16.6 | 7,368.0 | 1.66 | 736.8 |
| Late (A.D. 0–1700) | | | 1.41 | 307.2 |
| Recent (A.D. 1700–1900) | 32.0 | 3,878.0 | 17.00 | 1,182.8 |
| New (A.D. 1900–present) | | | 6.00 | 168.6 |

Source: Table 7.4.

may undertake a variety of measures to encourage the survival and productivity of the wild species they exploit: protection from habitat destruction or from overgrazing and overbrowsing by livestock, thinning, weeding, and other methods. There is scarcely a domesticate grown today that was not at one time harvested from the wild; and the gradient of care—ranging from neglect and indifference (apart from the harvest) through degrees of protoculture to the complex of propagation, selection, improvement, and cultivation that we know as agriculture and horticulture—can make it difficult to determine when a crop was domesticated. Other phenomena compound this difficulty. Some of them are fundamental to the problem of determining the importance of wild species as the source of new domesticates; others are largely definitional but will be addressed since they have obscured discussion of the subject elsewhere. The main phenomena are predomestication, transdomestication, multidomestication, polycrop species, polyspecies crops, inventions and surprises, metamorphoses, and incipient domestication.

*Predomestication*

Many of the wild species used by people are adapted to open, naturally disturbed habitats. The areas disturbed by humans are a home away from home for such species that soon spread there. This extension of their range is quite natural, although people and their livestock may aid the dispersal. Oil palm (*Elaeis guineensis*) is an example. Its natural habitat in West Africa is the forest edge—it does not tolerate shade well and so occurs along watercourses, in openings in the forest, and where forest meets savanna. As shifting cultivation (slash and burn) opened up the forest, the oil palm followed. Whenever the secondary vegetation was cleared, the palms were allowed to remain because the villagers valued them for their fruit. So larger and larger stands of oil palm developed without anyone sowing a seed (G-149, Y-23, Y-81). This fostering of useful wild species by tolerating or encouraging their spread into what might be called the cohabitat—habitat that is neither built on nor farmed but is shared by people, their domesticates, and wild species adapted to disturbance—is one phase of predomestication. Another is the alteration of gene frequencies through harvesting certain forms of a species in preference to others. The thickness of the shell surrounding the kernel of the oil palm fruit is controlled by a gene, one form of which gives a fruit with a thick shell (called *dura*), the other form giving a fruit with no shell at all (called *pisifera*). In hybrids between the two a third form appears that is intermediate in thickness (called *tenera*). *Pisiferas* are usually female sterile, so the frequency of that form of the gene would be expected to decline. However, in West Africa (where the plants are native) people tend to harvest the *teneras* and *pisiferas* for oil and to tap the *duras* for wine. Persistent tapping kills the palm; hence the frequency of the *dura* form is reduced while that of the other two is increased (G-147, G-150, G-163, S-186).

## Transdomestication

The term *transdomestication* was coined by Hymowitz (G-742) to explain the domestication of guar (*Cyamopsis tetragonoloba*). Guar is a cultigen. It has never been found in the wild, existing only as a domesticate. It originated on the Indian subcontinent, where it is still grown, yet wild *Cyamopsis* species that might have been involved in its ancestry occur only in Africa. Hymowitz suggests that *C. tetragonoloba* is a form of *C. senegalensis*, a species native to the Sahel zone from Senegal to Saudi Arabia. Between the ninth and thirteenth centuries A.D. there was a considerable horse trade between the Arabs and the Indians. The horses would have had to be fed on the sea journey, and *C. senegalensis* was probably taken on board as fodder. Once the plants arrived in the semiarid northwestern part of the subcontinent (with ecological conditions similar to the native area and where any unconsumed fodder might have been sold or discarded) they could easily have become established there. Transdomestication, then, is defined by Hymowitz as "the movement by man of a wild species from its indigenous area to another region where it is subsequently domesticated" (G-742). Other examples of transdomestication are macadamia (*Macadamia* spp.)—wild in Australia, domesticated in Hawaii (S-720); coffee (*Coffea arabica*)—wild in Ethiopia, domesticated in Yemen (D-148, V-78); and probably tomato (*Lycopersicon esculentum*)—truly wild forms of which are believed to be native only to Ecuador and Peru and to have been spread from there to Mexico, where they were domesticated (J-14).

## Multidomestication

Some species have been domesticated more than once independently. Cocoa (*Theobroma cacao*) seems to have been first domesticated by the Maya of what is now southern Mexico, northern Guatemala, and Belize about 3,000 years ago (A-1415, S-181, S-183). The Central American Criollo form domesticated by the Maya reputedly makes the finest chocolate but yields poorly and is in danger of extinction (G-809, S-181). Most of the cocoa grown today is the Amazonian Forastero form, which Brazilian growers first took into cultivation from the wild (or semiwild) state in about 1740 (A-1415).

*Polycrop Species*

Some species are the source of several crops arising at different times. From *Brassica oleracea*, for example, we have (a) thousand-head kale and brussels sprouts; (b) collards and leafy kales, Portuguese kale, red and white cabbage, savoy cabbage, marrow stem kale, and kohlrabi; and (c) sprouting broccoli (calabrese) and cauliflower. The crops are grouped thus because each of (a), (b), and (c) are believed by Helm (G-830 cited by P-322) to have been independently domesticated from wild cabbage, *B. oleracea sylvestris*. Thousand-head kale, thought to be the oldest cultivated type, may have been domesticated in the first millennium B.C. by the Celts in western Europe, by the Ligurians and Iberians of the Mediterranean, or by both. Shortly afterward, sprouting broccoli and the progenitor of the cabbage and collards group were developed from the wild stock, probably in the Mediterranean (P-322). The cabbages, collards, and leafy kales were early (B.C.) elaborations of domesticated line (b). The other crops were developed later: brussels sprouts—either in the fourteenth (P-322) or eighteenth century (S-279, S-686) from domesticated line (a); kohlrabi and cauliflower some time during the Middle Ages (G-334, S-279, S-686) from domesticated lines (b) and (c), respectively.

*Polyspecies Crops*

Conversely, many crops are combinations of different species domesticated at different times. Generally, they are perennial tree crops, in which the scion (fruiting) variety can be one species and the rootstock cultivar another. As an example, the wine grape (*Vitis vinifera*) was domesticated in the fourth millennium B.C. (M-324). It was grown on its own roots until the devastating pest *Phylloxera vitifoliae* struck Europe's vineyards in the mid-nineteenth century. In the 1870s, 1880s, and 1890s French viticulturalists discovered the *Phylloxera* resistance of the American species *V. berlandieri*, *V. riparia*, and *V. rupestris* and brought them into cultivation as hybrids with one another, or with *V. vinifera*, or (with the exception of *V. berlandieri*) as species in their own right (G-707). In California two other species, *V. champini* and *V. longii*, were brought into cultivation in the 1880s and 1890s as rootstock sources of resistance to nematodes (J-453, J-468). A number of ornamentals might also be regarded as polyspecies crops because they are traded by the genus although the crops themselves comprise more than one species; they include *Begonia*, *Narcissus*, and *Rhododendron*.

*Inventions and Surprises*

Implicit in the term *new domesticate* is the notion that the source material of the crop in question is wild. But wild populations are not the only sources of new crops. New crops may be developed directly from already domesticated crops (as in the *Brassica* polycrop species), or they may arise, by design or accident, from the hybridization of two domesticated species. By definition these are not "new" domesticates. We have chosen to call those that arise by design "inventions" and those that arise by accident "surprises."

Perhaps the best known example of an invention is triticale from the cross between wheat (*Triticum* spp.) and rye (*Secale cereale*). Hybrids between wheat and rye frequently occur spontaneously but most are sterile; the development of triticale as a potential crop effectively began in 1937 with the discovery of colchicine as a means of doubling the chromosome number of the hybrids (G-67, J-183). A commercially more successful invention is the tangelo, originated in Florida at the turn of this century by the citrus scholar Walter T. Swingle and his colleague Herbert J. Webber from a cross between a grapefruit (*Citrus* × *paradisi*) and a mandarin orange (*C. reticulata*) (A-870). Citrange (*Poncirus trifoliata* × the sweet orange (*C. sinensis*) and tangor (mandarin × sweet orange) are other inventions. The grapefruit itself is a surprise, appearing in Jamaica in the eighteenth century, presumably as the result of a spontaneous cross between pummelo (*C. grandis*) and a sweet orange. Since it is a derivative of early domesticates, we classify the grapefruit too as early (A-367; B. C. Stone, pers. comm., 28 October 1981).

Perhaps the most delightful surprise in the history of crop evolution is the modern strawberry (*Fragaria* × *ananassa*). It was discovered in France in the mid-eighteenth century, a plant with unusually large and fragrant fruits that the botanist Duchesne subsequently demonstrated was the progeny of *F. chiloensis* pollinated by *F. virginiana*. Many authorities describe *F.* × *ananassa* as a recent domesticate; but since the Mapuche and Huilliche Indians appear to have been cultivating *F. chiloensis* in Chile (origin of the French plants) at least since the fourteenth century and *F. virginiana* had been introduced from North America in the seventeenth century, it is strictly speaking a spontaneous derivative of a late domesticate (D-452, V-342).

*Metamorphoses*

The evolution and development of domesticates usually are gradual processes, but occasionally an event or quick succession of events will transform the crop genetically, economically, or both. Such metamorphoses often occur when a crop is grown outside its center of origin. The North American sunflower (*Helianthus annuus*) was developed as a high-yielding oil crop by the Soviets (P-461). The East Asian soybean (*Glycine max*) was transformed into an industrial crop in the United States.

The story of the soybean in North America illustrates how dramatic these metamorphoses can be. The soybean was domesticated in China during the first millennium B.C. A major source of vegetable protein as well as a valuable flavoring, it has long been a very important crop in East Asia. It did not begin to be grown in the United States until the latter half of the nineteenth century, when it was grown in Illinois for hay or to restore soil fertility. It was not universally acclaimed. Hymowitz and Newell (G-798) quote one commentator in 1899 who stated that "the Soya bean has been but recently introduced from Japan into our Northern States. It is not a success in the South. . . . The hay is inferior to that of the Cowpea on account of its heavy woody stems and because the leaves rapidly fall off. Like the Cowpea also, the roots are small and not much of value as a fertilizer." The acreage and value of the crop increased, however, until by the early 1920s soybean was grown on more than a million acres and farm sales were worth more than $10 million. Three-quarters of the crop was for forage; only a quarter for oil and meal. Soybean reached its peak as a forage crop in 1940, when 4.8 million acres were grown for hay. The next year was the first in which bean (oil and meal) acreage was greater than hay acreage. Today, the soybean is the most valuable domesticated plant in the United States with annual farm sales of more than $11 billion. More soybean is grown in Illinois alone than in all of China. Scarcely any of the crop is for hay—virtually all of it being grown for edible and industrial oils, lecithin (an emulsifier), and high protein meal for livestock and poultry (P-491).

The soybean provides an example of a crop in which economic metamorphoses have resulted in the proliferation of uses. It remains a major human food in East and Southeast Asia and has become an outstanding industrial and animal feed crop in the United States. In other cases metamorphosis has relegated an original use to minor status. The macadamia nut tree started life in Hawaii as an ornamental and a means of controlling erosion (S-720). Similarly the oil palm, introduced to Indonesia in 1848, was first planted there and in Malaysia as an ornamental: plantations for oil were not established until 1911 in Indonesia and 1917 in Malaysia (A-89, A-931, G-147, G-148, G-189, S-186).

*Incipient Domestication*

Domestication is a slow process. A product need must be identified; a species—and eventually particular forms of the species—must be found that meet the need better than do alternatives; and then cultivars have to be developed that are sufficiently productive and easily grown for farmers to grow them instead of, or in addition to, alternative crops. Domestication requires the development of both a market and a source of supply. Like any other human activity it does not always go smoothly. The first three introductions of quinine (*Cinchona calisaya*) to Southeast Asia were unsuccessful. The first introduction (made in 1840) failed outright, and the alkaloid content of the second and third introductions was too low to survive competition from the fourth introduction made in

1865. This accession was so superior that it enabled the Dutch to establish a virtual monopoly of quinine supplies until World War II (G-187, G-188, J-321).

An extreme example of the problems facing a potential domesticate is that of guayule (*Parthenium argentatum*), a desert shrub growing wild in northern Mexico and the Big Bend area of Texas. Wild Mexican guayule was once a commercial source of rubber. Its heyday was in the first decade of this century but overexploitation devastated the wild stands and ruined the industry. Domestication began in the United States in 1912. It was enthusiastically fostered as the way to ensure the supply of a strategic raw material during World War II and was summarily abandoned in 1946. Research continued for a while longer but ended in the 1950s. By the late 1970s there were no commercial plantations anywhere in the world. Mexico, however, continued work with its wild stands, which today are the only commercial source of guayule (M-231). Recently, breeding work began again in the United States, and in 1983 Tysdal and his colleagues released four guayule germplasms, two of them from crosses with related wild species *P. fruticosum* and *P. tomentosum* (S-834). (A germplasm is two developmental stages removed from a cultivar; the intervening stage is a parental line.)

The term *new domesticate* implies not only newly taken in from the wild but also a degree of success. With respect to the U.S. economy we have chosen a combined dockside and farmgate value of $1 million as the threshold between incipient domestication and establishment as a new, if minor, domesticate. Some new domesticates may never cross this threshold, instead joining the hundreds of microcrops that are grown for personal pleasure or for a highly specialized market. Others may eventually cross this threshold but only after many more years of effort. Comparing the tasks of the contemporary plant domesticator and the breeder working with established domesticates, Jain (J-633) writes: "In many established crops, from 3,000 to 10,000 generations of selection have provided a broad genetic base of cultivated materials for crop improvement in addition to the variation found in the wild and weedy relatives." Breeding work for most of the potential domesticates, he comments, is currently at the phase of selection of the most promising species for further research.

Most of the crops that from time to time are publicized as new do not qualify as new domesticates in the strict sense defined here. Rapeseed (*Brassica campestris* and *B. napus*) introduced to Canada in 1936 is an early (*B. campestris*) to recent (*B. napus*) domesticate (P-322). Safflower (*Carthamus tinctorius*), introduced to the United States in the 1940s, is also early (J-137). These are clearly old crops newly introduced to North America. Other rediscoveries are psyllium (*Plantago ovata*), the amaranths (*Amaranthus* spp.), and kenaf (*Hibiscus cannabinus*) (D-14, M-317, S-26). Others (such as guayule, already discussed) are still in the early stages of domestication. We look first at some genuinely new domesticates before considering a selection of incipient ones.

## New Domesticated Vascular Plants (other than timber trees)

Six crops—cashew, highbush blueberries, wild rice, lavender and lavandin, wheatgrasses, and kiwi fruit—taken into cultivation this century have become sufficiently important to the U.S. economy to be classed as new domesticates.

*Cashew* (Anacardium occidentale)

The cashew is economically the most important of the new domesticates. Native to the dry tropical forests of northeastern Brazil, wild cashew stands are still exploited there to an extent we have been unable to determine. The bulk of the cashew in international trade comes from cultivated plants; the main exporters to the United States are India (35%), Mozambique (27%), Brazil (26%), and Tanzania (5%). The crop is an example of both transdomestication and multidomestication. The Portuguese introduced the cashew to India in the sixteenth century and to Africa at an early but unknown date, possibly because they thought it had potential as a cash crop (J-365). The fruit, relished by birds and mammals as well as people, spread rapidly. It became widely naturalized, particularly in dry coastal regions, spreading much as the oil palm did in West Africa but on a pantropical scale. The cashew's value as a crop for small holdings was first realized in India at the beginning of this century when the domestication of the species effectively began (J-365). Feral plants in East Africa and Madagascar and wild and feral plants in Brazil were independently taken into cultivation shortly afterward, mostly by smallholders but in Brazil and Madagascar also as a plantation crop. The crop has been little developed, and it consists largely of seedling populations indistinguishable from feral/wild trees (M-266, V-389).

United States imports of cashew products are worth $116.1 million a year. Cashew nuts account for $108.5 million and cashew nut shell liquid (CNSL) for $7.6 million. Cashews are the most important (in both volume and value) of imported nuts consumed as nuts. (The number one nut import—coconut—is largely used as an industrial raw material.) Around 75% of the cashew nuts are sold salted in the snack-food trade; the balance are used in bakery and confectionery. They are very popular, more being sold in cashew-only packs than in mixes. In mixes, they act as the bait that sells the mix—apparently if cashews make up less than half the mix, sales fall (V-389). Almost all the CNSL (probably more than 90%) is processed into resins for use in brake linings and (a minor use) clutch facings. CNSL resins are used as fillers and binders in drumbrake lining compounds, performing more cost effectively than asbestos as a filler and linseed oil as a binder. In disc-brake pads they are used only as a filler, for which they are favored because they are cheaper and give a quieter braking action than synthetic phenolic resins (which are the preferred material for binders since they outperform CNSL at high temperatures) (V-389).

*Highbush Blueberries* (Vaccinium australe *and* V. corymbosum)

As we saw in chapter 6, a substantial supply of blueberries still comes from the wild. Almost all of these are lowbush blueberries (*V. angustifolium* and *V. myrtilloides*). The highbush blueberries, annual farm sales plus imports of which are worth $44 million, are new domesticates.

We are fortunate that the domesticator of the blueberry, Frederick V. Coville, wrote an account of his work shortly before he died in 1937. Coville worked for the U.S. Department of Agriculture, where he was principal botanist for the Bureau of Plant Industry's Division of Plant Exploration and Introduction. The domestication of the blueberry was his crowning achievement and well exemplifies the time and effort required between the first notion that a species might be brought into commercial cultivation and its establishment as a successful domesticate.

Coville began research on the biology of the species—which is the first stage in domestication—in 1906. After two years he had determined that blueberries require an acid soil (a fact that seems obvious enough today but was not known prior to Coville's experiments). From 1908 to 1910 he gained an understanding of pollination biology and propagation and developed the techniques needed for a series of breeding experiments. He discovered that blueberry plants are self-incompatible (cannot be pollinated with their own pollen) and determined some of the crossing relationships among blueberry species.

The second stage of the process of domestication (overlapping the first) is selection of suitable parental material. Coville realized, as some plant collectors and introducers have not, that selection of the right species for domestication is only half the battle; the other half is the selection of superior genotypes within the species. Coville was emphatic that his blueberries should taste good, and he destroyed even highly productive plants if they did not come up to his standards of deliciousness. His first selection, therefore, was for outstanding flavor. He found it in 1908 in a large-berried plant of *V. corymbosum* growing wild on a farm at Greenfield, New Hampshire. "The flesh was firm and juicy," Coville wrote. ". . . In flavor the berry was exceptionally good. It was sweet, but sufficiently acid to be decidedly superior to the mild-flavored fruit of the lowbush blueberry (*V. angustifolium* Ait.), yet not sour like the Canada blueberry, (*V. canadense* Kalm) [now *V. myrtilloides* Michx.], and it possessed in a high degree the flavoring ester that is the special characteristic of the best wild blueberries of New England" (A-909). This first selection from the wild he called Brooks after the owner of the farm.

Coville made five other important selections from the wild: Russell, a lowbush blueberry (*V. angustifolium*) (which he collected in 1909, also from Greenfield, New Hampshire), which he used for its earliness; and Sooy, Rubel, Chatsworth, and Grover, all of which are *V. australe* collected from the pine barrens of New Jersey in 1911. These six selections provided the raw material of Coville's improvement program. They were the parents of cultivars that either are still grown today—such as Jersey (Rubel × Grover; released 1928 and still, in 1976, the top cultivar in Michigan) and Stanley ([Brooks × Sooy] × Rubel; released 1930)—or have been used in subsequent improvement programs. In the course of domesticating the blueberry, Coville successfully combined in the cultivars he introduced the individual qualities of his wild selections: good flavor, earliness, desirable color (light blue), large berries, ease of picking, firm flesh, and good keeping (A-909).

Coville began crossing his selections (the third stage of domestication) in 1911 and released his first cultivar, Pioneer, in 1920 (from a cross between Brooks and Sooy made in 1912), 14 years after he initiated his investigations. As a domesticate, however, the highbush blueberry still needed improvement. Between 1920 and 1936 Coville introduced, in all, 15 improved varieties: they provided the foundation of a commercial crop that achieved farm sales of $3.5 million by 1949, topping the $1 million mark during the 1940s, some two decades after the introduction of Pioneer. From a glint in a domesticator's eye to the status of a minor domesticate was a matter of 35 years; from minor domesticate (>$1 million) to medium domesticate (>$10 million) took another 20 years. The highbush blueberry is still going strong and is now the third most valuable berry fruit in North America, after strawberry and cranberry.

*Wild Rice* (Zizania aquatica)

It is time to change the name of wild rice. "Rice" is not the problem: although not a true rice (genus *Oryza*), the *Zizania* species are in the same subfamily (Oryzoideae) of the grass family, and among the crops the true rices are its closest relatives (S-825). The problem is "wild." Most of the wild rice produced in the United States is domesticated. Of the nation's annual average production of 6.0 million pounds (unprocessed), 4.1 million pounds (68%) comes from cultivated paddies (note 2).

The earliest recorded commercial planting of wild rice was made in 1950 by James Godward and Gerald Godward of Merrifield, Minnesota (E. A. Oelke, pers. comm., 17 September 1981). They used seed from wild stands, as did other growers who began developing paddies during the 1960s. The first important event in the story of wild rice domestication occurred in the paddy of one of these growers, Al Johnson, who started in 1962. In his northern Minnesota site in 1963, two researchers (Paul Yagya and Erwin Brooks) at the University of Minnesota discovered a few plants with reduced seed shattering (M-654).

When the seeds of wild rice mature, the seed-heads shatter (as do those of other wild grasses), scattering the grains. This is a necessary survival mechanism in the wild plants, but it is a serious nuisance in cultivated plants because much of the production is thereby lost, and harvesting, particularly mechanized harvesting, is made very difficult. Shatter resistance is therefore a key characteristic in the domestication of a cereal like wild rice. Although research ended in 1965 due to lack of funds, Johnson increased the partially shatter-resistant seed and by 1968 was growing 20 acres of it (M-654). The discovery, increase, and distribution of this seed transformed wild rice from an incipient to a new domesticate. The average harvest from the wild is about 50 pounds/acre (M-264). Use of the partially shatter-resistant seed enabled commercial paddy yields to increase to 151 pounds/acre by 1969 and to continue increasing until the average today is 315 pounds/acre (E. A. Oelke, pers. comm., 17 September 1981). Minnesota's paddy acreage grew as well: from 908 acres in 1968 to 2,645 in 1969, 5,202 in 1970, 8,705 in 1971, to an average annual acreage since then of 15,000 acres (E. A. Oelke, pers. comm., 17 September 1981).

Wild rice achieved the status of minor domesticate in 1972, only two decades since its cultivation was first attempted and a mere decade since work on its improvement began. Since then progress has been disappointing, reflecting the lack of initial research. Today, more than another decade later, production remains at about 4 million pounds a year. We estimate that the annual average value of farm sales of domesticated wild rice is $2.8 million. The equivalent values of domestic production and imports (from Canada) of wild wild rice are $1.3 million and $1.9 million, respectively (a total of $3.2 million). Looking back, Oelke observes: "Considerable economic losses have occurred in the growing of wild rice because research in breeding and production was not started soon enough. Ideally, extensive research should have started 10 years ago before millions of dollars were invested in commercial growing of wild rice" (M-654). As it was, the Minnesota State Legislature did not begin to allocate funds for research until 1971. Since then the Agricultural Experiment Station at the University of Minnesota has had a wild rice research program covering plant breeding (to develop cultivars that are resistant to disease and shattering and that mature earlier); soils (to determine fertility requirements); production and seed (to determine cultural requirements); diseases; harvesting (to develop better methods and equipment); and processing (to obtain a more uniform and better quality product). Lacking the results of such research, growers apparently have suffered substantial economic losses to disease, principally brown spot (caused by the fungus *Bipolaris oryzae*), as well as the frustrations of cultivating a plant that morphologically, behaviorally, and genetically is still wild (A-1393, D-519, M-654).

*Lavender* (Lavandula angustifolia) *and lavandin* (L. angustifolia × latifolia)

The United States imports $2.6 million of "lavender oil," a category comprising the oils of lavender *L. angustifolia*, spike lavender *L. latifolia*, and lavandin, the natural hybrid of the two. On the basis of the returns from our supplier survey (described in chap. 6) we assume that imports from Spain ($0.6 million) are largely of wild spike lavender oil and those from France ($1.7 million) of lavender and lavandin oils, both wild and domesticated. According to Arctander (A-90), about 10 times as much lavandin oil is produced than lavender oil. Until the 1920s all essential oils of the lavender group came entirely from the wild (spike lavender oil still does). Then in the first decade of this century the French lavender harvest became erratic; the plants showed poor or no recovery, either because of overexploitation or for some other (undetermined) cause. In an effort to obtain a more reliable supply, a number of distillers started experimental plantations of *L. angustifolia* in 1910, but cultivation did not become established until the 1930s. Domestication of lavandin also began in the 1920s and 1930s (G-76). Today virtually all lavandin oil comes from domesticated plants (A-90). True lavender oil presents a more complicated picture, however. The "petite" or "fine lavande" growing wild up to an altitude of 1,300 meters in southeastern France is reputed to be of a higher quality than the cultivated form (G-76). Since lavandin has replaced lavender as a source of low-cost oil for perfuming soaps (A-90), the remaining demand for lavender is for use in expensive lotions, colognes, and perfumes and is probably rather price elastic. Hence, although much of the lavender oil that the United States imports is from plantation sources, we expect that a significant proportion—destined for use in the most expensive products—still comes from the wild.

Given these considerations, we estimate that domesticated lavandin and lavender (largely the former) account for about $2 million of U.S. imports of lavender oils. Arctander has described the domestication of lavandin in particular as a "tremendous success" (A-90). Prior to the late 1920s the oil was scarcely known; by the 1950s it had become one of the top ten essential oils (in volume) from natural sources. Cultivation assured a large and reliable supply, and the price per pound fell dramatically—from $3 in 1954 to about $0.80 in 1959. As a low-cost source of a popular fragrance it is widely used not only in soaps but also in detergents, liquid cleaners, and dishwasher liquids (A-90).

*Wheatgrasses* (Agropyron *spp.*)

Several species of wheatgrass have been newly domesticated for turf, pasture, hay, and erosion control. They include five introduced and four native species (the year in brackets is when the first cultivar was released):

Fairway wheatgrass *A. cristatum* (1927) from the USSR;
Crested wheatgrass *A. desertorum* (1953) from Turkmenia, USSR;
Tall wheatgrass *A. elongatum* (1937) from the USSR and Turkey;
Intermediate wheatgrass *A. intermedium* (includes *A. trichophorum*) (1945) from Manchuria (People's Republic of China), the USSR, and Turkey;
Siberian wheatgrass *A. sibiricum* (1953) from the USSR;
Streambank wheatgrass *A. riparium* (1954) from Oregon;

Bluebunch wheatgrass *A. spicatum* (includes *A. inerme*) (1946) from
Washington and Idaho;
Western wheatgrass *A. smithii* (1970) from Kansas;
Slender wheatgrass *A. trachycaulum* (1946) from Montana and
Saskatchewan.

The most important of these are perhaps *A. cristatum*, *A. desertorum*, and *A. intermedium* of the introduced species, and *A. smithii*, *A. spicatum*, and *A. trachycaulum* of the native species. Many of the cultivars for which certified seed is available are not cultivars in the strict sense but are named selections from the wild: some have been increased and released after observation and testing without further ado—for example, *A. cristatum* cv Fairway (1927), *A. desertorum* cv Summit (1953), and *A. smithii* cv Barton (1970); others after "improvement" by mass selection and elimination of aberrants—for example, *A. intermedium* cv Luna (1963) and *A. riparium* cv Sodar (1954). The most domesticated of the wheatgrass species is *A. intermedium*. Certified seed is available of several cultivars that have been developed after two or more generations of polycrossing (through mass pollination) ecotypically and phenotypically similar accessions and their progeny, selecting superior lines, and combining them as synthetic varieties (G-142).

*Kiwi Fruit* (Actinidia chinensis)

The kiwi fruit, also known as the Chinese gooseberry and in its native China as *mihoutao* (monkey peach), may be an example of a multidomesticate. Its cultivation may have begun in China in the Tang dynasty, for the poet Cen Can (714–770) mentioned an arbor of kiwi fruit in a courtyard in what is now Shaanxi Province. Later writers, however, consistently describe the kiwi fruit as a wild plant (a plant of the mountains), indicating that cultivation can never have been very extensive. Even today there is only very limited cultivation in China—large quantities of kiwi fruit are collected from the wild and sold in the markets as well as supplying a considerable canning industry. A. R. Ferguson (Department of Scientific and Industrial Research, New Zealand), who is preparing a history of the kiwi fruit and has generously given us access to a draft, tells us that, according to Tsuin Shen of Beijing, 100,000 tons of kiwi fruit are collected from the wild each year (pers. comm., 9 June 1983). By comparison New Zealand's annual production (1983) is 40,000–50,000 tons (A. R. Ferguson, pers. comm., 16 May 1983); and California's annual production (1978) is only about 800 tons (S-798).

Whether or not *A. chinensis* was domesticated at some time somewhere in China, it has been independently domesticated in New Zealand. The kiwi fruit was introduced to the non-Chinese world by the French missionary Paul Guillaume Farges, who sent seed to France in 1898. Although the arboretum at

Les Barres raised plants from the seed, apparently nothing came of these. Today's cultivars can be traced back to the English plant collector E. H. Wilson, who was sent to China by the British nursery Veitch & Sons to collect the legendary handkerchief tree (*Davidia involucrata*) (A. R. Ferguson, pers. comm., 9 June 1983). Wilson ended up introducing 1,500 species to the West, among them *A. chinensis*, which he found in 1900. Wilson's base was at Ichang, a city on the Yangtze River just downriver from the botanically rich Yangtze Gorges. European residents there were so unfamiliar with the fruit that they called it Wilson's gooseberry (A-1377), though this may have been a reflection more of the lack of awareness of the Europeans than of the unusualness of the fruit. Besides sending seed of the wild kiwi fruits he collected to England, Wilson also gave samples to interested foreigners in Ichang. The kiwi fruit is dioecious, bearing male and female flowers on different plants. Veitch & Sons advertised plants from Wilson's first consignment of seed in 1904. Unfortunately all were male; by the time Veitch's was able to sell female plants (1912), English horticulturalists had apparently lost interest in the species. The first successful introduction to the United States (in 1904) came from Wilson-collected material given to an American resident in Ichang but also proved to consist entirely of male plants. The first female plants arrived, from Veitch & Sons, in 1913. The commercial potential of the species went unrecognized, however (A. R. Ferguson, pers. comm., 9 June 1983).

All the kiwi fruit cultivars grown in New Zealand—indeed all the kiwi fruit grown commercially throughout the world—derive from plants grown by Alexander Allison, a sheepfarmer at Wanganui on the North Island of New Zealand (A-921, J-392, S-497; A. R. Ferguson, pers. comm., 9 June 1983). The source of these plants has not been established with certainty, but it is known that in 1904 Allison was given kiwi fruit seed by Isobel Fraser, the headmistress of a local school. Miss Fraser was given the seed by her sister Katie, a missionary at Ichang, on a visit to China in 1903. It is likely that the seed came from plants collected by Wilson. For more than 30 years after its introduction into New Zealand the kiwi fruit was grown as a novelty by a few keen gardeners. They contributed significantly to the development of the crop, however, by raising many seedlings and selecting several superior fruiting types (S-497). Around 1940 several plantings came into production, and for the first time the potential of *A. chinensis* was seriously considered. World War II delayed further progress, and it was not until 1958, following a survey of all the plantings, that types showing most promise for commercial production were identified and cultivars named (A-921, S-497). Acreage remained small (fewer than 350 acres) until about 1967, when it began rising rapidly until by 1981 the crop was being grown on more than 16,500 acres (it is still increasing). New Zealand exports more than three-quarters of its production, mostly (around 70%) to Germany and Japan. The United States is the third largest customer (6%) followed by the Netherlands and Belgium (4% each) (A-921). The value of the 1,046 tons of kiwi fruit that the United States imports each year (1,034 tons, or 99%, of which is from New Zealand) is $1.8 million. We have no figures for the value of U.S. domestic production of about 800 tons a year, but on a pro rata basis it would exceed $1 million.

Of the six crops domesticated this century that are grown or imported by the United States, one (cashew) has achieved major status, one (highbush blueberry) medium status, and the rest (wild rice, lavender and lavandin, wheatgrasses, and kiwi fruit) minor status. Three have been domesticated in North America (blueberry, wild rice, and wheatgrass) and three elsewhere: kiwi fruit in New Zealand, lavandin and lavender in France, and cashew in several countries (principally India and Brazil). Although new as domesticates, none is a new resource, all being used in the wild form prior to their domestication. Wheatgrasses were and still are important range grasses, and the other crops were well-established, if minor, wild resources. Even the kiwi fruit, the only novelty to North America, has a long history of use in China. The wonder is not that these species have been domesticated but that their domestication should have taken so long. Another interesting aspect is that there is nothing exotic or "advanced" about the types of product they supply: a pasture/turf grass; a fragrance; four foods (two fruits, a nut, and a grain). Cashew provides CNSL—an industrial raw material—but that was not the reason for its domestication. It is evident that we are still domesticating the same sorts of plants that our forebears did when they began the process some 9,000 years ago.

The stimulus to domestication and the impact of domestication on the wild resource vary. Only the domestication of cashew and of lavender/lavandin appear to have been in response to commercial demand. With the other crops, market development has been an integral part of the domestication process. Wild rice may be an exception in that, although contracting of acreage by Uncle Ben Incorporated in 1965 has been described as "the real beginning . . . of commercial production" (M-654), domestication has not resulted in an expansion of supply large enough to change, or to require changing, the market. Table 7.6 shows that the price per pound of wild wild rice fluctuates according to the availability of the wild product and is not significantly affected by availability of the domesticated product. Apart from home use by native Americans, wild rice remains (whether wild or not) a luxury, gourmet item.

By contrast, the market for kiwi fruit is entirely new; that for wheatgrass is part of the relatively recent development of forage grasses and the replacement of wild range by sown pasture; and the market for domesticated blueberries is a dramatic expansion of the original market for wild blueberries. Whereas the availability of domesticated lavender and lavandin has apparently reduced demand for their wild counterparts, this has not happened with the other species. There was no equivalent market for wild wheatgrasses; and the Chinese market for wild kiwi fruit was and is entirely independent of the modern international trade in the cultivated fruit. Cashew production is not well enough known to

Table 7.6 **Changes in price per pound of wild wild rice in relation to wild wild rice production and total wild rice production in Minnesota, 1976–1981**

| | PRODUCTION (POUNDS UNPROCESSED) | | | CHANGE (%) | | PRICE PER POUND OF WILD WILD RICE | |
|---|---|---|---|---|---|---|---|
| | Wild | Domesticated | Total | Wild | Total | $ | Change (%) |
| 1976 | 1,500,000 | 3,750,000 | 5,250,000 | — | — | 0.70 | — |
| 1977 | 2,600,000 | 3,000,000 | 5,600,000 | +73.7 | +6.7 | 0.60 | −14.3 |
| 1978 | 450,000 | 4,200,000 | 4,650,000 | −82.7 | −17.0 | 1.10 | +83.3 |
| 1979 | 850,000 | 4,600,000 | 5,450,000 | +88.9 | +17.2 | 1.00 | −9.1 |
| 1980 | 3,700,000 | 4,300,000 | 8,000,000 | +335.3 | +46.8 | 0.65 | −35.0 |
| 1981 | 600,000 | 4,000,000 | 4,600,000 | −83.8 | −42.5 | 1.25 | +92.3 |

Source: E. A. Oelke, pers. comm., 17 September 1981.

say with confidence that demand for the wild product has been reduced, increased, or is unaffected by availability of supplies from smallholders and plantations. Given the informality of production and the lack of improvement of cultivars, it seems most likely that it is unaffected. Wild wild rice, as we have seen, is also unaffected.

The period of incipience (the interval between the first introduction from the wild and establishment of the crop as a new domesticate) varies: about 20 years for wild rice and lavandin/lavender; 35 years for blueberry; 60 years for wheatgrass; 65 years for kiwi fruit. (We have no data for cashew.) No doubt the period of incipience for kiwi fruit would have been shorter had selection of superior fruiting types begun before 1930 and cultivar identification and naming before 1958. It is clear, however, that even in the most favorable circumstances (diverse, readily available germplasm; imaginative and dedicated scientific effort; effective product development and marketing—the highbush blueberry story being the outstanding example of this combination), domestication of a new crop takes many years.

## Some Incipient Crops

We noted in our discussion of tables 7.4 and 7.5, the sharp increase in the number of plant species domesticated in the last two centuries and the relatively low value of the crops domesticated in this century. The low value of the new crops is to be expected because of the length of time it takes for a new domesticate to become established. As we have seen, the period of incipience is 20–65 years, and it may take as long or longer for a crop to go from minor to medium status. Most crops will not make major: only 42 (19%) of the 226 macrocrops ($1 million or more) grown or imported by the United States are major and only 15 (7%) are super. Some of this century's domestications may be overspill from those of the recent period. The great increase in domestications in the last two centuries is attributable to the Industrial Revolution. There may have been similar surges in the ancient and early millennia (which cannot be detected from the archaeological record), and there may be similar surges in the future. Declining oil supplies may stimulate a shift from petrochemicals to botanochemicals and a consequent explosion of new commodity crops.

Of the 34 recent macrocrops (crops with an annual value of $1 million or more) grown or imported by the United States, 18 (53%) are commodity crops, 9 (26%) are animal feed/forage crops, 4 (12%) are food crops, and 3 (9%) are ornamentals (note 3). Of the 6 major crops ($100 million–$1,000 million) among them—collectively worth $2,023.7 million a year, or 86% of the total annual value of recent crops—3 are commodity crops (oil palm, jute, and rubber), 2 are feed/forage crops (Bermuda grass and timothy), and 1 is a food crop (pecan). The spur to the domestication of most of the commodity crops was almost certainly the mercantile impact of the Industrial Revolution, which led to the development of many plantation and smallholder cash crops that formerly were obtained from the wild. Examples are the following 5 fragrance crops: ylang ylang (*Cananga odorata*—plantations first established in Réunion in 1892); geranium (*Pelargonium* spp.—domesticated early in the nineteenth century); citronella (*Cymbopogon winterianus*—domesticated in the 1890s); patchouli (*Pogostemon cablin*—cultivated in Southeast Asia since 1834); and eucalyptus (*Eucalyptus globulus*—introduced into Spain and Portugal, the main suppliers of the United States, in the eighteenth century) (G-76).

## Feed/Forage Crops

Very few forage crops were domesticated before the middle of the nineteenth century, when the introduction of fertilizers prompted scientific research into pasture productivity (A-266, S-751, V-365). This development, together with the earlier (seventeenth century) discovery of the value of mixing legumes with grasses to form a pasture (S-751, V-365), led to the eighteenth- and nineteenth-century domestications of, among others, orchard grass (*Dactylis glomerata*), the fescues (*Festuca* spp.), and timothy (*Phleum pratense*) (A-266, A-1397, A-1411, G-142), birdsfoot trefoil (*Lotus corniculatus*), white clover (*Trifolium repens*), and crimson clover (*T. incarnatum*) (D-105, J-594, S-731). The process is still continuing, but it is difficult to determine the impact of incipient forage crops because of the dearth of statistics. Forage is consumed by livestock as either hay or living pasture; but the last year for which the U.S. Department of Agriculture compiled hay production data by type of hay was 1970, and the 1978 census of agriculture has not filled that gap (S-798). Our estimates of forage crop value are drawn from statistics of seed production (still published for alfalfa, red clover, ladino and white clover, crimson clover, lespedeza, vetch, orchard grass, fescue, timothy, Kentucky bluegrass, bentgrass, and ryegrass) and thus considerably understate the economic contribution of forage crops both individually and in totality.

Even so, it is clear that forage crop domestication in North America is still going on, although possibly at a slower rate than during the previous two centuries or than in some other regions (such as Australia). According to 1981–1983 registrations in *Crop Science* of new forage and feed-crop cultivars, germplasms, and parental lines, most work is being done with species whose domestication began—either in North America or elsewhere—before this century. Besides the crops mentioned in the preceding paragraph, they include sainfoin (*Onobrychis viciifolia*), sweet clover (*Melilotus* spp.), and lupine (*Lupinus* spp.). In addition, cultivars developed in other countries are being directly introduced into the United States. An example is subterranean clover (*Trifolium subterraneum*) introduced from Australia in 1920 and now grown on some 150,000 acres, largely in western Oregon but also in northern California and in Mississippi. All the cultivars being grown are Australian, and all were selected from naturalized populations introduced to Australia from the Mediterranean region in the last century (A-523, A-717, J-581).

Among the feed and forage crops whose domestication began this century are desmodium (*Desmodium canum* and *D. heterocarpon*), coastal panic grass (*Panicum amarum*), klein grass (*P. coloratum*), Bahia grass (*Paspalum notatum*), phalaris (*Phalaris aquatica*), and indian grass (*Sorghastrum nutans*). *Desmodium* is a mainly tropical and subtropical genus, several species of which are being domesticated as pasture legumes (A-678). *Desmodium canum* is apparently still under trial (A-678), but cultivar Florida has been developed for use in southern Florida from an introduction of *D. heterocarpon* from Uttar Pradesh, India (J-628). *Paspalum notatum*, a grass introduced from Brazil in 1914 (G-142), may in fact qualify as a new rather than an incipient domesticate. The annual value of seed production was $913,000 in 1974, when 3.9 million pounds of seed were harvested from 38,099 acres (S-831). By 1978 both the quantity harvested and the seed acreage had fallen to 2.6 million pounds from 22,329 (the value of which was not stated) (S-798), but the crop is well established (G-142). *Sorghastrum nutans* and *Panicum amarum* are two native species: several cultivars of the former have been selected from natural stands in Oklahoma, Nebraska, Kansas, New Mexico, North Dakota, South Dakota, and Texas (G-142, J-629), Atlantic, the first cultivar of *P. amarum* to be released, was selected from a stand in the Back Bay Wildlife Refuge (near Princess Anne, Virginia) and is intended mainly for stabilizing disturbed sites (A-1410).

## Commodity Crops

The surge of commodity crop domestications in the eighteenth and nineteenth centuries seems to have ended—or at least to have paused—with the twentieth-century domestication of lavender/lavandin. This domestication is in the pattern of ylang-ylang, geranium, and other minor commodities and appears to be an echo of the past rather than a portent of the future. Potential commodities are the crops that attract the greatest interest, but whether the many that are being discussed will be successfully developed remains to be seen. Of the 12 that are considered most promising, judging from five recent reviews (J-633, P-448, P-489, V-366, V-392), one is a fiber, one an insecticide, three are latexes, and seven are prospective oil crops.

The fiber (kenaf, *Hibiscus cannabinus*) can be excluded, since it has long been domesticated. So has the insecticide source, *Tephrosia vogelii*, a legume cultivated in East Africa as a fish poison and molluscicide as well as an insecticide (D-246). The three potential latex crops are guayule (*Parthenium argentatum*), copaiba (*Copaifera langsdorffi*), and the gopher plant (*Euphorbia lathyris* and other *Euphorbia* species). Interest in guayule is as a source of rubber; interest in the other two species is as a source of hydrocarbons for fuel and chemical feedstock. The seven prospective oil crops are buffalo gourd (*Cucurbita foetidissima*), jojoba (*Simmondsia chinensis*), meadowfoam (*Limnanthes alba*), crambe (*Crambe abyssinica*), vernonia (*Vernonia anthelmintica*), Stokes' aster (*Stokesia laevis*), and bladderpod (*Lesquerella* spp.).

The success or failure of these potential crops depends largely on two factors: the development of a market large enough to justify their existence, and the availability of germplasm with which breeders can develop superior cultivars. The prospects of several of these incipient domesticates are poor because they face stiff competition from well-established sources of supply: guayule from natural rubber from *Hevea brasiliensis* and synthetic rubber from petroleum; crambe and/or meadowfoam are intended to replace imported rapeseed ($3.9 million a year, mostly from Canada and Poland) as a botanical source of long-chain fatty acids for industrial production of polymers, lubricants, and plasticizers; bladderpod is intended to replace imported castor oil ($40.5 million a year, almost entirely from Brazil and India) as a source of hydroxy fatty acids; vernonia and Stokes' aster face competition from soybean oil as a source of epoxy fatty acids for the production of plastics and coatings; buffalo gourd is a potential source of edible polyunsaturated oil but has been too little studied to know how it might compare with current sources such as sunflower (M-229, P-448, P-489).

Although the promoters of a new crop may claim that it will protect the nation from the vulnerability of relying on imports, the reasoning is economically spurious. Unless the new crop has some special price or quality advantage over established sources of the product (whether imported or not), it is unlikely to succeed against them. If crambe and meadowfoam oil are simply intended as substitutes for rapeseed oil, then on the basis of current rapeseed oil consumption, at best one or the other will become a minor crop; at worst neither will become a crop at all. They are exposed to competition not only from imported rapeseed but also from U.S.-grown rapeseed, the cultivated area of which has increased from 828 acres in 1974 (S-831) to 50,099 acres in 1978 (S-798). The extent of crambe was 187 acres in 1974 (S-831) and about 1,000 in 1976 (V-392). (Crambe was not covered in the 1978 census of agriculture [S-798].)

The oil-yielding plant most likely to succeed as a new domesticate is probably jojoba (*Simmondsia chinensis*). This is because its oil is unique, and well-defined markets are being developed for it. Native to the Sonora Desert, the shrub grows wild in the American and Mexican states of Arizona, California, Baja California, and Sonora (A-697, A-969, D-100, G-20, M-229, M-563, M-663, S-69, V-380). For centuries the Indians of the Southwest used jojoba oil for treating wounds, soothing burns, conditioning hair, and supplementing their diet (A-1343, D-100, S-69). In 1933, two University of Arizona researchers discovered that the liquid contained in jojoba seeds differed radically from all other known seed oils and was, in fact, chemically a liquid wax (D-100).

The only other known source of a natural liquid wax is the sperm whale (*Physeter catodon*). Sperm whale oil is used extensively in lubricants that must withstand extreme pressures and temperatures, such as in machinery gears and car and tractor transmissions (A-697, D-100, G-20, M-229, M-563, M-663, V-380, Y-80). The addition of sulfurized sperm whale oil is said to turn ordinary transmission oil into automotive Courvoisier (D-100). The tanning industry is the other major industry that relies heavily on sperm oil. The oil is particularly favored for the production of soft, nongreasy leathers and special surface effects—such as sheen on suede surfaces. In addition, sperm whale oil imparts "run" to leathers so that they do not shrink back again after the stretching which takes place in the manufacturing process—an important feature in high quality gloves (V-380).

The possibility of using jojoba as a substitute for sperm whale oil in heavy industry began to be raised when whale harvesting was cut back with the outbreak of World War II (D-100). The first commercial planting of jojoba (320 acres) was made in Arizona in 1943 by the Durkee Famous Food Company. The company abandoned the project three years later because of extensive damage done to the seedlings by rodents and cattle. Another plantation, only half an acre in size, was started in California in 1944 but this too was abandoned eventually (A-164, Y-80). When World War II ended, the supply of sperm whale oil became plentiful again, and interest in jojoba subsided (D-100).

Sperm whale oil, classified as a strategic material in the United States because of its value to American industry, was stockpiled against national emergencies (M-229, M-563). Hunting of sperm whales continued, with the world catch reaching a peak of more than 30,000 animals killed in 1963 (V-298). Concern began to be expressed over the declining numbers of sperm whales, and in 1971 the United States banned all further importation of sperm whale oil (D-100). This rekindled American interest in jojoba.

It has been estimated that the wild jojoba stands in the Sonora Desert yield more than 100 million pounds of seed each year, but most of this goes to waste because of the difficulties of harvesting over such a wide area and under such harsh climatic conditions (M-563, V-380). Harvests, therefore, have been very small to date—for example 87,000 pounds of seed or 44,000 pounds of wax in

1972, and 500,000 pounds of seed or 250,000 pounds of wax in 1981 (M-663; J. Kazansky, pers. comm., 8 October 1982)—especially in comparison with competitive oils and waxes such as sperm oil, carnauba wax, and candelilla wax (table 7.7). The development of jojoba into a multimillion dollar international industry depends on its ability to offer a competitive alternative to these and other existing, well-established oils and waxes by assuring a plentiful, reliable supply at comparable prices. This means wide-scale cultivation.

In 1974, jojoba began to be planted in the United States and Mexico. The United States started with a 35–40-acre plot of nursery-grown jojoba on Indian land in southern California (A-164, M-563). More plantations in both California and Arizona followed. By 1979 a special report of World Market Perspective recommended jojoba plantations as "by far the most attractive enterprise investment available in the world today" (D-100). Jojoba was proclaimed the liquid gold of the West. Even the arid land—called everything from marginal to just plain ugly—on which wild jojoba grows turned a profit, with real estate prices shooting from $800 to $4,100 an acre (S-69). By 1982, 20,000 acres in California and Arizona were planted to jojoba (A-697; H. S. Gentry, pers. comm., 13 July 1981; J. Kazansky, pers. comm., 8 October 1982). In addition, commercial jojoba plantations have been established or are being considered in Mexico, Costa Rica, Venezuela, Kenya, Ghana, Libya, Egypt, Sudan, Saudi Arabia, Israel, Iran, Jordan, India, Thailand, and Australia. It is reported that Israel is now cultivating the most productive and genetically consistent strains of jojoba in the world (D-100, M-601). According to our supplier survey, the United States already is importing some jojoba from both Israel and Mexico.

As it takes 4–6 years from seed to bearing in jojoba and from 8 to 12 years for full mature production, it will be the late 1980s before plantation-grown jojoba begins to contribute significantly to overall production (A-697, D-100, S-69,

Table 7.7   **World production and U.S. imports of sperm whale oil, carnauba wax, and candelilla wax**

| OIL/WAX | WORLD PRODUCTION (Average annual pounds per period) | U.S. IMPORTS AS PERCENTAGE OF WORLD PRODUCTION (Average annual pounds per period) |
|---|---|---|
| Sperm whale oil | 300 million (1963–1967) | 59 million (18%) (1963–1967) |
| Carnauba wax | 23 million (1972–1976) | 8 million (33%) (1972–1976) |
| Candelilla wax | 5 million (1972–1976) | 3 million (57%) (1972–1976) |

Source: V-380.

Y-12, Y-80; J. Kazansky, pers. comm., 8 October 1982). At that time it is estimated that supply could meet the present demand (D-100). The cosmetic industry is the current major market for jojoba. It is used in soaps, shampoos, hair
conditioners, cleansing creams, moisturizers, body lotions, depilatories, sun-
screens, lipsticks, and bath liquids (A-697, D-100; J. Kazansky, pers. comm., 8
October 1982). But the restricted supply of jojoba limits its use even in cosmetics. In the 1970s, Avon was on the verge of releasing a skin lotion containing 5%
jojoba oil, but the company was forced to reformulate the product when it could
not secure an annual supply of 20,000–40,000 pounds (D-100).

The real challenge for jojoba is to penetrate the vast and lucrative market of
transmission lubricants—at present still being supplied by reserved stores of
sperm whale oil (A-697, D-100, Y-12) as well as by substitutes synthesized from
castor and other oils (P-490)—and other industrial applications. So far, the only
automobiles that can afford to use jojoba in their crankcases are high-speed
racing cars competing for prestige and big prize money (D-100).

The potential of copaiba and the gopher plant is as sources of fuel and depends
on the price and processing advantages that they may have not merely vis-à-vis
petroleum (which is likely to decline in availability and rise in price) and coal
(which may become a competitive liquid fuel source and remain so for a long
time) but also with other plants such as cassava. Their future as possible domesticates is thus highly speculative. Copaiba oil is composed entirely of hydrocarbons and is very similar to diesel oil. The gopher plant contains a mixture of
hydrocarbons that, when subjected to catalytic cracking, yields products that
are almost identical to those from naphtha, one of the main raw materials of the
chemical industry (V-366). Hence there are grounds for investigating both species. Unfortunately, the field of botanical fuels is as rich in hyperbole as it is in
hydrocarbons. In a review of the domestication and breeding of new crop plants,
Jain in fact points to the gopher plant as "a good example of the need for careful
scientific studies prior to raising high hopes and unhelpful publicity." Gopher
plant promoters have painted visions of "oil farms" and "petroleum plantations" of the species, but test plantings have shown that "much work is needed
on variation and improvement by breeding as well as the development of suit
able cultural practices" (J-633).

The identification, testing, and use of a variety of genetic materials suitable
for different applications are necessities if crop developers are to help create and
respond to breakthroughs in the market. With such variety an incipient domesticate that appears economically marginal now can take advantage of eventual
changes in market conditions and make the leap forward to new crop status.
Without a diverse germplasm base, its prospects are even bleaker. The development of both vernonia and crambe has been hampered by lack of the genetic
materials needed to incorporate seed retention in vernonia and higher yields,
disease resistance, and adaptation to specific production areas in crambe
(V-392). By contrast, there is considerable useful variation available in guayule,

jojoba, meadowfoam, bladderpod, and Stokes' aster (A-292, G-763, J-633, V-392).
This confirms the hopeful outlook for jojoba and could improve that for the
other species.

Against a background of great interest and some uncertainty over the domestication of new commodity crops, new food crops continue to be domesticated
at a modest but steady rate—pecan, cranberry, macadamia, and blackberry in
the last century; blueberry, wild rice, and kiwi fruit in this. Although there may
be few significant food plants now left for domestication, the record suggests
that the current rate could continue. Already Brazil nut is an incipient domesticate, and food plants currently obtained exclusively from the wild—such as
maple and fiddleheads—are candidates for domestication. There are also several
wild fruits and vegetables that will be increasingly difficult to forage for and may
disappear from farmers' markets unless they are domesticated. Wild onions
(*Allium* spp.) are dug up on such a scale in Gatineau Park, Quebec, that officials
now impose fines of up to $500 in an effort to stop the poaching (V-270). Once
domesticated, these or other vegetables might command a North American
market of $1 million or more, earning them the status of yet another new, if
minor, food crop.

## The Third Forest: The Domestication of Timber Trees

The first forest was the one that greeted Europeans when they arrived in North
America. They cut it down. The second forest arose largely on agricultural land
abandoned around the turn of the century. The forest regenerated naturally, in
most places untended and uncared for, until it reached an age when it too could
be, and was, felled. The second forest is being replaced by a rather different kind
of forest: this, the third forest, is being established through a mixture of more or
less managed natural regeneration and artificial regeneration (Y-82). Although
many stands in the third forest are direct descendants of the first and some are
completely wild, the emphasis is heavily on management. Consequently, even
in those stands that are regenerating naturally, the species composition and age
structure may be very different from what they would have been if natural
succession had been allowed to proceed. The timber trees of North America are
being domesticated.

The domestication of timber trees is almost as old as agriculture but was for
long so limited that it had no impact on the market. Silviculture on any scale
probably began in Japan in the sixteenth century and in Europe in the seventeenth century (D-141). It was not introduced into North America until the late
nineteenth century, when in 1889 the first commercial forest plantation was
started at Biltmore, North Carolina (A-1416).

The timber industry in the nineteenth century was nomadic. It moved from
New England to the Middle Atlantic states; then on to the Lake states, and

finally, in the early 1900s, to the South and the Pacific Northwest. It was a cut-and-run business. As the timber of one region was cut out, the industry moved on to another. The lumber companies cut the trees down because they were there, a resource for the taking. Once they reached the South and the Pacific coast, U.S. logging's last frontiers, they had nowhere else to go (A-1416). A company interested in staying in the timber business, rather than in investing its capital opportunistically in whatever industry might be booming at the time, has to get into silviculture. This was not evident in the last days of the first forest. It did not make good economic sense then, just as it would not now, to spend money growing a tree for 20 years when huge stands of 200-year-old trees were there for the felling. The third forest could not have begun, and did not begin, until the first and second forests were out of the way.

Plantings more or less followed the ax. They accounted for 1% of the commercial forest land in the North (New England, Middle Atlantic, Lake, and Central states) by the late 1930s; in the South (South Atlantic and Gulf states) by 1950; and in the West (Pacific region and Rocky Mountains) by the late 1950s. They reached the 1% mark for the whole of the United States in the late 1940s (table 7.8). Essentially, then, domestication of timber trees in the United States did not become a factor in commercial timber production until well into the twentieth century; and the species involved are, at the earliest, new domesticates, many still in the incipient stage.

The rate of artificial regeneration (planting and direct seeding) remained low during the first half of this century, not reaching a million acres a year until 1957 (S-800). Since then it has continued to increase and currently averages more than 2 million acres a year (A-1419), or 0.4% of the total area of commercial timberland in the United States (482.5 million acres: S-818). Estimates of the cumulative acreage regenerated artificially were last published for 1960 (see table 7.8) and gave a total of 18.3 million acres for the United States. Excluding wind-barrier plantings (which do not count as forest land) the total then was 17.2 million acres (or 3.6% of all commercial forest land), 9.4 million acres of which were in the South (5% of the South's total commercial forest acreage), 6 million acres in the North (3.6% of its total), and 1.8 million acres were in the West (1.4% of its total). At the rate of artificial regeneration since then, the total plantation area would have more than doubled by 1977—to 41.8 million acres or 8.7% of all commercial forest land, with 24.3 million acres in the South, 10.0 million acres in the North, and 7.5 million acres in the West (S-800).

These figures overestimate the current plantation acreage because they assume that all plantings had a 100% success rate and that none of them was logged. There are no statistically reliable data on plantation success rates, but estimates suggest that seedling survival in the South, where conditions are most favorable, is 70–75%. Survival is lower in the North and West (S-800). Until 1950, USDA Forest Service planting statistics had a column showing the cumulative acreage of "successful plantations," and this claimed higher success

Table 7.8 **Cumulative acreage of forest plantings in the United States, 1925–1976/77**

| REGION | CUMULATIVE ACREAGE OF FOREST PLANTINGS (1,000 ACRES) | | | | | | | | | | | TOTAL AREA OF COMMERCIAL FOREST LAND (1,000 acres) |
|---|---|---|---|---|---|---|---|---|---|---|---|---|
| | 1925T | 1930T | 1935S | 1940S | 1945S | 1950T | 1950S | 1955T | 1960T | 1965T | 1976/77T | |
| North | 1,357 | 1,385 | 1,615 | 2,658 | 2,862 | 4,420 | 3,363 | 5,646 | 6,039 | 7,418 | 9,962 | 166,141 |
| South | 30 | 65 | 111 | 877 | 945 | 1,944 | 1,645 | 3,859 | 9,443 | 13,726 | 24,264 | 188,046 |
| West | 240 | 342 | 227 | 315 | 411 | 743 | 577 | 1,067 | 1,762 | 3,150 | 7,538 | 128,299 |
| U.S. TOTAL | 1,627 | 1,792 | 1,953 | 3,850 | 4,218 | 7,107 | 5,585 | 10,572 | 17,245 | 24,295 | 41,765 | 482,486 |

Sources: 1925–1960: annual summaries of forest plantings in the United States, 1925–1932, 1934–1941, 1945–1960, compiled by U.S. Department of Agriculture Forest Service, Washington, D.C.; 1961–1976/77: S-800; total area: S-818.

Notes: Data rounded to nearest thousand; data may not add due to independent rounding. T = total acreage, S = successful acreage, 1925–1955 data include wind-barrier plantings, 1960–1976/77 data exclude wind-barrier plantings.

rates: 85% in the South, 76% in the North, 78% in the West, and an average for the United States of 79% (see table 7.8). We have been generous and assumed an average of 80% for the nation. This would reduce the current U.S. plantation area to 33.4 million acres (or 6.9% of the total). Except in the South, which has much shorter rotation rates than the rest of the country, very little of the plantation acreage would have been logged. We have therefore assumed that all new and successful plantings have added to the total plantation acreage (rather than simply replacing logged plantation trees) and accordingly that the cumulative acreage figures provide a reasonably realistic estimate of the total acreage of domesticated timber trees today.

We have not been able to determine precisely the species composition of the current plantation acreage. The consensus of opinion appears to be that in the South they consist almost entirely of southern yellow pines; in the North the main species are pines and spruces—chiefly red pine (*Pinus resinosa*), white pine (*P. strobus*), jack pine (*P. banksiana*), and white spruce (*Picea glauca*); in the West the main species is douglas fir (*Pseudotsuga menziesii*), although the earliest plantings were largely of pines—ponderosa pine (*Pinus ponderosa*), jeffrey pine (*P. jeffreyi*), and western white pine (*P. monticola*).

Of all these species the fastest growing are the southern yellow pines in the South, which can be grown on a 25-year rotation. Thinnings are harvested sooner than this. In Louisiana at Crown Zellerbach's Tickfaw Managed Forest (which is grown on a 28-year rotation with 90% natural regeneration), the first thinning is at age 15 (and yields pulpwood logs) and the second is at age 20 (and yields lumber for the stud mill). The final harvest produces sawlogs and transmission poles (W. E. Eberhardt, pers. comm., 11 August 1982). Until recently, the trend was to reduce the rotation ages of pine plantations, especially those established during the Soil Bank Program (1956–61). This program paid farmers to retire cropland during a period of low prices for farm products and encouraged them to plant the retired lands with pines (S-800). In recent years, managers of plantations operated by the timber industry have tended to prolong the rotation ages of pine plantations to obtain the higher returns available from veneer and sawtimber (compared with pulpwood) (D. L. Cromley, pers. comm., 11 July 1983). However, a 25-year rotation with a first thinning at 15 may be considered typical (Y-82). This means that plantings made after 1955 would make a small contribution (thinnings for pulp) to current (1980) timber harvests, while those made after 1965 would make no contribution at all.

In the North the rotations are longer, ranging from 45–60 years for jack pine to 80–120 years for red pine and white pine, with first thinnings from age 35 (red pine and white pine) to 40–50 (the spruces) (J. D. Murphy, pers. comm., 23 June 1983). First thinnings can therefore be expected to be a component of the current harvest from those plantings made by 1945; jack pine plantations established between 1920 and 1935 would make their full contribution; but generally speaking the plantations of the North are unlikely to be significant sources of timber until later this century.

The situation in the West is similar. A typical rotation for douglas fir is 80 years, although some may be harvested as early as age 50. However, major plantings of douglas fir did not begin until the late 1940s, which effectively removes them from the current supply picture (J. Edgren, pers. comm., 21 June 1983; J. Fiske, pers. comm., 21 June 1983). The early plantings were mostly of pine with rotation ages of 30–50 (Fiske, 21 June 1983). Accordingly, pine plantations established by 1950 are likely to be the only significant contributors of domesticated timber to current production.

We have used these considerations in estimating the proportion of U.S. timber production accounted for by artificially regenerated trees. We have assumed for calculation purposes that all plantations of harvest age in the South are southern yellow pines; in the North white pine, red pine, and jack pine; and in the West ponderosa, jeffrey, western white, and sugar pines. The area of commercial timberland in the South under the loblolly-shortleaf and longleaf-slash pine communities is 63.3 million acres, that in the North under the white-red-jack pine community is 11.5 million acres, and that in the West under the ponderosa and western white pine communities is 27.1 million acres (S-818).

In 1955 the cumulative plantation area (excluding wind barriers) in the South was 3.9 million acres. If we assume an 80% success rate, this figure is reduced to 3.1 million acres. An additional 10.0 million acres were planted between 1955 and 1965, providing (again assuming 80% success) 8.0 million acres. If all the former acreage and half the latter (thinnings) were harvested in 1980, this would mean that effectively 7.1 million acres—or 11.2% of the total southern pine acreage—supplied that year's production. In 1945 the cumulative successful plantation acreage (including wind barriers) in the North was 2.9 million acres. The 1945 plantings are the youngest that would supply current production, and since only thinnings would be taken, we have assumed that only half that acreage would be harvested—1.5 million acres, or 13.0% of white-red-jack pine acreage. In 1950 the cumulative successful plantation acreage (including wind barriers) in the West was 0.6 million—or 2.2% of the ponderosa-western white pine acreage. As shown in table 2.16, the southern yellow pines contributed 31.1% of total timber removals; eastern white and red pines 1.4%; and the western pines (ponderosa, jeffrey, white, and sugar) 6.3%. On the basis of the appropriate percentages of each (11.2% of southern pine, 13.0% of eastern pine, and 2.2% of western pine), we conclude that about 4% of current (1980) U.S. timber production comes from domesticated trees; wild trees provide just over 96%. The figures are summarized in table 7.9. The cumulative plantation acreages cited above are from table 7.8. We estimate that the annual value of this plantation production is $700 million: $654 million from the South, $14 million from the North, and $32 million from the West. The value of production in the

Table 7.9  **Apparent contribution of silviculture to U.S. domestic timber production, 1976–1980**

| | 1<br>TOTAL AREA<br>(million acres) | 2<br>HARVESTABLE AREA<br>UNDER SILVICULTURE<br>(million acres) | 3<br>YEAR<br>OF LATEST<br>PLANTING | 4<br>COLUMN 2<br>AS PERCENTAGE<br>OF 1 | 5<br>PERCENTAGE<br>OF TOTAL<br>REMOVALS | 6<br>COLUMN 4<br>AS PERCENTAGE<br>OF 5 |
|---|---|---|---|---|---|---|
| SOUTH<br>Southern pines | 63.3 | 3.1<br>50% of 8.0<br>7.1 | 1955<br>1965 | 11.2 | 31.1 | 3.5 |
| NORTH<br>White-red-jack pines | 11.5 | 50% of 2.9<br>1.5 | 1945 | 13.0 | 1.4 | 0.2 |
| WEST<br>Ponderosa-western pines | 27.1 | 0.6 | 1950 | 2.2 | 6.3 | 0.1 |
| U.S. TOTAL | | | | | | 3.8 |

West is higher than that in the North because western pines are more valuable than northern pines and spruces (P-498, S-797, S-817).

The contribution of artificially regenerated trees to U.S. imports is almost certainly no more than it is to U.S. production. A report on plantations in Canada shows that in 1965 they occupied only 1.9 million acres—0.3% of Canada's productive forest land (A-1356). Most of the trees had been planted in the 1950s and 1960s, and 20% of them were in wind barriers and therefore not a likely source of commercial timber. We estimate (table 7.10) that 0.2 million acres of plantations—or 0.03% of the total area—are old enough to contribute to current Canadian production. Estimated pro rata at 0.03% of $6,405 million (the annual value of timber imports from Canada), the annual value of U.S. imports of Canadian plantation products would be $1.9 million. Excluded from this calculation is an additional $5.9 million a year of Christmas trees imported from Canada—of which some 65%, or $3.8 million a year, comes from domesticated trees (primarily balsam fir, *Abies balsamea*) (S-835).

Canada accounts for 85% of U.S. timber imports by value (chap. 2). The remaining 15% comes largely from Southeast Asia, Europe, and tropical America. On the basis of those imports identified by species group and counting "don't knows" as domesticated, not more than 25% of non-Canadian imports comes from plantation trees (table 7.11 and note 4). This means that, at most, 4% of U.S. timber imports comes from artificially regenerated trees.

Without further study it is not possible for us to identify more than a sampling of the timber species that might qualify as new domesticates. Much the most important new domesticates in the United States are the southern yellow pines. They account for more than 90% of current production from plantation trees (table 7.9), which would give them an annual value of $654 million. The

Table 7.10    **Estimated acreage of artificially regenerated timber in Canada available for harvest in 1980**

| SPECIES GROUP | FIRST THINNINGS At age | FIRST THINNINGS Acreage available | WHOLE HARVEST At age | WHOLE HARVEST Acreage available | TOTAL* Acreage available |
|---|---|---|---|---|---|
| Douglas fir | 50 | 42,000 | 80 | 0 | 21,000 |
| Spruces | 40 | 94,000 | 60 | 5,000 | 52,000 |
| Pines | 35 | 173,000 | 60 | 16,000 | 102,500 |
| Other conifers | 35 | 68,000 | 60 | 8,000 | 42,000 |
| Poplars | — | — | 40 | 8,000 | 8,000 |
| TOTAL | | 377,000 | | 37,000 | 225,500 |

Sources: Acreages and rotation (whole harvest) ages: A-1356; first thinnings ages: main text.
*Fifty percent of acreage available for first thinnings + 100% of acreage available for whole harvest.

Table 7.11  **Timber imports by the United States identified by species group and coming from countries other than Canada, 1976–1980**

| SPECIES GROUP | EXPORTING COUNTRY | AVERAGE ANNUAL VALUE ($1,000) | | |
|---|---|---|---|---|
| | | Wild | Plantation | ? |
| SOFTWOODS | | | | |
| *Araucariaceae* | | | | |
| *Araucaria angustifolia* | Brazil | 1,472 | 1,472 | |
| Paraná pine | Other | | 102 | |
| *Cupressaceae* | | | | |
| *Thuja plicata* | Other | | 275 | |
| Red cedar | | | | |
| *Pinaceae* | | | | |
| *Abies* spp. | Other | | | 31 |
| Firs | | | | |
| *Larix* spp. | New Zealand | | 12 | |
| Larches | Other | | | 29 |
| *Picea* spp. | Denmark | | | 52 |
| Spruces | Other | | | 565 |
| *Pinus caribaea* and *P. oocarpa* | Mexico | 28,519 | | |
| Central American pines | Honduras | 4,048 | | |
| | Nicaragua | 612 | | |
| | Bahamas | 472 | | |
| *P. contorta* | Other | | 193 | |
| Lodgepole pine | | | | |
| *P. resinosa* and *P. strobus* | Mexico | | 94 | |
| Eastern red and white pines | Other | | 10 | |
| *P. sylvestris* | USSR | | | 25 |
| European red pine | Other | | | 25 |
| *Pinus* spp. | New Zealand | | 286 | |
| Pines | Other | | | 312 |
| *Pseudotsuga menziesii* | Other | | 22 | |
| Douglas fir | | | | |
| *Tsuga* spp. | United Kingdom | | 109 | |
| Hemlocks | Other | | 47 | |
| HARDWOODS | | | | |
| *Aceraceae* | | | | |
| *Acer* spp. | Other | | | 117 |
| Maples | | | | |
| *Araliaceae* | | | | |
| *Acanthopanax ricinofolius* | Japan | | | 32,143 |
| Sen | Taiwan | | | 3,375 |
| | Republic of Korea | | | 273 |
| | Other | | | 34 |

(*continued*)

Table 7.11  (*Continued*)

| SPECIES GROUP | EXPORTING COUNTRY | AVERAGE ANNUAL VALUE ($1,000) | | |
| --- | --- | --- | --- | --- |
| | | *Wild* | *Plantation* | ? |
| **Betulaceae** | | | | |
| *Betula* spp. | Japan | | | 25,133 |
| Birches | Finland | | | 8,391 |
| | USSR | | | 1,845 |
| | Poland | | | 16 |
| | Other | | | 12,538 |
| **Dipterocarpaceae** | | | | |
| *Parashorea, Pentacme,* and | Philippines | 57,337 | | |
| *Shorea* spp. | Other Southeast Asia | 8,774 | | |
| Lauan or Philippine | Republic of Korea | 82,812 | | |
| mahogany | Taiwan | 63,707 | | |
| | Other | 1,638 | | |
| **Ericaceae** | | | | |
| *Erica arborea* and *E. scoparia* | Greece | 910 | | |
| Brierroot | Spain | 467 | | |
| | Italy | 311 | | |
| | Other | 14 | | |
| **Fagaceae** | | | | |
| *Fagus* spp. | Denmark | | | 126 |
| Beeches | Other | | | 36 |
| *Quercus* spp. | Japan | | | 150 |
| Oaks | Sweden | | | 35 |
| | Other | | | 120 |
| **Juglandaceae** | | | | |
| *Juglans* spp. | Taiwan | | | 843 |
| Walnuts | Japan | | | 329 |
| | Republic of Korea | | | 237 |
| | Other | | | 38 |
| **Meliaceae** | | | | |
| *Cedrela* spp. | Brazil | 299 | | |
| Spanish cedars | Nicaragua | 195 | | |
| | Other | 83 | | |
| *Khaya* spp. | Ivory Coast | 457 | | |
| Mahoganies | Ghana | 460 | | |
| | Other West Africa | 218 | | |
| | Other | 19 | | |
| *Swietenia* spp. | Brazil | 10,232 | | |
| Mahoganies | Bolivia | 3,037 | | |
| | Other South America | 327 | | |
| | Central America | 691 | | |
| | Other | 1,150 | | |

Table 7.11  (*Continued*)

| SPECIES GROUP | EXPORTING COUNTRY | AVERAGE ANNUAL VALUE ($1,000) | | |
|---|---|---|---|---|
| | | *Wild* | *Plantation* | *?* |
| **Bombacaceae and Verbenaceae** | | | | |
| *Ochroma lagopus* | Ecuador | 1,342 | 1,342 | |
| Balsa | Belize | 38 | | |
| | Honduras | 26 | | |
| | Suriname | 84 | | |
| *Tectona grandis* | Thailand | 7,182 | 378 | |
| Teak | Burma | 2,363 | 124 | |
| | India | 85 | 4 | |
| | Indonesia | | 954 | |
| | Malaysia | | 130 | |
| | Taiwan | | 84 | |
| | China | | 52 | |
| | Ivory Coast | | 59 | |
| | Subtotal | (9,630) | (1,785) | |
| | Hong Kong | 1,302 | 248 | |
| | Singapore | 404 | 77 | |
| | Macao | 13 | 2 | |
| Either balsa or teak | Brazil | | | 64 |
| | Other | | | 559 |
| **Ebenaceae, Meliaceae, and Zygophyllaceae** | | | | |
| *Diospyros* spp. | Mexico | 172 | | |
| Ebony | Brazil | 132 | | |
| *Cedrela* spp. | Peru | 99 | | |
| Spanish cedar | Bolivia | 63 | | |
| *Guaiacum* spp. | Guatemala | 35 | | |
| Lignum vitae | India | 35 | | |
| | Other | 419 | | |
| **Aceraceae, Fagaceae, and Ulmaceae** | | | | |
| *Acer* spp. Japanese maple *Quercus* spp. Japanese oak | Japan | | | 44 |
| *Phyllostylon brasiliensis* Boxwood | Brazil | 39 | | |
| Any of the above | Other | | | 29 |
| TOTAL | | 282,094 | 6,076 | 87,514 |

Note: Explanation and sources are in note 4.

Table 7.12  **Composition of the southern yellow pines**

| SPECIES | | PERCENTAGE OF VOLUME OF COMMERCIAL SOUTHERN YELLOW PINE GROWING STOCK |
|---|---|---|
| Pinus taeda | Loblolly pine | 46.6 |
| P. echinata | Shortleaf pine | 24.4 |
| | | 71.0 |
| P. palustris | Longleaf pine | 9.3 |
| P. elliottii | Slash pine | 8.5 |
| | | 17.8 |
| P. virginiana | Virginia pine | 5.7 |
| P. serotina | Pond pine | 2.6 |
| P. rigida | Pitch pine | 1.7 |
| P. glabra | Spruce pine | 0.8 |
| P. pungens | Table Mountain pine | 0.2 |
| P. clausa | Sand pine | 0.1 |
| | | 11.1 |
| | | 99.9 |

Sources: S-733, S-818.

southern yellow pines comprise 10 species (table 7.12). The top four species—loblolly pine (*Pinus taeda*), shortleaf pine (*P. echinata*), longleaf pine (*P. palustris*), and slash pine (*P. elliottii*)—produce almost 90% of the commercial growing stock volume, but the two chief domesticates are loblolly and slash pine. Slash pine was the most popular species from the 1920s, when plantings in the South began, until the early 1970s (V-289; O. O. Wells, pers. comm., 11 August 1982). Since then, loblolly has far outstripped it. Although slash pine is still the major plantation species in Florida (Y-82), elsewhere in the South most plantings now—particularly of improved stock—are of loblolly (note 5). It seems likely that slash and loblolly together account for $500 million of current production from southern pine plantations, the balance being produced by shortleaf, longleaf, Virginia (*P. virginiana*), and pond pine (*P. serotina*).

Except during the era of the Soil Bank Program, when farmers and other private landowners outside the timber industry planted extensive acreages of these species, most of the impetus to the domestication of the southern pines has come from industry. The first plantation in the South was established in 1920 by the Great Southern Lumber Company, which also started the first nursery in 1923 at Bogalusa, Louisiana (A-1416; T. Vermillion, pers. comm., 11 August 1982). Of the 63.3 million acres of southern pines in the South, the timber industry owns 17.1 million acres (27%) while other private landowners own 39.8 million acres (63%); federal and state governments own the remaining 10% (S-818). About half the industry-owned and -operated pine forest land (the industry operates some of its land under long-term leases from other private owners [S-800]) has been artificially regenerated (see note 5). By contrast, on nonindustrial private lands only about 15% of the acreage is being planted to pines, the rest being allowed to revert to hardwoods (D. L. Cromley, pers. comm., 11 July 1983).

The most influential development in the domestication of southern pines occurred in the 1950s with the start of selection and breeding programs. Prior to that time, plantation seed was collected from wild trees—seldom with sufficient attention to the suitability of the seed for the planting site (V-289, Y-82). The programs are organized as three cooperatives, combining the efforts of universities, industry (chiefly pulp and paper companies), and state and federal forest services. The North Carolina State University–Industry Cooperative Tree Improvement Program covers the Carolinas, Virginia, Georgia, Alabama, and Mississippi. The Florida Tree Improvement Cooperative (based at the University of Florida) covers that state. The Western Gulf Forest Tree Improvement Program (based at Texas A&M University) covers Louisiana, Texas, Arkansas, and Oklahoma (R. J. Weir, pers. comm., 12 July 1982; O. O. Wells, pers. comm., 11 August 1982).

The impact of these programs can be illustrated by the North Carolina State University–Industry Cooperative. By June 1982 the cooperative, formed in 1955, included 25 forest-based industries and the forestry organizations of three states (North Carolina, South Carolina, and Virginia) (A-942). Data from the cooperative (see note 5) show that plantations have been established on just over half (53%) of the pine forest lands operated by its industry members. Just over half (54%) of this plantation acreage has been regenerated with improved trees. The remainder has been regenerated with seed from wild trees or from unimproved plantation trees (one generation from the wild). The most important plantation species by far is loblolly, followed by slash pine, the two making up 83% and 11%, respectively, of the cooperative's southern yellow pine seed orchard acreage. These two species also comprise the only second-generation seed orchard acreage (441 acres of loblolly and 16 acres of slash), the remaining 3,248 acres being of first-generation trees. Between 1977 and 1981 these seed orchards produced enough improved seed to regenerate 3.6 million acres (A-937, A-949). The additional revenue provided by increased yields from acreage regenerated with genetically improved seedlings is expected to be greater than $80 million a year.

The improvement programs have used the genetic variation within the loblolly and slash pine species to improve quality and increase yields. The quality improvements include straighter trees (enabling more of the trees to be harvested for high value purposes, such as sawlogs and transmission poles), higher wood specific gravity, and manipulation of tracheids (the tubelike cells of softwoods). Higher wood specific gravity means that the wood is denser and can yield more pulp per unit of wood; using parents with short tracheids and thin cell walls enables the production of softwood trees with a pulping quality similar to that of hardwoods, thereby increasing the flexibility of timber operations where hardwoods are in short supply (A-949, Y-82; R. J. Weir, pers. comm., 12 July 1982).

Yield improvements include better adaptability, faster growth, and disease resistance. Loblolly pines have been developed with greater drought tolerance, thereby helping to make marginal lands capable of growing profitable crops of trees. The improved loblollies can be grown to merchantable size sooner, reducing a 25-year rotation to 23 years. Faster growth also means that bigger, more valuable trees can be harvested in a given period of time. The resulting yield increases of 10–15% more wood per acre have been estimated to raise the value of production per acre by 18–32% (A-937, A-949).

The natural range of loblolly is from southern Delaware in a wide (roughly 200 mile) arc through southern Maryland, Virginia, the Carolinas, Georgia, northern Florida, Alabama, Mississippi, and eastern Louisiana to the Mississippi River, with a western outlier in southeast Texas, western Louisiana, and southern Arkansas (J-342, S-733). A 25-year study of variation in the species has demonstrated inherent variation in both growth rate and disease resistance. The western outlier population is slower growing, more drought resistant, and more resistant to fusiform rust (caused by the fungus *Cronartium fusiforme*) than are populations east of the Mississippi. Among the eastern populations, those of the coastal plain are faster growing, more susceptible to ice and cold, and less drought resistant than are populations from areas with a more continental climate, such as northern Georgia or the piedmont of South Carolina. The study shows that, with a few important exceptions, local seed is best. The most important exception is the high fusiform rust area of southern and central Mississippi, Alabama, and Georgia (V-309).

Fusiform rust was considered merely a curiosity at the turn of the century and generally a minor economic problem during the 1940s and 1950s. By the 1970s, however, the disease had become so serious in the high rust area that intensive silviculture could not be practiced (V-289). Fusiform rust has destroyed or damaged as much as 20–75% of planted unimproved slash pine and 20% of loblolly (S-800). Fortunately, loblolly populations that are highly resistant to *Cronartium fusiforme* have been found west of the Mississippi, on the eastern shore of Maryland, and in the panhandle of Louisiana north of New Orleans (V-290, V-291). The Texas and Arkansas (west of the Mississippi) populations are slow growing (in fact, Atlantic coastal loblolly grow faster in Arkansas than do the local trees [V-309]). The best combination of high rust resistance and fast growth is found in the Louisiana panhandle populations—particularly in Livingston Parish—and these are now the recommended source for planting in the high rust area and in coastal South Carolina, where rust is a serious problem. On high hazard sites in the piedmont of Alabama, Georgia, and South Carolina the more cold-resistant population of the eastern shore of Maryland is the recommended source. About 100,000 pounds of rust-resistant loblolly seed has been collected from wild stands in southeastern Louisiana, and some 300,000 acres of rust-resistant loblolly (largely originating from Livingston Parish) have been planted in the high rust area (V-289–V-291; O. O. Wells, pers. comm., 11 August 1982). Loblolly losses to rust have been reduced from 20 to 3%, and sites that were once marginal because of the presence of *C. fusiforme* can now be made productive (S-800).

The remaining 10% of current production from U.S. plantations (with an estimated annual value of $48 million) comes largely from pines and spruces in the North and pines in the West. On the basis of current plantings the main species in the North is red pine (*Pinus resinosa*), followed by eastern white pine (*P. strobus*), white spruce (*Picea glauca*), jack pine (*Pinus banksiana*), shortleaf and loblolly pine, and two introduced species—Scotch pine (*P. sylvestris*) and Norway spruce (*Picea abies*) (data supplied by J. D. Murphy, pers. comm., 23 June 1983). The native species are new domesticates; the introduced species are recent domesticates, their domestication beginning in Europe (V-376). The introduced domesticates account for 10% of current pine and spruce plantings in the North. On a pro rata basis this means that production from native domesticates in the North is worth $14 million a year, $1.4 million coming from the introduced domesticates. In the West the estimated $32 million a year contributed by plantations comes largely from western white pine (*Pinus monticola*), sugar pine (*P. lambertiana*), and ponderosa pine (*P. ponderosa*)—all new domesticates. Sources of resistance to blister rust in eastern white pine, western white pine, and sugar pine have been used to breed resistant forms of the latter two species, which have been planted in California, Idaho, Montana, Oregon, and Washington, thus rescuing pine plantations in the northern Rocky Mountains from almost certain destruction (D-396, S-800).

The only hardwood species that are being planted in the United States on a commercial scale are cottonwood (*Populus* spp.) and black walnut (*Juglans nigra*). Crown Zellerbach is the leader in cottonwood planting; it established a plantation on a former soybean farm in the early 1970s and planted 2,000–3,000 acres a year on a 20-year rotation (cottonwood being a good source of pulp for the manufacture of high gloss paper) (O. O. Wells, pers. comm., 11 August 1982). Black walnut growing is a farm woodlot operation in which the trees are grown for nuts as well as for veneer logs. At present wild trees continue to be the chief source of veneer logs (black walnut is the most valuable native veneer), but enough seed and seedlings are being sold to establish 7,000 acres of new plantations each year. Cottonwood growing is a twentieth-century development but the domestication of black walnut began in the last century (D-504, P-82).

The contribution of plantation trees in the United States and Canada to U.S. timber supplies is bound to grow as existing plantation acreage comes into production and as new acreage is established. In the United States southern pines will probably remain the most important domesticated species—most

(58%) of the existing acreage is in the South, and most (65%) new plantings are there too (table 7.8; A-1419). Douglas fir (*Pseudotsuga menziesii*), however, is the major incipient domesticate, since it is now the chief plantation species both in the U.S. West and (with white spruce) in Canada (A-1356, D-396, S-800). Nevertheless, it does not seem likely that artificially regenerated trees will become a bigger producer of timber than wild trees. As we saw in chapter 2, hardwoods are making a growing contribution to total timber production due to the resurgence of fuelwood and their greater use in the manufacture of pulp and panel products. Virtually all the hardwoods will probably be left to regenerate naturally (as they are on nonindustrial private lands in the South) because they do so easily and quickly (S-800). In the South, even in the forests managed for pure pine, volunteer hardwoods occupy 25–30% of the stand (W. E. Eberhardt, pers. comm., 11 August 1982). Throughout the United States the most typical problem of forest managers is the failure of southern pines, douglas fir, or other softwoods to regenerate due to competition from hardwoods (S-800). At the same time, managed, naturally regenerated softwood forests will continue to contribute substantial volumes of timber to the nation, and it will not be cost effective to replace more than a fraction of them with plantations. The emerging role of wild timber trees in North America is a dual one: as a substantial renewable source of raw materials, and as the basic germplasm resource for the domestication and improvement of plantation trees.

## New and Incipient Animal Domesticates

Far fewer animal species than plant species have been domesticated. Eighteen livestock species contribute roughly the same annual sum ($60 billion) to the U.S. economy as do 226 crop species. Tables 7.13 and 7.14 show that most of the species were domesticated in the ancient and early periods. The two most important livestock species—cattle and pigs—were domesticated during the ancient period and account for 84% of the annual value of livestock produced or imported by the United States. (The ancient period is given as 9000–5000 B.C. in tables 7.13 and 7.14 rather than 7000–5000 B.C. as in tables 7.1, 7.4, and 7.5 because of the earlier evidence of animal domestication [A-1413, S-323].) After the early period, domestications of land animals almost petered out but began again toward the end of the last century.

In the latter part of the nineteenth and the early part of the twentieth centuries demand for furs was so high that heavy pressure was put on some of the major furbearing species. In response, fox farms were started in Canada before the turn of the century, and others followed in the United States and Europe (notably in Scandinavia) (A-924). Two of the three new livestock species—mink and chinchilla—are furbearers whose domestication was part of this process. The main fox species farmed is the silver form of the red fox (*Vulpes vulpes*). The

Table 7.13   **Periods of domestication of 18 livestock species raised or imported by the United States with a minimum annual value of $1 million**

| PERIOD OF DOMESTICATION | VALUE CATEGORY* | LIVESTOCK SPECIES | COMBINED VALUE (U.S.$ million) |
|---|---|---|---|
| Ancient (9000–5000 B.C.) | Super | 2 | 50,757.2 |
| | Major | 1 | 807.8 |
| | Medium | 1 | 78.3 |
| | Minor | 0 | 0.0 |
| | | 4 | 51,643.3 |
| Early (5000–0 B.C.) | Super | 2 | 7,950.1 |
| | Major | 2 | 512.4 |
| | Medium | 1 | 64.2 |
| | Minor | 4 | 13.8 |
| | | 9 | 8,540.5 |
| Late (A.D. 0–1700) | Super | 0 | 0.0 |
| | Major | 0 | 0.0 |
| | Medium | 1 | 19.8 |
| | Minor | 0 | 0.0 |
| | | 1 | 19.8 |
| Recent (A.D. 1700–1900) | Super | 0 | 0.0 |
| | Major | 0 | 0.0 |
| | Medium | 1 | 18.5 |
| | Minor | 0 | 0.0 |
| | | 1 | 18.5 |
| New (A.D. 1900–present) | Super | 0 | 0.0 |
| | Major | 1 | 160.2 |
| | Medium | 1 | 17.1 |
| | Minor | 1 | 1.4 |
| | | 3 | 178.7 |
| TOTAL | | 18 | 60,400.8 |

Source: Table 7.17.

* Super = more than $1,000 million; major = $100–$1,000 million; medium = $10–$100 million; minor = $1 $10 million

early success of this domestication, coupled with rapidly rising demand for mink, encouraged the first mink (*Mustela vison*) ranches in the early 1900s, and there were many mink farms in Canada by 1913. The favored sources of breeding stock from the wild were the Pacific coast and Alaska because the animals there are larger and darker in color (P-408). While fox has declined in popularity, mink has become a domesticate of major importance—the first (as far as the North American economy is concerned) since the turkey was domesticated more than 2,000 years ago. The annual value of U.S. farm-raised mink is $84.5 million (S-798); average imports are worth almost as much—$75.7 million a year (S-450–S-454).

Table 7.14  **Apparent rates of domestication of 18 livestock species raised or imported by the United States with a minimum annual value of $1 million**

| PERIOD OF DOMESTICATION | APPARENT RATE PER MILLENNIUM | | APPARENT RATE PER CENTURY | |
|---|---|---|---|---|
| | *Livestock species* | *Combined value ($ million)* | *Livestock species* | *Combined value ($ million)* |
| Ancient (9000–5000 B.C.) | 1.0 | 12,910.8 | 0.10 | 1,291.1 |
| Early (5000–0 B.C.) | 1.8 | 1,708.1 | 0.18 | 170.8 |
| Late (A.D. 0–1700) | 2.5 | 108.5 | 0.06 | 1.2 |
| Recent (A.D. 1700–1900) | | | 0.50 | 9.3 |
| New (A.D. 1900–present) | | | 3.00 | 178.7 |

Source: Table 7.13.

The domestication of the chinchilla (*Chinchilla laniger*) has its origins in the closing decade of the last century; the first reported captive birth was in 1896 in Santiago, Chile. However, large-scale commercial breeding did not begin until the 1920s, when there was an intense demand from fur farms for live wild animals as breeding stock (S-625). Hence we regard the chinchilla as a new rather than a recent domesticate. It is a minor one: almost 52,000 U.S.-farm raised chinchilla pelts were sold in 1978 (compared to 3.1 million U.S.-farm raised mink pelts) worth $1.4 million (S-798).

Several other furbearing species are in the early phases of domestication. Commercial farming of beaver (*Castor canadensis*) began in the United States in the 1950s; and farming of sable (*Martes zibellina*) in the USSR was launched in 1929 in response to the species' near extinction in the wild due to excessive trapping. Three other furbearers whose domestication has begun in Europe are Arctic fox (*Alopex lagopus*), nutria (*Myocastor coypus*), and raccoon dog (*Nyctereutes procyonoides*) (IUCN Conservation Monitoring Centre, pers. comm., April 1984).

The medium-level new domesticate—earthworms—is a polyspecies stock. Earthworm farms for bait were started some 50 years ago (J. P. Martin, pers. comm., 20 September 1983). In 1978 U.S. worm farms sold about 3 million pounds of worms with a sales value of $7.7 million (S-798). The United States also imports an average of $9.4 million worth of worms a year, almost exclusively from Canada (S-450–S-454). The main worm-producing states are California (27% of sales), Florida (10%), Texas (9%), and Wisconsin (9%) (S-798). Farm-raised earthworms are sold largely as bait for freshwater sport fishing; some are also sold to gardeners for soil improvement and composting of organic refuse (M-494). In Lufkin, Texas, the sewage treatment plant is apparently saving about $100,000 a year by progressively substituting worms for electricity and diesel fuel. Red wiggler worms are placed in greenhouse-like cells where they eat the sludge, digest it, and excrete castings that can be used as fertilizer or planting material. The worms breed quickly and operating costs are negligible: "All you need," Lufkin city manager Harvey Westerholm told *Newsweek* magazine, "is a worm wrangler to look after the worms" (A-219). Such exotic uses are at present only a very small part of the domesticated earthworm market. For most buyers the earthworm's place is on a hook. The most commonly farmed worms—accounting for 80–90% of commercial production—are manure worms (also known as angleworms, bandlings, or red wigglers) and red worms. Both belong to the Lumbricidae family (M-494).

There is clearly a modest but significant resurgence in animal domestication, and we can expect additional successful domestications in the coming years. Two incipient livestock species are red deer (*Cervus elaphus*) and musk deer (*Moschus moschiferus*). Red deer are being domesticated in New Zealand, where they were introduced from Europe in the 1850s. With no predators, few parasites, and an ideal environment the deer proliferated and quickly became a pest. Because they were so destructive of vegetation, red deer were officially declared vermin and hunters were paid to destroy them (V-387). The economic worth of red deer began to be recognized in the 1960s. There are lucrative markets for venison in Europe (particularly in the Federal Republic of Germany and in Switzerland) and for antlers in East Asia and the USSR. The first deer farm started in 1970. Since then deer farms have multiplied as rapidly as did the deer a century earlier: there are now more than 2,000 deer farms in New Zealand, and the number of farmed animals is more than 180,000 (V-387). The domestication of red deer is incipient with respect to its impact on the United States, which imports very little venison: an average of $610,000 worth a year (S-450–S-454), of which $453,000 (74%) comes from New Zealand. We suspect that there is a significantly greater market for venison in North America—made up of people who like eating it but not hunting it—which could be opened up if New Zealand were to market its venison with the energy and skill with which it sells its lamb.

The odoriferous substance called musk is produced by the musk deer (*Moschus moschiferus*), which is native to Pakistan, India, Bhutan, Nepal, Tibet, the People's Republic of China, and Burma (A-90, A-924, J-337, S-426, Y-76). Only the male has the musk-producing gland (often called a pod), which is under the abdomen between the scrotum and the navel (Y-76). In the past, the animals were simply hunted and killed, and the musk pod was removed and dried (S-426). This resulted in a major population reduction of musk deer not only because of the number of males that were killed to supply the much sought after musk, but also because of the number of females indiscriminately killed—since sex identification in the field is difficult as both males and females are without antlers (A-90, S-426, Y-76). At present, more and more musk is collected from live captive males (J-337). We will use the Chinese experience in musk deer farming to illustrate this fairly recent development.

An experimental musk deer farm was established in China in 1958—an outcome of a State Council directive that declared it was desirable to "actively and systematically convert wild animals and plants used in medicines into those which can be raised and grown domestically (as) a basic step in developing the production of traditional Chinese medicines and resolving the problem of supply of traditional Chinese materia medica." Other farms followed. Over 25 years, China's musk deer farming has grown from small scale to large scale. However, "although there are several large-scale musk deer farms in the country which rely on breeding in captivity, nevertheless, live capture of wild musk deer also has a certain significance." Three reasons are given by the Chinese for the continued take of wild deer: to prevent too much inbreeding in the domesticated deer, to raise disease resistance in the domesticated deer, and to raise production performance in the domesticated deer (Y-76).

The productive musk years for males held in captivity in China are from age 3 to 13. The average amount of musk produced over the 10-year period is 100–150 grams per animal. Collection is best made twice a year—in China the recommended months are March/April and June/July. The collector inserts a spoon into the pod and draws out the grains of musk (Y-76).

While musk continues to be used in Chinese medicine, the major Western use is in perfumery (especially oriental and heavy-floral types) (A-90, A-924, J-337, V-234). It is also used for its "rounding off" effect in nut, caramel, and fruit-type flavors in major food products (J-337). Between 1976 and 1980, the United States imported on average each year $165,000 worth of musk from unspecified countries (table 6.3).

The North American bison (*Bison bison*) is another incipient livestock species. Commercial farming of bison began in the 1950s; in 1983 there were estimated to be more than 60,000 head on private farms and ranches. The National Buffalo Association was formed in 1966 and had some 800 members by 1982. Bison are productive under conditions that are suboptimal for cattle and require less care. Their meat is low in fat and high in protein and so commands a premium among dieters and gourmets alike (S-1271).

## Aquaculture

The first known document on aquaculture is "Fish Breeding," which was written in 473 B.C. by Fan Li, who started breeding and raising common carp (*Cyprinus carpio*) about that time (S-362). It is possible that aquaculture began earlier than this: carp raising may have started as early as 2000 B.C. in China, and it has been suggested that some of the ancient civilizations of West Asia raised *Tilapia* species as far back as 2500 B.C. Yet, although aquaculture is almost as old as agriculture, very few aquatic species have been domesticated. Once the carp had been domesticated in China, and independently in Europe sometime during the late period, no other species was domesticated until trout raising began in the eighteenth century. Many authorities regard only two aquatic species as being completely domesticated: the common carp and the rainbow trout (*Salmo gairdneri*) (A-1150).

Much that is called aquaculture involves the management, at various levels of effort, of wild species rather than their domestication. Bardach, Ryther, and McLarney (A-1150) have classified seven types of aquaculture according to the level of management involved; and Reay (P-291) has classified eight types according to the degree of biological manipulation. In table 7.15 we have adapted the two classifications to illustrate their relationship to the two variables we have chosen to distinguish wild and domesticated species: natural vs. artificial regeneration of (1) the species itself and (2) its critical habitats. We list only six of Reay's eight types because two of them (III, seed not supplied from hatcheries and no holding facility provided but stock fed by farmer; VII, seed supplied from hatcheries and stock fed by farmer but no holding facility provided) are improbable.

In this book we treat populations in categories 1 and 2 (wild and semiwild) as wild and those in 3 and 4 (semidomesticated and domesticated) as domesticated. Table 7.16 shows that the domesticated component of eight groups of aquatic species raised or imported by the United States and with a minimum annual value of $1 million have a combined average annual value of $212.1 million. Table 7.16 begins with the recent period because the only species domesticated before that (the carp) is economically insignificant in North America.

The oldest aquatic domesticates of importance to the U.S. economy are the rainbow trout (*Salmo gairdneri*), brown trout (*S. trutta*), and brook trout (*Salvelinus fontinalis*). Of these three the rainbow trout is the main commercial species. The first trout hatchery was started in Germany in 1741, but commercial trout culture was not attempted until the nineteenth century—in 1853 in the United States, perhaps earlier in Europe (A-1150). The average annual value of domesticated trout production in the United States is currently (1976–1980) $29.5 million (P-434, S-798); imports, chiefly from Japan, are worth another $0.5 million (S-450–S-454). Salmon culture might have followed soon after, but although the Pacific salmon (*Oncorhynchus*) species in particular were enthusiastically propagated during much of the latter half of the last century, lack of knowledge about their life histories meant that efforts were largely wasted. A technique for hatchery propagation was first developed in Canada around 1857 and soon spread to the United States. The programs failed largely because of overstocking of the fresh waters into which the fry were released. It was not until the 1940s that it was discovered that chinook (*O. tshawytscha*) —which was one of the two main species involved (the other was coho [*O. kisutch*]) — spend the first three months to two years of life after the egg in fresh water (A-1150).

This discovery was the breakthrough that led to success. The main emphasis,

Table 7.15   **Main types of aquaculture from management of wild species to raising of domesticated species**

1. WILD (species regenerates without human assistance in a habitat that is also self-regenerating)
   a. Seed supply from hatcheries? No. Holding facility provided? No. Stock fed by farmer? No. Activity: transplantation of organisms to better growing conditions. Example: oysters in Prince Edward Island, Canada.
   Type 1 of Bardach et al.   Type I of Reay.
   b. Seed supply from hatcheries? No. Holding facility provided? Yes. Stock fed by farmer? No. Activity: trapping of fish and invertebrates in enclosures where they are kept until harvest. Examples: shrimp in Southeast Asia; bluefin tuna in Nova Scotia, Canada.
   Types 3 and 4 of Bardach et al.   Type II of Reay.
   Activity: raft culture of naturally reproducing invertebrates. Example: oysters in Japan.
   Type 7 (in part) of Bardach et al.   Type II of Reay.
   c. Seed supply from hatcheries? No. Holding facility provided? Yes. Stock fed by farmer? Yes. Activity: pond culture of naturally reproducing fishes and invertebrates. Examples: eels and yellowtail in Japan; freshwater crayfish in United States.
   Type 6 (in part) of Bardach et al.   Type IV of Reay.
2. SEMIWILD (species regenerates with partial human assistance)
   a. Seed supply from hatcheries? No. Holding facility provided? No. Stock fed by farmer? No. Activity: increasing recruitment of wild fish by capturing fish at spawning time and raising and releasing young. Example: sturgeon in USSR.
   Type 2 (in part) of Bardach et al.   Type V (in part) of Reay.
3. SEMIDOMESTICATED (species regenerates with human assistance; critical habitats mixed natural and artificial)
   a. Seed supply from hatcheries? Yes. Holding facility provided? No. Stock fed by farmer? No. Activity: hatchery raised fish released to wild to grow to maturity, returning to hatchery for propagation. Example: Pacific salmon in the United States and Canada.
   Type 2 (in part) of Bardach et al.   Type V (in part) of Reay.
4. DOMESTICATED (species' entire life cycle carried out under human management)
   a. Seed supply from hatcheries? Yes. Holding facility provided? Yes. Stock fed by farmer? No. Activity: pond and raft culture. Example: nori (seaweed) culture in Japan.
   Types 5 (in part) and 7 (in part) of Bardach et al.   Type VI of Reay.
   b. Seed supply from hatcheries? Yes. Holding facility provided? Yes. Stock fed by farmer? Yes. Activity: pond culture. Examples: catfish in the United States; shrimp in Japan.
   Type 6 (in part) of Bardach et al.   Type VIII of Reay.

Sources: Bardach et al. (A-1150); Reay (P-291).

Table 7.16 **Periods and apparent rates of domestication of 8 groups of aquaculture species raised or imported by the United States with a minimum annual value of $1 million**

| PERIOD OF DOMESTICATION | VALUE CATEGORY* | SPECIES | COMBINED VALUE ($ million) | APPARENT RATE PER CENTURY | |
|---|---|---|---|---|---|
| | | | | Species | Combined value ($ million) |
| Recent (A.D. 1700–1900) | | | | | |
| | Super | 0 | 0.0 | | |
| | Major | 0 | 0.0 | | |
| | Medium | 1 | 30.0 | | |
| | Minor | 0 | 0.0 | | |
| | | 1 | 30.0 | 0.5 | 15.0 |
| New (A.D. 1900–present) | | | | | |
| | Super | 0 | 0.0 | | |
| | Major | 0 | 0.0 | | |
| | Medium | 3 | 165.7 | | |
| | Minor | 4 | 16.4 | | |
| | | 7 | 182.1 | 7.0 | 182.1 |
| TOTAL | | 8 | 212.1 | | |

Source: Table 7.17.

*Super = more than $1,000 million; major = $100–$1,000 million; medium = $10–$100 million; minor = $1–$10 million.

and biggest achievement, has been the use of hatcheries and artificial spawning channels to augment the natural populations. This effort has been so successful that several populations have ceased to be natural. It is estimated that by 1974 hatchery-reared fish contributed 60 million pounds (30%) of the total U.S. catch of Pacific salmon (201 million pounds) (A-1227, G-625). The main species are still chinook and coho (G-625). In addition to the release of hatchery-reared fish to natural waters—a condition of semidomestication—an average of 5 million pounds of farmed and ranched fish is being produced each year (P-434). These fish are either raised in pens or are harvested on their return to the hatchery (G-625). Hence the Pacific salmon fishery now consists of a mixture of wild, semidomesticated, and domesticated populations. On the basis of their contributing 30% of current production, the average annual value of semidomesticated salmon production is $90.8 million (including $4.5 million of imports from Canada), whereas that of domesticated salmon is $2.2 million (P-434).

The two other new aquaculture domesticates (besides Pacific salmon) in the medium category ($10 million–$100 million a year) are catfish and oysters. Experimental catfish culture began in the United States in the 1920s, and some

Table 7.17 **Periods of domestication and average annual values (1976–1980) of 18 livestock species and 8 groups of aquaculture species raised or imported by the United States**

| DOMESTICATE | | | PERIOD WHEN DOMESTICATED | | | | | AVERAGE ANNUAL VALUE 1976–1980 (U.S.$ MILLION) | | | |
|---|---|---|---|---|---|---|---|---|---|---|---|
| *Phylum* CLASS | *Order* FAMILY | SPECIES | *Ancient/ before 5000 B.C.* | *Early/ 5000– 0 B.C.* | *Late/ A.D. 0– 1700* | *Recent/ A.D. 1700– 1900* | *New/ A.D. 1900 on* | U.S. farm sales | U.S. imports (customs value) | Total farm sales and imports | Category |
| *Chordata* MAMMALIA Mammals | | | | | | | | | | | |
| | *Artiodactyla* BOVIDAE | *Bos taurus* Cattle | A-1413 | | | | | 40,154.0 | 1,877.5 | 42,031.5 | Super |
| | | *Bubalus bubalis* Buffalo | | A-1413 | | | | — | 8.2 | 8.2 | Minor |
| | | *Capra hircus* Goat | A-1413 | | | | | 32.5 | 45.8 | 78.3 | Medium |
| | | *Ovis aries* Sheep | A-1413 | | | | | 517.7 | 290.1 | 807.8 | Major |
| | CAMELIDAE | *Camelus bactrianus* Camel | | A-1413 | | | | — | 3.0 | 3.0 | Minor |
| | SUIDAE | *Sus domestica* Pig | A-1413 | | | | | 8,238.3 | 487.4 | 8,725.7 | Super |
| | *Carnivora* CANIDAE | *Vulpes vulpes* Red fox | | | | A-924 | | 0.2 | 18.3 | 18.5 | Medium |
| | MUSTELIDAE | *Mustela vison* American mink | | | | | P-408 | 84.5 (1978 only) | 75.7 | 160.2 | Major |
| | *Lagomorpha* LEPORIDAE | *Oryctolagus cuniculus* Rabbit | | | A-1413 | | | 6.8 (1978 only) | 13.0 | 19.8 | Medium |
| | *Perissodactyla* EQUIDAE | *Equus asinus* Donkey | A-1413 | | | | | 1.5 (1978 only) | <0.1 | 1.5 | Minor |
| | | *Equus caballus* Horse | A-1413 | | | | | 275.0 (average of 1979 and 1980 only; includes mules) | 90.2 | 365.2 | Major |

| | Family | Species / Common name | Reference | | | | Category |
|---|---|---|---|---|---|---|---|
| **Rodentia** CHINCHILLIDAE | | *Chinchilla laniger* Chinchilla | S-625 | 1.4 (1978 only) | — | 1.4 | Minor |
| AVES Birds | | | | | | | |
| **Anseriformes** ANATIDAE | | *Anser anser* Goose | S-323 | ? | 1.1 | 1.1 | Minor |
| **Galliformes** MELEAGRIDIDAE | | *Meleagris gallopavo* Turkey | A-1413 | 1,075.4 | <0.1 | 1,075.4 | Super |
| PHASIANIDAE | | *Gallus gallus* Chicken | A-1413 | 6,870.2 | 4.5 | 6,874.7 | Super |
| OSTEICHTHYES Bony fishes | | | | | | | |
| **Salmoniformes** SALMONIDAE | | *Oncorhynchus* spp. Pacific salmon | A-1150 | 88.5 | 4.5 | 93.0 | Medium |
| | | *Salmo gairdneri* Rainbow trout | A-1150 | 29.5 | 0.5 | 30.0 | Medium |
| **Siluriformes** ICTALURIDAE | | *Ictalurus punctatus* Channel catfish; *I. furcatus* Blue catfish | A-1150 | 36.9 | — | 36.9 | Medium |
| **Annelida** OLIGOCHAETA | | Earthworms | Page 264 | 7.7 (1978 only) | 9.4 | 17.1 | Major |
| **Arthropoda** CRUSTACEA Crustaceans | | | | | | | |
| **Decapoda** PALAEMONIDAE | | *Macrobrachium rosenbergii* Giant river prawn | J-651 | 1.2 | — | } 2.1 | Minor |
| PENAEIDAE | | *Penaeus japonicus* Kuruma shrimp | A-1150 | — | 0.9 | | |
| INSECTA Insects | | | | | | | |
| **Hymenoptera** APIDAE | | *Apis mellifera* Honey bee | S-349 | 122.2 | 25.0 | 147.2 | Major |

(continued)

# Table 7.17 (Continued)

| DOMESTICATE | | | PERIOD WHEN DOMESTICATED | | | | | AVERAGE ANNUAL VALUE 1976–1980 (U.S.$ MILLION) | | | |
|---|---|---|---|---|---|---|---|---|---|---|---|
| **Phylum** CLASS | **Order** FAMILY | SPECIES | *Ancient/ before 5000 B.C.* | *Early/ 5000– 0 B.C.* | *Late/ A.D. 0– 1700* | *Recent/ A.D. 1700– 1900* | *New/ A.D. 1900 on* | *U.S. farm sales* | *U.S. imports (customs value)* | *Total farm sales and imports* | *Category* |
| | **Lepidoptera** BOMBYCIDAE | *Bombyx mori* Silkworm | | V-26 | | | | — | 64.2 | 64.2 | Medium |
| **Mollusca** BIVALVIA Bivalve molluscs | **Pterioida** OSTREIDAE | *Crassostrea gigas* Pacific oyster *C. virginica* Atlantic oyster | | | | | A-1150 | 35.8 | — | 35.8 | Medium |
| | **Veneroida** VENERIDAE | *Mercenaria mercenaria* Hardshell clam, quahog | | | | | A-1150 | 9.9 | — | 9.9 | Minor |
| **Phaeophyta** Brown algae | | *Eucheuma* spp. *Gracilaria cornopifolia* *Hypnea* spp. Industrial seaweeds for agar | | | | | A-1150 | — | 1.8 | 1.8 | Minor |
| | | *Lamanaria* spp. Kombu | | | | | A-1150 | | | | |
| | | *Undaria pinnatifida* Wakame | | | | | A-1150 | — | 2.6 | 2.6 | Minor |
| **Rhodophyta** Red algae | | *Porphyra* spp. Nori | | | | | A-1150 | | | | |

Notes: — = none or negligible; ? = not determined; super = more than $1,000 million; major = $100–$1,000 million; medium = $10–$100 million; and minor = $1–$10 million. See note 6 for explanation and sources of value data.

small farms were operating by the 1950s. Commercial culture of any significance, however, did not begin until after 1960, when spawning of channel catfish (*Ictalurus punctatus*) became commercially feasible for the first time. Initially, catfish were not well accepted and restaurants tried to pass them off to customers as "tenderloin of trout"; now they are popular and the vendors of less esteemed fish, such as wolffish (*Anarhichas* spp.) and Brazilian catfish (several genera), try to pass them off as channel catfish (A-1150). Domesticated catfish production in the United States is now worth $36.9 million a year (P-434, S-798), most of the production being in Mississippi (57% of sales), Arkansas (12%), and Alabama (11%) (S-798). Catfish breeding is in its infancy. Inbreeding has been implicated in the rising incidence of deformities and other hereditary disorders in domesticated channel catfish. Besides the need to increase the genetic base, breeding goals include more efficient feed conversion, resistance to low dissolved oxygen concentrations, and fish with smaller heads in relation to body (fillet) size. Crosses between male blue catfish (*I. furcatus*), the second most frequently raised catfish species, and female channel catfish have shown 11–65% faster growth, as well as more uniform growth, than either parent (A-1150).

Raft and tray culture of wild oysters has a long history. The Japanese, the most sophisticated practitioners of the art, have been doing it since the seventeenth century. In Japan the breeding population consists of natural beds of oysters (A-1150). In the United States, where hatcheries using artificially induced spawning were developed in the 1940s, oyster production is a combination of completely wild (the public oyster fishery), cultured wild (type 1b of table 7.15), and domesticated (from hatchery seed sources), the latter two comprising the private fishery. The oyster aquaculture statistics correspond closely to the statistics for the private fishery and therefore combine wild and domesticated production as we define them. Hence they exaggerate the contribution of domesticated oyster production to total supply—valued at $35.8 million a year (P-434). The species concerned are *Crassostrea virginica* on the Atlantic coast and *C. gigas* on the Pacific coast (G-625).

The four minor new domesticates are clams, shrimp, edible seaweeds, and industrial seaweeds. Hatchery propagation of clams began at about the same time as did that of oysters and used the same techniques. The only domesticated species at present is *Mercenaria mercenaria*, the hardshell clam, known as littleneck or cherrystone when small and quahog when large (A-1150, G-625). The average annual value of aquaculture production is estimated to be $9.9 million (P-434). Shrimp domestication was pioneered by the Japanese, who have been commercially propagating and raising the kuruma shrimp (*Penaeus japonicus*) since 1959 (A-1150). We have assumed, for the purposes of calculation, that all Japanese shrimp supplies to the United States (average annual value of $0.9 million) are of domesticated kuruma. Commercial efforts to farm U.S. shrimp began in the 1970s with three major Gulf of Mexico species—the white shrimp (*Penaeus setiferus*), the brown shrimp (*P. aztecus*), and the pink shrimp

(*P. duorarum*)—and later with the eastern Pacific species *P. vannamei* and *P. stylirostris* (G-625). Difficulties have been experienced with propagation and, as far as we can tell, the stock still comes from the wild. Efforts in Hawaii with the freshwater prawn *Macrobrachium rosenbergii* have been much more successful. The domestication of this species (native to Southeast Asia and the western Pacific) began at Penang, Malaysia, in the 1950s. Propagation problems were overcome when in 1961 Shao-Wen Ling discovered that the larval shrimp need dilute seawater to survive and develop (in the wild they are swept by the river current down to the brackish waters of mangrove forests and estuaries) (J-651). Two berried females were sent from Penang to Hawaii in 1965. Annual production of their descendants in both Hawaii and Florida is worth $1.2 million (G-625, P-434).

Seaweed culture began in Japan in the seventeenth century, but it was a type 1b form of culture (table 7.15). Artificial regeneration of seaweeds was initiated in 1950, and since then a growing proportion of seaweed production—particularly of the edible seaweeds nori, wakame, and konbu—has been from domesticated sources (A-1150). Information on these, and on domesticated seaweeds producing agar for industry, is given in chapter 6. Our estimate of the average annual value of U.S. imports of domesticated edible seaweeds is $2.6 million, and of agar from domesticated industrial seaweeds (chiefly *Eucheuma* species in the Philippines) is $1.8 million.

## Conclusion

The domestication process is as important a part of the human economy as it ever was. The combined U.S. farm sales and import value of all new domesticates is already $1,236 million a year: $168.6 million from new crops; $706.6 million from newly domesticated timber trees (note 7); $178.7 million from new livestock; and $182.1 million from new aquaculture species. Their contribution is sure to grow as production from them increases and as yet more wild species are brought into the ranks of humanity's domesticates.

# 8

# Wild Genetic Resources

Wildlife is both the source of new domesticates and a reservoir of genetic resources for the improvement of domesticates. The gene pools of wild plants and animals are a new resource, but already they have made a major economic contribution and their importance is growing. The term *wild genetic resource* is sometimes used as a synonym for wild species, but this is to rob it of meaning. Our definition of the phrase is as follows: any heritable characteristic of a wild plant or animal that is of actual or potential use to people. The characteristic may be disease resistance, the presence or absence of a chemical, or any other yield or quality factor. As long as it is or is likely to be of economic or social value, is found in a wild species, and is transmitted genetically, it qualifies as a wild genetic resource. These three features of the definition—wildness, heritability, and utility—are of equal weight.

By definition the domestication of a new species is a use of a wild genetic resource. Until recently, however, domesticators have paid scant attention to the genetic variation within the species being domesticated. Aquaculturalists, for example, have tended to use whatever stocks are most readily to hand, without first investigating which gene pools within the species concerned might have the characteristics needed for successful domestication. By contrast, silviculturalists are devoting increasing efforts to the identification, selection, and combination of superior genetic stocks within the species they are domesticating. (This growing use of the wild genetic resources of timber trees is considered in chapter 7.) This chapter is devoted to wild genetic resources in agriculture. Since no commercial use has been made of wild germplasm (genetic material) in livestock improvement, the chapter is concerned exclusively with the contributions of wild genetic resources to agricultural and horticultural crops. We examine the nature of current contributions, estimate their value, consider patterns and trends in the use of wild germplasm, and outline some potential contributions.

## Current Contributions of Wild Genetic Resources

There is a huge and growing literature on the successful transfer of useful genes from wild plants to their domesticated relatives. Three recent reviews of this literature cite many examples covering a wide range of crops (G-167, P-270, S-196). They leave the impression that most of these transfers have resulted in improved commercial cultivars, which is not the case. It is one thing to transfer wild germplasm to a domesticate but quite another to develop a successful cultivar, one that is superior to other cultivars with respect to the characteristics incorporated from the wild and at least as good with respect to all other important characteristics. The number of crops that currently benefit from wild genetic resources is not small, but it is substantially smaller than might be inferred from the literature.

Table 8.1 lists the 23 nontimber crops grown or imported by the United States of which 1% or more of annual production is accounted for by cultivars with characteristics inherited from wild relatives. The characteristics fall into two groups: those that help to maintain or increase yields and those that improve quality. Yield characteristics have been successfully incorporated into 20 of the crops. Quality characteristics from the wild are less common—only 7 of the 23 crops have been improved this way.

### Disease and Pest Resistance

The most widely obtained yield characteristic is disease and pest resistance. Resistance to at least one pathogen or pest has been transferred to 15 (65%) of the 23 crops improved with wild genes. In many of the crops (sugar beet, highbush blueberry, oats, bread wheat, cotton, bell pepper, and potato) it is the only characteristic yet derived from the wild. In others (sunflower, sugarcane, tomato, and cacao) it was the first characteristic to be obtained, and it stimulated breeders to seek other types of improvement from the crops' wild relatives.

The use of wild genetic resources in crop improvement owes its origins to the quest for disease and pest resistance. The first successful examples—the development of grape rootstock cultivars resistant to the aphid *Phylloxera vitifoliae* and the nematodes *Meloidogyne* spp.—antedate the development of the science of genetics by several decades. Today 90–95% of California's north coast grape acreage is grown on the rootstock cultivars St. George and AXR 1; and 20% of the San Joaquin Valley and southern California grape acreage is grown on the rootstock cultivars 1613, Harmony, Freedom, Salt Creek, and Dogridge (A. N. Kasimatis, pers. comm., 22 June 1982). St. George and AXR 1 are *Phylloxera*-resistant rootstocks. St. George is a selection of wild *Vitis rupestris* collected in the nineteenth century (date and precise origin unknown); AXR 1 is a cross between *V. rupestris* and the wine grape (*V. vinifera*) made in 1879 (G-707). The rootstocks grown in the San Joaquin Valley are *Meloidogyne*-resistant. Cultivar 1613 is a cross between *V. longii* and cultivar Othello (*V. labrusca* × *riparia* ×

Table 8.1 **Crops grown or imported by the United States that have been significantly improved by wild species**

| CROP | TYPE OF IMPROVEMENT (Table reference) | | WILD SOURCE OF IMPROVEMENT |
|---|---|---|---|
| **CANNABIDACEAE** | | | |
| Hops (*Humulus lupulus*) | Yield: dpr | (8.2) | *H. lupulus* |
| | Yield: other | (8.3) | *H. lupulus* |
| | Quality | (8.4) | *H. lupulus* |
| **CHENOPODIACEAE** | | | |
| Sugar beet (*Beta vulgaris*) | Yield: dpr | (8.2) | *B. maritima* |
| **COMPOSITAE** | | | |
| Sunflower (*Helianthus annuus*) | Yield: dpr | (8.2) | *H. annuus* |
| | Yield: other | (8.3) | *H. annuus + H. petiolaris* |
| Lettuce (*Lactuca sativa*) | Yield: other | (8.3) | *L. virosa* |
| | Quality | (8.4) | *L. virosa* |
| **ERICACEAE** | | | |
| Highbush blueberry (*Vaccinium australe* and *V. corymbosum*) | Yield: dpr | (8.2) | *V. australe* |
| **GRAMINEAE** | | | |
| Oats (*Avena sativa*) | Yield: dpr | (8.2) | *A. sterilis* |
| Smooth brome (*Bromus inermis*) | Yield: other | (8.3) | *B. pumpellianus* |
| Bermuda grass (*Cynodon dactylon*) | Quality | (8.4) | *C. nlemfuensis* |
| Sugarcane (*Saccharum officinarum*) | Yield: dpr | (8.2) | *S. spontaneum* |
| | Yield: other | (8.3) | *S. spontaneum + S. robustum* |
| Bread wheat (*Triticum aestivum*) | Yield: dpr | (8.2) | *Aegilops umbellulata + T. turgidum dicoccoides + Agropyron elongatum* |
| **IRIDACEAE** | | | |
| Spanish iris (*Iris xiphium*) | Yield: other | (8.3) | *I. tingitana* |
| | Quality | (8.4) | *I. tingitana* |
| **LEGUMINOSAE** | | | |
| Alfalfa (*Medicago sativa*) | Yield: dpr | (8.2) | *M. falcata* |
| | Yield: other | (8.3) | *M. falcata* |
| Sweet clover (*Melilotus alba* and *M. officinalis*) | Quality | (8.4) | *M. dentata* |
| **LILIACEAE** | | | |
| Tulip (*Tulipa gesneriana*) | Quality | (8.4) | *T. fosteriana* |
| **MALVACEAE** | | | |
| Cotton (*Gossypium barbadense*) | Yield: dpr | (8.2) | *G. anomalum* |
| Cotton (*Gossypium hirsutum*) | Yield: dpr | (8.2) | *G. tomentosum* |
| | Quality | (8.4) | *G. thurberi* |

(*continued*)

Table 8.1   (*Continued*)

| CROP | TYPE OF IMPROVEMENT (*Table reference*) | | WILD SOURCE OF IMPROVEMENT |
|---|---|---|---|
| PALMAE | | | |
| Oil palm (*Elaeis guineensis*) | Yield: other | (8.3) | *E. guineensis* |
| ROSACEAE | | | |
| Strawberry (*Fragaria × ananassa*) | Yield: other | (8.3) | *F. chiloensis* |
| SOLANACEAE | | | |
| Bell pepper (*Capsicum annuum*) | Yield: dpr | (8.2) | *C. annuum* |
| Tomato (*Lycopersicon esculentum*) | Yield: dpr | (8.2) | *L. esculentum* var. *cerasiforme* + *L. pimpinellifolium* + *L. hirsutum* + *L. peruvianum* |
| | Quality | (8.4) | the above + *L. cheesmanii* + *L. chmielewskii* |
| Tobacco (*Nicotiana tabacum*) | Yield: dpr | (8.2) | *N. debneyi* + *N. glutinosa* + *N. longiflora* + *N. plumbaginifolia* + *N. tomentosa* |
| Potato (*Solanum tuberosum*) | Yield: dpr | (8.2) | *S. demissum* |
| STERCULIACEAE | | | |
| Cacao (*Theobroma cacao*) | Yield: dpr | (8.2) | *T. cacao* |
| | Yield: other | (8.3) | *T. cacao* |

Notes: dpr = disease and pest resistance; (8.2) = details in table 8.2, (8.3) = details in table 8.3, (8.4) = details in table 8.4.

*vinifera*) made in 1881 (G-707, J-468). Dogridge and Salt Creek are selections of wild *V. champini* collected before 1900 (J-453, J-468). Both Freedom and Harmony are crosses between 1613 and Dogridge that were made in 1956 and 1955, respectively (J-453).

All these rootstocks get their pest resistance from wild grapes; all the parent species were collected in the last century. A similar situation prevails in other grape-growing countries. In France, for example, more than 70% of the grape acreage is grown on *Phylloxera*-resistant rootstocks derived from wild North American species (mostly *V. berlandieri*, *V. riparia*, and *V. rupestris*) (note 1). In every case the original collections from the wild were made in the last century. We therefore regard the main grape rootstock species as recent domesticates and do not include them in our evaluation of current contributions of wild genetic resources. The fact that breeders have not needed to return to wild species for additional sources of resistance to *Phylloxera* or *Meloidogyne* is testimony to the effectiveness and durability of the original collections. New collections of

wild grape germplasm have been made and are being developed into new cultivars, but they are being used for their resistance to other pests, for disease
resistance, and for particular environmental adaptations. They include rootstock cultivars of potential importance in major grape-growing areas such as
California, and Champagne and Cognac in France, and scion cultivars in minor
areas with special problems for the grape grower such as Florida. They are
discussed in the section Potential Contributions of Wild Genetic Resources.

The results of what Gregor Mendel modestly described as "one isolated experiment" (seven years' work with more than 30,000 pea plants) were rediscovered in 1900; the term *genetics* was coined in 1906 and *gene* in 1909
(M-498). Thereafter the science of genetics and its application in plant and
animal breeding developed rapidly. The sugarcane and potato breeders were
among the earliest to follow in the footsteps of the grape breeders and turn to
wild species for resistance to the parasites of their crops.

The spur for sugarcane breeders was a viral disease, mosaic (SCMV). First
observed in Java (Indonesia) in the early 1890s, it spread rapidly and caused
devastating economic losses in almost every sugarcane-producing country.
SCMV reached Louisiana in about 1914 (probably in stem cuttings of cane
cultivars). Coming on top of two fungal diseases, red rot and root rot, it cut
production from an average of more than 200,000 tons a year to 47,000 tons in
1926. Losses to the Louisiana sugar industry were estimated at $100 million and
it was forsaken as a business risk by almost all financing institutions (A-273).
The industry was rescued from the brink of ruin only by the introduction of
cultivars with SCMV-resistance from the wild species *Saccharum spontaneum*
(A-1, A-273).

The key event in this story occurred in 1911, when Miss G. Wilbrink, the
sugarcane pathologist at the Proefstation Oost Java (in Java, Indonesia), crossed a
plant called Kassoer with the cultivar P.O.J. 100. Kassoer was found on an
extinct volcano, Gunung Tjereme, near the town of Tjirebon (then written
Cheribon) in Java. It was subsequently established that the plant was a natural
hybrid between cultivar Black Cheribon and wild *S. spontaneum* growing on the
mountain (A-273, A-359, M-288). Wilbrink's cross—called P.O.J. 2364—became one of the parents of P.O.J. 2878 (M-288), which was bred in 1921 and
described as "the greatest cane of all" (S-119). By obtaining P.O.J. 2364, Wilbrink
demonstrated the utility and crossability of *S. spontaneum* and initiated a "new
era in sugarcane breeding" (M-288).

In 1912, the year after Wilbrink achieved P.O.J. 2364, C. A. Barber at the
Sugarcane Breeding Institute in Coimbatore, southern India, crossed the local *S.
spontaneum* with the cultivar Ashy Mauritius (A-412, P-238, S-345). Remark-
ably, the first-generation progeny were of commercial standard requiring no
further improvement; two cultivars were released from this cross, Co205 and
Co206 (A-273, A-412). Together, the two sources of *S. spontaneum*—from Java
and from Coimbatore—have provided sugarcane with resistance to five major

diseases, without which resistance "there would most probably not be a viable sugarcane industry any place in the world" (J. D. Miller, pers. comm., 16 July 1981).

Table 8.2 summarizes the current contribution of wild species to the disease or pest resistance of crops grown or imported by the United States. Column K shows the kingdom of organism to which the pathogen or pest belongs. The fungi are by far the most numerous. Resistance to fungal pathogens has been transferred to 13 of the 15 crops. Resistance to bacterial and viral pathogens has been transferred to 5 and 4 crops, respectively; and resistance to animal pests to only 3 crops. This is almost certainly not a reflection of the distribution of traits in the wild species but rather of the importance of the group of organisms and of the role of breeding in their control. The most important group, in terms of the losses it causes in total world potential crop production, is that of animal pests (insects, nematodes, mites, slugs, birds, and small mammals), causing losses estimated at more than 25%. Next come the fungal diseases, which cause losses estimated at more than 20% of total world potential production. We have no estimates for the damage caused by viruses and bacteria, but viruses are the third most important group of parasites; bacterial diseases are generally much less damaging than fungal or viral diseases (P-214).

In general the breeding of resistant cultivars is just one of several methods of controlling pests, viruses, and bacteria. The other methods include chemical seed treatments and eradication of diseased plants in the case of bacteria; chemical control of insect vectors and appropriate crop rotations in the case of viruses; and chemical control, the use of predators and parasites, and cultural methods such as changing crop combinations and the timing of sowing in the case of pests (P-214). Fungal diseases are the exception. Although the use of resistant cultivars may be only part of an integrated control program—for example, control of late blight of potatoes, in which moderately resistant cultivars are used in combination with fungicides—resistance breeding makes a far bigger contribution overall to the control of fungi than it does to the control of other pathogens or of pests. In many cases—notably stem and leaf rust of wheat in the United States—resistance to particular fungi is a more important breeding objective than improvement of yield or quality (P-214). These two factors—that fungi are more destructive than any other group of organisms except animals and that resistance breeding is in the front line of their control—are the likely explanation for the predominance of fungal diseases in table 8.2.

There is a gradient of vulnerability to a pathogen or pest ranging from immunity (in which the plant cannot be attacked at all) to complete susceptibility (in which it has no defense at all). In between are varying degrees of resistance qualified by terms such as high, moderate, and low. A highly resistant cultivar is one that, although not immune to attack, is attacked very little. A moderately resistant cultivar will have a higher number of parasitized individuals than will a highly resistant cultivar and a higher number of individuals that resist attack

(*text continued on page 290*)

**Table 8.2  Yield characteristics from wild species in commercial cultivars of crops grown or imported by the United States: disease and pest resistance**

| CROP | PATHOGEN OR PEST | K | SOURCE OF RESISTANCE | LEVEL OF RESISTANCE | TYPE OF RESISTANCE | MODE OF INHERITANCE |
|---|---|---|---|---|---|---|
| CANNABIDACEAE | | | | | | |
| Hops | Downy mildew caused by *Pseudoperonospora humuli* | | *Humulus lupulus* from Bavaria (1) | Tolerant (2) | Durable (3) | Polygenic (3) |
| | | F | *H. lupulus* from Slovenia (4) | Resistant (5) | Durable (3) | Polygenic (3) |
| | | | *H. lupulus* from Manitoba (6) | Moderate (7) | Durable (3) | Polygenic (3) |
| | Wilt caused by *Verticillium albo-atrum* | F | *H. lupulus* from Manitoba and California (6) | High/tolerant (8) | Transient (9) | Not determined (10) |
| CHENOPODIACEAE | | | | | | |
| Sugar beet | Leaf spot caused by *Cercospora beticola* | F | *Beta maritima* from Italy (11) | Moderate-high (12) | Durable (13) | Polygenic (14) |
| COMPOSITAE | | | | | | |
| Sunflower | Downy mildew caused by *Plasmopara halstedii* | F | *Helianthus annuus* from Texas (15) | Resistant (16) | Not known (17) | Monogenic, dominant (18) |
| | Rust caused by *Puccinia helianthi* | F | *H. annuus* from Texas (19) | Moderate-high (20) | Transient (17) | Monogenic, dominant (21) |
| ERICACEAE | | | | | | |
| Highbush blueberry | Stem canker caused by *Botyosphaeria corticis* | F | *Vaccinium australe* from N. Carolina (22) | Moderate/tolerant (23) | Apparently transient (24) | Not determined (24) |
| GRAMINEAE | | | | | | |
| Oats | Crown rust caused by *Puccinia coronata* | F | *Avena sterilis* from Algeria, Israel, and Portugal (25) | Moderate/resistant (26) | Transient (27) | Monogenic, dominant (27) |

*(continued)*

# Table 8.2  (*Continued*)

| CROP | PATHOGEN OR PEST | K | SOURCE OF RESISTANCE | LEVEL OF RESISTANCE | TYPE OF RESISTANCE | MODE OF INHERITANCE |
|---|---|---|---|---|---|---|
| Sugarcane | Gummosis caused by *Xanthomonas vasculorum* | B | *Saccharum spontaneum* from Java and India (28) | High (28) | ? | ? |
| | Red rot caused by *Colletotrichum falcatum/ Physalospora tucumanensis* | F | *S. spontaneum* from India (29) | Moderate (29) | Transient in some; durable in others (29) | Monogenic, recessive? polygenic? (29) |
| | Root rot caused by *Pythium arrhenomanes* | F | *S. spontaneum* from Java and India (30) | Resistant (30) | ? | ? |
| | Smut caused by *Ustilago scitaminea* | F | *S. spontaneum* from Java (31) | Resistant (31) | ? | ? |
| | Sugarcane mosaic (SCMV) | V | *S. spontaneum* from Java (32) | Resistant-high (32) | Transient (33) | ? |
| | | | *S. spontaneum* from India (32) | Tolerant (32) | ? | ? |
| Bread wheat | Stem rust caused by *Puccinia graminis* | F | *Agropyron elongatum* (34) | Resistant (34) | Transient (34) | Monogenic, dominant (34) |
| | Leaf rust caused by *Puccinia recondita* | F | *Aegilops umbellulata* (35) | Resistant (35) | Transient (35) | Monogenic, dominant (35) |
| LEGUMINOSAE Alfalfa | Common leafspot caused by *Pseudopeziza medicagensis* | F | *Medicago falcata* (36) | Moderate (36) | ? | ? |
| | Yellow leaf blotch caused by *P. jonesii* | F | *M. falcata* (37) | Tolerant (37) | ? | ? |
| MALVACEAE Cotton (*G. barbadense*) | Bacterial blight caused by *Xanthomonas malvacearum* | B | *Gossypium anomalum* (38) | Resistant (38) | ? Transient | Monogenic, dominant (39) |
| Cotton (*G. hirsutum*) | Lygus bugs *Lygus* spp. | Ai | | | | |
| | Cotton fleahopper *Psallus seriatus* | Ai | | | | |

| | | | Resistance level | Durability | Inheritance |
|---|---|---|---|---|---|
| Cotton leafworm *Alabama argillacea* | Ai | | | | |
| Tobacco budworm *Heliothis virescens* | Ai | | | | |
| Cotton bollworm *Heliothis zea* | Ai | *Gossypium tomentosum* from Hawaii (40) | Moderate (41) | Durable (41) | Oligogenic, recessive (41) |
| Pink bollworm *Pectinophora gossypiella* | Ai | | | | |
| Cabbage looper *Trichoplusia ni* | Ai | | | | |
| Boll rot caused mostly by *Alternaria tenuis*, *Fusarium moniliforme*, *F. oxysporum* | F F F | | | | |
| **SOLANACEAE** | | | | | |
| **Bell pepper** | | | | | |
| Leaf spot caused by *Xanthomonas vesicatoria* | B | *Capsicum annuum* (42) | Resistant (42) | ? Transient | ? |
| **Tomato** | | | | | |
| Root-knot nematodes *Meloidogyne* spp. (except *M. hapla*) | An | *Lycopersicon peruvianum* (43) | Resistant (44) | ? Durable | Monogenic, dominant (45) |
| Bacterial canker caused by *Corynebacterium michiganense* | B | *L. pimpinellifolium* (46) | Moderate-high (46) | ? | Oligogenic (47) |
| | | *L. hirsutum* from Peru and Ecuador (48) | Resistant (46) | ? | Oligogenic (47) |
| | | *L. peruvianum* from Peru and Chile (48) | Resistant (46) | ? | Oligogenic (47) |
| Bacterial wilt caused by *Pseudomonas solanacearum* | B | *L. pimpinellifolium* from Peru (49) | Moderate (50) | Transient (50) | ? (50) |
| Leaf mold caused by *Cladosporium fulvum* | F | *L. pimpinellifolium* from Peru and Ecuador (51) | Resistant-immune (52) | Transient (52) | Monogenic, dominant (52) |
| | | *L. hirsutum* (52) | Resistant-immune (52) | Transient (52) | Monogenic, dominant (52) |

*(continued)*

# Table 8.2 (*Continued*)

| CROP | PATHOGEN OR PEST | K | SOURCE OF RESISTANCE | LEVEL OF RESISTANCE | TYPE OF RESISTANCE | MODE OF INHERITANCE |
|---|---|---|---|---|---|---|
| Tomato (*continued*) | Fruit anthracnose caused by *Colletotrichum coccodes* | K | *L. peruvianum* (52) | Resistant-immune (52) | Transient (52) | Monogenic, dominant (52) |
| | Wilt caused by *Fusarium oxysporum* | F | *L. esculentum* var. *cerasiforme* (53) | Resistant (53) | ? | ? |
| | | | *L. pimpinellifolium* from Peru (54) | High (55) | Transient (56) | Monogenic, dominant (57) |
| | Corky root caused by *Pyrenochaeta lycopersici* | F | *L. hirsutum* (53) | Resistant (53) | ? | ? |
| | | | *L. peruvianum* (53) | Resistant (53) | ? | ? |
| | Leaf spot caused by *Septoria lycopersici* | F | *L. pimpinellifolium* (58) | Moderate (58) | | Monogenic, dominant (58) |
| | | | *L. hirsutum* (58) | Moderate (58) | ? | Monogenic, dominant (58) |
| | Gray leaf spot caused by *Stemphylium solani* | F | *L. pimpinellifolium* from Peru (59) | Resistant (59) | ? | Monogenic, dominant (59) |
| | Wilt caused by *Verticillium albo-atrum* | F | *L. esculentum* var. *cerasiforme* from Peru (60) | Resistant (60) | ? | Monogenic, dominant (60) |
| | Curly top (CTV) | V | *L. peruvianum* (61) | ? Moderate | Durable (61) | Polygenic (61) |
| | Spotted wilt (SWV) | V | *L. pimpinellifolium* (62) | Resistant (62) | ? | Oligogenic (62) |
| | Tobacco mosaic (TMV) | V | *L. peruvianum* (63) | Resistant (63) | ? | Possibly monogenic, dominant (64) |
| Tobacco | Root-knot nematode *Meloidogyne incognita* | An | *Nicotiana tomentosa* or *N. tomentosiformis* (65) | Resistant (65) | Transient (66) | Monogenic, dominant (66) |
| | Wildfire caused by *Pseudomonas tabaci* | B | *N. longiflora* (67) | Resistant (67) | Transient (68) | Monogenic, dominant (66) |
| | Black shank caused by *Phytophthora parasitica* | F | *N. longiflora* (69) | High (70) | Transient (70) | Monogenic, dominant (66) |
| | | | *N. plumbaginifolia* (71) | High (70) | Transient (70) | Monogenic, dominant (66) |

| | K | Source | Resistance | Durability | Genetics |
|---|---|---|---|---|---|
| Black root rot caused by *Thielaviopsis basicola* | F | *N. debneyi* from Australia (72) | Immune (66) | Durable (73) | Monogenic, dominant (66) |
| Tobacco mosaic (TMV) | V | *N. glutinosa* from Peru (74) | Resistant (75) | Durable (76) | Monogenic, dominant (76) |
| Potato  Late blight caused by *Phytophthora infestans* | F | *Solanum demissum* from Mexico (77) | Moderate/field (78) | Durable (78) | Polygenic (78) |
| **STERCULIACEAE** Cacao  Sudden wilt caused by *Ceratocystis fimbriata* | F | *Theobroma cacao* from Peru (79) | Resistant (80) | ? | ? |
| Witches' broom caused by *Crinipellis perniciosa* | F | *T. cacao* from Peru (79) | Moderate (81) | Transient (81) | ? |
| Pod rot (black pod) and bark canker from *Phytophthora palmivora* | F | *T. cacao* from Peru (79) | Moderate (82) | ? | ? |
| Swollen shoot (CSSV) | V | *T. cacao* from Peru (79) | Moderate (83) | ? | ? Polygenic |

Notes: K = kingdom (of organism) to which the pathogen or pest belongs; A = animal (Animalia); i = insect, n = nematode; B = bacteria (Monera); F = fungi (Fungi); V = virus. Explanation of other columns is in text.

*Hops*

1. H. Ehrmaier, pers. comm., 22 Sept. 1981.
2. Cultivars Huller Bitterer, Hallertauer Gold, Perle, and Emerald, grown in West Germany (ibid.; V-348).
3. R. A. Neve, pers. comm., 24 Feb. 1981.
4. T. Wagner, pers. comm., 20 Jan. 1982.
5. The Super Styrian A cultivars: Ahil, Apolon, Atlas, and Aurora, grown in Yugoslavia (V-348).
6. S-9, S-10; R. A. Neve, pers. comm., 24 Feb. 1981.
7. Cultivars Bullion, Brewer's Gold, and Galena; grown in the United States (P-421, V-348).
8. Cultivars Brewer's Gold, Northern Brewer, and Record, highly resistant to strains in West Germany (M-243); Huller Bitterer and Perle tolerant (V-348).
9. This source of resistance is apparently race-specific since, although effective against strains of *Verticillium* in West Germany, it is ineffective against those in the United Kingdom (M-243); new more virulent strains are likely to appear (R. A. Neve, pers. comm., 24 Feb. 1981).
10. M-243.

*Sugar Beet*

11. M-198; R. K. Oldemeyer, pers. comm., 15 July 1981.
12. Hybrid cultivars derived from GW and MONO HY cultivars grown in the United States; Alba cultivars grown in Italy (R. K. Oldemeyer, pers. comm., 15 July 1981, and 5 Nov. 1981); moderately to highly resistant (P-214).

*(continued)*

# Table 8.2 (*Continued*)

13. R. K. Oldemeyer, pers. comm., 15 July 1981, and 5 Nov. 1981.
14. Ibid.; P-214.

*Sunflower*

15. D-150.
16. Amost all the hybrid cultivars grown in North America (W. Dedio, pers. comm., 2 Sept. 1981).
17. Y-88.
18. $Pl_2$ gene provides effective resistance to the race of *Plasmopara halstedii* occurring in North America (D-150).
19. P-76.
20. Almost all the hybrid cultivars grown in North America are moderately to highly resistant to race 1, the predominant race in the main sunflower producing area of North America (Y-35, Y-88; W. Dedio, pers. comm., 2 Sept. 1981).
21. Genes $R_1$ or $R_2$ (P-422).

*Highbush Blueberry*

22. M-633, V-355.
23. Moderate resistance (V-355); tolerance (M-633).
24. V-355.

*Oats*

25. A-718, A-1361, D-156, M-207.
26. Cultivar Bond and its derivatives (e.g., Clintford, Clinton, Diana, Garland, Grundy, Holden, Jaycee, Kota, Lodi, Newton, and Otter) grown in the United States have $Pc_3$ and $Pc_4$ genes (A-718, S-128). These are apparently still useful but are ineffective against most races of *Puccinia coronata* in North America. Multilines E68, E69, E70, M68, M69, M70, E72, E74, M72, and M73, grown in the United States, together have eight genes conditioning either resistance or moderate resistance to races 216, 264, 264B, 290, 305, 325, 326, 330, and 332 (D-156, D-181, D-479, D-480; K. J. Frey, pers. comm., 11 Nov. 1981). Cultivars TAM-0-301 and TAM-0-312 grown in the United States have, respectively, the $Pc_{58}$ and $Pc_{59}$ gene for resistance to many races of *P. coronata* (M-608, M-609, S-128). Cultivars Coker 227 and 234 grown in the United States have, respectively, the genes $Pc_{60}$ and $Pc_{61}$ for resistance to many races (S-128).
27. Sources cited in table note 26.

*Sugarcane*

28. A-1, G-394.
29. Some cultivars with *S. spontaneum* germplasm (e.g., Co. 421 and Co. 281) are moderately resistant to red rot. In some the resistance appears to be race-specific and transient, in others a more durable field resistance. There is an apparent additive effect of certain *S. sinense/S. spontaneum* combinations, e.g., in cultivar Co. 281 (A-1, A-2, A-412).
30. A-1, A-412.

31. T. L. Tew, pers. comm., 31 Aug. 1981.
32. A-412.
33. A-606.

*Bread Wheat*

34. Australian cultivars Eagle, Kite, and Jabiru have gene $Sr_{26}$ for stem rust resistance from *Agropyron elongatum* (M-98) from the translocation made by Knott (J-127). U.S. cultivars Agent and its derivatives [Blueboy II, Cloud, Fox, Osage, Parker 76, Sage, and W-332] and U.S. cultivar Payne have linked genes $Sr_{24}$ for stem rust resistance and $Lr_{24}$ for leaf rust resistance from another source of *A. elongatum* [A-1384, A-1392, G-740, M-98, M-618, P-436, S-824). Cultivar Agatha has linked genes $Sr_{25}$ for stem rust resistance and $Lr_{19}$ for leaf rust resistance from *A. elongatum* (M-98) from the translocation made by Sharma and Knott (S-82). Genes $Sr_{24}$ and $Lr_{24}$ are effective against a broad range of stem and leaf rust strains (M-98, S-824).
35. U.S. cultivar Riley 67 and its derivatives (Abe, Arthur 71, Oasis, Springfield, Sullivan, and Twin) have the $Lr_9$ gene for leaf rust resistance transferred by Sears (A-1384, A-1392, J-132; P-425, P-426; G. Fedak, pers. comm., 19 Nov. 1981; D. R. Knott, pers. comm., 30 Sept. 1981; T. E. Miller, pers. comm., 22 July 1981).

*Alfalfa*

36. Some U.S. cultivars (e.g., Teton) have moderate resistance from this source (G-636, J-621).
37. The resistance from this source in U.S. cultivars such as Teton and Vernal is variously described as tolerance and field resistance (A-621, J-621).

*Cotton (G. barbadense)*

38. Virtually all cultivars grown in Sudan (F. D. Wilson, pers. comm., 17 Aug. 1981).
39. A-1249.

*Cotton (G. hirsutum)*

40. M-136.
41. Two recessive genes $ne_1$ and $ne_2$ for nectarilessness (absence of leaf and extrafloral nectaries) are transferred from *G. tomentosum* to U.S. cultivar Stoneville 825 (M-136; F. D. Wilson, pers. comm., 17 Aug. 1981). Main text gives details.

*Bell Pepper*

42. U.S. cultivar Florida VR-2 has resistance to the less common of the two races of *Xanthomonas vesicatoria* occurring in Florida but not to the main one. Resistance is from wild *C. annuum* P.I.163192 (Z-490; A. A. Cook, pers. comm., 15 July 1981, and 1 Dec. 1981).

*Tomato*

43. G-31.
44. Larvae can penetrate roots but are unable to develop due to hypersensitivity reaction of plant's cells (J-185).
45. Single dominant gene *Mi* (G-31); incompletely dominant (J-185).
46. J-388, J-414, J-462.
47. Resistance is under the control of several "major quantitative" genes influenced by the action of modifying genes (J-462).

*(continued)*

287

Table 8.2 (*Continued*)

48. S-290.
49. J-462.
50. Genetics of bacterial wilt resistance is complex: partially dominant in the seedling stage, recessive in mature plants; expression of resistance varies both with increasing age and with changes in temperature (P-214).
51. G-74, P-51.
52. All sources of resistance are race-specific and conditioned by single dominant genes: $Cf_1$ from the domesticate confers resistance to races 1, 5, 7, and 9; $Cf_2$, $Cf_3$, and $Cf_5$ from *L. pimpinellifolium* confers resistance to four races and immunity to two; $Cf_4$ found in *L. pimpinellifolium*, *L. hirsutum*, and *L. peruvianum*, confers immunity or high resistance to race 6. Another unnamed gene, probably $Cf_9$, has been found in *L. pimpinellifolium* (J-89; E. A. Kerr, pers. comm., 14 Sept. 1981). Many races of *Cladosporium fulvum* that have combined virulence to more than one resistance gene are very widely distributed (P-214).
53. P-463.
54. A-260, P-50.
55. Almost all cultivars have *Fusarium* resistance from *L. pimpinellifolium* (E. A. Kerr, pers. comm., 14 Sept. 1981). Resistance is described as highly resistant/immune (A-260, P-50, P-214).
56. Main text gives details.
57. Single dominant gene with modifier genes (A-260, P-50, P-214).
58. A-40, J-222.
59. G-230.
60. S-38.
61. P-214.
62. Finlay identified five genes controlling resistance to prevailing strains of SWV: two allelic dominant genes $SW_1$a and $SW_1$b and three independent recessive genes $sw_2$, $sw_3$, and $sw_4$. *L. pimpinellifolium* is the source of $SW_1$a and the three recessive genes and provides resistance to all known strains of SWV except $TB_2$ (D-506).
63. Almost all cultivars have TMV resistance from *L. peruvianum* (E. A. Kerr, pers. comm., 14 Sept. 1981).
64. A-25.

*Tobacco*

65. *N. tomentosa* or possibly *N. tomentosiformis* is the source of *Meloidogyne* resistance in Kostoff (S-202) used in cultivars P.D.611 and NC95 (H. E. Heggestad, pers. comm., 15 Oct. 1981) and SC72 (G-94) grown in the United States.
66. S-202.
67. Cultivars Burley 21, Burley 37, Burley 49, Burley, 64, Va509, Ky165, Ky170, Ky171, Havana 501, Havana 503, Pennbel 69, and Pennleaf (J. F. Chaplin, pers. comm., 14 Aug. 1981); Ky9, Ky14, Ky15, and Ky17 (G. B. Collins, pers. comm., 16 July 1981).
68. S-202; however, although races of *Pseudomonas tabaci* have been discovered against which the *N. longiflora* source of resistance is ineffective, these have not been an important problem (P-214).

69. Burley hybrid cultivars in the United States using the L8 breeding line (E. A. Wernsman, pers. comm., 16 July 1981).

70. Cultivars with the *N. longiflora* and *N. plumbaginifolia* sources of resistance practically immune to race 0 of *Phytophthora parasitica*; moderately to highly susceptible to race 1 (S-202).

71. U.S. cultivar NC2326 (J. L. Apple, pers. comm., 16 July 1981; J. F. Chaplin, pers. comm., 14 Aug. 1981).

72. U.S. cultivars Burley 49, Burley 64, and Ky171 (J. F. Chaplin, pers. comm., 14 Aug. 1981); Ky15, Ky17, and Ky170 (G. B. Collins, pers. comm., 16 July 1981).

73. "Although variability in *T. basicola* is well documented, a race of the fungus pathogenic on *N. debneyi* and tobacco cultivars with *N. debneyi* immunity has not been reported. However, cultivars with the *N. debneyi* immunity have not yet been widely grown due to the difficulty in combining desirable yield and quality with immunity. This difficulty and the stability of the resistance suggested that immune tobaccos contain a considerable segment of the pertinent *N. debneyi* chromosome" (S-202).

74. G-27.

75. All TMV-resistant cultivars get their resistance from *N. glutinosa* (S-202). They include SC71, SC72, Burley 21, Burley 49, Burley 64, DF 516, Ky165, Ky170, Ky171, MR (mosaic resistant) Little Crittenden, MR Madole, MR Black Mammoth, MR Little Wood, Havana 425, Havana 501, Havana 503, Pennbel 69, and Maryland 10 (J. F. Chaplin, pers. comm., 14 Aug. 1981); Ky9, Ky10, Ky14, Ky15, Ky17, Ky151, and Ky160 (G. B. Collins, pers. comm., 16 July 1981); Va509, Va528, Burley 37, Coker 86, and NC628 (E. A. Wernsman, pers. comm., 16 July 1981); and Va770 (H. E. Heggestad, pers. comm., 15 Oct. 1981).

76. S-202; main text gives details.

*Potato*

77. A-455, G-196, G-835.

78. Polygenic, race-independent field resistance to *Phytophthora infestans* from *S. edinense* (natural F$_1$ hybrid of *S. tuberosum* and *S. demissum*) was transferred to the German W races, a seedling of which is in the parentage of U.S. cultivar Kennebec and its derivatives (Hudson, Nooksack, and Centennial Russet) (A-21, A-161, G-202, G-293, P-141, P-186, P-189). *S. demissum* is also in Canadian cultivar Keswick (A-161, P-141) and, via W races, in U.S. cultivars Early Gem and Pungo (G-293, P-141). Main text gives details.

*Cacao*

79. Pound's Upper Amazon collections Text note 2 discusses their origins and wildness.

80. A-1409.

81. D-109.

82. G-97.

83. Nanay and Iquitos Upper Amazon clones appear to be moderately resistant (J-83, J-196, J-237). Resistance factors from different cocoa populations can be accumulated, thus building up resistance (J-83) West African F$_3$ hybrids with only Nanay and Iquitos clones in parentage are T72, T73, T85, and T87 (J-125, S-301). Presumably these show resistance to CSSV.

than a completely susceptible cultivar. Tolerance is quite different from resistance. Tolerant cultivars may be susceptible to attack, but their yield and
quality are not reduced by it or are reduced only slightly. We are not sure that
these terms are always used as carefully as they should be. In the "level of
resistance" column of table 8.2, it may be that "tolerant" sometimes means
"not highly but sufficiently (moderately) resistant" and that "immune" is used
where "highly resistant" is more accurate. In many cases the term *resistant* is
used without qualification, and we have recorded that term alone. Sometimes
different workers have described different levels of resistance (for example:
moderate and high resistance to the fungal agent of rust in sunflower; moderate
resistance to, and tolerance of, stem canker in highbush blueberry; resistance
and immunity to the leaf mold fungus in tomato). In some of the cases, the
different terms probably reflect real differences in the field; in others, they
simply reflect differences in the way the terms are used. We are not in a position
to judge.

The columns "type of resistance" and "mode of inheritance" should be read
together, since often there is a close connection between the two. In the former,
there are two possibilities: durable or transient. The terms are not entirely
satisfactory. *Durable* implies a permanence that may be illusory; and *transient*
implies a uselessness that is often not the case. Analogous terms are van der
Plank's "horizontal resistance" and "vertical resistance" (P-36). Vertical resistance is race specific: a cultivar with vertical resistance is one that is resistant
to some variants of a pathogen and susceptible to others. Horizontal resistance
is non-race-specific: a cultivar with this type of resistance is resistant to all
variants of a pathogen. Russell comments that "horizontal" and "non-race
specific" must be applied cautiously because it is never possible to test cultivars
against all possible variants of a pathogen or pest (P-214). Resistance can therefore be said to be non-race-specific only for as long as no race emerges against
which it is ineffective. We use the term *durable* to mean that, as far as we know,
the source of resistance is still effective against the variants of the pathogen or
pest prevailing in the United States and/or countries supplying the United
States with the crop concerned. *Durable* therefore means "so far, so good." We
use the term *transient* to mean that the source of resistance is ineffective
against one or more of the prevailing variants of the pathogen or pest (although
the variant or variants against which it is effective may still be important).

Transient resistance can be much more useful than the term implies. An
example is the high resistance to *Fusarium oxysporum* conditioned by the I gene
from *Lycopersicon pimpinellifolium*. The first tomato cultivar with resistance
from this source (and in fact the first with *Fusarium*-resistance) was Pan America, which was released in 1941 (P-50). Resistance enabled "ten successive crops
of tomato to be produced on sand land in Florida where two crops would have
been the limit with other more susceptible varieties because of a build-up of *F.
oxysporum* in the soil" (V-388 cited by P-214). Subsequently it was shown that

the I gene was effective only against race 1 of *F. oxysporum*. However, although race 2 was discovered in 1945, it did not cause serious damage to race 1-resistant cultivars in Florida until the early 1960s. Another dominant gene, apparently independent of gene I, was found in *L. pimpinellifolium*. This gene is effective against race 2 and has been used in several cultivars, notably Walter, grown on more than 75% of Florida's tomato acreage during the early 1970s. A third race (race 3) of *F. oxysporum* was reported in 1955, and no doubt additional races will be discovered. Nevertheless, race 1 is "still the most widely distributed and economically important race" (P-214). Although the I gene resistance is transient, it provided effective control in Florida for 20 years, is still useful there, and remains effective in many other tomato-growing areas.

The terms *monogenic, oligogenic*, and *polygenic* mean, respectively, involving one gene, few genes, and many genes. In monogenically inherited resistance the resistance is determined by a single gene, although there may be modifier genes at work that can alter the expression of resistance, as in the case of the *Lycopersicon pimpinellifolium* source of resistance to *Fusarium* wilt in tomato (A-260, P-50, P-214). Where resistance is inherited oligogenically, the action of more than one gene is necessary. The absence of leaf and extrafloral nectaries in the wild Hawaiian cotton *Gossypium tomentosum* is conditioned by two recessive genes $ne_1$ and $ne_2$ (M-136). These genes for nectarilessness have been transferred to the cultivar Stoneville 825 (F. D. Wilson, pers. comm., 17 August 1981). Absence of extrafloral nectaries (nectaries just outside the flowers) lowers the incidence of those forms of boll rot caused by organisms entering the boll via the extrafloral nectaries—chiefly the fungi *Alterneria tenuis, Fusarium moniliiforme*, and *F. oxysporum* (A-383). Lack of both leaf and extrafloral nectaries (the domesticated cotton plant usually has three kinds of nectary—in the flower, just outside the flower, and under the leaf) reduces pest populations because of the reduction in nectar on which the adult insects feed. Populations of the Hemiptera lygus bugs and cotton fleahopper, Lepidoptera cotton leafworm, tobacco budworm, cotton bollworm, pink bollworm, and cabbage looper, listed in table 8.2, are substantially reduced in this way (J-247–J-249, M-138). This does not eliminate the need for pesticides, but it does mean that they can be applied later, less often, and in smaller doses. It is a means of cutting down pest populations that is well suited to integrated pest control programs, since it does not damage predator populations (M-138).

Polygenic resistance is determined by many genes, generally so many that not all of them can be identified. Just as it is difficult for geneticists to identify all the genetic actors in polygenically inherited resistance, so it is difficult for pathogens and pests to circumvent this type of resistance. In the six cases listed in table 8.2 in which disease resistance is known to be polygenically inherited, the resistance is durable. By contrast, in almost all of the 15 cases in which disease resistance is known to be monogenically inherited and in which the type of resistance is also known, the resistance is transient. Highly variable pathogens such as *Puccinia* and other fungi can easily develop new races against which single genes are ineffective. This is particularly so when, as is common, there is a gene for gene relationship between cultivar and pathogen—a gene for virulence in the pathogen being matched by one for susceptibility in the cultivar, and conversely a gene for resistance in the cultivar being matched by one for avirulence in the pathogen.

Oat breeders in the United States have used a succession of single gene sources of resistance to the crown rust pathogen *Puccinia coronata*. Between 1919 and 1938, when there were no *Puccinia*-resistant cultivars, average annual losses to crown rust in the United States were at least 2%, or 23 million bushels a year, probably much more. During the 1930s the cultivars Victoria and Bond were discovered to be highly resistant to all except a few rare and little known races of the fungus (M-205). Cultivars with *Puccinia* resistance derived from Victoria were introduced in 1941 and occupied 80% of U.S. oat acreage by 1945. Bond derivatives began to be introduced in 1946 as races of the pathogen against which the Victoria type of resistance was ineffective became more important. By 1951 the most famous Bond derivative—Clinton (in its three versions, Clinton, Clinton 11, and Clinton 59)—was grown on more than two-thirds of the U.S. oat acreage, "doubtless . . . the most widely grown single oat variety ever produced in North America" (A-1361).

The Bond genes for resistance to *Puccinia coronata* are believed to have come from an Algerian introduction of the wild oat *Avena sterilis* (A-718, A-1361). This species has become an increasingly important source of *Puccinia* resistance genes as new races of the fungus continue to be discovered. During the 1950s, despite their resistance obtained from Bond, Victoria, and other cultivars, crown rust caused an estimated loss of 3.7% of U.S. oat production (M-207). Toward the end of that decade the newly discovered race 264 of *P. coronata* became a problem. The search began for resistance genes but none was found in the crop (D-180). Fortunately, many were found in *Avena sterilis*, which has supplied genes for resistance to the cultivars listed in table 8.2 (note 26).

Wheat breeders in the United States have had a similar experience, although they have not yet reached the point where wild species are the only source of resistance genes effective against new variants of a pathogen. Useful genes are available within the bread wheat crop (*Triticum aestivum*) and in other domesticated wheats, notably macaroni wheat (the *durum* form of *T. turgidum turgidum*), emmer (*T. turgidum dicoccon*), and *T. timopheevi timopheevi*, as well as in wild species. The three species of *Puccinia*—*P. graminis*, *P. recondita*, and *P. striiformis*—that cause the three most serious diseases of wheat—respectively stem rust, leaf rust, and stripe rust—are highly variable. For example, more than 300 races of *P. graminis* have been identified. Even apparently simple monogenic resistance can prove very complex. Some types of adult plant resistance to *P. recondita* are apparently non-race-specific, while others are race-specific; some resistance genes can continue to confer moderate resistance to a wide range of races even after virulent races have appeared to which they are susceptible; maximum expression of resistance can require the presence of modifying genes in addition to the identified resistance genes; and the expression of resistance genes can be affected by the cytoplasm (P-214).

Because of these complicating factors it has not been possible to predict the durability of resistance. So far most cultivars with resistance to *P. graminis* have "given only a localized, intermittent control of stem rust. The pathogen has been able to produce new physiologic races capable of attacking one previously resistant variety after another" (P-214). Even so, a succession of resistant cultivars together with the use of fungicides has given relatively good control of rusts during the past two decades. Better, more durable control awaits the right combination of major resistance genes with polygenes conditioning a high level of field resistance in the adult plants (P-214).

Use of single gene resistance is like being on a treadmill but it has its advantages. It is simply inherited and clearly expressed, so it is easy to transfer to cultivars and to select for in subsequent generations. Any linkages between the resistance gene and genes for undesirable agronomic characteristics (such as poor milling or baking quality in bread wheat) are, by and large, easy to break. Polygenes come as a complex of genes from which it is generally difficult, and frequently impossible, to disentangle genes that are not wanted.

An example comes from the resistance of tobacco to tobacco mosaic virus (TMV), the most damaging viral disease in the United States, which caused losses of $10–$40 million in the mid-1970s (S-202). Following the discovery announced in 1933 that the Colombian cultivar Ambalema was resistant to TMV, intensive efforts were made in the United States and elsewhere to transfer resistance from this source. Ambalema's TMV resistance is inherited oligogenically via two independent recessive genes. These efforts were abandoned in the 1950s because of failure to break the linkage between the resistance genes and genes influencing plant type: lines derived from Ambalema had the undesirable habit of wilting severely on hot days after a period of rapid growth (V-3). Meanwhile in 1938 Francis O. Holmes had reported the successful transfer from the wild *Nicotiana glutinosa* of the dominant gene N governing a hypersensitive reaction to the virus (the leaf tissue dies around the point where the virus invades, so restricting its spread) (G-276). Although this source of resistance is associated with quality defects that severely limit its use in flue-cured cultivars, it does not have the linkage problems of Ambalema. Consequently the N gene from *N. glutinosa* is the only source of TMV resistance in use today and is found in essentially all burley tobacco cultivars grown in the United States (S-202; E. A. Wernsman, pers. comm., 16 July 1981). Although monogenically inherited, the resistance appears to be durable. The tobacco mosaic virus is highly variable, yet a strain that is virulent on *N. glutinosa* or on cultivars with *N. glutinosa* resistance has not been found (S-202).

Tobacco's TMV resistance from *N. glutinosa* and *Thielaviopsis basicola* (black root rot fungus) resistance from *N. debneyi* are the only cases we know of durable monogenically inherited disease resistance from wild species in currently grown commercial cultivars. The more usual experience is that of potato's resistance to the late blight fungus (*Phytophthora infestans*). R genes for *Phytophthora* resistance were first used on a large scale in Europe in the 1920s. During field trials in 1925 the German W varieties with the single dominant gene $R_1$ from wild *Solanum demissum* survived an epidemic of late blight without a trace of the disease (P-36). During the 1930s, however, races of *P. infestans* appeared that were unaffected by the $R_1$ gene. Other R genes were identified and used, only to be rendered redundant by the emergence of yet more races of the pathogen (P-186, P-189). Monogenically inherited resistance from *S. demissum* ceased to be effective by about 1936; subsequently, however, it was shown that potato cultivars with *S. demissum* in their parentage were often more resistant to late blight in the field than were cultivars without *S. demissum* due to the actions of polygenes (P-186, P-189; D. R. Glendinning, pers. comm., 14 July 1981). North American cultivars with this type of resistance are listed in table 8.2 (note 78). Field resistance to *P. infestans* is also available within the crop species (*S. tuberosum*), but this source has the limitation of being associated with late maturity, which is not the case with field resistance from *S. demissum* (S-302). Resistance from *S. demissum* and other species native to central Mexico (where *P. infestans* originates and is most diverse) is also likely to be more effective than that derived from Andean material, such as *S. tuberosum* (M-249, S-302). Even so, the polygenically inherited resistance is incomplete, and it is often necessary to apply fungicides even to field-resistant cultivars.

The practical value of field resistance lies in its durability, in the fact that field-resistant cultivars need be sprayed less thoroughly and less often than susceptible cultivars and still be adequately protected against blight (M-249), and that fungicides are more effective on field-resistant cultivars than on susceptible ones (P-214). Field resistance can be increased by crossing and selfing cultivars with *S. demissum* in their parentage, so accumulating the polygenes that are otherwise scattered at random throughout the breeding material (P-186, S-302). As a bonus, cultivars with *S. demissum* have been found to be resistant to potato leaf roll virus and to show heterosis in vigor and yield (P-186, P-189).

*Other Yield Characteristics*

Cacao (*Theobroma cacao*) is prominent among the crops for which the search for disease resistance was the spur to breeding with wild gene pools. Yet, although resistance to several serious diseases has been found in wild populations and has been transferred to the crop, it has not had the impact of other yield characteristics, notably heterosis, high yield potential, precocity, and environmental adaptability. Table 8.3 lists the yield characteristics (other than disease

# Table 8.3 Yield characteristics (other than disease and pest resistance) from wild species in commercial cultivars of crops grown or imported by the United States

| CROP | High yield potential | Vigor | Heterosis | Environmental adaptations | Other factors | SOURCE OF CHARACTERISTICS |
|---|---|---|---|---|---|---|
| **CANNABIDACEAE** Hops | (1) | (2) | | | | Humulus lupulus from Manitoba (1, 2) |
| | (3) | | | | | H. lupulus from Utah (3) |
| **COMPOSITAE** Sunflower | | | Expressed through use of CMS/GFR (4) | | CMS (5) | Helianthus petiolaris from Missouri (5) |
| | | | | | GFR (6) Recessive branching (7) | H. annuus from Texas (6, 7) |
| Lettuce | | More robust root system (8) | | | | Lactuca virosa (8) |
| **GRAMINEAE** Smooth brome | | | | Winter hardiness (9) | | Bromus pumpellianus from Alaska and Arctic Canada (9) |
| Sugarcane | (10) | Improved ratooning ability (11); good tillering (12) | (13) | Hardiness (14); cold tolerance (15); drought resistance (16) | Stalk thickness (17) | Saccharum spontaneum from Java and India (10–16) S. robustum from Papua New Guinea (10, 12, 13, 17) |
| **IRIDACEAE** Spanish iris | | | | | Earliness and ease of forcing (18) | Iris tingitana from Morocco (18) |
| **LEGUMINOSAE** Alfalfa | (19) | | | Winter hardiness (20) | Plant habit (20) | Medicago falcata from USSR (19, 20) |

*(continued)*

# Table 8.3  (*Continued*)

| CROP | CHARACTERISTICS | | | | | SOURCE OF CHARACTERISTICS |
|---|---|---|---|---|---|---|
| | High yield potential | Vigor | Heterosis | Environmental adaptations | Other factors | |
| **PALMAE** <br> Oil palm | (21) | | | | | *Elaeis guineensis* from Zaire, Ivory Coast, and Nigeria (21) |
| **ROSACEAE** <br> Strawberry | | (22) | | (22) | | *Fragaria chiloensis* from California (22) |
| **STERCULIACEAE** <br> Cacao | (23) | (23) | (24) | Drought tolerance (25) | Precocity (26) | *Theobroma cacao* from Peru (23–26) |

Notes: CMS = cytoplasmic male sterility, GFR = genetic fertility restoration.

*Hops*

1. In cultivar Brewer's Gold (grown in the United States and West Germany) (V-348).
2. Same as 1.
3. In cultivar Comet grown in the United States (V-348).

*Sunflower*

4. In hybrid cultivars accounting for 90% of North American production (D-150). Main text gives details.
5. D-150, J-396. Main text gives details.
6. D-150. Main text gives details.
7. D-406, P-356. Main text gives details.

*Lettuce*

8. In cultivars Salinas, Vanguard (and Vanguard derivatives), and Winterhaven, grown in the United States (S-286; E. J. Ryder, pers. comm., 30 July 1981).

*Smooth Brome*

9. In cultivar Polar (grown in the United States) (G-142, G-821).

*Sugarcane*

10. D-3, G-412, P-235, P-237. Closely linked to improved ratooning and tillering (table notes 11 and 12 below) and heterosis (table note 13).
11. Improved ratooning means higher capacity for regenerating canes from the underground parts of the plant, thus extending the useful life of the plant; in Hawaii, e.g., from three to five crops are obtained from each planting of "seed" cane (sugarcane is propagated vegetatively with cuttings of cane stalks) (A-1383, P-225). Improved ratooning is a characteristic of cultivars with *S. spontaneum* germplasm (P-225, P-235, P-237, S-345).
12. Tillering means the production of stems or stalks; whereas ratooning refers to the capacity for regeneration, tillering refers to the number of stalks per plant. *S.*

296

*spontaneum*'s tillering ability has made a valuable contribution to increased yields in tropical countries and has probably been indispensable in subtropical and temperate areas (such as Hawaii, Florida, and Louisiana). This is because the wild species' tillering ability, transferred to the crop, has enabled it to respond productively to the relatively low sola-energy levels of these subtropical and temperate areas (P-225). Good tillering has also been transferred from *S. robustum* (T. L. Tew, pers. comm., 24 Jan. 1982).

13. T. L. Tew, pers. comm., 24 Jan. 1982.
14. P-235, P-237, S-345.
15. D-3, J-564.
16. D-3, P-225.
17. T. L. Tew, pers. comm., 24 Jan. 1982

### Spanish Iris

18. Dutch cultivars Ideal, Hildegarde, White Wedgwood, Purple Sensation, Wedgwood, and possibly Professor Blaauw can be produced year round as a result of earliness and ease of forcing derived from Morccan *Iris tingitana* (J. P. van Eijk, pers. comm., 30 Apr. 1980).

### Alfalfa

19. High seed and forage yield in U.S. and Canadian cultivars such as Rhizoma, Narragansett, and Vernal (A-621).
20. The main contributions of *Medicago falcata* have been winter hardiness and desirable plant habit (spreading growth, broad crowns, and creeping roots) (A-621, A-1408). More than 70 cultivars have been grown in North America with 1% or more *M. falcata* germplasm. In the United States, major cultivars with 10% or more *M. falcata* germplasm include Rhizoma (50%), Teton (50%), Rambler (45%), Glacier (33%), Travois (33%), WL202 (17%), Vernal (16%), 525 (16%), Progress (16%), 522 (16%), Narragansett (15%), Mark II (15%), Iroquois (15%), and A-59 (10%) (A-1408).

### Oil Palm

21. Since about 1957 most commercial plantings in Malaysia have been of the *tenera* type of oil palm obtained by crossing *dura* cultivars with wild *pisifera* material (G-148, G-150). In Indonesia, planting of *tenera* (*dura × pisifera*) seed began in 1957, and *tenera* has been the only type planted since 1971 (J-242). Between 1950 and 1960 almost all plantation companies in both Southeast Asia and West Africa switched to *dura × pisifera* seed, and as a result almost all plantations in the two oil-palm-producing regions consist of *teneras*; the transformation will soon be complete, since during the last 15 years 100% of new plantings have been of the *dura × pisifera* hybrid (M. A. Adansi, pers. comm., 27 Apr. 1982; G. Blaak, pers. comm., 19 Oct. 1981). The Zaire *pisifera* material comes from wild palm groves near Eala and Yawenda, although one of the plants came from the Eala Botanical Garden (G-148, S-186; G. Blaak, pers. comm., 19 Oct. 1981). Other wild material comes from a wild palm grove near Bingerville, Ivory Coast (the La Me selections) and from semiwild groves in eastern Nigeria (Aba, Calabar, and Ufuma) and midwestern Nigeria (Benin) (A-931, G-101, G-150; M. A. Adansi, pers. comm., 27 Apr. 1982; G. Blaak, pers. comm., 19 Oct. 1981). Additional information is in the main text and in text note 3.

### Strawberry

22. Vigor and environmental adaptations (hardiness, earliness, and drought resistance) of cultivars Tioga and Fresno (grown in the United States) derived from Californian *Fragaria chiloensis* via Ettersburg 121 (V-342).

### Cacao

23. G-97, J-125, S-301, S-380. Main text gives details.
24. A-208, J-125, S-184, S-380. Main text gives details.
25. G-97. Main text gives details.
26. G-97, J-125, S-301, S-380. Main text gives details.

and pest resistance) that cacao and nine other crops have derived from wild germplasm. In cacao the combination of high yield potential, vigor, heterosis, drought tolerance, and precocity has increased yields substantially. In West Africa, Upper Amazon clones crossed with one another yielded 20% more (in terms of weight of dry cocoa per acre over a 10-year period) than the standard West African Amelonado cultivars. Upper Amazons crossed with Amelonados yielded 50% more than the Upper Amazons alone and 72% more than the Amelonados alone (G-95) (note 2). Several factors contribute to these yield increases, and it is not possible to distinguish their individual contributions. Heterosis means hybrid vigor. It is caused by the interaction of two distinct genotypes (homozygous parental lines) and is expressed in high yield potential, vigor, and other characteristics, such as precocity. Vigor itself is expressed in several ways, such as ease of establishment and recovery from stress. Clearly, the effects of heterosis will overlap with those of factors for high yield and vigor operating independently of heterosis.

Populations of *Theobroma cacao* in the area of the species' greatest diversity (northeastern Peru and eastern Ecuador) seem to be uniformly self-incompatible; away from this area, self-compatible trees can occur (A-452). Particular genotypes appear to be restricted to particular valleys, and individual populations are "uniform if not homozygous" for the genes determining their distinguishing characteristics (A-208). The wild and semiwild Upper Amazon clones used in breeding possess the multi-allelic system of incompatibility that is the feature of populations from the area; this system has been exploited by breeders in West Africa in the development of hybrid cultivars (A-208, J-125, S-184, S-380). The four main populations used have been Iquitos (IMC), Nanay (NA), Parinari (PA), and Scavina (SCA) (G-96, G-97, J-125, S-184, S-301). In addition to the heterosis obtained from interpopulational crosses (for example, West African $F_3$ T63: Parinari 35 × Nanay 32), the individual populations themselves provide particular yield factors. NA, PA, and SCA each contributes rapid rate of growth, high yields, and early commencement of bearing (G-97).

The last factor means that the trees begin bearing fruit in the third or fourth year rather than in the fifth (as is the case with Amelonado types), a characteristic described in table 8.3 as precocity. NA and PA contribute high fat contents, while NA and SCA contribute vigor, and PA and SCA drought tolerance (G-97). Drought tolerance is a valuable characteristic under the marginal rainfall conditions and severe dry season of large areas of western Nigeria (S-301).

The contribution of wild germplasm to the increased yield potential of oil palm is more straightforward. Wild and semiwild *pisifera* oil palms from Zaire (and to a lesser extent from the Ivory Coast and Nigeria) have contributed a higher proportion of oil-bearing mesocarp in the fruit. The *dura* oil palms, which provided the foundation material of the Malaysian and Indonesian plantations, have fruit that are 25–45% shell and 20–65% mesocarp. The *tenera* cultivars that have replaced them (produced by crossing *dura* with *pisifera*) have fruit that are 4–20% shell and 60–90% mesocarp (note 3). Although *teneras* have fewer fruit per bunch than have *duras*, they yield more oil per bunch because of the greater proportion of mesocarp in each fruit (G-147).

The Southeast Asian oil palm plantations are derived from only four *dura* plants introduced into the Botanical Garden at Bogor, Java, in 1848. The plants are believed to have come from the same parent (G-189). Plantations were first established in Indonesia (Sumatra) in 1911 and in Malaysia in 1917. The plants that were grown yielded 1.2 tons of oil per hectare in Indoncsia. The first selections for yield, made in 1920, brought an increase by about 65% to 2 tons per hectare. Subsequent generations of selection raised yields by another 35%, and improved plantation practices added a 50% increase to that, boosting yields to 4 tons per hectare (S-186). The introduction of *tenera* cultivars has enabled these impressive yield increases to continue. Oil yield per hectare has been raised by 25% again, bringing the average plantation yield to 5 tons per hectare (S-186). In experimental plantations oil yields are almost 7 tons per hectare, suggesting that further yield increases are likely (G-147).

Oil palm provides an example of a crop that has obtained a specific yield factor (more oil-bearing mesocarp) from the wild gene pool. Sunflower provides a contrasting example of the wild gene pool providing the means for breeders to take full advantage of heterosis. The growing of $F_1$ hybrids, produced by combining two different homozygous lines, fixes the expression of heterosis and hence provides growers with higher yields every growing season. To obtain hybrid seed, the seed producer must ensure that line A is pollinated only by line B, that individuals in line A do not pollinate onc another. This can be done by emasculating (cutting out the pollen-bearing organ of) the members of line A, but this is an expensive, labor intensive operation. A simpler and far cheaper method—and in fact the only practical possibility in crops like sunflower—is to ensure that the pollen of line A is sterile. Cytoplasmic male sterility (CMS) provides just such a method.

Cytoplasmic male sterility is so called because the gene for male (pollen) sterility occurs not on a chromosome but in the cytoplasm (roughly, the material of the cell, excluding the cell wall and the nucleus). The phenomenon has been found in 80 species, 25 genera, and 6 families of plants, so it is quite widespread; but stable CMS that is 100% effective under a wide range of conditions is rare (G-764). A stable source of CMS in sunflower, obtained from the wild *Helianthus petiolaris*, was first reported by Leclerq in 1969 (J-396). In 1970 Kinman reported a source of genetic fertility restoration (GFR)—necessary to restore fertility to the crop so that it sets seed—in wild *Helianthus annuus*. Since then three other sources of CMS have been discovered—all in wild species—and many more sources of GFR have been found, both in wild species and in the crop (D-150) (note 4).

Hybrids produced with the *H. petiolaris* source of CMS and wild *H. annuus* sources of GFR were grown commercially in the United States for the first time in 1972. They transformed sunflower from a minor U.S. crop to a major crop and currently account for 90% of North American sunflower production (D-150). The hybrids yield from 18 to 25+% more than the open-pollinated cultivars they have replaced (D-150, W. Dedio, pers. comm., 28 September 1981).

Production of hybrid sunflower seed is facilitated by a further contribution from wild *H. annuus:* a recessive gene for branching. Domesticated sunflower has been selected to bear one huge inflorescence on a single branch in contrast to the wild plants that have many flowering branches. The heads of branching plants mature at different times, which increases the duration and cost of harvesting. Consequently, breeding lines and cultivars with the usual dominant gene for branching have been discarded. Eric Putt discovered a recessive gene for branching in wild Texan *H. annuus* (P-356), which has been incorporated into the male GFR lines used in hybrid seed production (D-406, G. N. Fick, pers. comm., 2 October 1981). In this particular application the branching characteristic is very useful because it extends the period of pollen production in seed fields and enables seed to be produced from female lines that flower much later than the male GFR lines. Branching does not appear in the hybrids grown by the farmer because the gene governing it is recessive (D-406).

## Quality Characteristics

Eight crops have had their quality improved through the use of wild germplasm: hops, lettuce, Bermuda grass, Spanish iris, sweet clover, tulip, cotton, and tomato. Table 8.4 shows that the main qualities obtained from the wild have been improvements in color (lettuce, Spanish iris, tulip, and tomato) and chemical content (hops, sweet clover, and tomato); followed by better aroma or flavor (hops and lettuce), and a variety of miscellaneous quality factors, such as increased soluble solids and harvesting adaptations in the tomato. Tulip, hops, and tomato provide representative examples of wild-derived improvements in, respectively, color, chemical content, and "other factors."

The most popular tulips grown today are the Darwin hybrids. Darwin hybrid cultivars account for more than 37% of tulip production in the Netherlands (the world's largest producer of tulip bulbs and the major supplier to the United States), compared with Triumph tulips, the next most popular group, which account for less than 28% (P-70). The popularity of the Darwin hybrids is due to the contribution of their male parent, *Tulipa fosteriana* (D-85), first collected from the wild near Bukhara in the southern USSR in 1904 (S-311). *Tulipa fosteriana* provided the cultivated tulip for the first time with the brilliance and intensity of color (as well as a fine stateliness of form) that make cultivars such as Apeldoorn (which alone accounts for 20% of Dutch tulip production) favorite ornaments of the garden (P-70; H. Q. Varekamp, pers. comm., 30 April 1980).

Hops contribute aroma and bitterness to beer, the bitterness coming from alpha acids. High alpha acid content (9.5+%) is therefore of great value to hop growers and the brewing industry. By far the most important sources of high

**Table 8.4 Quality characteristics from wild species in commercial cultivars of crops grown or imported by the United States**

| CROP | CHARACTERISTICS | | | | SOURCE OF CHARACTERISTICS |
|---|---|---|---|---|---|
| | *Aroma/flavor* | *Chemical content* | *Color* | *Other factors* | |
| CANNABIDACEAE Hops | (1) | High alpha acids (2) | | | *Humulus lupulus* from Slovenia, Yugoslavia (1); *H. lupulus* from Bavaria, West Germany (1); *H. lupulus* from Manitoba, Canada (2); *H. lupulus* from California, United States (2) |
| COMPOSITAE Lettuce | (3) | | (4) | Adaptation to marketing (5) | *Lactuca virosa* (3, 4, 5) |
| GRAMINEAE Bermuda grass | | | | Increased digestibility and feeding value (6) | *Cynodon nlemfuensis* from Kenya (6) |
| IRIDACEAE Spanish iris | | | (7) | | *Iris tingitana* from Morocco (7) |
| LEGUMINOSAE Sweet clover | | Low coumarin (8) | | | *Melilotus dentata* from Russia, USSR (8) |
| LILIACEAE Tulip | | | (9) | Good form (10) | *Tulip fosteriana* from Tadzhik SSR, USSR (9,10) |
| MALVACEAE Cotton | | | | Fiber strength and elongation (11) | *Gossypium thurberi* from Arizona, United States (11) |
| SOLANACEAE Tomato | | High vitamin C (12); high beta-carotene (13) | (14) | High soluble solids (15); adaptation to harvesting (16) | *Lycopersicon peruvianum* (12); *L. hirsutum* (13, 14); *L. pimpinellifolium* (14); *L. chmielewskii* from Peru (14, 15); *L. cheesmanii* from Ecuador (16) |

*(continued)*

Table 8.4  (*Continued*)

Notes

*Hops*

1. Wild Slovenian hops have contributed improved aroma quality to the Super Styrian A cultivars grown in Yugoslavia: Ahil, Apolon, Atlas, and Aurora (T. Wagner, pers. comm., 20 Jan. 1982). Wild Bavarian hops are the likely source of the pleasant aroma of cultivars Huller Bitterer, Perle, and Emerald (grown in West Germany), although it could also have been cultivar Canterbury Golding (A. Haunold, pers. comm., 24 May 1983).

2. Cultivars Brewer's Gold and Bullion and their derivatives (Galena, Eroica, Ahil, Apolon, and Atlas), grown in the United States and Yugoslavia, get their high alpha acid content from BB1, a wild hop from Manitoba (G-583, G-584, M-243, S-9, V-348; A. Haunold, pers. comm., 20 Aug. 1981; T. Wagner, pers. comm., 20 Jan. 1982). Cultivar Northern Brewer and its derivatives (Record, Huller Bitterer, Perle, and Aurora), grown in West Germany and Yugoslavia, get their high alpha acid content from BB1 and also from OY1, a wild hop from California (G-583, M-243, S-10, V-348; T. Wagner, pers. comm., 20 Jan. 1982). Further information is in main text.

*Lettuce*

3. The sweeter flavor and tendency to remain sweet for a longer period of the crisphead (iceberg) cultivars Salinas, Vanguard (and Vanguard derivatives), and Winterhaven, grown in the United States, are attributed to wild *Lactuca virosa* (E. J. Ryder, pers. comm., 29 Sept. 1981).

4. The dull green exterior color and the preferred creamy yellow interior (rather than white) of the cultivars listed in table note 3 above are attributed to the same source (ibid.).

5. The softer leaf texture, a useful marketing adaptation since it reduces damage from breaking, of the cultivars listed in table note 3 above is attributed to the same source (ibid.).

*Bermuda Grass*

6. Cultivar Coastcross 1 (grown in the United States) is a cross between cultivar Coastal and a collection of wild *Cynodon nlemfuensis* var. *robustus*, deriving from the latter its increased digestibility and feeding value. Dry matter digestibility of Coastcross 1 is more than 60% compared with that of Coastal, which is 53.5%, an increase of more than 12%. Liveweight gains of livestock fed on Coastcross 1 are 717 grams/day/animal compared with 553 grams for Coastal, an increase of almost 30% (A-678, G-142).

*Spanish Iris*

7. Dutch cultivars Ideal, Hildegarde, Purple Sensation, and Wedgwood get their blue color from *Iris tingitana* (J. P. van Eijk, pers. comm., 30 Apr. 1980).

*Sweet Clover*

8. *Melilotus alba* cultivars Azumar, Cumino, Denta, and Polara, and *M. officinalis* cultivar Norgold have the gene *cu* for low coumarin from *M. dentata* G-102, G-107; B. P. Goplen, pers. comm., 2 Sept. 1981; R. R. Smith, pers. comm., 15 Oct. 1981). Low coumarin is important because coumarin causes sweet clover disease. In poorly preserved sweet clover hay or silage, coumarin may change to dicoumarol, a potent anticoagulant. Livestock eating dicoumarol-contaminated fodder often bleed to death from the slightest internal or external injury because the blood is prevented from clotting. Use of low coumarin cultivars of sweet clover eliminates this problem (G-53, G-111).

*Tulip*

9. The Darwin hybrid cultivars get their brilliance of color from *Tulipa fosteriana*. Tulips were not brilliant before *T. fosteriana* (H. Q. Varekamp, pers. comm., 30 Apr. 1980). Main text gives details.

10. *T. fosteriana* has also contributed its stateliness of form to the Darwin hybrids (ibid.).

*Cotton (G. hirsutum)*

11. Longer fibers and high fiber strength are contributed by Arizona *Gossypium thurberi* to cultivars Acala SJ-1, Acala SJ-2, Acala SJ-4, and Acala SJ-5 (grown in the United States) (A-450; L. S. Stith, pers. comm., 31 July 1981), as well as to several minor cultivars grown in the United States, such as MO-DEL, AZ64, and SC-1 (F. D. Wilson, pers. comm., 17 Aug. 1981). This is an example of an unexpected contribution, since *G. thurberi* is a wild diploid cotton and, like most of the wild diploids, has no lint and therefore could not be expected to have a gene for lint strength (S-28).

*Tomato*

12. U.S. cultivars Hi-C and Doublerich have increased vitamin C from *Lycopersicon peruvianum* (P-463).

13. U.S. cultivar Caro-Red has almost ten times the beta-carotene (provitamin A) content of common tomatoes (such as Rutgers), derived from *L. hirsutum* (S-296). Other cultivars also have much increased levels of beta-carotene from this source (P-463).

14. Both red-fruited species (*L. pimpinellifolium*) and green-fruited species (*L. hirsutum* and *L. chmielewskii*) have contributed to intensification of internal and external color (P-134, P-463).

15. G-831, P-134, P-140, P-263. Main text gives details.

16. P-449, P-450, P-463. Main text gives details.

alpha acids in currently grown cultivars have been two collections of wild hops (*Humulus lupulus*), one from Manitoba, the other from California. BB1, the hop from Manitoba, was sent to British hop breeder E. S. Salmon in 1918. It flowered, bore seeds, and promptly died. Two seedlings from this inauspicious beginning were raised the next year, and these produced the cultivars Brewer's Gold, released in 1934, and Bullion, released in 1938 (S-9). OY1, the hop from California, was collected in 1914. Salmon crossed it with Brewer's Gold and then crossed one of the resulting seedlings with the cultivar Canterbury Golding to produce the cultivar Northern Brewer, which was released in 1944 (S-10). Norther Brewer therefore has OY1 as a grandparent and BB1 as a great-grandparent.

All three cultivars became, and remain, major high alpha hops. Brewer's Gold and Bullion are important in the United States; Northern Brewer and Brewer's Gold are important in West Germany. In addition, either Brewer's Gold or Northern Brewer is in the parentage of almost every one of the other high or medium alpha acid cultivars grown in the United States, West Germany, and other hop-producing countries (note 5). BB1 is generally believed to be the main source of high alpha acids in these cultivars (G-584), though in the case of cultivars with Northern Brewer parentage, OY1 is a likely contributor as well (M-243).

Two wild tomato species have made striking quality contributions: *Lycopersicon chmielewskii* from Andean Peru has increased the soluble solids of tomatoes for processing; *L. cheesmanii* from the Galapagos Islands (Ecuador) has provided an adaptation for mechanized harvesting. Soluble solids consist mainly of fructose, glucose, and other sugars. They are of great importance to the tomato processing industry, since the bulk of Californian cannery tomatoes are used in products that are sold on the basis of their solids content (P-134). It has been estimated that each 0.5% increase in soluble solids is worth a million dollars to the processing industry (G-831). Addition of *L. chmielewskii* germplasm to processing tomato cultivars increased their soluble solids content by more than 2% (P-134). *L. cheesmanii*'s contribution is gene $j_2$, the gene that prevents the formation of a joint on the pedicel (the stalk of the fruit). Cultivars with a jointed pedicel are not adapted to harvesting with machines because the fruit tend to drop off and too much stalk stays on (P-449). Charles Rick, who discovered gene $j_2$ and transferred it to the crop, writes that it "has been incorporated in several cultivars and is being exploited widely in the breeding of mechanically harvested cultivars and in other situations in which vine retention of fruits and/or complete elimination of the pedicel stub are important" (P-463).

### Value of Wild Genetic Resources

We have tried to estimate the value of wild genetic resources in a way that would produce figures comparable with those for logging, fishing, trapping, and collecting. In a strict sense, the supply of a genetically controlled characteristic is not comparable with that of a consumable commodity, such as timber or seafood, so the results of such an evaluation can be only approximate. To arrive at a total value of wild consumable commodities, we added the harvested value of U.S.-produced timber, the landed value of U.S.-produced fish, the equivalent (point-of-first-sale) value of other (trapped or collected) U.S.-produced wild commodities, and the customs value of imported wild commodities. These values include the costs of obtaining the commodities from the wild (felling the trees, catching the fish, trapping the furbearers, and so on). Some of the import values (for example, the value of newsprint or of canned sardines) also include the costs and value-added of processing. The United States imports very little of its wild-derived raw materials in completely raw form. Most enter the country processed to some extent. In our judgment, to exclude imports of processed materials would distort the contribution of wild commodities to the U.S. economy more than if they were included.

The equivalent values of the agricultural crops improved by wild germplasm are the farm sales value of U.S.-grown crops and the customs value of imported crops (both processed and unprocessed, excluding manufactured articles). However, only a proportion of the characteristics that make a crop valuable are heritable: other factors—environmental inputs such as fertilizers and cultivation practices—also make a contribution. At most, therefore, the value of a genetic resource will be some proportion of the value of the crop. In the case of a wild genetic resource, the upper limit of this proportion is set by the proportion of the crop that is supplied by cultivars improved with wild germplasm. The value of a wild genetic resource is $f\%$ of $p\%$ of the value of the crop, $p\%$ being the proportion of the crop supplied by cultivars with wild germplasm, and $f\%$ being the proportion of the value of those cultivars accounted for by factors controlled by wild germplasm.

We have estimated $f\%$ in three ways, depending on whether the factor controlled by wild germplasm is disease and pest resistance, other yield characteristics, or quality characteristics. The value of disease or pest resistance is taken to be the value of that proportion of the crop that is likely to have been lost had the resistance not been obtained. An exception to this is the case of resistance to a disease or pest that is as readily controlled by some other means (such as a pesticide) as by breeding for resistance. In such a case the value of the wild genetic contribution is interpreted to be the savings of the cost of the alternative method of control.

We regard the value of other yield characteristics (high yield potential, vigor, heterosis, environmental adaptations) as being the value of the increased yield obtained by them. Essentially, we see disease and pest resistance as maintaining yields that otherwise would be lost, and other yield factors as generating additional yields. We have not attempted to apply this principle consistently because there are obvious exceptions to it. Newly obtained disease resistance can

(text continued on page 314)

**Table 8.5  Estimated average annual value of the contributions of wild genetic resources to crops grown or imported by the United States, 1976–1980**

| CROP | SOURCE | AVERAGE ANNUAL VALUE (U.S.$ million) | ESTIMATED PERCENTAGE OF SUPPLY FROM CVS WITH WGR [p] | ESTIMATED ANNUAL VALUE (U.S.$ million) | ESTIMATED ANNUAL VALUE OF CONTRIBUTIONS OF WGR (U.S.$ million) [f] Yield factors | Quality factors | Total |
|---|---|---|---|---|---|---|---|
| **CANNABIDACEAE** | | | | | | | |
| Hops | United States | 63.8 | 17 (1) | 10.8 | ? | 6.4 (3) | 6.4 |
| | Imports | 21.5 | 43 (2) | 9.2 | ? (4) | 5.5 (3) | 5.5 |
| **CHENOPODIACEAE** | | | | | | | |
| Sugar beet | United States | 710.9 | 15–20 (5) | 106.6–142.2 | 3.0–3.25 (7) | na | 3.0–3.25 |
| | Imports | 40.0 | — (6) | — | — | na | — |
| **COMPOSITAE** | | | | | | | |
| Sunflower | United States | 391.4 | 90 (8) | 352.3 | 88.1 (10) | na | 88.1 |
| | Imports | 2.0 | 75 (9) | 1.5 | 0.4 (10) | na | 0.4 |
| Lettuce | United States | 526.2 | 52 (11) | 275.6 | ? | ? | ? |
| | Imports | 1.1 | ? | | | | |
| **ERICACEAE** | | | | | | | |
| Highbush blueberry | United States | 41.6 | 11 (12) | 4.6 | ? (13) | na | ? |
| | Imports | 2.4 | 0 (12) | | | | |
| **GRAMINEAE** | | | | | | | |
| Oats | United States | 301.3 | 5–25 (14) | 15.1–75.3 | 0.6–2.3 (16) | na | 0.6–2.3 |
| | Imports | 2.9 | ? (15) | | | | |
| Smooth brome | United States | 1.1* | >1 (17) | | — | na | — |
| Bermuda grass | United States | 130.0† | >1 (18) | 1.3 | na | 0.4 (19) | 0.4 |
| Sugarcane | United States | 485.9 | 69 (20) | 338.1 | 33.8 (22) | na | 33.8 |
| | Imports | 1,236.6 | 69 (21) | 855.6 | 85.6 (22) | na | 85.6 |
| Bread wheat | United States | 6,450.5 | 10 (23) | 651.5 | 35.3 (24) | na | 35.3 |
| | Imports | 24.6 | ? | | | | |
| **IRIDACEAE** | | | | | | | |
| Spanish iris | United States | 5.0 | ? | | | | |
| | Imports | 1.6 | 31 (25) | 0.5 | ? | ? | ? |

| | | | | | | |
|---|---|---|---|---|---|---|
| LEGUMINOSAE | | | | | | |
| Alfalfa | United States | 1,053.6 | 30 (26) | 316.1 | ? (27) | na | ? |
| | Imports | — | | | | | |
| Sweet clover | United States | 1.0* | 1 (28) | — | na | — | : |
| | Imports | 1.6 | 1 (28) | — | na | — | — |
| LILIACEAE | | | | | | | |
| Tulip | United States | 9.4 | ? | | na | | ? |
| | Imports | 11.9 | 38 (29) | 4.6 | | ? | |
| MALVACEAE | | | | | | | |
| Cotton G. *barbadense* | United States | 45.0 | 0 (30) | | ? | na | ? |
| | Imports | 30.0‡ | 10 (30) | 3.0 | ? | na | ? |
| Cotton G. *hirsutum* | United States | 3,794.0 | 20 (31) | | | na | |
| | Imports | 439.0‡ | 0 (31) | 758.8 | | na | |
| PALMAE | | | | | | | |
| Oil palm | Imports | 143.3 | 90 (32) | 129.0 | 32.3 (33) | na | 32.3 |
| ROSACEAE | | | | | | | |
| Strawberry | United States | 218.9 | 49 (34) | 106.5 | ? (34) | na | ? |
| | Imports | 33.0 | ? | | | | |
| SOLANACEAE | | | | | | | |
| Bell pepper | United States | 104.4 | 2 (35) | 1.8 | — (36) | na | — |
| | Imports | 53.7 | 0 (35) | | | | |
| Tomato | United States | 893.0 | 90 (37) | 803.7 | ? (38) | ? (38) | ? |
| | Imports | 158.0 | 90 (37) | 142.2 | | | |
| Tobacco | United States | 2,437.8 | 35 (39) | 851.0 | 1.9 (41) | na | 1.9 |
| | Imports | 413.6 | ? (40) | | | | |
| Potato | United States | 1,195.8 | 11 (42) | 132.7 | ? | na | ? |
| | Imports | 10.2 | 26 (43) | 2.7 | ? | na | ? |
| STERCULIACEAE | | | | | | | |
| Cacao | Imports | 1,016.0 | 7 (44) | 70.0 | 49.0 (45) | na | 49.0 |
| TOTAL (46) | | | | 6,040.6 | | | 342.3 |

(continued)

# Table 8.5 (*Continued*)

Notes: ? = we do not know; — = less than $100,000; na = not applicable; CVS = cultivars, WGR = wild genetic resources.

* Seed; data for 1974.

† Hay; data for 1974.

‡ Cotton import value inclues raw cotton, cotton lintners and cotton waste, cotton yarns and thread and cotton cordage, cottonseed oilcake and meal, and cotton fabrics (but not clothing or other finished articles of cotton fabric).

## Hops

1. Bullion and Brewer's Gold 15% of U.S. production + Comet, Galena, and Eroica 2% (A-1385–A-1390; U.S. Hop Administrative Committee via A. Haunold, pers. comm., 24 May 1983).

2. Imports come from West Germany (71% of value), Yugoslavia (13%), Czechoslovakia (8%), and Poland (4%). Cultivars with WGR grown in West Germany are Huller Bitterer (8.5% of area), Record (3%), Perle (0.4%), Northern Brewer (31.9%), and Brewer's Gold (12.2%). Cultivars with WGR grown in Yugoslavia are Super Styrians (25% of area). (Cultivar area data are from A-1385–A-1390, supplemented by H. Ehrmaier, pers. comm., 24 Feb 1981). There are no WGR in Czech cultivars (R. A. Neve, pers. comm., 24 Feb. 1981). Cultivars with WGR are a small proportion of Poland's production (A-1385–A-1390, G-583).

3. The contribution of high alpha acids content is estimated as follows: 1981 premium prices for alpha acid content were 20 cents (U.S.) per 1% above base of 9.5%. Additional income to U.S. growers is upwards of $500/acre, sometimes as high as $2,000/acre. Average yields are in excess of 2,000 pounds/acre, and the average alpha acid content of the cultivars with WGR is 10–14%. On the basis of 2% increased alpha acids content above 9.5%, the calculation is $0.40/lb × 2,000 lbs/acre × 8,000 acres (average acreage) = $6.4 million. The contribution of high alpha acids with respect to imported hops is estimated pro rata. No estimate has been made of the value of the contribution of aroma.

4. Data are insufficient for estimating the value of disease resistance, high yield potential, or vigor. In West Germany, *Verticillium* wilt is such a problem that cultivars susceptible to wilt (notably Hallertau) are being replaced by tolerant cultivars such as Perle (A-1389).

## Sugar Beet

5. Hybrid cultivars are derived from GW and MONO HY cultivars grown on 200,000–250,000 acres (R. K. Oldemeyer, pers. comm., 15 July 1981, and 5 Nov. 1981). Average acreage 1976–1980: 1,252,000 acres (S-448, S-449, S-699).

6. Imports come from Canada (57% of value), France (20%), and Belgium (8%). Italy is a minor supplier. Alba cultivars are grown on 20,000–30,000 acres in Italy (Oldemeyer, 15 July 1981). Average Italian acreage 1976–1980: 669,000 acres (S-448, S-449, S-699).

7. The value of WGR-derived *Cercospora* leafspot resistance is in the saving of spraying costs, calculated by R. K. Oldemeyer (pers. comm., 5 Nov. 1981) to be $3 million–$3.25 million/year.

## Sunflower

8. D-150.

9. Imports come largely (82% of value) from Canada. The proportion of Canadian sunflower production accounted for by hybrids is similar to that of the United States. Hybrids are also widely used elsewhere, but we have excluded non-North American supplies from our estimates.

10. Direct substitution of adapted and tested hybrids is estimated to have resulted in yield increases "in excess of 25%" (D-150). The yield advantage of the hybrids over open-pollinated cultivars has been found to average 18% (W. Dedio, pers. comm., 28 Sept. 1981). The only effective control of downy mildew and rust is to use resistant cultivars (D-150, Y-88). Almost all the hybrids have downy mildew resistance from WGR, estimated to result in an additional 5% increase in yield. Hybrids occupying 10–15% of U.S. acreage and 20% of Canadian acreage have the R₁ gene for rust resistance; virtually all of the remainder have the R₂ gene (W. Dedio, pers. comm., 2 Sept. 1981). This has prevented yield reductions from rust infection, which occurs sporadically particularly in the United States. We have assumed that prevention of such reductions is the equivalent of an additional 2%. This brings the total WGR-derived yield increase to 25%. No estimate has

been made of the value of recessive branching. The overall importance of these contributions "is reflected in terms of growth of the sunflower industry [in the United States]. The crop grew from only several thousand acres in 1970 to over 4 million acres currently. This growth was made possible primarily by the development of hybrids, the keys of course being the identification of cytoplasmic male sterility and fertility restoration in the wild species" (G. N. Fick, pers. comm., 2 Oct. 1981).

*Lettuce*

11. Salinas accounts for 48% of California production, Vanguard, Vanguard 75, and other Vanguard derivatives for 19% of California production; Winterhaven 10% of California production (E. J. Ryder, pers. comm., 29 Sept. 1981). California accounts for 68% of U.S. production (value of farm sales) (S-724, S-726–S-728).

*Highbush Blueberry*

12. As a new domesticate, 100% of the U.S. and imported highbush blueberry crop is derived from wild germplasm. This entry refers only to the return to WGR for resistance to/tolerance of stem canker. It applies to the North Carolina crop only, where virtually all production is accounted for by cultivars with *Botryosphaeria* resistance or tolerance from local wild *Vaccinium australe* (M-633). North Carolina accounts for just over 11% of U.S. production (value of farm sales) (S-726–S-728).

13. Data are insufficient for estimating value. It will be a high proportion of the value of the North Carolina crop, since stem canker is the limiting factor in production (M-633) and use of resistant/tolerant cultivars is the only practical means of control (V-355).

*Oats*

14. The high percentage (25%) includes cultivars derived from Bond, which were grown on an average of 32% of the oat acreage of seven states surveyed: California, Illinois, Iowa, Minnesota, North Dakota, South Dakota, and Wisconsin. The low percentage (5%) excludes these cultivars; it includes only the E and M Multilines (grown on 5% of the oat acreage of the seven states), TAM 0-301, TAM 0-312, Coker 227, and Coker 234 (not grown in any of the seven states but grown in Texas and the Carolinas, which are not major oat producers). The seven states surveyed account for 63% of U.S. production (value of farm sales) (S-724, S-726–S-728).

15. Imports come from Canada (64% of value) and Colombia (29% of value). Apparently no WGR were in the cultivars grown in Canada in 1976–1980. We do not know the cultivar composition of oat production in Colombia.

16. Estimated on the assumption that *Puccinia coronata* resistance derived from WGR secures 3% of the yield of cultivars with that resistance. Crown rust is probably the most destructive of all oat diseases in the United States, having caused an estimated average annual loss of 3.7% of U.S. oat production during the 1950s (M-207). Some of the *Avena sterilis* source of resistance via Bond may still be useful (e.g., cultivar Lyon is "moderately resistant to moderately susceptible" to races of *P. coronata* and apparently "possesses some generalized resistance to crown rust" [S-826]; Noble "has resistance to most of the older races of crown rust . . . but is susceptible to the predominant newer races" [M-674]. The most widely grown cultivars with WGR-derived resistance to this latter group of races appear to be the E (early) and M (midseason) Multilines, which were grown on 1% of the South Dakota oat acreage, 5% of the Minnesota oat acreage, and 19% of the Iowa oat acreage during the period under review.

*Smooth Brome*

17. There are no data on the relative importance of cultivar Polar. We assume it is at least 1%.

*Bermuda Grass*

18. There are no data on the relative importance of cultivar Coastcross 1. We assume it is at least 1%.

*(continued)*

309

## Table 8.5  (Continued)

19. Increase in productivity (in terms of liveweight gains of livestock fed on the hay) over cultivars without WGR almost 30% (A-678). The contribution of WGR is estimated to be 30% of the value of the hay.

### Sugarcane

20. Cultivars with WGR account for 57% of production in Florida (S-356), 83% of production in Hawaii (G-829), and 70% of production in Louisiana and Texas (P-488). These states account, respectively, for 38, 37, 21, and 4% of U.S. production (value of farm sales) (S-724, S-726–S-728). Hence cultivars with WGR make up 69% of U.S. sugarcane production by value.

21. *Saccharum spontaneum* germplasm is probably as widely distributed in the cultivars grown in the countries exporting cane sugar to the United States (mainly, in order of value, the Dominican Republic, Brazil, the Philippines, Australia, Guatemala, Peru, Argentina, Panama, South Africa, and Colombia). We have used the 69% figure for imports as well.

22. In Hawaii the most serious disease is smut, which in fields with 30% infection can reduce yields by 10%. According to T. L. Tew (pers. comm., 24 Jan. 1982), it is fair to say that smut-resistant cultivars have prevented losses of this magnitude. In Louisiana sugarcane mosaic (SCMV) is the most serious disease. Although new races of the virus have emerged to which the main cultivars are susceptible, the degree of resistance and/or tolerance derived from wild germplasm has been sufficient to maintain yields near peak levels (apart from a 10% drop during the early 1970s). In Florida, Hawaii, and Louisiana, yields per ton of sugar per acre have plateaued, but they are significantly higher than they would have been in the absence of improved cultivars, and they are substantially higher than they were 40 years ago: 16% higher in the case of Florida, 36% higher in Hawaii, and 48% higher in Louisiana. (Texas is not included in the discussion because it did not become a sugarcane growing state until the 1970s.) From 50% (idem) to more than 75% (G-412) of increased yields are due to improved varieties. The known genetic contribution of wild species to these varieties ranges from 3 to 15% (S-356, T. L. Tew, pers. comm., 31 Aug. 1981). On average, it seems likely that the contribution to current yields of genes from *S. spontaneum* (and in Hawaii also *S. robustum*) for disease resistance and other yield factors (better ratooning and tillering, heterosis, environmental adaptations) is roughly 10%. We have used this percentage as the basis for our estimate.

### Bread Wheat

23. Cultivars with *Aegilops umbellulata* (Abe, Arthur 71, Oasis, Springfield, Sullivan, and Twin) are grown on 5.89% of the U.S. wheat acreage. Cultivars with *Agropyron elongatum* (Agent, Blueboy II, Cloud, Fox, Osage, Parker 76, Payne, Sage, and W-332) are grown on 4.21% of the U.S. wheat acreage. Cultivar acreage data are from A-1412.

24. From 1951 to 1960, average annual production losses to stem rust in the United States were more than 4%. However, U.S. cultivars with stem rust resistance from WGR are winter wheat varieties, and in the winter wheat belt, freedom from stem rust is mostly due to a climate unfavorable to rust development and escape from the disease due to early maturity of the cultivars. "Earliness is effective because the wheat usually matures before weather becomes favorable for stem rust development" (J-611). Cultivars with stem rust resistance from WGR are grown on 4.2% of U.S. wheat acreage. We assume that this resistance secures 1% of production from that area (25% of 4%, the balance being derived from earliness). We have no overall estimates of average annual losses to leaf rust, but losses of 20–25% are not unusual. "The most effective and cheapest method for control of leaf rust . . . has been breeding of resistant varieties" (J-611). Cultivars with leaf rust resistance from WGR are grown on 10.1% of U.S. wheat acreage, but the resistance is effective only against certain races of the pathogen. For example, cultivars with the $Lr_{24}$ gene from *Agropyron elongatum* are resistant to most of the prevalent North American races of *Puccinia recondita* except for race LR23 (A-1384). We assume that WGR-derived resistance to leaf rust secures 5% of production. Calculation: 1% of 4.2% = $2.7 million; 5% of 10.1% = $32.6 million; total: $35.3 million.

310

*Spanish Iris*

25. Imports come largely from the Nethe-lands (66% of value: bulbs) and France (26% of value: orris oil). In the Netherlands cultivars Ideal (38.5%), Hildegarde (2%), White Wedgwood (2.5%), Purple Sensation (4%), and Wedgwood (1%) are grown on 48% of the production area. Cultivar Professor Blaauw is grown on an additional 36%, but it is not certain that *Iris tingitana* is in its parentage, and we have excluded it from our calculations. Cultivar area data are from A-1379–A-1382.

*Alfalfa*

26. In 1969 cultivars with germplasm from *Medicago falcata* accounted for 30% of the U.S. alfalfa acreage. Germplasm content data are from A-1408, cultivar acreage data from P-479. On average *M. falcata* is estimated to have contributed 16% of the germplasm of these cultivars (A-1408). The proportion of *M. falcata* germplasm in the crop today "should be similar now as in 1969" (D. K. Barnes, pers. comm., 18 May 1982).

27. Yields of alfalfa hay production have increased from 2.7 tons per acre (annual average, 1966–1970) to 3.0 tons per acre (annual average, 1976–1980), an increase of 11.1% (calculated from S-699). We do not know how much of this is due to varietal improvement. In any case the yield characteristics from *M. falcata* (disease resistance, winter hardiness, and spreading plant habit) are likely to contribute more to yield maintenance than to yield increase. We have no basis for estimating *M. falcata*'s contribution to this.

*Sweet Clover*

28. There are no data on the relative importance of cultivars with WGR. We assume it is at least 1%.

*Tulip*

29. Imports come largely (98% of value) from the Netherlands. The Darwin hybrids are grown on 37% of the Netherlands' tulip production area. *Tulipa fosteriana* (the contributor of WGR to the Darwin hybrids) is also grown as a "botanical species" variety (it is the second most popular botanical species after *T. greigii* ) on an additional 2% of the Dutch tulip area. Cultivar acreage data are from P-70.

*Cotton (G. barbadense)*

30. As far as we know, the only *G. barbadense* cultivars improved with WGR are those grown in the Sudan, which supplies the United States with 10% (by value) of the *G. barbadense* cotton and cotton thread it imports.

*Cotton (G. hirsutum)*

31. Stoneville 825, grown on 7.1% of the U.S. upland cotton acreage in 1980 (A-1378). The annual average for 1976–1980 is estimated to be 3.5%. Acala SJ-2, Acala SJ-4, and Acala SJ-5 are grown on 16.5% of the U.S. upland cotton acreage (annual average, 1976–1980) (A-1378, A-1422–A-1424). As far as we know, there are no WGR in *G. hirsutum* cultivars grown in countries that export cotton to the United States.

*Oil Palm*

32. Imports come from Malaysia (81.5% of value), Indonesia (5%), Singapore (2%, probably produced in Sabah, Malaysia), the Netherlands (6%, probably produced in Indonesia), and West Africa (1%). Almost all current production in Malaysia and Indonesia is of *tenera* types, as is most of the plantation production in West Africa (see table 8.3, note 21).

33. The yield increase of 25% is directly attributable to WGR (see Other Yield Characteristics section in text).

311

*(continued)*

## Table 8.5 (Continued)

### Strawberry

34. Fresno (1%), Tioga (47%), and Tufts (19%) accounted for 67% of the California strawberry acreage (annual average, 1976–1980) (M-614). California accounted for $159.0 million (73%) of U.S. farm sales of strawberries during this period (S-724, S-726–S-728). We have no information on the varietal makeup of production in the countries from which the United States imports strawberries, mainly Mexico (87% by value) and Poland (8%).

### Bell Pepper

35. Florida VR-2 accounts for about 4% of Florida bell pepper sales (A. A. Cook, pers. comm., 15 July 1981, and 1 Dec. 1981) and hence for 2% of U.S. pepper and chili production (by value) (S-724, S-726–S-728).

36. Resistance is to one of two races of *Xanthomonas vesicatoria*, which are indistinguishable in the field (Cook, 1 Dec. 1981).

### Tomato

37. We have been unable to obtain adequate data on cultivars to determine precisely the proportions of U.S. production and imports accounted for by cultivars with WGR. However, the influence of wild germplasm is widespread in the crop; E. A. Kerr writes that "almost all tomatoes now have resistance to Fusarium wilt obtained from *L. pimpinellifolium* and tobacco mosaic resistance from *L. peruvianum*" (pers. comm., 14 Sept. 1981). It is on this basis that we assign the figure of 90%.

38. We lack adequate data to estimate the value of yield and quality factors from WGR.

### Tobacco

39. U.S. cultivars with disease resistance from WGR are listed in table 8.2 (notes 65–76). Together they account for 97% of U.S. burley tobacco production, about 10% of U.S. fire-cured tobacco production, about 50% of U.S. cigar filler tobacco production, and 100% of U.S. cigar binder tobacco production (J. F. Chaplin, pers. comm., 14 Aug. 1981). The value of this proportion of the crop is $851 million, broken down as follows: 97% of burley ($805 million), 10% of fire-cured ($4 million), 50% of cigar filler ($10 million), and 100% of cigar binder ($32 million) (S-448, S-449, S-699).

40. We lack sufficient data on cultivars grown outside the United States to estimate this.

41. From 1974 to 1976 black shank caused losses of $60 million, black root rot losses of $55 million, nematodes and mosaic losses of $10–$40 million each, and wildfire caused losses described as localized but serious (less than $2 million). Conservatively, these amount to annual losses of $20 million to black shank, $18 million to black root rot, $3 million to nematodes, $3 million to mosaic, and $0.5 million to wildfire. Most black-shank-resistant cultivars get their resistance from within the crop (cultivar Florida 301) (S-202). Only 7% of the burley crop (worth $58 million) gets its resistance to one of the races of the pathogen from WGR (J. F. Chaplin, pers. comm., 14 Aug. 1981). Similarly, black-root-rot-resistant cultivars get their resistance from within the crop (S-202); WGR-derived resistance occurs in only a few, not very successful, cultivars (Chaplin, 14 Aug. 1981). WGR are a major source of resistance to root-knot nematodes, but only a few cultivars have been released (H. E. Heggestad, pers. comm., 15 Oct. 1981). The most successful contributions of WGR have been mosaic and wildfire resistance. WGR are the only sources of resistance to these diseases (S-202): mosaic and wildfire resistance have been transferred to 97% of the burley crop, 10% of the fire-cured crop, 50% of the cigar filler crop, and 100% of the cigar binder crop (Chaplin, 14 Aug. 1981, plus additional data from G. B. Collins, pers. comm., 16 July 1981; and cultivar registration notices). If we assume that the annual losses of $3.5 million to these two diseases are borne by the 65% of the crop without resistance, this would indicate that the resistance of the remaining 35% of the crop saves $1.9 million a year. The proportion of the total tobacco crop with WGR-derived resistance to the other diseases is very much smaller: 2%. However, the diseases are more expensive. It seems likely that the resistance is worth within the region of $0.5–$1 million, but lacking adequate data on the relative importance of crop-derived resistance, we have not included this sum in our estimate.

42. Kennebec (8.3%), Centennial Russet (2.0%), Pungo (0.4%), Nooksack (0.2%), and Early Gem (2.0%) account for 11.1% of the U.S. potato acreage (estimated on the basis of seed potato acreage data from A-1394).

43. Imports come largely from Canada (82% of value) and the Netherlands (14%; includes potato flour and starch). Kennebec (32.2%), Nooksack (0.1%), and Keswick (0.1%) account for 32.4% of the Canad an potato acreage (estimated on the basis of seed potato acreage data from A-1394). Of 81 cultivars listed in the Netherlands in 1978, *Solanum demissum* was in the parentage of 25, *S. demissum* + *S. vernei* in another 7, and *S. stoloniferum* in the parentage of 1 (P-189, P-214). Lacking acreage data on these cultivars, we have not included them in this estimate.

44. Imports come largely from Brazil (24% of value), the Ivory Coast (16%), Ecuador (9%), Nigeria (8%), the Dominican Republic (7%), Ghana (7%), Papua New Guinea (2%), Mexico (2%), and Costa Rica (2%). Other major cacao-producing countries from which the United States may obtain cacao in the form of manufactured chocolate from Europe are Cameroon and Malaysia (D-386). "The bulk of the world's cocoa is still produced from old and ageing plantations of unimproved seedlings" (A-452). Improved cultivars have been successfully developed using Upper Amazon clones in Brazil (P. de T. Alvim, pers. comm., 7 May 1982), the Ivory Coast (A-238; H. Toxopeus, pers. comm., 10 Nov. 1981), Nigeria (S-301; Toxopeus, 10 Nov. 1981), and Malaysia (Toxopeus, 10 Nov. 1981). Attempts to use the Upper Amazons in Ecuador apparently have not been successful (D-109). We do not know the situation in the Dominican Republic, Papua New Guinea, Mexico, Costa Rica, or Cameroon. We can say, however, that Upper Amazon germplasm is in cultivars grown in countries supplying the United States with 55% of its cacao imports by value ($1,016.0 million; the average annual value of U.S. imports, includes cocoa beans, $492.2 million; cocoa, cocoa cake, and cocoa bean shells, $195.3 million; cocoa butter, $129.8 million  unsweetened chocolate, $140.5 million; sweetened chocolate, $22.3 million; candy and confectioners' coatings containing cocoa or chocolate, $35.8 million; and theobromine, $0.1 million).

G. Lockwood informs us that in Ghana, the first country to use Upper Amazon material (in 1954), "it is widely believed that Upper Amazon based varieties occupy about 20% of the total cocoa area . . . but the distribution is highly uneven" (pers. comm., 3 Nov. 1981). Plantings in Brazil, the Ivory Coast, Nigeria, and Malaysia began about a decade later: Upper Amazon–based material now occupies virtually all (say 90%) of Malaysia's cacao acreage (H. Toxopeus, pers. comm., 10 Nov. 1981). We assume that they occupy at least 10% of the cacao acreage of the other three countries. If these assumptions are correct, the Upper Amazon–based cultivars now account for about 7% of the U.S. supply.

H. Toxopeus has kindly given us his estimate of the current contribution of the Upper Amazon material. "The new hybrid seed became available for large scale planting (more than say a few 1000s of ha [hectares] per country per year) at the end of the 1960s in most cases; let us say in the past 12–14 years. A conservative guesstimate could be 250,000 ha [of] successful plantings, excluding Malaysia. A reasonable estimate of the production per ha of these plantings would be 300 kg/ha average, considering that plantings would reach the bearing stage in the 4th year after planting and it takes another 4 years to reach maturity and an average production of 1,000 kg/ha. This accounts for 75,000 ha [metric] tons of cocoa excluding Malaysia, where practically all cocoa is produced by hybrid varieties—so its total production of 25,000 tons [28,000 in our period] may be added. This adds up to 100,000 tonnes [metric tons]" (pers. comm., 10 Nov. 1981). It so happens that 100,000 metric tons is 6.4% of average annual world production for the period (1978–1980) of 1,553,000 metric tons (D-386).

45. A yield increase of 70% is attributable to WGR (see Other Yield Characteristics section in text).

46. The total of the estimated annual value of percentage (p columns) includes the higher figure in an entry with a range. For example, oats: 15.1–75.3; 75.3 is the figure added. The total of the estimated annual value of contributions of WGR (f columns) includes the lower figure in an entry with a range. For example, oats: 0.6–2.3; 0.6 is the figure added.

increase yields above a particular base level. Similarly, an environmental adaptation that enables a crop to be grown successfully in areas where otherwise it would be marginal has the function of maintaining yields rather than of increasing them. By and large, however, we have estimated the value of disease and pest resistance in terms of losses prevented, and the value of other yield factors in terms of gains achieved.

We consider the value of quality characteristics to be the increase in price that the quality realizes. Higher alpha acids in hops is worth an extra 20 cents per 1% above a base of 9.5%. Higher soluble solids in tomato is worth $1 million to the processing industry per 0.5% increase. Unfortunately, few examples are as clear cut as these, and generally we have decided not to try to estimate the value of quality factors.

Table 8.5 presents our estimates of the value of current contributions of wild genetic resources to crops grown or imported by the United States. We have had to make some quite large assumptions in making these estimates. These assumptions are described in the numbered notes to table 8.5. We have reasonable confidence in the $p$ columns of the table (those that estimate the proportion of the crop supplied by wild germplasm), and a lower confidence in the $f$ columns (those that estimate the value of the yield and quality factors contributed by the wild germplasm). In several cases we lack adequate data to make any estimate at all. Even so, we conclude (on the basis of the $p$ columns) that wild genetic resources have made yield and quality contributions to U.S.-grown or -imported crops worth a total of $6 billion a year and (on the basis of the $f$ columns) that the contributions are worth in the region of $340 million a year.

## Patterns and Trends in the Use of Wild Genetic Resources

To assess the predictability of use of wild genetic resources, we have compared four features of the U.S.-grown or -imported crops that have been improved with wild germplasm: the size category of the crop (in terms of average annual value of farm sales and imports), the age of the crop (how long the species has been domesticated), the type of crop, and the mode of reproduction of the crop species. These features are presented in table 8.6.

Eight of the 23 crops are super, 8 major, 4 medium, and 3 minor (the notes to table 8.6 define these terms). The number of nontimber crops in the U.S. economy in these categories is 15 super, 42 major, 85 medium, and 84 minor. It follows that 53% of super crops, 19% of major crops, 5% of medium crops, and 4% of minor crops have been improved with wild germplasm. In other words, wild genetic resources are 2–3 times more likely to be used to improve super crops than major crops, and 3–4 times more likely to be used to improve major crops than medium and minor crops. Even if we promoted smooth brome and sweet clover to the status of medium crops (a reasonable move since their

## Table 8.6 Features of U.S.-grown or -imported crops improved by wild genetic resources

| CROP | SIZE CATEGORY (Annual average, 1976–1980) | PERIOD OF DOMESTICATION | TYPE OF CROP | | MODE OF REPRODUCTION[*] |
|---|---|---|---|---|---|
| **CANNABIDACEAE** | | | | | |
| Hops | Medium | Late | Commodity | F | ob/cl |
| **CHENOPODIACEAE** | | | | | |
| Sugar beet | Major | Recent (from early) | Commodity | S | ob/sd |
| **COMPOSITAE** | | | | | |
| Sunflower | Major | Early | Commodity | O | ob/sd |
| Lettuce | Major | Early | Food | veg. | ib/sd |
| **ERICACEAE** | | | | | |
| Highbush blueberry | Medium | New | Food | fruit | ob/cl |
| **GRAMINEAE** | | | | | |
| Oats | Major | Early | Feed | grain | ib/sd |
| Smooth brome | Minor | Recent | Feed | grass | ob/sd |
| Bermuda grass | Major | Recent | Feed | grass | ob/cl |
| Sugarcane | Super | Early | Commodity | S | ob/cl |
| Bread wheat | Super | Ancient | Food | cereal | ib/sd |
| **IRIDACEAE** | | | | | |
| Spanish iris | Minor | Late | Ornamental | | ob/cl |
| **LEGUMINOSAE** | | | | | |
| Alfalfa | Super | Early | Feed | legume | ob/sd |
| Sweet clover | Minor | Recent | Feed | legume | ob/sd |
| **LILIACEAE** | | | | | |
| Tulip | Medium | Late | Ornamental | | ob/cl |
| **MALVACEAE** | | | | | |
| Cotton *G. barbadense* | Medium | Early | Commodity | T | ibob/sd |
| Cotton *G. hirsutum* | Super | Early | Commodity | T | ibob/sd |
| **PALMAE** | | | | | |
| Oil palm | Major | Recent | Commodity | O | ob/sd |
| **ROSACEAE** | | | | | |
| Strawberry | Major | Late | Food | fruit | ob/cl |
| **SOLANACEAE** | | | | | |
| Bell pepper | Major | Early | Food | veg. | ib/sd |
| Tomato | Super | Early | Food | veg. | ib/sd |
| Tobacco | Super | Early | Commodity | M | ib/sd |
| Potato | Super | Ancient/early | Food | root | ob/cl |
| **STERCULIACEAE** | | | | | |
| Cacao | Super | Early | Commodity | F | ob/sdcl |

[*]Definitions and most data in this column from S-123.

Notes: Super = farm sales + imports worth $1,000 million+, major = farm sales + imports worth $100 million+, medium = farm sales + imports worth $10 million+, minor = farm sales + imports worth $1 million+. Ancient = before 5000 B.C., early = 5000–0 B.C., late = A.D. 0–1700, recent = A.D. 1700–1900, new = after A.D. 1900. Commodity: F = flavoring, O = oil, M = miscellaneous, S = sweetener, T = textile fiber; food = primarily consumed as food by humans; feed = primarily consumed as fodder or forage by animals. ib = inbreeder (usually/always selfed, tolerant of inbreeding), ob = outbreeder (habitually crossed, suffers inbreeding depression), cl = clonally propagated, sd = seed propagated.

categorization as minor is based on the 1974 sales of their seed only and takes no account of their value as feed), these conclusions would not be materially changed. The proportion of medium crops improved with wild germplasm would be increased from 5 to 7%; it would still be 2–3 times more likely for wild genetic resources to be used to improve major crops than medium crops.

By contrast, the period of the crop's domestication seems to be unimportant. Two of the 23 crops are ancient (counting potato as ancient rather than early); 12 are early (including the sugar beet, since although the sugar beet itself is recent, it is simply a development of the beetroot, which is early); 4 are late; 4 are recent; and 1 is new. We have been able to determine the period of domestication of 160 of the crops in our U.S. sample: 13 ancient, 83 early, 24 late, 34 recent, and 6 new. If we assume that these figures are representative of the sample total of 226 crops, it appears that 15% of ancient crops, 14% of early crops, 17% of late crops, 12% of recent crops, and 17% of new crops have been improved with wild genetic resources.

Nine of the 23 crops are commodities, 7 are food crops, 5 are animal feed crops, and 2 are ornamentals. We classify 74 of our sample of 226 crops as commodities, 75 as food crops, 22 as animal feed crops, and 55 as ornamentals. Accordingly, 12% of the commodity crops, 9% of the food crops, 23% of the animal feed crops, and 2% of the ornamentals have been improved with wild germplasm. The small proportion of ornamentals may be more apparent than real because of lack of data, but the high proportion of animal feed (including forage) crops that have been improved using wild genetic resources is significant. Possibly it reflects the growing importance of pasture and feed species to the North American economy as a result of the intensification of livestock production.

Fifteen (65%) of the 23 crops are outbreeders; 6 (26%) are inbreeders (the remaining 2 are mixed). Fourteen (61%) are seed propagated; 8 (35%) are clonally propagated (the remaining one is both). All the clonally propagated crops are outbreeders; all the inbreeders are seed propagated. It may be that outbreeders are more likely to suffer from the effects of a narrowing genetic base than are inbreeders, in which case exotic germplasm would be needed more in the improvement of the former than the latter. However, the technical problems of recovering desirable characteristics from the crop parent in a crossing program and eliminating deleterious characteristics from the wild parent are greater with outbreeders than with inbreeders. The preponderance of outbreeders among the 23 crops suggests that the rewards of using wild genetic resources outweigh the difficulties.

The likelihood that a wild genetic resource will be used is a function of the importance of the plant or animal to be improved (which generally determines the scale of the improvement program), the rarity of the characteristic (it may be the only source of resistance to a disease or it may be one of many), and the ease with which it can be transferred to the domesticate—in other words, its genetic compatibility. Two University of Illinois professors, Jack Harlan and Jan de Wet, have devised an informal system for classifying wild species according to the ease with which they can be crossed with the domesticate to which they are related (G-175). The system is of great practical value because it provides a framework for comparing the wild gene pools of domesticated species and their actual and potential contributions to crop and livestock improvement.

The term *gene pool* means the total number of genes within a group of interbreeding plants or animals, that is, the pool of genes within a population. Harlan and de Wet have given the term a second meaning: the total number of genes within a domesticate and its wild relatives, that is, the pool of genes that is potentially available for the improvement of the domesticated plant or animal. They divide this gene pool into three categories, primary, secondary, and tertiary, depending on the ease of gene exchange.

The primary gene pool (GP1) consists of the domesticated species plus those wild forms that are interfertile and hybridize readily with it. Among the components of the primary gene pool, "crossing is easy; hybrids are generally fertile with good chromosome pairing; gene segregation is approximately normal and gene transfer is generally easy" (G-175). GP1 corresponds to the traditional concept of the biological species.

The secondary gene pool (GP2) consists of those biological species that can be crossed with the domesticated species using conventional breeding methods to produce at least some fertile progeny. Gene transfer from GP2 species is possible but there are barriers to crossing, chromosomes pair poorly or not at all, many or most hybrids are sterile, and some may be weak and difficult to bring to maturity; but there are at least some fertile $F_1$s (first-generation offspring), and the gene pool can be used without resorting to the radical techniques required with GP3 species.

The tertiary gene pool (GP3) consists of those species that can be crossed with the domesticate but from which gene transfer is possible only through the use of special techniques. "Hybrids tend to be anomalous, lethal or completely sterile. Gene transfer is either not possible with known techniques or else rather extreme or radical measures are required," such as embryo culture, grafting or tissue culture to obtain hybrids, doubling the chromosome number, or using bridging species (G-175).

Harlan and de Wet stress that their system is informal. It should not be applied rigorously; GP3 in particular is a highly flexible concept, defining "the extreme outer limit of potential genetic reach" (G-163), which is almost certain to expand with advances in genetic engineering. Nonetheless, the system is an extremely helpful way of describing the genetic relationships of crops and the wild species used in their improvement.

In table 8.7 we assign gene pool designations for the wild species used in the improvement of crops of economic importance to the United States. Of the 23 crops, 12 have been improved with wild germplasm from the crop's primary

Table 8.7 **Wild gene pools used in the improvement of crops grown or imported by the United States**

| CROP | WILD SPECIES | GENE POOL |
|------|-------------|-----------|
| CANNABIDACEAE | | |
| Hops | *Humulus lupulus* | GP1 |
| CHENOPODIACEAE | | |
| Sugar beet | *Beta maritima* | GP1 |
| COMPOSITAE | | |
| Sunflower | *Helianthus annuus* | GP1 |
| | *H. petiolaris* | GP1 |
| Lettuce | *Lactuca virosa* | GP3 |
| ERICACEAE | | |
| Highbush blueberry | *Vaccinium australe* | GP1 |
| GRAMINEAE | | |
| Oats | *Avena sterilis* | GP1 |
| Smooth brome | *Bromus pumpellianus* | GP2 |
| Bermuda grass | *Cynodon nlemfuensis* | GP3 |
| Sugarcane | *Saccharum robustum* | GP1* |
| | *S. spontaneum* | GP2* |
| Bread wheat | *Aegilops umbellulata* | GP3 |
| | *Agropyron elongatum* | GP3 |
| | *Triticum turgidum dicoccoides* | GP2† |
| IRIDACEAE | | |
| Spanish iris | *Iris tingitana* | GP3 |
| LEGUMINOSAE | | |
| Alfalfa | *Medicago falcata* | GP1 |
| Sweet clover | *Melilotus dentata* | GP3 |
| LILIACEAE | | |
| Tulip | *Tulipa fosteriana* | GP2 |
| MALVACEAE | | |
| Cotton *G. barbadense* | *Gossypium anomalum* | GP3 |
| Cotton *G. hirsutum* | *G. tomentosum* | GP2 |
| | *G. thurberi* | GP3 |
| PALMAE | | |
| Oil palm | *Elaeis guineensis* | GP1 |
| ROSACEAE | | |
| Strawberry | *Fragaria chiloensis* | GP1 |
| SOLANACEAE | | |
| Bell pepper | *Capsicum annuum* | GP1 |
| Tomato | *Lycopersicon esculentum* var. *cerasiforme* | GP1 |
| | *L. cheesmanii* | GP1 |
| | *L. pimpinellifolium* | GP1 |
| | *L. chmielewskii* | GP2 |
| | *L. hirsutum* | GP2 |
| | *L. peruvianum* | GP3 |

Table 8.7   (*Continued*)

| CROP | WILD SPECIES | GENE POOL |
|---|---|---|
| Tobacco | *Nicotiana debneyi* | GP2 |
| | *N. glutinosa* | GP2 |
| | *N. longiflora* | GP2 |
| | *N. plumbaginifolia* | GP2 |
| | *N. tomentosa* | GP2 |
| Potato | *Solanum demissum* | GP2 |
| STERCULIACEAE | | |
| Cacao | *Theobroma cacao* | GP1 |

*$Saccharum$ *spontaneum* is a polyploid complex with 40–128 chromosomes. In the Javan and Indian forms used in breeding, $2n = 112$ and 64, respectively; the chromosomes apparently do not pair with those of the crop species, *S. officinarum* ($2n = 80$). We therefore assign those forms to GP2. The Papua New Guinea *S. robustum* is more closely related to the crop ($2n = 80$ also) and is GP1 (A-971, J-274, P-6, P-66, P-67, P-224, S-119).

†Used as a bridging species between *Aegilops umbellulata* and the crop (*Triticum aestivum*) (J-132).

gene pool (hops, sugar beet, sunflower, highbush blueberry, oats, sugarcane, alfalfa, oil palm, strawberry, bell pepper, tomato, and cacao); 7 have been improved with wild germplasm from the crop's secondary gene pool (smooth brome, sugarcane, tulip, *G. hirsutum* cotton, tomato, tobacco, and potato); 8 have been improved with wild germplasm from the crop's tertiary gene pool (lettuce, Bermuda grass, bread wheat, Spanish iris, sweet clover, *G. barbadense* and *G. hirsutum* cotton, and tomato).

The total number of crops adds up to 27 rather than 23 because sugarcane and *G. hirsutum* cotton breeders have successfully resorted to two gene pools (GP1 and GP2 of sugarcane and GP2 and GP3 of cotton) and tomato breeders to all three gene pools.

These results suggest that, other things being equal, breeders are likely to use GP1 material about 1.5 times more than they would GP2 or GP3 material, but no more likely to use GP2 material than they would GP3 material. The preference for GP1 germplasm is explained by its greater availability (germplasm from GP2 and GP3 generally being poorly represented in collections [P-484]) and the complete interfertility of wild GP1 species with the crop species. The latter feature makes it easier for the breeder to transfer to the crop the desired characteristic of the wild species. Prior to this analysis we thought that the preference for GP1 would be even more strongly expressed than it is. Apparently "other things" seldom are equal: GP2 and GP3 materials combined have been used in as many crops as has GP1 material. Breeders will take superior yield and quality factors where they find them.

Three trends reveal whether the use of wild genetic resources is rising, falling,

Table 8.8  **Rate of use of new sources of wild germplasm in the improvement of crops grown or imported by the United States**

DECADE OF INTRODUCTION OF FIRST COMMERCIAL CULTIVAR WITH WILD GERMPLASM AND SOURCE OF WILD GERMPLASM

| CROP | 1870s to 1890s | 1900s | 1910s | 1920s | 1930s | 1940s | 1950s | 1960s | 1970s |
|---|---|---|---|---|---|---|---|---|---|
| CANNABIDACEAE |  |  |  |  |  |  |  |  |  |
| Hops *Humulus lupulus* |  |  |  |  | Manitoba *H. lupulus* (1) | California *H. lupulus* (2) |  |  | Bavaria, Slovenia, and Utah *H. lupulus* (3) |
| CHENOPODIACEAE |  |  |  |  |  |  |  |  |  |
| Sugar beet *Beta vulgaris* |  |  |  |  |  |  | Italy *B. maritima* (4) |  |  |
| COMPOSITAE |  |  |  |  |  |  |  |  |  |
| Sunflower *Helianthus annuus* |  |  |  |  |  |  | Texas *H. annuus* (5) |  | Missouri *H. petiolaris* (6) |
| Lettuce *Lactuca sativa* |  |  |  |  |  |  | *L. virosa* (7) [Russia *L. serriola*] (8) |  |  |
| ERICACEAE |  |  |  |  |  |  |  |  |  |
| Highbush blueberry *Vaccinium australe* and *V. corymbosum* |  |  |  |  |  |  | North Carolina *V. australe* (9) |  |  |
| GRAMINEAE |  |  |  |  |  |  |  |  |  |
| Oats *Avena sativa* |  |  |  |  |  | Algeria *A. sterilis* (10) |  |  | Israel and Portugal *A. sterilis* (11) |
| Smooth brome *Bromus inermis* |  |  |  |  |  |  |  | Alaska and Canada *B. pumpellianus* (12) |  |
| Bermuda grass *Cynodon dactylon* |  |  |  |  |  |  |  | Kenya *C. nlemfuensis* (13) |  |
| Sugarcane *Saccharum officinarum* |  |  | Java and India *S. spontaneum* (14) |  |  | Papua New Guinea *S. robustum* (15) |  |  |  |

| | | | | |
|---|---|---|---|---|
| **Bread wheat**<br>*Triticum aestivum* | | | | *Aegilops umbellulata* [16]<br>*Agropyron elongatum* [17] |
| **Maize**<br>*Zea mays* | | | | *(Tripsacum dactyloides)* [18] |
| IRIDACEAE<br>Spanish iris<br>*Iris xiphium* | Morocco<br>*I. tingitana* [19] | | | |
| LEGUMINOSAE<br>Alfalfa<br>*Medicago sativa* | USSR<br>*M. falcata* [20] | | | |
| Sweetclover<br>*Melilotus alba* and<br>*M. officinalis* | | | Russia, USSR<br>*M. dentata* [21] | |
| LILIACEAE<br>Tulip<br>*Tulipa gesneriana* | *T. greigii* [22]<br>*T. kaufmanniana* [22]<br>*T. fosteriana* [23]<br>*T. praestans* [23] | *T. fosteriana* [24] | | |
| MALVACEAE<br>Cotton<br>*Gossypium barbadense* | | | | *G. anomalum* [25] |
| Cotton<br>*G. hirsutum* | | | Arizona<br>*G. thurberi* [26] | Hawaii<br>*G. tomentosum* [27] |
| PALMAE<br>Oil palm<br>*Elaeis guineensis* | | | Zaire<br>*E. guineensis* [28] | |
| ROSACEAE<br>Strawberry<br>*Fragaria × ananassa* | California<br>*F. chiloensis* [29] | | | |
| SOLANACEAE<br>Bell pepper<br>*Capsicum annuum* | | | | *C. annuum* [30] |

*(continued)*

# Table 8.8 (Continued)

DECADE OF INTRODUCTION OF FIRST COMMERCIAL CULTIVAR WITH WILD GERMPLASM AND SOURCE OF WILD GERMPLASM

| CROP | 1870s to 1890s | 1900s | 1910s | 1920s | 1930s | 1940s | 1950s | 1960s | 1970s |
|---|---|---|---|---|---|---|---|---|---|
| Tomato Lycopersicon esculentum | | | | | L. pimpinellifolium (31) | | L. esculentum var. cerasiforme (32) L. hirsutum (33) | L. peruvianum (34) | L. cheesmanii (35) L. chmielewskii (36) |
| Tobacco Nicotiana tabacum | | | | | | | N. glutinosa (37) N. longiflora (38) N. tomentosa (39) | N. debneyi (40) N. plumbaginifolia (41) | |
| Potato Solanum tuberosum | | | | | | S. demissum (42) | | | |
| STERCULIACEAE Cacao Theobroma cacao | | | | | | | | Peru T. cacao (43) | |
| VITIDACEAE Grape Vitis vinifera | V. berlandieri (44) V. champini (45) V. longii (45) V. riparia (44) V. rupestris (44) | | | | | | | | |
| TOTAL CROPS using wild germplasm for first time | 2 | — | 2 | 2 | 2 | 3* | 7 | 6 | 2 |
| TOTAL NEW SOURCES of wild germplasm | 7 | 2 | 2 | 3 | 2 | 5 | 12 | 11 | 11 |

*Tulip counted twice (see text).

Notes:

**Hops**

1. Brewer's Gold (S-9).
2. Northern Brewer (S-10).
3. Bavaria: Huller Bitterer (H. Ehrmaier, pers. comm., 22 Sept. 1981). Slovenia: Super Styrian A cultivars (T. Wagner, pers. comm., 20 Jan. 1982); Utah: Comet (Y-74).

**Sugar Beet**

4. GW cultivars (R. K. Oldemeyer, pers. comm., 15 July 1981).

**Sunflower**

5. Beacon (P-76).
6. Hybrid cultivars (D-150).

**Lettuce**

7. Vanguard (P-219).
8. Valverde (P-220).

**Highbush Blueberry**

9. North Carolina cultivars (M-633).

**Oats**

10. Bond derivatives (A-1361).
11. Multiline E and M cultivars (D-181, D-542).

**Smooth Brome**

12. Polar (G-821).

**Bermuda Grass**

13. Coastcross 1 (G-142).

**Sugarcane**

14. Java: P.O.J. 2878 (S-119).
15. India: Co 213 (D-220).

**Bread Wheat**

16. Riley 67 (D. R. Knott, pers. comm., 30 Sept. 1981).
17. Agent (A-1392).

**Maize**

18. Texas 42SX and Texas 30A (A-153, A-154).

**Spanish Iris**

19. Wedgwood (P-203).

**Alfalfa**

20. Sevelra (A-1408).

**Sweet Clover**

21. Acumar and Cumino (B. P. Goplen, pers. comm., 2 Sept. 1981).

**Tulip**

22. P-204.
23. P-204, S-311.
24. Dardanelles, Elizabeth Arden, and Hollands Glorie (P-204).

**Cotton (G. barbadense)**

25. F. D. Wilson, pers. comm., 17 Aug. 1981.

**Cotton (G. hirsutum)**

26. MO-DEL (ibid.).
27. Stoneville 825 (ibid.).

**Oil Palm**

28. Tenera cultivars (G-148, G-150, J-242).

**Strawberry**

29. Ettersburg 121 (V-342).

**Bell Pepper**

30. Florida VR-2 (A-490).

**Tomato**

31. Vetomold (E. A. Kerr, pers. comm., 14 Sept. 1981).
32. S-38.
33. Vagabond (E. A. Kerr, pers. comm., 14 Sept. 1981).
34. Vantage (ibid.).
35. P-463.
36. P-463.

**Tobacco**

37. Burley 21 (J. R. Chaplin, pers. comm., 14 Aug. 1981).
38. Burley 21 (ibid.).
39. P.D. 611 (H. E. Heggestad, pers. comm., 15 Oct. 1981).
40. Burley 49 (J. F. Chaplin, pers. comm., 14 Aug. 1981).
41. NC 2326 (J. L. Apple, pers. comm., 16 July 1981).

**Potato**

42. Kennebec (A-21).

**Cacao**

43. $F_3$ Amazon hybrid cultivars (S-827).

**Grape**

44. Text note 1.
45. Dogridge, Salt Creek, and 1613 C (G-707, J-453, J-468).

or stable: the rate at which wild germplasm is used to improve a crop for the first time, the rate at which new sources of wild germplasm are used, and changes in the proportion of each crop accounted for by cultivars improved with wild germplasm.

Table 8.8 is concerned with the first two of these trends. It provides data on grapes and corn in addition to the 23 crops discussed throughout this chapter. As noted earlier, we excluded grapes from our analysis of the contribution of wild genetic resources because we count the nineteenth-century development of rootstock cultivars from wild *Vitis* species as a recent domestication. We include them here because their introduction marks the beginning of the trend in wild germplasm use and illustrates how nothing succeeds like success. The resistance to *Phylloxera* aphids and *Meloidogyne* nematodes obtained from the wild *Vitis* species has been so effective and durable that for almost a century there has been no need to return to the wild for new sources of germplasm.

By contrast, corn (*Zea mays*) was excluded from discussion hitherto because the contribution of wild germplasm to the crop was a passing one. Parental line Tx203-2, from a cross between line Tx203 and *Tripsacum dactyloides* (a wild relative in the secondary gene pool of corn), was used in the development of two hybrid cultivars, Texas 42SX and Texas 30A. According to A. J. Bockholt, who bred the cultivars, *T. dactyloides* contributed higher yields and the absence of top firing (killing of upper leaves during hot weather) and chlorophyll breakdown. The two cultivars were among the most popular hybrids in the southwestern United States and northern Mexico, being planted on an estimated 250,000–500,000 acres a year during the late 1960s and early 1970s. However, their popularity "has greatly diminished in the last 10 years with the emphasis on early maturing," and by 1981 they were planted on "only a very few acres" (A. J. Bockholt, pers. comm., 14 July 1981, and 22 October 1981; A-153, A-154, P-116).

Sources of wild germplasm that have ceased to influence 1% or more of the crop grown or imported by the United States are included in table 8.8 in parentheses. There is one source besides *T. dactyloides: Lactuca serriola*. A collection of *Lactuca serriola* from Russia provided the California lettuce cultivars Valverde, Calmar, and derivatives with the $Dm_8$ gene for resistance to downy mildew (caused by the fungus *Bremia lactucae*). Calmar, released in 1960, was the dominant cultivar in California for about 10 years. However, the $Dm_8$ gene is no longer effective, and no lettuce cultivar currently grown in California is resistant to downy mildew (A-506, A-507, J-28, P-220; E. J. Ryder, pers. comm., 30 July 1981).

Table 8.8 shows an apparent peak in the 1950s in the rate at which wild germplasm is successfully used for the first time in the improvement of a particular crop. The rate was two crops per decade (excluding the second counting of tulip in the 1940s, which is explained below) until the 1950s, when it rose to seven crops. It stayed roughly the same (six crops) in the 1960s, and then dropped back to two crops in the 1970s. This is probably a fair reflection of the U.S. situation. There are two reasons. First, the number of crops with a high probability of being improved with wild germplasm that have not yet been so improved becomes smaller with each decade. If we include grapes and corn, 10 (67%) of the 15 super crops, and 8 (19%) of the 42 major crops have already benefited from wild genetic resources. Second, it is too soon to tell whether some of the first-time uses of wild germplasm in the 1970s have been successful; examples are apple and rubber (see note 4).

We have counted tulip twice in the totals of crops using wild germplasm for the first time because the use in the 1940s is entirely different from those in the 1870s–1900s. With the introduction of *Tulipa greigii* in the 1870s and *T. kaufmanniana* in the 1890s (P-204, S-311) the tulip effectively became a polyspecies crop (this term is defined on p. 229). The species tulips form a particlar category of the crop distinct from traditional *T. gesneriana* tulips and their derivatives. The introduction in the 1900s of *T. eichleri*, *T. fosteriana*, and *T. praestans* (with *T. greigii* and *T. kaufmanniana* the most widely grown of the species tulips [P-70]) was part of this phenomenon. In addition, as we saw in the section Quality Characteristics, *T. fosteriana* has contributed its germplasm to the mainstream of the crop in the form of the Darwin hybrids. As far as we know, the first Darwin hybrids to be introduced were cultivars Dardanelles, Elizabeth Arden, and Hollands Glorie, all in 1942 (P-204).

Like the rate of first-time use of wild germplasm, the rate of use of new sources of wild germplasm peaked in the 1950s. Unlike the first trend, this trend has not declined but appears to be continuing at around the peak level. This is due to crop breeders returning to the wild for additional sources of germplasm. More than one source has been used in the improvement of hops, sunflower, lettuce, oats, sugarcane, cotton, tomato, and tobacco. Only in the case of oats has this been due to the transience of the disease resistance obtained from an earlier germplasm source (in this case the crown rust resistance obtained from Algerian *Avena sterilis* via the cultivar Bond). In the other cases the new sources of wild germplasm provided additional characteristics. For example, Bavarian, Slovenian, and Utah wild *Humulus lupulus* contributed yield and quality characteristics required for hop growing in West Germany, Yugoslavia, and the United States, respectively; Missouri *Helianthus petiolaris* provided a source of cytoplasmic male sterility to the sunflower crop (which had previously obtained disease resistance from Texas *H. annuus*, also a source of genetic fertility restoration); and Hawaii *Gossypium tomentosum* conferred nectarilessness on the cotton crop that previously had obtained stronger and longer fibers from Arizona *G. thurberi*.

We do not have the production or acreage data needed to determine trends in the proportion of each crop accounted for by cultivars improved with wild germplasm. We have been able to draw tentative conclusions for a selection of crops (table 8.9). In eight out of nine the proportion is rising or stable. The

Table 8.9 **Changes in the percentage of selected crops grown or imported by the United States accounted for by cultivars with wild genetic resources**

CANNABIDACEAE

| Hops | United States | 16.7% of production from cultivars with WGR, annual average 1976–1980; rising from 10.7% in 1976 to 22.0% in 1980 [1] 24.3% in 1981 [1] RISING |
| --- | --- | --- |
| | West Germany | 56.0% of area grown to cultivars with WGR, annual average 1976–1980; rising from 55.5% in 1976 to 58.0% in 1980 [2] 54.6% in 1981 [2] STABLE |
| | Yugoslavia | 24.8% of area grown to cultivars with WGR, annual average 1976–1980; rising from 14.1% in 1976 to 34.9% in 1980 [2] 36.8% in 1981 [2] RISING |

COMPOSITAE

| Sunflower | United States and Canada | Hybrids produced using wild sources of CMS and GFR introduced in 1972; accounted for an estimated 80+% of acreage by 1976 and 90% by 1977 [3] STABLE |
| --- | --- | --- |

GRAMINEAE

| Sugarcane | United States (Hawaii) | 82.8% of area grown to cultivars with WGR in 1980 [4] 86.7% of plantings with cultivars with WGR, annual average 1976–1980; rising from 77.8% in 1976 to 89.7% in 1980, with a peak of 91.5% in 1979 [4] STABLE |
| --- | --- | --- |
| Bread wheat | United States | 0.1% of acre grown to cultivars with WGR in 1969 [5] 4.4% of area grown to cultivars with WGR in 1974 [5] 10.1% of area grown to cultivars with WGR in 1979 [5] RISING |

IRIDACEAE

| Spanish iris | Netherlands | 47.7% of area grown to cultivars with WGR, annual average 1976–1980; 46.6% in 1976, 49.3% in 1977, 46.3% in 1980 [6] STABLE |
| --- | --- | --- |

Table 8.9　(*Continued*)

LEGUMINOSAE
Alfalfa　　　　United States　　30.0% of area grown to cultivars with WGR in
　　　　　　　　　　　　　　　　1969 (7)
　　　　　　　　　　　　　　　　1980s percentage said to be about the same (7)
　　　　　　　　　　　　　　　　STABLE

LILIACEAE
Tulip　　　　　Netherlands　　　40.1% of area grown to cultivars with WGR,
　　　　　　　　　　　　　　　　annual average 1976–1980; 39.8% in 1976,
　　　　　　　　　　　　　　　　41.4% in 1977, 38.4% in 1980 (8)
　　　　　　　　　　　　　　　　STABLE

MALVACEAE
Cotton　　　　United States　　20% of area grown to cultivars with WGR,
*G. hirsutum*　　　　　　　　　　annual average 1976–1980; 21.6% in 1976,
　　　　　　　　　　　　　　　　18.3% in 1980 (9)
　　　　　　　　　　　　　　　　25% of area grown to cultivars with WGR in
　　　　　　　　　　　　　　　　1982 (9)
　　　　　　　　　　　　　　　　RISING

SOLANACEAE
Potato　　　　United States　　11.1% of area grown to cultivars with WGR in
　　　　　　　　　　　　　　　　1980 (10)
　　　　　　　　　　　　　　　　10.5% of area grown to cultivars with WGR in
　　　　　　　　　　　　　　　　1982 (10)
　　　　　　　　　　　　　　　　FALLING
　　　　　　　Canada　　　　　32.4% of area grown to cultivars with WGR in
　　　　　　　　　　　　　　　　1980 (10)
　　　　　　　　　　　　　　　　31.6% of area grown to cultivars with WGR in
　　　　　　　　　　　　　　　　1982 (10)
　　　　　　　　　　　　　　　　FALLING

Notes:

*Hops*

1. U.S. Hop Administrative Committee via A. Haunold, pers. comm., 24 May 1983.
   Supplemented by data from A-1385–A-1391.
2. A-1385–A-1391.

*Sunflower*

3. D-150.

*Sugarcane*

4. G-829 and unpublished data from Experiment Station, Hawaiian Sugar Planters'
   Association.

*Bread Wheat*

5. A-1412, P-119.

(*continued*)

Table 8.9  (*Continued*)

*Spanish Iris*

 6. A-1379–A-1382.

*Alfalfa*

 7. P-479; D. K. Barnes, pers. comm., 18 May 1983.

*Tulip*

 8. P-70.

*Cotton* (G. hirsutum)

 9. A-1378, A-1422–A-1426.

*Potato*

10. A-1394–A-1396.

stability of the proportions of the sunflower and sugarcane crops grown to cultivars with wild germplasm is probably due to saturation, since 90% of the former and 80% of the latter (in Hawaii) are grown to them. The same applies to oil palm (not included in table 8.9), since 100% of plantings now are of *tenera* clones derived in part from the wild (discussed earlier in section Other Yield Characteristics). The stability of Spanish iris, alfalfa, and tulip suggests that current sources of wild germplasm have provided all they can.

The clearest evidence of rising proportions accounted for by cultivars with wild germplasm comes from hops in the United States and Yugoslavia and bread wheat in the United States. There has been vigorous development of new hop cultivars in both countries that makes use of local wild forms (particularly in Yugoslavia); and the rise in acreage is evidence of their success. In the United States as well, greater use is being made of the English cultivars Bullion and Brewer's Gold. The small but growing proportion of U.S. wheat acreage cultivars with wild germplasm is due to increases in the number of cultivars with rust resistance from *Aegilops umbellulata* and *Agropyron elongatum* and in the acreages grown to the top cultivars among them, Arthur 71 (2.61% in 1974, 3.16% in 1979), Sage (0.1% in 1974, 3.07% in 1979), and Abe (0.36% in 1974, 1.88% in 1979) (A-1412).

The general conclusion we draw from tables 8.8 and 8.9 is that use of wild genetic resources in crop improvement is fairly stable. The rate at which new sources of germplasm are being successfully used is high but is neither rising nor falling. Cultivars with wild germplasm have quickly and thoroughly taken over some crops (sunflower, sugarcane, oil palm, and tomato). Their contributions to other crops (such as alfalfa, Spanish iris, tulip, and tobacco), although substantial, are not so overwhelming. In only one crop (potato) does the proportion accounted for by cultivars with wild germplasm appear to be falling, and even this drop may be more apparent than real (being small and over a short period). At the same time, in only few crops (notably hops and bread wheat) is the proportion rising dramatically. The role of wild genetic resources in crop breeding is thus well established, making a considerable but stable contribution to some crops and a modest but growing contribution to others. Moreover, the list of crops that have been successfully improved with wild genetic resources continues to grow, albeit at a lower rate than in the 1950s and 1960s. Some of the crops that are likely to be next on the list are discussed in the next section.

## Potential Contributions of Wild Genetic Resources

The net benefit of wild genetic resources to U.S. crop production and imports is likely to continue growing, even though the growth rate may be slower than in previous decades. To give an impression of the direction of that growth, we outline below some potential contributions of wild gene pools to the 15 super crops. We discuss them crop by crop in order of importance to the U.S. economy (as listed in table 7.2).

*Soybean* (Glycine max)

The genetic base of the U.S. crop is very narrow, the same germplasm being used repeatedly to develop the main cultivars (A-681). Thus there is considerable unexploited variation within the crop (G-319, G-836). Soybean has one wild relative (*G. soja*) in its primary gene pool, no secondary gene pool, and a tertiary gene pool that is expected to comprise all 7 species in the subgenus *Glycine* (potential sources of disease resistance) (V-489). Highly productive, high protein lines have been developed with *G. soja* as the nonrecurrent parent in a backcrossing program (G-836), but they have not yet been used in the breeding of any U.S. cultivars (T. Hymowitz, pers. comm., 14 July 1981).

*Corn* (Zea mays)

The most promising source of wild germplasm for corn improvement is the newly (1977) discovered *Zea diploperennis*, a wild perennial species in the crop's primary gene pool (G-361). This species is immune to the two most serious viral diseases of corn in the United States: maize chlorotic dwarf virus and maize chlorotic mottle virus. No other source of immunity to either virus is known. Resistance to maize chlorotic dwarf virus and to strain B of maize dwarf mosaic virus (another serious viral disease in the United States) has been transferred to the crop, and efforts are now under way to fix this resistance in a homozygous condition in inbred parental lines. Hybrid cultivars produced from these parental lines should be available to farmers by the early 1990s. In addition, *Z. diploperennis* may provide resistance to other diseases and to pests such as corn earworms, stalk borers, and rootworms. Other possible contributions are genes for greater stalk and root strength, multiple ears per plant, and toler-ance of poorly drained soil (M-237).

*Wheat* (Triticum aestivum *and* T. turgidum turgidum)

The wild relatives of wheat are potential sources of drought resistance, winter hardiness, heat tolerance, salt tolerance, earlier ripening, higher productivity, and increased protein content (D-197). Their main interest for U.S. and Canadi-an breeding programs, however, appears still to be as sources of disease and pest resistance. Resistance to the nematodes *Meloidogyne incognita* and *M. jav-anica* was transferred from *Aegilops squarrosa* (in the tertiary gene pool of *T. aestivum*) to bread wheat in 1978 (cultivars from this breeding line have yet to be released [G. Waines, pers. comm., 14 August 1981]). Additional sources of resistance to stem rust (caused by the fungus *Puccinia graminis*) and leaf rust (caused by the fungus *P. recondita*) have been found in *A. squarrosa* and *A. speltoides* (also in the tertiary gene pool) and transferred to breeding stocks; but, again, no cultivars have yet been released for commercial production (E. R. Kerber, pers. comm., 10 September 1981).

*Cotton* (Gossypium hirsutum)

The search for resistance to diseases and pests continues to be a major stimulus to work with wild cotton species. For example, resistance to root-knot nema-todes (*Meloidogyne* spp.) has been transferred from a wild form of *G. hirsutum* (primary gene pool) to the breeding stock Auburn 623 RNR (F. D. Wilson, pers. comm., 17 August 1981). An even greater prize, to which both public and private breeders are devoting great energy, is cytoplasmic male sterility. Attempts to exploit first-generation heterosis on a commercial scale through the production of hybrids using the CMS system began in 1946 (L. S. Stith, pers. comm., 7 October 1982). Sources of CMS were found by Meyer and Meyer in the domesti-cated species *G. arboreum* and the wild species *G. anomalum* and *G. harknessii* (M-138, M-139). *Gossypium harknessii* (in the tertiary gene pool) has proved to be the most promising (M-138; L. S. Stith, pers. comm., 31 July 1981, and 7 October 1982); but none of the initial sources has been sufficiently stable to be commercially useful. The effects of the cytoplasm were modified by environ-mental factors, particularly changes in temperature (M-137, M-139). If the daily temperature reached 75°F, which it does not do every day in Mississippi (where the Meyers worked), then 19 days later when the flowers bloomed they would be sterile. If the temperature did not reach 75°F, the flowers were fertile (Stith, 7 October 1982).

This problem was overcome when in 1972 Vesta Meyer obtained a second source of CMS from *G. harknessii*, which proved to be stable. Since then, the objective has been to find a source of genetic fertility restoration (GFR) that is 100% reliable. The restorer material that Lee Stith (a cotton breeder at the

University of Arizona) is working with includes five species—the domesticated *G. barbadense* and *G. hirsutum*, and the wild *G. harknessii*, *G. raimondii*, and *G. thurberi* (Stith, 7 October 1982). Success is close at hand, and then the only remaining problem will be ensuring an adequate supply of suitable insect pollinators in the seed production fields (P-269; discussed in chap. 9). Successful production of hybrids using the CMS/GFR system will have as revolutionary an effect on the cotton industry as it has had on the sunflower industry, the potential contribution being more than $500 million a year (Stith, 31 July 1981).

## Coffee (Coffea arabica *and* C. canephora)

In Colombia, wild forms of *C. arabica* (primary gene pool) are being used to provide resistance to coffee rust (caused by the fungus *Hemileia vastatrix*) and to a much lesser extent to provide resistance to coffee berry disease (caused by the fungus *Colletotrichum coffeanum*); wild forms of *C. liberica* (secondary gene pool) are also being used as a source of resistance to coffee rust (G. Moreno Ruíz, pers. comm., 11 August 1981).

## Tobacco (Nicotiana tabacum)

Disease and pest resistance continues to be the main objective of using wild germplasm. The limiting factor has been undesirable changes in leaf color, a frequent by-product of interspecific gene transfers. In flue-cured tobacco (which makes up about 58% of U.S. production by value [S-699]), the leaf is cured by enzymatic breakdown of the chlorophyll pigments followed by moderately rapid drying. The result is a leaf that is bright yellow or orange. Transfer of germplasm from other species often results in green-brown mottling that the industry finds unacceptable. This does not matter with burley tobaccos (which account for some 34% of U.S. production by value [S-699]) because they are air cured. Air curing produces a brown leaf, which masks any unwanted off-color. The color problem is the reason why wild-derived disease resistance is found almost exclusively in burley and other air-cured cultivars and scarcely at all in bright or flue-cured cultivars (E. A. Wernsman, pers. comm., 16 July 1981).

Another problem has been the difficulty of transferring resistance from some of the better sources. An example is *N. repanda* (tertiary gene pool), which is said to be resistant to more diseases of *N. tabacum* than any of the other 63 species in the genus (A-304). *Nicotiana repanda* is the most promising source of resistance to root-knot nematodes (*Meloidogyne* spp.) and to *Cercospora nicotianae*, the fungus that causes frog-eye leaf spot. Immunity to both has been successfully transferred to tobacco germplasm using *N. sylvestris* as a bridging species and colchicine treatment to restore fertility to the $F_1$s. The development of stabilized, immune breeding lines is likely to require continued backcrossing and selfing for many generations with no assurance that the genes governing resistance to one or both parasites will not be lost in the process (S-203).

In the 1970s two apparently new species of *Nicotiana* were discovered, bringing the probable total number of species in the genus up to 66. *N. kawakamii* was found by Japanese explorers in the Andes of South America (S-836). *N. africana* was discovered by German botanists on several isolated mountains in Namibia. Until its discovery it was believed that *Nicotiana* species occurred naturally only in the Americas, Australia, and the southwestern Pacific (J-244; S-836). In preliminary tests *N. africana* has shown immunity to potato virus Y, a serious disease of tobacco in the United States, so this species may eventually make a valuable contribution to the crop (J-244).

## Sugarcane (Saccharum officinarum)

Despite the critical role that the wild relatives of sugarcane have played in the crop's commercial survival, only three sources of wild germplasm have been used on any scale: the Javan form of *S. spontaneum*, the Coimbatore form of Indian *S. spontaneum*, and *S. robustum* from Papua New Guinea (P-224). This conservatism is due to the difficulty that breeders have had in crossing sugarcane and *S. spontaneum* because the flowering times of the two species could not be synchronized (A-971). Some *S. spontaneum* clones flower in July, while in northern latitudes the earliest commercial cultivars do not begin flowering until mid-November. Similarly, many backcross progeny of *S. spontaneum* × commercial hybrid flower before the intended recurrent commercial parent. The transfer of desirable characteristics from the wild species to commercial stocks is clearly impossible if the two groups flower at different times. This obstacle can now be overcome by using artificial lighting to increase the photoperiod and interrupt the dark period, so delaying the flowering of the *S. spontaneum* clones (J-7).

Many forms of *S. spontaneum* are now being used in breeding programs and can be expected to maintain the major contribution wild species make to the crop. In Louisiana, resistance to sugarcane mosaic virus (SCMV) continues to be a prime objective. Widespread adoption of resistant cultivars bred at Canal Point, Florida, effectively reduced SCMV to a minor disease during the 1940s and 1950s. Then in 1956 a new strain, H2, was identified—which spread during the 1960s and helped to cause a drop in yield (from an average of 2.21 tons of sugar per harvested acre in 1966–1970 to an average of 1.99 tons in 1971–1975 [A-1383], the first since the late 1940s (A-606, A-1383). By 1973 the incidence of strain H2 in Louisiana was 78–94%, and since then two more strains (I9 and M8) have been identified (A-606). High resistance to strains A, B, D, H, and I has been found in a clone of *S. spontaneum* from Thailand, and there is hope of producing cultivars that will enable Louisiana sugarcane growers to stay ahead of the disease (D-207). Other aims are greater cold tolerance and higher cane tonnage through improved tillering and ratooning (see table 8.3, notes 11 and 12). Outstanding sources of cold tolerance have been found in *S. spontaneum* from Afghanistan and the Ryukyu Islands of Japan, and exceptional tillering and ratooning in *S. spontaneum* from Afghanistan, the Ryukyu Islands, and India (D-207).

Since 1978 in Hawaii one-third of the biparental sugarcane crosses have been with *S. spontaneum* from northern Thailand, a good source of vigor and of adaptation to high elevations (T. L. Tew and K. K. Wu, pers. comm., 24 January 1982). Some work is also being done with the yellow Sepik form of *S. robustum*, both for its vigor and because its cane surface is hard and very difficult to gnaw—hence an excellent means of rat proofing. A disadvantage of *S. robustum* is that it is highly fibrous—although this can be quite advantageous in areas such as Hawaii, where the industry fuels itself (burning of sugarcane wastes contributes 10% of the state's energy supply, as much as 35% on the islands of Kauai and Maui, and 45% on Hawaii) (T. L. Tew, pers. comm., 24 January 1982).

*Grape* (Vitis vinifera)

The beginning of the end of a 60-year gap in the use of new sources of wild germplasm for grape rootstocks came in 1961 with the collecting expedition of the French viticulturalist M. Rives to Missouri, Arkansas, Oklahoma, and Texas (P-367). In Texas, Rives collected material of *V. berlandieri* (primary gene pool), which has been used in the breeding of a new rootstock cultivar for France's Champagne and Cognac regions (P-363, P-368). The wine grape cannot be grown on its own roots in these regions because of its vulnerability to the *Phylloxera* aphid and to downy mildew caused by the fungus *Plasmopara viticula*. Unfortunately, most rootstock species cannot be grown there either, because they suffer from chlorosis (an iron deficiency disease) on the regions' calcareous soils. The only suitable rootstock species that is resistant to chlorosis is *V. berlandieri*. The problem with *V. berlandieri* is that it is so difficult to root that it must first be crossed with another species; the main rootstock cultivar in Charente (Cognac) and Marne (Champagne), 41 B, is a cross between *V. berlandieri* and *V. vinifera* (G-707, P-363). French breeders sought a rootstock superior to 41 B in rooting capacity and resistance to *Phylloxera* and chlorosis. They achieved their aim with the new cultivar Fercal (obtained by crossing the Texan clones of *V. berlandieri* with 41 B and other *V. vinifera* × *berlandieri* combinations, such as 333 EM, followed by a program of backcrossing and selection) (P-363).

Meanwhile in Napa County, California, the dagger nematode (*Xiphinema index*) has become a significant threat to production, both in its own right (it damages roots) and as a vector of fanleaf virus (J-458, M-499). Some 5,000 acres are affected, the pest causing losses of about 10,000 tons a year, or half the average annual production (A. N. Kasimatis, pers. comm., 26 October 1982). In infested areas the economic life of a vineyard can be reduced from 30 years to 10 (ibid.). Apart from the use of resistant rootstocks the only methods of control are leaving the soil fallow for up to ten years (which is economically unattractive) and soil fumigation (which is expensive, insufficiently effective to prevent the establishment of the fanleaf virus, and heavily regulated) (M-499). New rootstocks have now been developed that are tolerant of the dagger nematode and resistant to fanleaf virus, the nematode tolerance being obtained from the wild *V. arizonica* and *V. rufotomentosa* (J-458, M-499). These are undergoing viticultural trials and are expected to be released shortly (L. A. Lider, pers. comm., 26 October 1982).

New scion cultivars using wild species have been bred in Florida, where conditions are unsuitable for *V. vinifera* cultivars. Instead two other grape domesticates are grown: bunch grapes (*Vitis labrusca* and *V. labrusca* hybrids, of which Concord is the best-known example) and muscadine grapes (*Muscadinia rotundifolia*), both recent domesticates (G-707, M-324). Cultivars comprising 95% of the Florida bunch grape acreage and 45% of its muscadine acreage get their resistance to cracking and rotting of the fruit during rainy weather and to disease—principally the bacterial Pierce's disease—from wild *Vitis* and *Muscadinia* species (note 6).

*Potato* (Solanum tuberosum)

There is a great diversity of useful characteristics in the wild relatives of potato. Employment of these characteristics appears to be more advanced in the Netherlands and West Germany than in the United States or Canada. In fact, some of the $1.4 million of potato starch imported each year by the United States from the Netherlands (S-450–S-454) may already come from cultivars improved with wild germplasm. Of 81 cultivars listed in the Netherlands in 1978, *S. demissum* was in the parentage of 25, *S. demissum* and *S. vernei* in another 7, and *S. stoloniferum* in the parentage of one (P-189). *Solanum vernei* was used for its resistance to some forms of the potato cyst nematodes *Globodera pallida* and *G. rostochiensis*, but in addition "high starch content turned up unexpectedly during breeding with this species" (P-189). The Dutch cultivar Corine gets its resistance to potato viruses A and Y from *S. stoloniferum* (P-189, P-214).

*Rice* (Oryza sativa)

Resistance to stem rot caused by the fungus *Sclerotium oryzae* is being transferred to rice from the wild perennial *O. rufipogon* (primary gene pool) (P-492). Resistance to the disease, which causes significant yield losses in California, is available only in the wild species (*O. nivara* and *O. spontanea* in the primary gene pool and *O. officinalis* in the secondary gene pool are other sources of resistance) (P-493).

*Sweet orange* (Citrus sinensis)

The most likely use of wild germplasm in orange (or any other *Citrus*) breeding is for rootstocks. One species that is being investigated is the newly discovered *Microcitrus papuana*, which is native to Papua New Guinea (V-280).

*Sorghum* (Sorghum bicolor)

Breeders have started to use the virgatum race of *S. bicolor arundinaceum* (primary gene pool) and *S. halapense* (tertiary gene pool) for pest and disease resistance. Resistance to biotype C of greenbug (*Schizaphis graminum*) has been transferred from the former. Immunity to maize dwarf mosaic virus (MDMV) has been obtained from the latter (which is also a potential source of resistance to biotype E of greenbug) (P. Bramel-Cox, pers. comm., 7 November 1985).

*Alfalfa* (Medicago sativa)

Several of the wild *Medicago* species appear to have traits that would be useful to the crop, especially disease and pest resistance, but they have been little investigated. At present the main emphasis appears to be on using the variation within the crop, along with continued, somewhat limited, use of *M. falcata* germplasm (A-1408).

*Tomato* (Lycopersicon esculentum)

The wild relatives of tomato are as great a source of resistance to insect pests as they are of resistance to diseases. They are potential sources of high level resistance or immunity to 16 insect pests, *L. hirsutum* alone being the only known source of resistance to 9 of them. Progress in exploiting this resistance has been slow due in part to the many technical difficulties of evaluating insect resistance and to the late start of research in this area (since the mid-1960s) (P-463). Other new yield characteristics expected from current and future work with the wild species are adaptations to heat, cold, drought, excessive moisture, and high soil salinity (D-115, P-265, P-268).

*Cacao* (Theobroma cacao)

Many of the world's cacao breeding programs are based on the Upper Amazon clones collected by Pound. There is evidence that these do not provide breeders with enough variation, particularly with respect to the major diseases (G-809, J-635). The main needs are better resistance to *Crinipellis perniciosa* (the fungus causing witches' broom), especially in Ecuador (D-109), *Phytophthora palmivora* (the fungus causing black pod), and swollen shoot virus (CSSV), especially in West Africa (J-635). Sources may be found in wild and semiwild forms of *T. cacao* or in other *Theobroma* species, which could make a significant contribution to the crop once crossing difficulties have been overcome (G-809).

It is evident from these examples of the 15 super crops that yield characteristics will be the most likely contributions of wild genetic resources in the future as in the recent past. Similarly, the most important yield characteristic seems almost certain to remain disease and pest resistance. It is also clear that crops that have already benefited from wild germplasm will be improved with additional genetic resources from the wild, and that few crops that have yet to be improved with wild germplasm will continue to go without. These conclusions are borne out by a look at the potential of wild genetic resources for the improvement of many of the major crops (see note 4).

# 9

# Pollination and Pest Control

As noted in chapter 1, most essential ecological services—from maintenance of biogeochemical equilibria to soil and water conservation—are provided by wildlife at the ecosystem level. The two chief exceptions—pollination of crops and control of crop pests, both ecological services provided at the species level—are discussed in this chapter.

## Pollination

Crop plants may require pollination for production, propagation, or both. Pollination is necessary for production when the crop is a fruit that is not produced parthenocarpically (as are, for example, pineapple and banana). It is necessary for propagation of any crop that is propagated by seed rather than clonally, by cuttings (for example, apple and many other fruit crops), or by other vegetative parts (such as tubers in the case of the potato). Self-compatible crops (inbreeders) often are able to pollinate themselves. Some are almost entirely self-pollinated, such as pea (*Pisum sativum*) and common bean (*Phaseolus vulgaris*) (D-252, P-284). Others, although self-fertile, require a vector to transport the pollen from anther to stigma. The vector may be inanimate—normally wind (as with wheat and many other grasses), rarely water (as with the seagrass *Zostera*) (P-284)—or it may be an animal. Crimson clover (*Trifolium incarnatum*), for example, is self-fertile but not self-pollinating, requiring insects for adequate fertilization (A-252, J-594). Self-incompatible crops (outbreeders), of course, also need a pollen vector—either wind (as with corn, *Zea mays*) or animal.

Table 9.1 lists the 60 crops grown or imported by the United States requiring animal pollination (strictly speaking, animal transport of pollen, since it is the plants that pollinate each other) for production, propagation, or both. Twenty-six of them need it for production, 23 for propagation, and 11 for both. The animal generally used is the domesticated honey bee (*Apis mellifera*). Bee pollination can also improve the quality of fruits and vegetables. High cross-pollination of fruits and melons, for example, may improve their sales value by

(text continued on page 345)

Table 9.1 Crops grown or imported by the United States requiring animal pollination for production, propagation, or both

| FAMILY CROP | PRODUCTION | PROPAGATION | WILD |
|---|---|---|---|
| **ACTINIDIACEAE** *Actinidia chinensis* Chinese gooseberry | Insects; honey bees recommended (J-392, M-95) | | |
| **ALLIACEAE** *Allium cepa* Onion | | Insects, mainly honey bees, but wild flies and bees significant (J-193, M-95) | (*) |
| **ANACARDIACEAE** *Anacardium occidentale* Cashew | (D-252, G-7, M-95, M-266); reported by some to be by wind, by others to be by insects (mainly flies and ants) (D-252, M-95); "as the pollen is sticky and adheres to the stigma, and no wind-blown pollen was caught on sticky traps, it seems that insect pollination is important" (D-252) | | * |
| *Mangifera indica* Mango | (D-252, M-95, M-186); insects, notably flies and bees (although wind and self-pollination occur) (M-95, M-186); local insect populations seem adequate (D-252) | | * |
| **BOMBACACEAE** *Ceiba pentandra* Kapok | Bats, but self-pollination common, especially in large plantations (Y-24) | | (*) |
| **COMPOSITAE** *Cichorium intybus* Chicory, witloof | | Honey bees (S-171) | |
| *Helianthus annuus* Sunflower | | Insects: honey bees and wild bees (G-595, M-95, P-496) | (*) |
| *Tagetes* spp. Marigolds | | Insects: honey bees and wild bees (personal observation) | (*) |
| **CRUCIFERAE** *Brassica oleracea* Cabbage and other cole crops | | Insects, mainly honey bees, but wild bees could be important supplementary pollinators (D-252, M-95) | (*) |

338

| Species / Common name | Pollination | |
|---|---|---|
| *Raphanus sativus* Radish | Honey bees (D-252, M-95) | |
| **CUCURBITACEAE** | | |
| *Citrullus lanatus* Watermelon | Honey bees the most important pollinators, although other bees have been observed (M-95) | |
| *Cucumis melo* Melon | Bees, primarily honey bees, are the major pollinating agents (M-95) | |
| *Cucumis sativus* Cucumber | Honey bees (except for cultivars that set fruit parthenocarpically, in which case pollination must be avoided) (M-95) — Honey bees (D-252, M-95) | |
| *Cucurbita* spp. Squash | Insects: honey bees and wild bees; some report that honey bees are the more important (M-95), others that wild bees are (D-252) | * |
| **ERICACEAE** | | |
| *Vaccinium australe* and *V. corymbosum* Highbush blueberry | Insects: mainly wild bees, but honey bees are needed to supplement them (M-95, S-704) | * |
| *V. macrocarpon* Cranberry | Insects: mainly wild bees, but honey bees are needed to supplement them (M-95, M-404) | * |
| **EUPHORBIACEAE** | | |
| *Vernicia fordii* and *V. montana* Tung | Honey bees (M-95); relative importance of wind and insects, and the insects concerned, not yet determined (D-252) | |
| **LAURACEAE** | | |
| *Cinnamomum aromaticum* and *C. burmannii* Cassia | *C. aromaticum* usually propagated clonally, but *C. burmannii* usually propagated from seeds; insect pollination necessary; believed to be by flies (P-256) | * |
| *C. verum* Cinnamon | Propagated by seeds or cuttings; probably pollinated by insects, especially flies (P-256) | |

(continued)

# Table 9.1 (Continued)

| FAMILY CROP | PRODUCTION | PROPAGATION | WILD |
|---|---|---|---|
| *Persea americana* Avocado | (A-1230); honey bees the main pollinators (A-1230, M-95) | | |
| LEGUMINOSAE | | | |
| *Acacia mearnsii* Black wattle | | (D-246, S-96); seems to be mainly by bees (S-96) | * |
| *Ceratonia siliqua* Locust bean, carob | Insects; use of honey bees advised (D-246, P-497) | | (*) |
| *Lotus corniculatus* Birdsfoot trefoil | | (A-252, D-246, M-95, S-62); wild bees and honey bees (A-252, M-95, S-62, S-731) | (*) |
| *Medicago sativa* Alfalfa | | Insects: mainly domesticated alfalfa leaf-cutter bees and honey bees but also wild bees (A-259, G-260, P-494; N. Waters, pers. comm., 22 July 1982) | (*) |
| *Melilotus alba* and *M. officinalis* Sweet clover | | Insects: honey bees and wild bees, wasps and flies (A-252, G-111, M-95) | (*) |
| *Phaseolus lunatus* Lima bean | Usually self-pollinated but honey bees increase seed yield (D-246) | | |
| *Trifolium incarnatum* Crimson clover | | Insects, mainly honey bees but also wild bees (A-252, J-594, M-95, S-62) | (*) |
| *T. pratense* Red clover | | Insects, mainly wild bees; honey bees used only where wild pollinators are few (A-252, D-105, D-246, M-95, S-62) | * |
| *T. repens* Ladino clover, white clover | | Insects: honey bees and wild bees (A-252, J-20, M-95, S-62) | (*) |

| Species / Family | Pollination notes | |
|---|---|---|
| *Vicia sativa* and *V. villosa*<br>Vetch | Insect pollination apparently beneficial, but pollination requirements need clarification (M-95) | |
| LILIACEAE<br>*Asparagus officinalis*<br>Asparagus | Propagated by seed or clonally; pollinated mainly by honey bees (M-95) | |
| MORACEAE<br>*Ficus carica*<br>Fig | Caprification (pollination) by the fig wasp necessary for Smyrna fig production and main crop San Pedro fig production; not necessary for the first crop San Pedro or for common fig production (M-95, S-228, S-716) | |
| MYRISTICACEAE<br>*Myristica fragrans*<br>Nutmeg | Insect pollination apparently needed for fruit set, but insects responsible not known (M-95, P-256) | |
| MYRTACEAE<br>*Psidium guajava*<br>Guava | Self and insect pollinated; insect pollination apparently increases yields (M-95) | (*) |
| ORCHIDACEAE<br>*Vanilla planifolia*<br>Vanilla | Pollinated by hand (P-257) | |
| PALMAE<br>*Cocos nucifera*<br>Coconut | Wind and wild insects (D-252, M-95) | |
| *Phoenix dactylifera*<br>Date | Pollinated by hand or mechanically (A-334, D-252, M-95, M-255, M-283) | (*) |
| POLYGONACEAE<br>*Fagopyrum esculentum*<br>Buckwheat | Insects, usually honey bees (A-369, M-95) | |

*(continued)*

Table 9.1  (*Continued*)

| FAMILY CROP | PRODUCTION | PROPAGATION | WILD |
|---|---|---|---|
| PROTEACEAE<br>*Macadamia integrifolia*<br>Macadamia | Partly self-pollinating; cross-pollination by insects apparently increases production (S-720); honey bees the most common pollinating insects [M-95] | | (*) |
| ROSACEAE<br>*Fragaria* × *ananassa*<br>Strawberry | Insect pollination necessary for high set of well-formed fruit; pollinated by honey bees and by wild bees and flies [M-676] | | (*) |
| *Malus pumila*<br>Apple | (A-1236); honey bees and wild bees and flies (D-252, M-95) | | |
| *Prunus armeniaca*<br>Apricot | "Insect pollination is required on self-sterile cultivars and is at least beneficial to the self-fertile cultivars. Honey bees are primary pollinating agents" [M-95] | | |
| *P. avium* and *P. cerasus*<br>Cherry | [M-95]; insects; honey bees and wild bees and flies (D-252) | | (*) |
| *P. domestica* and *P. salicina*<br>Plum | Most *P. salicina* and many *P. domestica* cultivars are self-incompatible and require cross-pollination for adequate fruit set; "in some orchards wild bees are present in sufficient numbers to assure good sets," but in most honey bees are needed [J-461] | | (*) |
| *P. dulcis*<br>Almond | Honey bees [J-578, J-579, M-95] | | |

342

| | | |
|---|---|---|
| *Pyrus communis*<br>Pear | Honey bees the most effective pollinators (M-95); wild bees also effective (D-252) | (*) |
| *Rubus idaeus*<br>and *R. occidentalis*<br>Raspberry | "Honey bees are the best pollinating agents" (M-95); "because raspberry crops are so attractive to insects, adequate pollination may be achieved without importing honey bee colonies, although an increased yield and better quality fruit are sometimes obtained when this is done" (D-252) | (*) |
| *R. laciniatus* and *R. ursinus*<br>Blackberry | Some cultivars self-fertile, others self-incompatible; likely that self-fertile cultivars still require pollination by insects but this not determined for all cultivars; honey bees and wild bees (M-95) | (*) |
| RUBIACEAE<br>*Cinchona* spp.<br>Cinchona, quinine | In Indonesia *C. calisaya* propagated clonally and grafted onto *C. pubescens* rootstocks; rootstocks propagated by seed; pollination by wild insects (G-187) | * |
| RUTACEAE<br>*Citrus reticulata*<br>Tangerine | Many cultivars require insect pollination; others, though self-fertile, benefit from it; the honey bee is "unquestionably the primary pollinating agent" (M-95) | |
| SOLANACEAE<br>*Nicotiana tabacum*<br>Tobacco | Production of F$_1$ hybrid seed of burley tobacco requires pollination by hand (V-359) | |
| *Solanum melongena*<br>Eggplant | Self-compatible and highly self-pollinating (G-421); insects play the major role in pollination, and fertilization largely depends on crossing, although the plants do seem to be self-compatible (P-495) | |

(*continued*)

343

Table 9.1 (*Continued*)

| FAMILY<br>CROP | PRODUCTION | PROPAGATION | WILD |
|---|---|---|---|
| STERCULIACEAE<br>*Theobroma cacao*<br>Cacao, cocoa | Insects: midges (D-252) | | * |
| THEACEAE<br>*Camellia sinensis*<br>Tea | | Propagated clonally and by seed; insects presumed to be the main pollinating agents (V-23, V-24) | (*) |
| UMBELLIFERAE<br>*Apium graveolens*<br>Celery | | Self-fertile but requiring pollination by insects; honey bees probably the most satisfactory (M-95) | |
| *Carum carvi*<br>Caraway | Insects (M-95) | Insects (M-95) | |
| *Coriandrum sativum*<br>Coriander | Partially self-fertile but bee visits increase set; honey bees are apparently ideal pollinators (M-95) | | |
| *Daucus carota*<br>Carrot | (M-95); wild insects important but honey bees also necessary (A-257) | | (*) |
| VERBENACEAE<br>*Tectona grandis*<br>Teak | | Pollinated by wild bees (G-568, G-805) | * |
| ZINGIBERACEAE<br>*Elettaria cardamomum*<br>Cardamom | Pollination by insects necessary, apparently by bees (P-257) | | * |

Notes: Text entry across both the Production and Propagation columns means that animal pollination is required for both. Wild column: * = wild animals are the main pollen vectors, (*) = wild animals are significant pollen vectors.

344

25% (D. Pimental, pers. comm., 23 January 1984). Not all honey bees are domesticated; there are many feral populations, but for the sake of comparison with
the pollination contribution of entirely wild species, we lump domesticated and
feral species together. Other domesticates used for pollination are human
beings themselves—who hand or mechanically pollinate vanilla (*Vanilla
planifolia*) (P-257), date (*Phoenix dactylifera*) (A-334, M-255, M-283) and hybrid
burley tobacco (*Nicotiana tabacum*) (V-359)—the fig wasp, and the alfalfa leafcutter bee. The fig wasp (*Blastophaga psenes*), like the honey bee, is an early
domesticate. Its habitat is the caprifig, the inedible form of the cultivated fig
(*Ficus carica*) (D-252, M-95, S-228, S-229, S-716). Smyrna fig growers have been
hanging caprifigs on their fig trees for many centuries, so that the fig wasps can
pollinate the crop (D-252). In effect the insects were domesticated inadvertently
in the course of the domestication of the fig itself, probably by the third millennium B.C. (Y-46).

The alfalfa leafcutter bee (*Megachile rotundata*) is a new domesticate. The
species was accidentally introduced to North America during the 1930s (its
native region is southwestern Asia and southeastern Europe). It spread west
from the eastern seaboard of the United States and by the mid-1950s was abundant and widespread in many farming areas of the western states (A-898). Its
economic potential as a pollinator of alfalfa was first recognized in the late
1950s (A-898; N. D. Waters, pers. comm., 22 July 1982). Initially, growers of
alfalfa for seed simply encouraged the bees by making nesting holes in farm
buildings. Today special nesting sites are made (in Idaho, Oregon, and Washington they are usually of boards drilled with holes and covered with a shelter),
and the bees are overwintered in refrigerated rooms (at about 35°F to protect the
larvae from predatory beetles, which are active at 40+°F) (N. D. Waters, pers.
comm., 22 July 1982).

Alfalfa leafcutter bees are considered the only reliable pollinators of alfalfa in
Canada (G-260). They are the main alfalfa pollinators in the U.S. Northwest, but
elsewhere in the United States honey bees are more important (A-898, P-494). In
1980, when alfalfa leafcutter bees sold for $200 a gallon (there are 10,000 bees to
a gallon), U.S. and Canadian sales combined were $6–7 million (N. D. Waters,
pers. comm., 22 July 1982). The price of the bees fluctuates greatly: it was $100 a
gallon in 1972 (A-898) and only $30 a gallon in 1982 (Waters, 22 July 1982). Even
so, the alfalfa leafcutter bee is clearly established as a valuable new domesticate,
owing to its efficiency as a pollinator of alfalfa and to the ease with which it can
be managed.

Wild animals are important pollen vectors for the production of 18 crops and
the propagation of 19 (table 9.1). In all but one case the animals concerned are
insects, the exception being kapok (*Ceiba pentandra*), which is pollinated by
bats (Y-24). Wild insects are the main pollinating agents in the production of 7
crops with a combined average annual value of $1,249.3 million: cashew, man-
go, highbush blueberry, cranberry, squash, cacao, and cardamom (tables 9.1 and

Table 9.2 **Average annual value (1976–1980) of crops grown or imported by the United States, production of which depends mainly or partly on pollination by wild animals**

| FAMILY<br>CROP | AVERAGE ANNUAL VALUE ($ MILLION) | |
|---|---|---|
| | *Pollen vectors mainly wild* | *Pollen vectors partly wild* |
| ANACARDIACEAE<br>*Anacardium occidentale*<br>Cashew | 116.1 | |
| *Mangifera indica*<br>Mango | 8.6 | |
| BOMBACACEAE<br>*Ceiba pentandra*<br>Kapok | | 3.7 |
| CUCURBITACEAE<br>*Cucurbita* spp.<br>Squash | 11.8 | |
| ERICACEAE<br>*Vaccinium australe* and *V. corymbosum*<br>Highbush blueberry | 44.0 | |
| *V. macrocarpon*<br>Cranberry | 51.8 | |
| LEGUMINOSAE<br>*Ceratonia siliqua*<br>Locust bean, carob | | 4.7 |
| MYRTACEAE<br>*Psidium guajava*<br>Guava | | 2.3 |
| PALMAE<br>*Cocos nucifera*<br>Coconut | | 314.3 |
| ROSACEAE<br>*Fragaria* × *ananassa*<br>Strawberry | | 251.9 |
| *Malus pumila*<br>Apple | | 814.6 |
| *Prunus avium* and *P. cerasus*<br>Cherry | | 147.7 |
| *P. domestica* and *P. salicina*<br>Plum | | 155.0 |
| *Pyrus communis*<br>Pear | | 145.6 |

Table 9.2 (***Continued***)

| FAMILY<br>CROP | AVERAGE ANNUAL VALUE ($ MILLION) | |
| --- | --- | --- |
| | *Pollen vectors*<br>*mainly wild* | *Pollen vectors*<br>*partly wild* |
| *Rubus idaeus* and *R. occidentalis*<br>Raspberry | | 16.6 |
| *R. laciniatus* and *R. ursinus*<br>Blackberry | | 10.3 |
| STERCULIACEAE<br>*Theobroma cacao*<br>Cacao, cocoa | 1,016.0 | |
| ZINGIBERACEAE<br>*Elettaria cardamomum*<br>Cardamom | 1.0 | |
| TOTAL | 1,249.3 | 1,866.7 |

Sources: Pollination, table 9.1; crop values, table 7.3.

9.2). They are the main pollination agents in the propagation of 8 crops with a combined average annual value of $193.9 million: cashew, squash, Indonesian cassia, black wattle, red clover, quinine (rootstocks only), teak and cardamom (tables 9.1 and 9.3).

Native wild bees are the main pollinators of highbush blueberry (*Vaccinium australe* and *V. corymbosum*) and cranberry (*V. macrocarpon*) (M-95). Pollination has been described as a very critical phase of blueberry production because a fruit set of about 80% is needed for a good commercial crop, compared to only 20% for apples and peaches. Although the blueberry is self-fertile, its flowers are adapted to cross-pollination by bees, and self-pollination is difficult or improbable. Cross-pollination results in larger, earlier-maturing berries (S-704). Wild bumblebees are particularly valuable because they have longer tongues and work faster than honey bees, and they also work at much lower temperatures (so pollination is not so dependent on good weather) (S-704, V-87). Unfortunately, bumblebee populations fluctuate from year to year, and growers cannot be certain that wild bee numbers will be enough to give an adequate fruit set. Bee populations apparently are also being reduced by destruction of their habitats due to forest fires, loss of nesting sites because of intensification of cultivation, and the general diminution of wild lands (S-704). Accordingly, honey bees are brought into the fields to supplement them (M-95, S-704).

The pollination picture for cranberries is similar. Bees are essential for an adequate fruit set, and bumblebees are the best bees for the job. However, bumblebee populations continue to decline in most cranberry growing areas, and honey bee colonies have to be brought in to give them a hand. The situation

Table 9.3 **Average annual value (1976–1980) of crops grown or imported by the United States, propagation of which depends mainly or partly on pollination by wild animals**

| FAMILY<br>CROP | AVERAGE ANNUAL VALUE ($ MILLION) | |
|---|---|---|
| | *Pollen vectors*<br>*mainly wild* | *Pollen vectors*<br>*partly wild* |
| ALLIACEAE<br>*Allium cepa*<br>Onion | | 286.9 |
| ANACARDIACEAE<br>*Anacardium occidentale*<br>Cashew | 116.1 | |
| COMPOSITAE<br>*Helianthus annuus*<br>Sunflower | | 393.4 |
| *Tagetes* spp.<br>Marigolds | | 25.4 |
| CRUCIFERAE<br>*Brassica oleracea*<br>Cabbage and other cole crops | | 365.2 |
| CUCURBITACEAE<br>*Cucurbita* spp.<br>Squash | 11.8 | |
| LAURACEAE<br>*Cinnamomum burmannii**<br>Indonesian cassia | 4.4* | |
| LEGUMINOSAE<br>*Acacia mearnsii*<br>Black wattle | 3.9 | |
| *Lotus corniculatus*<br>Birdsfoot trefoil | | 1.3 |
| *Medicago sativa*<br>Alfalfa | | 1,053.7 |
| *Melilotus alba* and *M. officinalis*<br>Sweet clover | | 2.6 |
| *Trifolium incarnatum*<br>Crimson clover | | 1.6 |
| *T. pratense*<br>Red clover | 17.1 | |
| *T. repens*<br>Ladino clover, white clover | | 4.6 |
| RUBIACEAE<br>*Cinchona* spp.†<br>Cinchona, quinine | 37.5† | |

Table 9.3   (*Continued*)

| FAMILY CROP | AVERAGE ANNUAL VALUE ($ MILLION) | |
|---|---|---|
| | *Pollen vectors mainly wild* | *Pollen vectors partly wild* |
| THEACEAE *Camellia sinensis* Tea | | 128.0 |
| UMBELLIFERAE *Daucus carota* Carrot | | 142.3 |
| VERBENACEAE *Tectona grandis* Teak | 2.1 | |
| ZINGIBERACEAE *Elettaria cardamomum* Cardamom | 1.0 | |
| TOTAL | 193.9 | 2,405.0 |

Sources: Pollination, table 9.1; value of teak, table 7.11; other crop values, table 7.3.
* U.S. cassia imports of $11.4 million consist of Chinese cassia (*Cinnamomum aromaticum* = *C. cassia*) and Indonesian cassia (*C. burmannii*). Imports of $5.0 million from China are presumed to be of the former (which is usually clonally propagated). Imports of $4.4 million from Indonesia are presumed to be of the latter (which is usually seed propagated). Imports of $2.0 million from other countries (chiefly Japan and the Bahamas) may be of either species but are not included here (P-256, S-450–S-454).
† Wild pollen vectors involved only in rootstock propagation, but value is of crop.

is in one respect worse for cranberry growers than for blueberry growers. Cranberry flowers seem to be poor producers of nectar and pollen, and as a result honey bees are not eager to work them (M-404). Bumblebees and other wild bees, however, work them well (M-95).

Bees are also the main pollinators of squash (*Cucurbita maxima, C. moschata,* and *C. pepo*), although there is debate over whether wild or domesticated bees are the more important. McGregor notes that some species of wild bees are most efficient pollinators of *Cucurbita* but states that they are "frequently so limited in number or in range as to be of no great economic significance." Only the honey bee, he concludes, is available in sufficient numbers for commercial squash production (M-95). Free disagrees. He describes observations of insects visiting squash flowers, in which the honey bees managed to scrape pollen off the anthers only with great difficulty and gathered pollen loads that were "very small compared with those of solitary bees of the genera *Peponapis* and *Xenoglossa* which visited the flowers earlier in the day when the pollen was first available" (D-252). Because of the difficulty honey bees have in collecting pollen, they are easily distracted by competing crops (including wild flowers) and will desert the squash fields. In Iowa only 2% of the Hymenoptera (bee and wasp family) visiting *C. maxima* and *C. pepo* were honey bees. The most important pollinating species were *Xenoglossa strenua* and *Peponapis pruinosa*. Free comments that these species superficially resemble honey bees, especially when covered with pollen, which might explain reports of many honey bees visiting squash flowers (D-252).

*Peponapis* and *Xenoglossa* bees are so well adapted to, and closely associated with, cucurbits that they are known as squash bees (D-252). They are found only in the Americas, and in North America were formerly limited to areas of native cucurbits, such as the buffalo gourd (*C. foetidissima*). The cultivation of squash has greatly increased their range, however (J-227). Unlike many insect-pollinated plants, squash pollen is available very early in the day, sometimes before daylight. The squash bees have the coadaptive trait of early rising, being able to fly at low temperatures and low light intensities to collect the pollen, synchronizing their activity with the opening of the flowers, and avoiding competition with less punctual species. Male bees and females that have not yet begun to nest also spend the night in squash flowers, so they start the day covered in pollen. Moreover, the squash bees are perfectly built to collect and carry the large pollen grains of cucurbits. Even where squash bees are few or absent, other wild bees—notably bumblebees, carpenter bees, and halictid bees—may account for most squash pollination (D-252).

Cacao (*Theobroma cacao*) is the most valuable crop whose production depends on pollination by wild insects. Some cultivars are self-compatible, others are self-incompatible, but all require insect pollination. The chief and most efficient pollen vectors are midges (*Forcipomyia* and *Lasiohelea* species) of the Ceratopogonidae family (D-252, M-95).

Red clover (*Trifolium pratense*) is a classic example of a crop whose propagation depends heavily on wild insects. The production of red clover seed is directly proportional to pollinator activity (M-95) and the species can be efficiently pollinated only by long-tongued bumblebees (*Bombus* species) (D-105). Honey bees are capable of pollinating red clover, but they are only half as efficient as bumblebees (M-95), and their use generally is confined to areas where the wild bees are in poor supply. In the eastern United States, most red clover is pollinated by native bumblebees (D-246). In Washington's Columbia basin, red clover pollination is mainly by honey bees since wild bees are not abundant; but in Lewis County, Washington, honey bee colonies are not placed in the fields because bumblebee populations (mostly of *Bombus occidentalis* and *B. californicus*) are usually sizable (S-62). Wild bees are also the main pollinating agents in the propagation of quinine (*Cinchona pubescens*) rootstocks, although butterflies are also significant during fine weather and smaller insects in rainy weather (G-187). The two most important pollinators of teak (*Tectona grandis*) in Thailand are the wild bees *Heriades binghami* (family Megachilidae) and *Ceratina hieroglyphica* (family Anthophoridae) (G-568, G-805).

Wild animals are also significant supplementary pollinators. As such they make lesser but important contributions to the production of 11 crops with a combined average annual value of $1,866.7 million: kapok, carob, guava, coconut, strawberry, apple, cherry, plum, pear, raspberry, and blackberry (tables 9.1 and 9.2). Similarly, they make valuable contributions to the propagation of another 11 crops with a combined average annual value of $2,405.0 million: onion, sunflower, marigolds, cabbages and other cole crops, birdsfoot trefoil, alfalfa, sweet clover, crimson clover, ladino clover, tea, and carrot (tables 9.1 and 9.3).

Modern strawberry (*Fragaria* × *ananassa*) cultivars are self-fertile but not completely self-pollinating (M-95). Insect visits appear to be essential for full pollination, which itself is necessary for a high set of well-formed fruit (M-676). Growers generally do not bring honey bee colonies to their fields, relying on whatever insects happen to visit the crop (M-95). A great diversity of insects visits strawberry flowers; and strawberries usually set a good crop of fruit without special provision for pollination unless the field is large. One study of strawberry fields in Utah recorded that the most important pollinators (importance being a function of efficiency and abundance) were honey bees, the syrphid flies *Eristalis tenax* and *E. brousii*, and the solitary bees *Osmia trevoris*, *O. nanula*, *Halictus rubicundus*, and *H. ligatus* (M-676).

Honey bee colonies are brought to orchards to pollinate apple (*Malus pumila*), cherry (*Prunus avium* and *P. cerasus*), plum (*P. domestica* and *P. salicina*), and pear (*Pyrus communis*), but wild insects often play a bigger role in the fertilization of these crops than is realized. Among the important apple pollinators are the wild bees of the genera *Andrena*, *Bombus*, *Halictus*, and *Osmia*. They are particularly useful in the apple growing areas of New England and Canada since they visit flowers at lower temperatures than do honey bees (A-251, M-95). Syrphid flies and blowflies are important in some localities as pollinators of pear (A-251).

The contribution of wild pollinators is underestimated probably because there are often too few of them to pollinate the crop by themselves. This is generally the case in areas where wild bee habitat is sparse. However, wild bees are probably more valuable than their numbers imply because many of them work faster, probably for longer hours, and under a greater range of weather conditions than do honey bees (D-252). They are often more efficient than honey bees, too. When the honey bee visits an apple blossom for nectar (collecting nectar and pollen are often separate activities), it can take the nectar without touching the anthers or stigma, so that pollen is neither taken from the anthers nor brushed onto the stigma. By contrast, the bumblebee clambers over the anthers and stigma when foraging and so cannot avoid transferring pollen from flower to flower (M-95).

The significant support role of wild insects in crop propagation is ex-emplified by onion (*Allium cepa*), cole crops (*Brassica oleracea*), and carrot (*Daucus carota*). Honey bees are the main pollinators of onion. In Idaho, Oregon, and Washington, where much of the United States' onion seed is pro-duced, it is estimated that 95% of the pollination is by honey bees, wild insects accounting for only about 5% (N. D. Waters, pers. comm., 22 July 1982). Honey bees are particularly effective pollinators of open-pollinated onions because both pollen and nectar are available on all flower heads. They are less effective in hybrid seed production, which involves the use of male-sterile plants, be-cause only the nectar collectors move freely from pollen-sterile to pollen-fer-tile plants (M-95). Onion flowers are not very attractive to honey bees, es-pecially if the sugar content of the nectar is below 55%, and they will readily leave them for flowers they prefer, such as sweet clover (*Melilotus*) (Waters, 22 July 1982). By contrast they are highly attractive to many wild insects, es-pecially halictid bees, syrphid flies, and drone flies (J-193). On small plots with plenty of nearby nesting sites, the wild pollinators are abundant; but on large fields entirely surrounded by row crops (a habitat that is not conducive to the wild insects), which is where most of the onion seed is produced, hives of honey bees are needed (J-193; Waters, 22 July 1982).

The cole crops present a similar picture. They are both self- and cross-pollinated, but cross-pollination by insects is favored and increases seed set (D-252). Insect pollination is also necessary to ensure maximum set possible by self-pollination (D-252). The honey bee is the chief pollinator of cole crops, but since the plants may bloom at temperatures below 55°F, the minimum at which honey bees fly, wild insects can be important supplementary pollinators (M-95). Most of the United States' cole crop seed is produced in Washington's Puget Sound area, where honey bees are not very abundant but where there are many syrphid and muscoid flies (A-251).

Carrot seed is produced in California, Idaho, and Washington. In Idaho, which produces a third of the U.S. supply, wild insects account for as much as 50% of the pollination (honey bees accounting for the other 50%). The main insect group is Hymenoptera (bees and wasps: 40%). Diptera (flies), Coleoptera (beetles), and Lepidoptera (butterflies and moths) make up most of the remain-ing 10%. Carrot flowers are so attractive to insects (including honey bees) that most carrot growers in Idaho do not bother to hire hives of honey bees, particu-larly if they are growing open-pollinated seed. Honey bees brought in to polli-nate onion will often fly off to carrot up to four miles away. Nonetheless, if the growers are producing hybrid carrot seed, they may hire honey bee colonies to ensure complete pollination of the crop (N. D. Waters, pers. comm., 22 July 1982).

As long as there is suitable habitat nearby and the seed carrot plantings are small (high ratio of wild insect habitat to crop), the pollination of carrot will generally be done well enough by wild insects. Without special measures to

bring honey bees to the crop, wild insects are unquestionably the most important pollinators. Bohart and Nye, in a four-year study of insect visitors to carrot
seed plots in Utah, have shown that some wild species are about as efficient
pollinators as are honey bees, and many wild species make up in numbers what
they lack in efficiency (A-257). Efficiency was determined by the amount of
loose pollen carried on the insects' bodies, their size, flightiness, and contact
with stamens and stigmas as they moved across the flower heads. Pollen-
collecting honey bees were the most efficient, followed by the sphecid wasp
*Tachytes utahensis*, with nectar-collecting honey bees, halictid bees, large syrphid flies, and soldier flies next in efficiency. However, honey bees were not
the most abundant visitors, being far outnumbered by the wild species. When
efficiency and abundance were combined in an index of pollination importance, the top pollinators proved to be the wild insects. Table 9.4 expresses the
index of pollination importance in percentages and shows that wild insects
account for almost 97%. Three groups—the sphecid wasps (28.4%), the larger
flies (21.8%), and the small syrphid fly *Syritta pipiens* (18.7%)—together make
up more than two-thirds (68.9%).

The fact that wild insects are seldom if ever responsible for the complete
pollination of a crop makes their contribution difficult to evaluate. Sunflower
(*Helianthus annuus*) is regarded as a crop that requires no insect pollination for
production and depends on the honey bee for propagation. The sunflower

Table 9.4   **Most important insect pollinators of carrot in Utah**

| INSECT GROUP | POLLINATION IMPORTANCE (%) |
|---|---|
| Wild insects | |
| Sphecid wasps (Sphecidae) | 28.4 |
| Bees | 15.6 |
| Other Hymenoptera (e.g., ichneumons and vespoid wasps) | 4.9 |
| HYMENOPTERA | 48.9 |
| *Syritta pipiens* | 18.7 |
| Soldier flies (Stratiomyidae) and other larger flies | 21.8 |
| Tiny flies (e.g., midges) | 2.4 |
| DIPTERA | 42.9 |
| COLEOPTERA (e.g., checkered beetles and ladybirds), HEMIPTERA (e.g., the boxelder bug *Leptocoris trivittatus*), and OTHERS | 5.1 |
| TOTAL | 96.9 |
| Honey bees | 3.1 |
| | 100.0 |

Source: A-257.

hybrid cultivars are highly self-compatible and can produce a full crop when self-pollinated.

Doubts have been expressed, however, about the adequacy of pollen distribution on the flower heads without insect activity, and bee visits may be needed to ensure pollination of late emerging stigmas (P-496). In the absence of honey bees (it being assumed they are unnecessary), the wild bees may be making an unsuspected contribution by working the flowers and helping to increase the set. By contrast, there is no question about the need for insect pollinators in the fields that produce hybrid seed for propagation. Honey bee hives are placed in these fields because the pollen must be carried from one line to the other, and the honey bee is the only species that can do the job, is available in the numbers necessary for adequate pollination, and is manageable. Because the wild insects cannot be relied upon to achieve adequate pollination alone and unaided, the domesticated bees are brought in. Because the domesticated bees are introduced, it is assumed they are doing most of the pollinating.

This may not be the case. Large numbers of several wild bee species have been observed on sunflower. In samplings of bees visiting commercial seed-growing fields in California, Hurd and his colleagues (G-595) collected few honey bees but many native bees (table 9.5). *Diadasia, Melissodes,* and *Svastra* were observed busily taking nectar and pollen, "sometimes in incredibly large numbers," but there were no pollen-gathering honey bees and few nectar-gathering ones. When taking nectar, the honey bees often did not enter the flower head; instead they rested on the ray florets around the edge and probed the nectar-bearing florets from the outside (G-595).

Hurd and his colleagues concede that their samplings of commercial sunflowers were superficial and largely limited to the edges of the fields, so the small number of honey bees they saw may have been misleading. Even so, there were large nesting sites of *Diadasia enavata* and *Svastra obliqua* on the edge of one commercial field "from which the females were actively returning with heavy loads of pollen"—leaving no doubt that "these species can be an important factor in sunflower seed production" (G-595). The wild species are also highly efficient sunflower pollinators. *Melissodes agilis,* for example, visits the flowers early in the morning when they first shed their pollen; honey bees make their visits later after much of the pollen has already been shed.

As a rule the relative importance of wild pollinators will be high when there is abundant habitat for them (A-251, A-256). Ladino or white clover (*Trifolium repens*), for example, is partly to nearly entirely pollinated by honey bees, depending on the prevalence of wild bees, which are in turn dependent on the proximity of good wild bee habitat (J-20, M-95). In southern Oregon, bumblebees are about one-third as numerous as honey bees, but in South Carolina they are only a tenth as numerous (A-252). Studying pollination of clovers raised for seed in Washington, Johansen found that wild species were

Table 9.5  **Four samplings of principal bee species visiting sunflower (*Helianthus annuus*) in California**

| BEE SPECIES | SAMPLE 1 (%) | SAMPLE 2 (%) | SAMPLE 3 (%) | SAMPLE 4 (%) |
|---|---|---|---|---|
| *Diadasia enavata* | 89.1 | 83.8 | 3.3 | 35.0 |
| *Melissodes agilis* | 0.9 | 5.7 | 21.3 | 23.9 |
| *Svastra obliqua* | 6.3 | 2.3 | 55.3 | 36.8 |
| Other wild bee spp. | 2.2 | 6.2 | 14.5 | 3.1 |
| TOTAL wild bee spp. | 98.5 | 98.0 | 94.4 | 98.8 |
| *Apis mellifera* Honey bee | 1.5 | 2.0 | 5.6 | 1.2 |

Source: G-595.

quite scarce in one location and that one colony of honey bees was used for each acre of white clover (J-20). In another location the wild bees were more abundant, and one colony of honey bees was sufficient for two acres. In a third location wild pollinators (chiefly bumblebees *Bombus bifarius, B. occidentalis,* and other *Bombus* species) plus naturally occurring honey bees were so numerous that honey bee colonies were not brought in at all.

According to Bohart, it is likely that—at least in the eastern half of the United States—wild bees are more abundant now than when Europeans first arrived (A-256). The fragmentation of the eastern forests has increased the area of suitable foraging and nesting sites. So, too, have the building of highways in desert and semidesert regions (which concentrates moisture along the road shoulders and provides ribbons of flowers along their edge); the introduction and spread of weedy plants such as sweet clover and sunflower that are favored by bees; the growing of crops that provide additional forage, and the irrigation of arid lands (A-256). Road cuts, embankments, outbuildings, and eroded areas provide additional nesting sites for ground-dwelling bees and wasps (A-251). These improvements in the lot of wild pollinators may be wholly or partly offset by the spread of concrete and asphalt, intensification of land use, and clean cultivation practices, which destroy nesting habitat and flowering weeds. Herbicides reduce available forage and insecticides pose a still more direct threat; many pollinators and other beneficial insects are killed inadvertently by efforts to control pests (A-251, A-256).

The key factor, however, is not the gross area of suitable habitat but the availability of suitable habitat within normal flight range of the crops to be pollinated. In Saskatchewan, Canada, alfalfa grown for seed used to be pollinated mainly by native leafcutter bees (Megachilidae), which nest in beetle burrows in the forest timber. A few acres of seed surrounded by forest usually had plenty of leafcutter bees and consequently good seed crops, but when the area was given over to extensive cultivation, "only a few seed fields next to the wild country were adequately pollinated" (A-251).

Alkali bees (*Nomia melanderi*) illustrate the vicissitudes of wild pollinators. The species is native to the United States from the Rocky Mountains westward but is most abundant in the intermountain states from central Utah to east central Washington. Its numbers are believed to have increased greatly with the development of farming in the West. Inefficient irrigation methods and lack of drainage provided ideal nesting areas for the alkali bees (so called because they nest in bare or lightly vegetated soil that is moist from the cell level to the surface and is alkaline due to the low rainfall of the area and an impermeable layer beneath the soil surface). The growth of crops such as alfalfa, sweet clover (*Melilotus* spp.), peppermint (*Mentha* × *piperita*), and spearmint (*M. spicata*), and of weeds in fields and waste places increased the food supply of the alkali bees (A-898, P-494).

In the mid-1940s and early 1950s, growers of alfalfa seed realized that the species was a highly effective pollinator of alfalfa, and they began to improve existing nesting sites and to establish artificial sites. For a time alkali bees made a substantial contribution to alfalfa seed production in the Northwest. Then in the mid-1960s severe kills by insecticides and spoilage of nests due to unseasonally heavy summer rains drastically reduced their populations. Although under ideal conditions alkali bees are capable of explosive population increases, their numbers have not returned to the previous high levels. One factor may be an improvement in drainage practices, which has eliminated many nesting areas. As a result, alkali bees have virtually ceased to be of economic significance in Utah, Idaho, and eastern Oregon; and their importance in east central Washington is diminishing (A-898, P-494; N. D. Waters, pers. comm., 22 July 1982).

In estimating the total value of the crops that depend on wild pollinators for production or propagation we have borne in mind two contradictory factors. One is a tendency to assume that honey bees are doing more of the pollination and wild insects less than may be the case. The other is the uncertain availability of sufficient nearby habitat to assure the supply of wild pollinators in significant numbers. It is probably conservative to suppose that wild animals account for the pollination of 70% of each crop listed in the "pollen vectors mainly wild" columns of tables 9.2 and 9.3, and of 10% of each crop listed in the "pollen vectors partly wild" columns. This being so, the average annual value of crops grown or imported by the United States whose *production* depends on wild pollinators would be $1,061.2 million; and that of the crops grown or imported by the United States whose *propagation* depends on wild pollinators would be $376.2 million. Subtracting $90.2 million to avoid double counting of cashew, squash, and cardamom (the three crops that depend on wild pollinators for both production and propagation), the combined value of the crops that are produced or propagated with the help of wild pollinators is $1,347.2 million a year.

Other crops will likely be added to those listed in tables 9.1–9.3 as knowledge of the pollination of crops in the field improves and with new developments in agriculture. An example of the latter would be the production of hybrid cotton. We noted in chapter 8 (in the section Potential Contributions of Wild Genetic Resources) that the achievement of a reliable source of cytoplasmic male sterility and fertility restoration for hybrid cotton production can be expected in the near future. Cotton cultivars are generally self-pollinating, and insects are not regarded as necessary for production of the crop (J-588). In the production of hybrid seed, however, bees are expected to be essential—and the bees in question will amost certainly be wild. Honey bees show a preference for the extrafloral nectaries of cotton and often seem reluctant to enter the cotton flower. Bumblebees and *Melissodes* bees are most effective cotton pollinators but cannot be managed as can the domesticated honey bees (M-95). Shortage of insect vectors of pollen is recognized as a major obstacle to the production of hybrid cotton seed (P-269). The solution may be to locate hybrid seed production in regions where efficient wild pollinators are abundant and to manage the seed production fields for high pollinator populations (for example, using small fields to keep nest habitat to field ratio high and ensuring that cultivation is compatible with bee nesting within the fields). In Arizona (which would be a good place for hybrid seed production), three species of *Melissodes* bees (*M. paroselae*, *M. tepida*, and *M. thelypodii*) are relatively abundant, nest in the cotton fields, and favor cotton as a source of pollen (A-311).

## Pest Control

The modern era of pest control began in the second half of the last century with devastating outbreaks in the United States of the Colorado beetle (*Leptinotarsa decemlineata*) and the cottony cushion scale (*Icerya purchasi*). The Colorado beetle is native to the eastern slopes of the Rocky Mountains. When potato farming began in the region in the 1850s, the beetle quickly became a serious pest, spreading eastward at a rate of some 90 miles a year. It posed such a severe threat to the nation's potato production that it was decided (after a great deal of heated debate) to spray the crop with arsenic in the form of Paris Green—the first time a human poison had been used to protect a human food crop (D-281).

The cottony cushion scale was introduced from Australia and was so destructive that in 1887 it almost killed off California's new citrus industry. The natural enemies of the pest in Australia were investigated, and in 1889 the citrus growers received their first shipment of the vedalia ladybird (*Rodolia cardinalis*). Within 15 months the ladybird—together with a tachinid fly *Crypt-*

*ochaetum iceryae*, also from Australia—had brought the cottony cushion scale under effective control and the citrus industry was saved (A-1429, D-281).

For the next half century biological control—the control of pests using predators, parasites, and pathogens—reigned supreme. Unfortunately, it was heavily oversold because many of its proponents knew little about the causes of pest outbreaks or the conditions required for successful control. By the time the first organochlorine pesticides were introduced in the early 1940s, people were thoroughly disillusioned with biological control. DDT and the other organochlorines, together with the organophosphorus compounds (introduced in the early 1950s) and the carbamates (introduced in the 1960s), were so successful that chemical control became the watchword. Interest in biological control was more or less restricted to the "muck and magic" school; most people in the mainstream of agriculture believed that chemicals could solve most pest problems (D-281, S-104).

With increasing public awareness of the harmful side-effects of many pesticides (killings of pollinators; buildup of residues in the food chain causing death and injury to nontarget organisms including, in some cases, people) came recognition that chemical control was also being oversold. Pesticides left unsolved many pest problems and created new ones. New and more damaging outbreaks of pests occurred as untimely or excessive applications of pesticides imposed selection pressures on invertebrate populations, thus favoring the emergence of resistant strains of established pests, promoting minor pests to major status, and eliminating the pests' more vulnerable natural enemies (A-1429, D-281, S-104).

There are still extreme advocates of chemical control alone, just as there are of biological control alone, but the mainstream philosophy appears now to be that of integrated pest control or pest management. This is a commonsense approach that combines chemical and biological controls in a program of measures that also includes use of resistant or tolerant cultivars, microbial pesticides, pheromones, sterilization, and cultural controls (such as field sanitation, crop rotation, crop diversification, and timing of planting and harvesting dates to avoid peak pest periods) (A-1429, D-281, S-104).

Historically, the major application of biological control has been in the suppression of introduced weeds and pests using parasites and predators from the target species' native areas. Three herbivorous insect species introduced from Argentina now control alligatorweed (*Alternanthera philoxeroides*), a South American aquatic weed that has become established in the southeastern United States (A-1433). The tachinid fly *Lixophaga sphenophora* successfully controls its compatriot the New Guinea sugarcane weevil, a pest of sugarcane introduced to Hawaii (G-839). In California the walnut aphid (*Chromaphis juglandicola*), introduced from Europe in 1909 and a serious pest of Persian, or English, walnut (*Juglans regia*), has been brought under control by two ecotypes of the parasitic wasp *Trioxys pallidus*. The first, introduced from France in 1959, was successful along the coast and nearby valleys but was not adapted to the relative heat and dryness of central California. This problem was overcome in 1968 with the introduction of a strain from Iran that was well adapted and is now established (A-1429, A-1433, P-454).

There is also growing recognition of the value of the native enemies of pests. Irrespective of the prevailing fashion in pest control, naturally occurring predators and parasites have always made a substantial contribution to the protection of crops, and without them crop destruction would be far greater. About 90% of the control of insect and mite problems on nut crops in North America is achieved naturally by wild animals and the weather; the 10% that gets away, however, causes heavy losses—estimated by Payne and Johnson to be at least 20% of the annual potential U.S. nut crop and, in some years, up to 50% (P-454).

Efforts are now being made to determine which species are the most effective enemies of pests, partly so that measures can be taken to increase their numbers, partly to avoid inadvertently reducing their numbers while applying other controls (D-409). Larvae of syrphid flies are important predators of the green peach aphid (*Myzus persicae*) on peach trees in Washington; in the autumn they are the only effective predators since they can work under cooler conditions than most other aphid predators, such as ladybird beetles (Coccinellidae) and green lacewings (Chrysopidae) (G-838). Syrphid fly numbers can be increased by ensuring a plentiful bloom of wild flowers, on which the adults depend for nectar and pollen. The flowers can be in nearby wild habitat, in the orchard, or better still both. Fifteen unsprayed apple orchards in Canada were classified as rich, average, or poor, depending on the abundance of nectar-producing flowers in the undergrowth. About 18 times as many tent caterpillar pupae were parasitized in rich orchards as in poor orchards, with the average orchards intermediate (G-839).

The coding moth nematode (*Neoaplectana carpocapsae*) is being successfully used against the western poplar clearwing moth (*Paranthrene robiniae*) and other plant-boring insects. Caterpillars of the western poplar clearwing have become a serious pest of birch, poplar, and willow trees in parks and residential areas. Using this nematode for pest control is a form of bacterial warfare. A bacterium, *Xenorhabdus nematophilus*, occurs in the nematode's gut and is released when the nematode invades the body of the caterpillar. The caterpillar dies from a bacterial infection 24 to 48 hours later; and the nematode dines on the bacterial cells (so reingesting them) and the tissues of the caterpillar. The nematode-bacterial association infects only insects and was recently exempted from registration by the U.S. Environmental Protection Agency. Other countries, notably Australia and France, are also using this association against tree-boring and soil-infesting insects (J-636).

The pests themselves, as well as their enemies, are of course also wild. Often the evident damage caused by the pests has led people to overlook the valuable contributions of the parasites and predators. One beneficial side-effect of the overuse of pesticides is that in suppressing the natural enemies more than it did the pests, it revealed how important the enemies were. In California the main insect pests of cotton are lygus bugs (mostly *Lygus hesperus*) and the cotton bollworm (*Heliothis zea*). In the early 1960s pesticides were used against these pests selectively and only when it was apparent that parasites, predators, and pathogens were no longer suppressing them. Then in 1965 the pink bollworm (*Pectinophora gossypiella*) invaded the San Joaquin Valley and caused severe losses. Growers responded with frequent applications of broad-spectrum insecticides. These almost totally eliminated the natural parasites and predators, and as a result several normally minor pests—such as the cotton leafperforator (*Psallus seriatus*)—soon reached destructive levels (A-1431).

Currently a more balanced form of pest management is being developed. Lygus bugs are being controlled through a combination of strip-cutting of nearby alfalfa fields and interplanting alfalfa strips in the cotton fields, and minimizing early and midseason insecticide applications to avoid injury to the natural enemies of lepidopterous pests (such as the armyworm *Spodoptera exigua* and the cabbage looper *Trichoplusia ni*) and spider mites (*Tetranychus* species) (A-1431). Alfalfa is an essential component of the program because it is the primary host plant of the lygus bugs. Once alfalfa is harvested, the bugs move to other crops; strip-harvesting reduces this migration. Interplanting alfalfa provides a trap crop, retaining the lygus bugs and so helping to protect the cotton (A-1432). Bollworm control is being improved by reducing the number and frequency of insecticide applications to allow greater survival of predators such as green lacewings (*Chrysopa* species) (A-1431, G-838).

The pest management picture of two other crops—alfalfa and grape—illustrates the scope and limitations of control by the wild enemies of pests. In both cases the most satisfactory control is achieved by a combination of resistant or tolerant cultivars, prudent and timely use of selective pesticides, native and introduced predators and parasites, and other measures.

The main insect pests of alfalfa are the alfalfa weevil (Coleoptera: *Hypera postica*), the pea aphid (Homoptera: *Acrythosiphon pisum*), the spotted alfalfa aphid (Homoptera: *Therioaphis trifolii*), and the alfalfa caterpillar (Lepidoptera: *Colias eurytheme*). The first three species are introduced (they are native to Europe, North Africa, and West Asia) (A-1430); the last, otherwise known as the orange sulfur butterfly, is native to North America (P-357) but is seldom a serious pest outside the Southwest (A-1430). The alfalfa weevil is controlled using pesticides and an introduced ichneumon, *Bathyplectes curculionis* (Hymenoptera). Introduced to California in 1933 and 1934, *B. curculionis* has proved an excellent parasite of the weevil and today totally controls the pest in the coastal valleys of central California; it is also important in Utah (A-1431, G-838). Its effectiveness elsewhere in the West is apparently being reduced by untimely use of insecticides. Studies in Colorado show that early treatments with carbofuran, widely applied to control the larvae of the alfalfa weevil, can reduce emergence of *B. curculionis* by about 60% (A-1429). In the East, however, insecticides may be the only effective means of control, since the eastern form of the alfalfa weevil may be immune to the parasite (A-1430).

A wide range of measures is now available against the two aphid species. There are many resistant cultivars (the resistance being derived mainly from Turkestan germplasm within the alfalfa crop) (A-1408). The primary native predators are ladybird beetles (Coleoptera: *Coccinella* and *Hippodamia* species), particularly *H. convergens* (A-1430, G-838). In addition, three parasitic wasps (Hymenoptera: *Aphelinus semiflavus*, *Praon palitans*, and *Trioxys utilis*) introduced from West Asia assist in the control of the spotted alfalfa aphid in California; and two introduced parasitic wasps (*Aphidius pulcher* and *A. smithi*—the latter imported from India) help suppress the pea aphid (A-1431). The combination of resistant cultivars and biological control generally keeps the crop free enough of aphids to avoid the use of insecticides (the value of the cultivars' contribution alone is estimated to be at least $35 million a year). The subordination of insecticides to control by natural enemies began in the late 1950s, when the spotted alfalfa aphid developed resistance to organophosphate insecticides and crop losses became critical. It was decided to apply an organophosphate (demetron) in low doses so that, although many of the aphids survived, "so did many of the natural enemies which had not been effective controls on their own but were now able to control the surviving aphids. Within one year of applying the integrated control programme, the crisis was over" (D-281).

The alfalfa caterpillar is normally limited in abundance by natural enemies, especially the braconid wasp *Apanteles medicaginis* (Hymenoptera), *Trichogramma semifumatum* (another member of the Hymenoptera), and a virus. The two insects are the key controls in southern California, and *A. medicaginis* is the main agent of suppression in California's Central Valley (A-1431, G-838). If parasitism by *A. medicaginis* is too late to provide effective control, the microbial insecticide *Bacillus thuringiensis* is recommended. Other significant alfalfa pests among the Lepidoptera that are wholly to partially (depending on conditions) controlled by native enemies (Diptera and Hymenoptera) are webworms (*Loxostege* spp.), the western yellow-striped armyworm (*Prodenia praefica*), and the beet armyworm (*Spodoptera exigua*). In all three cases, the natural enemies are conserved by proper timings and dosages of selective insecticides that may have to be used for these or other pests (A-1431).

Among the main pests of grape in California are the aphid *Phylloxera vitifoliae*, the nematodes *Meloidogyne* species and *Xiphinema index*, the grape leafhopper (Homoptera: *Erythroneura elegantula*), the omnivorous leafroller (Lepidoptera: *Platynota stultana*), and the Pacific spider mite (Acarina: *Tetranychus pacificus*). The first two are effectively controlled through the use of resistant rootstocks (see chap. 8: Disease and Pest Resistance) and the third will be shortly (see chap. 8: Potential Contributions of Wild Genetic Resources). The recommended means of dealing with the omnivorous leafroller is through a combination of cultural measures (removal of trash in which the larvae overwinter) and carefully timed applications of insecticides; no effective natural enemy has been identified (A-1431).

Chemical control has been the major tool of suppression of both the grape leafhopper and the Pacific spider mite. Growers have used a succession of insecticides on both species, which responded by becoming resistant to one insecticide after another. Rates and dosages of applications were increased to no avail. An otherwise important predator of the spider mite—*Typhlodromus occidentalis* (Acarina: another mite, but in a different family)—was so reduced in numbers (due both to its being killed by pesticides and to loss of prey) that outbreaks of the Pacific spider mite increased. An integrated control program has been started (involving 10–20% of vineyards in California's San Joaquin Valley) that consists of using insecticides to control the grape leafhopper until the population reaches a threshold of 20 nymphs per leaf in the first brood or 15 nymphs per leaf in the second brood, and of reducing insecticide use during April and May to allow *T. occidentalis* to increase for spider mite control and to conserve the most effective parasite of the grape leafhopper—the wasp *Anagrus epos* (Hymenoptera) (A-1431).

The great value of *Anagrus epos* was recognized when it was shown that large acreages of grapes planted near stands of wild blackberries (*Rubus* spp.) usually had so few grape leafhoppers that insecticides were not needed. The species parasitizes the eggs of grape leafhopper and blackberry leafhopper (*Dikrella californica*). The latter is economically unimportant except for the fact that its eggs are present throughout the year on wild *Rubus*, and these eggs are the mainstay of *A. epos* during the winter—enabling it to survive in sufficient numbers for it to control the grape leafhopper. In the early spring the wasp moves from the *Rubus* to the vineyards to parasitize eggs laid by overwintering grape leafhoppers. Recently *A. epos* was discovered parasitizing the leafhopper *Edwardsiana prunicola* in prune orchards. *E. prunicola* is not considered a serious pest by prune growers, and it has the advantage of overwintering in the egg stage, providing another source of winter sustenance for *A. epos*. Together wild *Rubus* and cultivated *Prunus* provide a reservoir of prey for the parasitic wasp, enabling it to persist as an effective control of the grape leafhopper (J-580). It is estimated that by regulating pesticide use to allow full participation by *T. occidentalis* against the spider mite and *A. epos* against the grape leafhopper, grape growers can cut their pesticide use by half and save $40–$60 per acre (A-1431).

# 10

# Recreational Fishing, Hunting, and Nonconsumptive Wildlife Use

According to two national surveys conducted by the U.S. Fish and Wildlife Service (S-585, S-688), Americans spend about $30 billion each year on wildlife-associated recreation: $16.25 billion fishing; $7.15 billion hunting; and $6.6 billion in nonconsumptive (or nonharvesting) ways such as whale watching, feeding wild birds, and photographing wild flowers (note 1). Canadian data are also available (note 2). Figure 10.1 depicts 1975 and 1980 U.S. participation and expenditure rates in these three basic categories. Our own survey (described in the Parks subsection of this chapter) found that $112–$140 million are spent each year by visitors to state and national parks in the United States. We do not know what percentage of this expenditure is included in the Fish and Wildlife surveys.

## Recreational Fishing

Each year 54 million Americans fish for pleasure (note 3). In so doing they spend $16.25 billion a year (average of 1975 and 1980). Tables 10.1 and 10.2 break down expenditures into travel and equipment costs for both fresh- and saltwater fishing.

*Freshwater Fishing*

In 1980, 86% of all Americans (aged 16 years and older) who fished went after freshwater species exclusively or at some time. They spent about $11 a day, or $214 a year (S-585). The top eight freshwater (and anadromous) fish families (or groups of fish) were panfish (several families), sunfish (Centrarchidae), salmon (Salmonidae), catfish (Ictaluridae), pike (Esocidae), perch (Percidae), temperate bass (Percichthyidae), and perch (several families) (table 10.3). Table 10.4 lists the kinds of habitat frequented by freshwater fishing fans.

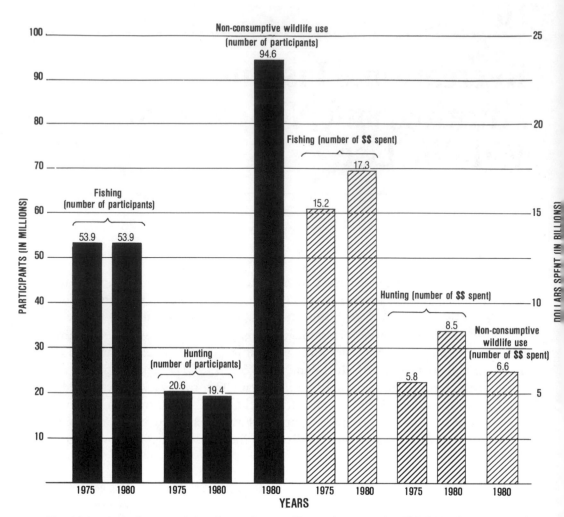

Fig. 10.1 American participation and expenditures in recreational fishing, hunting, and nonconsumptive wildlife use, 1975, 1980. Solid bars: millions of participants, shaded bars: billions of dollars spent. Sources: S-585, S-688

Table 10.1 Expenditures ($15.2 billion) by Americans on recreational fishing, 1975

|  | TRAVEL | EQUIPMENT | PERCENTAGE OF TOTAL EXPENDITURE |
|---|---|---|---|
| Freshwater | $8,739,824,000 | $1,670,617,000 | 69 |
| Saltwater (includes sea run) | $3,767,525,000 | $740,786,000 | 30 |
| Percentage of total expenditure | 82 | 16 | * |

Source: S-688.
Note: Figures are exclusive of licenses.
*Percentages do not add to 100 because of missing data.

Table 10.2  Expenditures ($17.⊟ billion) by Americans on recreational fishing, 1980

| | TRAVEL | EQUIPMENT | SPECIAL EQUIPMENT* | MISCELLANEOUS† | PERCENTAGE OF TOTAL EXPENDITURE |
|---|---|---|---|---|---|
| Freshwater | $5,929,768,000 | $1,864,441,000 | — | — | 45 |
| Saltwater (includes sea run) | $1,820,449,000 | $628,253,000 | — | — | 14 |
| Unspecified fishing | — | — | $6,449,230,000 | $632,515,000 | 41 |
| Percentage of total expenditure | 45 | 14 | 37 | 4 | 100 |

Source: S-585.

*Includes boats, vans, and similar vehicles.

†Includes magazine subscriptions, membership dues, land leasing, and ownership.

Table 10.3  **Freshwater (and anadromous) families fished recreationally by more than 1 million American participants, 1975 and 1980**

| FAMILY | PERSONS FISHING, 1975 | PERSONS FISHING, 1980 | SPECIES |
|---|---|---|---|
| "PANFISH" (Several families) | 27,000,000 | 19,500,000 | Several species such as *Fishus delicious* |
| CENTRARCHIDAE (Sunfish) | 15,500,000 | 19,000,000 | Several species such as *Micropterus salmoides* (Largemouth bass) and *M. dolomieui* (Smallmouth bass), two most important species |
| SALMONIDAE (Salmon) | No comparable data | 15,000,000 | Several species such as *Salmo clarki* (Cutthroat trout) *S. gairdneri* (Steelhead trout) *S. trutta* (Brown trout) *S. salar* (Atlantic salmon) *Salvelinus namaycush* (Lake trout) *S. fontinalis* (Brook trout) *Oncorhynchus gorbuscha* (Pink salmon) *O. tshawytscha* (Chinook salmon) *O. kisutch* (Coho salmon) *O. nerka* (Sockeye salmon) *O. keta* (Chum salmon) |
| ICTALURIDAE (Catfish) | 15,500,000 | 14,000,000 | Several species such as *Ictalurus* spp. |
| ESOCIDAE (Pike) | 7,000,000 | 5,000,000 | Several species such as *Esox lucius* (Northern pike) *E. masquinongy* (Muskie) *E. niger* (Chain pickerel) |

Table 10.3   (*Continued*)

| FAMILY | PERSONS FISHING, 1975 | PERSONS FISHING, 1980 | SPECIES |
|---|---|---|---|
| PERCIDAE (Perch) | 5,500,000 | 5,000,000 | Several species such as *Stizostedion vitreum* (Walleye) *S. canadense* (Sauger) |
| PERCICHTHYIDAE (Temperate bass) | No comparable data | 4,500,000 | Several species such as *Morone saxatilis* (Striped bass) *M. chrysops* (White bass) *M. americana* (White perch) |
| "PERCH" (Several families) | No comparable data | 1,500,000 | Several species such as *Perca flavescens* (Yellow perch) |

Sources: S-585, S-688.

Table 10.4   **Freshwater habitats fished by Americans in 1980**

| PERCENTAGE FISHING | KINDS OF HABITAT FISHED |
|---|---|
| 43 | Rivers and streams |
| 40 | Natural lakes and ponds |
| 40 | Artificial lakes and reservoirs (10 acres or bigger) |
| 23 | Artificial lakes and reservoirs (10 acres or smaller) |

Source: S-585.

*Saltwater Fishing*

In 1980, 29% of all Americans (aged 16 years and older) who fished went after saltwater species exclusively or at some time. They spent about $16 a day or $200 a year (S-585). In 1979, the top ten saltwater (and anadromous) fish families of the U.S. Atlantic and Gulf coasts were drum (Sciaenidae), bluefish (Pomatomidae), porgy (Sparidae), right-eye flounder (Pleuronectidae), sea catfish (Ariidae), sea bass (Serranidae), flounder (Bothidae), grunt (Pomadasyidae), snapper (Lutjanidae), and mackerel and tuna (Scombridae) (table 10.5). No recent national study on U.S. Pacific coast recreational fishing has been published. Saltwater fishing habitat preferences are described in table 10.6.

Table 10.5  **Marine (and anadromous) families (catches more than 1 million) fished recreationally by Americans on the Atlantic and Gulf coasts, 1979**

| FAMILY *(Number fish caught)* | GENUS/SPECIES | FISH CAUGHT BY GENUS/SPECIES |
|---|---|---|
| SCIAENIDAE Drum (75,562,000) | *Cynoscion* spp. | 26,857,000 |
| | *Leiostomus xanthurus* (Spot) | 18,480,000 |
| | *Micropogon undulatus* (Atlantic croaker) | 16,505,000 |
| | *Menticirrhus* spp. | 4,498,000 |
| | *Sciaenops ocellata* (Red drum) | 4,113,000 |
| | *Pogonias cromis* (Black drum) | 2,665,000 |
| | Others | 2,444,000 |
| POMATOMIDAE Bluefish (27,332,000) | *Pomatomus saltatrix* (Bluefish) | 27,332,000 |
| SPARIDAE Porgy (26,983,000) | *Lagodon rhomboides* (Pinfish) | 12,811,000 |
| | *Stenotomus* spp. | 7,601,000 |
| | Others | 6,571,000 |
| PLEURONECTIDAE Righteye flounder (22,554,000) | *Pseudopleuronectes americanus* (Winter flounder) | 22,554,000 |
| ARIIDAE Sea catfish (20,727,000) | *Bagre marinus* (Gafftopsail) *Arius felis* (Sea catfish) } | 20,727,000 |
| SERRANIDAE Sea bass (18,227,000) | *Centropristis* spp. | 8,301,000 |
| | *Morone americana* (White perch) | 5,494,000 |
| | *Diplectrum formosum* (Sand perch) | 1,834,000 |
| | Others | 1,417,000 |
| | *Morone saxatilis* (Striped bass) | 1,181,000 |
| BOTHIDAE Flounder (17,878,000) | *Paralichthys dentatus* (Summer flounder) *P. albigutta* (Gulf flounder) *P. lethostigma* (Southern flounder) } | 16,095,000 |
| | Others | 1,315,000 |
| | *Scophthalmus aquosus* (Windowpane) | 468,000 |

Table 10.5  (*Continued*)

| FAMILY<br>*(Number fish caught)* | GENUS/SPECIES | FISH CAUGHT<br>BY GENUS/SPECIES |
|---|---|---|
| POMADASYIDAE<br>Grunt<br>(10,598,000) | Others | 4,733,000 |
| | *Haemulon plumieri*<br>(White grunt) | 3,873,000 |
| | *Orthopristis chrysoptera*<br>(Pigfish) | 1,992,000 |
| LUTJANIDAE<br>Snapper<br>(9,363,000) | *Lutjanus campechanus*<br>(Red snapper) | 4,254,000 |
| | Others | 2,850,000 |
| | *Lutjanus griseus*<br>(Gray snapper) | 1,748,000 |
| | *Rhomboplites aurorubens*<br>(Vermillion snapper) | 511,000 |
| SCOMBRIDAE<br>Mackerel and tuna<br>(8,889,000) | *Scomber scombrus*<br>(Atlantic mackerel) | 4,043,000 |
| | *Scomberomorus maculatus*<br>(Spanish mackerel) | 2,209,000 |
| | *S. cavalla*<br>(King mackerel) | 994,000 |
| | *Sarda sarda*<br>(Atlantic bonito) | 578,000 |
| | *Euthynnus alletteratus*<br>(Little tunny) | 546,000 |
| | Others | 519,000 |
| MUGILIDAE<br>Mullet<br>(8,414,000) | *Mugil* spp. | 8,414,000 |
| LABRIDAE<br>Wrasse<br>(6,218,000) | *Tautogolabrus adspersus*<br>(Cunner) | 3,335,000 |
| | *Tautoga onitis*<br>(Tautog) | 2,883,000 |
| CLUPEIDAE<br>Herring<br>(6,109,000) | Several genera such as<br>*Alosa*<br>*Clupea*<br>*Brevoortia*<br>*Dorosoma*<br>*Harengula* | 6,109,000 |
| GADIDAE<br>Codfish<br>(6,023,000 +?) | *Gadus morhua*<br>(Atlantic cod) | 2,627,000 |
| | *Pollachius virens*<br>(Pollock) | 2,547,000 |
| | *Microgadus tomcod*<br>(Atlantic tomcod) | 849,000 |
| | Others | ? |

(*continued*)

Table 10.5  (*Continued*)

| FAMILY<br>(*Number fish caught*) | GENUS/SPECIES | FISH CAUGHT<br>BY GENUS/SPECIES |
|---|---|---|
| CARANGIDAE<br>Jack<br>(4,664,000) | Others<br>*Caranx hippos*<br>(Crevalle jack)<br>*C. crysos*<br>(Blue runner) | 1,810,000<br>1,556,000<br><br>1,298,000 |
| TRIGLIDAE<br>(3,757,000) | *Prionotus* spp.<br>*Bellator* spp. | 3,757,000 |
| CORYPHAENIDAE<br>Dolphin<br>(2,828,000) | *Coryphaena* spp. | 2,828,000 |
| BATRACHOIDIDAE<br>Toadfish<br>(1,313,000) | *Opsanus* spp. | 1,313,000 |

Source: S-687.

Table 10.6  **Saltwater habitats fished by Americans in 1980**

| PERCENTAGE FISHING | KINDS OF HABITAT FISHED |
|---|---|
| 55 | Surf and shore |
| 43 | Saltwater sounds, bays, tidal inlets, and streams |
| 37 | Deep sea |

Source: S-585.

## Recreational Hunting

Approximately 20 million Americans hunt annually (note 4). They spend $7.5 billion a year (average of 1975 and 1980). Tables 10.7 and 10.8 break down expenditures for travel and equipment costs for big game hunting, small game hunting, and migratory birds.

We conducted our own mail survey (described in chap. 4) of the 50 state, 10 provincial, and 2 territorial wildlife agencies in North America. (Appendix A lists the names and addresses of the respondents: only the State of Maryland and the Yukon Territory did not respond to the survey.) The 96.8% response to our wildlife survey provided all the tabulated information on the species hunted and the numbers killed. It should be noted that these numbers are only approximate (and largely underestimated) harvest figures due to uneven and incomplete data maintained by the agencies concerned.

Table 10.7  **Expenditures ($5.8 billion) by Americans on recreational hunting, 1975**

|  | TRAVEL | EQUIPMENT | PERCENTAGE OF TOTAL EXPENDITURE |
|---|---|---|---|
| Big game* | $1,767,437,000 | $794,127,000 | 44 |
| Small game* | $1,087,310,000 | $606,459,000 | 29 |
| Migratory birds* | $611,062,000 | $338,012,000 | 16 |
| Other game† | $231,582,000 | $125,451,000 | 6 |
| Percentage of total expenditure | 63 | 32 | ‡ |

Source: S-688.
*Exclusive of licenses.
†Exclusive of licenses and fees.
‡Percentages do not add to 100 because of missing data.

Table 10.9 lists the nine North American families in which more than 1 million animals were killed yearly by recreational hunters in Canada and the United States. They are—in order of importance—partridge, quails and pheasants (Phasianidae), doves and pigeons (Columbidae), ducks, geese, and swans (Anatidae), squirrels (Sciuridae), rabbits and hares (Leporidae), grouse (Tetraonidae), deer, elk, and moose (Cervidae), woodcock and snipe (Scolopacidae), and frogs (Ranidae).

Families in which fewer than 1 million animals were harvested annually appear in table 10.10. These eleven are coots and rails (Rallidae), crows and magpies (Corvidae), turkey (Meleagrididae), pigs (Suidae), pronghorn antelopes (Antilocapridae), peccaries (Tayassuidae), bears (Ursidae), cranes (Gruidae), softshell turtles (Trionychidae), goats, sheep, and bison (Bovidae), and porcupines (Erithizontidae).

## Nonconsumptive Wildlife Use

About 94.5 million Americans (or one in two) participate each year in some kind of nonconsumptive wildlife use. (By nonconsumptive we mean nonharvesting.) They spend $6.6 billion annually (fig. 10.1). While the number of participants in this nonconsumptive category is larger than the sum of all those persons who fish and who hunt, the expenditures are the least. This is not surprising. It costs very little to share one's lunch with pigeons and squirrels in the park or to stand on a river bank watching the salmon run or turn the TV channel to a show on giant pandas or observe the changing colors of autumn maple leaves.

Three questions are central to this discussion of nonconsumptive wildlife use in North America. First, where do people engage in the activity—at home or

(text continued on page 382)

**Table 10.8 Expenditures ($8.5 billion) by Americans on recreational hunting, 1980**

| | TRAVEL | EQUIPMENT | SPECIAL EQUIPMENT* | MISCELLANEOUS† | PERCENTAGE OF TOTAL EXPENDITURE |
|---|---|---|---|---|---|
| Big game | $1,670,227,000 | $1,119,424,000 | — | — | 32.5 |
| Small game | $958,596,000 | $704,840,000 | — | — | 19.5 |
| Migratory birds | $405,679,000 | $232,270,000 | — | — | 7.5 |
| Other game | $151,122,000 | $100,237,000 | — | — | 3.0 |
| Unspecified hunting | $245,779,000 | $2,260,000 | $2,518,402,000 | $436,311,000 | 37.5 |
| Percentage of total expenditure | 40 | 25 | 30 | 5 | 100 |

Source: S-585.

*Includes boats, vans, and similar vehicles.

†Includes magazine subscriptions, membership dues, land leasing, and ownership.

Table 10.9  North American nonfurbearing families with average annual harvest of more than 1 million animals, 1976–1980

| FAMILY (Mean harvest) | SPECIES | UNITED STATES + CANADA (Mean harvest) | UNITED STATES* (Mean harvest) | CANADA* (Mean harvest) |
|---|---|---|---|---|
| PHASIANIDAE (27,075,023) | *Colinus virginianus* Bobwhite quail | 11,744,134 | 11,744,134 | ND |
| | *Phasianus colchicus* Ring-necked pheasant | 7,418,413 | 7,334,764 | 83,649 |
| | Unspecified quails | 5,863,173 | 5,863,173 | ND |
| | *Alectoris chukar* Chukar partridge | 746,020 | 746,020 | ND |
| | *Perdix perdix* Gray partridge | 703,653 | 614,593 | 89,060 |
| | Unspecified pheasants | 465,344 | 465,344 | ND |
| | *Laphortyx gambelii* Gambel's quail | 67,579 | 67,579 | NO |
| | *Lophortyx californicus* California quail | 47,467 | 47,467 | ND |
| | *Callipepla squamata* Scaled quail | 17,452 | 17,452 | NO |
| | *Francolinus erckelii* Erckel's partridge | 659 | 659 | NO |
| | *Francolinus pondicerianus* Gray francolin | 531 | 531 | NO |
| | *Francolinus francolinus* Black partridge | 371 | 371 | NO |
| | *Coturnix japonica* Japanese quail | 227 | 227 | NO |

(continued)

Table 10.9  (*Continued*)

| FAMILY (Mean harvest) | SPECIES | UNITED STATES + CANADA (Mean harvest) | UNITED STATES* (Mean harvest) | CANADA* (Mean harvest) |
|---|---|---|---|---|
| COLUMBIDAE (27,045,149) | Unspecified doves | 13,570,427 | 13,570,427 | ND |
| | *Zenaida macroura* Mourning dove | 13,013,927 | 13,011,420 | 2,507 |
| | *Zenaida asiatica* White-winged dove | 299,243 | 299,243 | ND |
| | Unspecified pigeons | 94,876 | 74,668 | 20,208 |
| | *Columba fasciata* Band-tailed pigeon | 66,022 | 62,151 | 3,871 |
| | *Geopelia striata* Barred ground dove | 491 | 491 | NO |
| | *Streptopelia chinensis* Spotted dove | 163 | 163 | NO |
| ANATIDAE† (20,194,076) | *Anas platyrhynchos* Mallard | 6,524,618 | 4,885,997 | 1,638,621 |
| | *Anas crecca* Green-winged teal | 1,994,987 | 1,779,195 | 215,792 |
| | *Branta canadensis* Canada goose | 1,515,711 | 1,120,831 | 394,880 |
| | *Anas acuta* Pintail | 1,387,920 | 1,226,217 | 161,703 |
| | *Aix sponsa* Wood duck | 1,313,113 | 1,190,618 | 122,495 |

374

| Species | | | |
|---|---|---|---|
| *Anas americana* American wigeon | 1,112,180 | 979,820 | 132,360 |
| *Anas cyanoptera* Cinnamon teal and | 958,989 | 825,843 | 133,146 |
| *Anas discors* Blue-winged teal | | | |
| *Anas strepera* Gadwall | 948,268 | 842,412 | 105,856 |
| *Anas rubripes* Black duck | 697,206 | 344,136 | 353,070 |
| *Anser caerulescens* Snow goose | 619,392 | 480,237 | 139,155 |
| *Aythya collaris* Ring-necked duck | 614,284 | 496,355 | 117,929 |
| *Aythya affinis* Lesser scaup | 530,520 | 410,113 | 120,407 |
| *Anas clypeata* Northern shoveler | 476,074 | 425,303 | 50,771 |
| *Bucephala albeola* Bufflehead | 211,070 | 146,267 | 64,803 |
| *Aythya americana* Redhead | 208,004 | 155,562 | 52,442 |
| *Bucephala* spp. Unspecified goldeneyes | 201,767 | 91,460 | 110,307 |

(*continued*)

Table 10.9 *(Continued)*

| FAMILY (Mean harvest) | SPECIES | UNITED STATES + CANADA (Mean harvest) | UNITED STATES* (Mean harvest) | CANADA* (Mean harvest) |
|---|---|---|---|---|
| ANATIDAE† (continued) | *Anser albifrons* White-fronted goose | 172,049 | 107,725 | 64,324 |
| | *Aythya marila* Greater scaup | 138,254 | 78,749 | 59,505 |
| | *Melanitta* spp. Unspecified scoters | 116,311 | 49,220 | 67,091 |
| | *Aythya valisineria* Canvasback | 114,027 | 84,731 | 29,296 |
| | *Mergus cucullatus* Hooded merganser | 98,230 | 62,844 | 35,386 |
| | *Mergus* spp. Unspecified mergansers | 73,023 | 31,292 | 41,731 |
| | *Oxyura jamaicensis* Ruddy duck | 66,100 | 61,422 | 4,678 |
| | *Somateria* spp. Unspecified eiders | 46,049 | 16,349 | 29,700 |
| | *Clangula hyemalis* Oldsquaw | 28,164 | 12,385 | 15,779 |
| | *Anser rossii* Ross's goose | 9,914 | 4,496 | 5,418 |
| | Unspecified ducks and geese | 7,633 | 7,633 | ND |
| | *Branta bernicla* Brant goose | 6,295 | 5,245 | 1,050 |

| | | | |
|---|---|---|---|
| *Anser canagicus*<br>Emperor goose | 2,674 | 2,674 | ND |
| *Cygnus columbianus*<br>Whistling swan | 1,052 | 1,052 | ND |
| *Histrionicus histrionicus*<br>Harlequin duck | 198 | ND | 198 |
| SCIURIDAE<br>(19,903,763) | | | |
| Unspecified squirrels | 12,987,002 | 12,987,002 | ND |
| *Sciurus carolinensis*<br>Eastern gray squirrel | 4,509,327 | 4,509,327 | ND |
| *Sciurus niger*<br>Eastern fox squirrel | 1,717,292 | 1,717,292 | ND |
| *Marmota monax*<br>Woodchuck | 412,879 | 380,853 | 32,026 |
| *Cynomys* spp.<br>Prairie dog | 201,486 | 201,486 | ND |
| *Marmota flaviventris*<br>Yellow-bellied marmot | 62,494 | 62,494 | ND |
| *Tamiasciurus hudsonicus*<br>American red squirrel | 13,149 | 13,149 | ND |
| *Sciurus aberti*<br>Tassel-eared squirrel | 134 | 134 | NO |
| LEPORIDAE<br>(19,522,601) | | | |
| Unspecified cottontail rabbits | 10,065,913 | 9,783,658 | 282,255 |
| Unspecified rabbits | 5,991,677 | 5,991,677 | ND |
| *Lepus americanus*<br>Snowshoe hare | 3,368,239 | 1,065,032 | 2,303,207 |
| *Sylvilagus aquaticus*<br>Swamp rabbit | 96,772 | 96,772 | NO |

(continued)

Table 10.9  (*Continued*)

| FAMILY (*Mean harvest*) | SPECIES | UNITED STATES + CANADA (*Mean harvest*) | UNITED STATES* (*Mean harvest*) | CANADA* (*Mean harvest*) |
|---|---|---|---|---|
| TETRAONIDAE (5,653,477) | *Bonasa umbellus* Ruffed grouse | 3,434,609 | 2,369,413 | 1,065,196 |
| | Unspecified grouse | 1,373,601 | 721,877 | 651,724 |
| | *Tympanuchus phasianellus* Sharp-tailed grouse | 429,137 | 309,436 | 119,701 |
| | *Centrocercus urophasianus* Sage grouse | 196,386 | 196,386 | ND |
| | *Dendrogapus obscurus* Blue grouse | 88,862 | 88,862 | ND |
| | *Dendrogapus canadensis* Spruce grouse | 65,104 | 24,400 | 40,704 |
| | *Tympanuchus cupido* Prairie chicken | 64,040 | 64,040 | ND |
| | *Lagopus leucurus* White-tailed ptarmigan | 1,738 | 1,738 | ND |

378

| | | Total | U.S. | Canada |
|---|---|---|---|---|
| CERVIDAE (2,436,905) | *Odocoileus virginianus* Whitetail deer | 1,689,184 | 1,570,023 | 119,161 |
| | *Odocoileus hemionus* Mule deer | 315,028 | 308,938 | 6,090 |
| | *Odocoileus* spp. Unspecified deer | 289,571 | 261,362 | 28,209 |
| | *Cervus elaphus* Wapiti | 84,486 | 80,913 | 3,573 |
| | *Alces alces* Moose | 53,875 | 6,289 | 47,586 |
| | *Rangifer tarandus* Caribou | 4,550 | 1,400 | 3,150 |
| | *Cervus axis* Spotted deer | 211 | 211 | NO |
| SCOLOPACIDAE (1,500,162) | *Scolopax minor* American woodcock | 1,182,052 | 1,050,388 | 131,664 |
| | *Gallinago gallinago* Common snipe | 318,110 | 230,637 | 87,473 |
| RANIDAE (1,110,405) | *Rana catesbeiana* Bullfrog | 1,110,405 | 1,110,405 | ND |

Notes: ND = no data, NO = does not occur.
*Source: Mail survey (Appendix A).
†Source: U.S. data on Anatidae: A-1134–A-1136; Canadian data on Anatidae: V-331, V-332.

Table 10.10  North American nonfurbearing families with average annual harvest of fewer than 1 million animals, 1976–1980

| FAMILY (Mean harvest) | SPECIES | UNITED STATES + CANADA (Mean harvest) | UNITED STATES (Mean harvest) | CANADA (Mean harvest) |
|---|---|---|---|---|
| RALLIDAE (665,317) | Fulica americana American coot | 661,633 | 628,842 | 32,791 |
| | Rallus longirostris Clapper rail | 3,684 | 3,684 | ND |
| CORVIDAE (314,792) | Corvus brachyrhynchos Common crow | 288,462 | 276,062 | 12,400 |
| | Pica pica Common magpie | 26,330 | 26,330 | ND |
| MELEAGRIDIDAE (175,616) | Meleagris gallopavo Turkey | 175,616 | 175,567 | 49 |
| SUIDAE (95,550) | Unspecified pig | 95,550 | 95,550 | ND |
| ANTILOCAPRIDAE (87,173) | Antilocapra americana Pronghorn | 87,173 | 84,641 | 2,532 |
| TAYASSUIDAE (18,989) | Tayassu tajacu Collared peccary | 18,989 | 18,989 | NO |
| URSIDAE (16,058) | Ursus americanus American black bear | 15,246 | 15,246 | ND |
| | Ursus arctos Brown bear | 812 | 812 | ND |
| GRUIDAE (8,551) | Grus canadensis Sandhill crane | 8,327 | 5,875 | 2,452 |
| | Unspecified cranes | 224 | 224 | ND |

| | First | Second | Third |
|---|---|---|---|
| **TRIONYCHIDAE** (7,000) | | | |
| *Trionyx spiniferus* Spiny softshell turtle | 7,000 | 7,000 | ND |
| **BOVIDAE** (6,520) | | | |
| *Oreamnos americanus* Mountain goat | 2,053 | 1,141 | 912 |
| *Ovis canadensis* American bighorn | 1,265 | 535 | 730 |
| *Ovis dalli* Dall sheep | 1,106 | 1,065 | 41 |
| Feral sheep | 717 | 717 | ND |
| Feral goats | 627 | 627 | ND |
| *Ovis dalli* Dall sheep and *Ovis canadensis* American bighorn | 485 | ND | 485 |
| *Ammotragus lervia* Barbary sheep | 102 | 102 | NO |
| *Bison bison* American bison | 83 | 83 | ND |
| *Ovis orientalis* Mouflon | 57 | 57 | NO |
| Unspecified oryx | 16 | 16 | NO |
| *Capra ibex* Ibex | 9 | 9 | NO |
| **ERITHIZONTIDAE** (6,363) | | | |
| *Erithizon dorsatum* North American porcupine | 6,363 | 6,038 | 325 |

Source: Mail survey (Appendix A).
Notes: ND = no data, NO = does not occur.

away from home? Second, what are the main activities carried out both at home and away from home? Third, what is the motivation behind pursuing nonconsumptive activities—a generalized interest in wildlife or targeted interests in particular species or groups of species?

The first and second questions can be answered together. The 1980 U.S. national survey showed that activities whose primary purpose was nonconsumptive wildlife use were undertaken by 79.7 million Americans (or 47% of the population) at home (defined as areas within one mile of the house) and 28.8 million Americans (or 17% of the population) away from home (S-585). Of this latter group, 90% stayed within the home state, 24% visited another state, and 4% traveled outside the United States. (Visits to state and national parks are discussed in the Parks subsection of this chapter.) Table 10.11 lists residential and nonresidential activities. From this table emerge the three largest activity categories—observing, feeding, and photographing wildlife.

A comparison between American and Canadian (represented by the Province of Quebec—the second most populated province in Canada) expenditures on nonconsumptive wildlife pursuits reveals the following strong consistencies (figs. 10.2 and 10.3): travel accounts for 61% of U.S. and 58% of Quebec expenditures; photography for 16% of U.S. and optics (photography plus binoculars, etc.) for 23% of Quebec expenditures; in both cases 9% is spent on wild birds for seed, feeders, nest boxes, and so forth.

This leads to the third question: Are the nonconsumptive activities the result of a generalized interest in wildlife or do people actively seek out particular

---

Table 10.11  **Primary nonconsumptive wildlife activities enjoyed by Americans in 1980**

| AT HOME | | AWAY FROM HOME | |
|---|---|---|---|
| *Percent** | *Activity* | *Percent** | *Activity* |
| 37 | Feeding wild birds | 99 | Observing wildlife |
| 33 | Observing wildlife | 34 | Feeding wildlife |
| 12 | Feeding wildlife other than birds | 20 | Photographing wildlife |
| 8 | Visiting parks and natural areas (within one mile of home) | 6 | Scouting activities |
| 7 | Photographing wildlife | | |
| 7 | Maintaining food plants and cover plants for wildlife | | |
| 6 | Maintaining natural areas ($\frac{1}{4}$ acre and larger) for wildlife | | |

Source: S-585.
*Percentages do not add to 100 because of multiple responses.

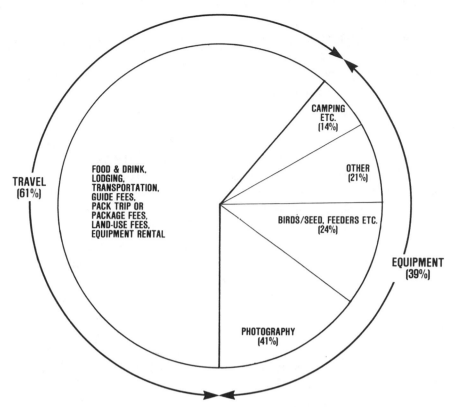

Fig. 10.2  **Expenditures of Americans ($6.6 billion) on recreational nonconsumptive wildlife use, 1980. Source: S-585**

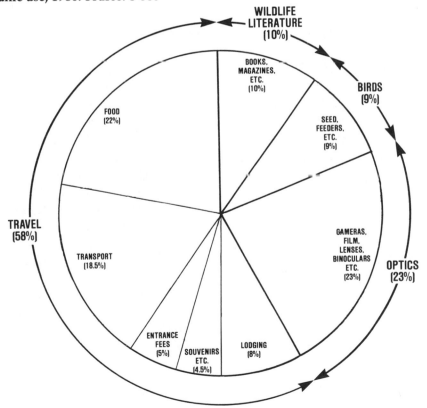

Fig. 10.3  **Expenditures of Quebec residents (Can $210.6 million) on recreational nonconsumptive wildlife use, 1980. Source: J-556**

species or groups of species to observe, feed, and photograph? The answer seems to be: It depends on the activity.

In the United States, 100 million persons attended zoos in 1979 (J-499). In fact more people visit the Bronx Zoo in the month of July than visit all the national parks of Africa in a year (A-772). A survey showed that for 24% of zoo visitors, the primary reason for visiting a zoo was a personal fascination with wild animals; for 11% the aesthetic appeal of the animals counted as the primary reason (J-499). These responses and others led the investigator, Stephen Kellert, to conclude that there were indications that visitors to zoos were motivated more by generalized affection for animals than by specific intellectual curiosity or attraction to wildlife and the out-of-doors. There are probably many more nonconsumptive activities that stem from a generalized affection for and appreciation of wildlife, such as a spring walk in the woods to enjoy the sights and smells of newly emerging flowers and foliage or a late summer's evening drive to spot whatever creatures might be up and about such as deer, jackrabbits, porcupine, raccoons, and owls.

There are also certain pleasures people pursue that are definitely geared if not to individual species, then to specific groups of species. Two of the more salient of these are bird watching and whale watching.

Whale watching became an internationally organized industry in 1971 (A-1201). In 1981 it was estimated to have generated between $5 and $6 million worth of business (A-1205). A 1983 paper reported that whale watching trips were now being offered in Argentina, the Bahamas, Canada, Mexico, New Zealand, Sri Lanka, St. Lucia, and the United States (M-667). (Also, trips to watch dolphins take place in the British colony of Gibraltar [A-1205, M-667].) The United States (in particular, the west coast) accounts for much of the whale watching business (A-1201). The states that offer whale watching trips are—on the Pacific side—California, Oregon, Washington, Alaska, and Hawaii; on the Atlantic side—New Hampshire, Maine, Massachusetts, and Maryland. The Canadian provinces include British Columbia in the west: Manitoba and the Northwest Territories in the north: Quebec, New Brunswick, and Newfoundland in the east (A-1205, M-667). The main whale species involved are minkes (*Balaenoptera acutorostrata*) in Atlantic Canada; humpbacks (*Megaptera novaeangliae*) in Atlantic Canada, the Atlantic United States plus Alaska and Hawaii; white whales or belugas (*Delphinapterus leucas*) in three Canadian regions—Hudson's Bay, Baffin Bay, and the Gulf of St. Lawrence; killer whales (*Orcinus orca*) in Washington state; gray whales (*Eschrichtius gibbosus*) from Alaska to Mexico.

Whale watching provides much needed steady revenue for individuals such as fishing boat operators whose boats during the winter season no longer have to lay idle, and even for cities. For example, in San Diego (California) the Chamber of Commerce promotes whale watching as a major attraction for the city and distributes brochures in all the hotels and tourist centers (J-562). For Churchill (Manitoba), not only beluga whales but also polar bears, snow geese, and rock ptarmigans are important tourist attractions that lure visitors from all over Canada, the United States, Europe, and Japan (G-448).

Wild birds seem to be at the receiving end of a great deal of enthusiastic nonconsumptive human activity, whether it is observation, feeding, or photography. As figures 10.2 and 10.3 illustrate, the amount of money spent annually on wild birds is a sizable percentage of the total expenditures on nonconsumptive wildlife use. No other class of animal figures so prominently. In the United States about $618 million are spent annually on wild birdseed, bird feeders, bird baths, birdhouses, and nest boxes (S-585); and in just one province in Canada over $17.3 million (converted to U.S.$) are spent each year in the same ways (J-556). These sums, impressive as they are, underestimate the total amount of money spent on wild birds, which would include the following: a percentage of all photographic equipment and film sold as well as film processing costs; a percentage of all binoculars sold (the percentage range indicated in table 10.12 may well be too high, underestimating the large proportion of binoculars bought for boating, watching football, and other activities not related to birds or other wildlife); sales of general books on birds; sales of field guides on birds; and membership fees in avian societies. Table 10.12 compares the total expenditures on wild birds estimated in a 1974 study (P-427) with expenditures in 1980 (S-585).

Birds are the class of animals most fed, most observed, and most photographed by the 79.7 million Americans who, from their homes, participate in activities primarily geared to nonconsumptive wildlife use (tables 10.13–10.15). (Again a reminder that the term *at home* includes areas within one mile of the house.) Among the birds, songbirds appear to be the most popular, closely followed by waterfowl and birds of prey. Nonavian species to which people are attracted include among the mammals—squirrels, chipmunks, rabbits, hares, deer, and raccoons; and among the arthropods—butterflies, spiders, and beetles.

For the 28.8 million Americans who travel away from home to observe, photograph, and feed wildlife, mammals slightly edge out birds as the objects on which the majority of eyes, lenses, and picnic basket contents are focused (table 10.16). Squirrels, chipmunks, deer, rabbits, and hares are the top mammals; waterfowl, songbirds, and birds of prey the top birds; butterflies, spiders, and beetles the top arthropods. In North America there are even famous areas—the coast region of Texas, Cape May in New Jersey, Point Pelee in Lake Erie, and strategic sites along the Pacific Coast—where the seasonal gathering of bird enthusiasts is an annual tourist event (A-1202).

It is interesting to compare these findings of the 1980 U.S. Fish and Wildlife Survey (S-585) on the wild animals most observed, fed, and photographed, with a list that emerged from Stephen Kellert's surveys on public preference for animal

*(text continued on page 391)*

Table 10.12  **Expenditures on wild birds by Americans, 1974 and 1980**

| EXPENDITURE CATEGORIES | 1974 EXPENDITURES*<br>*(Rounded U.S.$)* | 1980 EXPENDITURES†<br>*(Rounded U.S.$)* |
|---|---|---|
| 4% of all photographic expenditures | 190,000,000 | ? |
| Birdseed | 170,000,000 | 517,000,000 |
| 50–66% of all binocular sales | 115,000,000 | ? |
| Bird feeders, houses, nestboxes | 15,000,000 | 75,000,000 |
| Bird baths | ? | 26,000,000 |
| General bird books | 4,000,000 | ? |
| Bird field guides | 3,000,000 | ? |
| Bird society fees | 3,000,000 | ? |
| TOTAL | 500,000,000 +? | 618,000,000 +? |

*Source: P-427.
†Source: S-585.

Table 10.13  **Wildlife fed by 83.3 million Americans at home, 1980**

| WILD ANIMALS FED<br>*(Persons feeding)* | KIND OF FOOD USED (%)*<br>*(Species fed)* |
|---|---|
| Birds<br>(62,463,000) | Crumbs and scraps (73.8)<br>(?) |
| | Seed (55.9)<br>(Sparrows, finches, grosbeaks, doves, etc.) |
| | Suet (16.2)<br>(Chickadees, titmice, jays, woodpeckers, etc.) |
| | Other (10.9)<br>(?) |
| | Sugar water (6.5)<br>(Hummingbirds) |
| Other wildlife<br>(20,833,000) | ? |

Sources: A-1202, S-585.
*Percentages do not add to 100 because of multiple responses.

Table 10.14  **Wildlife observed by 55.9 million Americans at home, 1980**

| CLASS | SPECIES/SPECIES GROUP | OBSERVERS (Percentage of total)* |
|---|---|---|
| AVES<br>Birds | Songbirds | 50,172,158<br>(89.8) |
| | Birds of prey | 17,208,268<br>(30.8) |
| | Waterfowl | 16,873,042<br>(30.2) |
| | Upland game birds | 13,576,653<br>(24.3) |
| | Shorebirds | 6,201,681<br>(11.1) |
| MAMMALIA<br>Mammals | Squirrels, chipmunks | 38,942,087<br>(69.7) |
| | Rabbits, hares | 28,941,178<br>(51.8) |
| | Raccoons | 11,174,200<br>(20) |
| | Deer | 10,727,232<br>(19.2) |
| | Other small mammals | 9,721,554<br>(17.4) |
| | Coyotes, wolves | 2,290,711<br>(4.1) |
| | Other large mammals | 893,936<br>(1.6) |
| SEVERAL CLASSES<br>Arthropods | Butterflies | 28,103,113<br>(50.3) |
| | Spiders, beetles, other insects | 23,912,788<br>(42.8) |
| AMPHIBIA AND REPTILIA<br>Amphibians and reptiles | Amphibians, reptiles | 17,822,849<br>(31.9) |
| SEVERAL CLASSES<br>Fish | Fish | 5,642,971<br>(10.1) |

Source: S-585.
*Percentages do not add to 100 because of multiple responses.

Table 10.15 **Wildlife photographed by 12,401 Americans at home, 1980**

| CLASS | SPECIES/SPECIES GROUP | PHOTOGRAPHERS *(Percentage of total)** |
|---|---|---|
| AVES<br>Birds | Songbirds | 6,615<br>(53.3) |
| | Waterfowl | 2,021<br>(16.3) |
| | Birds of prey | 1,251<br>(10.1) |
| | Shorebirds | 780<br>(6.3) |
| | Upland game birds | 675<br>(5.4) |
| MAMMALIA<br>Mammals | Squirrels, chipmunks | 3,888<br>(31.4) |
| | Rabbits, hares | 1,918<br>(15.5) |
| | Deer | 1,182<br>(9.5) |
| | Raccoons | 717<br>(5.8) |
| | Other small mammals | 531<br>(4.3) |
| | Other large mammals | 186<br>(1.5) |
| SEVERAL CLASSES<br>Arthropods | Butterflies | 1,232<br>(9.9) |
| | Spiders, beetles, other insects | 806<br>(6.5) |
| AMPHIBIA AND REPTILIA<br>Amphibians and reptiles | Amphibians, reptiles | 170<br>(5.7) |
| SEVERAL CLASSES<br>Fish | Fish | 466<br>(3.8) |

Source: S-585.
*Percentages do not add to 100 because of multiple responses.

Table 10.16 **Wildlife fed, observed, or photographed by 28.8 million Americans away from home, 1980**

| CLASS | SPECIES/SPECIES GROUP | PARTICIPANTS *(Percentage of total)** |
|---|---|---|
| MAMMALIA<br>Mammals | Squirrels, chipmunks | 19,800,714<br>(68.7) |
| | Deer | 15,073,906<br>(52.3) |
| | Rabbits, hares | 15,045,084<br>(52.2) |
| | Other small mammals | 9,568,904<br>(33.2) |
| | Coyotes, wolves | 3,314,530<br>(11.5) |
| | Marine mammals | 2,911,022<br>(10.1) |
| | Other large mammals | 2,363,404<br>(8.2) |
| | Bears | 2,248,116<br>(7.8) |
| | Elk | 1,988,718<br>(6.9) |
| AVES<br>Birds | Waterfowl | 18,936,054<br>(65.7) |
| | Songbirds | 18,129,038<br>(62.9) |
| | Birds of prey | 14,266,890<br>(49.5) |
| | Upland game birds | 10,174,166<br>(35.3) |
| | Shorebirds | 8,531,312<br>(29.6) |
| SEVERAL CLASSES<br>Arthropods | Butterflies | 12,191,706<br>(42.3) |
| | Spiders, beetles, other insects | 11,499,978<br>(39.9) |
| SEVERAL CLASSES<br>Fish | Other fish | 8,012,516<br>(27.8) |
| | Trout, salmon | 4,323,300<br>(15) |
| AMPHIBIA AND REPTILIA<br>Amphibians and reptiles | Amphibians, reptiles | 11,874,664<br>(41.2) |

Source: S-585.
*Percentages do not add to 100 because of multiple responses.

**Table 10.17  Order of preference of Americans for selected animal species, 1978**

| LIKE | | MIXED FEELINGS | | DISLIKE | |
|---|---|---|---|---|---|
| Domesticated | Wild | Domesticated | Wild | Domesticated | Wild |
| 1 Dog | 3 Swan | | 21 Wolf | | 25 Skunk |
| 2 Horse | 4 Robin | | 22 Coyote | | 26 Shark |
| | 5 Butterfly | | 23 Crow | | 27 Vulture |
| | 6 Trout | | 24 Lizard | | 28 Bat |
| | 7 Salmon | | | | 29 Rattlesnake |
| | 8 Eagle | | | | 30 Wasp |
| | 9 Elephant | | | | 31 Rat |
| | 10 Owl | | | | 32 Mosquito |
| | 11 Turtle | | | | 33 Cockroach |
| 12 Cat | 13 Ladybug | | | | |
| | 14 Raccoon | | | | |
| | 15 Moose | | | | |
| | 16 Whale | | | | |
| | 17 Walrus | | | | |
| | 18 Bear | | | | |
| | 19 Frog | | | | |
| | 20 Gorilla | | | | |

Source: J-75.

390

species (J-75). Participants were given a list of the names of 33 domesticated and wild animals. The response range to each name went from "strongly like" to "strongly dislike." The preferred wild species were swans, robins, butterflies, trout, salmon, eagles, elephants, owls, turtles, ladybugs, raccoons, moose, whales, walruses, bears, frogs, and gorillas. Mixed feelings were expressed about wolves, coyotes, crows, and lizards. Disliked species included skunks, sharks, vultures, bats, rattlesnakes, wasps, rats, mosquitoes, and cockroaches (table 10.17).

Of course it is not possible to know the reason behind each person's affection for, or attraction to, a particular wild species or group of wild species, but broad predictions can be made on at least five stimuli that most certainly are at work in many cases: familiarity with a species; approachability of a species; aesthetic appeal of a species; cultural/symbolic/historic value of a species; and capability of a species to elicit empathy.

The first stimulus is familiarity with a species. Several wild species (for example, robins, pigeons, sparrows, and squirrels) have the ability not just to survive but to thrive in habitats that are not only heavily altered but are densely populated with humans, such as inner city parks and the suburbs. For many urban and semiurban dwellers, these familiar species represent the core of pleasurable wildlife (as opposed to threatening—rats—or repugnant—cockroaches—or irritating—mosquitoes) with which they will have a constant, close, and comfortable association for much of their lives. The second stimulus is approachability of a species or, to adapt the "user-friendly" terminology of computer jargon, its ability to be observer-friendly and feeder-friendly. A wild bird feeding from the hand really does seem to be worth two in the bush. The third stimulus is the aesthetic appeal of a species. This may be an especially important factor in the favorable attitude of humans to certain invertebrates such as butterflies, ladybugs, sea cucumbers, and starfish; to vertebrates such as frogs, lizards, and snakes; and to plants such as cacti and redwoods.

The fourth stimulus is the cultural or historic value of a species. This may influence many North Americans' positive feelings about predatory birds such as golden and bald eagles, game species such as trout, salmon, and moose, fur species such as beaver and fox. The symbolic relationship that certain species have with the wild applies here as well—such as bighorn sheep and the high Rockies, walrus and the Arctic, waterfowl and marshes, whales and the deep oceans. Certain animal sounds have become particularly evocative of North American wild places—the howling of wolves, the yapping of coyotes, the honking of Canada geese. The fifth stimulus is the range of behavior exhibited by wild animals with which people can identify—playfulness and deadliness, curiosity and shyness, carelessness and concentration, dexterity and clumsiness, courage and fearfulness, stillness and speed, selfishness and altruism, endurance and frailty, power and vulnerability.

## Parks

In 1872 the world's first national park was established at Yellowstone, Wyoming. Thirteen years later Canada opened its first national park in Banff, Alberta (D-482). In the 100 years that have passed since then, visits to state, provincial/territorial, and national parks have grown into a major form of outdoor recreation for millions of Americans and Canadians. Wildlife consumptive activities such as fishing are enjoyed as well as nonconsumptive activities such as nature walks.

We conducted a mail survey of the 50 state park agencies in the United States and the 12 provincial and territorial park agencies in Canada. Appendix D lists the respondents. Only Alabama, Georgia, New Jersey, and Saskatchewan would not participate in the survey. The 93.5% response provided all of the subnational park attendance and revenue data. Information on national parks was contributed by the National Parks Service in Washington and Parks Canada in Ottawa.

Table 10.18 **Fifteen American states with average annual attendance in state parks of more than 10 million persons, 1976–1980**

| STATE | STATE PARK ANNUAL ATTENDANCE* | STATE POPULATION† |
|---|---|---|
| California | 55,159,857 | 23,668,000 |
| New York | 41,087,000 | 17,558,000 |
| Ohio | 40,413,949 | 10,798,000 |
| Washington | 36,688,072 | 4,132,000 |
| Pennsylvania | 35,936,048 | 11,864,000 |
| Oregon | 32,740,766 | 2,633,000 |
| Illinois | 30,925,390 | 11,427,000 |
| Kentucky | 29,815,397 | 3,661,000 |
| Michigan | 22,044,798 | 9,262,000 |
| Oklahoma | 19,578,266 | 3,025,000 |
| Hawaii | 16,843,000 | 965,000 |
| Tennessee | 16,247,257 | 4,591,000 |
| Texas | 14,674,685 | 14,229,000 |
| Iowa | 14,546,336 | 2,914,000 |
| South Carolina | 11,059,909 | 3,122,000 |

Note: Attendance data not supplied by the following five respondents: Alaska, Louisiana, Massachusetts, Rhode Island, and Wyoming.
*Source: Mail survey (Appendix D).
†Source: S-799.

**Table 10.19  Twenty-seven American states with average annual attendance in state parks of fewer than 10 million persons, 1976–1980**

| STATE | STATE PARK ANNUAL ATTENDANCE* | STATE POPULATION† |
|---|---|---|
| Missouri | 9,607,690 | 4,917,000 |
| Wisconsin | 8,539,226 | 4,706,000 |
| Indiana | 7,475,493 | 5,490,000 |
| Nebraska | 7,428,000 | 1,570,000 |
| Connecticut | 7,395,757 | 3,108,000 |
| Utah | 6,571,616 | 1,461,000 |
| West Virginia | 6,506,548 | 1,950,000 |
| Minnesota | 6,387,342 | 4,076,000 |
| Maryland | 5,680,809 | 4,217,000 |
| Colorado | 5,661,902 | 2,890,000 |
| Arkansas | 5,629,063 | 2,286,000 |
| Kansas | 4,646,870 | 2,364,000 |
| North Carolina | 4,639,181 | 5,882,000 |
| New Hampshire | 4,037,389 | 921,000 |
| Mississippi | 3,875,986 | 2,521,000 |
| New Mexico | 3,351,015 | 1,303,000 |
| Florida | 3,159,237 | 9,746,000 |
| Virginia | 3,156,750 | 5,347,000 |
| Nevada | 3,004,558 | 800,000 |
| Delaware | 2,738,911 | 594,000 |
| Montana | 2,551,795 | 787,000 |
| Arizona | 2,192,501 | 2,718,000 |
| Idaho | 1,941,769 | 944,000 |
| Maine | 1,885,350 | 1,125,000 |
| South Dakota | 1,168,644 | 691,000 |
| North Dakota | 1,036,390 | 653,000 |
| Vermont | 848,927 | 511,000 |

Note: Attendance data not supplied by the following five respondents: Alaska, Louisiana, Massachusetts, Rhode Island, and Wyoming.
*Source: Mail survey (Appendix D).
†Source: S-799.

Table 10.20  **Ratio of the average annual number of visitors to state parks in the United States to the population of those same states, 1976–1980**

| STATE | RATIO: PERSONS ATTENDING STATE PARKS TO PERSONS LIVING IN STATE |
|---|---|
| Hawaii | 18:1 |
| Oregon | 12:1 |
| Washington | 9:1 |
| Kentucky | 8:1 |
| Oklahoma | 7:1 |
| Delaware | 5:1 |
| Iowa | 5:1 |
| Nebraska | 5:1 |
| Utah | 5:1 |
| Ohio | 4:1 |
| Nevada | 4:1 |
| New Hampshire | 4:1 |
| South Carolina | 4:1 |
| Tennessee | 4:1 |
| Arkansas | 3:1 |
| Illinois | 3:1 |
| Montana | 3:1 |
| New Mexico | 3:1 |
| Pennsylvania | 3:1 |
| West Virginia | 3:1 |
| California | 2:1 |
| Colorado | 2:1 |
| Connecticut | 2:1 |
| Idaho | 2:1 |
| Kansas | 2:1 |
| Maine | 2:1 |
| Michigan | 2:1 |
| Minnesota | 2:1 |
| Mississippi | 2:1 |
| Missouri | 2:1 |
| New York | 2:1 |
| North Dakota | 2:1 |
| South Dakota | 2:1 |
| Vermont | 2:1 |
| Wisconsin | 2:1 |
| Indiana | 1:1 |
| Maryland | 1:1 |
| Texas | 1:1 |
| Virginia | 1:1 |
| Arizona | State park attendance less than state population |
| Florida | State park attendance less than state population |
| North Carolina | State park attendance less than state population |

Sources: Tables 10.18, 10.19.

Table 10.21   **Eighteen American states with state parks' average annual revenue of more than $1 million, 1976–1980**

| STATE | AVERAGE ANNUAL REVENUE (U.S.$) |
|---|---|
| California | 13,395,091 |
| Oklahoma | 9,701,142 |
| Tennessee | 8,432,266 |
| Michigan | 8,293,246 |
| Maryland | 5,859,187 |
| Arkansas | 3,681,888 |
| Texas | 3,633,680 |
| Indiana | 3,149,626 |
| Ohio | 3,129,178 |
| Wisconsin | 2,877,000 |
| New York | 2,836,200 |
| Oregon | 2,757,224 |
| New Hampshire | 2,658,211 |
| South Carolina | 2,500,000 |
| Minnesota | 2,213,000 |
| Mississippi | 2,085,144 |
| Washington | 1,816,928 |
| Colorado | 1,446,114 |

Source: Mail survey (Appendix D).
Note: Revenue data not supplied by the following eight respondents: Alaska, Florida, Kentucky, Louisiana, Massachusetts, North Carolina, Pennsylvania, and Utah.

Tables 10.18–10.22 list state park attendance and revenue figures state by state. Between 1976 and 1980, annual attendance at state parks (for 12 states) averaged 538,879,449 persons. Roughly projected to 50 states, this figure would rise to 640 million persons. Both actual and projected state park attendance figures are double the average annual number of visitors (160,777,142) recorded during 1978, 1979, and 1980 at the following National Park System classes of areas: National Lakeshores, National Monuments, National Parks, National Parkways, National Preserves, National Recreation Areas, National Rivers, National Seashores, National Scenic Trails, National Capital Parks, and Parks—Other (S-734–S-736).

The most visited state parks are not necessarily within the most populated states, as table 10.20 demonstrates. The ratio of state park visitors to the resident population of a state may be regarded as an attraction index. Attraction

Table 10.22  **Twenty-one American states with state parks' average annual revenue of less than $1 million, 1976–1980**

| STATE | AVERAGE ANNUAL REVENUE (U.S.$) |
|---|---|
| Delaware | 957,953 |
| Nebraska | 942,745 |
| Illinois | 924,532 |
| Connecticut | 896,948 |
| Vermont | 868,923 |
| Missouri | 780,053 |
| Rhode Island | 766,122 |
| Kansas | 625,578 |
| Iowa | 615,445 |
| Virginia | 583,603 |
| New Mexico | 566,000 |
| Arizona | 503,608 |
| Maine | 498,318 |
| Hawaii | 419,712 |
| South Dakota | 397,357 |
| Nevada | 368,918 |
| West Virginia | 194,745 |
| North Dakota | 176,636 |
| Idaho | 176,069 |
| Montana | 78,677 |
| Wyoming | 55,879 |

Source: Mail survey (Appendix D).
Note: Revenue data not supplied by the following eight respondents: Alaska, Florida, Kentucky, Louisiana, Massachusetts, North Carolina, Pennsylvania, and Utah.

indices of Hawaii, Oregon, Washington, Kentucky, Oklahoma, Delaware, Iowa, Nebraska, and Utah are at least five—state park visitors outnumbering the state population by at least five times. Why state parks in these states are so much more attractive than those elsewhere is not known. Reasons (other than better attendance records) might include particular scenery or wildlife; activities such as excellent swimming, fishing, and cross-country skiing; a popular range of accommodations from camping to four-star hotels; easy access; and effective promotion.

Only surveys of park visitors could determine what attracts the public to a

Table 10.23    **Synopsis of Florida's 1981 Myakka River State Park visitor wildlife observation survey**

Number of respondents 628
Mean time in park 2 hours 39 minutes
Mean distance traveled to reach park 45 miles

| Reason for visit | | |
|---|---|---|
| | (1) to observe wildlife | 44% |
| | (2) other reason | 31 |
| | (3) to picnic | 11 |
| | (4) to day hike | 8 |
| | (5) to fish | 4 |
| | (6) to camp | 2 |

Wildlife species expected to be seen in park in priority order
        (1) alligators
        (2) deer
        (3) feral pigs
        (4) birds
        (5) armadillo
        (6) raccoon

Most commonly observed species during visit
        (1) alligators
        (2) deer
        (3) birds
        (4) feral pigs
        (5) squirrels

| Rating of wildlife observation in park | | |
|---|---|---|
| | (1) good | 39% |
| | (2) satisfactory | 26 |
| | (3) outstanding | 23 |
| | (4) disappointing | 11 |
| | (5) very disappointing | 1 |

particular park or system of parks. In our mail survey of park agencies, we asked for the findings of any visitor interest surveys that had been conducted. Of the findings we received, just one—for Florida's Myakka River State Park—was specifically targeted to nonconsumptive wildlife use (in particular to wildlife observation). A synopsis of some of the Myakka River results is found in table 10.23.

The average annual revenue generated by the state park systems of 39 states was $91,862,946. Roughly projected to 50 states, this sum would climb to $118 million. State park revenue is several times greater than the $20,739,601 generated annually by the National Park System. The combined revenue of the state and national systems is $113–139 million a year.

In Canada, average annual provincial park attendance figures for the period 1976–1980 are as follows: 35,555,231 persons (reported by nine provinces) or

Table 10.24 **Average annual attendance in the provincial parks of nine Canadian provinces, 1976–1980**

| PROVINCE | PROVINCIAL PARK ANNUAL ATTENDANCE* | PROVINCIAL POPULATION† |
|---|---|---|
| British Columbia | 11,933,974 | 2,744,467 |
| Ontario | 9,598,637 | 8,625,107 |
| Alberta | 3,922,682‡ | 2,237,724 |
| New Brunswick | 2,944,558 | 696,403 |
| Newfoundland | 2,795,323 | 567,681 |
| Manitoba | 2,693,174 | 1,026,241 |
| Quebec | 868,544 | 6,438,403 |
| Prince Edward Island | 653,883 | 122,506 |
| Nova Scotia | 144,456 | 847,442 |

Note: Attendance data not supplied by the following two respondents: Northwest Territories and Yukon Territory.
*Source: Mail survey (Appendix D).
†Source: S-698.
‡1979–1980 average.

Table 10.25 **Average annual revenue from provincial/territorial parks of seven Canadian provinces/territories, 1976–1980**

| PROVINCE/TERRITORY | AVERAGE ANNUAL REVENUE (U.S.$) |
|---|---|
| British Columbia | 2,772,505 |
| Manitoba | 577,899 |
| Alberta | 459,638 |
| Prince Edward Island | 328,202 |
| Newfoundland | 267,590 |
| Nova Scotia | 196,524 |
| Northwest Territories | 4,459 |

Source: Mail survey (Appendix D); Canadian dollars converted to U.S. dollars at exchange rate of 0.91, which was average annual rate for the period of 1976–1980 (D-450).
Note: Revenue data not supplied by the following four respondents: New Brunswick, Ontario, Quebec, and Yukon Territory.

Table 10.26   **Ratio of the average annual number of visitors to provincial parks in Canada to the population of those same provinces, 1976–1980**

| PROVINCE | RATIO: PERSONS ATTENDING PROVINCIAL PARKS TO PERSONS LIVING IN PROVINCE |
|---|---|
| Prince Edward Island | 5:1 |
| Newfoundland | 5:1 |
| New Brunswick | 4:1 |
| British Columbia | 4:1 |
| Manitoba | 3:1 |
| Alberta | 2:1 |
| Ontario | 1:1 |
| Quebec | Provincial park attendance less than provincial population |
| Nova Scotia | Provincial park attendance less than provincial population |

Source: Table 10.24.

47,406,974 persons (projected to 12 provinces and territories) (table 10.24). Like their United States' counterparts, provincial and territorial parks welcome about twice the number of visitors who attend Canadian national parks (calculated to be about 19,164,553 annually) (P-447). Unlike the United States, national parks in Canada take in more money than do the provincial and territorial parks. Average annual park revenue generated by seven provinces and territories was $4,606,817 ($8 million if projected to 12 provinces and territories) (table 10.25). National park revenue was $10,073,700. (Canadian dollars were converted to U.S. dollars at the average annual exchange rate for 1976–1980 of 0.91 [D-450].) The combined revenue of the provincial, territorial, and national systems is $15–18 million a year. Again provincial park attendance does not necessarily reflect population size (table 10.26). Prince Edward Island and Newfoundland have the highest provincial park attraction indices in Canada.

# 11

# Toward a Biogeography of Wildlife Use

Throughout this book we have considered North American uses of wildlife sector by sector: timber, fisheries, trapping, medicine, agriculture, recreation, and so on. As we noted in the introduction, the very business of using wildlife can bring these sectors together—a single ecosystem supplying resources for several different interest groups.

The ecosystem is the unifying concept both biologically (as the system in which wild species interact with one another) and for management purposes (as the system in which the users of wildlife interact with one another as well as with the wild species). Hence it is of value to know what are the most important ecosystems economically and what are the main sectors using the wildlife associated with particular ecosystems. The aim of a biogeography of wildlife use would be to provide this information.

As a first step in the development of such a biogeography we have organized our economic data on U.S. use of wild plants by bioregion. For the purposes of this chapter a bioregion is that part of a biome (the largest ecological subdivision of the biosphere) occurring in a particular realm (the largest biogeographical subdivision of the biosphere). We have restricted this analysis to land plants (seaweeds are excluded) and hence to terrestrial bioregions. We follow Udvardy (S-839) in defining the biogeographical realms. In defining the biomes, we have merged the systems of Bailey (A-1434, A-1435) and of Udvardy (S-839), following a modified version of the former for the Nearctic and of the latter for the rest of the world.

The eight realms (with their approximate geographical scope) are as follows:

Nearctic (North America, including Greenland and northern Mexico)
Neotropics (rest of the Americas, including the Caribbean and Bermuda)
Palearctic (Europe, Asia [except for Indomalaya, below], and North Africa including the Sahara)
Afrotropics (Africa south of the Sahara)
Indomalaya (the Indian subcontinent and southeast Asia)
Oceania (Melanesia, Micronesia, and Polynesia except New Zealand)

Australia

Antarctica (Antarctica, Southern Ocean islands, and New Zealand)

Our 16 biomes (with their equivalents in the Bailey and Udvardy systems) are listed below:

| BIOME | BAILEY DIVISION | UDVARDY BIOME |
|---|---|---|
| 1. Icecap | 110 | 9 (in part) |
| 2. Tundra | 120 | 9 (in part) |
| 3. Boreal forest and taiga | 130 | 3 |
| 4. Temperate mixed forest | 210 | — |
| 5. Temperate broadleaf forest | 220 | 5 (in part) |
| 6. Temperate maritime forest | 240 | 2 (in part) |
| 7. Subtropical forest | 230 | 2 (in part) + 5 (in part) |
| 8. Tropical dry forest (including monsoon forest) | 410 (in part) | 4 |
| 9. Tropical rain forest | 420 | 1 |
| 10. Mediterranean type | 260 | 6 |
| 11. Prairie (including parkland) | 250 | 11 |
| 12. Savanna | 410 (in part) | 10 |
| 13. Steppe | 310 | 8 |
| 14. Desert (including semidesert) | 320 | 7 |
| 15. Mountains | H210 + H310 | 12 |
| 16. Islands | — | 13 |

Table 11.1 shows the contributions of these bioregions to the U.S. economy in terms of their supply of harvested resources (wild timber plus wild plants used for medicine, food, and industry). The value of new timber domesticates is included with wild timber (note 1).

Because timber is the most important wild resource and because most of the timber consumed by the United States grows in the Nearctic, the Nearctic realm is much the most important, providing 97% of the value of wild harvested resources. The main Nearctic biomes are the temperate maritime forest (coastal western North America from Kodiak Island to San Francisco Bay) and the subtropical forest (the southern pine region of southeastern United States), which account for 37 and 27%, respectively, of the value of Nearctic wild plant production. Outside the Nearctic, the biggest contribution comes from tropical rain forests (79% of the wild plant supply from other realms), largely because of the dipterocarp trees of Southeast Asia.

The four biomes that have made the biggest contributions of wild germplasm are the tropical rain forest (the new domesticate balsa, and the wild relatives of sugarcane, oil palm, and cacao); the Mediterranean type (the new domesticate lavender, and the wild relatives of oats, wheat, and iris); the prairie (the new domesticate wheatgrass, and the wild relatives of hops, sunflower, and sweet clover); and the mountains (the new domesticates wheatgrass and kiwi fruit, and the wild relatives of hops, tulip, tomato, and potato).

Table 11.1 **Terrestrial bioregions contributing wild plant resources produced or imported by the United States: average annual value, 1976–1980 (U.S.$ million)**

| BIOME | NEARCTIC REALM | OTHER REALMS | TOTAL |
|---|---|---|---|
| 1. Icecap | — | — | — |
| 2. Tundra | — | — | — |
| 3. Boreal forest and taiga | 1,405.1 | — | 1,405.1 |
| 4. Temperate mixed forest | 2,193.9 | — | 2,193.9 |
| 5. Temperate broadleaf forest | 1,377.6 | 2.2 | 1,379.8 |
| 6. Temperate maritime forest | 8,353.7 | — | 8,353.7 |
| 7. Subtropical forest | 6,176.7 | 6.5 | 6,183.2 |
| 8. Tropical dry forest | — | 50.9 | 50.9 |
| 9. Tropical rain forest | — | 576.4 | 576.4 |
| 10. Mediterranean type | 502.3 | 27.0 | 529.3 |
| 11. Prairie | 65.0 | — | 65.0 |
| 12. Savanna | — | — | — |
| 13. Steppe | 0.3 | 1.5 | 1.8 |
| 14. Desert | 3.3 | 8.2 | 11.5 |
| 15. Mountains | 2,719.4 | 56.3 | 2,775.7 |
| 16. Islands | — | 1.2 | 1.2 |
| TOTAL | 22,797.3 | 730.2 | 23,527.5 |

NEARCTIC   U.S.$ 22,797.3 million                                      U.S.$ million

3. Boreal forest and taiga
    timber from Canada      1,402.1
    f&i    blueberry      2.1
            wild rice      0.9
                                     1,405.1
    wgr    *Bromus pumpellianus* (Alaska and Canada)

4. Temperate mixed forest
    timber from United States      470.0
    timber from Canada      1,688.9
    med    ginseng      0.4
    f&i    sugar maple      21.4
            blueberry      10.6
            wild rice      2.3
            cedar leaf oil      0.3
                                     2,193.9
    nd    highbush blueberry (with 5) [$\frac{1}{2}$ of $44.0 million]
            wild rice [$2.8 million]

5. Temperate broadleaf forest
    timber from United States      1,353.4
    timber from Canada      15.0
    med    ginseng      7.7
    f&i    sugar maple      1.5
                                     1,377.6

|  | | U.S.$ million |
|---|---|---|
| nd | highbush blueberry (with 4) [½ of $44.0 million] | |
| wgr | *Vaccinium australe* (North Carolina) | |

6. Temperate maritime forest
    timber from United States — 6,638.3
    timber from Canada — 1,715.4
    8,353.7

    wgr    *Fragaria chiloensis* (California)

7. Subtropical forest
    timber from United States — 6,167.5
    f&i    pecan — 9.2
    6,176.7

10. Mediterranean
    timber from United States — 502.3
    502.3

    wgr    *Humulus lupulus* (California)

11. Prairie
    timber from United States — 51.9
    med    ginseng — 0.4
    f&i    pecan — 12.7
    65.0

    nd    wheatgrasses (with 13 + 15) [part of $1.9 million]
    wgr    *Humulus lupulus* (Manitoba)
            *Helianthus annuus* (Texas)
            *Helianthus petiolaris* (Missouri)

13. Steppe
    f&i    oregano — 0.3
    0.3

    nd    wheatgrasses (with 11 + 15) [part of $1.9 million]
    wgr    *Gossypium thurberi* (Arizona)

14. Desert
    f&i    istle/tampico — 2.4
            candelilla wax — 0.6
            oregano — 0.3
    3.3

15. Mountains
    timber from United States — 1,230.5
    timber from Canada — 1,485.5
    f&i    istle/tampico — 2.4
            candelilla wax — 0.7
            oregano — 0.3
    2,719.4

    nd    wheatgrasses (with 11 + 13) [part of $1.9 million]
    wgr    *Humulus lupulus* (Utah)

(*continued*)

Table 11.1　(*Continued*)

| | | | U.S.$ million |
|---|---|---|---|
| INDOMALAYA　U.S.$ 523.7 million | | | |

**8. Tropical dry forest**

| | | |
|---|---|---|
| timber | teak | 10.0 |
| med | strychnos | 0.4 |
| f&i | karaya | 3.8 |
| | palmarosa | 0.2 |
| | | 14.4 |

**9. Tropical rain forest**

| | | |
|---|---|---|
| timber | hardwoods nspf | 221.3 |
| | dipterocarps | 214.3 |
| | veneer nspf | 11.8 |
| | teak | 1.3 |
| f&i | rattan | 53.2 |
| | jelutong | 4.3 |
| | guttas | 3.1 |
| | | 509.3 |

| | |
|---|---|
| wgr | *Saccharum spontaneum* (Java) |
| | *Saccharum spontaneum* (India) |

NEOTROPICS　U.S.$ 160.2 million

**7. Subtropical forest**

| | | |
|---|---|---|
| timber | parana pine | 2.9 |
| f&i | Brazilian sassafras | 1.1 |
| | | 4.0 |
| unallocated* | | 2.5 |
| | | 6.5 |

**8. Tropical dry forest**

| | | |
|---|---|---|
| timber | mahogany | 7.7 |
| | Central American pines | 2.3 |
| | pine chemicals | 0.4 |
| | Spanish cedar | 0.1 |
| f&i | carnauba | 5.4 |
| | quebracho | 4.6 |
| | Peru balsam | 1.1 |
| | allspice | 0.2 |
| | styrax natural balsam | 0.2 |
| | Tolu balsam | 0.1 |
| | | 22.1 |
| unallocated* | | 14.2 |
| | | 36.3 |
| nd | cashew [$116.1 million] | |

**9. Tropical rain forest**

| | | |
|---|---|---|
| timber | mahogany | 7.7 |
| | balsa | 2.8 |

|  |  |  | U.S.$ million |
|---|---|---|---|
| f&i | Brazil nut | 17.2 ⎫<br>0.5 ⎭ | 17.7 |
|  | chicle |  | 4.1 |
|  | leche-caspi |  | 3.1 |
|  | bois de rose |  | 1.0 |
|  | hearts of palm |  | 0.4 |
|  | allspice |  | 0.4 |
|  | babassu |  | 0.4 |
|  | guttas |  | 0.3 |
|  | Tolu balsam |  | 0.1 |
|  | tonka bean |  | 0.1 |
|  |  |  | 38.1 |
| | unallocated* |  | 23.6 |
|  |  |  | 61.7 |
| wgr | *Theobroma cacao* (Peru) |  |  |

14. Desert
  wgr  *Lycopersicon pimpinellifolium* (Peru)
       *Nicotiana glutinosa* (Peru)

15. Mountains

| timber | Central American pines |  | 30.8 |
|---|---|---|---|
|  | pine chemicals |  | 2.4 |
|  | Spanish cedar |  | 0.1 |
| f&i | styrax natural balsam |  | 0.2 |
|  |  |  | 33.5 |
| | unallocated* |  | 21.0 |
|  |  |  | 54.5 |
| wgr | *Lycopersicon chmielewskii* |  |  |
|  | *Solanum demissum* |  |  |

16. Islands

| timber | Central American pines |  | 0.5 |
|---|---|---|---|
| f&i/id | allspice |  | 0.7 |
|  |  |  | 1.2 |
| wgr | *Lycopersicon cheesmanii* |  |  |

Unallocated neotropical*

| timber | hardwoods nspf |  | 37.2 |
|---|---|---|---|
|  | pulp products (Brazil) |  | 23.8 |
|  | Spanish cedar (Brazil) |  | 0.3 |
|  |  |  | 61.3 |
| wgr | *Capsicum annuum* |  |  |
|  | *Lycopersicon esculentum* var. *cerasiforme* |  |  |
|  | *Lycopersicon peruvianum* |  |  |
|  | *Nicotiana longiflora* |  |  |
|  | *Nicotiana plumbaginifolia* |  |  |
|  | *Nicotiana tomentosa* |  |  |

(*continued*)

Table 11.1  (*Continued*)

| PALEARCTIC   U.S.$ 32.5 million | U.S.$ million |
|---|---|
| 5. Temperate broadleaf forest | |
|    timber casks, barrels (France) | 2.1 |
|     med   ginseng | 0.1 |
| | 2.2 |
|     nd   kiwi fruit (with 7 + 15) [part of $1.8 million] | |
| 7. Subtropical forest | |
|     nd   kiwi fruit (with 5 + 15) [part of $1.8 million] | |
| 10. Mediterranean | |
|    timber brierroot | 1.7 |
|        pine chemicals | 0.8 |
|     f&i   cork | 17.7 |
|        oregano | 1.9 |
|        sage | 1.5 |
|        rosemary | 0.9 |
|        thyme | 0.7 |
|        lavender | 0.6 |
|        pine nuts | 0.5 |
|        bay leaf | 0.4 |
|        valonia | 0.2 |
|        savory | 0.1 |
| | 27.0 |
|     nd   lavender [$2.0 million] | |
|     wgr  *Avena sterilis* (Algeria, Israel, Portugal) | |
|        *Aegilops umbellulata* (in part) | |
|        *Agropyron elongatum* (in part) | |
|        *Iris tingitana* (Morocco) | |
| 11. Prairie | |
|     nd   wheatgrasses (with 13) [part of $1.9 million] | |
|     wgr  *Melilotus dentata* (Russia) | |
| 13. Steppe | |
|     f&i   tragacanth | 1.5 |
| | 1.5 |
|     nd   wheatgrasses (with 11) [part of $1.9 million] | |
|     wgr  *Aegilops umbellulata* (in part) | |
|        *Agropyron elongatum* (in part) | |
| 15. Mountains | |
|     f&i   tragacanth | 1.5 |
|        pine nuts (China) | 0.3 |
| | 1.8 |
|     nd   kiwi fruit (with 5 + 7) [part of $1.8 million] | |
|     wgr  *Humulus lupulus* (Bavaria) | |
|        *Humulus lupulus* (Slovenia) | |
|        *Beta maritima* (Italy) | |
|        *Tulipa fosteriana* | |

|  | U.S.$ million |
|---|---:|

*Tulipa praestans*
*Tulipa eichleri*
*Tulipa urumiensis*

Unallocated palearctic
    wgr    *Lactuca virosa*
                *Medicago falcata*

AFROTROPICS   U.S.$ 13.8 million

8. Tropical dry forest
    f&i    gum acacia                      0.2
                                                          0.2

    wgr    *Cynodon nlemfuensis* (Kenya)

9. Tropical rain forest
    timber hardwoods nspf                  4.3
    mahogany                               1.1
                                                          5.4

    wgr    *Elaeis guineensis* (Zaire)

14. Desert
    f&i    gum acacia                      8.2
                                                           8.2

    wgr    *Gossypium anomalum*

OCEANIA

9. Tropical rain forest
    wgr    *Saccharum robustum* (Papua New Guinea)

16. Islands
    wgr    *Gossypium tomentosum* (Hawaii)

AUSTRALIA

Unallocated
    wgr    *Nicotiana debneyi*

Notes: med = medicine (chap. 5), f&i = food and industrial products (chap. 6), id = incipient domesticates (chap. 7), nd = new domesticates (chap. 7), wgr = wild genetic resources (chap. 8). *Unallocated neotropical timber products are assigned to biomes as shown, in proportion to the total value of timber products coming from those biomes.

# 12

# Conclusion

The contribution of wildlife to the U.S. economy is substantial. It is possible that $1 in every $22 generated in the United States—or 4.5% of the gross domestic product (GDP)—is attributable to wild species. The basis for this conclusion is given in table 12.1, which summarizes the findings of chapters 2–10. Wild harvested resources (timber, fisheries, and other wild products) are worth $27 billion a year. The contributions of wild timber and fisheries to the GDP are 3.8 and 0.3%, respectively. That of other wild products is probably less than 0.1%, so we conclude that the combined contribution to GDP of wild harvested resources is 4.1%.

The value of wild germplasm as the source of new domesticates and for crop improvement is obviously less than the total value of the domesticates concerned ($7 billion a year). In chapter 8, we valued the contributions of wild genetic resources at around $340 million (or 6% of the value of the crops improved). It is more difficult to assign a value to the contribution of wild germplasm to a new domesticate. In a sense it is 100%. We leave it at that, since it is unnecessary to attempt an evaluation that is equivalent to that for harvested resources. We are not able to trace the contributions of the domesticates concerned through the economy from farmgate or dockside to the final consumer and so cannot provide an objective assessment of GDP. We note, however, that it takes $604 million of timber production to contribute each 0.1% of timber's GDP, and $1,330 million of fisheries production to contribute each 0.1% of fisheries' GDP. On the basis of the latter ratio, the combined contributions of wildlife-supported agriculture would be 0.2%. It seems fair to claim that about 0.1% of the GDP can be attributed to the contributions of wild germplasm to agriculture. On the same basis wild pollinators may contribute another 0.1%.

The economic impact of wildlife-based recreation is assessed on a completely different basis, that of consumer expenditures. As such, the figures for recreation bear no relationship to those for the other contributions of wild species. For the sake of completeness, however, we suggest a nominal 0.1% as the contribution of wildlife-based recreation to GDP.

Table 12.1  **Contributions of wildlife to the U.S. economy, annual average, 1976–1980 (U.S.$ million)**

| CONTRIBUTION | VALUE OF RESOURCE | VALUE OF DOMESTICATE | EXPENDITURE |
|---|---|---|---|
| Harvested resources | | | |
| Timber | 22,954 | | |
| Fisheries | 3,991 | | |
| Other wild products | 441 | | |
| Total | 27,386 | | |
| Biological diversity | | | |
| New domesticates | | 1,236 | |
| Wild genetic resources | | 6,036 | |
| Total | | 7,272 | |
| Ecological services | | | |
| Pollination | | 1,347 | |
| Total | | 1,347 | |
| Recreation | | | |
| Consumptive | | | 23,458 |
| Nonconsumptive | | | 6,626 |
| Total | | | 30,084 |
| TOTAL | 27,386 | 8,619 | 30,084 |

We should stress that the three groups of contribution (harvested resources, biological diversity and ecological services, and recreation) are not comparable. The GDP contributions of timber and fisheries have been estimated on the basis of detailed assessments by qualified economists, which we are not. The GDP estimates for wildlife-supported agriculture and wildlife-based recreation are intended simply to help provide a synoptic picture of the overall contribution of wildlife to the U.S. economy, which may be stated as follows: $1 of every $22 generated in the United States is attributable to wildlife—91 cents of that dollar comes from wild harvested resources, 7 cents comes from wild-supported agriculture, and 2 cents from wildlife-based recreation.

Another way of looking at the economic contribution of wild plants and animals is as a part of the nation's living resource base—the sum total of produced and imported, domesticated and wild plants, animals, and other organisms, which provides (along with people, nonliving resources, and energy) the raw material of all economies. Figure 12.1 and table 12.2 show that wild resources make up 17% of the U.S. living resource base and that wild species support an additional 5% of the resource base through the provision of new domesticates, wild genetic resources, and wild pollinators.

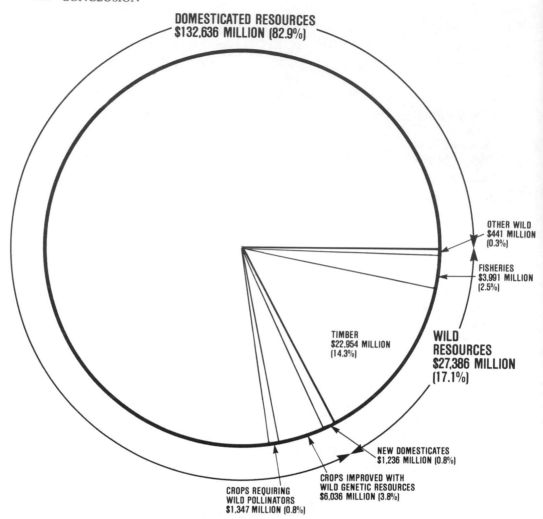

Fig. 12.1   **Contributions of wildlife to the U.S. living resource base: annual average value (1976–1980) $160,022 million**

## Trends in Wildlife Uses

Currently the six main uses of wildlife may be ranked as follows in terms of impact on the U.S. economy: logging, fishing (commercial), use of wild germ-plasm (domestication and crop improvement), recreation, pollination and pest control, and trapping and collecting. Each of these uses faces four possible fates that will determine whether their overall and relative importance will change significantly in the future: obsolescence, domestication, extinction, and sustainable use.

Logging is the activity most likely to decline. This is not because timber will play less of a part in the lives of North Americans. On the contrary, lower wood

Table 12.2  **Living resource base of the United States, annual average, 1976–1980 (U.S.$ million)**

| SECTOR | U.S. PRODUCTION | | U.S. IMPORTS | |
|---|---|---|---|---|
| | *Domesticated* | *Wild* | *Domesticated* | *Wild* |
| Agriculture | | | | |
| Plants | 56,065 | — | 13,368 | — |
| Animals | 57,762 | — | 3,716 | — |
| Subtotal | 113,827 | — | 17,084 | — |
| Fungi | 305 | — | 224* | — |
| Total | 114,132 | — | 17,308 | — |
| Forestry: Plants | 700 | 15,714 | 284 | 7,240 |
| Fisheries: Animals | 202 | 1,706 | 10† | 2,285 |
| Trapping: Animals‡ | — | 119 | — | 84 |
| Collecting: Plants‡ | — | 53 | — | 185 |
| TOTAL | 115,034 | 17,592 | 17,602 | 9,794 |

Total domesticated
| Plants | 70,417 |
| Animals | 61,690 |
| Fungi | 529 |
| All | 132,636 |

Total wild
| Plants | 23,192 |
| Animals | 4,194 |
| All | 27,386 |

LIVING RESOURCE BASE 160,022

*Includes some wild.
†Includes $4 million from domesticated seaweeds.
‡Includes medicine, food, and industry.

consumption is being more than offset by slightly higher pulp consumption and the sharp recovery of fuelwood consumption. The main factor is domestication. Plantations, now accounting for only 4% of output, are coming into production and can be expected to provide a much greater proportion of domestic supply, particularly of southern pines but also of other important softwoods. Nonetheless, wild trees will probably continue to be the source of the bulk of U.S. timber production. Natural regeneration in the North and South (particularly of hardwoods) currently exceeds removals, and this favorable supply situation is expected to persist until well into the next century. In the West removals exceed regeneration, but only because much of the timber being cut comprises the last vestiges of the first forest and hence is what foresters quaintly call "overmature" or "decadent" (S-800). Additional factors are an easing in demand for softwoods due partly to their high price compared with hardwoods, partly to the recession and the consequent relapse of the construction industry, and partly to the growing demand for hardwoods discussed in chapter 2. The proportion of U.S. timber consumption accounted for by hardwoods is projected to continue growing until it reaches about a third.

The supply situation is less favorable among the main timber exporters to the United States. In Canada annual allowable cuts (the amount that can be taken sustainably) of softwoods had to be reduced by about 20% in 1981, in response to a combination of unexpectedly high losses to pests and fire, poor management in the past (and consequent neglect of forest renewal), and the introduction of better management practices. The latter include restrictions on logging adjacent to streams and lakes as well as on steeper slopes or higher elevations. The Canadian Forest Service concludes that "the limits are in sight for premium softwood sawlogs in many locations. . . . Pulpwood shortages are emerging in local communities across the country. Only a fraction of our forests are being managed for sustained production, even today" (A-1871).

In Southeast Asia, present rates of logging the dipterocarps are predicted to exhaust accessible supplies within the next 10–15 years. The main hope for their economic survival is domestication (provided biological problems such as lack of seed dormancy and irregular flowering can be overcome), the development of sustainable mixed agrisilvicultural systems, or a combination of the two. Similarly, in Africa and tropical America, the mahoganies (*Khaya* and *Swietenia* spp.), Spanish cedar (*Cedrela* spp.), and other valuable members of the Meliaceae family have been heavily overexploited. Constant "creaming" of the best trees in Central and South America have reduced trees of good form to rarities in inaccessible places, and the same process is occurring rapidly and widely in Africa and Asia (S-833). The evidence suggests that outside the United States at least wild timber supplies will decline due to inadequate regeneration of wild trees and greater production from plantations.

Although the contribution of wild timber is declining, it will probably stabilize at a substantially higher level than that of other wildlife uses. Other uses that appear to have stabilized already are consumptive recreation and commercial fisheries. Expenditures on hunting and fishing are rising, but the numbers of participants in either sport did not change significantly between 1975 and 1980. More people are involved in nonconsumptive recreation but their per capita economic impact is lower.

Although per capita consumption of seafood is growing, the growth is small compared with consumption levels of meat, and the economic impact of wild fisheries (as a percentage of GDP) has remained fairly steady. Consumers of fish and shellfish seem to be rather conservative; the most important species groups used as food are high and medium value resources such as shrimp, tuna, and salmon—so dramatic changes in use patterns are unlikely. We doubt, too, that aquaculture will make inroads on wild fisheries equivalent to the effect that plantation silviculture will have on the proportion of timber supplied from the wild. Public sector involvement in aquaculture will probably continue to be concerned largely if not exclusively with enhancement of stocks that essentially are wild. Private sector involvement will be restricted to organisms that either can be managed from cradle to grave (oysters, trout, and catfish) or are programmed biologically to return to their owners after a period of ocean foraging (salmon). A distinctive feature of wild fisheries to which the industry seems unable to adapt is its periodicity. Populations of species as diverse as king crab, Pacific salmons, capelin, and herring boom and bust with changes in their environment, the busts exacerbated by excessive fishing pressure brought on by the booms. Producers of competing aquaculture resources may find it difficult to operate in a market that fluctuates between oversupply and undersupply.

Whereas consumptive recreation and commercial fisheries appear to have stabilized (for the time being) at high and intermediate levels, respectively, trapping and collecting (including the supply of wild medicines, foodstuffs, and industrial materials) have apparently stabilized at low economic levels. The lists of species supplying medical ingredients in chapter 5 illustrate an interesting phenomenon of wildlife use: persistence in the face of obsolescence. An astonishing variety of wild plants and animals continues to be used in the preparation of over-the-counter and prescription drugs. Both collectively and individually their economic impact is small: a major native drug species such as cascara (*Rhamnus purshiana*) has an annual production value of perhaps $1 million and a final market (retail) value of some $75 million. Their physiological and psychological contributions, however, may be high. In any case, although their value is small compared with other wild resources, their collection continues to provide income and employment to many rural people in North America and elsewhere.

Use of wild germplasm for the development of new domesticates and the improvement of established domesticates is the wildlife use most likely to go on growing. Historically high numbers of wild plant and animal species have been domesticated in this century for agriculture, silviculture, and aquaculture. Although the value of these new domesticates is modest compared with the totality of domesticated resources, it is growing and almost certainly will continue to grow—especially the new forage and timber domesticates. The rate of domestication will no doubt subside to historically conventional levels eventually, but it could well remain high for the next few decades. In addition, although the rate at which established domesticates are being improved with wild genetic resources is now apparently constant, the value of the contributions of wild genetic resources is increasing—owing to improved cultivars accounting for higher proportions of the crops concerned and to additional crops being improved with wild germplasm. Besides their expanding contribution to agriculture, wild genetic resources are likely to assume increasing importance in silviculture and aquaculture. As we noted in chapter 7, use of wild germplasm has been the key to the successful development of improved plantation pines; the future of aquaculture also lies in large measure in the effective use of wild gene pools. Under the circumstances there is a good chance that use of wild germplasm will displace commercial fisheries as the number two wildlife use after timber.

On the evidence presented in this book three generalizations can be made about the predictability of wildlife use. First, in general terms it is highly predictable. There is nothing unexpected about the main types of use: new uses are often old uses rediscovered (for example, the scientific discovery of reserpine, *Rauvolfia serpentina*, an Indian folk treatment for hypertension); the wild plants and animals that are being domesticated today yield products that are much the same as those provided by earlier domesticates; and the wild gene pools most likely to be used in crop improvement are those related to high value crops. Second, in specific terms (by contrast) predictability is low. It does not seem possible to predict the plants and animals that will become new wild resources or the next new domesticates, or which particular wild genotype will be incorporated successfully in a crop. Fusiform rust was once a disease of no consequence to growers of loblolly pines, so that the rust-resistant populations of Livingston Parish, Louisiana, were of no interest. Today they are of great value. The rust pathogen is potentially highly virulent and could evolve new pathotypes: new sources of resistance may (or may not) be needed (V-289). The biological variables are compounded by economic and social variables. Even with hindsight, for example, it is difficult to explain the success of the kiwi fruit. The third generalization about predictability is that a wild resource can be declining into oblivion and then be revived by a sudden change in socioeconomic conditions. The first fuel—wild wood—was a rustic curiosity until the energy crisis returned it to importance.

These three generalizations suggest that we should prepare for unpredictable events, both biological and socioeconomic. The best preparation in the context of wildlife use is to have a safety net of diversity—maintaining as many gene pools as possible, particularly within those wild species that are economically significant or are likely to be (for example, important resource species and relatives of major and super crops). This will require increasing emphasis on the conservation of within-species diversity in situ (or on site) in parks, reserves, and other protected areas—which in turn calls for close cooperation among the various users of wild species (foresters, wildlife conservationists, and others). The first resource can continue to make a major contribution to the lives of North Americans, provided it is conserved and provided its use is managed with the needs of all users (consumptive and nonconsumptive, urban and rural, indigenous and nonindigenous) in mind.

# Appendix A

## Names and Affiliations of Respondents to State/Provincial/Territorial Wildlife Agency Survey (Listed Alphabetically by State/Province/Territory)

Mr. Archie D. Hooper
Dept. of Conservation & Natural
  Resources
Montgomery, Alabama 36130

Mr. Sam L. Spencer
Dept. of Conservation & Natural
  Resources
Montgomery, Alabama 36130

Mr. William F. Kelly
Game and Fish Division
Jacksonville, Alabama 36265

Dr. Ronald O. Skoog
Department of Fish & Game
Juneau, Alaska 99801

Mr. Herbert Melchior
Department of Fish & Game
Fairbanks, Alaska 99701

Mr. Mike Watson
Dept. of Energy & Natural Resources
Edmonton, Alberta T5K 2C9
Canada

Mr. Bob Barsch
Department of Game and Fish
Phoenix, Arizona 85023

Ms. Kathy L. Heller
Game and Fish Commission
Little Rock, Arkansas 72205

Mr. Jim McCrossan
Ministry of Environment
Victoria, British Columbia V8W 2H1
Canada

Ms. Loti E. Calliga
Department of Fish and Game
Sacramento, California 95814

Mr. Dave Lemons
Dept. of Natural Resources Planning
Denver, Colorado 80216

Mr. Richard L. Norman
Dept. of Natural Resources Planning
Denver, Colorado 80216

Mr. Frank L. Disbrow
Dept. of Environmental Protection
Hartford, Connecticut 06115

Mr. Thomas W. Whittendale, Jr.
Dept. of Natural Resources &
  Environmental Control
Dover, Delaware 19901

Mr. Thomas M. Goodwin
Dept. of Natural Resources
Tallahassee, Florida 32301

Mr. Leon A. Kirkland
Dept. of Natural Resources
Atlanta, Georgia 30334

Mr. J. Gibson Johnston, Jr.
Dept. of Natural Resources
Atlanta, Georgia 30334

Mr. Timothy Sutterfield
Dept. of Land & Natural Resources
Honolulu, Hawaii 96813

Mr. Kenji Ego
Dept. of Land & Natural Resources
Honolulu, Hawaii 96813

Mr. Jerry M. Conley
Department of Fish and Game
Boise, Idaho 83707

Mr. Roger M. Williams
Department of Fish and Game
Boise, Idaho 83707

Mr. Richard A. Rogers
Department of Conservation
Springfield, Illinois 62706

Mr. Duane L. Shroufe
Dept. of Natural Resources
Indianapolis, Indiana 46204

Mr. Richard A. Bishop
Iowa Conservation Commission
Des Moines, Iowa 50319

Mr. Verlyn Ebert
Fish and Game Commission
Pratt, Kansas 67124

Mr. James S. Durell
Dept. of Fish & Wildlife Resources
Frankfort, Kentucky 40601

Mr. John D. Newsom
Dept. of Wildlife & Fisheries
Baton Rouge, Louisiana 70898

Mr. Art Ritter
Dept. of Inland Fisheries & Wildlife
Augusta, Maine 04333

Mr. Ross C. Thompson
Dept. of Natural Resources
Winnipeg, Manitoba R3H 0W9
Canada

Mr. Carl S. Prescott
Dept. of Fisheries, Wildlife &
   Recreational Vehicles
Boston, Massachusetts 02202

Ms. Kristine L. Corey
Division of Fisheries and Wildlife
Westboro, Massachusetts 01581

Mr. Lawrence A. Ryel
Dept. of Natural Resources
Lansing, Michigan 48909

Mr. Jack Skrypek
Dept. of Natural Resources
St. Paul, Minnesota 55155

Mr. Arthur R. Peterson
Dept. of Natural Resources
St. Paul, Minnesota 55155

Mr. John H. Phares
Dept. of Wildlife Conservation
Jackson, Mississippi 39205

Mr. Edwin H. Glaser
Dept. of Conservation
Jefferson City, Missouri 65102

Mr. Vern Craig
Dept. of Fish and Game
Helena, Montana 59601

Mr. Kim G. Poole
Dept. of Renewable Resources
Yellowknife, N.W.T. X1A 2L9
Canada

Mr. Kenneth L. Johnson
Game and Parks Commission
Lincoln, Nebraska 68503

Mr. Norm Dey
Game and Parks Commission
Lincoln, Nebraska 68503

Mr. George K. Tsukamoto
Department of Wildlife
Reno, Nevada 89520

Mr. David J. Cartwright
Department of Natural Resources
Fredericton, New Brunswick E3B 5H1
Canada

Ms. Patricia R. Fleurie
Department of Fish and Game
Concord, New Hampshire 03301

Mr. Frank Tourine
Dept. of Environmental Protection
Trenton, New Jersey 08625

Mr. Harold F. Olson
Department of Game and Fish
Santa Fe, New Mexico 87503

Mr. George W. Merrill
Department of Game and Fish
Santa Fe, New Mexico 87503

Ms. Elizabeth McLellan
Department of Game and Fish
Sante Fe, New Mexico 87503

Mr. Kenneth F. Wich
Dept. of Environmental Conservation
Albany, New York 12233

Mr. Norman J. VanValkenburgh
Dept. of Environmental Conservation
Albany, New York 12233

Mr. Stuart L. Free
Dept. of Environmental Conservation
Albany, New York 12233

Mr. David G. Pike
Dept. of Culture, Recreation & Youth
Pleasantville, Newfoundland A1C 5T7
Canada

Mr. John H. C. Pippy
Dept. of Fisheries and Oceans
St. John's, Newfoundland A1C 5X1
Canada

Mr. W. C. Parkinson
Dept. of Rural, Agricultural & Northern
    Development
St. John's, Newfoundland A1C 5T7
Canada

Mr. Eric Baggs
Department of Development
St. John's, Newfoundland A1C 5T7
Canada

Mr. Richard B. Hamilton
Wildlife Resources Commission
Raleigh, North Carolina 27611

Mr. Arlen Harmoning
Department of Game and Fish
Bismarck, North Dakota 58505

Mr. Merrill Prime
Dept. of Lands and Forests
Kentville, Nova Scotia B4N 3X3
Canada

Mr. Steven H. Cole
Dept. of Natural Resources
Columbus, Ohio 43224

Mr. John Skeen
Dept. of Wildlife Conservation
Oklahoma City, Oklahoma 73105

Dr. J. Douglas Roseborough
Ministry of Natural Resources

Toronto, Ontario M7A 1W3
Canada

Mr. Ron E. Shay
Dept. of Fish and Wildlife
Portland, Oregon 97208

Mr. Allan P. Godfrey
Dept. of Community Affairs
Charlottetown, P.E.I. C1A 7N8
Canada

Mr. Fred Johnson
Fish Commission
Harrisburg, Pennsylvania 17120

Mr. Glenn L. Bowers
Game Commission
Harrisburg, Pennsylvania 17120

Mr. Larry Shaffer
Fish Commission
Harrisburg, Pennsylvania 17120

Mr. Dale E. Sheffer
Game Commission
Harrisburg, Pennsylvania 17120

Mr. Luc Samson
Ministere du Loisir, de la Chasse et de la
    Peche
Quebec, Quebec G1R 4Y1
Canada

Mr. John M. Cronan
Division of Fish and Wildlife
Wakefield, Rhode Island 02879

Mr. Harold B. Strom
Dept. of Tourism & Renewable
    Resources
Prince Albert, Saskatchewan S6V 1B5
Canada

Mr. G. W. Pepper
Dept. of Tourism & Renewable
    Resources
Regina, Saskatchewan S4S 5W6
Canada

Mr. Sumter Moore
Wildlife & Marine Resources
    Department
Columbia, South Carolina 29202

Mr. Charles Backlund
Department of Game, Fish & Parks
Pierre, South Dakota 57501

Mr. Clifton J. Whitehead, Jr.
Wildlife Resources Agency
Nashville, Tennessee 37204

Mr. Charles D. Travis
Parks and Wildlife Department
Austin, Texas 78744

Mr. Edwin V. Rawley
Dept. of Natural Resources
Salt Lake City, Utah 84116

Mr. Edward F. Kehoe
Agency of Environmental Conservation
Montpelier, Vermont 05602

Mr. John Hall
Fish & Game Dept.
Montpelier, Vermont 05602

Mr. R. H. Cross, Jr.
Commission of Game & Inland Fisheries
Richmond, Virginia 23230

Mr. Rick Lawrence
Department of Game
Olympia, Washington 98504

Mr. Robert L. Miles
Dept. of Natural Resources
Charleston, West Virginia 25305

Mr. Kenneth B. Knight
Dept. of Natural Resources
Elkins, West Virginia 26241

Mr. Walter S. Kordek
Department of Natural Resources
Elkins, West Virginia 26241

Mr. Dennis A. Schenborn
Dept. of Natural Resources
Madison, Wisconsin 53707

Mr. John M. Keener
Dept. of Natural Resources
Madison, Wisconsin 53707

Mr. Douglas M. Crowe
Game and Fish Department
Cheyenne, Wyoming 82002

# Appendix B

## Names and Affiliations of Respondents to Industrial Supplier Survey
## (Listed Alphabetically by Company)

Mr. Andrew J. Dahlke
Abbey Colour & Chemical Co., Inc.
Philadelphia, Pennsylvania 19134

Mr. Richard DeGraf
Abbot, Cole & DeGraf, Inc.
San Francisco, California 94107

Mr. Richard L. Sheffer
Acme Hardesty Co., Inc.
Jenkintown, Pennsylvania 19046

Mr. Joseph F. Naughton
Archer Daniels Midland Co.
Decatur, Illinois 62525

Mr. L. M. Argueso, Jr.
M. Argueso & Co., Inc.
Mamaroneck, New York 10543

Mr. W. V. Symons
Arizona Chemical Co.
Fair Lawn, New Jersey 07410

Mr. M. Blum
Atomergic Chemetals Corp.
Plainview, New York 11803

Mr. Robert A. Baldini
Robert A. Baldini & Co., Inc.
Millburn, New Jersey 07041

Mr. Jean W. Baer
Baromatic Corporation
Great Neck, New York 11022

Mr. Chester H. Ziemiecki
The E. Berghausen Chemical Co.
Cincinnati, Ohio 45232

Mr. F. Berlage
Fred Berlage Co.
Mount Kisco, New York 10549

Mr. William Bernstein
William Bernstein Co., Inc.
New York, New York 10038

Mr. Dennis Meyers
Bio Serv Inc.
Frenchtown, New Jersey 08825

Mr. Robert Quatman
Botanicals International, Inc.
Long Beach, California 90810

Mr. Christopher Parnell
Braco Farms Ltd.
Trelawny, Jamaica
West Indies

Ms. Elsie B. Brady
Bradshaw-Praeger & Co.
Chicago, Illinois 60632

Mr. M. Blum
Burlington Bio-Medical Corp.
Plainview, New York 11803

Mr. Sol Kaminsky
Celanese Plastics & Specialties Company
Louisville, Kentucky 40202

Mr. Louis Braganti
Pierre Chauvet S.A.
83440 Fayence
France

Mr. J. Alan Sheridan
Clayton & Jowett Ltd.
Liverpool L1 4AH
England

Mr. Nicolas Hrab
Cominso (Canada) Ltd.
Montreal, Quebec H2Y 1L9
Canada

Mr. Hagop S. Touloukian
Cornhill Commercial Co. Inc.
New York, New York 10118

Mr. Ed McKeon
Costec, Inc.
Palatine, Illinois 60067

Ms. Elizabeth C. Bergin
Crosby Chemicals, Inc.
New Orleans, Louisiana 70130

Mr./Ms. G. Himelwright
Gerard J. Danco International Corp.
Convent Station, New Jersey 07961

Dr. Hartmut von Kienle
Degussa AG
6450 Hanau 1
West Germany

Mr. M. Kovacevic
Dominant Flavors & Aromatics Co.
Bethpage, New York 11714

Mr. Martin Strauss
Durachem Division of Dura
  Commodities Corp.
Harrison, New York 10528

Mr. Eric H. Rothouse
EM Industries Co., EM Chemicals, Inc.
Hawthorne, New York 10532

Messrs. F. Bagan & B. Kull
Emil Flachsmann Ltd.
8038 Zurich
Switzerland

Sales Manager
Food Materials Corp.
Chicago, Illinois 60618

Mr. F. D. Poholsky
Frank Enterprises, Inc.
Columbus, Ohio 43219

Mr. Philip Wechsler
Frigid Food Products, Inc.
Detroit, Michigan 48207

Mr. Robert J. Eiserle
Fritzsche Dodge & Olcott, Inc.
New York, New York 10011

Mr. Claude E. Bird
FRP Co.
Baxley, Georgia 31513

Mr. R. Galland
H. Wm. Galland Corp.
Islip, New York 11751

Mr. Greg Kaiser
Gamma Foods
Wapato, Washington 98951

Mr. William J. Ludlum
Givaudan Corp.
Clifton, New Jersey 07014

Mr. Sol Reiss
Globe Extracts, Inc.
Hauppauge, New York 11788

Mr. R. M. Brewer
The C. P. Hall Company
Stow, Ohio 44224

Mr. H. R. Harkins
H. R. Harkins, Inc.
Pleasant Valley, New York 12569

Mr. L. S. Simon
Hercules Incorporated
Wilmington, Delaware 19899

Mr. Herbert G. Roskind, Jr.
Holtrachem, Inc.
Natick, Massachusetts 01760

Mr. Proctor W. Houghton
Houghton Chemical Corp.
Allston, Massachusetts 02134

Mr. Richard Micali
ICN Nutritional Biochemicals
Cleveland, Ohio 44128

Mr. Richard O. Innes
O. G. Innes Corporation
New York, New York 10016

Mr. P. H. Semler
International Flavors & Fragrances
   (Canada) Ltd.
Concord, Ontario L4K 1B6
Canada

Mr. Frank J. Clarke
International Wax Refining Co., Inc.
Valley Stream, New York 11582

Mr. John Y. Abe
Ishihara Corp. (USA)
San Francisco, California 94111

Mr. Keith Mantell
Isogenics, Inc.
Westwood, New Jersey 07675

Mr. Kelley Dwyer
Jojoba Commodities Group
North Hollywood, California 91603

Ms. Laure Moutet
JPM Imports, Inc.
Astoria, New York 11103

Mr. H. Cripps
Kalsec, Inc.
Kalamazoo, Michigan 49005

Sales Manager
Lebermuth Company
South Bend, Indiana 46624

Mr. Edward J. Iorio
Marine Products Co.
Boston, Massachusetts 02127

Mr. Trevor D. Lloyd
McLaughlin Gormley King Co.
Minneapolis, Minnesota 55427

Mr. Joseph L. Kanig
Edward Mendell Co., Inc.
Carmel, New York 10512

Mr. Kurt Schoen
David Michael & Co., Inc.
Philadelphia, Pennsylvania 19154

Verne L. Rhodes
Monsanto Plastics & Resins Co.
St. Louis, Missouri 63166

Mr. Ed Morse
Morse Chemical
San Gabriel, California 91776

Mr. Robert L. Schuette
Natrochem Inc.
Savannah, Georgia 31402

Mr. Gerhart S. Suppiger, Jr.
Nikken Food Corp./G. S. Suppiger Co.
St. Louis, Missouri 63102

Mr. Richard Shutt
Noris Chemical Corporation
Huntington Beach, California 92647

Ms. Patricia Coyle
P.A.T. Products, Inc.
Bangor, Maine 04401

Mr. W. B. Parker
Parker Trading Corp.
Staten Island, New York 10314

Mr. Richard A. Gruhl
Pascal Co., Inc.
Bellevue, Washington 98004

Mr. Rod Paterson
A. S. Paterson Co. Ltd.
Toronto, Ontario M4P 2C8
Canada

Mr. H. C. Peterson
Perny, Inc.
Ridgewood, New Jersey 07451

Ms. Penelope McCain
Polarome International Company
New York, New York 10013

Sales Manager
Carl Rasmussen A/S
N-5064 Straumsgrend
Norway

Mr. Paul Adams
Robertet, Inc.
Oakland, New Jersey 07436

Mr. Bernard Pompeo
Frank B. Ross Co., Inc.
Jersey City, New Jersey 07304

Mr. Gary Selander
Roussel Corp.
New York, New York 10017

Sales Manager
Samrak Chemical
Bronxville, New York 10708

Mr. Samuel Kruty
Santell Chemical Co.
Chicago, Illinois 60616

Mr. Hugh Harkins
E. L. Scott & Company, Inc.
New York, New York 10048

Mr. Waldemar Meckes, Jr.
Werner G. Smith, Inc.
Cleveland, Ohio 44113

Mr. Joseph Snowiss
Snowiss Fur Co.
Williamsport, Pennsylvania 17701

Mr. Paul Burg
Spectrum Chemical Mfg. Corp.
Gardena, California 90248

Mr. Paul C. Stievater
Spencer Kellogg Div. of Textron Inc.
Buffalo, New York 14240

Mr. J. Stauber
Stauber Chemical, Inc.
La Habra, California 90631

Mr. Robert Q. Behrer
Strahl & Pitsch, Inc.
West Babylon, New York 11704

Mr. Anthony Colavito
Synfleur
Paramus, New Jersey 07652

Mr. Melvin Teal
Teal's Evergreens Inc.
Bark River, Michigan 49807

Managing Director
Techno Chemical Industries Ltd.
Calicut 673 001
India

Mr. Barry L. Lewis
Tenneco Chemicals, Inc.
Piscataway, New Jersey 08854

Sales Manager
Tri-K Industries, Inc.
Westwood, New Jersey 07675

Mr. Karl M. Poehlmann
George Uhe Co., Inc.
New York, New York 10011

Mr. Joe Linder
Ungerer & Co.
Lincoln Park, New Jersey 07035

Mr. J. M. Ralston
Union Camp Corporation
Savannah, Georgia 31402

Mr. Robert C. Koch
Universal Flavors
Indianapolis, Indiana 46241

Mr. Herbert Ravitz
Universal Preservachem, Inc.
Brooklyn, New York 11211

Mr. Gregory S. Lermond
John D. Walsh Co., Inc.
Glen Rock, New Jersey 07452

Dr. R. E. Erickson
Warner-Jenkinson Co.
St. Louis, Missouri 63106

Mr. Chuck Stevens
Whole Herb Co.
Mill Valley, California 94941

Mr. R. H. Hawxhurst
S. Winterbourne & Co., Inc.
Rahway, New Jersey 07065

Mr. E. T. Gendron
William Zinsser & Co., Inc.
Somerset, New Jersey 08873

# Appendix C

## Names and Affiliations of Persons (Other Than Those Listed in Appendixes A, B, and D) Who Provided Help and Information (Listed Alphabetically by Family Name)

Dr. M. A. Adansi
Oil Palm Research Centre
Kade
Ghana

Dr. Quazi Akhter Ahmed
Bangladesh Jute Research Institute
Dacca-7
Bangladesh

Dr. Hannu Ahokas
University of Helsinki, Department of
  Genetics
SF-00100 Helsinki 10
Finland

Dr. H. T. Allen
Agriculture Canada, Lacombe Research
  Station
Lacombe, Alberta T0C 1S0
Canada

Dr. W. S. Alles
Department of Minor Export Crops
Matale
Sri Lanka

Dr. M. N. Alvarez
International Institute of Tropical
  Agriculture (IITA)
Ibadan
Nigeria

Dr. Paulo de T. Alvim
Centro de Pesquisas do Cacau, CEPLAC
Itabuna, B.A.
Brazil

Dr. Mesfin Ameha
Institute of Agricultural Research
Addis Ababa
Ethiopia

Mr. Jack Andarrusman
C. V. Primaco Indonesia
Jakarta Timur
Indonesia

Dr. Hugh Harris Anderson
Pacific Rubber Growers
South Pasadena, California 91030

Ir. P. Angkapradipta
Balai Penelitian Perkebunan Bogor
Bogor
Indonesia

Dr. J. L. Apple
North Carolina State University,
  Agricultural Research Service
Raleigh, North Carolina 27650

Dr. M. H. Arnold
Plant Breeding Institute, Sugar Beet
  Department
Cambridge CB2 2LQ
England

Dr. David D. Baltensperger
University of Florida, Agronomy
  Department
Gainesville, Florida 32611

Dr. O. Banga
Wageningen
Netherlands

Dr. D. K. Barnes
University of Minnesota, Agronomy &
 Plant Genetics Department
St. Paul, Minnesota 55108

Dr. R. F. Barnes
The University of the West Indies,
 Department of Biological Sciences
St. Augustine
Trinidad

Dr. Duane P. Bartholomew
University of Hawaii, Agronomy & Soil
 Science Department
Honolulu, Hawaii 96822

Dr. Bernard R. Baum
Agriculture Canada, Biosystematics
 Research Institute
Ottawa, Ontario K1A 0C6
Canada

Mr. Vincent S. Bavisotto
Miller Brewing Company
Milwaukee, Wisconsin 53208

Dr. P. R. Beal
Division of Primary Industry, Redlands
 Horticultural Research Station
Ormiston, Queensland 4163
Australia

Dr. Benjamin H. Beard
University of California, Agronomy &
 Range Science
Davis, California 95616

Dr. Dorothea Bedigian
University of Illinois at Urbana-
 Champaign, Department of Agronomy
Urbana, Illinois 61801

Dr. D. F. Beech
CSIRO, Division of Tropical Crops &
 Pastures
St. Lucia, Queensland 4067
Australia

Dr. Jose R. Benero
University of Puerto Rico, Food
 Technology Laboratory
Mayaguez
Puerto Rico 00708

Dr. Bob O. Bergh
University of California, Botany and
 Plant Sciences Department
Riverside, California 92521

Dr. N. R. Bhagat
National Research Centre for Groundnut
 (ICAR)
Junagadh—PIN 362002
India

Dr. L. S. Bird
Texas A & M University, Plant Sciences
 Department
College Station, Texas 77843

Ir. G. Blaak
Department of Agricultural Research
1092 AD Amsterdam
Netherlands

Dr. A. J. Bockholt
Texas A & M University, Soil and Crop
 Sciences Department
College Station, Texas 77843

Dr. John C. Bouwkamp
University of Maryland, Horticulture
 Department
College Park, Maryland 20742

Dr. Paula Bramel-Cox
Kansas State University, Department of
 Agronomy
Manhattan, Kansas 66506

Dr. Terry F. Branson
USDA, Northern Grain Insects Research
 Laboratory
Brookings, South Dakota 57006

Dr. Ricardo Bressani
INCAP
Guatemala City
Guatemala

Dr. Lee W. Briggle
USDA-SEA
Beltsville, Maryland 20705

Mr. David A. Browne
US Department of the Interior, National
 Park Service
Washington, D.C. 20240

Mr. L. J. Brunette
Parks Canada, Finance and
  Administration
Ottawa, Ontario K1A 1G2
Canada

Dr. Lawrence G. Burk
USDA, Tobacco Research Laboratory
Oxford, North Carolina 27565

Dr. Jeffery Burley
Commonwealth Forestry Institute
Oxford OX1 3RB
England

Dr. Byron L. Burson
USDA, Grassland, Soil and Water
  Research Laboratory
Temple, Texas 76503

Dr. William J. Cable
University of the South Pacific, School of
  Agriculture
Apia
Western Samoa

Dr. David W. Cain
Clemson University, Horticulture
  Department
Clemson, South Carolina 29631

Dr. J. W. Cameron
University of California, Botany and
  Plant Sciences Department
Riverside, California 92521

Dr. Carl W. Campbell
University of Florida, Agricultural
  Research and Education Center
Homestead, Florida 33031

Mr. Robert T. Carter
Crown Zellerbach, Southern Timber &
  Wood Products Division
Bogalusa, Louisiana 70427

Dr. Alcides Carvalho
IAC, Secao de Genetica
13100 Campinas, Sao Paulo
Brazil

Dr. John E. Casida
University of California, Entomological
  Sciences
Berkeley, California 94720

Dr. James F. Chaplin
USDA, Tobacco Research Laboratory
Oxford, North Carolina 27565

Dr. P. S. Cocks
South Australia Department of
  Agriculture
Adelaide, South Australia 5001
Australia

Dr. Gerald E. Coe
USDA, Field Crops Laboratory
Beltsville, Maryland 20705

Dr. G. B. Collins
University of Kentucky, Agronomy
  Department
Lexington, Kentucky 40546

Dr. A. A. Cook
University of Florida, Plant Pathology
  Department
Gainesville, Florida 32611

Mr. Roberto E. Coronel
University of the Philippines at Los
  Banos, College of Agriculture
Laguna
Philippines

Mr. D. G. Coursey
Tropical Products Institute
London WC1X 8LU
England

Dr. Stan Cox
International Crops Research Institute
  for the Semi-Arid Tropics (ICRISAT)
Andhra Pradesh 502324
India

Dr. Dermot P. Coyne
University of Nebraska, Horticulture
  Department
Lincoln, Nebraska 68583

Dr. D. L. Craig
Agriculture Canada, Kentville Research
  Station
Kentville, Nova Scotia B4N 1J5
Canada

Dr. Julian C. Crane
University of California, Pomology
  Department
Davis, California 95616

Dr. Peter Crisp
National Vegetable Research Station
Wellesbourne, Warwick CV35 9EF
England

Mr. D. Lee Cromley
USDA—Forest Service
Atlanta, Georgia 30367

Ms. Patricia A. Crosley
CTFA, Inc.
Washington, D.C. 20005

Dr. I. R. Crute
National Vegetable Research Station
Wellesbourne, Warwick CV35 9EF
England

Dr. James N. Cummins
New York State Agricultural Experiment
  Station
Pomology and Viticulture Department
Geneva, New York 14456

Dr. H. Daday
CSIRO, Division of Plant Industry
Canberra City, A.C.T. 2601
Australia

Mr. Oliva Daigle
Oyster Culture Station
Ellerslie, Prince Edward Island C0B 1J0
Canada

Mr. Chuck L. Darsono
Jakarta Barat
Indonesia

Dr. W. Ellis Davies
Welsh Plant Breeding Station, Herbage
  Breeding Department
Plas Gogerddan, Aberystwyth SY23 3EB
Wales

Dr. Ir. P. W. F. de Waard
Department of Agricultural Research
1092 AD Amsterdam
Netherlands

Dr. J. M. J. de Wet
University of Illinois at Urbana-
  Champaign, Agronomy Department
Urbana, Illinois 61801

Dr. W. Dedio
Agriculture Canada, Morden Research
  Station
Morden, Manitoba R0G 1J0
Canada

Dr. Lanre Denton
National Horticultural Research Institute
Ibadan
Nigeria

Dr. Lionel Dessureaux
Agriculture Canada, Research Branch
Ottawa, Ontario K1A 0C5
Canada

Dr. Douglas R. Dewey
USDA, Crops Research Laboratory
Logan, Utah 84322

Mr. J. G. Disney
Tropical Products Institute
London WC1X 8LU
England

Dr. H. Doggett
Wye, Kent TN25 5BV
England

Dr. V. F. Dorofeev
N. I. Vavilov All-Union Scientific
  Research Institute of Plant Industry
Leningrad 190000
USSR

Dr. Ross W. Downes
CSIRO, Division of Plant Industry
Canberra City, A.C.T. 2601
Australia

Dr. R. K. Downey
Agriculture Canada, Saskatoon Research
  Station
Saskatoon, Saskatchewan S7N 0X2
Canada

Dr. Arlen Draper
USDA, Plant Genetics and Germplasm
  Institute
Beltsville, Maryland 20705

Dr. Pierre Dublin
GERDAT, Laboratoire de Culture in
  Vitro
34032 Montpellier Cedex
France

Dr. James A. Duke
USDA, Economic Botany Laboratory
Beltsville, Maryland 20705

Mr. W. E. Eberhardt
Crown Zellerbach, Southern Timber &
    Wood Products Division
Livingston, Louisiana 70754

Mr. J. Edgren
USDA—Forest Service
Portland, Oregon 97208

Dr. Herbert Ehramaier
Hopfenforschung und Hopfenberatung
8069 Wolnzach
West Germany

Dr. S. Ellerstrom
The Swedish University of Agricultural
    Sciences
Department of Crop Genetics & Breeding
S-268 00 Svalov
Sweden

Dr. C. R. Elliott
Agriculture Canada, Beaverlodge
    Research Station
Beaverlodge, Alberta T0H 0C0
Canada

Ir. Jan Engels
CATIE, Unidad de Recursos Geneticos
Turrialba
Costa Rica

Dr. Gustavo A. Enriquez
CATIE
Turrialba
Costa Rica

Dr. B. A. C. Enyi
West Africa Rice Development
    Association (WARDA)
Monrovia
Liberia

Dr. Emanuel Epstein
University of California, Land, Air &
    Water Resources Department
Davis, California 95616

Dr. W. Hardy Eshbaugh
Miami University, Department of Botany
Oxford, Ohio 45056

Dr. James Estes
University of Oklahoma, Robert Bebb
    Herbarium
Norman, Oklahoma 73019

Dr. Alice M. Evans
Cambridge University, Department of
    Applied Biology
Cambridge
England

Dr. Norman R. Farnsworth
University of lllinois at the Medical
    Center
Department of Pharmacognosy &
    Pharmacology
Chicago, Illinois 60680

Mr. Peter Faulkner
Statistics Canada, Library
Ottawa, Ontario K1A 0T6
Canada

Dr. George Fedak
Agriculture Canada, Research Branch
Ottawa, Ontario K1A 0C6
Canada

Dr. Laurie B. Feine
18 Mill Street
Cazenovia, New York 13035

Dr. Moshe Feldman
Weizmann Institute of Science,
    Department of Plant Genetics
Rehovot
Israel

Dr. A. R. Ferguson
DSIR, Division of Horticulture &
    Processing
Auckland
New Zealand

Dr. L. M. Fernie
Trout Cottage
Priory Lane
Frensham, Farnham
Surrey GU10 3DW
England

Dr. Richard L. Fery
USDA, Vegetable Laboratory
Charleston, South Carolina 29407

Dr. Gerhardt N. Fick
Sigco Research Inc.
Breckenridge, Minnesota 56520

Dr. Ralph E. Finkner
USDA, Agricultural Experiment Station
Clovis, New Mexico 88101

Mr. John Fiske
USDA—Forest Service
San Francisco, California 94111

Dr. Harold W. Fogle
USDA, Fruit Laboratory
Beltsville, Maryland 20705

Dr. G. Sam Foster
Crown Zellerbach, Southern Timber &
    Wood Products Division
Bogalusa, Louisiana 70427

Dr. Thomas R. Francis
Northrup King Co.
Ilderton, Ontario N0M 2A0
Canada

Dr. W. A. Frazier
3225 N.W. Crest Drive
Corvallis, Oregon 97330

Dr. Kenneth J. Frey
Iowa State University of Science and
    Technology, Agronomy Department
Ames, Iowa 50011

Dr. George F. Freytag
Mayaguez Institute of Tropical
    Agriculture
Mayaguez
Puerto Rico 00709

Mr. Adelard Gallant
Fisheries and Oceans
Charlottetown, Prince Edward Island
    C1A 7M8
Canada

Dr. Howard Scott Gentry
Gentry Experimental Farm
Murrieta, California 92362

Dr. Peter J. Gerone
Delta Regional Primate Research Center
Covington, Louisiana 70433

Dr. D. U. Gerstel
North Carolina State University, Crop
    Science Department
Raleigh, North Carolina 27650

Ir. F. M. A. Geurts
Department of Agricultural Research
1092 AD Amsterdam
Netherlands

Dr. J. S. Gladstones
Western Australia Department of
    Agriculture
South Perth 6151, Western Australia
Australia

Dr. D. R. Glendinning
45 Morningside Drive
Edinburgh
Scotland

Dr. H. J. Gooding
The West of Scotland Agricultural
    College, Department of Horticulture &
    Beekeeping
Auchincruive, Ayr KA6 5AE
Scotland

Dr. Major M. Goodman
North Carolina State University,
    Statistics Department
Raleigh, North Carolina 27650

Dr. B. P. Goplen
Agriculture Canada, Saskatoon Research
    Station
Saskatoon, Saskatchewan S7N 0X2
Canada

Dr. C. L. Green
Tropical Products Institute
London WC1X 8LU
England

Dr. Walter H. Greenleaf
Auburn University, Horticulture
    Department
Auburn, Alabama 36830

Dr. Ir. G. J. H. Grubben
Department of Agricultural Research
1092 AD Amsterdam
Netherlands

Dr. S. K. Hahn
International Institute of Tropical
  Agriculture (IITA)
Ibadan
Nigeria

Dr. Ivan V. Hall
Agriculture Canada, Kentville Research
  Station
Kentville, Nova Scotia B4N 1J5
Canada

Dr. R. A. Hamilton
University of Hawaii, Horticulture
  Department
Honolulu, Hawaii 96822

Dr. Ray O. Hammons
USDA, Crops Research Unit
Tifton, Georgia 31793

Dr. P. Hanelt
Zentralinstitut fur Genetik und
  Kulturpflanzenforschung
Akademie der Wissenschaften der DDR
D-4325 Gatersleben
East Germany

Dr. Wayne W. Hanna
USDA, Coastal Plain Experiment Station
Tifton, Georgia 31793

Dr. J. J. Hardon
Ministerie van Landbouw en Visserij
6708 PA Wageningen
Netherlands

Dr. Jack R. Harlan
University of Illinois at Urbana-
  Champaign, Department of Agronomy
Urbana, Illinois 61801

Dr. Hugh C. Harries
Dami Oil Palm Research Station
Kimbe, West New Britain Province
Papua New Guinea

Mr. Haji Alui Hashim
Firma Hasco
Jakarta Pusat
Indonesia

Dr. Alfred Haunold
Oregon State University, Crop Science
  Department
Corvallis, Oregon 97331

Dr. C. Jack Hearn
USDA, Horticultural Research
  Laboratory
Orlando, Florida 32803

Dr. H. E. Heggestad
USDA, Crops Research Division
Beltsville, Maryland 20705

Dr. Charles B. Heiser Jr.
Indiana University, Department of
  Biology
Bloomington, Indiana 47405

Mr. J. S. Hemingway
Reckitt & Colman Ltd.
Carrow, Norwich NR1 2DD
England

Dr. E. F. Henzell
CSIRO, Division of Tropical Crops &
  Pastures
St. Lucia, Queensland 4067
Australia

Mr. John B. Heppes
Canadian Wildlife Service, CITES
Ottawa, Ontario K1A 0E7
Canada

Dr. Anthony Hepton
Castle & Cooke Foods, Hawaii Pineapple
  Division
Honolulu, Hawaii 96801

Dr. Clair H. Hershey
Centro Internacional de Agricultura
  Tropical (CIAT)
Cali
Colombia

Dr. Claron O. Hesse
2251 W. Browning Avenue
Fresno, California 93711

Dr. Walter H. Hodge
3 Cayuga View Road
Trumansburg, New York 14886

Dr. J. A. Hoes
Agriculture Canada, Morden Research
  Station
Morden, Manitoba R0G 1J0
Canada

Dr. LeMoyne Hogan
University of Arizona, Department of
Plant Sciences
Tucson, Arizona 85721

Dr. Miguel Holle
CATIE, Programa de Cultivos Anuales
Turrialba
Costa Rica

Dr. Shigemi Honma
Michigan State University, Horticulture
Department
East Lansing, Michigan 48824

Dr. Art Hooker
Pfizer
St. Louis, Missouri 63141

Dr. Donald L. Hopkins
Agricultural Research Center
Leesburg, Florida 32748

Mr. William K. Howell
Miller Brewing Company
Milwaukee, Wisconsin 53208

Dr. Richard E. Hunter
USDA, Pecan Field Station
Brownwood, Texas 76801

Dr. Theodore Hymowitz
University of Illinois at Urbana-
Champaign, Agronomy Department
Urbana, Illinois 61801

Dr. Hugh H. Iltis
University of Wisconsin, Department of
Botany
Madison, Wisconsin 53706

Dr. Ernest Imle
USDA, International Programs Division
Hyattsville, Maryland 20782

Professor N. Lindsay Innes
National Vegetable Research Station
Wellesbourne, Warwick CV35 9EF
England

Dr. Amr A. Ismail
University of Maine at Orono,
Department of Plant & Soil Sciences
Orono, Maine 04469

Dr. Thomas J. Jacks
USDA, Agricultural Research Southern
Region
New Orleans, Louisiana 70179

Dr. G. V. H. Jackson
Ministry of Home Affairs & National
Development
Honiara
Solomon Islands

Dr. M. Jacquot
Institut de Recherches Agronomiques
Tropicales (IRAT)
34032 Montpellier Cedex
France

Mr. S. Jaima
Sabah Rotan Corporation Sdn. Bhd.
Kota Kinabalu, Sabah
Malaysia

Dr. Subodh K. Jain
University of California, Agronomy and
Range Science Department
Davis, California 95616

Mr. Stephen W. James
Canadian Wildlife Service
Ottawa, Ontario K1A 0E7
Canada

Mr. C. G. Jarman
Tropical Products Institute
London WC1X 8LU
England

Dr. Richard A. Jaynes
Connecticut Agricultural Experiment
Station
New Haven, Connecticut 06504

Dr. D. L. Jennings
Scottish Crop Research Institute
Invergowrie, Dundee DD2 5DA
Scotland

Mr. Suren Jhaveri
Health and Welfare Canada, Drug
Information Division
Vanier, Ontario K1A 1B8
Canada

Dr. A. G. Johnson
National Vegetable Research Station
Wellesbourne, Warwick CV35 9EF
England

Dr. Alfred Jones
USDA, Vegetable Laboratory
Charleston, South Carolina 29407

Dr. Quentin Jones
USDA, SEA
Beltsville, Maryland 20705

Dr. J. Helms Jorgensen
Riso National Laboratory
DK-4000 Roskilde
Denmark

Mr. A. N. Kasimatis
University of California, Viticulture &
    Enology Department
Davis, California 95616

Mr. Jeff Kazansky
Desert Whale Jojoba Co.
Tucson, Arizona 85717

Dr. Elizabeth Keep
East Malling Research Station
Maidstone, Kent ME19 6BJ
England

Dr. William R. Kehr
University of Nebraska, Agronomy
    Department
Lincoln, Nebraska 68583

Dr. E. R. Kerber
Agriculture Canada, Winnipeg Research
    Station
Winnipeg, Manitoba R3T 2M9
Canada

Dr. E. A. Kerr
Horticultural Experiment Station
Simcoe, Ontario N3Y 4N5
Canada

Dr. Tanaveer N. Khan
Western Australia Department of
    Agriculture, Plant Research Division
South Perth, Western Australia 6151
Australia

Dr. P. P. Khanna
National Bureau of Plant Genetic
    Resources
New Delhi—110012
India

Dr. Gurdev S. Khush
International Rice Research Institute
Manila
Philippines

Dr. Gordon Kimber
University of Missouri, Agronomy
    Department
Columbia, Missouri 65211

Dr. D. R. Knott
University of Saskatchewan, Crop
    Science Department
Saskatoon, Saskatchewan S7N 0W0
Canada

Dr. A. J. Kostermans
Herbarium Bogoriense
Bogor
Indonesia

Dr. Jose Antonio C. Laborde
INIA, Unit of Genetic Resources
Celaya, GT0
Mexico

Mr. Thomas D. Landis
USDA—Forest Service
Lakewood, Colorado 80225

Dr. Russell E. Larson
ACRI
State College, Pennsylvania 16801

Dr. Francis J. Lawrence
Oregon State University, Department of
    Horticulture
Corvallis, Oregon 97331

Dr. Richard E. C. Layne
Agriculture Canada, Harrow Research
    Station
Harrow, Ontario N0R 1G0
Canada

Mr. P. H. Leeuwenburg
Department of Agricultural Research
1092 AD Amsterdam
Netherlands

Dr. L. A. Lider
University of California, Viticulture &
  Enology Department
Davis, California 95616

Dr. G. Lockwood
Plant Breeding Institute
Cambridge CB2 2LQ
England

Dr. Roland Loiselle
Agriculture Canada, Research Station
Ottawa, Ontario K1A 0C6
Canada

Dr. William D. Loub
University of Illinois at the Medical
  Center
Department of Pharmacognosy &
  Pharmacology
Chicago, Illinois 60680

Dr. F. G. H. Lupton
Plant Breeding Institute, Cereals
  Department
Cambridge CB2 2LQ
England

Dr. R. C. F. Macer
The Plant Royalty Bureau Ltd.
Ely, Cambridge CB7 4ND
England

Mr. David Mack
Traffic (USA)
Washington, D.C. 20009

Dr. Don H. Maggs
CSIRO, Division of Horticultural
  Research
Merbein, Victoria 3505
Australia

Dr. W. F. Mai
Cornell University, Plant Pathology
  Department
Ithaca, New York 14853

Dr. Robert Marechal
Universite de Gembloux, Faculte des
  Sciences Agronomiques
B 5800 Gembloux
Belgium

Dr. Franklin W. Martin
University of Puerto Rico, Horticulture
  Department
Mayaguez
Puerto Rico 00708

Dr. J. P. Martin
University of California, Soil &
  Environmental Sciences Department
Riverside, California 92521

Dr. John W. Maxon Smith
Glasshouse Crops Research Institute
Littlehampton BN16 3PU
England

Ms. Maxine McCloskey
Whale Center
Oakland, California 94610

Dr. Gilbert D. McCollum
USDA, Vegetable Laboratory
Beltsville, Maryland 20705

Dr. J. S. McFarlane
US Agricultural Research Station,
  Sugarbeet Production Research Unit
Salinas, California 93915

Dr. R. I. H. McKenzie
Agriculture Canada, Winnipeg Research
  Station
Winnipeg, Manitoba R3T 2M9
Canada

Mr. Prince Meadors
Route 3
Box 101
Williamsburg, Kentucky 40769

Mr. Lou Messmer
Grays Harbor College, Biology
  Department
Aberdeen, Washington 98520

Dr. J. D. Miller
USDA, Sugarcane Field Station
Canal Point, Florida 33438

Dr. Jerry F. Miller
North Dakota State University
Fargo, North Dakota 58105

Mr. T. E. Miller
Plant Breeding Institute
Cambridge CB2 2LQ
England

Dr. Richard M. Mitchell
US Fish and Wildlife Service, Office of
the Scientific Authority
Washington, D.C. 20240

Dr. M. Kader Mohideen
Horticultural Research Station
Perumbarai-624212
Tamilnadu
India

Dr. J. L. Molina-Cano
La Cruz del Campo, S.A.
Department of Barley Breeding
Sevilla 7
Spain

Dr. John A. Mortensen
University of Florida, Agricultural
Research Center
Leesburg, Florida 32748

Dr. Julia F. Morton
University of Miami, Morton
Collectanea
Coral Gables, Florida 33124

Dr. John G. Moseman
USDA, Agricultural Research Center
Beltsville, Maryland 20705

Dr. Koichiro Mukade
Tohoku National Agricultural
Experimental Station
Shimo-Kuriyagawa
Morioka 020-01
Japan

Dr. Sunilkumar K. Mukherjee
University of Calcutta, University
College of Agriculture
Calcutta 700019
India

Mr. Bill Murphy
Fisheries and Oceans
Charlottetown, Prince Edward Island
C1A 7M8
Canada

Mr. John D. Murphy
USDA—Forest Service
Milwaukee, Wisconsin 53203

Mr. Abdul Rahman Mustafa
SAFODA
Kota Kinabalu, Sabah
Malaysia

Mr. Gary Nabhan
Meals for Millions Foundation
Tucson, Arizona 85733

Dr. J. Nabney
Tropical Products Institute
London WC1X 8LU
England

Dr. M. K. Nair
Central Plantation Crops Research
Institute
Calicut 673 012
Kerala
India

Dr. H. Y. Nakasone
University of Hawaii at Manoa,
Horticulture Department
Honolulu, Hawaii 96822

Dr. Lowell R. Nault
Ohio Agricultural Research and
Development Center, Entomology
Department
Wooster, Ohio 44691

Dr. N. M. Nayar
Central Plantation Crops Research
Institute
Kasaragod 670 124
Kerala
India

Mr. Larry K. Neuman
Miller Brewing Company
Milwaukee, Wisconsin 53208

Dr. R. A. Neve
Wye College, Department of Hop
Research
Ashford
Kent
England

Dr. Sadao Nishi
Vegetable and Ornamental Crops
  Research Station
Tsu-City
Japan

Dr. Ervin A. Oelke
University of Minnesota, Department of
  Agronomy and Plant Genetics
St. Paul, Minnesota 55108

Dr. Ian S. Ogilvie
L'Assomption Experimental Farm
L'Assomption, Quebec J0K 1G0
Canada

Dr. H.-I. Oka
National Chung Hsing University,
  Agronomy Department
Taichung
Taiwan

Dr. Robert K. Oldemeyer
The Great Western Sugar Co.,
  Agricultural Research Center
Longmont, Colorado 80501

Dr. Harold P. Olmo
University of California, Viticulture &
  Enology Dept.
Davis, California 95616

Dr. James R. Olson
University of Kentucky, Department of
  Forestry
Lexington, Kentucky 40546

Dr. R. T. Opena
International Agricultural Development
  Service
Balittan Lembang
Indonesia

Mr. John Overstreet
Robinson Forest
Clayhold, Kentucky 41317

Mr. E. R. Palmer
Tropical Products Institute
London WC1X 8LU
England

Dr. Jose Pardales Jr.
Visayas State College of Agriculture
Philippine Root Crop Research &
  Training Center

Baybay
Leyte 7127
Philippines

Dr. J. E. Parlevliet
Agricultural University, Institute of
  Plant Breeding (IVP)
6700 AJ Wageningen
Netherlands

Dr. Victor Manuel Patino
Instituto Vallecaucano de Investigaciones
  Cientificas
Cali
Colombia

Dr. Gordon Patterson
Hershey Foods Corporation, Technical
  Center
Hershey, Pennsylvania 17033

Dr. Erwin S. Penn
National Marine Fisheries Services,
  Office of Utilization Research
Washington, D.C. 20235

Dr. O. S. Peries
Rubber Research Institute of Sri Lanka
Dartonfield
Agalawatta
Sri Lanka

Dr. Robert B. Phelps
USDA—Forest Service
Washington, D.C. 20013

Dr. Barbara Pickersgill
University of Reading, Department of
  Agricultural Botany
Whiteknights, Reading RG6 2AJ
England

Dr. V. Sukumara Pillay
Kerala Agricultural University, Pepper
  Research Station
Panniyur, Taliparamba 670 141
India

Dr. D. Pimental
Cornell University, Entomology
  Department
Ithaca, New York

Dr. Donald L. Plucknett
CGIAR
Washington, D.C. 20433

Dr. E. Pochard
INRA, Centre de Recherches
  Agronomiques d'Avignon
84140 Montfavet
France

Mr. Kok Kian Poh
Sabah Rotan Corporation Sdn. Bhd.
Kota Kinabalu, Sabah
Malaysia

Mr. Pairoj Polprasid
Department of Agriculture, Division of
  Horticulture
Bangkok 9
Thailand

Dr. M. E. D. Poore
Commonwealth Forestry Institute
Oxford OX1 3RB
England

Dr. John Popenoe
Fairchild Tropical Garden
Miami, Florida 33156

Ms. Jan R. Potts
CTFA, Inc.
Washington, D.C. 20005

Dr. Jerrel B. Powell
USDA, Agricultural Research Center
Beltsville, Maryland 20705

Dr. Phil B. Price
South Dakota State University, Plant
  Science Department
Brookings, South Dakota 57007

Dr. Richard B. Primack
Boston University
Boston, Massachusetts 02215

Dr. Gordon M. Prine
University of Florida, Agronomy
  Department
Gainesville, Florida 32611

Dr. Claude Py
Institut de Recherches sur les Fruits et
  Agrumes (IRFA)
34032 Montpellier Cedex
France

Dr. K. O. Rachie
The Rockefeller Foundation
New York, New York 10036

Dr. N. Rajanaidu
PORIM
Serdang, Selangor
Malaysia

Dr. S. S. Randhawa
Indian Agricultural Research Institute,
  Regional Station
Simla 171004
India

Mr. John T. Reznor
International Flavours & Fragrances
  (Australia) Pty. Ltd.
Dee Why, New South Wales 2099
Australia

Dr. A. M. Rhodes
University of Illinois at Urbana-
  Champaign, Horticulture Department
Urbana, Illinois 61801

Dr. Billy B. Rhodes
Agricultural Experiment Station
Blackville, South Carolina 29817

Mr. Norman R. Richardson
CCTFA
Toronto, Ontario M4S 1A1
Canada

Dr. Charles M. Rick
University of California, Vegetable Crops
  Department
Davis, California 95616

Dr. W. W. Roath
Zambian Agricultural Research &
  Extension
Lusaka
Zambia

Dr. C. R. Roberts
University of Kentucky, Horticulture &
  Landscape Art
Lexington, Kentucky 40506

Dr. R. W. Robinson
New York State Agricultural Experiment
  Station, Seed & Vegetable Sciences
  Department
Geneva, New York 14456

Dr. C. J. Rodriguez Jr.
Centro de Investigacao das Ferrugens do
  Cafeeiro
Oeiras
Portugal

Dr. Charles E. Rogers
USDA, Conservation & Production
  Research Laboratory
Bushland, Texas 79012

Dr. Inocencio A. Ronquillo
Bureau of Fisheries & Aquatic Resources,
  Division of Research
Manila
Philippines

Prof. Dr. Hans Ross
Dompfaffenweg 33
D-5000 Koln 30
West Germany

Dr. Phillip Rowe
United Fruit Company, Division of
  Tropical Research
La Lima
Honduras

Dr. German Moreno Ruiz
Centro Nacional de Investigaciones de
  Cafe
Chinchina, Caldas
Colombia

Dr. J. N. Rutger
University of California, Agronomy and
  Range Science
Davis, California 95616

Dr. Edward J. Ryder
USDA, Agricultural Research Station
Salinas, California 93915

Dr. W. E. Sackston
McGill University, Plant Science
  Department
Ste. Anne de Bellevue, Quebec H9X 1C0
Canada

Dr. Satoshi Sakamoto
Kyushu National Agricultural
  Experiment Station
Nishigoshi
Kumamoto 861-11
Japan

Dr. Setijati Sastrapradja
National Biological Institute
Bogor
Indonesia

Dr. Jonathan D. Sauer
University of California, Department of
  Geography
Los Angeles, California 90024

Dr. Helen Savitsky
USDA-ARS
Salinas, California 93901

Dr. M. C. Saxena
ICARDA
Aleppo
Syria

Dr. A. B. Schooler
North Dakota State University,
  Agronomy Department
Fargo, North Dakota 58105

Dr. G. J. Sharp
Fisheries and Oceans, Resource Branch
Halifax, Nova Scotia B3J 2S7
Canada

Dr. John R. Shelly
University of Kentucky, Department of
  Forestry
Lexington, Kentucky 40546

Dr. Raymond L. Shepherd
Auburn University, Crop Science
  Research
Auburn, Alabama 36849

Dr. Wayne Sherman
University of Florida, Fruit Crops
  Department
Gainesville, Florida 32611

Dr. N. W. Simmonds
Edinburgh School of Agriculture
Edinburgh EH9 3JG
Scotland

Dr. Marr D. Simons
Iowa State University of Science and
  Technology
Ames, Iowa 50011

Dr. W. V. Single
Agricultural Research Centre
Tamworth, New South Wales 2340
Australia

Dr. Willis Skrdla
Iowa State University, North Central
  Plant Introduction Station
Ames, Iowa 50010

Dr. J. Smartt
University of Southampton, Department
  of Biology
Southampton S09 5NH
England

Mr. Emil J. Smith, Jr.
Department of Fish and Game, Marine
  Resources Branch
Sacramento, California 95814

Dr. M. V. Smith
University of Guelph, Environmental
  Biology Department
Guelph, Ontario N1G 2W1
Canada

Dr. R. R. Smith
University of Wisconsin, Agronomy
  Department
Madison, Wisconsin 53706

Dr. Sven Snogerup
Universitetets Botaniska Museum
S-223 61 Lund
Sweden

Dr. Wertit Soegeng Reksodihardjo
Pioneer Agricultura Ltda.
Londrina, Paraná
Brazil

Dr. R. K. Soost
University of California, Botany and
  Plant Sciences Department
Riverside, California 92521

Dr. Jorge Soria V.
Instituto Interamericano de Cooperacion
  para la Agricultura
San Jose
Costa Rica

Dr. James Soule
University of Florida
Fruit Crops Department
Gainesville, Florida 32611

Baron Benkt Sparre
Curator-Regnellian Herbarium
Stockholm 50
Sweden

Dr. Pinhas Spiegel-Roy
The Volcani Center, Agricultural
  Research Organization
Bet-Dagan
Israel

Dr. G. F. Sprague
University of Illinois, Agronomy
  Department
Urbana, Illinois 61801

Mr. Michael Srago
USDA—Forest Service
San Francisco, California 94111

Dr. Harold St. John
Bishop Museum
Honolulu, Hawaii 96819

Dr. R. E. Stafford
USDA-SEA
Bushland, Texas 79012

Dr. H. Thomas Stalker
North Carolina State University, Crop
  Science Department
Raleigh, North Carolina 27650

Dr. Jack Stanford
Brownwood, Texas 76801

Dr. Ian Staples
Department of Primary Industries
Mareeba, Queensland 4880
Australia

Dr. Lee S. Stith
University of Arizona, Plant Sciences
  Department
Tucson, Arizona 85721

Dr. Benjamin C. Stone
Universiti Malaya
Kuala Lumpur
Malaysia

Dr. W. B. Storey
University of California, Botany & Plant
  Sciences Department
Riverside, California 92521

Dr. Deon D. Stuthman
University of Minnesota, Agronomy &
Plant Genetics Department
St. Paul, Minnesota 55108

Dr. R. Subramanya
University of Florida, Agricultural
Research and Education Center
Belle Glade, Florida 33430

Dr. Norman L. Taylor
University of Kentucky, Agronomy
Department
Lexington, Kentucky 40546

Dr. Thomas L. Tew
Hawaiian Sugar Planters' Association
Aiea, Hawaii 96701

Dr. E. M. Thain
Tropical Products Institute
London WC1X 8LU
England

Ir. J. P. Thijsee
Department of Agricultural Research,
Agronomy & Information Services
Division
1092 AD Amsterdam
Netherlands

Mr. B. G. Thompson
U.S. Department of Commerce, National
Marine Fisheries Service
Washington, D.C. 20235

Dr. Sue Thompson
University of Illinois, Crop Evolution Lab
Urbana, Illinois 61801

Dr. T. E. Thompson
USDA, Pecan Field Station
Brownwood, Texas 76801

Dr. Bill D. Thyr
University of Nevada, Plant, Soil &
Water Science Dept.
Reno, Nevada 89557

Dr. T. F. Townley-Smith
Agriculture Canada, Swift Current
Research Station
Swift Current, Saskatchewan S9H 3X2
Canada

Dr. Hille Toxopeus
Stichting voor Plantenveredeling SVP
6700 AC Wageningen
Netherlands

Shri Phub Tshering
Ministry of Development, Agriculture
Department
Thimphu
Bhutan

Dr. John H. Turner Jr.
Shafter, California 93263

Dr. Jaap van Tuyl
Instituut voor de Veredeling van
Tuinbouwgewassen (IVP)
6700 AA Wageningen
Netherlands

Dr. Ramon V. Valmayor
Philippine Council for Agriculture &
Resources Research
Los Banos, Laguna
Philippines

Dr. L. J. G. van der Maesen
University of Illinois at Urbana-
Champaign, Agronomy Department
Urbana, Illinois 61801

Dr. T. van der Zwet
USDA, Fruit Laboratory
Beltsville, Maryland 20705

Dr. Joop P. Van Eijk
Instituut voor de Veredelingvan
Tuinbouwgewassen (IVT)
6700 AA Wageningen
Netherlands

Dr. Ir. A. M. van Harten
Agricultural University, Institute of
Plant Breeding
Wageningen
Netherlands

Dr. Thierry Vanderborght
Centro Internacional de Agricultura
Tropical (CIAT)
Cali
Colombia

Mr. Henk Varekamp
Instituut voor de Veredeling van
   Tuinbouwgewassen (IVP)
6700 AA Wageningen
Netherlands

Dr. P. G. Veeraraghavan
Kerala Agricultural University, Cashew
   Research Station
Trichur—680654
Kerala
India

Mr. Tom Vermillion
Crown Zellerbach, Southern Timber &
   Wood Products Division
Bogalusa, Louisiana 70427

Mr. Jose Vicente-Chandler
USDA, Agricultural Experiment Station
Rio Piedras
Puerto Rico 00928

Dr. Roland von Bothmer
The Swedish University of Agricultural
   Sciences, Department of Crop Genetics
   & Breeding
S-268 00 Svalov
Sweden

Prof. Dr. Tone Wagner
Institut za hmeljarstvo in pivovarstvo
63310 Zalec
Yugoslavia

Dr. I. Wahl
Tel Aviv University, Botany Department
Tel Aviv
Israel

Dr. Giles Waines
University of California, Botany and
   Plant Sciences
Riverside, California 92521

Dr. Helmut Wakeham
Philip Morris Incorporated
Richmond, Virginia

Dr. Norman D. Waters
University of Idaho, College of
   Agriculture
Parma, Idaho 83660

Dr. Ray Watkins
East Malling Research Station
Maidstone, Kent ME19 6BJ
England

Dr. Jay F. Watson
US Fish and Wildlife Service
Portland, Oregon 97232

Dr. Raymond E. Webb
USDA, Agricultural Research Center
Beltsville, Maryland 20705

Mr. Robert J. Weir
North Carolina State University, School
   of Forest Resources
Raleigh, North Carolina 27607

Dr. Osborn O. Wells
Forest Sciences Laboratory
Gulfport, Mississippi 39503

Dr. E. A. Wernsman
North Carolina State University, Crop
   Science Department
Raleigh, North Carolina 27650

Dr. M. N. Westwood
Northwest Plant Germplasm Repository
Corvallis, Oregon 97333

Dr. Thomas W. Whitaker
USDA-SEA
La Jolla, California 92038

Dr. George A. White
USDA, Agricultural Research Center
Beltsville, Maryland 20705

Dr. T. C. Whitmore
Commonwealth Forestry Institute
Oxford OX1 3RB
England

Dr. Garrison Wilkes
University of Massachusetts—Boston
Boston, Massachusetts 02125

Dr. David Williams
Maui Pineapple Company
Kahului, Hawaii 96732

Dr. Paul H. Williams
University of Wisconsin, Plant Pathology
   Department
Madison, Wisconsin 53706

Dr. F. D. Wilson
USDA, Western Cotton Research
  Laboratory
Phoenix, Arizona 85040

Dr. G. P. M. Wilson
Agricultural Research Station
Grafton, New South Wales 2460
Australia

Dr. Hugh D. Wilson
Texas A & M University, Biology
  Department
College Station, Texas 77843

Dr. Donald L. Woods
Agriculture Canada, Saskatoon Research
  Station
Saskatoon, Saskatchewan S7N 0X2
Canada

Dr. K. K. Wu
Hawaiian Sugar Planters' Association
Aiea, Hawaii 96701

Dr. Tomosaburo Yabuno
University of Osaka Prefecture, College
  of Agriculture
Sakai, Osaka Prefecture
Japan

Dr. D. M. Yermanos
University of California, Botany and
  Plant Sciences
Riverside, California 92521

Dr. Pooi Kong Yoon
Rubber Research Institute of Malaysia
Kuala Lumpur 01-02
Malaysia

Dr. George A. Zentmyer
University of California, Department of
  Plant Pathology
Riverside, California 92521

Dr. Ir. A. C. Zeven
Agricultural University, Institute of
  Plant Breeding
6700 AJ Wageningen
Netherlands

# Appendix D

## Names and Affiliations of Respondents to State/Provincial/Territorial Park Agency Survey (Listed Alphabetically by State/Province/Territory)

Ms. Barbara A. Johnson
Dept. of Natural Resources
Anchorage, Alaska 99501

Mr. Donn E. Cline
Recreation and Parks
Edmonton, Alberta T5J 3N4
Canada

Mr. Richard R. Perfrement
Recreation and Parks
Edmonton, Alberta T5J 3N4
Canada

Mr. James Neidigh
Arizona State Parks
Phoenix, Arizona 85007

Mr. Joe T. Fallini
Land Department
Phoenix, Arizona 85007

Mr. Robert T. McKittrick
Boyce Thompson Southwestern
   Arboretum
Superior, Arizona 85273

Mr. William C. Beattie
Department of Parks and Tourism
Little Rock, Arkansas 72201

Mr. George Trachuk
Ministry of Lands, Parks & Housing
Victoria, B.C. V8W 2Y9
Canada

Mr. Pete Dangermond, Jr.
Dept. of Parks and Recreation
Sacramento, California 95811

Mr. Randy Jamison
Dept. of Parks and Recreation
Sacramento, California 95811

Mr. Jim Cole
Division of Parks & Outdoor Recreation
Denver, Colorado 80203

Mr. William F. Miller
Dept. of Environmental Protection
Hartford, Connecticut 06115

Mr. Earl R. Fenton
Dept. of Natural Resources and
   Environmental Control
Dover, Delaware 19901

Mr. James W. O'Neill
Dept. of Natural Resources and
   Environmental Control
Dover, Delaware 19901

Mr. Jim Stevenson
Dept. of Natural Resources
Tallahassee, Florida 32303

Mr. Roy K. C. Sue
Dept. of Land and Natural Resources
Honolulu, Hawaii 96809

Mr. Merl Mews
Dept. of Parks and Recreation
Boise, Idaho 83720

Mr. Charles L. Tamminga
Dept. of Conservation
Springfield, Illinois 62706

Mr. Vernon M. Kleen
Dept. of Conservation
Springfield, Illinois 62706

Mr. Jeffrey B. Seidenstein
Dept. of Natural Resources
Indianapolis, Indiana 46204

Ms. Barbara Kent-Stafford
Division of Outdoor Recreation
Indianapolis, Indiana 46204

Mr. James E. Scheffler
Iowa Conservation Commission
Des Moines, Iowa 50319

Mr. Edward J. Unrein
State Park & Resources Authority
Topeka, Kansas 66601

Mr. Ed Henson
Department of Parks
Frankfort, Kentucky 40601

Mr. Kirk Carney
Dept. of Culture, Recreation and
    Tourism
Baton Rouge, Louisiana 70821

Mr. Herbert Hartman
Department of Conservation
Augusta, Maine 04333

Ms. Christina C. Hammond
Department of Conservation
Augusta, Maine 04333

Mr. Ed G. Wong
Dept. of Mines, Natural Resources &
    Environment
Winnipeg, Manitoba R3C 1T5
Canada

Ms. Barbara Newnam
Dept. of Natural Resources
Annapolis, Maryland 21401

Mr. Gilbert A. Bliss
Dept. of Environmental Management
Boston, Massachusetts 02202

Mr. Roland F. Nagel
Dept. of Natural Resources
Lansing, Michigan 48909

Mr. Raleigh W. Hosfield
Dept. of Natural Resources
St. Paul, Minnesota 55155

Mr. Aubrey D. Rozzell
Dept. of Natural Resources
Jackson, Mississippi 39209

Mr. John King
Department of Natural Resources
Jackson, Mississippi 39209

Mr. John Karel
Dept. of Natural Resources
Jefferson City, Missouri 65102

Mr. Greg F. Iffrig
Department of Natural Resources
Jefferson City, Missouri 65102

Mr. Paul R. Pacini
Dept. of Fish, Wildlife and Parks
Helena, Montana 59620

Mr. Charles Livingston
Dept. of Economic Development and
    Tourism
Yellowknife, N.W.T. X1A 2L9
Canada

Mr. James H. Fuller
Game and Parks Commission
Lincoln, Nebraska 68503

Ms. Kathleen Foote
Game and Parks Commission
Lincoln, Nebraska 68503

Mr. Marshall Humphreys
Dept. of Conservation & Natural
    Resources
Carson City, Nevada 89710

Mr. R. B. Armstrong
Dept. of Tourism
Fredericton, New Brunswick E3B 5C3
Canada

Mr. Eric G. Hadley
Dept. of Tourism
Fredericton, New Brunswick E3B 5C3
Canada

Ms. Gail A. Stickland
Dept. of Resources and Economic
  Development
Concord, New Hampshire 03301

Mr. Mark K. Sideris
Natural Resources Department
Santa Fe, New Mexico 87504

Mr. Vincent J. Moore
Adirondack Park Agency
Ray Brook, New York 12977

Mr. Robert W. Reinhardt
New York State Parks and Recreation
Albany, New York 12238

Ms. Sandra Meier
Dept. of Environmental Conservation
Albany, New York 12233

Mr. Donald G. Hustins
Dept. of Culture, Recreation & Youth
Pleasantville, Newfoundland A1C 5T7
Canada

Mr. Jim Stevens
Dept. of Natural Resources and
  Community Development
Raleigh, North Carolina 27611

Mr. Neal A. Shipman
Parks and Recreation Department
Bismarck, North Dakota 58502

Mr. A. Dale Smith
Department of Lands and Forests
Belmont, Nova Scotia B0M 1C0
Canada

Mr. Barry N. Diamond
Department of Lands and Forests
Belmont, Nova Scotia B0M 1C0
Canada

Mr. Donald G. Olson
Dept. of Natural Resources
Columbus, Ohio 43224

Mr. Clay McDermeit
Tourism & Recreation Dept.
Oklahoma City, Oklahoma 73105

Mr. Norm R. Richards
Ministry of Natural Resources
Toronto, Ontario M7A 1W3
Canada

Mr. John Elliott
Dept. of Transportation
Salem, Oregon 97310

Planning Division
Dept. of Highways & Public Works
Charlottetown, P.E.I. C1A 7N8
Canada

Mr. William C. Forrey
Dept. of Environmental Resources
Harrisburg, Pennsylvania 17120

Mr. Richard W. Eberle
Department of Environmental Resources
Harrisburg, Pennsylvania 17120

Mr. Gilles Barras
Ministere du Loisir, de la Chasse et de la
  Peche
Quebec, Quebec G1R 4Y2
Canada

Mr. Jacques Hebert
Ministere du Loisir, de la Chasse et de la
  Peche
Quebec, Quebec G1R 4Y2
Canada

Mr. William F. Ryan
Dept. of Environmental Management
Providence, Rhode Island 02903

Ms. Beth McClure
Dept. of Parks, Recreation and Tourism
Columbia, South Carolina 29201

Mr. David A. Kruger
Department of Game, Fish & Parks
Pierre, South Dakota 57501

Mr. Don Charpio
Department of Conservation
Nashville, Tennessee 37203

Ms. Linda Drees
Department of Conservation
Nashville, Tennessee 37203

Mr. David H. Riskind
Parks and Wildlife Department
Austin, Texas 78744

Mr. Jeff McCusker
Natural Resources and Energy
Salt Lake City, Utah 84116

Mr. Edward J. Koenemann
Dept. of Forests, Parks & Recreation
Montpelier, Vermont 05602

Mr. Dennis R. Baker
Dept. of Conservation and Economic
  Development
Richmond, Virginia 23219

Ms. Yvonne Ferrell
Washington State Parks and Recreation
  Commission
Olympia, Washington 98504

Mr. Donald R. Andrews
Dept. of Natural Resources
Charleston, West Virginia 25305

Mr. Loren M. Thorson
Dept. of Natural Resources
Madison, Wisconsin 53707

Mr. Joe Bonds
Recreation Commission
Cheyenne, Wyoming 82002

Mr. Manfred Hoefs
Dept. of Renewable Resources
Whitehouse, Yukon Y1A 2C6
Canada

# Notes

**Chapter 2 Logging**

1. The trade figures are the means (rounded to the nearest billion) of the import and export figures. The precise figures are $39,601,916,000 for world trade in timber products (D–384) and $11,833,487,000 for world trade in fishery products (D–288, D–385).

2. Table 2.1 shows the volume (roundwood equivalent) and estimated value in current dollars of U.S. timber production for the years 1976–1980 and the annual average value for that period. Data on volume come from S-817. The values have been calculated by us as shown in tables 2.3–2.5. Table 2.3 shows the values, volumes, and average prices for 1972 of each of the main timber-product groups (sawlogs, veneer logs, pulpwood, other products) from each section of the United States (North, South, West). These data are from P-475 and serve as our base. Table 2.3 also shows our estimate of the percent increase or decrease in unit price for each product group from each section for each of the years 1976–1980 together with the resulting average price. The average prices have been weighted according to the proportion of each product group from each section. The price calculations are derived from the data given in tables 2.4 and 2.5. Since some species and component products contribute more to a given product group than do others (e.g., southern pines are more important than hardwoods as a source of sawlogs in the South), where possible we have weighted the averages used to calculate the percent change in price. This is shown in the appropriate column.

3. Import values are customs import values (the value of imports as appraised by the U.S. Customs Service). Sources for the years 1976–1980 are S-450–S-454. The figure of $7.5 billion (the precise figure is $7,524,859,000) is the average annual value for the period of imported timber products and derived silvichemicals in the following categories of the U.S. International Trade Commission (S-816):

| | |
|---|---|
| Schedule 1. | Animal and vegetable products |
| Part 15. | Other animal and vegetable products |
| | Wood naval stores and Christmas trees *only* |
| Schedule 2. | Wood and paper; printed matter |
| Part 1. | Wood and wood products |
| Part 3. | Wood veneers, plywood and other wood-veneer assemblies, and building boards, *except* gypsum or plaster building boards and lath |
| Part 4. | Paper, paperboard, and products thereof |
| Schedule 3. | Textile fibers and textile products |
| Part 1. | Textile fibers and wastes; yarns and threads |
| | Yarns of paper only |

Part 3.   Woven fabrics
             Woven fabrics of paper yarns

Schedule 4.   Chemicals and related products

Part 1.   Benzenoid chemicals and products: C. Finished organic chemical products
             Vanillin *only*

Part 3.   Drugs and related products: B. Alkaloids, antibiotics, barbiturates, hormones, vitamins, and other drugs and related products
             Haarlem oil and terpin hydrate *only*

Part 7.   Aromatic or odoriferous substances; perfumery, cosmetics, and toiletry preparations: A. Aromatic or odoriferous substances
             Anethol and terpineol *only*

Part 8.   Surface-active agents; soap and synthetic detergents: A. Surface-active agents
             Carboxymethyl cellulose salts and lignin sulfonic acid and its salts *only*

Part 9.   Dyeing and tanning products; pigments and pigmentlike materials; inks, paints, and related products: C. Inks, paints, and related products
             Varnishes, cellulose derivative *only*

Part 13.   Fatty substances, camphor, chars and carbons, isotopes, waxes, and other products: A. Fatty substances
             Fatty acids from tall oil *only*
             B. Camphors, chars and carbons, isotopes, waxes, and other products
             Cellulose compounds, synthetic camphor, pitch and tar from wood, salicin and tall oil *only*

4. Gross product and value added are essentially the same. They equal the gross output (value of goods and services sold) less intermediate inputs (raw materials, energy, and other utilities). In the United States there is no source of comprehensive data on gross output or intermediate inputs by industry except for the U.S. Department of Commerce Bureau of Economic Analysis's five-year series of input-output analysis. The latest series available is for 1973–1977. The only source of data on gross domestic product for the years 1976–1980 is the Bureau of Economic Analysis's National Income and Product Accounts of the United States (NIPA) and supporting material (S-819–S-822). In NIPA reports gross product equals the sum of employee compensation plus net interest plus profit type income plus net indirect business taxes plus capital consumption allowances.

NIPA reports are organized on an industry-by-industry basis according to the Standard Industrial Classification (SIC) (D-381, D-382). It is not possible to identify from NIPA reports the contribution of timber to the gross product of a nontimber sector, such as the construction industry, or the contribution of other intermediate inputs in a timber sector, such as paper and allied products. Hence it is not possible to calculate the value added attributable to timber. Fortunately, Robert B. Phelps of the Demand, Price, and Trade Analysis Group, Forest Resources Economics Research Staff, USDA Forest Service, has calculated the value added attributable to timber for the years 1963, 1967, and 1972. Unfortunately, his industry groupings do not correspond exactly with those of NIPA, and even when they are close, the figures for gross product are significantly different. It is therefore possible to use the Phelps study to interpret NIPA only in a rather indirect and approximate way.

Our approach is shown in table 2.6. We have arranged Phelps's industry groupings according to the industry groupings of NIPA. For each industry grouping we show the gross product according to NIPA reports and the value added attributable to timber, according to Phelps, and its percentage of gross product for the years 1963, 1967, and

1972. We have used the resulting series of percentages to arrive at a percentage for the annual average of 1976–1980. If a 1963–1972 series is declining, we continue the decline ("Furniture and fixtures" is an example). If a series fluctuates, we choose a percentage between those of 1967 and 1972, but closer to 1972 than to 1967 ("Construction" is an example). This decision is based on the performance of the two NIPA sectors, lumber and wood products (24) and paper and allied products (26), whose gross products are almost entirely attributable to timber. This performance is shown in figure 2.1 and is summarized as a percentage of the gross domestic product in 1963, 1967, 1972, and the annual average in 1976–1980 as follows:

|  | U.S.$ MILLION | | | PERCENTAGE OF GDP |
|---|---|---|---|---|
|  | *Lumber and wood products* | *Paper and allied products* | *Lumber + paper* |  |
| 1963 | 4,444 | 6,316 | 10,760 | 1.818 |
| 1967 | 5,569 | 8,132 | 13,701 | 1.726 |
| 1972 | 9,623 | 11,413 | 21,036 | 1.790 |
| 1976–80 annual average | 17,469 | 20,676 | 38,145 | 1.788 |

The combined gross product of the two sectors for the 1976–1980 annual average as a percentage of the total gross domestic product is slightly lower than that of 1972 but not as low as that of 1967. This seems to us to be a reasonable indicator of timber's overall contribution to the U.S. economy during the period under review.

5. The USDA Forest Service (S-800) defines growing stock volume as net volume in cubic feet of live sawtimber and poletimber trees from stump to a minimum four-inch top (of central stem) outside bark or to the point where the central stem breaks into limbs. Commercial timberland is forest land that is producing or is capable of producing industrial wood at a rate in excess of 20 cubic feet per acre per year in natural stands and that is not withdrawn from timber utilization by statute or administrative regulation. Currently inaccessible and inoperable areas are included.

## Chapter 4 Trapping and Collecting

1. The average annual value (for 1976–1980) of U.S. imports of fur and skin products strictly from the wild was estimated to be $51,103,000. This was calculated as follows: 0% of the value of all imports listed under ? (unknown) in the source column of tables 4.2 and 4.3; 100% of the value ($23,381,000) of the 12 imports listed under W (wild) in the source column of tables 4.2 and 4.3. The 12 W import categories (all reptile and sharkskin imports plus lynx, marten, beaver, carpincho, otter, squirrel, seal, ocelot, and leopard) cover species that are not farmed commercially at all or whose commercial farm populations made negligible contributions to fur and skin supplies during 1976–1980. The main text (p. 81) discusses the confusion of the terms *wild, ranched,* and *farmed* with respect to the more important of these species. The import entries under W + D (wild and domesticated) in the source column of tables 4.2 and 4.3 were evaluated individually. In five import categories (all in table 4.2) we assumed that all furs from exporting countries other than Canada were from domesticated species and, therefore, had a 0% wild fur value. Of the Canadian exports, we calculated 65% to be from wild sources. This percentage represents the average annual percentage of Canada's total fur production for 1976–1980 that came from wild species (S-554–S-558). These five categories are: mink fur skin ($8,499,000 from the wild in Canada); fur skins nspf ($3,657,000 from the wild in Cana-

da); fox skins except silver, black, platinum ($1,392,000 from the wild in Canada); beaver, ocelot, wolf, sable, and other skins ($440,000 from the wild in Canada); and fur wearing apparel nspf of mink skins ($693,000 from the wild in Canada). The total value of wild furs in these five categories was estimated to be $14,681,000. The three remaining W + D entries were estimated as follows:

a. Hides and skins except fur skins nspf; leather and leathers nspf. This category includes wild rhea skins from South America and wild ungulate and domesticated ostrich skins from Africa (D. Mack, personal communication, 26 Jan. 1984), as well as other non-fur, non-reptile skins from unspecified wild or domesticated animals. Among the wild skins originating in Southeast Asia are probably those of pangolin (*Manis* spp.). The South American component may include wild peccary skins, since the United States is a significant importer of skins of both the white-lipped peccary (*Tayassu peccari*) and the collared peccary (*T. tajacu*) (A-2023). (Wild peccary skins could also enter the country under the category of pig and hogskins.) Because the South American contribution to this category is more than 36% and because the bulk of this contribution comes from wild animals, we estimate that a minimum of 25% of this entry may be attributed to the wild ($8,158,000).

b. Sable fur skins. The sable (*Martes zibellina*) is a new domesticate (see chap. 7). Supplies from the USSR come from both wild and domesticated animals. Canadian supplies are probably marten (*Martes americana*), marketed as Canadian sable (data on file from IUCN Conservation Monitoring Centre, April 1984). We estimate that 50% of this entry can be attributed to the wild ($4,285,000).

c. Deer, buck, doe skins. Reindeer is an established domesticate. Red deer and several other deer species are new or incipient domesticates (see chap. 7), but they are also harvested from the wild. We have assumed that the wild component is 50% of this entry ($598,000).

2. Not enough precise supply information was available in the literature for an estimate of the wild component of the following four import categories in table 4.1: feathers and down ($55,342,000); live plants nspf and orchids ($17,876,000); alpaca, llama, and vicuña hair ($580,000); and articles of bone, horn, hoof, whalebone, and quill ($534,200).

3. In the following eight categories (table 4.1) we estimated that 100% of the species/products concerned came from the wild: crude shells, shell articles ($10,980,000); raw ivory, worked ivory ($6,369,000); crude coral, worked coral, and cameos ($4,895,000); natural pearls and pearl parts ($1,880,000); sponges, sponge articles ($1,029,000); ornamental hydroids ($727,000); tussah, or wild silk ($66,000); and live turtles ($31,000).

4. The import value of $7,989,000 for wild fish for the aquarium trade was calculated as follows: all imports from South and East Asia considered 0% wild, except for 80% of those from Thailand (A-757) ($2,377,000), 100% of those from the Philippines (G-432) ($1,419,000), and 50% of those from Indonesia (G-1184) ($96,000); imports from South America and the Caribbean 100% wild ($3,677,000); imports from Africa 100% wild ($374,000); imports from unspecified other countries 0% wild.

5. The import value of $4,888,000 for wild birds for the pet trade was calculated as follows: 81.5% of $5,997,000, the average percentage of U.S. imports of wild birds in 1971 and 1972 (77 and 86%, respectively) (A-1197, A-1198).

6. The import value of $807,000 for wild live animals nspf represents the proportion of this category coming from tropical Africa, America, and Asia. Many of the unspecified live animals from these regions are likely to be reptiles (other than turtles) for the pet trade. In 1980, for example, the United States imported some 400,000 such reptiles,

including 55,000 iguanas (*Iguana iguana*), 25,000 house geckos (*Cosymbotus platyurus*), 20,000 boa constrictors (*Boa constrictor*), and 13,000 spectacled caimans (*Caiman crocodilus*) (G-1182).

## Chapter 5 Medicine

1. The government of Canada (G-727) defines a drug as "any substance or mixture of substances manufactured, sold or represented for use in:

a. the diagnosis, treatment, mitigation or prevention of a disease, disorder, abnormal physical state, or the symptoms thereof, in man or animal,
b. restoring, correcting or modifying organic functions in man or animal, or
c. disinfection in premises in which food is manufactured, prepared or kept, or for the control of vermin in such premises."

## Chapter 6 Food and Industrial Products

1. According to USDA publications (S-448, S-449, S-699), the average annual production of all pecans in the United States during the period 1976–1980 was 196,900,000 pounds. Of this, 62% (or 121,860,000 pounds) was derived from improved varieties and 38% (or 75,040,000 pounds) from native and seedling varieties. Of the 75,040,000 pounds from native and seedling varieties, 62.4% (or 46,800,000 pounds) came from five states in which, according to the literature (J-342, M-624), the wild pecan is especially abundant: Texas (23,200,000 pounds), Louisiana (12,160,000 pounds), Oklahoma (7,800,000 pounds), Mississippi (2,200,000 pounds), and Arkansas (1,440,000 pounds). We assumed, therefore, that 62.4% of the pecans harvested from native and seedling varieties was from the wild.

In these same USDA publications, 70% of the average annual dollar value of pecans was attributed to improved varieties, 30% to native and seedling varieties. These percentages were applied to U.S. farm sale dollar values for pecans for 1976–1980 (S-724, S-726–S-728). The average annual farm sale value for all pecans was $121,575,000—of which $85,103,000 (or 70%) came from improved varieties and $36,472,000 (or 30%) from native varieties and seedlings. We then calculated 60% (a rounding of 62.4%—the percentage by weight of wild pecans) of $36,472,000. This gave an average annual dollar value for wild pecans of $21.9 million.

2. The proportion of domesticated to wild blueberries produced by the United States was estimated on the basis of acreage and quantity data for 1978 (S-798). This proportion was then applied to average annual farm sales value for blueberries as reported in USDA publications (S-724, S-726–S-728). The proportion of wild blueberry imports from Canada was based on A. D. Draper, pers. comm., 9 October 1981.

3. Our method of calculating the proportion of domesticated to wild wild rice and the average annual value of U.S. production for 1976–1980 is discussed on page 450.

4. We estimated the import value of wild rattan to be $53,244,000. This was calculated as follows: Indonesia supplies 90% of the world trade, and cultivated sources account for only ⅙ of Indonesian production (G-428). We assumed, therefore, that 90% of the imports from Hong Kong, Taiwan, the People's Republic of China, Singapore, and Macao came from Indonesia. This sum ($29,562,300) was then added to imports directly from Indonesia ($1,347,000). Only ⅙ of $30,909,300 (or $5,151,550) could be attributed

to cultivated sources (as rattan from the other exporters—the Philippines, Thailand, Malaysia, and India—is largely native and wild).

5. We arbitrarily assigned 75% as an appropriate proportion from the wild in every import category for which a description of "mostly wild" was derived from our research.

6. Only 1% of Brazil's Brazil nut production comes from cultivated sources (V-208). Brazil nuts from 2% of the exporting countries—Turkey, Cameroon, Tanzania, and Mozambique—either are from plantations or are misidentified.

7. As there is some cultivation of gutta in Indonesia (V-277), we considered only non-Indonesian imports to be from the wild.

8. We arbitrarily assigned 25% as an appropriate proportion from the wild in every import category for which a description of "partially wild" was derived from our research.

9. We arbitrarily assigned 50% as an appropriate proportion from the wild in every import category for which "mostly wild" seemed too liberal an assessment and "partially wild" too conservative.

10. The bulk of Jamaican allspice is cultivated, whereas the bulk of Mexican, Guatemalan, and Honduran allspice comes from wild trees (P-164, P-183, P-256).

### Chapter 7 New Domesticates

1. Our sample of 160 species consists of those of the 226 crops in table 7.3 whose period of domestication we have been able to determine. The 226 crops are all the domesticated vascular plant species (excluding timber trees) for which U.S. production or import statistics are published and whose combined domestic (farm sales) plus import (customs) value is $1 million or more a year. Unless otherwise indicated, the values are average annual values for 1976–1980. U.S. farm sales data are from USDA's state farm income and balance sheet statistics (S-724, S-726–S-728) for the years 1976–1980. For crops not included in these statistics, we have obtained 1978 data from the 1979 census of horticultural specialties (S-832), and 1974 data from the 1974 census of agriculture (S-831). The 1978 census (S-798) does not provide values for the crops it reports on except for the horticultural crops reported in S-832. All import data are for the years 1976–1980 and are from the U.S. Department of Commerce's U.S. imports for consumption and general imports (S-450–S-454). Import data include crop products imported in processed as well as raw form but not in final manufactured form (e.g., the cotton import data include raw cotton and cotton fabric but not cotton shirts or sheets). They are therefore not strictly equivalent to the U.S. production (farm sales) data.

Table 7.2 lists the 226 crops in order of their combined annual value. It shows the family to which each crop belongs and so can be used as an index to table 7.3. Table 7.3 presents our data base, listing the crop species in alphabetical order by family and, within each family, in alphabetical order by scientific name of the species. Family names are according to Willis (V-232). We obtained from the sources indicated estimated dates of domestication for 160 of the 226 crop species. The total annual value of all 226 crop species is $65,679.8 million; that of the 160 crop species is $62,360.9 million (95%); and that of the 66 crop species not included in our discussion of domestication rates is $3,318.9 million (5%).

2. Annual volume and value data for wild wild rice production in Minnesota and annual volume data for domesticated wild rice production in Minnesota were supplied by E. A. Oelke (pers. comm., 17 Sept. 1981). Values of Minnesota domesticated wild rice

production were calculated on the basis of those for wild wild rice. The average annual figures for 1976–1980 are as follows:

|  | VOLUME (pounds) | VALUE (U.S.$) |
|---|---|---|
| Minnesota wild wild rice | 1,820,000 | 1,272,000 |
| Minnesota domesticated wild rice | 3,970,000 | 2,775,000 |

The remainder (less than 5%) of U.S. production of wild wild rice comes from Wisconsin (idem). We therefore rounded up the Minnesota volume figure to 1,900,000 pounds (+4.4%) to take account of this and increased the value figure pro rata to $1,328,000. The remainder of U.S. production of domesticated wild rice comes from California, Wisconsin, and Idaho (idem). Their combined production in 1978 was 49,700 pounds according to the 1978 census of agriculture (S-798). We assume that this is the processed weight, since the census gives 1,859,339 as the corresponding figure for Minnesota. Our data are unprocessed weights, and the 1978 figure for Minnesota is 4,200,000. Accordingly, we have used the 1978 data to determine the percentage contribution of Minnesota (97.4%) to total U.S. production and thereby establish U.S. figures of 4,075,000 pounds (volume) and $2,849,000 (value). Thus our estimates of average annual (1976–1980) production of wild rice in the United States are as follows:

|  | VOLUME (pounds) | VALUE (U.S.$) | PERCENT |
|---|---|---|---|
| Wild wild rice | 1,900,000 | 1,328,000 | 31.8 |
| Domesticated wild rice | 4,075,000 | 2,849,000 | 68.2 |
| TOTAL | 5,975,000 | 4,177,000 | 100.0 |

3. We classify the 34 recent crop species as follows:

18 COMMODITY CROPS

| 5 fragrance crops | ylang ylang *Cananga odorata* (MI)<br>geranium *Pelargonium graveolens* and other *Pelargonium* spp. (MI)<br>citronella *Cymbopogon winterianus* and *C. nardus* (MI)<br>patchouli *Pogostemon cablin* (MI)<br>eucalyptus *Eucalyptus globulus* (MI) |
|---|---|
| 4 fiber crops | jute *Corchorus capsularis* (MA)<br>sisal *Agave sisalana* (MI)<br>cork *Quercus suber* (MI; bulk of crop is wild)<br>rattan *Calamus* spp. (MI; bulk of crop is wild) |
| 3 flavor crops | peppermint *Mentha* × *piperita* (ME)<br>cinnamon *Cinnamomum verum* (MI)<br>cardamom *Elettaria cardamomum* (MI) |
| 3 miscellaneous crops | rubber *Hevea brasiliensis* (MA)<br>pyrethrum *Chrysanthemum cinerariifolium* (ME)<br>black wattle *Acacia mearnsii* (MI) |
| 2 medicinal crops | American ginseng *Panax quinquefolium* (ME; also wild)<br>quinine *Cinchona* spp. (ME) |

| | |
|---|---|
| 1 oil crop | oil palm *Elaeis guineensis* (MA) |
| 9 ANIMAL FEED OR FORAGE CROPS | bermuda grass *Cynodon dactylon* (MA) |
| | timothy *Phleum pratense* (MA) |
| | brome grass *Bromus* spp. (MI) |
| | orchard grass *Dactylis glomerata* (MI) |
| | fescue *Festuca* spp. (ME) |
| | birdsfoot trefoil *Lotus corniculatus* (MI) |
| | sweet clover *Melilotus alba* and |
| |    *M. officinalis* (MI) |
| | ladino clover, white clover *Trifolium repens* |
| |    (MI) |
| | crimson clover *T. incarnatum* (MI) |
| 4 FOOD CROPS | pecan *Carya illinoensis* (MA; also wild) |
| | cranberry *Vaccinium macrocarpon* (ME) |
| | macadamia *Macadamia integrifolia* (ME) |
| | blackberry *Rubus laciniatus* and |
| |    *R. ursinus* (ME) |
| 3 ORNAMENTAL CROPS | begonia *Begonia* spp. (ME) |
| | zinnia *Zinnia elegans* (MI) |
| | fuchsia *Fuchsia* spp. (MI) |

Note: MA = major, ME = medium, MI = minor.

4. U.S. timber imports identified by species group and coming from countries other than Canada are listed in table 7.11. Species that are not native to the exporting country are assumed to be domesticated. They comprise all the entries in the domesticated column except for *Araucaria angustifolia* (paraná pine) from Brazil, *Ochroma lagopus* (balsa) from Ecuador, and the *Tectona grandis* (teak) entries. Paraná pine from Brazil is both wild and cultivated (M-258). For the purposes of calculation we have assumed that U.S. supplies come in equal proportion from both sources. Balsa production in Ecuador was described in 1951 as principally from wild trees but with plantations becoming more important (D-416). Again, we have assumed that by now U.S. supplies come in equal proportion from both. U.S. import statistics combine balsa and teak. It is not difficult to distinguish the two, except in the case of unidentified countries (Other) and Brazil, which has teak plantations and may also be a source of balsa. Teak is native to Thailand, Burma, and India. It has been cultivated for some time, but acreages of wild teak are much larger than of plantation teak. In Thailand, India, and probably Burma, plantations account for less than 5% of total teak acreage. For these three countries we have estimated that 95% of exports to the United States come from the wild and 5% from plantations. Teak is cultivated in Malaysia, Taiwan, China, and the Ivory Coast; in Indonesia there is some dispute over whether the large (1.9 million acres) "natural" stands are indigenous or were established by Hindu settlers, possibly as early as the seventh century A.D. (G-805). We count them as cultivated. Supplies from the entrepreneurial centers of Hong Kong, Singapore, and Macao are estimated to be 84% wild and 16% domesticated, the proportions obtained from the subtotal of the entries from producing countries.

Non-Canadian imports coming entirely from the wild are the Central American pines (*Pinus caribaea* and *P. oocarpa*) (G-91, G-451, J-170; A. Greaves, pers. comm., 10 Feb. 1981); lauan or Philippine mahogany (*Parashorea, Pentacme,* and *Shorea* spp.) (A-1420; T. C. Whitmore, pers. comm., 10 Feb. 1981); brierroot (*Erica arborea* and *E. scoparia*) (A-90); Spanish cedar (*Cedrela* spp. mainly *C. odorata*) (A-863; G. E. Chaplin, pers.

comm., 10 Feb. 1981); the mahoganies (*Khaya* spp. and *Swietenia* spp.) (S-833); and ebony (*Diospyros* spp.), lignum vitae (*Guaiacum* spp.), and Brazilian boxwood (*Phyllostylon brasiliensis*) (T. C. Whitmore, pers. comm., 10 Feb. 1981).

5. The contribution of pine plantations as a proportion of total pine forest land operated by the 25 industry members of the North Carolina State University–Industry Cooperative Tree Improvement Program is shown below. Also shown are the contribution of improved seedling as a proportion of total acres planted annually, and the relative importance of different species as indicated by the proportion of seed orchard acreage they account for.

| FOREST LANDS | ACRES | (%) |
|---|---|---|
| Operated by the industries | 17.9 million | |
| Classified as pine land | 13.1 million | (73) |
| Pine plantations established | 6.9 million | (53) |
| Planted and direct-seeded annually | 476,000 | |
| Planted annually with improved seedlings | 256,000 | (54) |

| SEED ORCHARDS | ACRES | |
|---|---|---|
| Established | 3,705 | |
| Southern yellow pines | 3,639 | (98.2) |
| White pine (*Pinus strobus*) | 61 | (1.6) |
| Fraser fir (*Abies fraseri*) | 5 | (0.1) |
| *Southern yellow pine seed orchards by species* | | |
| Loblolly pine (*Pinus taeda*) | 3,011 | (82.7) |
| Slash pine (*P. elliottii*) | 404 | (11.1) |
| Longleaf pine (*P. palustris*) | 84 | (2.3) |
| Virginia pine (*P. virginiana*) | 79 | (2.2) |
| Pond pine (*P. serotina*) | 29 | (0.8) |
| Shortleaf pine (*P. echinata*) | 23 | (0.6) |
| Pitch pine (*P. rigida*) | 4 | (0.1) |
| Spruce pine (*P. glabra*) | 4 | (0.1) |
| Sand pine (*P. clausa*) | 1 | (—) |
| *Second-generation seed orchard* | 457 | |
| Loblolly | 441 | (96.5) |
| Slash | 16 | (3.5) |
| *First-generation seed orchard* | 3,059 | |
| Loblolly | 2,399 | (78.4) |
| Slash | 370 | (12.1) |
| Other | 290 | (9.5) |
| *Disease-resistant and other specialty seed orchard* | 189 | |
| Loblolly | 171 | (90.5) |
| Slash | 18 | (9.5) |

Source: A-937.

6. Our sample of 18 livestock species and 8 groups of aquaculture species is listed in table 7.17. These are all the domesticated animal and nonvascular plant species for which U.S. production or import statistics are published and whose combined domestic (farm sales) plus import (customs) value is $1 million or more a year.

Unless otherwise indicated, the farm sales values for mammals, birds, and insects are average annual values for 1976–1980 obtained from data in USDA's state farm income and balance sheet statistics (S-724, S-726–S-728). Unless otherwise indicated, farm sales values for fishes, crustaceans, and molluscs are average annual values for 1978–1980 obtained from data in the 1978 census of agriculture (S-798) and the U.S. Department of Commerce's current fishery statistics (P-434). Values for 1978 only are from the 1978 census of agriculture (S-798). All import values are average annual values for 1976–1980 and are from the U.S. Department of Commerce's U.S. imports for consumption and general imports (S-450–S-454).

The 1978 census of agriculture gives production statistics for ducks, geese, pigeons (squab), pheasants, and quails. In the absence of corresponding value data, only geese have been included in table 7.17 because their average annual import value is more than $1 million.

Farm sales values for cattle include dairy products; for sheep include wool; for goats are for mohair only; for chickens include eggs; and for bees include honey and beeswax. Import values for cattle comprise live animals, meat, dairy products, hides, and leather; for buffalo comprise hides and leather; for goats comprise live animals, meat, skins, leather, and hair; for sheep comprise live animals, meat, dairy products, skins, leather, wool grease, wool cordage, and wool fabrics; for pigs comprise live animals, meat, and leather; for camels comprise hair; for fox and mink comprise furskins; for rabbits comprise meat, furskins, and hair; for horses and mules comprise live animals, meat, hides, and hair; for geese comprise goose liver products; for chickens comprise meat and eggs; for bees comprise honey and beeswax; and for silkworm comprise silk yarns, raw silk, silk waste, silk roving, silk cordage, and silk fabrics.

7. We calculate the $706.6 million from newly domesticated timber trees as follows:

$700 million from U.S. plantations less $1.4 million from introduced recent domesticates in the North = $698.6 million

+ $1.9 million from Canadian plantations + $3.8 million domesticated Christmas trees from Canada = $5.7 million; less 10% (same percentage as for U.S. North) for introduced recent domesticates (*Picea abies* and *Pinus sylvestris*), or $0.6 million, = $5.1 million

+ $1.6 million from imports of domesticated paraná pine (*Araucaria angustifolia*) and $1.3 million of domesticated balsa (*Ochroma lagopus*), plantings of which began in 1940 (D-416), = $2.9 million.

> *(U.S.$ million)*
> | | |
> |---|---|
> | 698.6 | U.S. plantation production |
> | 5.1 | imports from Canadian plantation production |
> | 2.9 | imports from other plantation production |
> | 706.6. | |

## Chapter 8 Wild Genetic Resources

1. Grapes are grown on rootstocks on an estimated 941,000 hectares (72%) of France's 1,310,000 hectares of vineyards (1976 data) (G-707, M-495). The main rootstock cultivars, the areas on which they are grown, and the year of their original cross or selection from the wild (if known) are listed by species or species combination, as follows:

| SPECIES AND CULTIVAR | AREA (1,000 hectares) | PERCENTAGE OF TOTAL AREA | YEAR OF ORIGINAL CROSS/SELECTION |
|---|---|---|---|
| *Vitis riparia* | | | |
| Gloire de Montpellier | 150 | 15.9 | Not known |
| *Vitis rupestris* | | | |
| St. George | 300 | 31.9 | Not known |
| *V. berlandieri* × *V. riparia* | | | |
| 161-49 C | 55 | | 1888 |
| SO 4 | 40 | | 1886* |
| 420 A | 18 | | 1887 |
| | 113 | 12.0 | |
| *V. berlandieri* × *V. rupestris* | | | |
| 99 R | 50 | | 1889 |
| 110 R | 30 | | 1889 (1874)† |
| 140 Ru | 15 | | 1890s |
| 1103 P | 15 | | 1892 |
| | 110 | 11.7 | |
| *V. berlandieri* × *V. vinifera* | | | |
| 41 B | 75 | 8.0 | 1882 |
| *V. berlandieri* × ? | | | |
| 5 BB | 20 | 2.1 | 1886* |
| *V. riparia* × *V. labrusca* | | | |
| Vialla | 14 | 1.5 | Not known |
| *V. riparia* × *V. rupestris* | | | |
| 3309 C | 130 | | 1881 |
| 101-14 Mgt | 9 | | 1882 |
| | 139 | 14.8 | |
| *V. riparia* × (*V. cordifolia* × *V. rupestris*) | | | |
| 44-53 M | 20 | 2.1 | Not known |
| TOTAL | 941 | 100.0 | |

Source: G-707

*SO 4 and 5 BB derive from a consignment of seed labeled *Berlandieri* sent by a French nurseryman to Sigmund Teleki in Hungary in 1886. *Vitis berlandieri* is so difficult to root that it is crossed with other species (P-363). It is known that SO 4 is a *berlandieri-riparia* cross. Galet (G-707) lists 5 BB as "*berlandieri*," but we presume there is another species in its parentage.

†The year of the original cross is 1889. The selection of *V. rupestris* involved was sent from Texas to France in 1874.

2. The only wild germplasm to have been used in cacao breeding with commercial result is the Upper Amazon material collected by F. J. Pound in 1937 and 1942. The Upper Amazon germplasm consists of six groups of clones labeled IMC, MO, NA, PA, SCA, and POUND (J-634). The first five were collected by Pound on his 1937–38 trip; the sixth on his 1942 trip. The origins of all groups except for SCA are reasonably well established.

The IMC clones are a mixed group of types from the large island in the River Amazon opposite Iquitos (P-482). IMC stands for Iquitos Mixed Calabacillo (J-634, P-481), Iquitos Mixed Collection (J-634), or possibly Iquitos Mid Channel (J-634). The MO clones come from the River Morona region, about 300 miles up the River Marañón from Iquitos. The NA clones come from the peninsula formed by the confluence of the River Nanay with the Amazon, just downriver from Iquitos. The PA clones come from just upriver from the town of Parinari on the River Marañón, about 100 miles upstream of Iquitos (P-482). The POUND clones come from four sources: Iquitos Island (same source as IMC), the River Nanay (same source as NA), the River Napo (which joins the Amazon below Iquitos), and Contamana on the River Ucayali (P-483).

The origin of the SCA clones is not known (J-634). They are not mentioned in Pound's two reports (P-482, P-483). SCA stands for Scavina, which several cacao workers have interpreted as being a misspelling of Scavinia, an estate in Ecuador (G-95, J-237, S-380). Posnette (P-481) disagrees with this interpretation: "I cannot support this because Pound told me that the Scavina progeny, all of which he labelled SCA and spelled the name so, was from the Amazon and he planted it with Upper Amazon types. In their uniformity, homozygosity, type of self-incompatibility and the heterosis shown by their progeny in crosses with other types, the Scavinas fit into the Upper Amazon mould." In his reports (P-482, P-483) Pound described six distinct Upper Amazon types, all but one of which correspond to types in current germplasm banks: the mixed Iquitos group (IMC); the Morona type (MO); the Nanay types (NA); the Parinari types (PA); the Napo type, which initially he was not sure about (P-482) but which he confirmed to be a distinct type on his second trip and included in the POUND clones (P-483); and a type from the River Ucayali. Pound described the typical Ucayali strain as "quite green, only moderately warty, possessing a definite but blunt point and lacking the bottle neck" and with beans with dark purple cotyledons. He visited a stand between Contamana and Pucallpa in which all the trees were of this type, "and there was no sign of [witches' broom] disease on any tree. Here then appears to be another highly resistant type of cacao" (P-482). Pound confirmed this high resistance of the Ucayali type on a return visit in 1942: "A rapid visit was made to the Rio Ucayali as far as the Rio Pacheata [which joins the Ucayali upriver from Pucallpa] and in this trip it was found that conditions as regards Witches' Broom had not changed. . . . Budwood was collected from one tree in Contamana noted to have been free of disease in 1938 and which was still free though growing near infected trees" (P-483). This was the only trip that Pound made away from the Iquitos area on his 1942 mission, and Pound was obviously impressed with the Ucayali type. It is strange that apparently it is represented only by one (the Contamana) clone of the 32 POUND clones; perhaps there is a Scavina somewhere on the Ucayali.

There are differences of opinion as to whether the Upper Amazon clones are wild. "Most of the Amazon cacao is found near river banks and it is possible that all plants were associated with former human settlements. In other words, there is no evidence of the existence of truly wild cacao" (A-208). Cacao "is generally considered to be of such ancient origin as a cultivated crop that no wild forms exist" (Q. Jones, pers. comm., 6 Aug. 1981). Other authorities report wild cacao in several areas of the Amazon basin (A-474, S-182), and Pound's Upper Amazon collections in particular are often referred to as wild or semiwild (S-183; G. Lockwood, pers. comm., 3 Nov. 1981 and 25 Jan. 1982; H. Toxopeus, pers. comm., 10 Nov. 1981). Pound himself described his Upper Amazon collections as "growing wild" (P-482, p. 57), with the exception of some of the POUND clones that are evidently from planted trees (P-483). It is clear from his reports, however, that many of his "wild" trees were growing in secondary vegetation or in groves of planted cacao (or mixtures of naturally regenerated and planted cacao). Some of the Nanay trees, for example, Pound regarded as "old monarchial trees . . . which are probably originals left from a native population" (P-482). Reviewing the evidence, Cheesman (A-1415) concluded that most of the Upper Amazons are "most appropriately called 'semi-wild.' In that region some at least of the cacao trees found in the forests are probably truly wild and indigenous, but the groups found along the river banks are influenced by man, if only to the extent that by leaving cacao trees standing when clearing a patch for his habitation, man has altered the ecological conditions governing survival." According to our definitions of the terms, some of the Upper Amazon clones would be wild and others semiwild.

3. Formation of the shell of the kernel of the oil palm fruit is governed by a gene *sh*, one allele of which (*sh+*) determines presence of a shell, and the other (*sh−*) absence of a shell. The *dura* type of oil palm is homozygous for *sh+* (both alleles are *sh+*) and has a thick shell. The *pisifera* type is homozygous for *sh−* (both alleles are *sh−*) and has no shell at all. The *tenera* type of oil palm (*dura* × *pisifera*) is heterozygous (one allele is *sh+*, the other is *sh−*) and has a thin shell. All three types (*dura*, *pisifera*, and *tenera*) occur naturally. *Tenera* is now the plantation type of choice because, being thin shelled, it has a correspondingly thick mesocarp—the fibrous material that surrounds the endocarp (shell + kernel) and is the main oil-yielding part of the fruit. Pure *tenera* lines cannot be achieved by crossing *tenera* with *tenera* since such crosses segregate in the ratio of 1 *dura*: 2 *tenera*: 1 *pisifera*. Instead, wholly *tenera* lines are achieved by crossing female *dura* with male *pisifera* (female *pisiferas* are generally sterile) (G-147, G-150, S-186).

4. Following are the potential contributions of wild genetic resources to selected major crops:

### Apple (Malus pumila)

Vf gene for resistance to apple scab (caused by the fungus *Venturia inaequalis*) transferred from *M. floribunda*. Six cultivars were released in the United States—Prima (1970), Priscilla (1972), Priam (1974), Sir Prize (1975), Liberty (1978), and Jonafree (1979); three cultivars in Canada—Macfree (1974), Nova Easygro (1975), and Novamac (1978) (J-174; H. W. Fogle, pers. comm., 24 Aug. 1981). It is too soon to tell how successful these will be.

### Sugar Beet (Beta vulgaris)

For some time, breeders have been attempting to transfer resistance to the sugar beet cyst nematode (*Heterodera schachtii*), perhaps the major pest of the crop, from the wild *B. procumbens*. This and two other species in crop's secondary (possibly tertiary) gene pool, *B. patellaris* and *B. webbiana*, are the only known sources of high resistance to the pest. In 25 years of work, breeders have had the greatest difficulty in ridding the few successful crosses of undesirable characteristics without also getting rid of the gene for cyst nematode resistance. Recently a satisfactory breeding line has been developed, and commercial cultivars with cyst nematode resistance should be released in due course (D-151, M-272, M-273, S-30–S-35, S-219; G. E. Coe, pers. comm., 28 Aug. 1981; J. S. McFarlane, pers. comm., 21 July 1981; H. Savitsky, pers. comm., 30 July 1981).

### Peanut (Arachis hypogaea)

*Arachis monticola* (primary gene pool) is in the parentage of cultivar Spancross and is deduced to be in the parentage of cultivar Tamnut 74; however, it is not known to have contributed any characteristic, useful or otherwise, to either cultivar (R. O. Hammons, pers. comm., 5 Aug. 1981; H. T. Stalker, pers. comm., 31 Aug. 1981). Considerable effort is under way to improve disease resistance (largely to the *Cercospora* leafspots) through the use of less closely related wild species (J. Smartt, pers. comm., 21 July 1981). Wild species are for the most part the only sources of resistance to the crop's major diseases and pests (A-204, G-136, M-178, M-675, V-363). They could also be used to increase oil content (V-363).

*Rubber* (Hevea brasiliensis)

Three clones have been developed in Malaysia using wild germplasm, two of which have been released: RRIM 725 (1969–1970) and IAN 873 (1980–1982). Both have wild collections of *H. brasiliensis* (primary gene pool) in their parentage, from which they get a measure of resistance to South American leaf blight (SALB, caused by the fungus *Mycrocyclus ulei*). This is precautionary resistance that, it is hoped, will not be needed (SALB does not occur outside the Americas). Since rubber is a perennial crop with a replacement cycle as long as 30 years, very limited plantings have so far been made of these cultivars (P. K. Yoon, pers. comm., 29 Aug. 1981). Most work with wild species has been done in Latin America (D-146, G-439, P-105), but the United States imports very little rubber ($0.4 million a year) from Latin America.

*Barley* (Hordeum vulgare)

*Hordeum spontaneum* (primary gene pool) shows promise for improving the crop's productivity (V-13) and for providing a source of cytoplasmic male sterility (A-1427).

*Lettuce* (Lactuca sativa)

*Lactuca saligna* (secondary gene pool) is expected to provide resistance to downy mildew and to the cabbage looper (*Trichoplusia ni*) (E. J. Ryder, pers. comm., 30 July 1981). The cabbage looper is among the most destructive pests of the late fall and winter lettuce crops of the inland desert valleys of California. Chemical control is effective but expensive, requiring as many as seven applications to cope with heavy infestations; so resistance would save growers a lot of money (P-220).

*Common Bean* (Phaseolus vulgaris)

Many valuable genes are available in the wild relatives of the common bean but have been inaccessible. Use of recently developed embryo culture techniques and improved knowledge of species barriers and incompatibilities should result in greater commercial use of these gene pools (G. F. Freytag, pers. comm., 6 Oct. 1981).

*Sunflower* (Helianthus annuus)

Because the hybrids that make up 90% of the North American sunflower crop share the same cytoplasm, much of the crop could be quickly destroyed if a disease broke out to which the cytoplasm was susceptible. Alternative cytoplasms—and hence alternative sources of cytoplasmic male sterility—are needed as insurance. Fortunately, three more sources have been discovered (all in wild species): Manitoba, Canada, populations of *H. giganteus* and *H. petiolaris*, and a North Dakota population of *H. annuus* (G-837, V-393). They are being bred into parental lines.

5. High and medium alpha acid cultivars of hops

|  | *Alpha acids levels (%)* |
|---|---|
| *Seedlings of BB1 (wild* H. lupulus *from Morden, Manitoba × unknown male)* | |
| Brewer's Gold | 6–12 |
| Bullion | 6–13 |

| Canterbury Golding × (Brewer's Gold × OY1, wild H. lupulus *from Mendocino, California)* Northern Brewer | *Alpha acids levels (%)* 7–12.5 |
|---|---|

*Cultivars with Brewer's Gold in parentage*

| Pride of Ringwood | 11–14.5 |
|---|---|
| Ahil | 9–15 |
| Apolon | 9–12.5 |
| Atlas | 8–12.5 |
| K 692266 | 12–14 |
| K 700216 | 13–16 |

*Cultivars with Northern Brewer in parentage*

| Aurora | 10–15.6 |
|---|---|
| Blisk | |
| Bobek | |
| Buket | |
| Dunav | 10.7 |
| Neoplanta | 10 |
| Vojvodenia | 11–12.8 |
| Record | 9–11 |
| Huller Bitterer | 7–10 |
| Perle | |
| Wye Challenger | 7–11.6 |
| Wye Northdown | 7.7–10.7 |
| Wye Target | 11 |

*Cultivars whose high alpha acids content has not come from BB1 or OY1*

| Columbia | 8–10.2 |
|---|---|
| Comet | 9–13.5 |

Source: G-584, supplemented with data from G-583, M-243, S-9, S-10, and V-348.

6. The main Florida bunch grape (*Vitis labrusca*) and muscadine grape (*Muscadinia rotundifolia*) cultivars with useful characteristics from wild genetic resources are as follows:

Stover — comprises 60% of Florida bunch grape acreage; originates from a cross made in 1956; released 1968; contains germplasm from *V. berlandieri, V. rupestris,* and *V. shuttleworthi* (source of resistance to Pierce's disease).

Blue Lake — comprises 20% of Florida bunch grape acreage; originates from a cross made in 1950; released 1960; contains germplasm from *V. lincecumi* and *V. smalliana* (source of resistance to Pierce's disease).

Lake Emerald — comprises 15% of Florida bunch grape acreage; originates from a cross made in 1945; released 1954; contains germplasm from *V. simpsoni* (source of resistance to Pierce's disease).

Noble — comprises about 25% of Florida muscadine grape acreage; originates from a cross made in 1946; released 1973; contains germplasm from *M. munsoniana*.

Dixie    comprises about 20% of Florida muscadine grape acreage; originates from a cross made in 1953; released 1976; contains germplasm from *M. munsoniana.*

Sources: M-171; J. A. Mortensen, pers. comm., 31 Aug. 1981.

## Chapter 10 Recreational Fishing, Hunting, and Nonconsumptive Wildlife Use

1. The figure of $30 billion was derived from the addition of the expenditure averages from 1975 and 1980 (S-585, S-688) for fishing ($16.25) and hunting ($7.15) and the 1980 expenditure (S-585) on nonconsumptive activities ($6.6).

2. In 1982, Statistics Canada conducted the first comprehensive national survey on Canadian attitudes to wildlife and Canadian participation and expenditures in wildlife-related activities. Preliminary results from this survey (D-537), in addition to results from a 1975 sportfishing survey (A-1376), indicate the following: 5.4 million Canadians fished recreationally in 1975 and spent about Can $662 million (U.S. $651 million at 1975 exchange rate of 0.983 [D-450]); 1.8 million Canadians hunted recreationally in 1981 and spent about Can $1.2 billion (U.S. $1 billion at 1981 exchange rate of 0.834 [D-549]). To date, no estimate is available on the number of Canadians who participated in all nonconsumptive wildlife-related activities, but expenditures in this area for 1981 totaled Can $3 billion (U.S. $2.5 billion) (S. W. James, pers. comm., 22 July 1983). This sum includes money spent on boats, snowmobiles, multiple terrain vehicles, and other equipment.

3. The annual fishing participation figure of 53.9 million Americans was derived from the average of the 1975 number (53,929,000 people 9 years old or older) (S-688) and the 1980 sum (42,100,000 people 16 years old and older plus 11,800,000 people 6–15 years old) (S-585).

4. The annual hunting participation figure of 19.9 million Americans was derived from the average of the 1975 number (20,591,000 people 9 years old or older) (S-688) and the 1980 sum (17,400,000 people 16 years old and older plus 2,000,000 people 6–15 years old) (S-585).

## Chapter 11 Toward a Biogeography of Wildlife Use

1. Values were obtained from the sources indicated in chaps. 5–8, except for timber values. U.S. timber values were extrapolated from the annual average for 1976–1980 $/1,000 board feet price of sawtimber stumpage sold from National Forests (P-498, S-797, S-817). These enabled us to estimate values with respect to data on removals by species group and region in the Forest Statistics of the United States, 1977 (S-800) and slightly more detailed statistics for the West (P-478). Equivalent data for Canadian timber production by species group and region were obtained from Canadian forestry statistics (S-512, S-574).

The country-by-country data (for supplies from outside North America) and state-by-state/province-by-province data (for supplies from within North America) fell into three groups. First are those in which the country, state, or province was entirely within one biome: for example, Indonesia (tropical rain forest) and Maine (temperate mixed forest). Second, the country, state, or province consisted of more than one bioregion, but it was possible to determine how much of the supply came from each: for example, timber from Washington and Oregon, production statistics for which distinguish between the douglas fir subregion (temperate maritime forest) and the pine subregion (mountains). Third, more than one bioregion was involved, and we were unable to determine how much of the product came from each: for example, mahogany from the Neotropics (tropical rain forest and tropical dry forest). In this third situation we apportioned the sum as equally as possible to each bioregion concerned.

All data are rounded to the nearest $0.1 million. Such low values are necessary to represent fairly the contributions of nontimber resources. However, the percentage points lend a spurious impression of precision to the timber figures that we disclaim. The timber data are our best estimates but they are rough.

# References (Listed numerically)

A-1. Abbott, E. V. 1953. Sugarcane and its diseases. In USDA, *Plant diseases: The yearbook of agriculture:* 526–535 [Reference S-434].

A-2. Abbott, E. V. 1953. Red rot of sugarcane. In USDA, *Plant diseases: The yearbook of agriculture:* 536–539 [Reference S-434].

A-5. Adamson, A. D., & J.-M. K. Bell. 1974. *The market for gum arabic.* Report G87. Tropical Products Institute. London. 99 pp.

A-21. Akeley, R. V., F. J. Stevenson, & E. S. Schultz. 1948. Kennebec, a new potato variety resistant to late blight, mild mosaic and net necrosis. *American Potato Journal* 25: 351.

A-25. Alexander, L. J. 1963. Transfer of a dominant type of resistance to the four known Ohio pathogenic strains of TMV from *Lycopersicon peruvianum* to *L. esculentum. Phytopathology* 53: 869.

A-40. Andrus, C. F., & G. B. Reynard. 1945. Resistance to *Septoria* leaf spot and its inheritance in tomatoes. *Phytopathology* 35: 16–24.

A-57. Anonymous. 1978. Furs: flying high. *Newsweek.* February 6.

A-61. Anonymous. 1979. Options for growers in *Solanum* cropping. *New Zealand Journal of Agriculture* 138: 33–34.

A-89. Arasu, N. T., & N. Rajanaidu. 1975. Conservation and utilization of genetic resources in the oil palm. In J. T. Williams, C. H. Lamoureux, & N. Wulijarni-Soetjipto (eds.). *South East Asian plant genetic resources:* 182–186 [Reference V-211].

A-90. Arctander, S. 1960. *Perfume and flavor materials of natural origin.* Steffen Arctander. Elizabeth (New Jersey). 736 pp.

A-109. Adamson, A. D. 1971. *Oleoresins production and markets with particular reference to the United Kingdom.* Report G56. Tropical Products Institute. London. 46 pp.

A-134. Allen, J. L., & C. E. F. Manning. 1969. *Notes on the market for patchouli, citronella and lemongrass oils.* Report G39. Tropical Products Institute. London.

A-153. Anonymous. 1968. *Texas 42 SX: A special cross yellow corn hybrid.* Texas A & M Agricultural Experiment Station. Publication L-768.

A-154. Anonymous. 1968. *Texas 30A: An improved Texas 30.* Texas Agricultural Experiment Station. Publication L-769.

A-161. Anonymous. 1980. North American varieties from which to choose. *American Potato Journal (Supplement)* 57: 11–15.

A-164. Anonymous. No date. *Preliminary recommendation on jojoba propagation.* University of Arizona Indian Jojoba Project. 3 pp.

A-171. Aalders, L. E., I. V. Hall, & A. C. Brydon. 1978. Yields of native clones of lowbush blueberry under cultivation. *Fruit Varieties Journal* 32(3): 64–67.

A-172. Aalders, L. E., I. V. Hall, & A. C. Brydon. 1979. A comparison of fruit yields of lowbush blueberry clonal lines and related seedling progenies. *Canadian Journal of Plant Science* 59: 875–877.

A-201. Banga, O. 1957. Origin of the European cultivated carrot. *Euphytica* 6: 54–63.

A-202. Banga, O., 1976. Radish. In N. W. Simmonds (ed.). *Evolution of crop plants*: 60–62 [Reference S-384].

A-204. Banks, D. J. 1976. Peanuts: Germplasm resources. *Crop Science* 16: 499–502.

A-208. Bartley, B. G. D. 1963. Exploration for *Theobroma* in the Amazon Valley. *Genetica Agraria* 17: 345–349.

A-211. Baum, B. R. 1977. *Oats: wild and cultivated. A monograph of the genus Avena L. (Poaceae).* Agriculture Canada. 463 pp.

A-219. Beck, M. 1979. Energy: The joys of thinking small. *Newsweek.* October 8.

A-233. Bergh, B. O. 1976. Avocado. In N. W. Simmonds (ed.). *Evolution of crop plants*: 148–151 [Reference S-384].

A-238. Besse, J. 1964. L'amelioration du cacaoyer en Cote d'Ivoire. *Cafe, Cacao, The* 8: 245–263.

A-248. Boardman, J. 1976. The olive in the Mediterranean: Its culture and use. *Philosophical Transactions of the Royal Society of London (Series B)* 275: 187–196.

A-251. Bohart, G. E. 1952. Pollination by native insects. *USDA Yearbook* 1952: 107–121.

A-252. Bohart, G. E. 1960. Insect pollination of forage legumes. *Bee World* 41: 57–64, 85–97.

A-256. Bohart, G. E. 1972. *Management of habitats for wild bees.* Proceedings of a Conference on Ecological Animal Control by Habitat Management. 25–27 February 1971. Tall Timbers Research Station. Tallahassee, Florida 3: 253–266.

A-257. Bohart, G. E., & W. P. Nye. 1960. *Insect pollinators of carrots in Utah.* Bulletin of the Utah Agriculture Experimental Station. No. 419. 16 pp.

A-259. Bohart, G. E., M. J. Moradeshaghi, & R. W. Rust. 1967. Competition between honey bees and wild bees on alfalfa. *XXI International Beekeeping Congress Preliminary Scientific Meeting Summary Paper* 32: 66–67.

A-260. Bohn, G. W., & C. M. Tucker. 1939. Immunity to *Fusarium* wilt in the tomato. *Science* 89: 603–604.

A-266. Borrill, M. 1976. Temperate grasses. In N. W. Simmonds (ed.). *Evolution of crop plants:* 137–142 [Reference S-384].

A-267. Bosemark, N. O. 1979. Genetic poverty of the sugarbeet in Europe. In A. C. Zeven & A. M. van Harten (eds.). *Proceedings of the conference broadening the genetic base of crops:* 29–35 [Reference Y-48].

A-273. Brandes, E. W., & G. B. Sartoris. 1936. Sugarcane: Its origin and improvement. *USDA Yearbook:* 561–623.

A-292. Brown, C. R., H. Hauptli, & S. K. Jain. 1979. Variation in *Limnanthes alba:* A biosystematic survey of germ plasm resources. *Economic Botany* 33: 267–274.

A-299. Buckner, R. C., & L. P. Bush (eds.). 1979. *Tall fescue.* American Society of Agronomy, Inc., Crop Science Society of America Inc., Soil Science Society of America. Madison. 351 pp.

A-304. Burk, L. G., & H. E. Heggestad. 1966. The genus *Nicotiana:* A source of resistance to diseases of cultivated tobacco. *Economic Botany* 20: 76–88.

A-311. Butler, G. D., F. E. Todd, S. E. McGregor, & F. G. Werner. 1960. *Melissodes bees in Arizona cotton fields.* Technical Bulletin of the Arizona Agriculture Experimental Station. No. 139. 11 pp.

A-314. Byers, D. S. (ed.). 1967. *The prehistory of the Tehaucan Valley. Volume 1. Environment and subsistence.* University of Texas Press. Austin (Texas).

A-316. Balick, M. J. 1979. Amazonian oil palms of promise: A survey. *Economic Botany* 33: 11–28.

A-317. Berry, C. D., K. J. Lessman, G. A. White, & F. R. Earle. 1970. Genetic diversity inherent in *Vernonia anthelmintica* (L.) Willd. *Crop Science* 10: 178–180.

A-324. Blunden, G., C. Culling, & K. Jewers. 1975. Steroidal sapogenins: A review of actual and potential plant sources. *Tropical Science* 17: 139–154.

A-325. Bose, P. K., Y. Sankaranarayanan, & S. C. Sen Gupta. 1963. *Chemistry of lac.* Indian Lac Research Institute Namkum Ranchi. Bihar (India). 225 pp.

A-330. Beard, B. H. 1981. The sunflower crop. *Scientific American* 244: 150–161.

A-332. Blaak, G. 1976. Pejibaye. *Abstracts on Tropical Agriculture* 2: 9–17.

A-334. Baradi, T. A. el. 1968. Date growing. *Tropical Abstracts* 23: 473–479.

A-342. Baradi, T. A. el. Pulses: 3. Pigeon peas. *Abstracts on Tropical Agriculture:* 9–23.

A-359. Brandes, E. W., & P. J. Klaphaak. 1925. Breeding of disease resisting sugar plants for America. *Reference Book of the Sugar Industry of the World* 3: 50–57.

A-363. Cal, M. de la. 1980. Ancient cork industry to undergo automation. *International Herald Tribune.* May.

A-367. Cameron, J. W., & R. K. Soost. 1976. *Citrus.* In N. W. Simmonds (ed.). *Evolution of crop plants:* 261–265 [Reference S-384]

A-368. Campbell, C. G. 1976. Buckwheat. In N. W. Simmonds (ed.). *Evolution of crop plants:* 235–237 [Reference S-384].

A-369. Campbell, C. G., & G. H. Gubbels. 1978. *Growing buckwheat.* Agriculture Canada. Publication 1468. Ottawa. 11 pp.

A-376. Carter, J. F. (ed.). 1978. *Sunflower science and technology.* American Society of Agronomy, Crop Science Society of America, Soil Science Society of America, Inc. Madison. 505 pp.

A-379. Casida, J. E. (ed.). 1973. *Pyrethrum: The natural insecticide.* Academic Press. New York, London. 329 pp.

A-383. Cauquil, J., & C. D. Ranney. 1967. *Studies on internal infection of green cotton bolls and the possibilities of genetic selection to reduce boll rot.* Mississippi Agricultural Experiment Station. Technical Bulletin 53. 24 pp.

A-387. Chambliss, C. E. 1940. The botany and history of *Zizania aquatica* L. (wild rice). *Journal of the Washington Academy of Sciences* 30 (5): 185–203.

A-390. Chang, T. T. 1976. Rice. In N. W. Simmonds (cd.). *Evolution of crop plants:* 98–104 [Reference S-384].

A-412. Chona, B. L. 1957. Sources of resistance to diseases in breeding varieties of sugarcane. *Indian Journal of Genetics and Plant Breeding* 17: 257–268.

A-413. Choudhury, B. 1976. Eggplant. In N. W. Simmonds (ed.). *Evolution of crop plants:* 278–279 [Reference S-384].

A-135. Coffman, F. A. (ed.) 1961. *Oats and oat improvement.* American Society of Agronomy. Madison. 650 pp.

A-443. Contant, R. B. 1976. Pyrethrum. In N. W. Simmonds (ed.). *Evolution of crop plants:* 33–36 [Reference S-384].

A-446. Cooke, G. B. 1948. Cork and cork products. *Economic Botany* 2: 393–402.

A-450. Cooper, H. B. Jr., A. H. Hyer, & J. H. Turner Jr. 1977. Cotton germplasm development. *California Agriculture* 31: 14–15.

A-452. Cope, F. W. 1976. Cacao. In N. W. Simmonds (ed.). *Evolution of crop plants:* 285–289 [Reference S-384].

A-455. Correll, D. S. 1962. *The potato and its wild relatives.* Texas Research Foundation. Renner (Texas). 606 pp.

A-474. Cuatrecasas, J. 1964. Cacao and its allies: A taxonomic revision of the genus *Theobroma. Contributions from the United States National Herbarium* 35: 379–614.

A-482. Cutler, H. C., & T. J. Whitaker. 1961. History and distribution of the cultivated cucurbits in the Americas. *American Antiquity* 26: 469–485.

A-490. Cook, A. A., H. Y. Ozaki, T. A. Zitter, & C. H. Blazquez. 1976. *Florida VR-2: A bell pepper with resistances to three virus diseases.* University of Florida. Gainesville. Circular S-242.

A-500. Chadwick, M. G. A. 1961. The market for gum arabic. *Tropical Science* 3: 31–39.

A-506. Crute, I. R., & A. G. Johnson. The development of a strategy for lettuce downy mildew resistance. *Proceedings of the Eucarpia meeting on leafy vegetables (Wageningen): 88–94.*

A-507. Crute, I. R., & A. G. Johnson. 1976. The genetic relationship between races of *Bremia lactucae* and cultivars of *Lactuca sativa. Annals of Applied Biology* 83: 125–137.

A-523. Cocks, P. S., M. J. Mathison, & E. J. Crawford. 1980. From wild plants to pasture cultivars: Annual medics and subterranean clover in southern Australia. In R. J. Summerfield & A. H. Bunting (eds.). *Advances in legume science:* 569–596 [Reference S-245].

A-532. Cooke, G. B. 1961. *Cork and the cork tree.* International series of monographs on pure and applied biology. Division botany. Volume 4. Pergamon Press. 121 pp.

A-606. Breaux, R. D., & H. Koike. 1977. Problems and progress in breeding sugarcane for mosaic resistance in Louisiana's sub-tropical environment. *ISSCT Proceedings of the 16th Congress (Brazil)* 1: 425–432.

A-621. Borstel, R. C. von, & K. Lesins. 1977. Chapter 5. On germ plasm conservation with special reference to the genus *Medicago.* In A. Muhammed, R. Aksel, & R. C. von Borstel (ed.). *Genetic diversity in plants:* 45–50 [Reference M-293].

A-642. Chang, J. C. 1977. Ginseng and cosmetics. *Cosmetics and Toiletries* 92 (5): 50–57.

A-649. Cherfas, J. 1980. Still no ban on green turtle imports. *New Scientist.* March 27.

A-661. Chapman, V. J. 1970. *Seaweeds and their uses.* Methuen & Co. Ltd. London. 304 pp.

A-662. Coursey, D. G. 1967. *Yams: An account of the nature, origins, cultivation and utilization of the useful members of the Dioscoreaceae.* Longmans, Green and Co. Ltd. London. 230 pp.

A-666. Applezweig, N. 1977. *Dioscorea*—the pill crop. In D. S. Seigler (ed.). *Crop resources:* 149–163 [Reference S-366].

A-671. Coppen, J. J. W. 1979. Steroids: From plants to pills—the changing picture. *Tropical Science* 21 (3): 125–141.

A-674. Brokaw, H. P. (ed.). 1978. *Wildlife and America: Contributions to an understanding of American wildlife and its conservation.* Council on Environmental Quality, U.S. Fish and Wildlife Service, U.S. Forest Service, National Oceanic and Atmospheric Administration. Washington, D.C. 532 pp.

A-678. Bogdan, A. V. 1977. *Tropical pasture and fodder plants (grasses and legumes).* Longman. London, New York. 475 pp.

A-681. Committee on Genetic Vulnerability of Major Crops, Agricultural Board. 1972. *Genetic vulnerability of major crops.* National Academy of Sciences. Washington, D.C. 307 pp.

A-686. American Institute of Homeopathy. 1979. *The homoeopathic pharmacopoeia of the United States.* 8th edition. American Institute of Homeopathy. Falls Church (Virginia). 721 pp.

A-687. American Pharmaceutical Association Project Staff. 1979. *Handbook of nonprescription drugs.* 6th edition. American Pharmaceutical Association. Washington, D.C. 488 pp.

A-697. Anonymous. 1981. Go, go jojoba: Growers bet on a desert bean. *Time.* July 27.

A-717. Barnard, C. 1972. *Register of Australian herbage plant cultivars.* CSIRO. Division of Plant Industry. Canberra. 260 pp.

A-718. Baum, B. R. 1972. *Material for an international oat register.* Agriculture Canada. Plant Research Institute Contribution No. 895. Ottawa. 266 pp.

A-732. Building Research Establishment. 1972. *Handbook of hardwoods.* 2d ed. Revised by R. H. Farmer. Her Majesty's Stationery Office. London. 243 pp.

A-736. Caldwell, B. E. (ed.). 1973. *Soybeans: Improvement, production, and uses.* American Society of Agronomy, Inc. Madison (Wisconsin). 681 pp.

A-739. Canadian Pharmaceutical Association. 1981. *Canadian self-medication: A reference for the health professions.* Canadian Pharmaceutical Association. Ottawa. 484 pp.

A-757. Conroy, D. A. 1975. *An evaluation of the present state of world trade in ornamental fish.* FAO Fisheries Technical Paper No. 146. FAO. Rome. FIRS/T146. 128 pp.

A-769. Banfield, A. W. F. 1977. *The mammals of Canada.* University of Toronto Press. Toronto, Buffalo. 438 pp.

A-772. Bendiner, R. 1981. *The fall of the wild—the rise of the zoo.* E. P. Dutton. New York. 196 pp.

A-797. Conant, R. 1975. *A field guide to reptiles and amphibians of eastern and North America.* 2d edition. Houghton Mifflin Company. Boston. 429 pp.

A-839. Bianchini, F., & F. Corbetta. 1977. *Health plants of the world—atlas of medicinal plants.* Newsweek Books. New York. 179 pp.

A-863. Chaplin, G. E. 1980. Progress with provenance exploration and seed collection of *Cedrela* spp. *11th Commonwealth Forestry Conference.*

A-870. Cooper, W. C., P. C. Reece, & J. R. Furr. 1962. *Citrus* breeding in Florida—past, present and future. *Proceedings of the Florida State Horticultural Society* 75: 5–13.

A-890. Baranov, A. 1966. Recent advances in our knowledge of the morphology, cultivation and uses of ginseng (*Panax ginseng* C. A. Meyer). *Economic Botany* 20: 403–406.

A-898. Bohart, G. E. 1972. Management of wild bees for the pollination of crops. *Annual Review of Entomology* 17: 287–312.

A-909. Coville, F. V. 1937. Improving the wild blueberry. *USDA Yearbook of Agriculture* 1937: 559–574.

A-912. Cunningham, J. 1981. The berries: John Bragg, a Cumberland Country boy, has turned a summer job picking blueberries into a frozen food empire with sales nearing $10 million a year. *Halifax Business.* October.

A-913. Almeyda, N., & F. W. Martin. 1980. *Cultivation of neglected tropical fruits with promise. Part 8. The pejibaye.* USDA. SEA. 10 pp.

A-915. Anonymous. No date. *Cascara.* Oregon State College Extension Service. 2 pp.

A-921. Bollard, E. G. 1981. *Prospects for horticulture: A research viewpoint.* New Zealand Department of Scientific and Industrial Research. Discussion Paper No. 6. Wellington (New Zealand). 212 pp.

A-922. Bratt, L. C. 1979. Wood-derived chemicals: Trends in production in the U.S. *Pulp & Paper* 53: 102–108.

A-923. Burley, J., & B. T. Styles (eds.). 1976. *Tropical trees: Variation, breeding and conservation.* Linnean Society Symposium Series Number 2. Academic Press. London, New York. 243 pp.

A-924. Burton, M. (ed.). 1981. *The new Larousse encyclopedia of animal life.* Bonanza Books. New York. 640 pp.

A-931. Adansi, M. A. 1978. *Exploration and exploitation of genetic resources of oil palms as a basis for improvement.* Invited paper for AAASA "Workshop on genetic conservation in Africa." IITA. Ibadan (Nigeria). 13 pp.

A-937. Anonymous. 1980. *North Carolina State University—industry cooperative tree improvement program: 24th annual report.* North Carolina State University. School of Forest Resources. Raleigh. 63 pp.

A-942. Anonymous. 1982. *North Carolina State University—industry cooperative tree improvement program: 26th annual report.* North Carolina State University. School of Forest Resources. Raleigh. 72 pp.

A-949. Anonymous. 1982. "North Carolina State University—industry cooperative tree improvement program: A report on program objectives, accomplishments and future development efforts." Mimeo. 14 pp.

A-969. Benson, L., & R. A. Darrow. 1981. *Trees and shrubs of the southwestern deserts.* University of Arizona Press. Tucson. 416 pp.

A-971. Bull, T. A., & K. T. Glasziou. 1979. Sugarcane. In J. V. Lovett & A. Lazenby (eds.). *Australian field crops: Volume 2:* 95–112 [Reference J-490].

A-982. Anonymous. 1981. Beaver chomps at capital. *Times-Colonist.* June 17.

A-1013. Bartsch, W. 1978. Gnaws—a Canadian sequal to "Jaws." *Maclean's.* October 23.

A-1027. Abbott, R. T. 1980. *The shell trade in Florida: Status, trade, and legislation.* Traffic (USA) Special Report 3. Washington, D.C. 85 pp.

A-1045. Chandler, R. A. 1973. *The sea scallop.* Environment Canada. Fisheries Fact Sheet No. 4. 4 pp.

A-1063. Anonymous. 1982. Wisconsin's oriental roots. *Newsweek.* November 8.

A-1079. Anderson, A. B. 1955. Recovery and utilization of tree extractives. *Economic Botany* 9: 108–140.

A-1098. Anonymous. 1982. The status of beaver in Canada. *International Wildlife.* September/October.

A-1100. Anonymous. 1982. Mariculture challenged: Saving turtles or whetting tastes? *Equinox.* March/April.

A-1120. Amo, S. R. del. 1979. *Plantas medicinales del estado de Veracruz.* Instituto Nacional de Investigaciones sobre Recursos Bioticos. Xalapa (Veracruz). 279 pp.

A-1134. Carney, S. M., M. F. Sorensen, & E. M. Martin. 1978. *Waterfowl harvest and hunter activity in the United States during the 1977 hunting season.* U.S. Fish and Wildlife Service. Office of Migratory Bird Management. Laurel (Maryland). 27 pp.

A-1135. Carney, S. M., M. F. Sorensen, & E. M. Martin. 1980. *Waterfowl harvest and hunter activity in the United States during the 1979 hunting season.* U.S. Fish and Wildlife Service. Office of Migratory Bird Management. Laurel (Maryland). 27 pp.

A-1136. Carney, S. M., M. F. Sorensen, & E. M. Martin. 1981. *Waterfowl harvest and hunter activity in the United States during the 1980 hunting season.* U.S. Fish and Wildlife Service. Office of Migratory Bird Management. Laurel (Maryland). 27 pp.

A-1150. Bardach, J. E., J. H. Ryther, & W. O. McLarney. 1972. *Aquaculture: The farming and husbandry of freshwater and marine organisms.* John Wiley & Sons. New York, Chichester, Brisbane, Toronto. 868 pp.

A-1170. Anonymous. Unpublished. "Naval stores—general notes." Tropical Products Institute. London. 8 pp.

A-1186. Bjerre-Petersen, E., J. Christensen, & P. Hemmingsen. 1973. Furcellaran. In R. L. Whistler (ed.). *Industrial gums: Polysaccharides and their derivatives:* 123–136 [Reference V-102].

A-1187. Argus, G. W. 1980. The export of American ginseng (*Panax quinquefolius*) from Canada. *Proceedings of the 2nd National Ginseng Conference (Jefferson City, Missouri):* 9–11.

A-1188. Argus, G. W. 1980. *The status of American ginseng (Panax quinquefolius) in Canada.* 6 pp.

A-1189. Corbet, G. B., & J. E. Hill. 1980. *A world list of mammalian species.* British Museum (Natural History). London. Cornell University Press. Ithaca. 226 pp.

A-1197. Clapp, R. B. 1975. *Birds imported into the United States in 1972.* United States Department of the Interior. Fish and Wildlife Service. Special Science Report—Wildlife No. 193.

A-1198. Clapp, R. B., & R. C. Banks. 1973. *Birds imported into the United States in 1971.* United States Department of the Interior. Bureau Sport Fisheries. Special Science Report—Wildlife No. 170.

A-1201. Ager, S. 1983. The big business of whales. *San Jose Mercury News.* January 16.

A-1202. Allen, D. L. 1978. The enjoyment of wildlife. In H. P. Brokaw (ed.). *Wildlife and America: Contributions to an understanding of American wildlife and its conservation:* 28–41 [Reference A-674].

A-1203. Anderson, N., E. Frenette, and G. Webster. 1977. *Global village! Global pillage: Irish moss from PEI in the world market.* Social Action Commission. Roman Catholic Diocese of Charlottetown. Charlottetown (Prince Edward Island). 102 pp.

A-1205. Anonymous. 1982. *The whalewatching industry.* Report presented at the 1982 meeting of the International Whaling Commission. 3 pp.

A-1206. Bell, T. (ed.). 1978. *Fisheries of the United States, 1977.* US Department of Commerce. Current Fishery Statistics No. 7500. Washington, D.C. 112 pp.

A-1207. Bell, W. 1981. *Irish moss.* Underwater World Factsheets. Fisheries and Oceans. Ottawa. 6 pp.

A-1227. Bell, T. I., & D. S. Fitzgibbon (eds.). 1976. *Fishery statistics of the United States, 1974.* U.S. Department of Commerce. Statistical Digest No. 68. Washington, D.C. 424 pp.

A-1228. Bell, T. I., & D. S. Fitzgibbon (eds.). 1978. *Fishery statistics of the United States, 1975.* U.S. Department of Commerce. Statistical Digest No. 69. Washington, D.C. 418 pp.

A-1229. Bell, T. I., & D. S. Fitzgibbon (eds.). 1980. *Fishery statistics of the United States, 1976.* U.S. Department of Commerce. Statistical Digest No. 70. Washington, D.C. 419 pp.

A-1230. Bergh, B. O. 1975. Avocados. In J. Janick & J. N. Moore (eds.). *Advances in fruit breeding:* 541–567 [Reference J-8].

A-1236. Brown, A. G. 1975. Apples. In J. Janick & J. N. Moore (eds.). *Advances in fruit breeding:* 3–37 [Reference J-8].

A-1249. Brinkerhoff, L. A. 1970. Variation in *Xanthomonas malvacearum* and its relation to control. *Annual Review of Phytopathology* 8: 85–110.

A-1273. Chapin, W. 1887–1888. *Vermont agricultural report.*

A-1343. Anonymous. 1982. Jojoba—the "super bean." *Airborne.* July/August.

A-1356. Cayford, J. H., & A. Bickerstaff. No date. *Man-made forests in Canada.* Department of Fisheries and Forestry. Forestry Branch Publication No. 1240.

A-1360. Cannon, T. B. 1980. Rattan: Enduring, exotic. *Contempo.* July/September.

A-1361. Coffman, F. A., H. C. Murphy, & W. H. Chapman. 1961. Oat breeding. In F. A. Coffman (ed.). *Oats and oat improvement:* 263–329 [Reference A-435].

A-1367. Chemical Sources Association. 1980. *Source listing of natural and synthetic raw materials.* Chemical Sources Association. Washington, D.C. 159 pp.

A-1368. Chemical Marketing Reporter. 1981. *1981–82 OPD chemical buyers directory.* Schnell Publishing Company. New York. 1216 pp.

A-1375. Carroll, M. N. 1981. Panel products. In E. J. Mullins & T. S. McKnight (eds.). *Canadian woods: Their properties and uses:* 245–264 [Reference M-370].

A-1376. Anonymous. 1978. *Sportfishing in Canada.* Fisheries and Environment Canada. Recreational Fisheries Branch. Ottawa.

A-1377. Allan, M. 1974. *Plants that changed our gardens.* David & Charles. Newton Abbot, North Pomfret (Vermont) & Vancouver (British Columbia). 208 pp.

A-1378. Anonymous. 1981. *US cotton handbook.* Cotton Council International & National Cotton Council of America. Memphis (Tennessee). 40 pp.

A-1379. Anonymous. 1977. *Statistiek van de beplante oppervlakte per 1 februari 1977 van hyacinten, narcissen, bol-irissen, crocussen, allium chionodoxa, muscari, puschkinia en scilla.* Bloembollenkeuringsdienst (BKD). Hillegom, Netherlands. 16 pp.

A-1380. Anonymous. 1978. *Statistiek van de beplante oppervlakte per 1 februari 1978 van hyacinten, narcissen, bol-irissen, crocussen, allium chionodoxa, muscari, puschkinia en scilla.* Bloembollenkeuringsdienst (BKD). Hillegom, Netherlands. 16 pp.

A-1381. Anonymous. 1979. *Statistiek van de beplante oppervlakte per 1 februari 1979 van hyacinten, narcissen, bol-irissen, crocussen, allium chionodoxa, muscari, puschkinia en scilla.* Bloembollenkeuringsdienst (BKD). Hillegom, Netherlands. 16 pp.

A-1382. Anonymous. 1980. *Statistiek van de beplante oppervlakte per 1 februari 1980 van hyacinten, narcissen, bol-irissen, crocussen, allium chionodoxa, muscari, puschkinia en scilla.* Bloembollenkeuringsdienst (BKD). Hillegom, Netherlands. 18 pp.

A-1383. Anonymous. 1981. *HSPA sugar manual 1981.* Hawaiian Sugar Planters' Association. Aiea (Hawaii). 41 pp.

A-1384. Anonymous. No date. *Wheat variety handbook.* USDA Extension Service & Agricultural Research Service.

A-1385. Anonymous. 1977. *Hops 1976/77.* Joh. Barth & Sohn. Nurnberg (West Germany). 20 pp.

A-1386. Anonymous. 1978. *Hops 1977/78.* Joh. Barth & Sohn. Nurnberg (West Germany). 20 pp.

A-1387. Anonymous. 1979. *Hops 1978/1979.* Joh. Barth & Sohn. Nurnberg (West Germany). 20 pp.

A-1388. Anonymous. 1980. *Hops 1979/80.* Joh. Barth & Sohn. Nurnberg (West Germany). 20 pp.

A-1389. Anonymous. 1981. *Hops 1980/81.* Joh. Barth & Sohn. Nurnberg (West Germany). 16 pp.

A-1390. Anonymous. 1982. *Hops 1981/82.* Joh. Barth & Sohn. Nurnberg (West Germany). 12 pp.

A-1391. Anonymous. 1983. *Hops 1982/83.* Joh. Barth & Sohn. Nurnberg (West Germany). 13 pp.

A-1392. Anonymous. 1972. *Wheat variety descriptions, 1964–1972.* USDA. Agricultural Research Service.

A-1393. Anonymous. 1981. *Minnesota wild rice research, 1980.* University of Minnesota Agricultural Experiment Station. St. Paul. 81 pp.

A-1394. Anonymous. 1981. *Certified seed edition (part 2): Seed report, 1980.* United Fresh Fruit and Vegetable Association. Potato Division. Alexandria (Virginia).

A-1395. Anonymous. 1981. *Certified seed edition: Seed report 1981.* United Fresh Fruit and Vegetable Association. Potato Division. Alexandria (Virginia).

A-1396. Anonymous. 1983. *Certified seed edition: Seed report 1982.* United Fresh Fruit and Vegetable Association. Potato Division. Alexandria (Virginia).

A-1397. Asay, K. H., R. V. Frakes, & R. C. Buckner. 1979. Breeding and cultivars. In R. C. Buckner & L. P. Bush (eds.). *Tall fescue:* 111–139 [Reference A-299].

A-1408. Barnes, D. K., E. T. Bingham, R. P. Murphy, O. J. Hunt, D. F. Beard, W. H. Skrdla, & L. R. Teuber. 1977. *Alfalfa germplasm in the United States: Genetic vulnerability, use, improvement, and maintenance.* USDA. ARS. Technical Bulletin Number 1571. Washington, D.C. 21 pp.

A-1409. Bartley, B. G. D. 1968. F. J. Pound and his contribution to cocoa improvement. In H. Toxopeus (ed.). *Archives of cocoa research:* 192–196 [Reference S-578].

A-1410. Belcher, C. R., W. C. Sharp, R. W. Duell, & F. H. Webb. 1982. Registration of Atlantic coastal panicgrass (reg. no. 82). *Crop Science* 22: 1262–1263.

A-1411. Buckner, R. C., J. B. Powell, & R. V. Frakes. 1979. Historical development. In R. C. Buckner & L. P. Bush (eds.). *Tall fescue:* 1–8 [Reference A-299].

A-1412. Briggle, L. W., S. L. Strauss, D. E. Hamilton, & G. H. Howse. 1982. *Distribution of the varieties and classes of wheat in the United States in 1979.* USDA. ARS. Statistical Bulletin Number 676. 107 pp.

A-1413. Brothwell, D. 1978. On the complex nature of man-animal relationships from the Pleistocene to early agricultural societies. In J. G. Hawkes (ed.). *Conservation and agriculture:* 45–59. [Reference G-201].

A-1415. Cheesman, E. E. 1944. Notes on the nomenclature, classification and possible relationships of cacao populations. In H. Toxopeus (ed.). *Archives of cocoa research:* 98–116 [Reference S-578].

A-1416. Clepper, H. 1971. *Professional forestry in the United States.* Resources for the Future. Washington, D.C.

A-1419. Anonymous. 1981. *Forest planting, seeding, and silvical treatments in the United States: 1980 report.* USDA. Forest Service. FS-368. 15 pp.

A-1420. Ashton, P. S. 1978. *The biological and ecological basis for the utilisation of dipterocarps.* Paper presented at Eighth World Forestry Congress. Jakarta (Indonesia) 16–28 October 1978. 14 pp.

A-1421. Bolton, J. L., B. P. Goplen, & H. Baenziger. 1972. World distribution and historical developments. In C. H. Hanson (ed.). *Alfalfa science and technology:* 1–34 [Reference G-460].

A-1422. Anonymous. 1977. *US cotton handbook.* Cotton Council International & National Cotton Council of America. Memphis (Tennessee). 34 pp.

A-1423. Anonymous. 1978. *US cotton handbook.* Cotton Council International & National Cotton Council of America. Memphis (Tennessee). 33 pp.

A-1424. Anonymous. 1979. *US cotton handbook.* Cotton Council International & National Cotton Council of America. Memphis (Tennessee). 38 pp.

A-1425. Anonymous. 1982. *US cotton handbook.* Cotton Council International & National Cotton Council of America. Memphis (Tennessee). 39 pp.

A-1426. Anonymous. 1983. *US cotton handbook.* Cotton Council International & National Cotton Council of America. Memphis (Tennessee). 38 pp.

A-1427. Ahokas, H., & E. A. Hockett. 1981. Performance tests of cytoplasmic male-sterile barley at two different latitudes. *Crop Science* 21: 607–611.

A-1428. Baenziger, P. S., J. G. Moseman, & R. A. Kilpatrick. 1981. Registration of barley composite crosses XXXVII-A, -B, and -C (reg. nos. GP55–GP57). *Crop Science* 21: 351–352.

A-1429. Andres, L. A., E. R. Oatman, & R. G. Simpson. 1979. Re-examination of pest control practices. In D. W. Davis, S. C. Hoyt, J. A. McMurtry, & M. T. AliNiazee (eds.). *Biological control and insect pest management:* 1–10 [Reference D-409]

A-1430. App, B. A., & G. R. Manglitz. 1972. Insects and related pests. In C. H. Hanson (ed.). *Alfalfa science and technology:* 527–554 [Reference G-460].

A-1431. AliNiazee, M. T., & E. R. Oatman. 1979. Pest management programs. In D. W. Davis, S. C. Hoyt, J. A. McMurtry, & M. T. AliNiazee (eds.). *Biological control and insect pest management:* 80–88 [Reference D-409].

A-1432. Bishop, G. W., D. W. Davis, & T. F. Watson. 1979. Cultural practices in pest management. In D. W. Davis, S. C. Hoyt, J. A. McMurtry, & M. T. AliNiazee (eds.). *Biological control and insect pest management:* 61–71 [Reference D-409].

A-1433. Andres, L. A., & J. A. McMurtry. 1979. Introduction of new species and biotypes. In D. W. Davis, S. C. Hoyt, J. A. McMurtry, M. T. AliNiazee (eds.). *Biological control and insect pest management:* 41–45 [Reference D-409].

A-1434. Bailey, R. G. 1981. *Ecoregions of North America (after the classification of J. M. Crowley).* USDA. Fish and Wildlife Service.

A-1435. Bailey, R. G. 1980. *Description of the ecoregions of the United States.* USDA. Forest Service. Miscellaneous Publication No. 1391. 77 pp.

A-1871. Canadian Forestry Service. 1981. "A forest sector strategy for Canada: Discussion paper."

A-2023. Broad, S. 1984. The peccary skin trade. *Traffic Bulletin* 6 (2): 27–28.

A-2029. Barton, G. M., and H. H. Brownell. 1981. The chemistry of wood. In E. J. Mullins & T. S. McKnight (eds.). *Canadian woods: Their properties and uses:* 97–127 [Reference M-370].

A-2038. Aderkas, P. von. 1984. Economic history of ostrich fern, *Matteuccia struthiopteris*, the edible fiddlehead. *Economic Botany* 38 (1): 14–23.

A-2040. Anonymous. 1983. International trade in skins of monitor and tegu lizards, 1975–1980. *IUCN Traffic Bulletin* 4 (6): 71–79.

A-2041. Caldwell, J. R. 1984. Recent developments in the raw ivory trade of Hong Kong and Japan. *IUCN Traffic Bulletin* 6 (2): 16–20.

A-2042. Barzdo, J. 1984. The worked ivory trade. *IUCN Traffic Bulletin* 6 (2): 21–26.

D-3. Daniels, J., P. Smith, & N. Paton. 1975. The origin of sugarcanes and centres of genetic diversity in *Saccharum*. In J. T. Williams, C. H. Lamoureux, & N. Wulijarni-Soetjipto (eds.). *South East Asian plant genetic resources:* 91–107 [Reference V-211].

D-12. De, D. N. 1974. Pigeon pea. In J. Hutchinson (ed.). *Evolutionary studies in world crops: Diversity and change in the Indian subcontinent:* 79–87. [Reference G-311].

D-14. Dempsey, J. M. 1975. *Fiber crops.* University Presses of Florida. Gainesville. 457 pp.

D-31. Doggett, H. 1976. Sorghum. In N. W. Simmonds (ed.). *Evolution of crop plants:* 112–117 [Reference S-384].

D-50. Dunnett, J. M. 1957. Variation in pathogenicity of the potato root eelworm (*Heterodera rostochiensis* Woll.) and its significance in potato breeding. *Euphytica* 6: 77–89.

D-68. Dransfield, J. 1981. The biology of Asiatic rattans in relation to the rattan trade and conservation. In H. Synge (ed.). *The biological aspects of rare plant conservation* [Reference S-257].

D-69. Dransfield, J. 1979. *A manual of the rattans of the Malay peninsula.* Malayan Forest Records 29. Forest Department. Ministry of Primary Industries. Malaysia. 270 pp.

D-70. Dransfield, J. 1977. *Calamus caesius* and *Calamus trachycoleus* compared. *Gardens' Bulletin* 30: 75–78.

D-81. Durbin, R. D. (ed.). 1979. *Nicotiana: Procedures for experimental use.* USDA. Technical Bulletin 1586. 124 pp.

D-85. Eijk, J. P. van, & H. Q. Varekamp. 1979. Collections of species and ancient cultivars of tulip (*Tulipa* L.) in the Netherlands. In A. C. Zeven & A. M. van Harten (eds.). *Proceedings of the conference broadening the genetic base of crops:* 139–143 [Reference Y-48].

D-100. ERC Publishing Company. 1979. *Jojoba: The "super bean" of the future.* Special report of World Market Perspective. November. 13 pp.

D-104. Evans, A. M. 1976. Beans. In N. W. Simmonds (ed.). *Evolution of crop plants:* 168–172 [Reference S-384].

D-105. Evans, A. M. 1976. Clovers. In N. W. Simmonds (ed.). *Evolution of crop plants:* 175–179 [Reference S-384].

D-109. Evans, H. C., D. F. Edwards, & M. Rodriguez. 1977. Research on cocoa diseases in Ecuador: Past and present. *PANS* 23 (1): 68–80.

D-115. Epstein, E., J. D. Norlyn, D. W. Rush, R. W. Kingsbury, D. B. Kelley, G. A. Cunningham, & A. F. Wrona. 1980. Saline culture of crops: A genetic approach. *Science* 210: 399–404.

D-118. Eck, P., & N. F. Childers (eds.). 1966. *Blueberry culture.* Rutgers University Press. New Brunswick (New Jersey). 378 pp.

D-135. Farnsworth, N. R., & R. W. Morris. 1976. Higher plants—the sleeping giant of drug development. *American Journal of Pharmacy* 148: 46–52.

D-141. Faulkner, R. 1976. Timber trees. In N. W. Simmonds (ed.). *Evolution of crop plants:* 298–301. [Reference S-384].

D-144. Feldman, M. 1976. Wheats. In N. W. Simmonds (ed.). *Evolution of crop plants:* 120–128 [Reference S-384].

D-146. Ferwerda, F. P. 1969. Rubber. In F. P. Ferwerda & F. Wit (eds.). *Outlines of perennial crop breeding in the tropics:* 427–458 [Reference D-257].

D-148. Ferwerda, F. P. 1976. Coffees. In N. W. Simmonds (ed.). *Evolution of crop plants:* 257–260 [Reference S-384].

D-150. Fick, G. N. 1978. Breeding and genetics. In J. F. Carter (ed.). *Sunflower science and technology:* 279–338 [Reference A-376].

D-151. Finkner, R. E., & J. F. Swink. 1956. Breeding sugar beets for resistance to nematodes. *Agronomy Journal* 48: 389–392.

D-156. Fleischmann, G., R. I. H. McKenzie, & W. A. Shipton. 1971. Inheritance of crown rust resistance genes in *Avena sterilis* collections from Israel, Portugal, and Tunisia. *Canadian Journal of Genetics and Cytology* 13: 251–255.

D-168. Frankel, O. H. (ed.). 1973. *Survey of crop genetic resources in their centres of diversity: First report.* FAO, IBPGR, & ICSU. 164 pp.

D-175. Frankel, O. H., & J. G. Hawkes (eds.). 1975. *Crop genetic resources for today and tomorrow.* International Biological Programme 2. Cambridge University Press. Cambridge, London, New York, Melbourne. 492 pp.

D-180. Frey, K. J. 1976. Plant breeding in the seventies: Useful genes from wild species. *Egyptian Journal of Genetics and Cytology* 5: 460–482.

D-181. Frey, K. J., J. A. Browning, & R. L. Grindeland. 1971. Registration of multiline E68, multiline E69, and multiline E70 oat cultivars. *Crop Science* 11: 939–940.

D-197. Feldman, M., & E. R. Sears. 1981. The wild gene resources of wheat. *Scientific American* 244: 98–109.

D-205. Davidson, J. 1942. *The cascara tree in British Columbia.* Province of British Columbia Bulletin No. A108. 32 pp.

D-207. Dunckelman, P. H., & R. D. Breaux. 1971. Breeding sugarcane varieties for Louisiana with new germ plasm. *ISSCT Proceedings of the 14th Congress (Louisiana):* 233–239.

D-220. Flores, S. C., & S. K. Osada. 1980. Sugarcane smut (*Ustilago scitaminea* Syd) in Belize and Mexico. *ISSCT Proceedings of the 17th Congress (Philippines)* 2: 1481–1484.

D-221. Fischbeck, C. L. 1967. Ethiopian civet. *American Perfumer and Cosmetics* 82 (12): 45–46, 48.

D-238. Farnsworth, N. R. 1969. Drugs from animals. *Tile & Till* 55 (4): 67–71.

D-242. FAO. 1976. *Appendixes.* Extracted from The marketing of tropical wood. C. Wood species from Southeast Asian tropical moist forests. FAO Forestry Department. FO:MISC/76/8. Rome.

D-245. FAO. 1980. *1979 yearbook of fishery statistics: Catches and landings.* FAO Fisheries Series. Volume 48. Rome. 384 pp.

D-246. Duke, J. A. 1981. *Handbook of legumes of world economic importance.* Plenum Press. New York, London. 345 pp.

D-248. Dransfield, J. 1979. *Report of consultancy on rattan development carried out in Thailand, Philippines, Indonesia and Malaysia.* 14 March–8 May 1979. For FAO Regional Office for Asia and the Far East. Bangkok. 40 pp.

D-252. Free, J. B. 1970. *Insect pollination of crop plants.* Academic Press. London, New York. 544 pp.

D-257. Ferwerda, F. P., & F. Wit (eds.). 1969. *Outlines of perennial crop breeding in the tropics.* Miscellaneous Papers 4. H. Veenman and Zonen, N. V. Wageningen, Netherlands. 511 pp.

D-268. Davidson, A. 1979. *North Atlantic seafood.* Macmillan London. 512 pp.

D-272. Duplaix, N. 1981. *River otter export and international trade.* Prepared for River Otter Educational Workshop. 5 December 1981. Hancock, New Hampshire. Traffic (USA). Washington, D.C. 16 pp.

D-281. Emden, H. F. van. 1974. *Pest control and its ecology.* Institute of Biology's Studies in Biology No. 50. Edward Arnold. London. 60 pp.

D-288. FAO. 1977. *1976 yearbook of fishery statistics: Fishery commodities.* Volume 43. FAO Fisheries Series. Rome. 336 pp.

D-320. Deems, E. F. Jr., & D. Pursley (eds.). 1978. *North American furbearers: Their management, research and harvest status in 1976.* International Association of Fish and Wildlife Agencies. College Park (Maryland). 171 pp.

D-322. Dorst, J., & P. Dandelot. 1972. *Guide des grands mammiferes d'Afrique.* Delachaux & Niestle S. A. Neuchatel, Paris. 286 pp.

D-339. Darrow, G. M. 1960. Blueberry breeding: Past, present, future. *American Horticultural Magazine* 39: 14–33.

D-366. Darrow, G. M. 1937. Blackberry and raspberry improvement. *USDA Yearbook of Agriculture* 1937: 496–533.

D-371. Duplaix, N. 1979. *Traffic (USA) report on the ivory trade in response to the proposed Elephant Protection Act of 1979, HR4685 before the Merchant Marine and Fisheries Committee.* Traffic (USA). Washington, D.C.

D-378. Dunn, L. 1942. *Cascara.* Oregon State College. School of Forestry. Corvallis (Oregon). 10 pp.

D-381. Executive Office of the President & Office of Management and Budget. 1972. *Standard industrial classification manual: 1972.* U.S. Department of Commerce. Washington, D.C. 649 pp.

D-382. Executive Office of the President & Office of Management and Budget. 1977. *Standard industrial classification manual: 1972: 1977 supplement.* U.S. Department of Commerce. Washington, D.C. 15 pp.

D-384. FAO. 1981. *1979 yearbook of forest products.* FAO Forestry Series. FAO Rome. 430 pp.

D-385. FAO. 1981. *1980 yearbook of fishery statistics: Fishery commodities.* FAO Fisheries Series. Volume 51. Rome. 178 pp.

D-386. FAO. 1981. *1980 FAO production yearbook.* FAO Statistics Series No. 34. Rome. 296 pp.

D-396. Ellis, G. No date. *Better trees for northwest forests: A brief look at tree improvement programs in western North America.* Forest Genetics Research Foundation. 19 pp.

D-404. Farnsworth, N. R. 1982. *The potential consequence of plant extinction in the United States on the current and future availability of prescription drugs.* Presented at a symposium on "Estimating the value of endangered species: Responsibilities and role of the scientific community." Annual meeting of the AAAS. Washington, D.C. 19 pp.

D-405. Fehr, W. R., & H. H. Hadley (eds.). 1980. *Hybridization of crop plants.* American Society of Agronomy and Crop Science Society of America. Madison (Wisconsin). 765 pp.

D-406. Fick, G. N., D. E. Zimmer, & T. E. Thompson. 1976. Wild species of *Helianthus* as a source of variability in sunflower breeding. *Proceedings of Sunflower Forum:* 4–5.

D-409. Davis, D. W., S. C. Hoyt, J. A. McMurtry, & M. T. AliNiazee (eds.). 1979. *Biological control and insect pest management.* University of California. Division of Agricultural Sciences. Priced Publication 4096. 102 pp.

D-414. Estes, J. R., R. J. Tyrl, & J. N. Brunken (eds.). 1982. *Grasses and grasslands: Systematics and ecology.* University of Oklahoma Press. Norman. 312 pp.

D-416. Fletcher, M. I. 1951. Balsa—production and utilization. *Economic Botany* 5: 107–125.

D-420. Fyles, F. 1920. *Wild rice.* Dominion of Canada. Department of Agriculture. Dominion Experimental Farms. Bulletin No. 42. Ottawa. 20 pp.

D-450. FAO. 1981. *1980 FAO trade yearbook.* FAO Statistics Series No. 35. Rome. 359 pp.

D-452. Darrow, G. M. 1966. *The strawberry: History, breeding and physiology.* Holt, Rinehart & Winston. New York, Chicago, San Francisco. 447 pp.

D-470. Duke, J. A., & C. F. Reed. No date. *Panax quinquefolius L. Araliaceae ginseng, sang.* 4 pp.

D-474. Domalain, J. Y. 1977. *The animal connection.* Transl. M. Barnett. William Morrow & Co. New York.

D-476. Eudey, A., & D. Mack. 1985. Use of primates and captive-breeding programs in the United States. In D. Mack & R. Mittermeier (eds.). *The international primate trade.* [Reference M-607].

D-479. Frey, K. J., & J. A. Browning. 1976. Registration of multiline E72, multiline E73, and multiline E74 oat cultivars (reg. nos. 268 to 270). *Crop Science* 16: 311–312.

D-480. Frey, K. J., & J. A. Browning. 1976. Registration of multiline M72 and M73 oat cultivars (reg. nos. 266 and 267) *Crop Science* 16: 311.

D-482. Dickenson, R. E. 1982. *Parks and preserves in the Nearctic Realm.* Keynote address session VIC (Nearctic). World National Parks Congress. Bali (Indonesia).

D-499. Fogle, H. W. 1975. Cherries. In J. Janick & J. N. Moore (eds.). *Advances in fruit breeding:* 348–366 [Reference J-8].

D-504. Funk, D. T. 1979. Black walnuts for nuts and timber. In R. A. Jaynes (ed.). *Nut tree culture in North America:* 51–73 [Reference J-306].

D-506. Finlay, K. W. 1953. Inheritance of spotted wilt resistance in the tomato. II. Five genes controlling spotted wilt resistance in four tomato types. *Australian Journal of Biological Sciences* 6: 153–163.

D-512. Dore, W. G. 1969. *Wild-rice.* Agriculture Canada. Research Branch Publication 1393. 84 pp.

D-519. Elliot, W. A., & E. A. Oelke. 1977. New era for wild rice. *Crops and Soils* 29: 8–11.

D-537. Filion, F. L., S. W. James, J.-L. Ducharme, W. Pepper, R. Reid, P. Boxall, & D. Teillet. 1983. *The importance of wildlife to Canadians: Highlights of the 1981 national survey.* Canadian Wildlife Service. Ottawa. 40 pp.

D-542. Frey, K. J., J. A. Browning, & R. L. Grindeland. 1971. Registration of Multiline M68, Multiline M69, and Multiline M70 oat cultivars (reg. no. 245–247). *Crop Science* 11: 940.

D-549. FAO. 1982. *1981 FAO trade yearbook.* Volume 35. FAO Statistics Series. Rome.

D-697. Fleisher, A., & N. Sneer. 1982. Oregano spices and *Origanum* chemotypes. *Journal of the Science of Food and Agriculture* 33 (5): 441–446.

D-804. Dobie, J. 1981. Residues. In E. J. Mullins & T. S. McKnight (eds.). *Canadian woods: Their properties and uses:* 321–334. [Reference M-370].

D-811. Dixon, A. M. 1984. The European trade in sealskins. *IUCN Traffic Bulletin* 6 (3/4): 54–65.

G-4. Galinat, W. C. 1971. The origin of maize. *Annual Review of Genetics* 5: 447–478.

G-5. Galinat, W. C. 1974. The domestication and genetic erosion of maize. *Economic Botany* 28: 31–37.

G-6. Galinat, W. C. 1977. The origin of corn. In G. F. Sprague (ed.). *Corn and corn improvement:* 1–47 [Reference S-190].

G-7. Garner, R. J., S. A. Chaudhri, & the Staff of the Commonwealth Bureau of Horticulture and Plantation Crops. 1976. *The propagation of tropical fruit trees.* Horticultural Review 4. Commonwealth Bureau of Horticulture and Plantation Crops. (East Malling, Maidstone, Kent). Commonwealth Agricultural Bureaux. 566 pp.

G-14. Genders, R. 1973. *Bulbs: A complete handbook.* Robert Hale. London. 622 pp.

G-20. Gentry, H. S. 1958. The natural history of jojoba (*Simmondsia chinensis*) and its cultural aspects. *Economic Botany* 12: 261–295.

G-27. Gerstel, D. U. 1945. Inheritance in *Nicotiana tabacum* crosses: The addition of *Nicotiana glutinosa* chromosomes to tobacco. *Journal of Heredity* 36: 197–206.

G-28. Gerstel, D. U. 1976. Tobacco. In N. W. Simmonds (ed.). *Evolution of crop plants:* 273–277 [Reference S-384].

G-31. Gilbert, J. C., & D. C. McGuire. 1956. Inheritance of resistance to severe root-knot from *Meloidogyne incognita* in commercial type tomatoes. *Proceedings of the American Society for Horticultural Science* 68: 437–442.

G-44. Glicksman, M., & R. E. Sand. 1973. Gum arabic. In R. L. Whistler (ed.). *Industrial gums, polysaccharides and their derivatives:* 197–263 [Reference V-102].

G-45. Goldstein, A. M., & E. N. Alter. 1973. Gum karaya. In R. L. Whistler (ed.). *Industrial gums, polysaccharides and their derivatives:* 273–287 [Reference V-102].

G-53. Goplen, B. P., & A. T. H. Gross. 1977. *Sweetclover production in western Canada.* Agriculture Canada. Publication 1613. Ottawa. 14 pp.

G-67. Gregory, R. S. 1975. The commercial production of *Triticale. Span* 18: 65–66.

G-69. Gregory, W. C., & M. P. Gregory. 1976. Groundnut. In N. W. Simmonds (ed.). *Evolution of crop plants:* 151–154 [Reference S-384].

G-74. Guba, E. F. 1960. *Red forcing tomatoes immune to Cladosporium leaf mold.* University of Massachusetts Agricultural Experiment Station. Bulletin 519. 20 pp.

G-76. Guenther, E. 1948–1952. *The essential oils.* Volumes 1–6. Van Nostrand. Princeton (New Jersey).

G-81. Grover, N. 1965. Man and plants against pain. *Economic Botany* 19: 99–112.

G-83. Greenhalgh, P. 1979. *The market for culinary herbs.* Report G121. Tropical Products Institute. London. 171 pp.

G-91. Greaves, A. 1979. *Descriptions of seed sources and collections for provenances of Pinus oocarpa.* Tropical Forestry Papers No. 13. 144 pp.

G-94. Graham, T. W., J. F. Chaplin, Z. T. Ford, & R. E. Currin III. 1972. *SC72, a new tobacco variety with resistance to mosaic and other diseases.* South Carolina Agricultural Experiment Station Circular 163. 6 pp

G-95. Glendinning, D. R. 1963. The CRI cocoa varieties. *Ghana Journal of Science* 3: 111–119.

G-96. Glendinning, D. R. 1967. New cocoa varieties in Ghana. *Cocoa Growers Bulletin* 8: 19–26.

G-97. Glendinning, D. R. 1966. Further developments in the breeding programme at the Cocoa Research Institute, Tafo. *Ghana Journal of Science* 6: 52–62.

G-101. Gascon, J. P., & C. de Berchoux. 1964. Caracteristiques de la production d'*Elaeis guineensis* (Jacq.) de diverses origines et de leurs croisements. *Oleagineux* 19: 75–84.

G-102. Goplen, B. P. 1981. Norgold-lc yellow-flowered sweetclover. *Agriculture Canada Biweekly Letter.* July 15.

G-107. Goplen, B. P. 1971. Polara, a low coumarin cultivar of sweetclover. *Canadian Journal of Plant Science* 51: 249–251.

G-111. Goplen, B. P. 1980. Sweetclover production and agronomy. *Canadian Veterinary Journal* 21: 149–151.

G-121. Hall, I. V. 1979. The cultivar situation in lowbush blueberry in Nova Scotia. *Fruit Varieties Journal* 33 (2): 54–56.

G-124. Hall, I. V., L. E. Aalders, N. L. Nickerson, & S. P. van der Kloet. 1979. The biological flora of Canada. I. *Vaccinium angustifolium* Ait., sweet lowbush blueberry. *Canadian Field Naturalist* 93: 415–430.

G-127. Hall, I. V., L. E. Aalders, C. L. Lockhart, L. P. Jackson, G. W. Wood, & R. W. Delbridge. 1979. *Lowbush blueberry production*. Agriculture Canada. Publication 1477. Ottawa. 39 pp.

G-136. Hammons, R. O. 1976. Peanuts: Genetic vulnerability and breeding strategy. *Crop Science* 16: 527–530.

G-142. Hanson, A. A. 1972. *Grass varieties in the United States*. USDA. ARS. Agriculture Handbook No. 170. 124 pp.

G-147. Hardon, J. J. 1976. Oil palm. In N. W. Simmonds (ed.). *Evolution of crop plants:* 225–229 [Reference S-384].

G-148. Hardon, J. J., & R. L. Thomas. 1968. Breeding and selection of the oil palm in Malaya. *Oleagineux* 23 (2): 85–90.

G-149. Hardon, J. J., & G. Y. Tan. 1969. Interspecific hybrids in the genus *Elaeis*. 1. Crossability, cytogenetics and fertility of $F_1$ hybrids of *E. guineensis* × *E. oleifera*. *Euphytica* 18: 372–379.

G-150. Hardon, J. J., M. Hashim, & S. C. Ooi. 1972. Oil palm breeding: A review. In *Advances in oil palm cultivation*. I. S. P. Kuala Lumpur. Malaysia: 1–12.

G-163. Harlan, J. R. 1975. *Crops and man*. American Society of Agronomy. Madison (Wisconsin). 295 pp.

G-167. Harlan, J. R. 1976. Genetic resources in wild relatives of crops. *Crop Science* 16: 329–333.

G-170. Harlan, J. R. 1976. Barley. In N. W. Simmonds (ed.). *Evolution of crop plants:* 93–98 [Reference S-384].

G-175. Harlan, J. R., & J. M. J. de Wet. 1971. Toward a rational classification of cultivated plants. *Taxon* 20: 509–517.

G-187. Harten, A. M. van. 1969. Cinchona: Cinchona spp. In F. P. Ferwerda & F. Wit (eds.). *Outlines of perennial crop breeding in the tropics:* 111–128 [Reference D-257].

G-188. Harten, A. M. van. 1976. Quinine. In N. W. Simmonds (ed.). *Evolution of crop plants:* 255–257 [Reference S-384].

G-189. Hartley, C. W. S. 1977. *The oil palm*. 2d edition. Longman. London, New York. 806 pp.

G-196. Hawkes, J. G. 1966. Modern taxonomic work on the *Solanum* species of Mexico and adjacent countries. *American Potato Journal* 43: 81–103.

G-201. Hawkes, J. G. (ed.). 1978. *Conservation and agriculture*. Gerald Duckworth London. 284 pp.

G-202. Hawkes, J. G. 1979. Genetic poverty of the potato in Europe. In A. C. Zeven & A. M. van Harten (eds.). *Proceedings of the conference broadening the genetic base of crops:* 19–27 [Reference Y-48].

G-219. Heiser, C. B. Jr. 1976. Sunflowers. In N. W. Simmonds (ed.). *Evolution of crop plants:* 36–38 [Reference S-384].

G-230. Hendrix, J. W., & W. A. Frazier. 1949. *Studies on the inheritance of Stemphylium resistance in tomatoes*. University of Hawaii Agricultural Experiment Station. Technical Bulletin No. 8. 24 pp.

G-260. Hobbs, G. A. 1973. *Alfalfa leafcutter bees for pollinating alfalfa in western Canada*. Agriculture Canada. Publication 1495. Ottawa. 30 pp.

G-263. Hodge, W. H., & H. H. Sineath. 1956. The Mexican candelilla plant and its wax. *Economic Botany* 10 (2): 134–154.

G-269. Hofstrand, R. H. 1970. Wild ricing. *Natural History* 79 (3): 50–55.

G-276. Holmes, F. O. 1938. Inheritance of resistance to tobacco-mosaic disease in tobacco. *Phytopathology* 28: 553–561.

G-293. Hougas, R. W., & R. W. Ross. 1956. The use of foreign introduction in breeding American potato varieties. *American Potato Journal* 33: 328–339.

G-300. Howes, F. N. 1949. *Vegetable gums and resins.* Chronica Botanica. Waltham (Massachusetts). 188 pp.

G-301. Howes, F. N. 1953. *Vegetable tanning materials.* Butterworths Scientific Publications. London. 325 pp.

G-311. Hutchinson, J. (ed.). 1974. *Evolutionary studies in world crops: Diversity and change in the Indian subcontinent.* Cambridge University Press. Cambridge. 175 pp.

G-317. Hymowitz, T. 1970. On the domestication of the soybean. *Economic Botany* 24: 408–421.

G-319. Hymowitz, T., & C. A. Newell. 1980. Taxonomy, speciation, domestication, dissemination, germplasm resources and variation in the genus *Glycine.* In R. J. Summerfield & A. H. Bunting (eds.). *Advances in legume science:* 251–264 [Reference S-245].

G-334. IBPGR. 1980. IBPGR secretariat consultation on the genetic resources of cruciferous crops. 17–19 November 1980. Rome. 42 pp.

G-361. Iltis, H. H., J. F. Doebley, R. M. Guzman, & B. Pazy. 1979. *Zea diploperennis* (Gramineae): A new teosinte from Mexico. *Science* 203: 186–188.

G-363. Ilyas, M. 1978. The spices of India—II. *Economic Botany* 32: 238–263.

G-368. Ingram, J. S. 1969. Saffron (*Crocus sativus* L.) *Tropical Science* 11: 177–184.

G-380. Iten, O. 1980. Chew chicle while you can. *Observer.* September 28.

G-391. IUCN. 1980. *World conservation strategy.* IUCN, UNEP, WWF. Gland and Nairobi.

G-394. Gard, K. R. 1953. The aims of the sugarcane breeding programme at Macknade, Queensland, with special reference to sugar content, vigour and disease resistance. *ISSCT Proceedings of the 8th Congress (British West Indies):* 423–429.

G-409. Goldsborough, J. 1977. Lo, the vanishing herring: Scarcity leads to total ban. *International Herald Tribune.* July 25.

G-412. Heinz, D. J. 1965. Wild *Saccharum* species for breeding in Hawaii. *ISSCT Proceedings of the 12th Congress (Puerto Rico):* 1037–1043.

G-416. Hodgson, R. E. (ed.). 1961. *Germ plasm resources.* A symposium presented at the Chicago meeting of the American Association for the Advancement of Science. 28–31 December 1959. AAAS. Washington, D.C.

G-421. Grubben, G. J. H. 1977. *Tropical vegetables and their genetic resources.* IBPGR. Rome. AGPE:IBPGR/77/23. 197 pp.

G-423. Gupta, R. 1981. *Genetic resources of medicinal plants in a world prospective.* FAO/UNEP/IBPGR Technical Conference on Crop Genetic Resources. 6–10 April 1981. Rome. 28 pp.

G-425. Interagency Primate Steering Committee. 1978. *National primate plan.* U.S. Department of Health, Education, and Welfare Publication (NIH) 80-1520. 81 pp.

G-428. IDRC. 1980. *Rattan: A report of a workshop held in Singapore.* 4–6 June 1979. IDRC-155e. 76 pp.

G-432. ITC. 1979. *International trade in tropical aquarium fish.* International Trade Centre. Geneva. 137 pp.

G-439. Imle, E. P. 1978. *Hevea* rubber—past and future. *Economic Botany* 32: 264–277.

G-448. Golden, F. 1981. A plethora of polar bears: Each fall the white beasts overrun Churchill, Manitoba. *Time.* December 21.

G-449. Grady, L., & N. Duplaix. 1980. *The harvest of northeastern furbearers, past and present.* Prepared for the Northeast Endangered Species Conference. 9–11 May 1980. Provincetown, Massachusetts. Traffic (USA). Washington, D.C. 33 pp.

G-451. Greaves, A. 1978. *Descriptions of seed sources and collections for provenances of Pinus caribaea.* Tropical Forestry Papers 12. Commonwealth Forestry Institute. Oxford. 98 pp.

G-452. Grey-Wilson, C. 1979. *The alpine flowers of Britain and Europe.* Collins. London. 384 pp.

G-453. Grieve, M. 1980. *A modern herbal.* Ed. C. F. Leyel. Penguin Books. 912 pp.

G-460. Hanson, C. H. (ed.). 1972. *Alfalfa science and technology.* American Society of Agronomy. Madison (Wisconsin). 812 pp.

G-461. Hardigree, P. A. 1977. *The free food seafood book.* Stackpole Books. Harrisburg (Pennsylvania). 228 pp.

G-463. Harris, P. M. (ed.). 1978. *The potato crop: The scientific basis for improvement.* Chapman & Hall. London. John Wiley & Sons. New York. 730 pp.

G-464. Hart, J. L. 1973. *Pacific fishes of Canada.* Fisheries Research Board of Canada Bulletin 180. Ottawa. 740 pp.

G-467. Hedrick, U. P. (ed.). 1972. *Sturtevant's edible plants of the world.* Dover Publications. New York. 686 pp.

G-478. Honegger, R. E. 1979. *IUCN red data book. Volume 3: Amphibia and Reptilia.* IUCN. Morges (Switzerland).

G-479. Hosie, R. C. 1979. *Native trees of Canada.* 8th ed. Fitzhenry & Whiteside. Don Mills (Ontario). 380 pp.

G-486. International Convention Advisory Commission. 1981. *CITES: The appendices arranged in taxonomic sequence and alphabetically by common and scientific names.* Traffic (USA). Washington, D.C. 127 pp.

G-527. Glicksman, M. 1969. *Gum technology in the food industry.* Academic Press. New York, San Francisco, London. 590 pp.

G-536. Harrington, T. A. 1969. Production of oleoresin from southern pine trees. *Forest Products Journal* 19: 31–36.

G-538. Hawkes, J. G., R. N. Lester, & A. D. Skelding (eds.). 1979. *The biology and taxonomy of the Solanaceae.* Linnean Society Symposium Series No. 7. Academic Press. London. 738 pp.

G-556. Gentry, H. S. 1957. Gum tragacanth in Iran. *Economic Botany* 11: 40–63.

G-568. Hedegart, T. 1973. Pollination of teak (*Tectona grandis* L.). 2. *Silvae Genetica* 22: 124–128.

G-573. Houston, A. W. 1980. *The American Heritage book of fish cookery.* American Heritage Publishing. New York. 224 pp.

G-583. Haunold, A. 1981. Hop production, breeding, and variety development in various countries. *Journal of the American Society of Brewing Chemists* 39: 27–34.

G-584. Haunold, A., S. T. Likens, & C. E. Horner. 1976. *The breeding and development of new hop varieties.* Proceedings of the scientific commission of the international hop grower's convention. 12–13 August 1976. Wye College.

G-589. Henkel, A. 1909. *American medicinal barks.* USDA Bulletin No. 139. Washington, D.C. 59 pp.

G-594. Hughes, P. 1972. *Pueblo Indian cookbook: Recipes from the Pueblos of the American southwest.* Museum of New Mexico Press. Sante Fe. 64 pp.

G-595. Hurd, P. D. Jr., W. E. LaBerge, & E. G. Linsley. 1980. *Principal sunflower bees of North America with emphasis on the southwestern United States (Hymenoptera: Apoidea).* Smithsonian Institution Press. Washington, D.C. 158 pp.

G-611. Ismail, A. A. No date. *Introduction to growing blueberries in Maine.* Blueberry information sheet. University of Maine at Orono. Cooperative Extension Service. 4 pp.

G-625. Glude, J. B. (ed.). 1977. *NOAA aquaculture plan.* U.S. Department of Commerce. Washington, D.C. 41 pp.

G-626. Gidney, N. 1981. Salmon stock is "stable": Outdoors expert testifies. *Times-Colonist.* May 15.

G-635. Haltenorth, T., & H. Diller. 1980. *A field guide to the mammals of Africa including Madagascar.* William Collins Sons. London, Glasgow, Sydney, Auckland, Toronto, Johannesburg. 400 pp.

G-636. Hanson, C. H. 1960. *Alfalfa varieties in the United States.* USDA. ARS. Agriculture Handbook No. 177. Washington, D.C. 30 pp.

G-683. Howes, F. N. 1950. Age-old resins of the Mediterranean region and their uses. *Economic Botany* 4: 307–316.

G-684. Humm, H. J. 1947. Agar—a pre-war Japanese monopoly. *Economic Botany* 1: 317–329.

G-697. Inskipp, T. P. No date. *All heaven in a rage: A study into the importation of birds into the United Kingdom.* Royal Society for the Protection of Birds. 41 pp.

G-707. Galet, P. 1979. *A practical ampelography: Grapevine identification.* Trans. and adapt. L. T. Morton. Cornell University Press. Ithaca, London. 248 pp.

G-724. Health and Welfare Canada. 1981. *Canadian drug identification code, 1981.* 8th edition. Ottawa.

G-727. Government of Canada. 1971. *An act respecting food, drugs, cosmetics and therapeutic devices.* Ottawa.

G-735. Held, J. R. 1982. "Nonhuman primates, their use in biomedical research." Paper presented at the Symposium on the use of nonhuman primates in exotic viral and immunologic diseases.

G-740. Heyne, E. G., & L. E. Browder. 1974. Registration of Cloud wheat (reg. no. 547). *Crop Science* 14: 909.

G-742. Hymowitz, T. 1972. The trans-domestication concept as applied to guar. *Economic Botany* 26: 49–60.

G-744. Galletta, G. J. 1975. Blueberries and cranberries. In J. Janick & J. N. Moore (eds.). *Advances in fruit breeding:* 154–196 [Reference J-8].

G-746. Gorer, R. 1970. *The development of garden flowers.* Eyre & Spottiswoode. London. 254 pp.

G-755. Hesse, C. O. 1975. Peaches. In J. Janick & J. N. Moore (eds.). *Advances in fruit breeding:* 285–335 [Reference J-8].

G-763. Gunn, C. R., & G. A. White. 1974. *Stokesia laevis:* Taxonomy and economic value. *Economic Botany* 28: 130–135.

G-764. Harvey, P. H., C. S. Levings III, & E. A. Wernsman. 1972. The role of extra-chromosomal inheritance in plant breeding. *Advances in Agronomy* 24: 1–27.

G-792. Gertler, P. E. 1980. *Convention on International Trade in Endangered Species of Wild Fauna and Flora: 1979 annual report for the United States of America.* U.S. Fish and Wildlife Service. Federal Wildlife Permit Office. Washington, D.C. 202 pp.

G-798. Hymowitz, T., & C. A. Newell. 1977. Current thoughts on origins, present status and future of soybeans. In D. S. Seigler (ed.). *Crop resources:* 197–209 [Reference S-366].

G-805. Hedegart, T. 1976. Breeding systems, variation and genetic improvement of teak (*Tectona grandis* L.f.). In J. Burley & B. T. Styles (eds.). *Tropical trees: Variation, breeding and conservation:* 109–123 [Reference A-923].

G-809. IBPGR. 1981. *IBPGR working group on genetic resources of cocoa.* IBPGR. AGP:IBPGR/80/56. Rome. 25 pp.

G-821. Hodgson, H. J., A. C. Wilton, R. L. Taylor, & L. J. Klebesadel. 1971. Registration of Polar bromegrass (reg. no. 15). *Crop Science* 11: 939.

G-828. Groombridge, B. 1982. *The IUCN Amphibia-Reptilia red data book: Part 1—Testudines, Crocodylia, Rhynchocephalia.* IUCN. Gland (Switzerland). 426 pp.

G-829. Heinz, D. J. (ed.). 1981. *Hawaiian Sugar Planters' Association experiment station annual report 1980.* Hawaiian Sugar Planters' Association. Aiea (Hawaii). 73 pp.

G-830. Helm, J. 1963. Morphologisch-taxonomische gliederung der kultursippen von *Brassica oleracea* L. *Die Kulturpflanze* 11: 92–210.

G-831. Iltis, H. H. 1982. Discovery of No. 832: An essay in defense of the National Science Foundation. *Desert Plants* 3: 175–192.

G-832. Greenhalgh, P. 1979. *The markets for mint oils and menthol.* Tropical Products Institute. G126. London. 171 pp.

G-833. Grigson, J. 1978. *Jane Grigson's vegetable book.* Penguin.

G-834. Harlan, J. R. 1979. On the origin of barley. In USDA. *Barley origin, botany, culture, winter hardiness, genetics, utilization, pests:* 10–36 [Reference S-334].

G-835. Hawkes, J. G. 1978. History of the potato. In P. M. Harris (ed.). *The potato crop: The scientific basis for improvement:* 1–14 [Reference G-463].

G-836. Hartwig, E. E. 1973. Varietal development. In B. E. Caldwell (ed.). *Soybeans: Improvement, production, and uses:* 187–210 [Reference A-736].

G-837. Heiser, C. B. Jr. 1982. Registration of Indiana-1 CMS sunflower germplasm (reg. no. GP6). *Crop Science* 22: 1089.

G-838. Hagen, K. S., & J. A. McMurtry. 1979. Natural enemies and predator-prey ratios. In D. W. Davis, S. C. Hoyt, J. A. McMurtry, & M. T. AliNiazee (eds.). *Biological control and insect pest management:* 28–40 [Reference D-409].

G-839. Hagen, K. S., & G. W. Bishop. 1979. Use of supplemental foods and behavioral chemicals to increase the effectiveness of natural enemies. In D. W. Davis, S. C. Hoyt, J. A. McMurtry, & M. T. AliNiazee (eds.). *Biological control and insect pest management:* 49–60 [Reference D-409].

G-1178. Hemley, G. 1984. World trade in tegu skins. *Traffic Bulletin* 5 (5/6): 60–62.

G-1199. Hemley, G. 1983. International reptile skin trade dependent on few species. *Traffic (USA)* 5 (2): 1, 8, 9, 12.

G-1200. Hemley, G., & G. Robertson. No date. *Travelling tropicals: A study of the US ornamental fish trade.* Preliminary draft. Traffic (USA).

G-1201. Inskipp, T. 1984. World trade in monitor lizard skins, 1977–1982. *IUCN Traffic bulletin* 6 (3/4): 51–53.

J-7. James, N. I. 1972. Delayed flowering of *Saccharum spontaneum* L. related hybrids. *Crop Science* 12: 425–427.

J-8. Janick, J., & J. N. Moore (eds.). 1975. *Advances in fruit breeding.* Purdue University Press. West Lafayette (Indiana). 622 pp.

J-14. Jenkins, J. A. 1948. The origin of the cultivated tomato. *Economic Botany* 2: 379–392.

J-17. Jennings, D. L. 1976. Raspberries and blackberries. In N. W. Simmonds (ed.). *Evolution of crop plants:* 251–254 [Reference S-384].

J-20. Johansen, C. 1966. Pollination of clovers raised for seed in Washington. *American Bee Journal* 106: 298–300.

J-21. Johannessen, C. L. 1966. Pejibayes in commercial production. *Turrialba* 16 (2): 181–187.

J-26. Johannessen, C. L. 1966. The domestication process in trees reproduced by seed: The peijibaye palm in Costa Rica. *Geographical Review* 56: 363–376.

J-28. Johnson, A. G., I. R. Crute, & P. L. Gordon. 1977. The genetics of race specific resistance in lettuce (*Lactuca sativa*) to downy mildew (*Bremia lactucae*). *Annals of Applied Biology* 86: 87–103.

J-51. Kaplan, L. 1965. Archaeology and domestication in American *Phaseolus* beans. *Economic Botany* 19: 356–368.

J-75. Kellert, S. R., & J. K. Berry. 1980. *Knowledge, affection and basic attitudes toward animals in American society: Phase III.* U.S. Department of the Interior. Fish and Wildlife Service. 162 pp.

J-83. Kenton, R. H., & G. Lockwood. 1977. Studies on the possibility of increasing resistance to cocoa swollen-shoot virus by breeding. *Annals of Applied Biology* 85: 71–78.

J-89. Kerr, E. A., & D. L. Bailey. 1964. Resistance to *Cladosporium fulvum* Cke. obtained from wild species of tomato. *Canadian Journal of Botany* 42: 1541–1554.

J-97. Khush, G. S. 1963. Cytogenetic and evolutionary studies in *Secale*. III. Cytogenetics of weedy ryes and origin of cultivated rye. *Economic Botany* 17: 60–71.

J-110. King, D. B., H. B. Wagner, & G. H. Goldsborough. 1962. *The outlook for naval stores.* 62 pp.

J-125. Knight, R., & H. H. Rogers. 1955. Recent introductions to West Africa of *Theobroma cacao* and related species. 1. A review of the first ten years. *Empire Journal of Experimental Agriculture* 23: 113.

J-127. Knott, D. 1961. The inheritance of rust resistance. VI. The transfer of stem rust resistance from *Agropyron elongatum* to common wheat. *Canadian Journal of Plant Science* 41: 109–123.

J-132. Knott, D., & J. Dvorak. 1976. Alien germplasm as a source of resistance to disease. *Annual Review of Phytopathology* 14: 211–235.

J-137. Knowles, P. F. 1976. Safflower. In N. W. Simmonds (ed.). *Evolution of crop plants:* 31–33 [Reference S-384].

J-164. Ladizinsky, G. 1979. Seed dispersal in relation to the domestication of Middle East legumes. *Economic Botany* 33: 284–289.

J-170. Lamb, A. F. A. 1973. *Fast growing timber trees of the lowland tropics.* No. 6. *Pinus caribea.* Volume 1.

J-174. Lamb, R. C., & H. Aldwinckle. 1981. Disease resistance in fruit crops. *Pennsylvania Fruit News 1981 Proceedings* 60: 55–59.

J-183. Larter, E. N. 1976. Triticale. In N. W. Simmonds (ed.). *Evolution of crop plants:* 117–120 [Reference S-384].

J-185. Laterrot, H. 1973. Selection de varietes de tomate resistantes aux *Meloidogyne*. *OEPP/EPPO Bulletin* 3 (1): 89–92.

J-193. Lederhouse, R. C., D. M. Caron, & R. A. Morse. 1968. Onion pollination in New York. *New York's Food and Life Sciences.* July–September 1968: 8–9.

J-196. Legg, J. T., & G. Lockwood. 1977. Evaluation and use of a screening method to aid selection of cocoa (*Theobroma cacao*) with field resistance to cocoa swollen shoot virus in Ghana. *Annals of Applied Biology* 86: 241–248.

J-213. Leung, A. Y. 1977. Cascara sagrada: New standards are needed. *Drug and Cosmetic Industry* 121 (6): 42–44, 143–145.

J-217. Lewis, W. H., & M. P. F. Elvin-Lewis. 1977. *Medical botany—plants affecting man's health.* John Wiley & Sons. New York, London, Sydney, Toronto. 515 pp.

J-222. Lincoln, R. E., & G. B. Cummins. 1949. *Septoria* blight resistance in the tomato. *Phytopathology* 39: 647–655.

J-225. Lindqvist, K. 1960. On the origin of cultivated lettuce. *Hereditas* 46: 319–349.

J-227. Linsley, E. G. 1958. The ecology of solitary bees. *Hilgardia* 27 (19): 543–599.

J-228. Little, E. L. Jr. 1979. *Important forest trees of the United States.* USDA. Forest Service. Agriculture Handbook No. 519. Washington, D.C. 70 pp.

J-235. Loewenfeld, C., & P. Back. 1974. *The complete book of herbs and spices.* Little, Brown. Boston, New York. 313 pp.

J-237. Longworth, J. F., & J. M. Thresh. 1963. The reaction of different cocoa types to infection with swollen shoot virus. *Annals of Applied Biology* 52: 117–125.

J-242. Lubis, A. U., & Kiswito. 1975. New perspectives in oil palm breeding in Indonesia. In J. T. Williams, C. H. Lamoureux, & N. Wulijarni-Soetjipto (eds.). *South East Asian plant genetic resources:* 187–195 [Reference V-211].

J-244. Lucas, G. B., G. V. Gooding Jr., J. N. Sasser, & D. U. Gerstel. 1980. Reaction of *Nicotiana africana* to black shank, granville wilt, root knot, tobacco mosaic virus, and potato virus Y. *Tobacco Science* 141: 64–65.

J-247. Lukefahr, M. J., & C. Rhyne. 1960. Effects of nectariless cottons on populations of three lepidopterous insects. *Journal of Economic Entomology* 53: 242–244.

J-248. Lukefahr, M. J., D. F. Martin, & J. R. Meyer. 1965. Plant resistance to five Lepidoptera attacking corn. *Journal of Economic Entomology* 58: 516–518.

J-249. Lukefahr, M. J., C. B. Cowan, T. R. Pfrimmer, & L. W. Noble. 1966. Resistance of experimental cotton strain 1514 to the bollworm and cotton fleahopper. *Journal of Economic Entomology* 59: 393–395.

J-252. Lundell, C. L. 1933. Chicle exploitation in the sapodilla forest of the Yucatan peninsula. *Field & Laboratory* November 2: 15–21.

J-256. Lutz, J. F. 1972. *Veneer species that grow in the United States.* USDA. Forest Service. Research Paper FPL 167. Washington, D.C. 127 pp.

J-268. Kirby, R. H. 1950. Seaweeds in commerce. Part I: Introduction. *Colonial Plant and Animal Products* 1 (3): 183–216.

J-274. Li, H. W., & S. Price. 1965. Chromosome numbers of some noble sugarcane clones. *ISSCT Proceedings of the 12th Congress (Puerto Rico):* 884–886.

J-292. King, F. W. 1978. The wildlife trade. In H. P. Brokaw (ed.). *Wildlife and America: Contributions to an understanding of American wildlife and its conservation:* 253–271 [Reference A-674].

J-306. Jaynes, R. A. (ed.). 1979. *Nut tree culture in North America.* Northern Nut Growers Association. Hamden (Connecticut). 466 pp.

J-310. Jones, E. 1981. *American food: The gastronomic story.* 2d edition. Vintage Books. New York. 516 pp.

J-321. Klein, R. M. 1979. *The green world: An introduction to plants and people.* Harper & Row. New York, Hagerstown, San Francisco, London. 437 pp.

J-322. Kluger, M. 1982. Fiddleheads. *Gourmet.* May.

J-325. Krochmal, A., & C. Krochmal. 1973. *A guide to the medicinal plants of the United States.* Quadrangle/New York Times Book Co. New York. 259 pp.

J-337. Leung, A. Y. 1980. *Encyclopedia of common natural ingredients used in food, drugs, and cosmetics.* John Wiley & Sons. New York, Chichester, Brisbane, Toronto. 409 pp.

J-338. Lesins, K. A., & I. Lesins. 1979. *Genus Medicago (Leguminosae): A taxogenetic study.* Dr. W. Junk bv Publishers. The Hague, Boston, London. 228 pp.

J-342. Little, E. L. Jr. 1971. *Atlas of United States trees.* Volume 1. Conifers and important hardwoods. USDA. Forest Service. Miscellaneous Publication No. 1146. Washington, D.C.

J-365. Johnson, D. 1973. The botany, origin and spread of the cashew *Anacardium occidentale* L. *Journal of Plantation Crops (India)* 1: 1–7.

J-388. Kuriyama, T., & K. Kuniyasu. 1974. [Studies on breeding disease-resistant tomatoes by means of interspecific hybridization. III. Selecting new material resistant to bacterial canker.] *Bulletin of the Vegetable and Ornamental Crops Research Station* A. No. 1: 93–107. *Plant Breeding Abstracts (1976).* Volume 46: No. 2943.

J-392. Larue, M. 1975. *L'Actinidia chinensis* et sa culture. *Fruits (France)* 30: 45–50.

J-396. Leclercq, P. 1969. Une sterilite male cytoplasmique chez le tournesol. *Annales de l'Amelioration des Plantes/Annales de l'Institut National de la Recherche Agronomique (B)* 19: 99–106.

J-414. Jong, J. de, & S. Honma. 1976. Inheritance of resistance to *Corynebacterium michiganense* in the tomato. *Journal of Heredity* 67: 79–84.

J-416. Kavasch, B. 1979. *Native harvests: Recipes and botanicals of the American Indian*. Vintage Books. New York. 202 pp.

J-436. Leenhouts, P. W. 1978. Systematic notes on the Sapindaceae—Nephelieae. *Blumea* 24: 395–403.

J-442. Kimball, Y., & J. Anderson. 1965. *The art of American Indian cooking*. Doubleday. Garden City (New York). 215 pp.

J-453. Kasimatis, A. N., & L. Lider. 1981. *Grape rootstock varieties*. University of California. Division of Agricultural Sciences. Leaflet 2780. 19 pp.

J-458. Kunde, R. M., L. A. Lider, & R. V. Schmitt. 1968. A test of *Vitis* resistance to *Xiphinema index*. *American Journal of Enology and Viticulture* 19: 30–36.

J-461. LaRue, J. H., & M. H. Gerdts. 1976. *Commercial plum growing in California*. University of California. Division of Agricultural Sciences. Leaflet 2458. 22 pp.

J-462. Laterrot, H., R. Brand, & M.-C. Daunay. 1978. La resistance a *Corynebacterium michiganense* chez la tomate: etude bibliographique. *Annales de l'Amelioration des Plantes* 28 (5): 579–591.

J-465. Lesser, M. A. 1950. Alginates in drugs and cosmetics. *Economic Botany* 4: 317–321.

J-468. Lider, L. A. 1960. Vineyard trials in California with nematode-resistant grape rootstocks. *Hilgardia* 30: 123–152.

J-472. Jamieson, G. S. 1981. *Underwater world: The sea scallop*. Fisheries and Oceans. Catalogue Fs41-33/5. Ottawa. 8 pp.

J-489. Laitin, J. 1982. Improving quality of U.S. seafood is no mean task. *National Fisherman*. July.

J-490. Lovett, J. V., & A. Lazenby (eds.). 1979. *Australian field crops: Volume 2: Tropical cereals, oilseeds, grain legumes and other crops*. Angus & Robertson.

J-499. Kellert, S. R., & J. K. Berry. 1980. *Activities of the American public relating to animals: Phase II*. U.S. Department of the Interior. Fish and Wildlife Service. 178 pp.

J-529. Lanner, R. M. 1981. *The piñon pine: A natural and cultural history*. University of Nevada Press. Reno. 208 pp.

J-550. Lewis, D. 1977. *The maple harvest cookbook*. Stein & Day. New York. 94 pp.

J-556. Lacasse, M., J.-L. Ducharme, & J. Pelletier. 1981. *Le loisir relie a l'utilisation de la faune au Quebec*. Ministere du Loisir, de la Chasse et de la Peche. Direction generale de la faune. Quebec. 321 pp.

J-562. Kaza, S. 1982. Recreational whalewatching in California: A profile. *Whalewatcher* 16: 6–8.

J-564. James, N. I. 1980. Sugarcane. In W. R. Fehr & H. H. Hadley (eds.). *Hybridization of crop plants:* 617–629 [Reference D-405].

J-567. Jaynes, R. A. 1979. Chestnuts. In R. A. Jaynes (ed.). *Nut tree culture in North America:* 111–127 [Reference J-306].

J-578. Kester, D. E. 1979. Almonds. In R. A. Jaynes (ed.). *Nut tree culture in North America:* 148–162 [Reference J-306].

J-579. Kester, D. E., & R. Asay. 1975. Almonds. In J. Janick & J. N. Moore (eds.). *Advances in fruit breeding:* 387–419 [Reference J-8].

J-580. Kido, H., D. L. Flaherty, D. F. Bosch, & K. A. Valero. 1983. Biological control of grape leafhopper. *California Agriculture* 37: 4–6.

J-581. Knight, W. E., C. Hagedorn, V. H. Watson, & D. L. Friesner. 1982. Subterranean clover in the United States. *Advances in Agronomy* 35: 165–191.

J-587. Layne, R. E. C., & H. A. Quamme. 1975. Pears. In J. Janick & J. N. Moore (eds.). *Advances in fruit breeding:* 38–70 [Reference J-8].

J-588. Lee, J. A. 1980. Cotton. In W. R. Fehr & H. H. Hadley (eds.). *Hybridization of crop plants:* 313–325 [Reference D-405].

J-593. Kaplan, L. 1981. What is the origin of the common bean? *Economic Botany* 35: 240–254.

J-594. Knight, W. E., & E. A. Hollowell. 1973. Crimson clover. *Advances in Agronomy* 25: 47–76.

J-598. Josephy, A. M. Jr. 1968. *The Indian heritage of America.* Bantam Books. Toronto, New York, London. 397 pp.

J-611. Loegering, W. Q., C. O. Johnston, & J. W. Hendrix. 1967. Wheat rusts. In K. S. Quisenberry & L. P. Reitz (eds.). *Wheat and wheat improvement:* 307–335 [Reference P-88].

J-620. Johnson, H. 1971. *The world atlas of wine: The classic guide to the wines and spirits of the world.* Simon and Schuster. New York. 288 pp.

J-621. Kehr, W. R., F. I. Frosheiser, R. D. Wilcoxson, & D. K. Barnes. 1972. Breeding for disease resistance. In C. H. Hanson (ed.). *Alfalfa science and technology:* 335–354 [Reference G-460].

J-624. Lachner, E. A., C. R. Robins, & W. R. Courtenay. 1970. Exotic fishes and other organisms introduced into North America. *Smithsonian Contributions to Zoology* 59: 1–29.

J-626. Korhonen, J. E. 1981. Other uses and processes. In E. J. Mullins & T. S. McKnight (eds.). *Canadian woods: Their properties and uses:* 285–302 [Reference M-370].

J-627. Lee, R. B., & I. DeVore (eds.). 1968. *Man the hunter.* Aldine. Chicago.

J-628. Kretschmer, A. E. Jr., J. B. Brolmann, G. H. Snyder, & S. W. Coleman. 1982. Registration of "Florida" carpon desmodium (reg. no. 24). *Crop Science* 22: 158–159.

J-629. Lorenz, D. G., & R. B. Heizer. 1982. Registration of "Lometa" indiangrass (reg. no. 79). *Crop Science* 22: 686.

J-633. Jain, S. K. No date. Domestication and breeding of new crop plants. In *Crop breeding.*

J-634. Lockwood, G., & M. M. O. Gyamfi. 1979. *The CRIG cocoa germplasm collection with notes on codes used in the breeding programme at TAFO and elsewhere.* Cocoa Research Institute (Ghana). Technical Bulletin No. 10. 62 pp.

J-635. Lockwood, G. 1973. "Report on a visit to cocoa centres in the United States of America, the Caribbean and Latin America for acquisition of germplasm of *Theobroma cacao* with particular reference to cocoa swollen-shoot disease." Cocoa Research Institute of Ghana. Mimeo.

J-636. Kaya, H. K., & J. E. Lindegren. 1983. Parasitic nematode controls western poplar clearwing moth. *California Agriculture* 37: 31–32.

J-651. Ling, S.-W. 1977. *Aquaculture in southeast Asia: A historical overview.* University of Washington Press. Seattle & London. 108 pp.

J-1039. Kumar, P., & N. S. Chauman. 1976. Problems and prospects in lac host breeding. *Indian Farming* 27: 31, 33.

M-5. MacKey, J. 1966. Species relationships in *Triticum. Hereditas Supplement* 2: 237–276.

M-22. Malstrom, H. L., G. D. Madden, & L. D. Romberg. 1978. Evolution of the pecan and origin of many cultivars. *Pecan Quarterly* 12: 24–28.

M-29. Mangelsdorf, P. C., R. S. MacNeish, & W. C. Galinat. 1967. Prehistoric wild and cultivated maize. In D. S. Byers (ed.). *The prehistory of the Tehaucan Valley. Volume 1. Environment and subsistence:* 178–200 [Reference A-314].

M-30. Manheimer, S. 1973. Essential oils of South America. *Cosmetics and Perfumery* 88 (6): 41–45.

M-33. Mann, J. D. 1978. Production of solasodine for the pharmaceutical industry. *Advances in Agronomy* 30: 207–245.

M-35. Manning, C. E. F. 1969. *The market for steroid drug precursors with particular reference to diosgenin.* Report G41. Tropical Products Institute. London.

M-48. Martin, F. W., & M. H. Gaskins. 1968. *Cultivation of sapogenin-bearing Dioscorea spp.* ARS. USDA. Production Research Report No. 103. 19 pp.

M-57. Masefield, G. B., M. Wallis, S. G. Harrison, & B. E. Nicholson. 1969. *The Oxford book of food plants.* Oxford University Press. Oxford. 206 pp.

M-83. McCollum, G. D. 1976. Onion and allies. In N. W. Simmonds (ed.). *Evolution of crop plants:* 186–190 [Reference S-384].

M-95. McGregor, S. E. 1976. *Insect pollination of cultivated crop plants.* USDA. ARS. Agriculture Handbook No. 496. Washington, D.C. 411 pp.

M-98. McIntosh, R. A., P. L. Dyck, & G. J. Green. 1976. Inheritance of leaf rust and stem rust resistance in wheat cultivars Agent and Agatha. *Australian Journal of Agricultural Research* 28: 37–45.

M-101. McLaughlin, G. A. 1973. History of pyrethrum. In J. E. Casida (ed.). *Pyrethrum: The natural insecticide:* 3–15 [Reference A-379].

M-102. McNaughton, I. H. 1976. Swedes and rapes. In N. W. Simmonds (ed.). *Evolution of crop plants:* 53–56 [Reference S-384].

M-107. Meer, G., W. A. Meer, & T. Gerard. 1973. Gum tragacanth. In R. L. Whistler (ed.). *Industrial gums, polysaccharides and their derivatives:* 289–299 [Reference V-102].

M-110. Meer, G. Jr., & W. A. Meer. 1962. Natural plant hydrocolloids—Part II. *American Perfumer* 77 (4): 49–52.

M-111. Meer, G. Jr., & W. A. Meer. 1962. Natural plant hydrocolloids—Part III. *American Perfumer* 77 (5): 49–56.

M-112. Meer, W. A., & G. Meer Jr. 1961. *Panax ginseng. American Perfumer* 76 (10): 29–30.

M-129. Merory, J. 1968. *Food flavorings—composition, manufacture, and use.* 2d edition. AVI Publishing Company. Westport (Connecticut). 478 pp.

M-133. Metcalf, C. L., & W. P. Flint. 1962. *Destructive and useful insects, their habits and control.* McGraw Hill. New York, London.

M-136. Meyer, J. R., & V. G. Meyer. 1961. Origin and inheritance of nectariless cotton. *Crop Science* 1: 167–169.

M-137. Meyer, V. G. 1969. Some effects of genes, cytoplasm, and environment on male sterility of cotton (*Gossypium*). *Crop Science* 9: 237–242.

M-138. Meyer, V. G. 1974. Interspecific cotton breeding. *Economic Botany* 28: 56–60.

M-139. Meyer, V. G., & J. R. Meyer. 1965. Cytoplasmically controlled male sterility in cotton. *Crop Science* 5: 444–448.

M-149. Ministerio de Agricultura: Instituto Nacional de Investgaciones Agrarias. 1978. *[Cork—a multi-purpose material.].* (In Spanish.) Communicaciones INIA. Recursos Naturales No. 6. 50 pp.

M-171. Mortensen, J. A. 1971. Breeding grapes for central Florida. *HortScience* 6: 7–11.

M-178. Moss, J. P. 1980. Wild species in the improvement of groundnuts. In R. J. Summerfield & A. H. Bunting (eds.). *Advances in legume science:* 525–535 [Reference S-245].

M-182. Mukherjee, S. 1949. The mango and its relatives. *Science and Culture* 15: 5–9.

M-186. Mukherjee, S. K. 1953. The mango—its botany, cultivation, uses and future improvement, especially as observed in India. *Economic Botany* 7: 130–162.

M-191. Mikherjee, S. K. 1972. Origin of mango (*Mangifera indica*). *Economic Botany* 26: 260–266.

M-198. Munerati, O. 1932. Sull incrocio della barbabietola coltivata con la beta selvaggia della costa adriatica. *Industria Saccarifera Italiana* 25: 303–304.

M-205. Murphy, H. C., T. R. Stanton, & F. A. Coffman. 1942. Breeding for disease resistance in oats. *Journal of the American Society of Agronomy* 34: 72–89.

M-207. Murphy, H. C., I. Wahl, A. Dinoor, J. D. Miller, D. D. Morey, H. H. Luke, D. Sechler, & L. Reyes. 1967. Resistance to crown rust and soil borne mosaic virus in *Avena sterilis. Plant Disease Reporter* 51: 120–124.

M-224. Narain, A. 1974. Rape and mustard. In J. Hutchinson (ed.). *Evolutionary studies in world crops: Diversity and change in the Indian subcontinent:* 67–70 [Reference G-311].

M-229. National Academy of Sciences. 1975. *Underexploited tropical plants with promising economic value.* National Academy of Sciences. Washington, D.C. 188 pp.

M-231. National Academy of Sciences. 1977. *Guayule: An alternative source of natural rubber.* National Academy of Sciences. Washington, D.C. 80 pp.

M-237. Nault, L. R., & W. R. Findley. 1981–82. *Zea diploperennis:* A primitive relative offers new traits to improve corn. *Desert Plants* 3 (4): 202–205.

M-238. Nayar, N. M. 1976. Sesame. In N. W. Simmonds (ed.). *Evolution of crop plants:* 231–233. [Reference S-384].

M-239. Nayar, N. M., & K. L. Mehra. 1970. Sesame: Its uses, botany, cytogenetics and origin. *Economic Botany* 24: 20–31.

M-243. Neve, R. A. 1976. Hops. In N. W. Simmonds (ed.). *Evolution of crop plants:* 208–211 [Reference S-384].

M-249. Niederhauser, J. S., J. Cervantes, & L. Servia. 1954. Late blight in Mexico and its implications. *Phytopathology* 44: 406–408.

M-252. Nirula, K. K., N. M. Nayar, K. K. Bassi, & G. Singh. 1967. Reaction of tuber-bearing *Solanum* species to root knot nematode, *Meloidogyne incognita. American Potato Journal* 44: 66–69.

M-255. Nixon, R. W., & J. B. Carpenter. 1978. *Growing dates in the United States.* USDA Agriculture Information Bulletin No. 207. 63 pp.

M-258. Ntima, O. O. 1968. *Fast growing timber trees of the lowland tropics No. 3. The Araucarias.* Commonwealth Forestry Institute. Oxford.

M-264. Oelke, E. H., W. A. Elliot, M. F. Kernkamp, & D. W. Noetzel. 1973. *Commercial production of wild rice.* University of Minnesota Agricultural Extension Service Folder 284.

M-266. Ohler, J. G. 1967. Cashew growing. *Tropical Abstracts* 22: 1–9.

M-272. Oldemeyer, R. K. 1954. Viable interspecific hybrids between wild species in the section Vulgares and species in the section Patellares in the genus *Beta. Proceedings of the American Society of Sugar Beet Technologists* 8: 153–156.

M-273. Oldemeyer, R. K. 1970. A sugarbeet × *Beta procumbens* hybrid and its backcross derivatives. *Journal of the American Society of Sugar Beet Technologists* 15: 641–646.

M-277. Oliveira, A. L. F. de, & E. da S. R. Goes. 1974. *[A study on grazed cork oak stands: Relations between the soil and the vegetation in the Pliocene areas south of the Tagus. 1. Soil. 2. Vegetation.]* In Portuguese. Publicacoes, Direccao Geral dos Servicos Florestais e Aquicolas 1962–65. Vol. XXIX a XXXII. 207 pp.

M-283. Oudejans, J. H. M. 1969. Date plam: *Phoenix dactylifera* L. In F. P. Ferwerda & F. Wit (eds.). *Outlines of perennial crop breeding in the tropics:* 243–257 [Reference D-257].

M-288. Mangelsdorf, A. J. 1959. Sugar-cane breeding methods. *ISSCT Proceedings of the 10th Congress (Hawaii):* 694–701.

M-293. Muhammed, A., R. Aksel, & R. C. von Borstel (eds.). 1977. *Genetic diversity in plants.* Plenum Press. New York, London. 506 pp.

M-307. Osol, A., & G. E. Farrar Jr. (eds.). 1960. *The dispensatory of the United States of America.* 25th edition. J. B. Lippincott. Philadelphia.

M-312. National Academy of Sciences. 1979. *Staff summary report: NAS participation in second Caribbean Commonwealth meeting on utilization of natural products.* 22–27 April 1979. Port-of-Spain. 66 pp.

M-313. Naylor, J. 1976. *Production, trade and utilization of seaweeds and seaweed products.* FAO Fisheries Technical Paper No. 159. FAO. Rome. FIPP/T159. 73 pp.

M-317. Morton, J. F. 1977. *Major medicinal plants: Botany, culture and uses.* Charles C. Thomas. Springfield (Illinois). 431 pp.

M-319. McNeely, W. H., & D. J. Pettitt. 1973. Algin. In R. L. Whistler (ed.). *Industrial gums: Polysaccharides and their derivatives:* 49–81 [Reference V-102].

M-324. Olmo, H. P. 1976. Grapes. In N. W. Simmonds (ed.). *Evolution of crop plants:* 294–298 [Reference S-384].

M-329. Mack, D., N. Duplaix, & S. Wells. 1979. *International trade in sea turtle products.* 2d edition. Traffic (USA). Washington, D.C. 84 pp.

M-332. Madlener, J. C. 1977. *The seavegetable book: Foraging and cooking seaweed.* Clarkson N. Potter. New York. 288 pp.

M-348. McClane, A. J. 1977. *The encyclopedia of fish cookery.* Holt, Rinehart & Winston. New York. 511 pp.

M-355. Medway, Lord. 1978. *The wild mammals of Malaya (peninsular Malaysia) and Singapore.* 2d edition. Oxford University Press. Kuala Lumpur, Oxford, New York, Melbourne. 128 pp.

M-358. Michanek, G. 1975. *Seaweed resources of the ocean.* FAO Fisheries Technical Paper No. 138. FIRS/T138. FAO. Rome.

M-367. Morris, P. A. 1973. *A field guide to shells of the Atlantic and Gulf coasts and the West Indies.* 3d edition. Houghton Mifflin. Boston.

M-370. Mullins, E. J., & T. S. McKnight (eds.). 1981. *Canadian woods: Their properties and uses.* 3d edition. University of Toronto Press. Toronto, Buffalo, London. 389 pp.

M-373. Nearing, H., & S. Nearing. 1970. *The maple sugar book: Together with remarks on pioneering as a way of living in the twentieth century.* Schocken. New York. 273 pp.

M-379. Nilsson, G., & D. Mack. 1980. *Macaws: Traded to extinction?* Traffic (USA). Washington, D.C. 136 pp.

M-403. Martin, F. W. 1972. Current status of the sapogenin-bearing yams. *Plants, Foods, Human Nutrition* 2: 139–143.

M-404. Marucci, P. E. 1967. Cranberry pollination. *American Bee Journal* 107: 212–213.

M-458. Mangelsdorf, P. C., R. S. MacNeish, & W. C. Galinat. 1964. Domestication of corn. *Science* 143: 538–545.

M-461. Martin, F. W. 1969. The species of *Dioscorea* containing sapogenin. *Economic Botany* 23: 373–379.

M-469. Mitchum, H. 1978. *Creole gumbo and all that jazz: A New Orleans seafood cookbook.* Addison-Wesley. Reading, Menlo Park, London, Amsterdam, Don Mills, Sydney. 271 pp.

M-477. Niethammer, C. 1974. *American Indian food and lore.* Collier Books. New York, London. 191 pp.

M-482. Ortiz, E. L. 1979. *The book of Latin American cooking.* Alfred A. Knopf. New York. 357 pp.

M-489. Nelson, J. S. 1976. *Fishes of the world.* John Wiley & Sons. New York, London, Sydney, Toronto. 416 pp.

M-494. Martin, J. P., J. H. Black, & R. M. Hawthorne. 1977. *Earthworm biology and production.* University of California. Division of Agricultural Sciences Leaflet 2828. 10 pp.

M-495. Mauron, P. 1977. La situation de la viticulture dans le monde en 1976. *Bulletin de l'O.I.V.* 50: 739–775.

M-498. Mayr, E. 1982. *The growth of biological thought: Diversity, evolution, and inheritance.* The Belknap Press of Harvard University Press. Cambridge (Massachusetts), London (England). 974 pp.

M-499. Meredith, C. P., L. A. Lider, D. J. Raski, & N. L. Ferrari. 1982. Inheritance to tolerance to *Xiphinema index* in *Vitis* species. *American Journal of Enology and Viticulture* 33: 154–158.

M-563. National Academy of Sciences. 1975. *Products from jojoba: A promising new crop for arid lands.* NAS. Washington, D.C. 30 pp.

M-566. Nelson, K. S. 1982. Pecans. *Cuisine.* November.

M-577. McMahan, L. 1981. *The trade, biology, and management of American ginseng Panax quinquefolius.* Traffic (USA). Washington, D.C.

M-579. Mendieta, R. M., & S. R. del Amo. 1981. *Plants medicinales del estado de Yucatan.* Instituto Nacional de Investigaciones sobre Recursos Bioticos. Xalapa (Veracruz). 428 pp.

M-601. Myers, N. 1983. *A wealth of wild species: Storehouse for human welfare.* Westview Press. Boulder (Colorado). 274 pp.

M-605. Mack, D. 1983. Trends in primate imports into the United States: 1982. *ILAR News.*

M-607. Mack, D., & R. Mittermeier (eds.). 1985. *The international primate trade.* Volume 1: Legislation, trade and captive breeding. World Wildlife Fund–US, Traffic (USA), and IUCN/SSC. 185 pp.

M-608. McDaniel, M. E. 1974. Registration of TAM 0-301 oats (reg. no. 256). *Crop Science* 14: 127–128.

M-609. McDaniel, M. E. 1974. Registration of TAM 0-312 oats (reg. no. 257). *Crop Science* 14: 128.

M-611. Myers, N. 1983. Land: One tusk of a dilemma. *Science Digest.* June.

M-614. National Council on Gene Resources. 1982. *Strawberry genetic resources: An assessment and plan for California.* National Council on Gene Resources. Berkeley. 252 pp.

M-616. Nilsson, G. 1977. *The bird business: A study of the importation of birds into the United States.* Animal Welfare Institute. Washington, D.C. 81 pp.

M-618. Merkle, O. G., E. C. Gilmore, & F. J. Gough. 1973. Registration of Fox wheat (reg. no. 524). *Crop Science* 13: 288.

M-624. Madden, G. 1979. Pecans. In R. A. Jaynes (ed.). *Nut tree culture in North America:* 13–34 [Reference J-306].

M-625. Madden, G. D., & H. L. Malstrom. 1975. Pecans and hickories. In J. Janick & J. N. Moore (eds.). *Advances in fruit breeding:* 420–438 [Reference J-8].

M-631. Millikan, D. F. 1979. Beeches, oaks, pines, and ginkgo. In R. A. Jaynes (ed.). *Nut tree culture in North America:* 175–187 [Reference J-306].

M-633. Moore, J. N. 1966. Breeding. In P. Eck & N. F. Childers (eds.). *Blueberry culture:* 45–74 [Reference D-118].

M-641. Ourecky, D. K. 1975. Brambles. In J. Janick & J. N. Moore (eds.). *Advances in fruit breeding:* 98–129 [Reference J-8].

M-644. Markley, K. S. 1971. The babassu oil palm of Brazil. *Economic Botany* 25: 267–304.

M-646. Metcalf, H. N., & J. N. Sharma. 1971. Germ plasm resources of the genus *Zinnia* L. *Economic Botany* 25: 169–181.

M-652. Moyle, J. B., & P. Krueger. 1968. *Wild rice in Minnesota.* Minnesota Department of Conservation. Division of Game and Fish. Information Leaflet 5. 10 pp.

M-653. Moyle, J. B. 1969. *Wild-rice—some notes, comments and problems.* Minnesota Department of Conservation. Division of Game and Fish. Special Publication No. 47. 10 pp.

M-654. Oelke, E. A. 1974. Wild rice domestication as a model. In G. F. Somers (ed.). *Seed-bearing halophytes as food plants:* 47–56 [Reference S-741].

M-663. Norman, C. 1975. Plenty of potential for jojoba oil. *Nature* 255: 272–273.

M-667. McCloskey, M. 1983. "Recreational whale-watching." Paper presented at the Global conference on the non-consumptive utilisation of cetacean resources. June 1983. Boston (Massachusetts). 20 pp.

M-674. Ohm, H. W., F. L. Patterson, J. J. Roberts, & G. E. Shaner. 1974. Registration of Noble oats (reg. no. 259). *Crop Science* 14: 906–907.

M-675. Norden, A. J. 1980. Crop improvement and genetic resources in ground nuts. In R. J. Summerfield & A. H. Bunting (eds.). *Advances in legume science:* 515–523 [Reference S-245].

M-676. Nye, W. P., & J. L. Anderson. 1974. Insect pollinators frequenting strawberry blossoms and the effect of honey bees on yield and fruit quality. *Journal of the American Society for Horticultural Science* 99: 40–44.

M-1021. McMahan, L. 1983. Cat skin trade shifts to smaller species. *Traffic* (USA) 5 (2): 3, 5.

M-1025. Morris, E. A. 1979. Turpentine for synthetic fragrance: A commercial appraisal. *Tropical Science* 21 (3): 197–206.

P-6. Panje, R. R., & C. N. Babu. 1960. Studies in *Saccharum spontaneum:* Distribution and geographical association of chromosome numbers. *Cytologia* 25: 152–172.

P-11. Parker, J. B. 1966. Gum arabic from Sudan exported to markets all over the world. *Foreign Agriculture* 4 (25): 7.

P-27. Pickersgill, B. 1969. The archaeological record of chili peppers (*Capsicum* spp.) and the sequence of plant domestication in Peru. *American Antiquity* 34: 54–61.

P-28. Pickersgill, B. 1969. The domestication of chili peppers. In P. J. Ucko & G. W. Dimbleby (eds.). *The domestication and exploitation of plants and animals:* 443–450 [Reference S-323].

P-36. Plank, J. E. van der. 1968. *Disease resistance in plants.* Academic Press. New York, San Francisco, London. 206 pp.

P-39. Plucknett, D. L., R. S. de la Pena, & R. Obrero. 1970. Taro (*Colocasia esculenta*). *Field Crop Abstracts* 23: 413–426.

P-50. Porte, W. S., & H. B. Walker. 1941. The Pan America tomato, a new red variety highly resistant to *Fusarium* wilt. *USDA Circular* 611: 1–6.

P-51. Porte, W. S., & H. B. Walker. 1945. A cross between *Lycopersicon esculentum* and disease resistant *L. peruvianum. Phytopathology* 35: 931–933.

P-66. Price, S. 1957. Cytological studies in *Saccharum* and allied genera. III. Chromosome numbers in interspecific hybrids. *Botanical Gazette* 118: 146–159.

P-67. Price, S. 1965. *Cytology of Saccharum robustum and related sympatric species and natural hybrids.* USDA. Technical Bulletin No. 1337. 47 pp.

P-70. Produktschap voor Siergewassen. 1980. *Tulpen: beplante oppervlakten 1976/1977+/m1979/1980.* Publicatie nr. 1980-4. Gravenhage, Netherlands. 19 pp.

P-76. Putt, E. D., & W. E. Sackston. 1957. Studies on sunflower rust. I. Some sources of rust resistance. *Canadian Journal of Plant Science* 37: 43–54.

P-82. Quigley, K. L., & R. D. Lindmark. 1967. *A look at black walnut timber resources and industries.* U.S. Forest Service Resource Bulletin. Northeastern Forest Experiment Station. No. NE-4. 29 pp.

P-88. Quisenberry, K. S., & L. P. Reitz (eds.). 1967. *Wheat and wheat improvement.* American Society of Agronomy. Madison. 560 pp.

P-100. Ramanujam, S. 1976. Chickpea. In N. W. Simmonds (ed.). *Evolution of crop plants:* 157–159 [Reference S-384].

P-105. Rands, R. D., & L. G. Polhamus. 1955. *Progress report on the co-operative rubber development program in Latin America.* USDA Circular 976. 79 pp.

P-108. Rasheed, M. A. el. 1970/1971. The production and role of gum arabic in the economy of the Sudan. *Y Coedwigwr* 6: 84–87.

P-116. Reeves, R. G., & A. J. Bockholt. 1964. Modification and improvement of a maize inbred by crossing it with *Tripsacum. Crop Science* 4: 7–10.

P-119. Reitz, L. P., & W. G. Hamlin. 1978. *Distribution of the varieties and classes of wheat in the United States in 1974.* USDA. Science and Education Administration. Statistical Bulletin No. 604. Washington, D.C. 98 pp.

P-124. Renfrew, J. M. 1969. The archaeological evidence for the domestication of plants: Methods and problems. In P. J. Ucko & G. W. Dimbleby (eds.). *The domestication and exploitation of plants and animals:* 149–172 [Reference S-323].

P-125. Rennie, N. 1978. *Solanum* cropping takes off in Taranaki. *New Zealand Farmer* August 24: 22–23.

P-126. Rennie, N. 1980. *Solanum* progress not so smooth. *New Zealand Farmer* December 11: 10–12.

P-134. Rick, C. M. 1974. High soluble-solids content in large-fruited tomato lines derived from a wild green-fruited species. *Hilgardia* 42: 493–510.

P-140. Rick, C. M., E. Kesicki, J. F. Forbes, & M. Holle. 1976. Genetic and biosystematic studies on two new sibling species of *Lycopersicon* from interandine Peru. *Theoretical and Applied Genetics* 47: 55–68.

P-141. Rieman, G. H., D. C. Cooper, & R. W. Hougas. 1954. Potato varieties derived from species hybrids. *American Potato Journal* 31: 1–11.

P-151. Robbins, S. R. J., & P. Greenhalgh. 1979. *The markets for selected herbaceous essential oils.* Report G120. Tropical Products Institute. London. 60 pp.

P-157. Robins, E. 1980. Cork that puts the pop in champagne. *International Herald Tribune.* 19–20 April.

P-164. Rodriquez, D. W. 1969. *Pimento—a short economic history.* Commodity Bulletin. Ministry of Agriculture & Fisheries. Kingston No. 3. 52 pp.

P-166. Rogers, D. J. 1963. Studies of *Manihot esculenta* Crantz and related species. *Bulletin of the Torrey Botanical Club* 90: 43–54.

P-167. Rogers, D. J., & S. G. Appan. 1973. *Flora Neotropica monograph no. 13: Manihot Manihotoides (Euphorbiaceae).* Hafner Press. New York. 272 pp.

P-171. Root, W. 1978. Ginseng's magic is mighty but its taste isn't much. *International Herald Tribune.* 16 February.

P-183. Rosengarten, F. Jr. 1969. *The book of spices.* Livingston Publishing. Philadelphia.

P-186. Ross, H. 1966. The use of wild *Solanum* species in German potato breeding of the past and today. *American Potato Journal* 43: 63–80.

P-189. Ross, H. 1979. Wild species and primitive cultivars as ancestors of potato varieties. In A. C. Zeven & A. M. van Harten (eds.). *Proceedings of the conference broadening the genetic base of crops:* 237–245 [Reference Y-48].

P-203. The Royal General Bulbgrowers' Association. 1975. *Classified list and international register of hyacinths and other bulbous and tuberous-rooted plants.* Hillegom, Netherlands. 277 pp.

P-204. The Royal General Bulbgrowers' Association. 1976. *Classified list and international register of tulip names.* Hillegom, Netherlands. 192 pp.

P-206. Royes, W. V. 1976. Pigeon pea. In N. W. Simmonds (ed.). *Evolution of crop plants:* 154–156 [Reference S-384].

P-214. Russell, G. E. 1978. *Plant breeding for pest and disease resistance.* Butterworths. London, Boston. 485 pp.

P-217. Ryder, E. J. 1976. Lettuce. In N. W. Simmonds (ed.). *Evolution of crop plants:* 39–41 [Reference S-384].

P-219. Ryder, E. J. 1979. "Salinas" lettuce. *HortScience* 14: 283–284.

P-220. Ryder, E. J., & T. W. Whitaker. No date. The lettuce industry in California: A quarter century of change, 1954–1979. *Horticultural Reviews* 164–207.

P-224. Price, S. 1965. Interspecific hybridization in sugarcane breeding. *ISSCT Proceedings of the 12th Congress (Puerto Rico):* 1021–1026.

P-225. Panje, R. R. 1971. The role of *Saccharum spontaneum* in sugarcane breeding. *ISSCT Proceedings of the 14th Congress (Louisiana):* 217–223.

P-235. Roach, B. T. 1971. Nobilisation of sugarcane. *ISSCT Proceedings of the 14th Congress (Louisiana):* 206–216.

P-237. Roach, B. T. 1977. Utilization of *Saccharum spontaneum* in sugarcane breeding. *ISSCT Proceedings of the 16th Congress (Brazil)* 1: 43–58.

P-238. Rao, J. T., & M. K. Krishnaswami. 1957. Assessing the breeding behavior of *Saccharum spontaneum* variants. *Indian Journal of Sugarcane Research and Development* 1 (3): 164–169.

P-245. Root, W. 1979. Sizing up the shrimp, a most variable creature. *International Herald Tribune.* July 31.

P-246. Root, W. 1979. Salmon: Captivity makes it insipid. *International Herald Tribune.* June 12.

P-248. Root, W. 1980. The herring: A homebody rises to the occasion. *International Herald Tribune.* September 30.

P-256. Purseglove, J. W., E. G. Brown, C. L. Green, & S. R. J. Robbins. 1981. *Spices. Volume 1.* Longman. London. New York. 439 pp.

P-257. Purseglove, J. W., E. G. Brown, C. L. Green, & S. R. J. Robbins. 1981. *Spices. Volume 2.* Longman. London, New York. 447–812 pp.

P-258. Robbins, S. R. J., & W. S. A. Matthews. 1974. Minor forest products. *Unasylva* 26 (106): 7–14.

P-260. Roet, E. C., D. S. Mack, & N. Duplaix. 1981. *Psittacines imported by the United States (October 1979–June 1980).* Proceedings of the ICBP Parrot Workshop. 15–19 April 1980. St. Lucia. Special report 7. 70 pp.

P-265. Rick, C. M. 1973. Potential genetic resources in tomato species: Clues from observations in native habitats. In A. M. Srb (ed.). *Basic life sciences. Volume 2:* 255–269 [Reference S-379].

P-268. Rick, C. M. 1979. Potential improvement of tomatoes by controlled introgression of genes from wild species. In A. C. Zeven & A. M. van Harten (eds.). *Proceedings of a conference broadening the genetic base of crops:* 167–173 [Reference Y-48].

P-269. Phillips, L. L. 1976. Cotton. In N. W. Simmonds (ed.). *Evolution of crop plants:* 196–200 [Reference S-384].

P-270. Prescott-Allen, R., & C. Prescott-Allen. 1981. *In situ conservation of crop genetic resources.* FAO/UNEP/IBPGR Technical Conference on Crop Genetic Resources. 6–10 April 1981. Rome.

P-275. Parry, J. W. 1969. *Spices. Volume I: The story of spices: The spices described.* Chemical Publishing Company. New York. 235 pp.

P-284. Proctor, M., & P. Yeo. 1973. *The pollination of flowers.* Collins. London. 418 pp.

P-291. Reay, P. J. 1979. *Aquaculture.* Institute of Biology's Studies in Biology No. 106. Edward Arnold. London. 60 pp.

P-302. Root, W. 1980. *Food: An authoritative and visual history and dictionary of the foods of the world.* Simon and Schuster. New York. 602 pp.

P-303. Root, W. (ed.). 1980. *Herbs and spices: The pursuit of flavor.* McGraw-Hill. New York, St. Louis, San Francisco. 191 pp.

P-304. Root, W., & R. de Rochemont. 1981. *Eating in America: A history.* Ecco Press. New York. 512 pp.

P-322. Prakash, S., & K. Hinata. 1980. Taxonomy, cytogenetics and origin of crop brassicas: A review. *Opera Botanica* 55: 57 pp.

P-323. Price, W. C. (ed.). 1961. *Proceedings of the 2nd Conference of the International Organization of Citrus Virologists.* University of Florida Press. Gainesville.

P-356. Putt, E. D. 1964. Recessive branching in sunflowers. *Crop Science* 4: 444–445.

P-357. Pyle, R. M. 1981. *The Audubon Society field guide to North American butterflies.* Alfred A. Knopf. New York. 916 pp.

P-363. Pouget, R. de. 1977. Obtention de nouveaux portes-greffes favorables a la qualite, la resistance a la chlorose et la maitrise de la vigueur. *Bulletin de l'O.I.V.* 50: 387–397.

P-365. Prescott-Allen, R., & C. Prescott-Allen. 1982. *What's wildlife worth? Economic contributions of wild plants and animals to developing countries.* Earthscan. London. 92 pp.

P-367. Rives, L. 1963. Prospection preliminaire des especes americaines du genre *Vitis.* *Annales de l'Amelioration des Plants* 13: 51–82.

P-368. Rives, M. 1974. Les vignes sauvages comme sources de genes pour l'amelioration. *Vitis* 13: 186–197.

P-373. Palmer, C. 1982. Berry market not-so-blue. *Maine Alumnus.* June.

P-391. Ricciuti, E. R. 1980. The ivory wars. *Animal Kingdom.* February/March.

P-403. Proulx, E. A. 1982. Homarus domesticus: Wild stocks dwindle alarmingly as Canadian researchers seek to tame the world's most toothsome crustacean. *Equinox.* July/August.

P-406. Roeper, N., & G. Hemley. 1982. *Crocodile and alligator trade by the United States 1981.* Traffic (USA). Washington, D.C. 23 pp.

P-408. Rue, L. L. III. 1981. *Furbearing animals of North America.* Crown. New York. 343 pp.

P-421. Romanko, R. R., J. Jaeger, G. B. Nickerson, & C. E. Zimmermann. 1979. Registration of Galena hop. *Crop Science* 19: 563.

P-422. Putt, E. D., & W. E. Sackston. 1963. Studies on sunflower rust. IV. Two genes, $R_1$ and $R_2$ for resistance in the host. *Canadian Journal of Plant Science* 43: 490–496.

P-425. Patterson, F. L., R. L. Gallun, J. J. Roberts, R. E. Finney, & G. E. Shaner. 1975. Registration of Arthur 71 and Abe wheat (reg. nos. 560 and 562). *Crop Science* 15: 736.

P-426. Patterson, F. L., J. J. Roberts, R. E. Finney, G. E. Shaner, R. L. Gallun, & H. W. Ohm. 1975. Registration of Oasis wheat. *Crop Science* 15: 736–737.

P-427. Payne, B. R., & R. M. DeGraaf. 1975. Economic values and recreational trends associated with human enjoyment of nongame birds. In D. R. Smith (technical coordinator). *Proceedings of the symposium on management of forest and range habitats for nongame birds*: 6–10 [Reference S-567].

P-430. Pringle, J. D., & G. J. Sharp. 1980. *An overview of the Maritime marine plant industry—1980.* Fisheries and Oceans. Resource Branch. Halifax (Nova Scotia).

P-432. Resource Statistics Division. 1979. *Fisheries of the United States, 1978.* U.S. Department of Commerce. Current Fishery Statistics No. 7800. Washington, D.C. 120 pp.

P-433. Resource Statistics Division. 1980. *Fisheries of the United States, 1979.* U.S.

Department of Commerce, Current Fishery Statistics No. 8000. Washington, D.C. 131 pp.

P-434. Resource Statistics Division. 1981. *Fisheries of the United States, 1980.* U.S. Department of Commerce. Current Fishery Statistics No. 8100. Washington, D.C. 132 pp.

P-435. Resource Statistics Division. 1982. *Fisheries of the United States, 1981.* U.S. Department of Commerce. Current Fishery Statistics No. 8200. Washington, D.C. 131 pp.

P-436. Robertson, L. D., & K. E. Miskin. 1974. Registration of W-332 wheat (reg. no. 534). *Crop Science* 14: 129.

P-439. Penn, E. S. 1980. "Consumer expenditures for and economic contributions from industrial fishery products in the United States, 1977–79." Draft report.

P-447. Parks Canada. 1982. *Park-use statistics, 1981–82.* Socio-Economic Division. SED 82-1. Ottawa. 361 pp.

P-448. Princen, L. H. 1982. Alternate industrial feedstocks from agriculture. *Economic Botany* 36: 302–312.

P-449. Rick, C. M. 1967. Fruit and pedicel characters derived from Galapagos tomatoes. *Economic Botany* 21: 171–184.

P-450. Rick, C. M., & J. F. Fobes. 1975. Allozymes of Galapagos tomatoes: Polymorphism, geographic distribution, and affinities. *Evolution* 29: 443–457.

P-454. Payne, J. A., & W. T. Johnson. 1979. Plant pests. In R. A. Jaynes (ed.). *Nut tree culture in North America:* 314–395 [Reference J-306].

P-461. Putt, E. D. 1978. History and present world status. In J. F. Carter (ed.). *Sunflower science and technology:* 1–29 [Reference A-376].

P-463. Rick, C. M. 1981. "The potential of exotic germplasm for tomato improvement." Unpublished.

P-475. Phelps, R. B. 1980. *Timber in the United States economy: 1963, 1967, and 1972.* USDA. Forest Service. General Technical Report WO-21. Washington, D.C. 90 pp.

P-476. Payne, R. J. 1981. Houses and structures. In E. J. Mullins & T. S. McKnight (eds.). *Canadian woods: Their properties and uses:* 265–284 [Reference M-370].

P-477. Perem, E., C. F. McBride, & C. T. Keith. 1981. Commercial woods. In E. J. Mullins & T. S. McKnight (eds.). *Canadian woods: Their properties and uses:* 9–40 [Reference M-370].

P-478. Ruderman, F. K. 1982. *Production, prices, employment, and trade in northwest forest industries, second quarter 1982.* USDA. Forest Service. Portland (Oregon). 64 pp.

P-479. Pauling, J. R. 1970. *Trends in forage crop varieties—1969.* USDA. Federal Extension Service.

P-481. Posnette, A. F. 1982. Note on the origin of Scavina. In H. Toxopeus (ed.). *Archives of cocoa research:* 13 [Reference S-578].

P-482. Pound, F. J. 1938. Cacao and witchbroom disease (*Marasmius perniciosus*) of South America. In H. Toxopeus (ed.). *Archives of cocoa research:* 20–72 [Reference S-578].

P-483. Pound, F. J. 1943. Cacao and witches' broom disease *(Marasmius perniciosus).* In H. Toxopeus (ed.). *Archives of cocoa research:* 73–92 [Reference S-578].

P-484. Prescott-Allen, R., & C. Prescott-Allen. 1983. *Genes from the wild.* Earthscan. London.

P-488. Reeves, S. A. Jr. 1975. Sugarcane varieties. In Texas Agricultural Experiment Station. *Texas sugarcane growers guide:* 1–22.

P-489. Princen, L. H. 1977. Potential wealth in new crops: Research and development. In D. S. Seigler (ed.). *Crop resources:* 1–15 [Reference S-366].

P-490. Pryde, E. H. 1977. Nonfood uses for commercial vegetable oil crops. In D. S. Seigler (ed.). *Crop resources:* 25–45 [Reference S-366].

P-491. Probst, A. H., & R. W. Judd. 1973. Origin, U.S. history and development, and world distribution. In B. E. Caldwell (ed.). *Soybeans: Improvement, production, and uses:* 1–15 [Reference A-736].

P-492. Rice Research Board. 1982. *Thirteenth annual report to the California rice growers.* California Food and Agriculture. Yuba City (California). 24 pp.

P-493. Rutger, J. N., R. K. Webster, & R. A. Figoni. 1983. Weedy species of rice show promise for disease resistance. *California Agriculture* 37: 7–9.

P-494. Pedersen, M. W., G. E. Bohart, V. L. Marble, & E. C. Klostermeyer. 1972. Seed production practices. In C. H. Hanson (ed.). *Alfalfa science and technology:* 689–720 [Reference G-460].

P-495. Quagliotti, L. 1979. Floral biology of *Capsicum* and *Solanum melongena.* In J. G. Hawkes, R. N. Lester, & A. D. Skelding (eds.). *The biology and taxonomy of the Solanaceae:* 399–419 [Reference G-538].

P-496. Robinson, R. G. 1978. Production and culture. In J. F. Carter (ed.). *Sunflower science and technology:* 89–143 [Reference A-376].

P-497. Rol, F. 1973. Locust bean gum. In R. L. Whistler (ed.). *Industrial gums: Polysaccharides and their derivatives:* 323–337 [Reference V-102].

P-498. Phelps, R. B. 1977. *The demand and price situation for forest products, 1976–77.* USDA. Forest Service. Miscellaneous Publication No. 1357. 95 pp.

P-788. Pennak, R. W. 1978. *Fresh-water invertebrates of the United States.* 2d edition. John Wiley & Sons. New York, Chichester, Brisbane, Toronto. 803 pp.

P-792. Pimentel, D., E. Garnick, A. Berkowitz, S. Jacobson, S. Napolitano, P. Black, S. Valdes-Cogliano, B. Vinzant, E. Hudes, & S. Littman. 1980. Environmental quality and natural biota. *BioScience* 30 (11): 750–755.

P-797. Parker, I. S. C., & E. B. Martin. 1983. Further insight into the international ivory trade. *Oryx* 17 (4): 194–200.

S-9. Salmon, E. S. 1938. Notes on hops. *Journal of the South-Eastern Agricultural College (Wye, Kent)* No. 42: 47–59.

S-10. Salmon, E. S. 1944. *Four seedlings of the Cantebury Golding.* South-Eastern Agricultural College, Wye. 8 pp.

S-13. Samarawira, I. 1972. Cardamom. *World Crops* 24: 76–78.

S-26. Sauer, J. D. 1976. Grain amaranths. In N. W. Simmonds (ed.). *Evolution of crop plants:* 4–7 [Reference S-384].

S-28. Saunders, J. H. 1970. Wild diploid species of *Gossypium* in cotton breeding. In M. A. Siddiq & L. C. Hughes (eds.). *Cotton growth in the Gezira environment: A symposium to mark the 15th anniversary of the Gezira Research Station:* 159–163 [Reference S-101].

S-30. Savitsky, H. 1973. Meiosis in hybrids between *Beta vulgaris* L. and *Beta procumbens* Chr. Sm. and transmission of sugarbeet nematode resistance. Proceedings of the International Congress on Genetics. *Genetics* 74 (2): 241.

S-31. Savitsky, H. 1975. Hybridization between *Beta vulgaris* and *B. procumbens* and transmission of nematode *(Heterodera schachtii)* resistance to sugarbeet. *Canadian Journal of Genetics and Cytology* 12: 197–209.

S-32. Savitsky, H. 1978. Nematode *(Heterodera schachtii)* resistance and meiosis in diploid plants from interspecific *Beta vulgaris* × *B. procumbens* hybrids. *Canadian Journal of Genetics and Cytology* 20: 177–186.

S-33. Savitsky, H. 1979. Improvement in the rate of nematode resistance transmission in diploid *Beta vulgaris–procumbens* hybrids. *Genetics* 91: Abstract S-112.

S-34. Savitsky, H. 1980. Nematode resistance transmission of diploid *Beta vulgaris–*

*procumbens* hybrids and the production of homozygous nematode-resistant plants. *Genetics* 94: Abstract S-93.

S-35. Savitsky, H. 1981. Production of homozygous nematode-resistant lines in diploid *Beta vulgaris–procumbens* hybrids. *Genetics* 97: Abstract S-94.

S-38. Schaible, L. W., O. S. Cannon, & V. Waddoups. 1951. Inheritance of resistance to *Verticillium* wilt in a tomato cross. *Phytopathology* 41: 986–990.

S-41. Schery. R. W. 1972. *Plants for man.* 2d edition. Prentice-Hall. Engelwood Cliffs (New Jersey). 657 pp.

S-55. Schultes, R. E. 1979. The Amazonia as a source of new economic plants. *Economic Botany* 33: 259–266.

S-62. Scullen, H. A. 1956. *Bees—for legume seed production.* Oregon Agricultural Experiment Station. Circular 554.

S-69. Seder, J. 1979. Jojoba: The miracle bean? *Spokesman Review.* March 18.

S-74. Seibert, R. J. 1950. The importance of palms to Latin America: Pejibaye a notable example. *Ceiba* 1 (2): 65–74.

S-82. Sharma, D., & D. Knott. 1966. The transfer of leaf rust resistance from *Agropyron* to *Triticum* by irradiation. *Canadian Journal of Genetics and Cytology* 8: 137–143.

S-96. Sherry, S. P. 1971. *The black wattle (Acacia mearnsii de Wild.)* University of Natal Press. Pietermaritzburg. 402 pp.

S-101. Siddiq, M. A., & L. C. Hughes (eds.). 1970. *Cotton growth in the Gezira environment: A symposium to mark the 15th anniversary of the Gezira Research Station. 6–9* January 1969. Agricultural Research Corporation. Wad Medani. Republic of the Sudan.

S-104. Simmonds, F. J. 1970. Biological control of pests. *Tropical Science* 12: 191–199.

S-119. Simmonds, N. W. 1976. Sugarcanes. In N. W. Simmonds (ed.). *Evolution of crop plants:* 104–108 [Reference S-384].

S-122. Simmonds, N. W. 1976. Bananas. In N. W. Simmonds (ed.). *Evolution of crop plants:* 211–215 [Reference S-384].

S-123. Simmonds, N. W. 1979. *Principles of crop improvement.* Longman. London, New York. 408 pp.

S-128. Simons, M. D., J. W. Martens, R. J. H. McKenzie, I. Nishiyama, K. Sadanaga, J. Sebesta, & H. Thomas. 1978. *Oats: A standardized system of nomenclature for genes and chromosomes and catalog of genes governing characters.* USDA. SEA. Agriculture Handbook No. 509. Washington, D.C. 40 pp.

S-131. Singh, D. P. 1976. Jute. In N. W. Simmonds (ed.). *Evolution of crop plants:* 290–291 [Reference S-384].

S-132. Singh, D. 1976. Castor. In N. W. Simmonds (ed.). *Evolution of crop plants:* 84–86 [Reference S-384].

S-171. Smith, P. M. 1976. Minor crops. In N. W. Simmonds (ed.). *Evolution of crop plants:* 301–324 [Reference S-384].

S-178. Somigliana, J. C. 1973. [Summary of the present economic state and development prospects of the quebracho tannin extract industry of Argentina.] In Spanish. *Revista Forestal Argentina* 17: 101–106.

S-181. Soria, J. V. 1973. Latin America: Primitive cultivars of cacao in America. In O. H. Frankel (ed.). *Survey of crop genetic resources in their centres of diversity: First report:* 119–125 [Reference D-168].

S-182. Soria, J. V. 1970. The latest cocoa expeditions to the Amazon basin. *Cacao* 15: 5–18.

S-183. Soria, J. 1975. Recent cocoa collecting expeditions. In O. H. Frankel & J. G. Hawkes (eds.). *Crop genetic resources for today and tomorrow:* 175–179 [Reference D-175].

S-184. Soria, J. V. 1978. The breeding of cacao (*Theobroma cacao* L.). *Tropical Agriculture Research Series* No. 11: 161–168.

S-186. Sparnaaij, L. D. 1969. Oil palm. In F. P. Ferwerda & F. Wit (eds.). *Outlines of perennial crop breeding in the tropics:* 339–387 [Reference D-257].

S-190. Sprague, G. F. (ed.). 1977. *Corn and corn improvement.* 2d edition. Monograph 18. American Society of Agronomy. Madison (Wisconsin). 774 pp.

S-196. Stalker, H. T. 1980. Utilization of wild species for crop improvement. *Advances in Agronomy* 33: 111–147.

S-202. Stavely, J. R. 1979. Disease resistance. In R. D. Durbin (ed.). *Nicotiana: Procedures for experimental use:* 87–110 [Reference D-81].

S-203. Stavely, J. R., G. W. Pittarelli, & L. G. Burk. 1973. *Nicotiana repanda* as a potential source for disease resistance in *N. tabacum. Journal of Heredity* 64: 265–271.

S-207. Steele, W. M. 1976. Cowpeas. In N. W. Simmonds (ed.). *Evolution of crop plants:* 183–185 [Reference S-384].

S-219. Stewart, D. 1950. Sugar beet × *Beta procumbens,* the $F_1$ and backcross generations. *Proceedings of the 6th General Meeting of the American Society of Sugar Beet Technologists:* 176–179.

S-226. Storey, W. B. 1969. Papaya: *Carica papaya* L. In F. P. Ferwerda & F. Wit (eds.). *Outlines of perennial crop breeding in the tropics:* 389–407 [Reference D-257].

S-228. Storey, W. B. 1976. Fig. In N. W. Simmonds (ed.). *Evolution of crop plants:* 205–208 [Reference S-384].

S-229. Storey, W. B., & I. J. Condit. 1969. Fig: *Ficus carica* L. In F. P. Ferwerda & F. Wit (eds.). *Outlines of perennial crop breeding in the tropics:* 259–267 [Reference D-257].

S-245. Summerfield, R. J., & A. H. Bunting (eds.). 1980. *Advances in legume science.* Volume 1 of the Proceedings of the International Legume Conference. 31 July–4 August 1978. Kew Royal Botanic Gardens. Kew. 667 pp.

S-257. Synge, H. (ed.). 1981. *The biological aspects of rare plant conservation.* John Wiley & Sons. Chichester, New York, Brisbane, Toronto. 586 pp.

S-279. Thompson, K. F. 1976. Cabbages, kales, etc. In N. W. Simmonds (ed.). *Evolution of crop plants:* 49–52 [Reference S-384].

S-286. Thompson, R. C., & E. J. Ryder. 1961. *Descriptions and pedigrees of nine varieties of lettuce.* USDA Agricultural Research Service Technical Bulletin No. 1244. 19 pp.

S-290. Thyr, B. D. 1969. Additional sources of resistance to bacterial canker of tomato (*Corynebacterium michiganense). Plant Disease Reporter* 53: 234–237.

S-296. Tomes, M. L., & F. W. Quackenbush. 1958. Caro-Red, a new provitamin A rich tomato. *Economic Botany* 12: 256–260.

S-301. Toxopeus, H. 1964. $F_3$ Amazon cocoa in Nigeria. *CRIN Annual Report* 1963/64. 13–23.

S-302. Toxopeus, H. J. 1964. Treasure digging for blight resistance in potatoes. *Euphytica* 13: 206–222.

S-311. Tubergen, C. G. van Ltd. 1947. *New bulbous and tuberous rooted plants introduced into cultivation by C. G. van Tubergen Ltd.* Leiden.

S-323. Ucko, P. J., & G. W. Dimbleby (eds.). 1969. *The domestication and exploitation of plants and animals.* Gerald Duckworth. London. 581 pp.

S-334. USDA. 1979. *Barley: Origin, botany, culture, winter hardiness, genetics, utilization, pests.* USDA. SEA. Agriculture Handbook No. 338. Washington, D.C. 154 pp.

S-337. Usher, G. 1974. *A dictionary of plants used by man.* Constable & Company. London. 619 pp.

S-345. Sundaresan, K., & S. Thangavelu. 1975. Study of co canes widely cultivated in India and their derivation. *ISSCT Sugarcane Breeders' Newsletter* 37: 72–86.

S-349. Sailer, R. I. 1961. Possibilities for genetic improvement of beneficial insects. In R. E. Hodgson (ed.). *Germ plasm resources:* 295–303 [Reference G-416].

S-356. Tai, P., & J. D. Miller. 1978. The pedigree of selected Canal Point (CP) varieties of sugarcane. *Proceedings of the American Society of Sugarcane Technologists* 8: 34–39.

S-359. Tseng, C. K. 1947. Seaweed resources of North America and their utilization. *Economic Botany.* 1: 69–97.

S-362. Tapiador, D. D., H. F. Henderson, M. N. Delmendo, & H. Tsutsui. 1977. *Freshwater fisheries and aquaculture in China.* FAO Fisheries Technical Paper No. 168. FIR/T168. FAO. Rome. 84 pp.

S-366. Seigler, D. S. (ed.). 1977. *Crop resources.* Proceedings of the 17th Annual Meeting of the Society for Economic Botany. 13–17 June 1976. Urbana, Illinois. Academic Press. New York, San Francisco, London. 233 pp.

S-369. Towle, G. A. 1973. Carrageenan. In R. L. Whistler (ed.). *Industrial gums: Polysaccharides and their derivatives:* 83–114 [Reference V-102].

S-370. Selby, H. H., & W. H. Wynne. 1973. Agar. In R. L. Whistler (ed.). *Industrial gums: Polysaccharides and their derivatives:* 29–48 [Reference V-102].

S-372. USDA. 1976. *Tree nuts.* USDA Foreign Agriculture Circular. July. FN 5-76.

S-373. Shane, M. 1977. The economics of a Sabah rattan industry. In W. W. Yen & M. Shane (eds.). *A Sabah rattan industry:* 43–53 [Reference Y-47].

S-379. Srb, A. M. (ed.). 1973. *Basic life sciences. Volume 2.* Plenum. New York.

S-380. Toxopeus, H. 1969. Cacao. In F. P. Ferwerda & F. Wit (eds.). *Outlines of perennial crop breeding in the tropics:* 79–109 [Reference D-257].

S-384. Simmonds, N. W. (ed.). 1976. *Evolution of crop plants.* Longman. London, New York. 339 pp.

S-407. Sokolov, R. 1981. *Fading feast: A compendium of disappearing American regional foods.* Farrar, Straus & Giroux. New York. 276 pp.

S-409. Statistics Canada. 1978. *Imports: Merchandise trade commodity detail: 1976–1977.* Statistics Canada. External Trade Division. Ottawa. Catalogue 65-207. 1242 pp.

S-410. Statistics Canada. 1980. *Imports: Merchandise trade commodity detail: 1979.* Statistics Canada. External Trade Division. Ottawa. Catalogue 65-207. 1286 pp.

S-411. Statistics Canada. 1981. *Imports: Merchandise trade commodity detail: 1980.* Statistics Canada. External Trade Division. Ottawa. Catalogue 65-207. 1272 pp.

S-413. Stobart, T. 1977. *Herbs, spices and flavourings.* Penguin Books. 320 pp.

S-422. Terrell, E. E. 1977. *A checklist of names for 3,000 vascular plants of economic importance.* USDA. ARS. Agriculture Handbook No. 505. Washington, D.C. 201 pp.

S-426. Thornback, J. 1978. *IUCN red data book. Volume I: Mammalia.* IUCN. Morges (Switzerland).

S-428. Traffic (USA). 1979. *Bobcat export and international trade.* Prepared for Bobcat Research Conference. 16–18 October 1979. Front Royal, Virginia. Traffic (USA). Washington, D.C. 9 pp.

S-429. Traffic (USA). 1980. *Neotropical psittacines in trade.* Traffic (USA). Washington, D.C. 27 pp.

S-433. Tyler, V. E., L. R. Brady, & J. E. Robbers. 1981. *Pharmacognosy.* 8th edition. Lea & Febiger. Philadelphia. 520 pp.

S-434. USDA. 1953. *Plant diseases: The yearbook of agriculture.* USDA. Washington, D.C. 940 pp.

S-448. USDA. 1979. *Agricultural statistics, 1979.* USDA. Washington, D.C. 603 pp.

S-449. USDA. 1980. *Agricultural statistics, 1980.* USDA. Washington, D.C. 603 pp.

S-450. U.S. Department of Commerce. 1977. *US imports for consumption and general imports: TSUSA commodity by country of origin.* Bureau of the Census. FT246/Annual 1976. Washington, D.C.

S-451. U.S. Department of Commerce. 1978. *US imports for consumption and general imports: TSUSA commodity by country of origin.* Bureau of the Census. FT246/Annual 1977. Washington, D.C.

S-452. U.S. Department of Commerce. 1980. *US imports for consumption and general imports: TSUSA commodity by country of origin.* Bureau of the Census. FT246/Annual 1978. Washington, D.C.

S-453. U.S. Department of Commerce. 1980. *US imports for consumption and general imports: TSUSA commodity by country of origin.* Bureau of the Census. FT246/Annual 1979. Washington, D.C.

S-454. U.S. Department of Commerce. 1981. *US imports for consumption and general imports: TSUSA commodity by country of origin.* Bureau of the Census. FT246/Annual 1980. Washington, D.C.

S-469. Society of Leather Trades' Chemists. 1956. *The chemistry of vegetable tannins: A symposium.* Croydon. (England). 160 pp.

S-475. Stockberger, W.W. 1935. *Drug plants under cultivation.* FB663. USDA. Washington, D.C. 37 pp.

S-478. Subramaniam, S. 1968. Performance of recent introductions of *Hevea* in Malaya. *Proceedings of the National Rubber Conference (Kuala Lumpur):* 11–18.

S-485. Thomas, H. K. 1956. Essential oils of the conifers. II. *American Perfumer and Aromatics* 68 (3): 44–46.

S-493. Unver, A. S. 1969. The history of tulips in Turkey. *Daffodil and Tulip Year Book* 34: 46–53.

S-497. Schroeder, C. A., & W. A. Fletcher. 1967. The Chinese gooseberry *(Actinidia chinensis)* in New Zealand. *Economic Botany* 21: 81–92.

S-503. Shiu, Y. H. 1976. The genus *Panax* (ginseng) in Chinese medicine. *Economic Botany* 30: 11–28.

S-512. Statistics Canada. 1981. *Canadian forestry statistics: 1979.* Catalogue 25-202. Ottawa. 64 pp.

S-517. Statistics Canada. 1978. *Production of maple products, 1978, and value of maple products, 1977.* Catalogue 22-204. Ottawa. 3 pp.

S-518. Statistics Canada. 1979. *Production of maple products, 1979, and value of maple products, 1978.* Catalogue 22-204. Ottawa. 5 pp.

S-519. Statistics Canada. 1980. *Production of maple products, 1980, and value of maple products, 1979.* Catalogue 22-204. Ottawa. 5 pp.

S-520. Statistics Canada. 1981. *Production of maple products, 1981, and value of maple products, 1980.* Catalogue 22-204. Ottawa. 5 pp.

S-554. Statistics Canada. 1978. *Fur production: Season, 1976–77.* Catalogue 23-207. Ottawa. 14 pp.

S-555. Statistics Canada. 1979. *Fur production: Season, 1977–78.* Catalogue 23-207. Ottawa. 17 pp.

S-556. Statistics Canada. 1980. *Fur production: Season, 1978–79.* Catalogue 23-207. Ottawa. 17 pp.

S-557. Statistics Canada. 1981. *Fur production: Season, 1979–80.* Catalogue 23-207. Ottawa. 18 pp.

S-558. Statistics Canada. 1982. *Fur production: Season, 1980–81.* Catalogue 23-207. Ottawa. 18 pp.

S-567. Smith, D. R. (technical coordinator). 1975. *Proceedings of the symposium on management of forest and range habitats for nongame birds.* 6–9 May 1975. Tucson,

Arizona. USDA Forest Service. General Technical Report WO-1. Washington, D.C. 343 pp.

S-574. Statistics Canada. 1982. *Canadian forestry statistics: 1980.* Catalogue 25-202. Ottawa. 43 pp.

S-578. Toxopeus, H. (ed.). 1982. *Archives of cocoa research.* Volume 1. American Cocoa Research Institute & International Office of Cocoa and Chocolate. 196 pp.

S-585. U.S. Fish and Wildlife Service & U.S. Bureau of the Census. 1982. *1980 national survey of fishing, hunting, and wildlife associated recreation: preliminary report.* U.S. Department of the Interior & U.S. Department of Commerce. Washington, D.C. 154 pp.

S-594. Stearn, W. T. 1970. A brief survey of lily literature. *Lily Year Book* 33: 186–198.

S-595. Stone, G., J. M. Stewart, D. Woods, D. Punter, & G. Beaubier. 1975. *Wild rice production in Manitoba.* Manitoba Department of Agriculture Publication 527.

S-622. Statistics Canada. 1977. *Production of maple products, 1977, and value of maple products, 1976.* Catalogue 22-204. Ottawa. 3 pp.

S-625. Thornback, J., & M. Jenkins. 1982. *The IUCN mammal red data book. Part 1.* IUCN. Gland (Switzerland). 516 pp.

S-671. Traffic (USA). 1982. *Trade in Latin American crocodiles.* Prepared for the "Second course on research, management and conservation of crocodilians for Latin American biologists." Traffic (USA). Washington, D.C. 10 pp.

S-682. U. S. Department of the Navy. 1965. *Poisonous snakes of the world: A manual for use by US amphibious forces.* Bureau of Medicine and Surgery. Washington, D.C. 212 pp.

S-683. USDA. 1981. *Ginseng.* Foreign Agriculture Circular FTEA 2-81. 16 pp.

S-684. Sheldon, S. 1980. Ethnobotany of *Agave lecheguilla* and *Yucca carnerosana* in Mexico's zona ixtlera. *Economic Botany* 34: 376–390.

S-685. Statistics Canada. 1983. *Fur production: season, 1981–82.* Catalogue 23-207. Ottawa. 20 pp.

S-686. Toxopeus, H., & P. Crisp. 1980. *Genetic resources of cruciferous crops in Europe.* IBPGR. Rome.

S-687. U.S. Department of Commerce & National Oceanic and Atmospheric Administration. 1980. *Marine recreational fishery statistics survey, Atlantic and Gulf coasts, 1979.* U.S. Department of Commerce & NOAA. Washington, D.C. 139 pp.

S-688. U.S. Fish and Wildlife Service. 1977. *1975 national survey of hunting, fishing and wildlife-associated recreation.* U.S. Department of the Interior. Washington, D.C. 91 pp.

S-691. Secretary of Agriculture. 1977. *Animal welfare enforcement, 1976: Report of the Secretary of Agriculture to the President of the Senate and the Speaker of the House of Representatives.* USDA. Washington, D.C.

S-692. Secretary of Agriculture. 1978. *Animal welfare enforcement, 1977: Report of the Secretary of Agriculture to the President of the Senate and the Speaker of the House of Representatives.* USDA. Washington, D.C.

S-693. Secretary of Agriculture. 1979. *Animal welfare enforcement FY 1978: Report of the Secretary of Agriculture to the President of the Senate and the Speaker of the House of Representatives.* USDA. Washington, D.C.

S-695. Secretary of Agriculture. 1980. *Animal welfare enforcement FY 1979: Report of the Secretary of Agriculture to the President of the Senate and the Speaker of the House of Representatives.* USDA. Washington, D.C.

S-696. Secretary of Agriculture. No date. *Animal welfare enforcement, FY 1980: Report of the Secretary of Agriculture to the President of the Senate and the Speaker of the House of Representatives.* USDA. Washington, D.C.

S-698. Statistics Canada. 1981. *Population counts: 1976–1981*. Catalogue 99-908. Ottawa.

S-699. USDA. 1981. *Agricultural statistics 1981*. USDA. Washington, D.C. 601 pp.

S-704. Shutak, V. G., & P. E. Marucci. 1966. Plant and fruit development. In P. Eck & N. F. Childers (eds.). *Blueberry culture:* 179–198 [Reference D-118].

S-708. Soost, R. K., & J. W. Cameron. 1975. Citrus. In J. Janick & J. N. Moore (eds.). *Advances in fruit breeding:* 507–540 [Reference J-8].

S-716. Storey, W. B. 1975. Figs. In J. Janick & J. N. Moore (eds.). *Advances in fruit breeding:* 568–589 [Reference J-8].

S-720. Thomson, P. H. 1979. Macadamia. In R. A. Jaynes (ed.). *Nut tree culture in North America:* 188–202 [Reference J-306].

S-724. USDA. 1980. *State farm income statistics: Supplement to statistical bulletin no. 627*. USDA. Economics, Statistics, and Cooperatives Service. Washington, D.C. 95 pp.

S-725. USDA. 1981. *Agricultural statistics 1981*. USDA. Washington, D.C. 601 pp.

S-726. USDA. 1981. *Economic indicators of the farm sector: State income and balance sheet statistics, 1979*. USDA. Economics and Statistics Service. Statistical Bulletin no. 661. Washington, D.C. 194 pp.

S-727. USDA. 1981. *Economic indicators of the farm sector: State income and balance sheet statistics, 1980*. USDA. Economics Research Service. Statistical Bulletin no. 678. Washington, D.C. 196 pp.

S-728. USDA. 1982. *Economic indicators of the farm sector: State income and balance sheet statistics, 1981*. USDA. Economics Research Service. ECIFS 1-2. Washington, D.C. 193 pp.

S-730. Scora, R. W. 1975. IX. On the history and origin of citrus. *Bulletin of the Torrey Botanical Club* 102: 369–375.

S-731. Seaney, R. R., & P. R. Henson. 1970. Birdsfoot trefoil. *Advances in Agronomy* 22: 119–157.

S-733. Sternitzke, H. S., & T. C. Nelson. 1970. The southern pines of the United States. *Economic Botany* 24: 142–150.

S-734. U.S. National Park Service. 1979. *National park statistical abstract: 1978*. U.S. Department of the Interior. 30 pp.

S-735. U.S. National Park Service. 1980. *National park statistical abstract: 1979*. U.S. Department of Interior. 39 pp.

S-736. U.S. National Park Service. 1981. *National park statistical abstract: 1980*. U.S. Department of the Interior. 41 pp.

S-741. Somers, G. F. (ed.). 1974. *Seed-bearing halophytes as food plants*. University of Delaware. Newark (Delaware).

S-744. Spencer, R. F., & J. D. Jennings. 1965. *The native Americans*. Harper & Row. New York, Evanston, London. 539 pp.

S-751. 't Mannetje, L., K. F. O'Connor, & R. L. Burt. 1980. The use and adaptation of pasture and fodder legumes. In R. J. Summerfield A. H. Bunting (eds.). *Advances in legume science:* 537–551 [Reference S-245].

S-780. Szczawinski, A. F., & N. J. Turner. 1980. *Wild green vegetables of Canada*. National Museums of Canada. Edible Wild Plants of Canada No. 4. Ottawa. 179 pp.

S-782. USDA. 1976. *Nuts*. Foreign Agriculture circular FN 1-76. Washington, D.C. 91 pp.

S-786. UNIDO. 1976. *Technical report: Production and marketing of rattan furniture in Indonesia*. Assistance to the National Agency for Export Development (NAFED), Ministry of Trade, in the field of the export product adaptation: IS/INS/74/030. UNIDO. Vienna. 58 pp.

S-796. Turner, N. J., & A. F. Szczawinski. 1979. *Edible wild fruits and nuts of Canada*. National Museums of Canada. Edible Wild Plants of Canada No. 3. Ottawa. 212 pp.

S-797. Ulrich, A. H. 1981. *US timber production, trade, consumption, and price statistics, 1950–80*. USDA Forest Service. Miscellaneous Publication No. 1408. Washington, D.C. 81 pp.

S-798. U.S. Department of Commerce. 1981. *1978 census of agriculture. Volume 1: Summary and state data. Part 51: United States*. Bureau of the Census. Washington, D.C.

S-799. U.S. Department of Commerce. 1983. *Statistical abstracts of the United States, 1982–83*. Bureau of the Census. Washington, D.C.

S-800. USDA Forest Service. 1982. *An analysis of the timber situation in the United States, 1952–2030*. USDA. Forest Resource Report No. 23. Washington, D.C.

S-801. USDA. 1972. *Agricultural statistics, 1972*. USDA. Washington, D.C.

S-803. Suto, S. 1974. Mariculture of seaweeds and its problems in Japan. *NOAA Technical Report NMFS Circ.* 388: 7–16.

S-805. Tsuji, S. 1980. *Japanese cooking: A simple art*. Kodansha International. Tokyo, New York, San Francisco. 517 pp.

S-806. U.S. Department of Commerce. 1977. *Canned fishery products, annual summary, 1976*. National Marine Fisheries Service. Current Fisheries Statistics No. 7201. Washington, D.C. 13 pp.

S-807. U.S. Department of Commerce. 1979. *Canned fishery products, annual summary, 1977*. National Marine Fisheries Service. Current Fisheries Statistics No. 7501. Washington, D.C. 13 pp.

S-808. U.S. Department of Commerce. 1979. *Canned fishery products, annual summary, 1978*. National Marine Fisheries Service. Current Fisheries Statistics No. 7801. Washington, D.C. 13 pp.

S-809. U.S. Department of Commerce. 1981. *Canned fishery products, annual summary, 1979*. National Marine Fisheries Service. Current Fisheries Statistics No. 8001. Washington, D.C. 12 pp.

S-810. U.S. Department of Commerce. 1982. *Canned fishery products, annual summary, 1980*. National Marine Fisheries Service. Current Fisheries Statistics No. 8101. Washington, D.C. 12 pp.

S-811. U.S. Department of Commerce. 1978. *Processed fishery products, annual summary, 1976*. National Marine Fisheries Service. Current Fisheries Statistics No. 7203. Washington, D.C. 39 pp.

S-812. U.S. Department of Commerce. 1979. *Processed fishery products, annual summary, 1977*. National Marine Fisheries Service. Current Fisheries Statistics No. 7503. Washington, D.C. 34 pp.

S-813. U.S. Department of Commerce. No date. *Processed fishery products, annual summary, 1978*. National Marine Fisheries Service. Current Fisheries Statistics No. 7803. Washington, D.C. 31 pp.

S-814. U.S. Department of Commerce. 1980. *Processed fishery products, annual summary, 1979*. National Marine Fisheries Service. Current Fisheries Statistics No. 8003. Washington, D.C. 33 pp.

S-815. U.S. Department of Commerce. 1982. *Processed fishery products, annual summary, 1980*. National Marine Fisheries Service. Current Fisheries Statistics No. 8103. Washington, D.C. 35 pp.

S-816. U.S. International Trade Commission. 1979. *Tariff schedules of the United States annotated, 1980*. USITC Publication 1011. Washington, D.C.

S-817. Ulrich, A.H. 1983. *US timber production, trade, consumption, and price statistics, 1950–1980*. USDA Forest Service. Miscellaneous Publication No. 1424. Washington, D.C.

S-818. USDA Forest Service. 1980. *Forest statistics of the US, 1977.* Revised version issued as appendix 3 of USDA Forest Service. *An analysis of the timber situation in the United States, 1952–2030.*

S-819. U.S. Department of Commerce. 1981. The national income and product accounts of the United States, 1929–1976. Supplement to *Survey of current business.* Bureau of Economic Analysis. Washington, D.C.

S-820. U.S. Department of Commerce. 1981. The national income and product accounts, 1976–1979. Special supplement to *Survey of current business.* Bureau of Economic Analysis. Washington, D.C.

S-821. U.S. Department of Commerce. 1981. Selected national income and product account tables, 1979–1980. *Survey of Current Business* 61: 22–28.

S-822. U.S. Department of Commerce. No date. *Unpublished data.* Bureau of Economic Analysis.

S-823. Statistics Canada. 1978. *Pulp and paper mills, 1976.* Catalogue 36-204. Ottawa.

S-824. Smith, E. L., E. E. Sebesta, H. C. Young Jr., H. Pass, & D. C. Abbott. 1981. Registration of Payne wheat (reg. no. 642). *Crop Science* 21: 636.

S-825. Stebbins, G. L. 1982. Major trends of evolution in the Poaceae and their possible significance. In J. R. Estes, R. J. Tyrl, & J. N. Brunken (eds.). *Grasses and grasslands— systematics and ecology:* 3–36 [Reference D-414].

S-826. Stuthman, D. D., M. B. Moore, P. G. Rothman, & R. D. Wilcoxson. 1978. Registration of Lyon oats (reg. no. 285). *Crop Science* 18: 356.

S-827. Toxopeus, H. 1964. F$_3$ Amazon cocoa in Nigeria. In H. Toxopeus (ed.). *Archives of cocoa research:* 179–191 [Reference S-578].

S-830. U.S. Department of Commerce. 1978. *1974 census of agriculture. Volume II: Statistics by subject. Part 5: Livestock, poultry, livestock and poultry products, fish.* Bureau of the Census. Washington, D.C. 184 pp.

S-831. U.S. Department of Commerce. 1978. *1974 census of agriculture. Volume II: Statistics by subject. Part 6: Crops, nursery and greenhouse products.* Bureau of the Census. Washington, D.C. 162 pp.

S-832. U.S. Department of Commerce. 1982. *1978 census of agriculture. Volume 5: Special reports. Part 7: 1979 census of horticultural specialties.* Bureau of the Census. Washington, D.C.

S-833. Styles, B. T., & P. K. Khosla. 1976. Cytology and reproductive biology of Meliaceae. In J. Burley & B. T. Styles (eds.). *Tropical trees: Variation, breeding and conservation:* 61–67 [Reference A-923].

S-834. Tysdal, H. M., A. Estilai, I. A. Siddiqui, & P. F. Knowles. 1983. Registration of four guayule germplasms (reg. no. GP1 to GP4). *Crop Science* 23: 189.

S-835. Stiell, W. M., & C. R. Stanton. 1981. *An introduction to Christmas tree growing in Canada.* Canadian Forestry Service Publication No. 1330. Ottawa. 32 pp.

S-836. Smith, H. H. 1979. The genus as a genetic resource. In R. D. Durbin (ed.). *Nicotiana: Procedures for experimental use:* 1–16 [Reference D-81].

S-837. Sorensen, E. L., M. C. Wilson, & G. R. Manglitz. 1972. Breeding for insect resistance. In C. H. Hanson (ed.). *Alfalfa science and technology:* 371–390 [Reference G-460].

S-838. Smith, D. L. 1978. Planting seed production. In J. F. Carter (ed.). *Sunflower science and technology:* 371–386 [Reference A-376].

S-839. Udvardy, M. D. F. 1975. *A classification of the biogeographical provinces of the world.* IUCN Occasional Paper No. 18. IUCN. Morges (Switzerland).

S-880. Steinhoff, R. J. 1979. *Variation in early growth of western white pine in north Idaho.* USDA. Forest Service Research Paper INT-222. 22 pp.

S-935. Trease, G. E., & W. C. Evans. 1983. *Pharmacognosy.* 12th edition. Bailliere Tindall. London. 812 pp.

S-1271. Thornback, J. 1983. *Wild cattle, bison and buffaloes: Their status and potential value.* IUCN Conservation Monitoring Centre. WWF, UNEP, & IUCN.

V-3. Valleau, W. D. 1952. Breeding tobacco for disease resistance. *Economic Botany* 6: 69–102.

V-13. Vega, U., & K. J. Frey. 1980. Trangressive segregation in inter- and intraspecific crosses of barley. *Euphytica* 29: 585–594.

V-23. Visser, T. 1969. Tea. In F. P. Ferwerda & F. Wit (eds.). *Outlines of perennial crop breeding in the tropics:* 459–493 [Reference D-257].

V-24. Visser, T. 1976. Tea. In N. W. Simmonds (ed.). *Evolution of crop plants:* 18–20 [Reference S-384].

V-26. Vries, C. A. de. 1974. Sericulture. *Tropical Abstracts* 29: No. 9.

V-46. Watkins, R. 1976. Apple and pear. In N. W. Simmonds (ed.). *Evolution of crop plants:* 247–250 [Reference S-384].

V-47. Watkins, R. 1976. Cherry, plum, peach, apricot and almond. In N. W. Simmonds (ed.). *Evolution of crop plants:* 242–247 [Reference S-384].

V-50. Watkins, R. 1979. "Plums, apricots, almonds, peaches, cherries (genus *Prunus*)." Unpublished paper.

V-62. Weathers, D., & J. Huck. 1979. Feathered friends. *Newsweek.* July 23.

V-70. Webster, G. L. 1967. The genera of Euphorbiaceae in the southeastern United States. *Journal of the Arnold Arboretum* 48: 303–361, 363–430.

V-78. Wellman, F. L. 1961. *Coffee: Botany, cultivation and utilization.* Leonard Hill (Books). London. Interscience Publishers. New York. 488 pp.

V-85. Werkhoven, J., & J. G. Ohler. 1968. Babassu. *Tropical Abstracts* 23: No. 12.

V-87. Westbury, J. 1971. Bumble bees as pollinators: Limiting factors. *American Bee Journal* 111: 342, 345.

V-96. Wet, J. M. J. de, & J. R. Harlan. 1971. The origin and domestication of *Sorghum bicolor. Economic Botany* 25: 128–135.

V-102. Whistler, R. L. (ed.). 1973. *Industrial gums, polysaccharides and their derivatives.* 2d edition. Academic Press. New York, San Francisco, London. 807 pp.

V-105. Whitaker, T. W. 1976. Cucurbits. In N. W. Simmonds (ed.). *Evolution of crop plants:* 64–69 [Reference S-384].

V-106. Whitaker, T. W., & I. C. Jagger. 1937. Breeding and improvement of cucurbits. *USDA Yearbook* 1937: 207–232.

V-108. White, N. J., & C. Robinson. 1979. A fly-by-night plot in Australia. *Newsweek.* October 1.

V-122. Wienk, J. F. 1969. Long fibre agaves: *Agave sisalana* Perr. and *A. fourcroydes* Lem. In F. P. Ferwerda & F. Wit (eds.). *Outlines of perennial crop breeding in the tropics:* 1–21 [Reference D-257].

V-123. Wienk, J. F. 1976. Sisal and relatives. In N. W. Simmonds (ed.). *Evolution of crop plants:* 1–4 [Reference S-384].

V-144. Wilkes, H. G. 1979. Mexico and Central America as a centre for the origin of agriculture and the evolution of maize. *Crop Improvement* 6: 1–18.

V-150. Williams, L. O. 1960. *Drug and condiment plants.* USDA. ARS. Agriculture Handbook 172. Washington, D.C.

V-166. Wit, F. 1976. Clove. In N. W. Simmonds (ed.). *Evolution of crop plants:* 216–218 [Reference S-384].

V-185. Wycherley, P. R. 1976. Rubber. In N. W. Simmonds (ed.). *Evolution of crop plants:* 77–81 [Reference S-384].

V-198. Wilson, B. 1979. High tide for seaweed profit. *The Observer.* March 18.

V-206. WHO. 1979. The selection of essential drugs. Second Report of the WHO Expert Committee. *WHO Technical Report Series 641.* 44 pp.

V-208. Woodroof, J. G. 1979. *Tree nuts: Production, processing, products.* 2d edition. AVI Publishing. Westport, Connecticut. 731 pp.

V-209. Whitmore, T. C. (ed.). 1973. *Tree flora of Malaya: A manual for foresters.* Volume 2. Longman. 444 pp.

V-211. Williams, J. T., C. H. Lamoureux, & N. Wulijarni-Soetjipto (eds.). 1975. *South East Asian plant genetic resources.* IBPGR, BIOTROP & LIPI. Bogor. 272 pp.

V-215. Vietmeyer, N. 1981. Man's new best friends. *Quest* January/February 5 (1): 43–49.

V-222. Warner, G. F. 1977. *The biology of crabs.* Paul Elek (Scientific Books). London. 202 pp.

V-223. Warner, W. W. 1977. *Beautiful swimmers: Watermen, crabs and the Chesapeake Bay.* Penguin Books. 304 pp.

V-224. Weiner, M. 1980. *Weiner's herbal: The guide to herb medicine.* Stein & Day. New York. 224 pp.

V-232. Willis, J. C. 1980. *A dictionary of the flowering plants and ferns.* 8th ed. Rev. H. K. A. Shaw. Cambridge University Press. Cambridge, London, New York, New Rochelle, Melbourne, Sydney. 1245 pp.

V-234. Windholz, M. (ed). 1976. *The Merck index: An encyclopedia of chemicals and drugs.* 9th edition. Merck & Co. Rahway (New Jersey).

V-270. Walmsley, A. 1982. A wild leguminous feast. *Maclean's.* March 15.

V-273. Wells, S. M. 1981. *International trade in corals.* IUCN Conservation Monitoring Unit. Cambridge. 18 pp.

V-274. Wells, S. M. 1981. *International trade in ornamental shells.* IUCN Conservation Monitoring Centre. Cambridge. 22 pp.

V-276. Williams, L. 1963. Laticiferous plants of economic importance. IV. Jelutong (*Dyera*) spp. *Economic Botany* 17: 110–126.

V-277. Williams, L. 1964. Laticiferous plants of economic importance. V. Resources of gutta-percha: *Palaquium* species (Sapotaceae). *Economic Botany* 18: 5–26.

V-280. Winters, H. F. 1976. *Microcitrus papuana,* a new species from Papua New Guinea (Rutaceae). *Baileya* 20: 19–24.

V-289. Wells, O. O. 1976. Provenance research and fusiform rust in the southern United States. *Proceedings 4th North American Forest Biology Workshop:* 23–28.

V-290. Wells, O. O., & G. L. Switzer. 1971. Variation in rust resistance in Mississippi loblolly pine. *Proceedings of the 11th Conference on Southern Forest Tree Improvement:* 25–30.

V-291. Wells, O. O., & G. L. Switzer. 1975. Selecting populations of loblolly pine for rust resistance and fast growth. *Proceedings of the 13th Southern Forest Tree Improvement Conference:* 37–44.

V-298. Watson, L. 1981. *Sea guide to whales of the world.* E. P. Dutton. New York. 302 pp.

V-309. Wells, O. O. Southwide pine seed source study—loblolly pine at 25 years. *Southern Journal of Applied Forestry.*

V-315. Williams, L. 1962. Laticiferous plants of economic importance. III. *Couma* species. *Economic Botany* 16: 251–263.

V-317. Wallis, B. E. 1980. *Marketing assistance programme for agricultural products from least developed countries: Market prospects for reptile leathers.* International Trade Centre. UNCTAD/GATT. ITC/DIP/12.

V-327. Vines, R. A. 1960. *Trees, shrubs and woody vines of the southwest: A guide for the states of Arkansas, Louisiana, New Mexico, Oklahoma, and Texas.* University of Texas Press. Austin, London. 1104 pp.

V-331. Wendt, J. S., W. Mortimer, & F. G. Cooch. 1979. *Migratory birds killed in Canada during the 1978 season.* Canadian Wildlife Service. Progress Notes No. 101. 45 pp.

V-332. Wendt, S., & C. Hyslop. 1981. *Migratory birds killed in Canada during the 1980 season.* Canadian Wildlife Service. Progress Notes No. 126. 42 pp.

V-336. Wiley, J. P. Jr. 1982. Phenomena, comment and notes. *Smithsonian.* March.

V-341. Whittaker, R. H. 1969. New concepts of kingdoms of organisms. *Science* 163: 150–160.

V-342. Wilhelm, S., & J. E. Sagen. 1974. *A history of the strawberry: From ancient gardens to modern markets.* University of California. Berkeley. 298 pp.

V-345. Veninga, L., & B. R. Zaricor. 1976. *Goldenseal/etc.* Ruka Publications. Santa Cruz (California). 193 pp.

V-347. Williams, L., & J. A. Duke. 1978. *Growing ginseng.* USDA. Farmers' Bulletin No. 2201. Washington, D.C. 8 pp.

V-348. Wagner, T. 1978. *Gene pools of hop countries.* Institut za Hmeljarstvo. Zalec (Yugoslavia). 83 pp.

V-350. Wolfle, T. L. 1983. Nonhuman primates in research: Trends in conservation, importation, production and use in the United States. *Lab Animal.* April.

V-355. Varney, E. H., & A. W. Stretch. 1966. Diseases and their control. In P. Eck & N. F. Childers (eds.). *Blueberry culture:* 236–279 [Reference D-118].

V-358. Weinberger, J. H. 1975. Plums. In J. Janick & J. N. Moore (eds.). *Advances in fruit breeding:* 336–347 [Reference J-8].

V-359. Wernsman, E. A., & D. F. Matzinger. 1980. Tobacco. In W. R. Fehr & H. H. Hadley (eds.). *Hybridization of crop plants:* 657–668 [Reference D-405].

V-363. Wynne, J. C., & W. C. Gregory. 1981. Peanut breeding. *Advances in Agronomy* 34: 39–72.

V-365. Walton, P. D. 1971. The origin and development of world forage crops. *Economic Botany* 25: 263–266.

V-366. Wang, S.-C., & J. B. Huffman. 1981. Botanochemicals: Supplements to petrochemicals. *Economic Botany* 35: 369–382.

V-367. Whistler, R. L. 1982. Industrial gums from plants: Guar and chia. *Economic Botany* 36: 195–202.

V-368. Whitaker, T. W. 1981. Archeological cucurbits. *Economic Botany* 35: 460–466.

V-376. Wright, J. W. 1976. *Introduction to forest genetics.* Academic Press. New York, San Francisco, London. 463 pp.

V-380. Walters, P. R., N. Macfarlane, & P. C. Spensley. 1979. *Jojoba: An assessment of prospects.* Tropical Products Institute G128. London. 32 pp.

V-382. Whistler, R. L. 1973. Factors influencing gum costs and applications. In R. L. Whistler (ed.). *Industrial gums: Polysaccharides and their derivatives:* 5–18 [Reference V-102].

V-387. Vietmeyer, N. 1983. A 10,000 year breakthrough. *International Wildlife.* May/June.

V-388. Walter, J. M. 1967. Hereditary resistance to disease in tomato. *Annual Review of Phytopathology* 5: 131.

V-389. Wilson, R. J. 1975. *The market for cashew-nut kernels and cashew-nut shell liquid.* Tropical Products Institute G91. London. 119 pp.

V-392. White, G. A. 1977. Plant introductions—a source of new crops. In D. S. Seigler (ed.). *Crop resources:* 17–24 [Reference S-366].

V-393. Whelan, E. D. P. 1981. Cytoplasmic male sterility in *Helianthus giganteus* L. × *H. annuus* L. *Crop Science* 21: 855–858.

V-489. Vaughan, D. A., & T. Hymowitz. 1983. Progress in wild perennial soyabean characterization. *Plant Genetic Resources Newsletter* 56: 7–12.

Y-10. Yen, D. E. 1976. Sweet potato. In N. W. Simmonds (ed.). *Evolution of crop plants:* 42–44 [Reference S-384].

Y-11. Yen, D. E., & E. J. Newhook. 1959. V548—a new glasshouse tomato for release in 1959. *New Zealand Journal of Agriculture* 98: 487–488.

Y-12. Yermanos, D. M. 1979. Jojoba—a crop whose time has come. *California Agriculture* 33: 4–7, 10–11.

Y-23. Zeven, A. C. 1967. *The semi-wild oil palm and its industry in Africa.* Agricultural Research Reports No. 689. Pudoc. Wageningen, Netherlands. 178 pp.

Y-24. Zeven, A. C. 1969. Kapok tree: *Ceiba pentandra* Gaertn. In F. P. Ferwerda & F. Wit (eds.). *Outlines of perennial crop breeding in the tropics:* 269–287 [Reference D-257].

Y-25. Zeven, A. C. 1976. Kapok. In N. W. Simmonds (ed.). *Evolution of crop plants:* 13–14 [Reference S-384].

Y-35. Zimmer, D. E., & D. Rehder. 1976. Rust resistance of wild *Helianthus* species of the north central United States. *Phytopathology* 66: 208–211.

Y-40. Zohary, D. 1972. The wild progenitor and the place of the origin of the cultivated lentil: *Lens culinaris. Economic Botany* 26: 326–332.

Y-46. Zohary, D., & M. Spiegel-Roy. 1975. Beginnings of fruit growing in the Old World. *Science* 187: 319–327.

Y-47. Yen, W. W., & M. Shane (eds.). 1977. *A Sabah rattan industry.* Transcript of meeting on prepolicy discussion on rattan in Sabah. 23 July 1977. SAFODA. Kota Kinabalu, Sabah.

Y-48. Zeven, A. C., & A. M. van Harten (eds.). 1979. *Proceedings of the conference broadening the genetic base of crops.* 3–7 July 1978. Wageningen, Netherlands. Pudoc. Wageningen. 347 pp.

Y-58. Zohary, D., & M. Hopf. 1973. Domestication of pulses in the Old World. *Science* 182: 887–894.

Y-74. Zimmermann, C. E., S. T. Likens, A. Haunold, C. E. Horner, & D. D. Roberts. 1975. Registration of Comet hop. *Crop Science* 15: 98

Y-76. Zhang, B. L., et al. 1979. *The farming of musk deer.* In Chinese. Trans. P. Jackson. Agriculture Publishing. Beijing.

Y-80. Yermanos, D. M. 1974. Agronomic survey of jojoba in California. *Economic Botany* 28: 160–174.

Y-81. Zeven, A. C. 1972. The partial and complete domestication of the oil palm *(Elaeis guineensis). Economic Botany* 26: 274–279.

Y-82. Zobel, B. J. 1971. The genetic improvement of southern pines. *Scientific American* 225. 93–103.

Y-83. Zohary, D., & J. Basnizky. 1975. The cultivated artichoke—*Cynara scolymus* its probable wild ancestors. *Economic Botany* 29: 233–235.

Y-88. Zimmer, D. E., & J. A. Hoes. 1978. Diseases. In J. F. Carter (ed.). *Sunflower science and technology:* 225–262 [Reference A-376].

# Index

Wild species, 2; economic impact of, 408–410; value of, 408. *See also* Species and species groups; Trends in wildlife uses
Willow, basket, 201, 222
Windowpane, 368
Wintergreen, 105, 133
Witch hazel, 113, 134
Witloof, 202, 206, 338
Wolf, 71, 78, 80
Wolffish, 65, 273
Wolverine, 75, 78
Woodchuck, 377
Woodcock, 371, 379
World Health Organization (WHO), 140
World Wildlife Fund, 68
Worms: earthworms, 264–265, 271; manure, 265; red wriggler, 265
Wrasse, 369

*Xanthomonas malvacearum. See* Bacterial diseases, blight
*Xanthomonas vasculorum. See* Bacterial diseases, gummosis
*Xanthomonas vesicatoria. See* Bacterial diseases, leaf spot

*Xenoglossa* spp. *See* Bees, honey
*Xenorhabdus nematophilus*, 359
Xiphiidae, 64

Yams, 138
Yarrow, 113, 132
Yellow dock, 118
Yew, ornamental, 199, 224
Ylang ylang, 202, 204, 242
Yohimbine, 105, 133
*Yucca carnerosana. See* Istle

*Zanthoxylum americanum. See* Ash, prickly
*Zanthoxylum clava-herculis. See* Ash, prickly
*Zea diploperennis. See* Maize
*Zea mays. See* Maize
*Zenaida asiatica. See* Doves, white-winged
*Zenaida macroura. See* Doves, mourning
Zingiberaceae, 202, 203, 224, 334, 347, 349
Zinnia, 201, 206
*Zinnia elegans. See* Zinnia
*Zizania aquatica. See* Wild rice
Zoos, 384
Zygophyllaceae, 257